# TZELTAL FOLK ZOOLOGY

The Classification of
Discontinuities in
Nature

**LANGUAGE, THOUGHT, AND CULTURE:** *Advances in the Study of Cognition*

*Under the Editorship of:* E. A. HAMMEL

DEPARTMENT OF ANTHROPOLOGY
UNIVERSITY OF CALIFORNIA
BERKELEY

# TZELTAL FOLK ZOOLOGY

## The Classification of Discontinuities in Nature

EUGENE S. HUNN

*Department of Anthropology*
*University of Washington*
*Seattle, Washington*

ACADEMIC PRESS   New York   San Francisco   London
*A Subsidiary of Harcourt Brace Jovanovich, Publishers*

ACADEMIC PRESS, INC.
111 Fifth Avenue, New York, New York 10003

*United Kingdom Edition published by*
ACADEMIC PRESS, INC. (LONDON) LTD.
24/28 Oval Road, London NW1

Library of Congress Cataloging in Publication Data

Hunn, Eugene S
    Tzeltal folk zoology.

    (Language, thought, and culture series)
    1.    Tzeltal Indians.    2.    Ethnozoology—Mexico—
Chiapas.    3.    Tzeltal language—Glossaries, vocabu-
laries, etc.    4.    Classification, Primitive.
I.    Title.
F1221.T8H86        591'.01'2        76-56205
ISBN 0-12-361750-2

*In memory of*
*SIERRA DYLAN HUNN*

And out of the ground
the Lord God formed every beast
of the field, and every fowl of the air;
and brought them unto Adam
to see what he would call them:
and whatsoever Adam called every living
creature, that was the name thereof.
    And Adam gave names to all cattle,
and to the fowl of the air,
and to every beast of the field; . . .

GENESIS 2: 19–20

---

We take as given the idea of distinction
    and the idea of indication,
    and that we cannot make an indication
without drawing a distinction.

We take, therefore, the form of distinction
    for the form.

. . .

Once a distinction is drawn, the spaces,
    states, or contents on each side
    of the boundary, being distinct,
can be indicated.

There can be no distinction without motive,
    and there can be no motive unless
    contents are seen to differ in value.

If a content is of value, a name can be taken
    to indicate this value.

Thus the calling of the name
    can be identified with
    the value of the content.

G. SPENCER BROWN
*Laws of Form* (1969:1)

# CONTENTS

## CHAPTER 1

### Context                                            1

## CHAPTER 2

### Methods                                            17

# PREFACE

My basic goal is to compile an encyclopedic dictionary of the zoological lexicon used by the Indians of Tenejapa, a *municipio** in the central highlands of the Mexican state of Chiapas. The definition of terms applied to the more than 500 distinct taxa of animals† that are distinguished by Tenejapanecos occupied the major portion of my effort. Descriptive and anatomical terminology, behavioral, ecological, and developmental vocabulary, and animal product names were systematically elicited from a few informants.

These Indians speak a dialect of Tzeltal, a language of the Mayan family without written tradition. Thus this dictionary provides a permanent record of one aspect of the intellectual achievement of these people. The folk-botanical study of this same Indian community by Berlin, Breedlove, and Raven (1974) together with this monograph constitute the closest approximation to a comprehensive description of a folk natural history in the anthropological literature. These data provide a vantage point from which we may better assess the achievements of modern science. They are also a tribute to primitive man, who is none other than ourselves without the perspectives and prejudices of civilization.

These data should be relevant to scholars in such fields as linguistics, psychology, ecology, biological systematics, and many areas of anthropology.

The gradually expanding body of folk-biological descriptions will eventually allow the testing of hypotheses concerning the function and evolution of lexicon. For example, the structure of the biological lexicon of hunting and gathering groups may differ consistently from that of agriculturalists such as the Tenejapa Tzeltal, and that in turn from systems described for citizens of industrial countries. The maximal number of taxonomic levels in folk classification systems may be a function of certain evolutionary processes as has been suggested by Berlin (1972). Alternatively that number may be a function of the total number of taxa in the domain, which in turn may vary directly or inversely with the approach to civilization.

A survey conducted in 25 geographic subregions of Tenejapa demonstrates the high degree of lexical variation one may find within a rather limited area. The analysis of such variation has important implications for understanding linguistic change and the communicative function of language.

Exciting recent trends in linguistics involve attempts to include semantic analysis in linguistic theory and generally to extend the rigor applied to phonology and grammar to the analysis of meaning (cf. Katz and Fodor 1963; Friedrich 1969). Plant and ani-

---

*A *municipio* is a political subdivision of a Mexican state. This unit has been translated as 'county' or 'town', the latter in regions of concentrated settlement.

†In English "animal" may refer either to the kingdom Animalia, thus including in principle all actively motile living things, or it may refer more specifically to a group of furred, four-legged animals, a group roughly equivalent to the class Mammalia. In this dissertation the unmarked usage implies the former; the more restricted sense will be indicated by a qualifying statement.

mal terminology is a logical starting point for such studies in that an "etic grid" exists in biological systematics for defining the denotata of these terms (see Chapter 3, Section 9). Proof of the existence of semantic universals, both structural and substantive, can only follow the collection of systematic data such as are presented here. Candidates for structural universals include the logic of taxonomies (for formal treatments see Gregg 1954, 1962; Kay 1971) and the unique psychological status of generic taxa (Bulmer 1970; Berlin, Breedlove, and Raven 1973). Substantive universals comparable to the basic color foci (Berlin and Kay 1969) may include foci of categories such as "tree" and "bird" (Berlin 1970:14–15).

Since linguistics is a science of certain mental functions and capacities, what is relevant to linguistics is also relevant to psychology. A dictionary, in fact, is not so much a list of words as an inventory of concepts, of psychological structures. In the tradition of modern ethnography, I will organize these concepts as far as possible according to Tzeltal principles of classification and notions of relatedness. The organization of the data is thus a hypothesis about cognitive structure.

A basic philosophical issue underlying these queries is the well-known problem of psychological reality. While it is, of course, not possible to climb inside an informant's head, it is certainly possible to discuss criteria for choosing among alternative cognitive models used to account for observable facts, such as naming behavior and informants' abilities to identify and, occasionally, to misidentify tokens of their categories. The data presented here do limit the range of acceptable explanatory models. The folk-biological ranks proposed by Berlin, Breedlove, and Raven (1973), for example, will be critically analyzed in terms of my data, and certain modifications proposed.

Though the basic data is lexicographic, collected by an anthropologist and analyzed from a psychological perspective, biologists with special interest in ecology and systematics may also profit from this presentation.

Ecological studies often avoid consideration of the role of human beings in ecological systems, since human behavior is difficult to predict in terms of the models employed by biologists to describe such systems. A better understanding of the human role in natural systems should follow from a detailed analysis of the conscious, cultural plans that guide human behavior (cf. Miller, Galanter, and Pribram 1960; Geoghegan 1974). This monograph does not attempt to describe such plans but analyzes a portion of the knowledge utilized in organizing behavior and provides some incidental information about the utilization by Tenejapanecos of their knowledge of natural history. The human impact on natural systems is in part a function of the knowledge of such systems available to the actors on the local cultural stage.

The controversy among biosystematists concerning the logical status of a biological classification (Simpson 1961:54–57, 114–119), in particular the nature of the "reality" of biological taxa and the role of inductive as opposed to deductive principles in such classifications (Cain 1958, 1959), is clarified by comparison with the folk system described here.

No general survey of Tenejapan culture and society has been published. The anthropologists who have so far done research in Tenejapa have focused on more specific topics. However, I hope that, where breadth is lacking, the attempt at complete coverage of the particular topic may compensate. Though plants and animals are not the sole concern of the Tenejapaneco, they are of far greater importance to him than to the average American. The accuracy and detail of most Tenejapanecos' knowledge of his natural environment is ample testimony to this fact.

We are presented with a paradox. Tenejapanecos are agriculturalists almost solely dependent on plant life for their subsistence. They do very little hunting and keep few domestic animals other than chickens, turkeys, and dogs (which they do not eat). Nevertheless they exhibit roughly comparable detail and accuracy in their zoological knowledge as in their botanical knowledge. This raises the question of the relative role of utilitarian as opposed to intellectual motives for knowing things (cf. Levi-Strauss 1966:2–9).

Animal and plant names have connotative as well as denotative meanings. My data are far from complete in this area; however, the association of animals with personal names, clan names, and geographical designations indicates that diverse aspects of the Tenejapan way of life are related to their knowledge of animals. The roles played by animal species in folk tales—and they play some role in the majority of a sample of more than 70 tales collected by K. Branstetter and myself—provide clues to aspects of Tenejapan world view and cosmology. The accurate identification of the animals named in folklore is, of course, essential to an accurate interpretation of the meaning of the tales.

More than 50 magical and medicinal uses of animals are known to Tenejapanecos (cf. Chapter 4, Section 5). Turkeys, for instance, are sacrificed to avoid soul loss, a serious condition that may be precipitated by a fall on a trail. Turkey feathers scattered alongside the trail, encountered whenever one travels the back country, are mute testimony to this belief. Thus domestic animals provide more than protein. Dogs, though poorly fed, are generally well treated and enjoyed. Few households are without them. A folktale recounts how house cats were first created from a ball of corn dough by the mother of the house to protect the family's corn stores from the ravages of the house rat, like the cat a foreign introduction. Owls and certain other animals foretell impending death, while ants are models of industry, much as they are for us. In short, in describing the zoological nomenclature and lore of Tenejapa the Indian community comes alive; a host of questions come to mind sufficient to occupy students of Tenejapan culture for years to come.

# ACKNOWLEDGMENTS

The essentially accidental events of personal history that affect the topics and sites of one's research are seldom stressed. My interest in folk zoology is due in large part to my birdwatching avocation. I found that I could put this interest to good use by comparing my skills as a birdwatcher with the powers of observation of the Tzeltal Indians. However, I went to Chiapas, México, to pursue this research only after encountering unexpected difficulties with my original research plan on another continent. The outcome was more than satisfactory. My "double motivation," professional and avocational, more than made up for my initial lack of familiarity with Meso-American ethnography.

I owe a double debt of gratitude to Brent Berlin. First, he introduced me to the field of folk science, and my work developed through his constant encouragement and criticism. Our disagreements have always been creative. Second he and his family have been friends in need, assisting unstintingly in the most difficult aspects of field work.

Other anthropological colleagues at the University of California, Berkeley, in particular those associated with the Language-Behavior Research Laboratory, provided a stimulating environment during the preparation of this work. I benefited especially from the comments of William Geoghegan, Paul Kay, and Robert Randall. When I first arrived in the field, Katherine Branstetter and Brian Stross were of considerable assistance, introducing me to the land and people of Tenejapa, and the "Field Dictionary of Tenejapa Tzeltal" compiled by Branstetter from data collected by Berlin and T. Kaufman was invaluable. I also benefited from the library facilities at Na Balom, San Cristòbal, Chiapas, and from conversations with Miguel Alvarez del Toro, Departmento de Zoología, Instituto de Historia Natural, Tuxtla Gutiérrez, Chiapas. John Atkins and Terence Hays, University of Washington, contributed much in the way of intellectual stimulation.

I am indebted to the following biologists for contributing their time and expertise to identifying the organisms collected: at the Museum of Vertebrate Zoology, University of California, Berkeley, James Patton (mammals) and James Lynch and James Stewart (herptiles); in the Division of Entomology, University of California, Berkeley, E. I. Schlinger (Coleoptera: Zopheridae; Diptera; Hymenoptera: Formicidae), H. V. Daly (Hymenoptera: Apoidea), J. T. Doyen (Hemiptera; Coleoptera), R. E. Dietz (Lepidoptera), S. Szerlip (Hemiptera: Reduviidae), and M. Bentzien (Araneida and miscellaneous arthropods). Peter Rauch of that division provided invaluable encouragement and assistance in providing equipment, preparing specimens, and organizing the data. R. M. Bohart, Department of Entomology, University of California, Davis, identified most of the wasps (Hymenoptera: Trigonalidae, Tiphiidae, Eumenidae, Vespidae, and Sphecidae). J. Pinto, Department of Entomology, University of California, Riverside, identified the Meloidae (Coleoptera), George Buxton, director, and Allan Hardy, entomologist, Laboratory Services, Division of Plant Industry, California Department of Foods and Agriculture, Sacramento, California, assisted with the Orthoptera. Allyn Smith (Mollusca) and D. D. Chivers (miscellaneous invertebrates), Department of Invertebrate Zoology, California Academy of Sciences, San Francisco, California, also provided identifications. Joseph F. Copp, Scripps Institute of Oceanography, LaJolla, California, made his personal collection of herpetological specimens available to me and to two of my informants. He also took an intense personal interest in the accuracy of all herpetological details. Dennis Breedlove, California Academy of Sciences, provided valuable assistance in the field. His unbounded energy was exemplary. Laurence Binford, Curator of Ornithology, California Academy of Sciences, and James Patton read portions of the manuscript and offered many helpful suggestions.

The map of the Chiapas highlands and the illustrations of traps and of anatomical terminology were drawn by Linda Stoner, Seattle, Washington. Illustrations of birds are reproduced from *Birds of Mexico: A Guide for Field Identification* by Emmet Reid Blake (1953). Blake's illustrations were drawn by Douglas E. Tibbitts. Permission to reproduce was granted by The University of Chicago Press. Game birds and mammals are illustrated in part by the work of Charles Schwartz, whose drawings appeared originally in A. Starker Leopold, *Wildlife of Mexico: The Game Birds and Mammals* (1959). Permission to reproduce was granted by The Regents of the University of California for the University of California Press. Other mammal illustrations are reproduced by permission of The Ronald Press Company, New York, from E. Raymond Hall and Keith R. Kelson, *The Mammals of North America* (1959). Most photos of reptiles and amphibians were generously loaned by the Museum of Natural History, University of Kansas; others were provided by Dennis E. Breedlove, Joseph F. Copp, and John H. Tashjian. The photographs of invertebrate specimens were obtained with the aid of Gerald Eck, Department of Anthropology, and Herman Real, Division of Entomology, University of California, Berkeley. Finally, *hʔaluš mentes ton* (Alonso Mendez Ton), *hciak mentes caʔpat* (Santiago Mendez Zapata), and *hšoš kusman c'uhkin* (José Guzman Gomez) provided a number of fine color pencil sketches, which I am pleased to be able to publish here. Alonso Mendez's drawings were kindly made available by Brent Berlin.

For financial assistance I would like to thank the National Institute of Mental Health, which generously supported the research through a Combination Fellowship and Research Grant (No. 1-F01-MH-49, 601-01). The Latin American Studies Center, University of California, Berkeley, offered timely assistance in the preparation of the dissertation version of the manuscript. The Graduate School of the University of Washington made possible the analysis of textual materials through a summer salary award, 1973.

The real authors of the dictionary assembled here are the Tenejapanecos, whose words I have assembled. *hciak mentes caʔpat* (SMZ) and *hšoš kusman c'uhkin* (JGG) were my constant companions, and the work would have been impossible without their energy and understanding. Thanks are also due to the then president of Tenejapa, *hʔaluš mentes ton*, who welcomed me and facilitated my work from the beginning.

And my wife Nancy was there through it all, keeping me alive.

# CONVENTIONS AND ABBREVIATIONS

All Tzeltal words are printed in bold face sans serif italics (e.g., **tenehapa**). Latin genus and species names are italicized, though names of higher taxa are not (e.g., Colubridae: *Boa constrictor*). If a Tzeltal expression is analyzed, the analysis is separated by brackets (e.g., **wamal čitam** ['bush' + 'pig']). Single quotes are used extensively to gloss Tzeltal words or phrases. These glosses are of two types, a true gloss or approximate English equivalent (e.g., **ʔaha čab** 'honeybee'), or a rough literal "translation" (e.g., **ʔaha čab** 'honey master' [< **ʔahaw** 'master' + **čab** 'honey']). It should be apparent from the context which is intended.

Abbreviations used are as follows:

| | |
|---|---|
| ag | agentive affix |
| cm | centimeters |
| dd | derivational desinence |
| gn | "gender" prefix, **h-** (male) and **š-** (female). It is not clear if such prefixes have any such semantic content in the context of animal and plant names. |
| iv | intransitive verb stem |
| km | kilometer |
| **kps** | **kol pahaluk sok** 'almost the same as', a Tzeltal expression used to indicate that an organism is most nearly that of the name specified. |
| KU No. | Museum of Natural History, University of Kansas, slide catalogue number |
| lit | "literally" |
| m | meter |
| mm | millimeter |
| ON | onomatopoetic constituent |
| OSp | Old Spanish (ca. sixteenth century) |
| pl | plural |
| pp | possessive prefix |
| redup | reduplication |
| rs | relational suffix |
| s | singular |
| sq km | square kilometer |
| sp. | an unspecified species of the genus |
| spp. | more than one unspecified species |
| sq | square |
| ssp. | an unspecified subspecies of the species |
| tv | transitive verb stem |
| UN | unanalýzable constituent |
| < | derived from |
| ⊂ | included in |
| + | morphemic juncture |

Table 0.1 indicates the orthographic conventions used for all Tzeltal words (indicated by boldface sans serif italics) throughout the text.

**Table 0.1**
TENEJAPA TZELTAL SEGMENTAL PHONEMES[a]

| | Consonants | | | | |
|---|---|---|---|---|---|
| | *Bilabial* | *Alveolar* | *Palatal* | *Velar* | *Glottal* |
| Simple stops | *p* | *t* | | *k* | *ʔ* |
| Glottalized stops, unvoiced | *p′* | *t′* | | *k′* | |
| Glottalized stop, voiced | *b* | | | | |
| Simple affricatives | | *c* | *č* | | |
| Glottalized affricatives | | *c′* | *č′* | | |
| Fricatives | | *s* | *š* | | |
| Nasals | *m* | | *n* | | |
| Lateral | | *l* | | | |
| Flap | | *r* | | | |
| Glides | *w*[b] | | *y* | | |

| | Vowels | | |
|---|---|---|---|
| | *Front* | *Central* | *Back* |
| High | *i* | | *u* |
| Mid | *e* | | *o* |
| Low | | *a* | |

[a]From Berlin 1962a:17.

[b]In the Tzotzil words cited, the **w** is more labio-dental and is written **v**. The simple voiced stops, /b/, /d/, and /g/, of Spanish, are sometimes used by bilingual Tzeltal informants. Their occurrence is noted in the text.

# FOLK SYSTEMATIC LIST
# OF THE FAUNA*

| | | | |
|---|---|---|---|
| UNIQUE BEGINNER: *čanbalam₁* 'animal' | ANIMALIA | 'animal' | p. 134 |
| LIFE FORM: *mut₁* | AVES | 'bird' | p. 135 |
| COVERT COMPLEX: waterbird | Podicipedidae<br>Ardeidae<br>Anatidae<br>Rallidae<br>Charadriidae<br>Scolopacidae<br>Laridae<br>(Alcedinidae) | | p. 136 |
| *peč'* | Anatidae:part | 'domestic duck' | p. 136 |
| *peč'ul ha?* | Podicipedidae<br>Anatidae:part<br>Rallidae:part<br>(Alcedinidae) | 'wild duck/grebe' | p. 137 |
| *c'u? lukum* | Charadriidae<br>Scolopacidae | 'shorebird' | p. 138 |
| *me? c'ahel* | Rallidae:part | 'rail' | p. 139 |
| *hti? čay* | Ardeidae<br>(Laridae) | 'heron/egret' | p. 139 |
| COVERT COMPLEX: vulture | Cathartidae | | p. 140 |
| *?usel* | *Sarcoramphus papa* | 'King Vulture' | p. 140 |
| *ca?los* | *Coragyps atratus* | 'Black Vulture' | p. 141 |
| *šulem* | *Cathartes aura* | 'Turkey Vulture' | p. 142 |

*Scientific taxa cited in parenthesis are included in the extended range of the corresponding Tzeltal taxon.

COVERT COMPLEX: bird of prey

| | | | |
|---|---|---|---|
| | Accipitridae | | p. 142 |
| | Falconidae | | |
| **kok mut** | *Harpia harpyja* | 'eagle' | p. 142 |
| **likawal** | Accipitridae:part | 'hawk' | p. 143 |
| [R] **likawal** | Accipitridae:part | | p. 143 |
| **šik likawal** | *Buteo magnirostris* | 'Roadside Hawk' | p. 144 |
| | *B. brachyura* | 'Short-tailed Hawk' | |
| **yan te?tikil likawal** | *Accipiter chionogaster* | 'White-breasted Hawk' | p. 144 |
| **liklik** | *Falco sparverius* | 'kestrel' | p. 145 |
| **me? k'ulub** | *Elanus leucurus* | 'White-tailed Kite' | p. 145 |
| **tešereš ne** | *Elanoides forficatus* | 'Swallow-tailed Kite' | p. 145 |

COVERT COMPLEX: turkey

| | | | |
|---|---|---|---|
| | Cracidae | | p. 146 |
| | Meleagrididae | | |
| **tuluk'** | *Meleagris gallopavo* | 'turkey' | p. 146 |
| **te?tikil tuluk'** | *Penelope purpurascens* | 'guan' | p. 148 |
| **?is mut** | *Crax rubra* | 'curassow' | p. 148 |
| **č'ekek** | *Penelopina nigra* | 'penelopina' | p. 149 |
| **hohkot** | *Ortalis vetula* | 'chachalaca' | p. 149 |
| **peya?** | *Psilorhinus morio* | 'Brown Jay' | p. 149 |
| **šulub mut** | *Calocitta formosa* | 'Magpie Jay' | p. 150 |
| **heš** | Corvidae:part | 'small jay' | p. 150 |
| **k'an heš** | *Cyanocorax yncas* | 'Green Jay' | p. 150 |
| **yaš heš** | *Cyanocitta stelleri* | 'Steller's Jay' | p. 150 |
| | *(Aphelocoma unicolor)* | | |
| **kastiyána heš** | *Cyanolyca pumilo* | 'Black-throated Jay' | p. 151 |
| **sak hol heš** | *C. cucullatus* | 'Azure-hooded Jay' | p. 151 |
| **mut$_2$** | *Gallus gallus* | 'Chicken' | p. 151 |
| **merikáno mut** | *G. gallus*:part | | p. 152 |
| **č'et** | *G. gallus*:part | | p. 152 |
| [R] **mut** | *G. gallus*:part | | p. 152 |

| | | | |
|---|---|---|---|
| COVERT COMPLEX: quail | Tinamidae<br>Phasianidae:part | | p. 152 |
| *šʔub* | Phasianidae:part | 'quail' | p. 152 |
| *č'in šʔub* | *Colinus virginianus* | 'bobwhite' | p. 153 |
| *muk'ul šʔub* | *Dactylortyx thoracicus* | 'Singing Quail' | p. 153 |
| *čiktawilon* | *Crypturellus cinnamomeus* | 'tinamou' | p. 153 |
| *šʔuman* | *Geococcyx velox* | 'roadrunner' | p. 154 |
| *k'ank'an mut* | *Piaya cayana* | 'Squirrel Cuckoo' | p. 155 |
| COVERT COMPLEX: dove | Columbidae | | p. 155 |
| *palomaš* | *Columba livia* | 'domestic pigeon' | p. 155 |
| *šč'a bikil* | *C. fasciata* | 'Band-tailed Pigeon' | p. 155 |
| *kuč kuutik wo* | *C. flavirostris* | 'Red-billed Pigeon' | p. 156 |
| *scumut* | Columbidae:part | 'dove' | p. 156 |
| *kašlan scumut* | *Zenaida asiatica* | 'White-winged Dove' | p. 156 |
| *yalem scumut* | *Z. macroura* | 'Mourning Dove' | p. 157 |
| *bac'il scumut* | *Leptotila verreauxi* | 'White-tipped Dove' | p. 157 |
| *špurowok* | *Scardafella* sp.<br>*Columbina* spp. | 'dovelet' | p. 157 |
| *kašlan špurowok* | *Scardafella inca* | 'Inca Dove' | p. 157 |
| *cahal špurowok* | *Columbina talpacoti* | 'Ruddy Ground Dove' | p. 157 |
| COVERT COMPLEX: owl | Strigiformes | | p. 158 |
| *kurunkuc* | *Otus* spp. | 'screech owl' | p. 159 |
| *toytoy* | *Glaucidium* spp.<br>*Aegolius* sp. | 'pygmy owl/<br>saw-whet owl' | p. 159 |
| *k'alel toytoy* | *Glaucidium brasilianum* | 'Ferruginous Pygmy Owl' | p. 159 |
| *ʔahk'ubal toytoy* | *Glaucidium gnoma*<br>*Aegolius ridgwayi* | 'Northern Pygmy Owl'<br>'Unspotted Saw-whet Owl' | p. 159 |
| *šoč'* | *Tyto alba* | 'Barn Owl' | p. 160 |
| *škuh* | *Ciccaba virgata* | 'Mottled Owl' | p. 160 |
| *k'ahk'al waš* | *Strix fulvescens* | 'Fulvous Owl' | p. 160 |
| *tuhkulum pukuh* | *Bubo virginianus* | 'Great Horned Owl' | p. 161 |
| COVERT COMPLEX: nightjar | Caprimulgidae:part | | p. 161 |
| *purkuwič'* | *Caprimulgus vociferus* | 'whip-poor-will' | p. 161 |
| *puʔkuy* | *Nyctidromus albicollis* | 'Pauraque' | p. 161 |
| *pum cis* | *Chordeiles* spp. | 'nighthawk' | p. 162 |

COVERT COMPLEX: swift–swallow

| | | | |
|---|---|---|---|
| | Apodidae | | p. 162 |
| | Hirundinidae | | |
| ʔulič | Hirundinidae | 'swallow' | p. 162 |
| sik' | Apodidae | 'swift' | p. 163 |
| muk'ul sik' | *Streptoprocne zonaris* | 'White-collared Swift' | p. 163 |
| č'in sik' | *Cypseloides* spp. | 'small swift' | p. 163 |
| | *Chaetura* sp. | | |
| | *Aeronautes* sp. | | |
| c'unun | Trochilidae | 'hummingbird' | p. 164 |
| c'ibal sit c'unun | *Hylocharis leucotis* | 'White-eared Hummingbird' | p. 164 |
| kašlan c'unun | *Colibri thalassinus* | 'Green Violet-Ear' | p. 164 |
| tešereš ne c'unun | *Doricha enicura* | 'Slender Sheartail' | p. 165 |
| ʔihk'al c'unun | *Lampornis amethystinus* | 'Amethyst-throated Hummingbird' | p. 165 |
| sakil c'unun | *Amazilia cyanocephala* | 'Azure-crowned Hummingbird' | p. 165 |

COVERT COMPLEX: parrot

| | | | |
|---|---|---|---|
| | Psittacidae | | p. 166 |
| puyuč' | Psittacidae:part | | p. 167 |
| periko | Psittacidae:part | 'large parrot' | p. 168 |
| lorotíro | Psittacidae:part | 'parakeet' | p. 168 |
| moʔ | *Ara* spp. | 'macaw' | p. 168 |
| pan | Ramphastidae | 'toucan' | p. 169 |

COVERT COMPLEX: trogon–motmot

| | | | |
|---|---|---|---|
| | Trogonidae | | p. 169 |
| | Momotidae | | |
| k'uk' | *Trogon* spp. | 'trogon' | p. 169 |
| šk'orin mut | *Aspatha gularis* | 'Blue-throated Motmot' | p. 170 |
| kuckuc | *Momotus momota* | 'Blue-crowned Motmot' | p. 170 |

COVERT COMPLEX: woodpecker

| | | | |
|---|---|---|---|
| | Picidae | | p. 170 |
| tukut | *Colaptes auratus* | 'flicker' | p. 171 |
| tiʔ | *Centurus aurifrons* | 'Golden-fronted Woodpecker' | p. 171 |
| k'oročoč | *Melanerpes formicivorus* | 'Acorn Woodpecker' | p. 171 |
| tuncerek' | *Dryocopus lineatus* | 'Lineated Woodpecker' | p. 172 |
| c'ihtil | Picidae:part | 'small woodpecker' | p. 172 |
| ʔihk'al c'ihtil | *Dendrocopos villosus* | 'Hairy Woodpecker' | p. 172 |
| c'irin c'ihtil | *D. scalaris* | 'Ladder-backed Woodpecker' | p. 172 |
| k'anal c'ihtil | *Piculus rubiginosus* | 'Golden-olive Woodpecker' | p. 172 |
| c'irin mut | *Certhia familiaris* | 'Brown Creeper' | p. 172 |
| c'uhkin mut | Dendrocolaptidae | 'woodcreeper' | p. 173 |

| | | | |
|---|---|---|---|
| COVERT COMPLEX: flycatcher | Tyrannidae<br>(Cotingidae:part) | | p. 174 |
| | Tyrannidae:part | | p. 174 |
| *wirin* | | | |
| *bac'il wirin* | *Myiarchus tuberculifer*<br>*Contopus pertinax* | 'Dusky-capped Flycatcher'<br>'Greater Pewee' | p. 175 |
| *č'in wirin* | *Contopus*:part | 'wood pewee' | p. 175 |
| *kašlan wirin* | *Tyrannus melancholicus* | 'Tropical Kingbird' | p. 175 |
| *ʔihk'al wirin* | *Sayornis nigricans* | 'Black phoebe' | p. 175 |
| *cahal wirin* | *Pyrocephalus rubinus* | 'Vermilion Flycatcher' | p. 175 |
| *p'itp'it* | *Empidonax* spp. | | p. 176 |
| *pahal mac'* | *Myiozetetes similis* | 'Social Flycatcher' | p. 177 |
| *cokoy* | *Campylorhynchus zonatus* | 'Band-backed Wren' | p. 177 |
| | | | |
| COVERT COMPLEX: wren | Troglodytidae:part | | p. 178 |
| *č'etet waš* | *Thryothorus* spp.<br>*Hemicorhina* spp. | 'wood wren' | p. 178 |
| *či ʔči ʔ bulbul* | *Troglodytes* spp. | 'house wren' | p. 178 |
| | | | |
| COVERT COMPLEX: mockingbird | Mimidae: part | | p. 179 |
| *čulin* | *Melanotis hypoleucus* | 'Blue-and-white Mockingbird' | p. 179 |
| *hti ʔ cuhkum* | *Mimus gilvus*<br>(*Coccyzus americanus*) | 'Tropical Mockingbird' | p. 179 |
| | | | |
| COVERT COMPLEX: thrush | Turdidae:part<br>Parulidae:part | | p. 179 |
| *toht* | *Turdus* spp. | 'robin' | p. 179 |
| *č'iš toht* | *Turdus rufitorques* | 'Rufous-collared Robin' | p. 180 |
| *k'an toht* | *T. grayi* | 'Clay-colored Robin' | p. 181 |
| *ʔihk'al toht* | *T. infuscatus* | 'Black Robin' | p. 181 |
| *yašal toht* | *T. plebejus* | 'Mountain Robin' | p. 181 |
| *cahal toht* | *T. migratorius* | 'American Robin' | p. 181 |
| *sian* | *Myadestes obscurus* | 'solitaire' | p. 182 |
| *šluš* | *Catharus frantzii*<br>*C. aurantiirostris* | 'nightingale thrush' | p. 182 |
| *šmayil* | *Seiurus* spp. | 'waterthrush' | p. 182 |
| *yaš mut* | *Sialia sialis* | 'bluebird' | p. 183 |
| *t'ok hol mut* | *Ptilogonys cinereus* | 'Gray Silky-Flycatcher' | p. 183 |
| *yihkac te ʔ* | *Cyclarhis gujanensis* | 'peppershrike' | p. 183 |

| | | | |
|---|---|---|---|
| COVERT COMPLEX: sparrow | Fringillidae:part<br>Ploceidae | | p. 190 |
| *tak'in sit mut* | *Junco phaeonotus* | `junco` | p. 190 |
| *čončiw* | | `sparrow` | p. 190 |
| *bac'il čončiw* | *Zonotrichia capensis* | `Rufous-collared Sparrow` | p. 190 |
| *meba čončiw* | *Melospiza lincolnii* | `Lincoln's Sparrow` | p. 190 |
| *me? čončiw* | *Aimophila rufescens* | `Rusty Sparrow` | p. 190 |
| *kašlan čončiw* | *Passer domesticus* | `House sparrow` | p. 190 |
| *solsol* | *Melozone biarcuatum* | `White-faced Ground Sparrow` | p. 191 |
| *k'usin* | *Atlapetes albinucha* | `White-naped Brush Finch` | p. 191 |
| *k'oweš* | *Pipilo erythrophthalmus* | `towhee` | p. 191 |
| *šep ?e mut* | *Loxia curvirostra* | `crossbill` | p. 192 |
| *wol ni? mut* | *Pheucticus* spp. | `grosbeak` | p. 192 |
| *pay sit mut* | *Chlorospingus ophthalmicus* | `bush tanager` | p. 192 |
| *kaptan mut* | *Piranga flava* | `Hepatic Tanager` | p. 193 |
| *čiboriáno* | *Sturnella magna* | `meadowlark` | p. 193 |
| *čohčowit* | *Saltator coerulescens* | `Grayish Saltator` | p. 193 |
| *čačalak' mut* | *S. atriceps* | `Black-headed Saltator` | p. 193 |
| COVERT COMPLEX: oriole | *Icterus* spp. | | p. 194 |
| *tu č'ič'* | Icterus:part | | p. 194 |
| *bac'il tu č'ič'* | *Icterus chrysater* | `Yellow-backed Oriole` | p. 194 |
| *meba tu č'ič'* | *I. galbula*<br>*I. sclateri*<br>(*I. spurius*) | `Northern Oriole`<br>`Streaked-backed Oriole` | p. 195 |
| *burúho mut* | *I. mesomelas*<br>(*I. wagleri*) | `Yellow-tailed Oriole` | p. 195 |
| *šč'e?* | *Dumetella carolinensis* | `catbird` | p. 195 |
| COVERT COMPLEX: black bird | Cuculidae:part<br>Corvidae:part<br>Icteridae:part | | p. 196 |
| *hti? sip* | *Crotophaga sulcirostris* | `ani` | p. 196 |
| *?ot?ot* | *Amblycercus holosericeus* | `Yellow-billed Cacique` | p. 196 |
| *wančil* | *Dives dives* | `Melodious Blackbird` | p. 196 |
| *kulkulína* | *Agelaius phoeniceus* | `Red-winged Blackbird` | p. 197 |
| *sanáte* | *Molothrus aeneus* | `cowbird` | p. 197 |
| *hoh mut* | *Cassidix mexicana* | `grackle` | p. 197 |
| *hoh* | *Corvus corax* | `raven` | p. 197 |
| *bak hol mut* | *Zarhynchus wagleri* | `oropendola` | p. 197 |

| | | | |
|---|---|---|---|
| NAMED COMPLEX: *č'o* `rat` | Soricidae<br>Cricetidae<br>Muridae | | p. 207 |
| ya?al be | Soricidae | `shrew` | p. 208 |
| sin | *Reithrodontomys* spp. | `harvest mouse` | p. 209 |
| šlumil č'o | *Mus musculus* | `house mouse` | p. 209 |
| COVERT GENERIC: `white-footed mouse` | *Peromyscus* spp. | `white-footed mouse` | p. 210 |
|    yašal č'o | | | |
|    sak ?eal č'o | | | |
|    k'alel č'o | | | |
| čitam č'o | *Sigmodon hispidus* | `cotton rat` | p. 212 |
| sabin č'o | *Oryzomys palustris* | `rice rat` | p. 212 |
| k'iwoč č'o | *Heteromys desmarestianus* | `pocket mouse` | p. 212 |
| moin te? č'o | *Nyctomys sumichrasti* | `vesper rat` | p. 212 |
| hse? te? | *Tylomys bullaris*<br>*Neotoma mexicana* | `climbing rat`<br>`wood rat` | p. 213 |
| karánsa | *Rattus rattus* | `black rat` | p. 214 |
| č'iš ?uhčum | *Coendu mexicana* | `porcupine` | p. 214 |
| halaw | *Cuniculus paca*<br>(*Dasyprocta* spp.) | `paca` | p. 215 |

| | | | |
|---|---|---|---|
| COVERT COMPLEX: dog | Canidae:part | | p. 215 |
| | Mustelidae:part | | |
| ʔok'il₁ | Canis latrans | 'coyote' | p. 215 |
| c'iʔ | C. familiaris | 'domestic dog' | p. 215 |
| bac'il c'iʔ | C. familiaris:part | | p. 216 |
| kašlan c'iʔ | C. familiaris:part | | p. 216 |
| polisia c'iʔ | C. familiaris:part | | p. 217 |
| haʔal c'iʔ | Lutra annectens | 'river otter' | p. 218 |
| waš | Urocyon cinereoargenteus | 'gray fox' | p. 218 |
| meʔel | Procyon lotor | 'raccoon' | p. 219 |
| kohtom | Nasua narica | 'coati' | p. 219 |
| ʔuyoh | Potos flavus | 'kinkajou' | p. 219 |
| sabin | Mustela frenata | 'weasel' | p. 220 |
| sak hol | Eira barbara | 'tayra' | p. 220 |
| c'uhc'uneh čab | Tamandua tetradactyla | 'tamandua' | p. 221 |
| pay | Mephitinae | 'skunk' | p. 221 |
| č'in pay | Spilogale angustifrons | 'spotted skunk' | p. 221 |
| muk'ul pay | Mephitis macroura | 'hooded skunk' | p. 221 |
| lem pat pay | Conepatus mesoleucus | 'hog-nosed skunk' | p. 222 |
| ʔik' sab | Felis yagouaroundi | 'jaguarundi' | p. 222 |
| COVERT COMPLEX: cat | Felis:part | | p. 222 |
| balam | Felis onca | 'jaguar' | p. 222 |
| čoh | F. concolor | 'cougar' | p. 223 |
| cahal čoh | F. pardalis | 'ocelot' | p. 223 |
| cis balam | F. wiedii | 'margay' | p. 224 |
| šawin | F. cattus | 'domestic cat' | p. 224 |
| cemen | Tapirus bairdii | 'tapir' | p. 224 |

COVERT COMPLEX: pig

| | | | |
|---|---|---|---|
| | Suiformes | | p. 225 |
| *čitam* | *Sus scrofa* | `domestic pig` | p. 225 |
| *bac'il čitam* | *S. scrofa*:part | | p. 225 |
| *merikáno čitam* | *S. scrofa*:part | | p. 226 |
| *škoen čitam* | *S. scrofa*:part | | p. 226 |
| *wamal čitam* | Tayassuidae | `peccary` | p. 226 |
| *niwak wamal čitam* | Tayassuidae:part | `adult peccary` | p. 226 |
| *bahk'al wamal čitam* | Tayassuidae:part | `juvenile peccary` | p. 226 |

COVERT COMPLEX: sheep

| | | | |
|---|---|---|---|
| | Cervidae<br>Bovidae:part | | p. 227 |
| *tunim čih* | *Ovis aries* | `domestic sheep` | p. 228 |
| *teʔtikil čih* | Cervidae | `deer` | p. 228 |
| *yašal teʔtikil čih* | *Odocoileus virginianus* | `white-tailed deer` | p. 228 |
| *cahal teʔtikil čih* | *Mazama americana* | `brocket` | p. 228 |
| *tencun* | *Capra hircus* | `domestic goat` | p. 229 |
| *wakaš* | *Bos taurus* | `domestic cattle` | p. 229 |
| *bac'il wakaš* | *Bos taurus*:part | | p. 229 |
| *merikáno wakaš* | *Bos taurus*:part | `zebu` | p. 230 |

COVERT COMPLEX: horse

| | | | |
|---|---|---|---|
| | Equidae | | p. 230 |
| *búro* | *Equus asinus* | `domestic donkey` | p. 230 |
| *kawáyu* | *E. caballus*<br>*E. caballus* X *E. asinus* | `horse`<br>`mule` | p. 230 |
| COVERT SPECIFIC: | *E. caballus* X *E. asinus* | `mule` | p. 230 |
| COVERT SPECIFIC: | *E. caballus* | `horse` | p. 231 |

(End of Life Form *čanbalam₂*)

| | | | |
|---|---|---|---|
| *mayil tiʔbal* | *Dasypus novemcinctus* | `armadillo` | p. 232 |
| *šʔahk'* | Testudinata | `turtle` | p. 232 |
| *šʔain* | Crocodilia | `crocodile` | p. 232 |

| | | | |
|---|---|---|---|
| COVERT COMPLEX: lizard | Lacertilia, Caudata | | p. 232 |
| š²iwána | *Iguana iguana* *Ctenosaura* spp. | 'iguana' | p. 234 |
| ²ečeh | *Basiliscus vittatus* | 'basilisk lizard' | p. 234 |
| k'intun | *Anolis* spp. | 'anole' | p. 235 |
| ²ohkoc | *Sceloperus* spp. | 'spiny lizard' | p. 235 |
| ²ohkoc čan | *Gerrhonotus liocephalus* | 'alligator lizard' | p. 236 |
| č'iš čikin | *Abronia lythrochila* | | p. 236 |
| k'alel čan | *Barisia moreletii* | | p. 236 |
| ²uhc'²uhc' ni² | *Leiolopisma incertum* | 'skink' | p. 237 |
| c'uhkuton | *Coleonyx elegans* *Bolitoglossa* spp. | 'gecko' 'salamander' | p. 237 |
| NAMED COMPLEX: čan₁ 'snake' | Ophidia | | p. 238 |
| masakwáto | *Boa constrictor* | | p. 238 |
| ²ahaw čan | *Crotalus durissus* *Pituophis lineaticollis* | 'rattlesnake' 'gopher snake' | p. 239 |
| kantil | *Agkistrodon bilineatus* | 'moccasin' | p. 240 |
| ²áwa kantil | *Drymarchon corais* | 'indigo snake' | p. 240 |
| c'in te² čan | *Bothrops godmani* | | p. 240 |
| ²ik'os čan | *B. nummifer* | | p. 240 |
| kantéla čan | *Micrurus* spp. | 'coral snake' | p. 241 |
| me² c'isim | *Lampropeltis triangulum* | 'king snake' | p. 241 |
| k'ančo | *Drymobius margaritiferus* | 'speckled racer' | p. 242 |
| ha²al čan | *Thamnophis* spp. | 'garter snake' | p. 242 |
| me² čenek' | *Ninia sebae* | | p. 242 |
| pacan sihk' | *N. diademata* | | p. 243 |
| me² ²išim | *Rhadinaea hempsteadae* | | p. 243 |
| me² k'apal | *Coniophanes imperialis* | | p. 243 |
| mokoč čan | *Adelphicos veraepacis* | | p. 243 |
| c'ibal čan | *C. schmidti* | | p. 244 |
| p'ahsum čan | *Tropidodipsas fischeri* | | p. 244 |
| šč'oš čan | *Oxybelis aeneus* | 'vine snake' | p. 244 |
| yaš ²itah čan | *O. fulgidus* *Leptophis* spp. | 'green vine snake' | p. 244 |
| p'ehel nuhkul čan | *Leptodeira septentrionalis* | 'cat-eyed snake' | p. 245 |
| čihil čan | *Spilotes pullatus* | | p. 245 |
| lukum čan | *Leptotyphlops phenops* | | p. 245 |

| | | | |
|---|---|---|---|
| NAMED COMPLEX: *čanul haʔ₁* water bug | Odonata (larvae)<br>Hemiptera:part<br>Corydalidae (larvae)<br>Coleoptera:part<br>Culicidae (pupae) | | p. 254 |
| *bac'ul haʔ* | Zygoptera (larvae) | 'damselfly larvae' | p. 254 |
| *šk'ohowil čan* | Anisoptera (larvae) | 'dragonfly larvae' | p. 254 |
| *špálu haʔ* | Corydalidae:part | 'hellgrammite' | p. 254 |
| *bosbos čan* | Culicidae (pupae) | 'mosquito pupa' | p. 254 |
| *šmeʔ šmut* | Belostomatidae | 'giant water bug' | p. 254 |
| *hawhaw čan* | Notonectidae<br>Corixidae | 'backswimmer'<br>'water boatman' | p. 254 |
| *mayil čan₁* | Gyrinidae | 'whirligig beetle' | p. 255 |
| *pošil nušel* | Veliidae<br>Gerridae | 'ripple bug'<br>'water strider' | p. 255 |

HYPOTHETICAL LIST: *čanul haʔ₁*                                                    p. 255

| | | | |
|---|---|---|---|
| COVERT COMPLEX: snail | MOLLUSCA:part | | p. 256 |
| *puy* | Thiaridae<br>Cyclophoridae | | p. 256 |
| *bac'il puy* | | | p. 256 |
| *šyaš puy* | | | p. 256 |
| *čikin puy* | | | p. 256 |
| *k'oʔ* | Helminthoglyptidae<br>Planorbidae | | p. 257 |
| *muk'ul k'oʔ* | *Lysinoe ghiesbreghti* | | p. 257 |
| *č'in k'oʔ* | *Taphius* cf *T. subpronus* | | p. 257 |
| *k'ohčin teʔ* | *Euglandina* spp. | | p. 257 |
| *yat naab* | Physidae | | p. 257 |
| *bak čikin* | Unionidae | | p. 257 |
| *nap'ak* | *Deroceras laeve* | 'slug' | p. 257 |

| COVERT COMPLEX: worm | PLATYHELMINTHES | | p. 258 |
|---|---|---|---|
| | ASCHELMINTHES | | |
| | ANNELIDA | | |
| *lukum* | | | p. 258 |
| [R] *lukum* | OLIGOCHAETA:part | 'earthworm' | p. 258 |
| *ha?al lukum* | OLIGOCHAETA:part | 'giant earthworm' | p. 258 |
| *k'ahk'et lukum* | ? | | p. 258 |
| *me? lukum* | CESTODA | 'tapeworm' | p. 258 |
| *slukumil č'uht* | *Ascaris* | 'round worm' | p. 258 |
| *č'uhč'ul lukum* | *Oxyuris* | 'pinworm' | p. 258 |
| *?ohcel* | HIRUDINEA | 'leech' | p. 258 |
| *cocil holol čan* | Gordioidea | 'horse-hair worm' | p. 258 |
| COVERT COMPLEX: ant | Formicidae | | p. 259 |
| | (Isoptera) | | |
| *šanič* | | | p. 259 |
| *bac'il šanič* | *Solenopsis* spp. | 'fire ant' | p. 260 |
| *meba šanič* | *Aphaenogaster* sp. | | p. 260 |
| *cihil šanič* | *Pseudomyrma* spp. | | p. 260 |
| | unidentified sp. | | |
| | *Tapinoma* sp. | | |
| *c'isim* | *Atta* spp. | 'leaf-cutting ant' | p. 262 |
| *bac'il c'isim* | *Atta*:part | | p. 262 |
| *meba c'isim* | *Atta*:part | | p. 262 |
| *yalem c'isim* | *Atta*:part | 'queen ant' | p. 262 |
| *k'ork'owe* | *Camponotus* spp. | 'carpenter ant' | p. 262 |
| *bah te?* | *Eciton*:part | 'army ant' | p. 262 |
| *muk'ul bah te?* | *Eciton*:part | | p. 262 |
| *meba bah te?* | *Eciton*:part | | p. 262 |
| *čikitoroš* | *Eciton*:part | 'army ant' | p. 263 |
| *ses* | *Pheidole* spp. | | p. 263 |
| *k'ečeč* | *Dorymyrmex* spp. | | p. 263 |
| | *Myrmecocystes* sp. | | |
| *bak yat* | Ponerinae:part | | p. 263 |
| *čil te? čan* | *Neoponeura* sp. | | p. 263 |
| *muy ?am* | Mutillidae | 'velvet ant' | p. 263 |

| | | | |
|---|---|---|---|
| COVERT COMPLEX: bee | Apoidea | | p. 271 |
| *honon* | *Bombus* spp. | 'bumblebee' | p. 272 |
| *meʔ honon* | *Bombus* sp. 1:queen | | p. 272 |
| *čʼin honon* | *Bombus* sp. 1:worker | | p. 272 |
| *cʼirin honon* | *Bombus* sp. 2:worker, male | | p. 272 |
| *honon teʔ* | *Eulaema* sp. | | p. 272 |
| *nucnuc* | *Xylocopa* spp. | 'carpenter bee' | p. 272 |
| *ʔaha čab* | *Apis mellifera* | 'honey bee' | p. 272 |
| *ʔinam čab* | *Trigona*:part | 'stingless bee' | p. 272 |
| *šenen čab* | *Trigona*:part | 'stingless bee' | p. 274 |
| *ʔus čab* | *Trigona*:part | 'stingless bee' | p. 274 |
| *sunul* | *Trigona*:part | 'stingless bee' | p. 274 |
| *šoy* | *Trigona*:part | 'stingless bee' | p. 274 |
| *suk* | Halictidae:part | 'sweat bee' | p. 274 |
| *šyaš ʔič* | Halictidae:part | 'sweat bee' | p. 274 |
| *suʔsiwal* | Halictidae:part Megachilidae Anthophoridae | 'assorted bees' | p. 275 |
| *šut* | Syrphidae:part | 'flower fly' | p. 275 |

| | | | |
|---|---|---|---|
| COVERT COMPLEX: 'fly' | Diptera:part<br>Braconidae | | p. 275 |
| ha | | | p. 275 |
| yaš ton haʔ | Calliphoridae | 'blow fly' | p. 276 |
| coc ʔit haʔ | Tachinidae:part | | p. 276 |
| ʔus | Diptera:part<br>Braconidae | | p. 278 |
| muk'ul ʔus | Muscidae<br>Sarcophagidae<br>Tachinidae:part | | p. 278 |
| k'an ʔus | Simuliidae:part? | | p. 278 |
| ʔihk'al ʔus | Simuliidae:part? | | p. 278 |
| sakil ʔus | *Drosophila* spp. | 'pomace fly' | p. 278 |
| p'oʔ č'in ʔus | Chloropidae | 'fruit fly' | p. 278 |
| k'unil ʔus | Platypezidae:part? | | p. 278 |
| yusil sac' | Braconidae | | p. 278 |
| šenen | Culicidae<br>Tipulidae:part | 'mosquito' | p. 279 |
| tiʔwal šenen | Culicidae:female | 'mosquito' | p. 279 |
| k'unil šenen | Culicidae:male<br>Tipulidae:part | | p. 279 |
| č'ikil | ? | | p. 279 |
| škač | Tabanidae | 'horse fly' | p. 279 |
| huk | Gasterophilidae<br>Cuterebridae<br>Oestridae | 'bot fly' | p. 279 |
| la lum | Tipulidae:part | 'crane fly' | p. 279 |
| čanul caʔ mut | Bibionidae<br>Sciaridae | 'march fly' | p. 280 |

| | | | |
|---|---|---|---|
| COVERT COMPLEX: butterfly-moth | Lepidoptera:adult | | p. 280 |
| *pehpen* | Lepidoptera:adult:part | | p. 281 |
| [R] *pehpen* | Lėpidoptera:adult:part | | p. 281 |
| *c'unun pehpen* | Sphingidae | 'sphinx moth' | p. 284 |
| *tultuš pehpen* | Heliconidae Ithomiidae | | p. 284 |
| *ne mut pehpen* | Hesperiidae:part | 'tailed skippers' | p. 284 |
| *pehpenul balam* | *Caligo memnon* | 'owl butterfly' | p. 284 |
| *me? sac'* | *Thysania agrippina* | | p. 284 |
| *supul* | Microlepidoptera Lithosiidae:part Arctiidae:part Noctuidae:part | 'mothlet' | p. 285 |
| *tultuš* | Odonata:adult | 'dragonfly' | p. 285 |
| [R] *tultuš* | Odonata:part | | p. 285 |
| *meba tultuš* | Zygoptera:part | 'damselfly' | p. 286 |
| *nen tultuš* | *Mecistogaster ornata* | | p. 286 |
| *hmah ha?* | Libellulidae Gomphidae | | p. 286 |
| *čikitin* | Cicadidae | 'cicada' | p. 287 |
| *meba čikitin* | Cicadidae:part | | p. 287 |
| *šk'anan čikitin* | Cicadidae:part | | p. 287 |
| *šč'oy čikitin* | Cicadidae:part | | p. 287 |
| *p'um te?* | Membracidae:adult (Cicadellidae) (Flatidae) | 'treehopper' | p. 287 |

| | | | |
|---|---|---|---|
| COVERT COMPLEX: beetle–bug | Coleoptera:adult<br>Hemiptera | | p. 295 |
| *kuhtum caʔ* | Scarabaeinae<br>Geotrupinae<br>(Cetoniinae) | 'dung beetle' | p. 295 |
| *čimol* | Dynastinae | 'rhinoceros beetle' | p. 295 |
| *čimolil teʔ* | Passalidae | 'bessbug' | p. 295 |
| *ʔumoh* | Melolonthinae<br>Rutelinae | 'June bug' | p. 295 |
| *kukai* | Lampyridae | 'firefly' | p. 296 |
| *šul ton* | Prioninae | 'long-horned beetle' | p. 296 |
| *hseʔ teʔ čan* | Cerambycidae:part | 'long-horned beetle' | p. 296 |
| *šp'ahk'in teʔ čan* | Elateridae | 'click beetle' | p. 298 |
| *wayway čan* | *Zopherus jourdani* | | p. 298 |
| *tuluk' čan* | *Meloe* spp. | 'oil beetle' | p. 298 |
| *tu cis čan* | Tenebrioninae | 'darkling beetle' | p. 298 |
| *cihil čan* | Pentatomidae<br>Coreidae<br>(other Hemiptera) | 'stink bug' | p. 298 |
| *čan₂* | Coleoptera:adult:part | | p. 299 |
| | | | |
| COVERT COMPLEX: weevil | | | p. 299 |
| *hmil mut čan* | Curculionidae:part | 'weevil' | p. 299 |
| *hoč'* | Curculionoidea:part | 'weevil' | p. 300 |
| *šhoč'ol čenek'* | Anthribidae | 'weevil' | p. 300 |
| *šhoč'ol ʔišim* | Curculionidae:part | 'weevil' | p. 301 |
| *šhoč'ol č'uh teʔ* | Curculionidae:part | 'weevil' | p. 301 |
| *šhoč'ol ʔič* | Curculionidae:part | 'weevil' | p. 301 |
| *škoen čan* | Isopoda | 'sowbug' | p. 301 |
| *butbut ʔit čan* | Myrmeleontidae:larva | 'antlion' | p. 301 |
| *čanul čenek'* | Alticinae:part | 'bean beetle' | p. 301 |
| *čanul karawánco* | Aphididae | 'aphid' | p. 301 |
| *čanul yabenal nahk* | Chrysomelidae:larva | | p. 301 |
| *čanul hi* | unidentified larva | | p. 301 |
| *čanul sakil bok* | unidentified larva | | p. 301 |
| *čanul teʔ* | Coleoptera:larva<br>Lepidoptera:larva<br>Diptera:larva | | p. 302 |
| *bac'il čanul teʔ* | | | p. 302 |
| [R] *čanul teʔ* | | | p. 302 |
| *k'olom* | Scarabaeidae:larva | 'grub' | p. 302 |

| | | |
|---|---|---|
| COVERT COMPLEX: caterpillar | Lepidoptera:larva:part<br>Diptera:larva:part | p. 303 |
| *cuhkum* | | 'woolly bear'    p. 304 |
| *bac'il c'uhkum* | Arctiidae:larva:part | p. 304 |
| *sak'al cuhkum* | | p. 304 |
| *cuhkumal cic* | | p. 304 |
| *č'ištul* | *Nymphalis antiopa*:larva | 'mourning cloak larva'    p. 304 |
| *šak tah* | Saturniidae:larva:part | p. 305 |
| *čup* | | p. 305 |
| *bac'il čup* | Limacodidae:larva:part | p. 305 |
| *šulub čup* | | p. 305 |
| *meʔ c'iʔ* | Arctiidae:larva:part | p. 305 |
| *buluk' sit* | Papilionidae:larva:part | p. 305 |
| *sac'* | Sphingidae:larva:part | p. 305 |
| *sac' čan* | Sphingidae:larva:part | p. 305 |
| *wah čan* | | p. 305 |
| *hohtiwaneh* | Geometridae:larva | 'inch worm'    p. 305 |
| *meʔ toyiw* | Diptera:larva:part | p. 306 |
| *meba meʔ toyiw* | Diptera:larva:part | p. 306 |
| *ʔihk'al meʔ toyiw* | | p. 306 |
| *yal ha* | Diptera:larva:part | 'maggot'    p. 306 |
| *bac'il yal ha* | | p. 306 |
| *syalhaul* [R] | | p. 306 |

| | | | |
|---|---|---|---|
| COVERT COMPLEX: parasite | Acarina<br>Mallophaga<br>Anoplura<br>Cimicidae<br>Membracidae:larva:part<br>Pseudococcidae<br>Eriococcidae<br>Siphonaptera | | p. 306 |
| *č'ak* | Siphonaptera | `flea` | p. 306 |
| *bac'il č'ak* | Pulicidae | `flea` | p. 306 |
| *ʔoč'em č'ak* | Tungidae | `chigoe flea` | p. 306 |
| *šohk* | Thrombidiformes:part | `chigger` | p. 308 |
| *sip* | Parasitiformes | `tick` | p. 308 |
| *sipul tuhkulum č'iš* | Membracidae:larva:part | | p. 308 |
| *ʔuč'* | Mallophaga<br>Anoplura | `louse` | p. 308 |
| *sak ʔuč'* | Pediculus h. humanus | `body louse` | p. 308 |
| *bac'il ʔuč'* | Pediculus h. capitis | `head louse` | p. 308 |
| *yuč' čitam* | Haematopinidae:part | | p. 308 |
| *yuč' wakaš* | Haematopinidae:part | | p. 308 |
| *ʔosol* | Mallophaga:part<br>Acarina:part<br>Homoptera:part | `louse` | p. 308 |
| *yosolil mut* | Menoponidae<br>Philopteridae | `bird louse` | p. 308 |
| *yosolil nep'* | Acarina:part | `crab louse` | p. 308 |
| *yosolil teʔ* | Pseudococcidae<br>Eriococcidae | `mealy bug` | p. 308 |
| *poč'* | Cimex sp. | `bed bug` | p. 308 |
| *yaʔal čan* | ? | | p. 308 |
| *hukulub* | Gasterophilidae:larva<br>Cuterebridae:larva<br>Oestridae:larva | `botfly larva` | p. 309 |
| COVERT COMPLEX: millipede | MYRIAPODA | | p. 309 |
| *mokoč* | DIPLOPODA | `millipede` | p. 309 |
| *šulub čan* | CHILOPODA | `centipede` | p. 310 |
| *cek* | Scorpionida | `scorpion` | p. 310 |

# CHAPTER 1

# Context

## 1  The Field of Folk Biology

This report is a study of folk science. The choice of folk science, rather than the more familiar "ethnoscience," is deliberate. The two concerns are related but distinct. Ethnoscience has come to imply a methodology and a critical stance within cultural anthropology. The method is above all systematic and verbal; its most radical proponents seem to disclaim the necessity for participant observation. The data of ethnoscience are words that stand for concepts. They are defined by regularities observed in their distribution among certain contexts, in particular, question and answer frames (Metzger and Williams 1963, 1966; Black and Metzger 1965) much as syntactic categories are defined by linguists. Linguistic techniques provide the analogical model for ethnoscience research. The concepts and their distributional regularities are, it is asserted, the essential content of culture. Ethnography is adequate, say the ethnoscientists, insofar as it meets the standards that linguists impose on their own descriptive analyses, their grammars.

Studies of folk science shift the emphasis from method to content. Metzger and Williams's ethnoscience classic, "Some Procedures and Results in the Study of Native Categories: Tzeltal Firewood" (1966), was certainly not motivated by an interest in firewood. Firewood was simply the vehicle for the methodological exercise. The works of Conklin (1954), Bulmer (1970; Bulmer and Tyler 1968), and Berlin, on the contrary, are clearly motivated by an interest in natural history shared by informant and ethnographer. The value of such research, I believe, is enhanced more by the ethnographer's desire to understand the role of man in nature than by his concern with methodological dogma. In fact, the techniques of ethnoscience, such as the strict reliance on native language question frames

for eliciting data, are used or not according to the nature of the task at hand in the study of folk science.

In like fashion the associated technique of componential analysis is only sporadically applied to define folk-scientific categories. It is inefficient and inaccurate as a model of the psychological reality underlying categories of organisms. Informants do not readily verbalize criterial features of most biological taxa, perhaps because such taxa are conceptually "primitive," i.e., they are not definable in terms of concatenations of conceptually prior "givens." Rather, it seems likely that such taxa are best characterized as defined by a single complex pattern or "gestalt," abstracted automatically from each perceived image, rather than as a set of values of several discrete dimensions of contrast or "features."

Despite these differences, folk-scientific research shares a basic interest with ethnoscience. Both seek to illuminate the nature of human knowledge, and both are predicated upon the belief that it is possible to make inferences about the structure of the human mind from behavioral and speech data.

The distinction between folk science and ethnoscience may be extended to the myriad compounds of ethno- plus the name of an academic specialty, e.g., ethnobiology, ethnopsychology, ethnolinguistics, ethnohistory, etc. (see Sturtevant 1964). Ethnobotany, for example, traditionally refers to a specialty within the field of botany concerned with discovering useful plant products by investigating how non-European peoples utilize their local floras. Recently the same term has been extended with reference to the basically psychological and semantic concerns of Conklin and Berlin. To avoid confusion, "folk botany" might be substituted for "ethnobotany" when referring to investigations into the nature of folk knowledge of the plant world. Analogously, folk psychology would involve analysis of folk systems of knowledge about regularities of human behavior, folk concepts of personality types, and folk theories of human motivation and character. Ethnopsychology may then retain its established meaning, "the psychology of races and peoples" (*Webster's Third New International Dictionary* 1967). Ethnohistory means "the interpretation of the meaning of archaeological artifacts by means of documentary material" (*Webster's Third New International Dictionary*). Folk history would then mean the description of a particular culture's knowledge and theory of history and historical causation. Likewise ethnozoology retains its traditional referent as "the animal lore of a race or people" (*Webster's Third New International Dictionary*), while folk zoology refers to the descriptive analysis of what is known within a particular community about animal classification, morphology, and behavior, and to the comparative study of such systems of knowledge.

It should be noted that all such terms have two interpretations. For example, folk zoology may refer to a focus of anthropological study, the comparative study of systems of knowledge about animals. On the other hand, it may refer to a particular system of such knowledge, e.g., the folk zoology of the Tenejapa Tzeltal. In the first instance, the status of folk systems as "sciences" is not an issue; the subject matter is defined external to particular cultures by reference to the domain treated by modern zoology. In the second instance one may question, on the one hand, whether zoology is a valid unit from the particular cultural viewpoint being described or, on the other hand, whether the system of knowledge being described is worthy of the title "science." Such questions deserve an empirical answer. In the Tzeltal case it is clear that the relationship of all animals to one another is recognized (see Chapter 5, Section 2), and thus we do not impose our frame of reference on their conception of reality by treating folk zoology as a unit. Furthermore their system of zoological knowledge may be called a science. Of the various definitions cited for "science" in *Webster's New World Dictionary* (1957)

the following are most appropriate, "systematized knowledge derived from observation, study, and experimentation carried on in order to determine the nature or principles of what is being studied" or "the systematized knowledge of nature and the physical world." The Tzeltal Indian's knowledge of nature is derived from close observation and study, at least, and it is systematic in that it is consistently based on inductive reasoning, as will be demonstrated later. However, Tzeltal science involves neither an explicit methodology nor an explicit purpose. In response to those who would argue that it is, therefore, not scientific I quote Radin on a related issue, i.e., does primitive philosophy exist?

I think most of my readers would say [ that the series of proverbs cited does not constitute a philosophical system ] for a simple reason. They really mean by philosophy a very special thing, namely the integrated philosophical systems which began in Western Europe with Plato and Aristotle. Naturally this cannot be found among primitive peoples. . . . The development of formal integrated philosophical systems is however only one form which the evolution of philosophy has taken. All the problems with which it is concerned can be adequately formulated without ever being integrated into a system. This should never be forgotten [ 1957: xxv–xxvi ].

Likewise I believe it would be unproductive to define folk science out of existence.

For present purposes I will define science as a system of knowledge conditioned simultaneously by physical reality and by the human mind perceiving that reality. If knowledge is not responsive to objective reality it cannot be called science. And human knowledge is inevitably a product of human thought. Thus folk science may be subsumed in the more inclusive field of cognitive anthropology (Tyler 1969). Cognitive anthropology is concerned not only with man's knowledge of his biophysical environment but also with his conceptualization of social reality, e.g., the logic of kinship and of social events.

The essential process common to all aspects of cognitive anthropology is the categorization and naming of phenomena. The categorization of phenomena is a characteristic shared by all living things, a fundamental requirement for life. This process in the human organism involves a quantum leap in complexity over the analogous process in other organisms. The use of names to symbolize categories is one revolutionary factor. Thus folk-scientific research begins with the elicitation of lexical sets exhaustive of a specified domain and the attempt to define the categories named.

The categories are also ordered with respect to one another. For this reason we speak of systems of knowledge. No doubt this organizational factor is necessary to ensure the efficient storage and retrieval of the huge quantities of information which, with the aid of language, man is able to learn. Several organizational principles have been described, such as the paradigm or attribute-feature matrix (as in componential analyses); taxonomies that involve relations of contrast and inclusion; the part–whole relations involved in folk-anatomical systems; life stage relations; spatial relations; etc. The eventual preparation of an exhaustive list of basic relational types should coincide with attempts at specifying all possible semantic contrasts (see Casagrande and Hale 1967).

The ultimate goal of cognitive anthropology and of folk science is to construct a theory that adequately accounts for the pan-human ability to form concepts and to organize them in efficient systems.

## 2 The Ethnographic Setting

Latitude 16° 50′ North and longitude 92° 30′ West meet near the center of the *municipio* of Tenejapa. The territory lies in the American tropics, in the mountains southwest of the Yucatan. The region is often referred to as southern Mexico, though Tenejapa itself is actually a bit north of Acapulco and Oaxaca. This confusion is due to the eastward trend of the continent here. Though tropical in latitude, the altitude creates temperate conditions. The land of the *municipio* ranges from 900 m at the northeast corner to over 2800 m in the southern *paraje*

of **macab**. The land drains to the northeast, the swift streams running underground through limestone caverns as readily as they do above. The Tanaté River marks the northern border of the *municipio* before turning northward. It vanishes into the ground, emerging as the Chacté River, which meets the Tlacotalpa River at Huitiupan (see Figure 1.1). Here it makes one last descent through high cliffs to the Gulf Coast plains, the Grijalva River, and the sea.

Since Tenejapa is located "over the hill" from San Cristóbal, that is, on the Gulf slope, it receives considerably more rain than the 1171 mm annual average recorded there (Vogt 1969a:6). The difference is reflected by obvious vegetational changes as one passes the drainage divide (see Berlin, Breedlove, and Raven 1974:5). This considerable rainfall comes between late May and December. Most of the early rain falls in thunderstorms of short duration. After August, however, *nortes* ('north') dominate. These dismal drizzles may last several days and are local reflections of hurricane conditions off the Mexican Gulf coast. The rains turn the trails to mud, making travel uncomfortable. But they clean the air of the smoky haze of March through May, caused by the burning of brush that is cut in preparing Indian corn fields for planting. A wide vista to the north and east is revealed to the hiker, and the rugged terrain of Tenejapa is seen at its clearest. The scenery is magnificent.

The limestone substratum is pocketed with basins where streams disappear into the mouths of caves. The Pueblo of Tenejapa (the "county seat") is built on the lip of one such *sumidero* ('sinkhole') in a long valley at the base of sheer cliffs several hundred feet high. Once over the crest of the ridge to the north of the Pueblo, practically all the land of Tenejapa may be taken in at a glance. *k'išin k'inal* 'hot country' lies in a crescent to the northeast. All around to the southeast and west are the high pine and oak clad ridges of **sikil k'inal** 'cold country'. To the west a microwave relay tower perches on top of **con te? wic** 'tree-moss mountain', at 2900 m the highest point in the central high-

Figure 1.1 The central highlands of Chiapas. [Adapted from The University of Chicago (1964).]

lands. Beyond **con te? wic** lie the better known Tzotzil-speaking communities of Chamula and Zinacantan.

The city of San Cristóbal (pop. ca. 25,000), headquarters for research and government in the highlands, is 30 km southwest of the Pueblo of Tenejapa over the southern shoulder of **con te? wic**. A new road, passable at any season, was (in the spring of 1972) expected to be opened soon as far as the Pueblo. The old road was scarcely passable at any season past the Chamula hamlet of Las Ollas during 1971. The 8-km hike to the Pueblo from Las Ollas over rough terrain contributed to Tenejapa's isolation and is partly responsible for the relative conservatism of the community.

The Indians of Tenejapa speak Tzeltal, a language of the Mayan family. They speak the language in a way characteristic of their community. Furthermore Tenejapan Indians can recognize a person from Cancuc as opposed to Oxchuc, two neighboring Tzeltal-speaking communities, by linguistic cues, in the absence of distinctive differences in clothing (Branstetter 1974). Thus we may speak of Tenejapa, Cancuc and Oxchuc dialects of Tzeltal, though speech within each of these communities is by no means uniform. Kaufman (1964) and Hopkins (1970) suggest dialect groupings within Tzeltal. In both systems, Tenejapan and Cancuc dialects form a cluster in contradistinction to all other dialects of the language.

Tenejapanecos also have Tzotzil-speaking neighbors in the communities of Huistan (to the southeast), Chamula (to the south and west). Mitontic (to the west), and Chenalhó (to the northwest). Though few Tenejapanecos speak Tzotzil, they can fairly readily understand this closely related language. I have traveled in unfamiliar Tzotzil country with Tenejapanecos as guides, and they were able to ask directions and understand the responses. Tenejapanecos also recognize regional differences within Tzotzil. They find some dialects of Tzotzil easier to understand than others.

Glottochronological estimates suggest that Tzeltalan, the hypothetical common protolanguage, began to differentiate about A.D. 300, and that Tzeltal began to differentiate internally by A.D. 1200 (Hopkins 1970:203).

Tojolabal is spoken to the east around Comitán and is only slightly removed from the Tzeltalan branch. At the northern edge of the highlands, Chol, yet another Mayan language, is spoken. In the town of Yajalón, both Tzeltal and Chol may be heard. West of the westernmost Tzotzil communities, where the Chiapas highlands drop off toward the Isthmus of Tehuántepec, yet still within the boundaries of the state of Chiapas (see Figure 1.1), are several thousand Zoque speakers. This language is at best but very distantly related to the Mayan family. These are the five major Indian languages of Chiapas. The number of speakers (including bilinguals) of each is given in Table 1.1. Spanish is spoken throughout by some 80,000 Ladinos (Berlin, Breedlove, and Raven 1974: 6–7) and by some Indians in every *municipio*.

The fact that all Mayan languages (with the exception of Haustec) form a compact, relatively unbroken distribution may indicate that the people who spoke these languages experienced relatively stable political conditions during the millennia since proto-Mayan began its differentiation and expansion (ca. 2600 B.C.). Central Mexico, by contrast, is a maze of interpenetrating pockets of distantly related or unrelated languages, testimony to the turbulent centuries of empire building staged on the Mexican plateau. Pockets of Uto-Aztecan

**Table 1.1**
THE MAJOR INDIAN LANGUAGES OF CHIAPAS ACCORDING TO RECENT ESTIMATES

| Language | Number of speakers | Source of data |
|---|---|---|
| Chol | 49,000 | Villa Rojas 1969 |
| Tojolabal | 40,000 | Montagu 1969 |
| Tzeltal | 78,000 | 1960 Mexican Census[a] |
| Tzotzil | 114,000 | Laughlin 1969 |
| Zoque | 15,000[b] | Foster 1969 |

[a]This same census records 80,000 Tzotzil speakers, far fewer than the more recent and accurate estimate of Laughlin given in the table. It is thus likely that Tzeltal speakers today also number well over 100,000.

[b]The figure is for 1930; it has been decreasing since then.

speech down the Pacific coast of Central America as far as Honduras mark the zenith of Central Mexican influence. Yet there are very few such pockets within the Mayan area.

The State of Chiapas is a first-order subdivision within the governmental hierarchy of Mexico. Chiapas is further subdivided into 111 *municipios* (Corzo 1946). Tenejapa is one such basic minimal unit of the governmental structure. In each such *municipio* a president and a *síndico* ('legal officer, second in command') are elected for 3-year terms, subject to the prior approval of the dominant *Partido Revolucionário Institucional* ('the Institutional Revolutionary Party'; PRI). The president then appoints his subordinate officials.

The *municipio* of Tenejapa (see Figure 1.2) is officially divided into 21 *parajes*, though local usage recognizes anywhere from 25 to 35 nonoverlapping, named localities to which the term *paraje* is loosely applied.* The

* Berlin, Breedlove, and Raven (1974:20) refer to the 21 officially constituted *parajes* as such. They distinguish named subdivisions of these as *barrios*. For example, *hušal ha?* is a *barrio* of the *paraje* **mahben čauk** in this version. However most informants treat both **hušal ha?** and **mahben čauk** as *parajes* which are coordinate in space. In this view **mahben čauk** refers only to a segment of the officially recognized *paraje* of that name. I see no indication that Tenejapanecos distinguish between 'parajes' and 'barrios'.

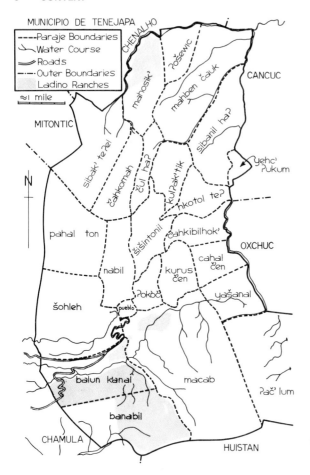

**Figure 1.2** Map of Tenejapa. [Adapted from Berlin, Breedlove, and Raven (1974).]

Indians are at home in the *parajes*, though the seat of local government is located in the Pueblo. Here, around the plaza, you find the church, the *cabildo* ('townhall'), which houses the one-room jail, the president's office, and the single telephone connection to San Cristóbal (see Figure 1.3). Tenejapan civil and religious officials reside in the Pueblo during their terms of office but return to their *parajes* after completing their service. The permanent residents of the Pueblo include no more than a few hundred Ladinos, most engaged in commerce, and a handful of ladinoized Indians. The Pueblo is a classic example of the "vacant towns" of the Mayan area.

The distinction between Indians and Ladinos is pervasive and basic to an understanding of Chiapas society. A Ladino in this part of Chiapas, as in Guatemala, is a native Spanish speaker. He never wears an Indian costume. He would be insulted if mistaken for an Indian. He traces his ancestry to the *conquistadores* regardless of the actual racial admixture and identifies himself with the nation rather than with the local community. An Indian may learn Spanish and put away his traditional clothing in favor of pants, shoes, and a jacket. Yet in his home territory he can only be an Indian. And by and large he has no desire to be otherwise. Thus one's identity in this regard is inherited (see Colby and van den Berghe 1961). Local Spanish terms for Indians range from insulting to euphemistic, e.g., *indio* (derogatory), *indito* (patronizing), or *indígena* (formal and neutral). The term *ladino* is disliked by Ladinos but is used here since no neutral term for this fundamental category is in current use.

**Figure 1.3**  The Pueblo of Tenejapa. Note the grid pattern of the Ladino section of town, the plaza and church in the upper right corner, the scattered wattle and daub, thatched houses of the Indians on the lower right. The cut for the new road from San Cristóbal via Chamula is visible in the center rear. [Color slide by the author.]

Viewing Tenejapa as a minimal unit of the Mexican governmental hierarchy is an external perspective. The social and political terrain looks quite different from the Indian point of view. In the first place, the political units of the Mexican hierarchy are not named in Tzeltal. Nation and state are relevant to very few Tenejapan Indians. Neither are *municipios*, as such, given nomenclatural recognition. The entities to which the Tzeltal terms *tenehapa*, *ʔoščuhk*, (Oxchuc), *čamoʔ* (Chamula), *soc'leb* (Zinacantan), etc., refer are not *municipios* but Indian communities. The geographical correspondence of these communities with current *municipio* boundaries is coincidental. Outside the highlands there is no such ready correspondence. Even in the highlands there are exceptions. *k'ankuhk* (Cancuc), for example, is not a *municipio* but rather an *agéncia*, a semiautonomous subdivision pertaining to the *municipio* of Ocosingo. The Tzotzil-speaking *municipio* of

Chenalhó actually encompasses three named units, three separate Indian communities. Each has its own vacant center, its own church and patron saint. In each one finds a separate hierarchy of *cargos* ('institutionalized social responsibility' or 'office') dedicated to the care of that saint and the other sacred personages associated with the whole community. However, two of these three communities are subordinated to the third for strictly political functions.

Thus the *municipio* and the Indian community are distinct though they may be coterminous on a map. Each has had a different origin and history and each still has clearly distinct functions and leadership. Ladinos live in and are subject to the *municipio* government. The municipal secretary is usually one of their number. They are not, however, considered acceptable marriage partners within the endogamous community of *tenehapa*. They hold no *cargo* positions in the Tenejapan religious hierarchy. They are, in fact, foreigners regardless of how many generations their families have lived on the Tenejapan land, and they will remain foreigners as long as **tenehapa**, the Indian community, exists.

To avoid confusion in future reference, **tenehapa** written with Tzeltal orthography will refer specifically to the Indian community rather than to the Mexican *municipio*. Tenejapa, the Spanish spelling, will be used whenever this specific distinction is unnecessary. However Tenejapan, as adjective, or Tenejapaneco, as personal noun, will be used to refer to the Indian community of **tenehapa** only.

**bac'il winik** 'true man' is an Indian man from Tenejapa. **bac'il ʔanc** 'true woman' is an Indian woman from Tenejapa. Indians of other communities are referred to as **winik X** or **ʔanc Y**, where X and Y stand for the Tzeltal name of the community.* Ladinos are **kašlan** (< Sp *castellano* 'a man from Castile'), though they are also **winiketik** 'men', in the broadest sense of this term.

## 2.1  THE COMMUNITY OF **tenehapa**: THE BASIC ETHNOGRAPHIC UNIT

Informants never tired of my joking reference to "the Republic of Tenejapa." Though pure hyperbole it captures their basic feelings toward their community. It is certainly the major focus of their identity in the larger highland region. My assistant, Santiago Mendez, was disgusted when Ladinos in Tehuántepec, Oaxaca, referred to him as a "Chamula"—the generic term for Chiapas Indians in much of Mexico.

As indicated earlier, Tenejapan Tzeltal is a distinct dialect. Tenejapanecos, however, are not able to distinguish the *paraje* of origin of their fellow citizens by linguistic cues. That there is, nevertheless, considerable intracommunity variation in speech has been well documented with regard to certain

phonological variants by Stross (n.d.). This variation exhibits no clear geographic pattern with the exception of that due to influences felt in border *parajes* from neighboring dialects of Tzeltal or Tzotzil. The remaining variation is most likely correlated with kin and neighbor networks that are not characterized by long-term geographical contiguity. Children of both sexes learn the bulk of their language while closely associated with their mothers (Stross 1973). Their mothers, as a rule, were raised in another *paraje* due to the prohibition of marriage between men and women with the same "clan" name and the tendency for such names to be localized.* The rule of community endogamy, on the other hand, practically eliminates the possibility that a Tenejapan child will learn any other dialect of the language. Thus marriage regulations minimize the probability of geographically based variants within the community while ensuring eventual systematic variation between communities.

**tenehapa** is a speech community not solely because of marriage rules. The concentration of marketing, ritual, and political functions in the Pueblo also contribute. Though other market centers are regularly visited by Tenejapanecos, notably **yočib** bordering Cancuc and Oxchuc and **ʔolil lum** in Mitontic, the weekly Sunday market in the Pueblo is undoubtedly the most frequently visited. Here the ancient community rituals are performed a dozen times each year while thousands of Tenejapanecos congregate to buy, sell, drink, talk, fight, and watch the fiesta. All serious disputes, such as marital problems, property claims, and physical attacks, require personal appearances in the Pueblo. Identity papers required for labor in the *fincas* ('plantations') and school registration also involve visiting the *cabildo*, often repeatedly. Thus

---

* **winik X** is normally abbreviated as **X**, e.g., a man from Zinacantan is typically referred to as **soc'leb**.

* There is one exception to the rule of "clan" exogamy, the **komes** "clan." According to informant JGG, members of this group simply decided to ignore the rule. Their failure to maintain exogamy is viewed by this informant with a mixture of amusement and a sense of superiority.

Tenejapanecos from all parts of the community have frequent opportunities to interact with their fellow citizens.

Interaction with Indians from other communities is largely restricted to external contacts, as in San Cristóbal or during occasional visits to markets or fiestas in other Pueblos. I was struck by the fact that informants were often ignorant of parts of other communities at distances of but a few miles from their homes. Indians simply do not wander beyond their well-established routes. In view of the foregoing it is easily seen how the Tenejapa dialect originated and is maintained. *tenehapa* is a speech community because it is also a religious, political, economic, and social unit. For the majority of highland Chiapas Indians, the community is a miniature nation.

## 2.2  THE COMMUNITY OF *tenehapa*: BASIC ECOLOGICAL DATA

Government census figures for 1950 underestimate both the total and the relative proportion of the Tenejapan Indian population. The census obviously underestimates the land area of the *municipio*. The official figure of 67 km² (Villa Rojas 1969:196) is certainly less than half of the true area. The 1500 Spanish-speaking citizens of a total of 7750 cited (Villa Rojas 1969:196) must be based on very lax criteria for defining "Spanish-speaking" as there are only 500 Ladinos resident in the municipio.* As for the number of Indians, I agree with Berlin, Breedlove, and Raven (1974:20) that the total is closer to 10,000.

If we assume a twofold difference in density between cold and hot country and that somewhat more than half the land area lies in cold country, approximate densities of settlement are 40 to 50 persons per km²

in highland areas and slightly more than 100 persons per km² on land below 1800 m. Since some 10% of the land area of the *municipio* is still in the hands of Ladinos, densities of Indian settlement will be somewhat greater than estimated above.

I have no basis for interpreting these densities as a proportion of some stable ecological limiting value.* However the fact that 20 of a sample of 25 adult male Tenejapanecos from all parts of the community have traveled to *fincas* as laborers, many on a regular basis, indicates that most Indian families supplement the productivity of their lands with a cash income from time to time. In addition, the absence of able-bodied males in the highland *paraje* of *macab* during a visit in early October of 1971, was striking. Practically all were in the *fincas*, and those remaining were planning to leave shortly. The harvest was still more than a month distant, and the women were reduced to making tortillas of store-bought flour. Despite this evidence of ecological cliff-hanging in certain areas and at certain times, there is little evidence that people have been forced to leave the land permanently.

The population is dispersed widely. Outside the Pueblo concentrations of houses appear to be due primarily to topographical factors, such as the need for a relatively level area for the house and yard. *Paraje* boundaries generally follow such features as ridges, streams, and declivities and are marked by trail crosses. The boundary regions are not, however, marked by otherwise usable land left vacant.

Land is controlled by male heads of

---

*This figure is an estimate based on my own impressions. It accords well with the figure of 517 persons resident in the Pueblo (Villa Rojas 1969:203), the great majority of whom are Ladinos. To this must be added no more than 25 Ladinos resident on ranches outside the Pueblo.

*The present estimates may be compared with estimates of the capacity of lowland swidden agriculture in the Mexican region. Heizer estimates 20/km² in the hinterland of La Venta, the major Olmec site of Late Formative times (1960:219). Cowgill estimates 60 mile² (ca. 10/km²) for northern Yucatan and 100–200/mile² (ca. 20–35/km²) for the southern Maya lowlands (1962:82). Palerm suggests that upland fallowing systems (*barbecho*) such as in Tenejapa are approximately twice as productive as lowland slash-and-burn agriculture (*roza*) (1955:30). Thus the estimated density for the entire *municipio* of Tenejapa (10,000/150 km²— ca. 70/km²) is close to the larger of the expected values.

households, and sons may control property in their own right, even though their father is still alive. Plots may be widely separated, and it is advantageous to have land at various elevations. In this way a variety of crops are raised and agricultural labor more evenly distributed throughout the year.

The main types of land, in terms of vegetative cover, result from the cycle of man's agricultural activities. A very few patches of virgin forest (*ha?mal*) remain. Most is cloud forest above 2400 m where land is marginally productive in corn. Higher lands are farmed in adjacent areas of Guatemala but are planted in potatoes (Oakes 1951), which is not a major crop in highland Chiapas. Wooded areas (*te?tikil*) cover land that has been allowed to regenerate for long periods following cultivation. These are found at all elevations and are characterized by pine, oak, and sweet gum. The most extensive wooded areas are found on Ladino properties or lands owned by wealthy Tenejapanecos. They can afford to leave the land vacant for extended periods. Every family needs access to certain amounts of such land, however, as a source of firewood and construction materials. In lowland areas (below 1500 m) wooded plots are maintained to provide shade for coffee trees, a cash crop which is on the increase.

Land cleared for *milpa* ('Indian corn field'; *k'altik* in Tzeltal) is used for several years before allowed to lie fallow. Such fallow land may be recognized by the dense brushy tangles (*wamaleltik*) covering it. Groves of fruit trees, such as bananas, mangoes, oranges, and other citrus fruits, commonly surround lowland homesteads or line lowland watercourses. Short grass (*?akiltik*) with scattered trees is characteristic of much Ladino land, as it is used exclusively for grazing cattle.

The local agriculture, devoted primarily to corn and several varieties of beans and squash, is described in some detail by Berlin, Breedlove, and Raven (1974:103–124). Crops grown primarily for sale include the peanut (for which Tenejapanecos are locally famous), coffee, chili peppers, and fruits

#### Table 1.2
NUMBERS OF DOMESTIC ANIMALS OWNED ACCORDING TO A GEOGRAPHICALLY REPRESENTATIVE SAMPLE OF TENEJAPAN HOUSEHOLDS[a]

| Species | Number responding | Own none | Median number owned, all ages |
|---|---|---|---|
| Chickens (*mut₂*) | 25 | 1 | 18 |
| Turkeys (*tuluk'*) | 23 | 8 | 2 |
| Dogs (*c'i?*) | 24 | 4 | 2 |
| Cats (*šawin*) | 19 | 11 | — |
| Bulls (*stat wakaš*) | 19 | 8 | 1 |
| Pigs (*čitam*) | 17 | 11 | — |

[a] In addition to the animals listed, there were reports of one duck and one mule being owned.

of various kinds. Hunting is clearly subordinate to *milpa* agriculture, as most of the land has been modified by agricultural activities, leaving little cover for the larger game animals.

Every family owns some domestic animals. Most commonly kept are chickens, turkeys, and dogs (see Table 1.2). Fowl and their eggs are luxury food items, ritual offerings, or sources of cash income. Dogs guard the homestead, may be used in hunting, and are enjoyed as pets. Cats are valued as rat catchers. Cattle and pigs are kept with increasing frequency. They are treated as investments. Bulls are bought young, fattened for a year or two, and sold. Much of the meat, as with pork and eggs, is sold to Ladinos in the Pueblo. Mules are preferred to horses as beasts of burden, for the trails are difficult, especially in the rainy season. Men do the bulk of the cargo hauling, however, and only a wealthy few own mules. No goats, sheep, or donkeys are kept by Indians in Tenejapa; it is simply not done. Occasional experimentation with domestic duck, pigeon, and rabbit is reported, but such experiments have not thrived.

Mud nests of certain stingless bees (Apidae: *Trigona* sp.: see *sunul*/bee) are established in pottery shards or hollow logs under the eaves of houses. Wild nests of other species of bees are raided for honey. Thus animal husbandry shades into categories of hunting and gathering. In general such food sources are sporadically utilized, either for the sake of variety or of necessity. Besides wild honey, certain large larval Lepidoptera (see *sac'*/caterpillar) are highly prized. Wasp larvae (see *šuš* complex), a large flying ant (see *c'isim*/ant), various Orthoptera, and certain aquatic invertebrates such as hellgrammites (see *špálu ha?*/waterbug) and crabs (see *nep'*) are also considered edible, as is one type of snail (see *puy*/snail). I never observed anyone actually eating invertebrates however. Their dietary role is clearly quantitatively marginal, though they may serve as emergency rations during poor crop years, and some are used to remedy pathological conditions (see Ruddle 1973).

Fishing by means of the preferred poisoning technique (see *čay* complex) is possible only at the height of the dry season, from late March to early May. Then the torrents are reduced to quiet pools. Fishing is generally restricted to the people of low country adjacent to the largest streams on Tenejapa's northern and eastern boundaries. Some fish, however, have recently been stocked in artificial pools in the highland *paraje* of **macab**.

A few men pride themselves on their hunting skills. Weapons include slingshots (**tirol**) for subadult play, shotguns (**bac'il tuhk'**) locally produced by Ladinos, a variety of traps (see Chapter 4, Section 4), and dogs. Most common prey include cottontail rabbit (**t'ul**), raccoon (**me?el**), opossum (**?uč**), and paca (**halaw**). Occasional weasels (**sabin**), pocket gophers (**ba**), gray foxes (**waš**), and large ground-dwelling birds are taken. Most mice and birds which I trapped were eagerly eaten, the smaller species being saved for the children. Larger game species such as deer (**te?tikil čih**) and peccary (**wamal čitam**) are no longer locally available, having retreated to unoccupied forest areas.

In sum, animal foods are not staples but provide variety or a hint of luxury, or they serve special ritual or medicinal needs. Their nutritional value remains to be accurately assessed.

The only source of cash income readily available, aside from the sale of surplus produce, is labor on the distant *fincas*. Such labor involves considerable hardship and pays minimally. A few Tenejapan Indians, male and female, have become schoolteachers. This requires a minimum of 7 years of schooling. The handful of civil government positions involve no direct remuneration but are nonetheless lucrative. Anthropologists pay better than average wages, but very few Indians obtain more than token amounts from this source. Within the last few years some Indians in practically every *paraje* have opened small shops. This development restricts the drain of Indian resources to outsiders but generates no new income for the community. The new road provides a few jobs. No income-producing crafts are regularly exploited, though the women are highly skilled at weaving and embroidery.

## 3 Zoogeography of the Region

Altitude, rainfall, and geographical barriers combine to define the major biotic regions in the tropics. The primary distinction is between highlands and lowlands. Though elevation is a continuous quantity, biologists generally recognize a relatively discrete boundary between biotic complexes at 1500–1800 m at the latitude of Chiapas (Edwards 1972:2). Thus the highland areas of Chiapas are split in two by the valley of the Grijalva River, each with quite distinct floral and faunal complexes. The Sierra Madre de Chiapas rises abruptly from the Pacific coastal plain to elevations of 2000 m in the west and to 4000 m on Volcán Tacaná at the Guatemalan border. This ridge forms the continental divide.

North, across the low, dry plain of the Río Grande de Chiapas, as this segment of the Grijalva is sometimes known, we find Tenejapa, near the summit of the central highland mass. East and west along the southern lip of this highland mass one finds a series of small mountain basins with subterranean drainage patterns. Here the Spaniards concentrated in colonial times, and here today are the major towns and cities of the highlands, such as San Cristóbal, Comitán, and Teopisca.

The central highland mass slopes gradually downward to the northeast. Narrow river valleys penetrate nearly to the center of the mass leaving high "islands" far to the north of the main ridge. One such "island" is Tumbalá, which at 2100 m looks directly out over the Gulf coastal plain. Despite the complexity of the terrain, and despite the fact that three physiographic regions are recognized within the central highland area (Vogt 1969b:134), the faunal distribution is fairly uniform, given equivalent elevations.

The Tenejapaneco is familiar with the central highland fauna, with a few exceptions, these due to lack of suitable habitat in his immediate vicinity. Many Gulf coast lowland forms extend into Tenejapa along the Tanaté River drainage, adding a tropical element to his experience. However, the great variety of tropical forest species— those adapted to virgin forest—are blocked by lack of such habitat near Tenejapa. Many of these forms are found near Ocosingo 30 trail miles north of Tenejapa. This provides the basis for the Tenejapanecos' sketchy, secondhand knowledge of the more distinctive animals of such habitat. Monkeys, tapirs, and parrots are known in Tenejapa only by hearsay or from captive specimens. Only a few Tenejapanecos remember aboriginal terms for parrots (see *puyuč'*/bird, parrot); most know only the terms borrowed from Spanish.

The fauna of the Grijalva valley and of the Pacific lowlands is likewise poorly known, since the Tenejapanecos' experience there is limited to occasional trips to work on the *fincas*. They have become acquainted with the iguanas and the Magpie Jay (*Calocitta formosa*) but do not seem familiar with the large and poisonous beaded lizard (*Heloderma horridum*) found throughout the Grijalva valley. Though Tenejapanecos may travel to coastal *fincas*, these trips are hardly sightseeing jaunts. Thus they may never have seen the ocean in dozens of trips to the Huixtla region and are ignorant, as well, of the unique Sierra Madre fauna.

Certain exotic animals are known through schoolbooks and traveling zoos. Thus bears, elephants, camels, African lions, and giraffes have been marginally incorporated into the Tenejapan repertoire. Elephants may be called *muk'ul cemen* 'big tapir'. The native American tapir is then *č'in cemen* 'small tapir' (see *cemen*/mammal). These two animals are equally foreign from the Tenejapan point of view, as tapirs are now very rare in Mexico and are restricted to tropical lowland forests (Alvarez del Toro 1952).

Within the large regions defined here, habitat types further restrict the occurrence of animal species. For example, Red-winged Blackbirds (*Agelaius phoeniceus*) and Eastern Meadowlarks (*Sturnella magna*), though common in the fields and marshes surrounding San Cristóbal, are confined to one corner of Tenejapa in the *colonia* of *ba nabil*. Names for these two species were elicited from a *ba nabil* informant but were not known elsewhere in Tenejapa. Likewise cloud forest and montane rain forest are rare in Tenejapa. Thus, the fauna restricted to such habitat is poorly known. Resplendent Quetzals (*Pharomachrus mocinno*), for example, occur at comparable elevations less than 80 km from Tenejapa, but are unknown locally, despite their paramount role in ancient Mayan ritual.

The faunal distribution is further complicated by seasonal factors, most notable among the migratory birds. A great variety of small, colorful wood warblers (Parulidae) pass through during spring and fall. Many remain for the winter and a few are year-round residents. The majority of the more than 40 species of this family that I recorded in and near Tenejapa are referred to simply as *šč'iht*, a name imitative of the call notes of many species of this family. Other migratory species, however, are well known. One such is the Gray Catbird (*Dumetella carolinensis*, see *šč'eʔ*/bird). Siskins (*Spinus* spp., see **me kʼin haʔal**/bird, siskin-seedeater) appear in large numbers during the fall months (though they are only locally migratory) and thus are called **meʔ kʼin haʔal** 'mother of the winter rains', which begin at this time.

Seasonal variation of occurrence is recognized also with reference to pocket gophers, snakes, certain caterpillars, and ants. In such cases, migration is not involved. The seasonal pattern of occurrence is due rather to behavioral or maturational patterns.

The numbers of species of some groups of animals are estimated in Table 1.3 to indicate the variety of animal life to which the Tzeltal are exposed.

**Table 1.3**

NUMBERS OF SPECIES OF CERTAIN KINDS OF ANIMALS KNOWN TO OCCUR IN THE STUDY REGION[a]

| Group | In Chiapas | In Tenejapa |
|---|---|---|
| Mammals | 150 | ca. 55 |
|   Bats | 60 | ca. 20 |
|   Rodents | 35 | ca. 20–25 |
| Birds | ca. 650 | ca. 200 |
|   Permanent resident | | ca. 140 |
|   Migrant, winter only | | ca. 60 |
| Amphibians | ca. 30 | ca. 15 |
| Reptiles | ca. 170 | ca. 40 |
|   Lizards | 65 | ca. 10 |
|   Snakes | 90 | ca. 15–25 |
| Total vertebrates (excluding fish) | ca. 1000 | ca. 300–325 |
| Lepidoptera alone | ca. 3000 | |

[a]Information abstracted from Hall and Kelson (1959); Alvarez del Toro (1971, 1973); Stuart (1963); miscellaneous sources; personal observations.

# Methods

*CHAPTER 2*

# Methods

## 1 The Basic Datum: The Identification

The denotata of folk names for categories of organisms are inferred from sets of events; each is an identification. An identification consists of the following: (a) an organism to be identified or a realistic representation of that organism; (b) the naming of the organism by the informant and the recording of that name by the ethnographer; (c) the identification of the same organism by the biologist. How many such identifications are required to establish the fact that a folk taxon and a scientific taxon are equivalent?

No theoretical value for the probability of events of this sort is calculable, thus an exact figure is unjustified. However a large sample is typically unnecessary. For example, consider the null hypothesis that the scientific classification and a particular folk classification of a set of organisms (an infinite but geographically bounded set) are independent. For the sake of exposition, let us assume that both classification systems consist of sets of 1000 mutually exclusive taxa and that organisms are equally likely to be assigned to any given taxon. The probability that organisms from the same scientific taxon will be placed in a single folk taxon on two independent occasions is 1/1000, the probability for three independent occasions is 1/1,000,000. Thus if an informant applies the same name to organisms of a single scientific taxon on several occasions—assuming that the name applied does not label a broadly inclusive taxon—one can be quite sure that the folk category and the scientific category are not defined independently of one another. This lends credence to the alternative hypothesis that either the folk taxon is a subset of the scientific taxon or vice versa.

A similar logic may be applied to the null hypothesis that informants classify independently of one another. The alternative hypothesis in this case is that the informants share a cultural system of classification. These null hypotheses are, of course, absurd. The question is not **whether** folk and scientific classifications of organisms are correlated, but how and to what extent (for a measure of the degree of this association see Chapter 3, Section 9).

Two important exceptions must be noted. First, if informants tend to disagree in naming the same kind of organism, further identifications are necessary to evaluate the nature of the disagreement and its extent (see discussion of informant variability, this chapter, Section 9). Second, if the same name is applied to diverse kinds of organisms as defined by the biologist, further sampling is necessary to clarify the classificatory principles employed in the folk system.

## 2 Establishing Category Correspondences from Identifications

Figure 2.1 illustrates the inferential structure involved in the interpretation of folk-biological data. Scientific categories are named according to explicit procedures. The naming of folk categories is not so predictable. Nevertheless, it is the categories rather than the names which are the sine qua non of the research. The correspondence between folk name and scientific name, as I have indicated, may be confidently established with a small sample of tokens (identifications). However the fact that the same folk name is consistently applied to organisms of a single scientific category is not sufficient evidence that the folk category is identical to the scientific category. Tokens one, two, and three establish the correspondence of part of the folk category with part of the scientific category. But how may we exclude the possibility that there may be tokens such as four and five, which are included in one category but not in the other? The following examples illustrate two major problems of this sort.

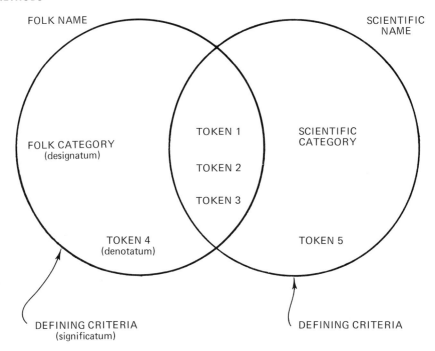

FOLK NAME

SCIENTIFIC
NAME

TOKEN 1

SCIENTIFIC
CATEGORY

FOLK CATEGORY
(designatum)

TOKEN 2

TOKEN 3

TOKEN 4
(denotatum)

TOKEN 5

DEFINING CRITERIA
(significatum)

DEFINING CRITERIA

**Figure 2.1**    Inferential structure of folk-biological definitions.

First is the problem of determining to which of several hierarchically related scientific taxa the folk taxon corresponds, a species, genus, family, etc. **stok'ob**, for example, is applied by informants to the common highland species of tree frog, *Hyla walkeri*. No other species of the Hylidae was collected in Tenejapa, though two different species of that family heard calling at a lower elevation some 80 km from the *municipio* (*H. microcephala* and *Smilisca baudini*) were collected. SMZ and JGG considered their calls unfamiliar but referred to them as **kol pahaluk sok stok'ob** 'almost the same as the tree frog'. An unidentified specimen of the Hylidae collected by Breedlove in the Sierra Madre de Chiapas, which was three times the size of typical *H. walkeri*, was shown to several informants. They named it **stok'ob** after close inspection, noting the slimness of the legs and the shape of the toes but expressing amazement at its large size. Finally, while SMZ and JGG were visiting in Berkeley, California, we found an example of the Pacific tree frog (*Hyla regilla*). They named it **stok'ob** without hesitation or qualification. How might we best translate this term? Does it denote *H. walkeri* only? May it refer to some but not all species of the genus *Hyla*, to the entire genus, or to the entire family? In short, the category is generalizable to include a range of variation never before encountered. An exact definition of a folk taxon should specify the **potential** range of the generalizing criteria defining the category. To specify this, one needs to understand the full range of variability viewed by the biologist and the **defining criteria** of the folk taxon. The latter type of data is rarely explicit.

The solution of the second problem involves knowing the referential range of all names applied within a folk domain. For example, the fact that informants consistently apply the name **š?uman** to the Lesser Roadrunner (*Geococcyx velox*) does not prove that **š?uman** is equivalent to the Lesser Roadrunner unless it can be shown that **š?uman** is not also applied to other organisms and that no other nonsynonymous term may be applied to organisms of that scientific taxon. An exhaustive accounting of the local terminology and of the local fauna is required to validate referential definitions.

## 3  Evaluating Identifications

### 3.1  QUALITY OF THE STIMULUS

The validity of identifications is variable. If an informant is to make an accurate identification of an organism, sufficient information for identification must be present in the stimulus situation. The ideal stimulus is the living organism in its natural habitat observed at close range and at length. Such ideal circumstances rarely obtain. Yet Tenejapanecos correctly identified many birds by voice alone, mice from animals dead in traps, and wasps by the form of their nests—information that the biologist may find insufficient. Of course the Tenejapanecos' recognition is facilitated by life-long familiarity.

Captive animals, herptile specimens in formalin, pinned insects, or skins of birds and mammals are often confusing to informants because of the absence of behavioral, vocal, or habitat cues from the stimulus. Two-dimensional representations, such as photographs, paintings, or drawings may be practically useless in some cases. The problem of scale for people unfamiliar with such a convention is a major difficulty. One informant insisted that a colored illustration of a large rail (Robbins, Bruun, and Zim 1966:104) was *c'unun* 'hummingbird'.

Even free-living birds can be misidentified in unfamiliar surroundings. For example, SMZ did not recognize the Social Flycatcher (*Myiozetetes similis*, see **pahal mac'**/bird, flycatcher) when we first encountered this species near Ocosingo, 50 km from his home. When we later saw the same species near his house, he named it with assurance. Near one's home the possibilities are well known. The same kind of animal in other surroundings is part of a different, partially unknown set of animals. In short, identifications should

take place in the informant's home territory and in familiar contexts whenever possible.

### 3.2  MISIDENTIFICATIONS

It is possible for an outside observer to recognize erroneous identifications on the part of his informants, and it is, of course, to his advantage to do so. Since it is a potential source of bias to exclude some data as incorrect while basing one's conclusions on the remainder, I will specify as clearly as possible the criteria employed in such judgments (cf. Wyman and Bailey 1964:20; Bulmer and Tyler 1968).

Two sources of misidentifications are readily distinguished. The first is the informant's ignorance of either the organisms or the criteria for naming them. Such error is to be expected when informants are confronted with unfamiliar organisms or prove to be unreliable with respect to animal identification. The latter case may be due to lack of interest in the subject or to disassociation from the local cultural environment due to schooling or ladinoization.

#### 3.2.1  Unfamiliar Forms

This example involves an unfamiliar extralimital form. SMZ and JGG identified a large, hirsute ant collected 80 km from Tenejapa at 600 m as an unfamiliar kind of **muy ʔam**. Within Tenejapa this taxon is monotypic and refers exclusively to species of velvet ants (Hymenoptera: Mutillidae, see **muy ʔam**), never to species of true ants (Hymenoptera: Formicidae, see ant complex). The strange ants were quite different from any kind found in Tenejapa and resembled velvet ants both in size and the hairiness of their bodies. Yet they differed from velvet ants in shape and color. In short, they were ambiguous with respect to the criteria utilized within Tenejapa for discriminating velvet ants from true ants. Given these circumstances, I believe it is best to consider this a case of misidentification, rather than an example of a lack of correspondence between the folk taxon *muy ʔam* and the scientific taxon Mutillidae.

Misidentifications may also occur close to home and with knowledgeable informants. SMZ identified a small black ant found just 3 km from his home as *cihil šanič* 'stinking ant'. Local enquiries revealed that the ant in question is widely known as *k'ečeč*. SMZ had heard this other term but apparently had never learned to apply it appropriately, i.e., as most of his immediate neighbors do. This interpretation, as opposed to the conclusion that SMZ's naming behavior is correct but idiolectally distinct, is based on the evidence that SMZ was unusually hesitant in his identification and that the nest building behavior of the ant in question contradicted SMZ's own prior statements about the nest building of *cihil šanič* (see Figure 5.194).

Other things being equal, the rarer the animal the more likely it is to be misidentified. Some animals are so distinctive that they can be correctly identified on first encounter (on the basis of information in prior verbal accounts), others are so subtly different from similar taxa as to remain difficult despite frequent experience. Animals that are both rare and similar to their congeners, therefore, will be prime subjects for errors.

An example is provided by the shorebirds (suborder Charadrii, see *c'uʔ lukum*/bird, waterbird), several species of which may occur with about equal probability in the restircted suitable habitat in and near Tenejapa. The Spotted Sandpiper (Scolopacidae: *Actitis macularia*) and the Killdeer (Charadriidae: *Charadrius vociferus*) are the most likely. The Solitary Sandpiper (Scolopacidae: *Tringa solitaria*) and the Pectoral Sandpiper (Scolopacidae: *Calidris melanotos*) only slightly less so. I have also observed Least Sandpipers (Scolopacidae: *Calidris minutilla*), Semipalmated Plovers (Charadriidae: *Charadrius semipalmatus*), and Wilson's Phalaropes (Phalaropodidae: *Steganopus tricolor*) nearby in the highlands. Several other species could just as well occur. SMZ was aware that several of these birds differed significantly, and he also knew several names that he considered appropriate for this type

of bird. Yet his use of the terms *čanul haʔ* 'water critter', *c'uʔ lukum* 'worm sucker', and *meʔ c'ahel* 'mother of the marsh' seemed inconsistent. He called the Spotted Sandpiper *čanul haʔ* on several occasions but *htiʔ čanul haʔ* 'water critter eater' when we found it feeding in mud. Least, Pectoral, and Solitary Sandpipers were all called *c'uʔ lukum* by SMZ, though the Pectoral was identified as *čanul haʔ* by AGM. On another occasion SMZ suggested that *čanul haʔ* was a more general term for all birds of marsh and shoreline habitat. Everyone agreed that the Killdeer was *c'uʔ lukum* par excellence. However no example of *meʔ c'ahel* was ever found. SMZ admitted that he had never seen the animal so named and suggested that the name might be synonymous with *c'uʔ lukum*, though other informants claimed to know both birds well.

In this case, distinct types of shorebirds are recognized by some Tenejapanecos, but only the names, not the categories to which the names refer, are widely known. The scarcity of suitable habitat and the number of related forms, all of which are equally rare, provide a poor basis for generalization for most Tenejapanecos. When anthropologists demand definite answers to questions that informants have not had the opportunity to answer for themselves, errors are as likely as correct responses.

Instead of falsely implying a stability of reference to such "loose names" (see this chapter, Section 9), it is best to specify the meaning of terms only when general agreement among informants is evident. Terms that are inconsistently applied in error-prone situations are discussed with reference to the general range of possible referents implied by the documented usages, and firm pronouncements are avoided.

### 3.2.2  Insufficient Information

The second common source of error is insufficient information. For example, SMZ heard the call of a Magpie Jay (*Calocitta formosa*, see *šulub mut*/bird) and asserted that it was *peyaʔ*, which properly refers to the Brown Jay (*Psilorhinus morio*). When the bird came into sight he realized his error and corrected himself. These two birds do sound alike. It is also true that Brown Jays are resident in Tenejapa and thus more familiar than the Magpie Jay, which is encountered only from the dry slopes of the Grijalva valley to the Pacific coast. The sound alone was an insufficient sample of the perceptible attributes in this case, since SMZ was not fully cognizant of the distributional factors involved.

A vexing example is that of the house mouse (*Mus musculus*, see *šlumil č'o*/rat), in that five of a total of seven potential identifications are in error. One might wonder if a term can be defined with such tenuous and contradictory evidence. An examination of each case in point is necessary.

Two of the erroneous identifications involved immature mice of the genus *Peromyscus*, which were labeled *šlumil č'o* 'ground mouse' (i.e., the house mouse) by AKČ'. It is interesting that these immature forms were not confused with harvest mice (*Reithrodontomys* spp., see *sin*/rat), the native form that is of house mouse size. Harvest mice, however, are common and well known, while *šlumil č'o* is restricted to the Pueblo and thus poorly known. The atypical immature *Peromyscus* were placed where current information provided no contradictory data, i.e., in the less familiar category of appropriate size.

The remaining identifications involve two specimens of the house mouse collected in and near my house in San Cristóbal. One was correctly identified by AGM and later by his father. However, SMZ insisted that both specimens were *yašal sin* 'gray harvest mouse'. He pointed to the belly and said that it was too pale for *šlumil č'o*. However he was forced to considerable ingenuity to explain what the animal was doing in my house, since it is commonly asserted that *sin č'o* is an animal of the fields, while *šlumil č'o* is typically found in houses. He suggested that perhaps it came in through the woodpile. SMZ, by his own admission, is not familiar with the house mouse. It is also true that

the habitat and morphological features as he understood them conflicted in this case. He gave priority to the morphological criteria—even though incorrectly—much as a zoologist would.

In this case the conclusion that *šlumil č'o* properly refers only to the house mouse is based on a consistent verbal description, i.e., *šlumil č'o* is the size of a harvest mouse but lives by preference about houses and is not native, rather than on inconsistent identifications.

A final example involves the common biological phenomenon of defensive mimicry. The Viceroy butterfly (*Limenitis archippus*), which is tasty, resembles the Monarch (*Danaus plexippus*), which is poisonous. This presumably has survival value. I have collected a variety of insects that informants identified as *ʔakoʔ* (see *šuš* 'wasp'). These include a fly (order Diptera), a potter wasp (Hymenoptera: Eumenidae), a digger wasp (Hymenoptera: Sphecidae), and a social Vespid wasp (Hymenoptera: Vespidae). What is the true meaning of the term? I have concluded that the first three were misidentified because it is commonly asserted that *ʔakoʔ* (1) stings and (2) builds a "paper" nest of specific size and shape. The fly, which is an able wasp mimic, does neither. The digger and potter wasps superficially resemble both the fly and the "true" *ʔakoʔ* but are not social, "paper"-nest building type wasps. Morphology in this case must be supplemented with behavioral information for accurate identification. Entomologists can specify purely morphological criteria for distinguishing these four forms, yet these criteria involve details of wing structure and venation that Tenejapanecos ignore.

In sum, informants do make errors and it is possible to recognize them. Several factors are weighed in evaluating such naming responses. First, how familiar is the informant with the organisms identified? Second, how difficult is the identification? Third, how sufficient is the information available to the informant? Fourth, does the appearance or behavior of the organism being identified contradict prior descriptions given by the same informant? Finally, how does the informant's style of response compare with his past performance? The recognition of errors, if well documented, should result in a clearer and more objective presentation of the facts, since one need not give equal credence to every identification.

## 4    Defining Terms in the Absence of Identifications

Some animals that are named are never observed despite one's efforts. In some such cases one may infer the designatum of the unidentified taxon from informants' descriptions. One must be aware of the total variety of forms that are likely to occur in the study region. Thus one knows not only which animals are named, but also which animals have not yet been accounted for in the folk system. One may then attempt to match the undefined terms with the unnamed animals, by comparison of folk and scientific descriptions of morphology and behavior. One may also frame questions designed with reference to scientific descriptions of the as yet unnamed animals (see Table 2.1).

**Table 2.1**
INTERROGATIVE FORMAT:
KINDS OF SNAKES

| Questions | Answers received |
|---|---|
| 1) **binti sbil huhuten čanetik** 'What are the names of all the kinds of snakes?' | a) **ʔahaw čan** 'master snake' <br> b) **kʾančo** <br> c) **kantéla čan** 'candle snake' |
| 2) **binti yilel** 'What does it look like?' | a) **yaš** 'green' <br> b) **sot sne** 'rattle-tailed' |
| 3) **binti snahtil** 'What is its length?' | a) **hun haw** 'one arm's breadth' <br> b) **čaʔ- ʔošhoht** '2–3 measures of thumb to extended second finger' |
| 4) **ya bal stakʾ smil winik** 'Can it kill a man?' | a) **yak, lom ya stiʔwan** 'yes, it really bites' <br> b) **huʔuk, mayuk smul** 'no, no crime' |

**Table 2.2**
FOLK DESCRIPTION: SLENDER SHEARTAIL
(*Doricha enicura*)

*tešereš ne cʾunun. ya spas sna ta suniltik,*
Scissor-tail hummingbird. Builds its nest in sunflowers,

*sok čʾin ščanul, naht sniʔ,*
small body, long beak,

*sok kʾankʾantik yihkʾal skʾukʾumal.*
yellowish-black feathers.

*melel yuʔun hun ta tešereš ne.*
Because it is one with scissor-like tail.

*ya spas snain na ʔam sok nič ʔak.*
Builds its house of spider web and grass flowers.

*kʾalal ʔalah yoʔtan ta ton, la spak ston smeʔ cʾunun.*
When its heart is ready, the female lays its eggs.

*ta hun wašakeb kʾal tohkiš čʾuhčʾul cʾunun ʔa.*
In one week the little hummingbirds are born.

*hič lom hun yoʔtan ya sle be weʔel yalatak.*
Thus it happily searches for food for its young.

*"han, han," ši ya škʾopoh.*[a]
"Han, han," it says.

[a]Informant was JGG.

Detailed descriptions of folk taxa may be elicited (see Table 2.2). In my experience, such descriptions rarely state what might be considered the criterial attributes of a taxon. In short, they are not **definitions**. Rather, one obtains a list of true statements about a given taxon, many of which may also be true for a number of other taxa. Morphological description is typically meager, while information on the animal's feeding habits, movements, nesting sites, and behavior relevant to human activities, e.g., "it stings," "it eats our crops," is stressed. Such information may provide useful clues if the ethnographer has access to details of the natural history of the animals that are potential referents of the undefined terms.

Inferred definitions are illustrated below.

1. **pehpen čuč** 'butterfly squirrel' (southern flying squirrel, *Glaucomys volans*). Flying squirrels are named in Zinacantan Tzotzil (R. Laughlin personal communication) and Tenejapa is within their range (Hall and Kelson 1959:406). However, no appropriate name for such an animal was elicited during the first 6 months in the field. My informant

sample at that point, however, was biased toward the lowlands, where typical flying squirrel habitat is scarce. Thus I made enquiries in several highland *parajes*. Two informants (SPE, ALS) in **macab** cited this term and described the animal as a small, reddish 'squirrel' which is able to glide from tree to tree. Since the term *čuč* is applied to all other squirrels known to occur in the region, I feel confident that this term can have no other referent.

2. *k'iwoč č'o* 'cheek-pocket mouse' (spiny pocket mouse, *Heteromys desmarestianus*). A sizable minority of informants cited this as a kind of *č'o* 'rat-mouse'. Most agreed that it preferred rocky situations and was of moderate size relative to other 'rats'. Its most distinctive character is that referred to in the name. Among small mammals only the pocket gophers (Geomyidae) and pocket mice (Heteromyidae) have external cheek pouches. The local species of pocket gopher is much larger and is called **ba**. Of the Heteromyidae only the species cited above is known to occur in the central highland region of Chiapas (Hall and Kelson 1959:545). Furthermore, the morphological and behavioral data cited by Hall and Kelson for this species accord well with the Tzeltal description. "This species is usually found at high elevations. . . . The habitat is tropical rain forest, especially in areas where rocky outcroppings occur [Hall and Kelson 1959:543]." In addition, other genera of small rodents known to occur in the region are attributable to other named taxa.

3. Owls were an especially difficult group to define. First, practically all are strictly nocturnal, and it is quite inappropriate to prowl about at night in Tenejapa. Second, owls are thought to be harbingers of evil. Third, many species are rare and local in distribution. Their calls, however, tend to be distinctive. This provided the best clues to the identification of the half dozen types named. I netted three small species and heard the fourth in the company of two informants. A tape recording of a fifth species (the Great Horned Owl, *Bubo virginianus*) was recognized as **tuh kulum pukuh**, the name being

onomatopoetic. The Barn Owl (*Tyto alba*, see *šoč'* bird, owl) was determined on the basis of consistent descriptions of its call (rendered invariably as *ššštt*) and color (**sak** 'white') given by over 20 informants. Two other types of owls are widely recognized, **škuh** (onomatopoetic) and **k'ahk'al waš** 'fierce fox', which barks like a fox. Both are large owls. Descriptions of typical vocalizations (Davis 1972) and data on abundance, habitat, and altitudinal preferences (Land 1970) eliminate several species that are either extremely rare (Striped Owl, *Rhinoptynx clamator*; Stygian Owl, *Asio stygius*) or are restricted to tropical lowland forests (Crested Owl, *Lophostrix cristata*; Spectacled Owl, *Pulsatrix perspicillata*; Black-and-white Owl, *Ciccaba nigrolineata*). Two large species remain unaccounted for. The Mottled Owl (*Ciccaba virgata*) is common and widespread to 2300 m (Land 1970:140). The description of its call ("hut"; Davis 1972:62) is roughly comparable to the onomatopoetic Tzeltal rendition, **škuh**. The barking call attributed to **k'ahk'al waš** would be quite appropriate for the Spotted Owl (*Strix occidentalis*), a close relative of the remaining possibility, the highland-resident Fulvous Owl (*Strix fulvescens*). Since these determinations remain speculative, the inferential argument is cited in detail.

In contrast, repeated attempts to elicit names that might apply to the cacomistle (Procyonidae: *Bassariscus sumichrasti*), grisón (Mustelidae: *Galictis allamandi*), both large and distinctive mammals, or the Resplendent Quetzal (Trogonidae: *Pharomachrus mocinno*), the most sacred bird of the ancient Maya, proved fruitless. I have concluded that these animals do not now occur near Tenejapa. This negative conclusion is in itself a fact of biological and lexicographic relevance.

## 4.1 THE DANGER OF CONTACT-LANGUAGE TRANSLATIONS

In the past, bilingual dictionaries typically consisted of "translations" of terms from one folk system into a second folk system. Inevitably some inaccuracy and considerable ambiguity resulted. For example, the Tzeltal term **hoh** is sometimes translated as 'crow' in the ethnographic literature. However no true crows occur in Chiapas. The bird involved is the Common Raven (Corvidae: *Corvus corax*), distinct from crows in both habits and habitat. The source of the error is the uncritical use of the Spanish term *cuervo*, which is applied to the raven in Chiapas but which is given as "crow" in Spanish–English dictionaries.

## 5    What Is a Name?

Names as a subset of all possible utterances are defined by two criteria. The first is contextual. The utterance must be appropriate as a response to a question such as **binti sbil** 'what is its name', whether explicitly formulated or implicit in the context of identification. Second, the utterance must be a single **lexeme**. A lexeme may be defined as a semantically endocentric construction, i.e., "what is essential is that its meaning cannot be deduced from its grammatical structure [Conklin 1962:121]." If all lexemes were single morphemes, the problem of recognizing lexemes would reduce to the nontrivial problem of recognizing morphemes. Monomorphemic lexemes (to be more precise, a lexeme with a single root morpheme) are termed unitary simple lexemes by Conklin (1962:121) and (unanalyzable) primary lexemes by Berlin, Breedlove, and Raven (1973:217). English examples include oak, bear, and swallow. Tzeltal examples include *čuč* 'squirrel', **toht** 'robin', and *ʔus* 'fly'.

Lexemes of a second type, unitary complex lexemes (Conklin 1962:121) or unproductive (analyzable) primary lexemes (Berlin, Breedlove, and Raven 1973), are also readily recognized. These consist of more than one root morpheme, but no part of the name refers to any superordinate taxon. English examples include pineapple, poison oak, and woodpecker. Tzeltal examples include *c'uʔ lukum* 'worm sucker', a kind of bird, and **muy ʔam**

'masticating? spider', the velvet ants, which are not thought to be a kind of spider.

Conklin's composite lexemes may require special techniques to distinguish them from polylexemic forms. Such lexemes consist of more than one root morpheme, and, in addition, part of the name labels a superordinate taxon. Such lexemes in English may be recognized by intonational patterns, e.g., the often cited distinction between bláck-bìrd (a composite lexeme) and blàck bírd (two lexemes). Unfortunately Tzeltal provides no comparable contrast for distinguishing such minimal pairs. I presented a number of colored illustrations of birds to one informant and requested their names. He was most obliging and used several forms that I had not previously encountered. I later shared these new "names" with other informants. They laughed uproariously. One of the terms was **spahk'oh ston c'unun** 'egg-laying hummingbird', the "name" applied to my picture of a female hummingbird sitting on its nest.

Berlin, Breedlove, and Raven (1974:49–51) suggest several techniques besides that of cultural consensus, as exemplified earlier, for evaluating the status of such names in Tzeltal. The application of possessive prefixes will distinguish lexemes from descriptive phrases, but this technique is of limited use in folk zoology, since the possession of wild animals is a semantic absurdity in Tzeltal.

A more generally applicable test involves the assumption that single lexemes as responses to the question **binti sbil** are likely to be more consistent over a number of naming instances than are polylexemic phrases, since such phrases consist of more than one unit each of which may occur independently. For example, the Green Jay (*Cyanocorax yncas*) is known universally as **k'an heš** 'yellow jay' in Tenejapa. It has a green back and a yellow breast, yet it is always 'yellow jay', never 'green jay'. This technique is difficult to apply when the animals named are rarely encountered.

A technique not discussed by Berlin and his colleagues involves the assumption that most taxa* are characterized by multiple criteria (cf. Bulmer 1970:1088). Descriptive phrases, on the other hand, refer to categories defined more simply, i.e., by the addition of the features implied by the parts of the phrase. Thus a blàck bírd is a bird that is black. Nothing more is implied. However, the term bláckbìrd, for me at least, implies a bird that is typically black, though not necessarily so, with a characteristic range of shape and size, distinctive vocalizations, distinctive habits, and perhaps other characteristics of which I am not consciously aware.

One can test this factor in ambiguous cases by enquiring about attributes other than those implied by the informant's naming response. For example, *k'anal pehpen* 'yellow butterfly' is a frequent response to the question *binti sbil huhuten pehpen* 'what are the names of all the kinds of butterflies?' I then asked about its size or habits, questions designed to test the multiplicity of the criteria associated with the response. Consistent further specification was considered evidence that the response was a name rather than a descriptive phrase.

Despite these techniques many cases remain ambiguous and are treated as potential names in the text with a discussion of the evidence pro and con.

## 5.1 THE COINING OF NEW TERMS

Names are readily coined for unfamiliar animals. The great majority of such coinages are composite, i.e., a productive attributive will be added to an established name, which is a primary lexeme. Such names were systematically rejected by Berlin in favor of the format *kol pahaluk sok X* 'almost the same as X', where X stands for the name of an established category. Though this format differentiates basic and extended ranges of terms (Berlin, Breedlove, and Raven 1974: 56–58), certain valuable information may be

*A taxon in the context of this discussion is a set of organisms which is an element of an inclusive taxonomic structure. Thus "edible plant" is typically not included, nor are categories of nonbiological entities.

lost. A token may be a "true member" of A, where A is a polytypic taxon, but may not be a "true member" of any established subcategory of A. One might encounter a new kind of fish or butterfly without being able to specify what kind of fish or butterfly it is. Nevertheless it is not necessarily "almost the same as" a trout or a monarch or any other specific variety we may know. Yet it **is** a fish or a butterfly.

For example, SMZ was unfamiliar with the Black Phoebe (*Sayornis nigricans*), the Vermilion Flycatcher (*Pyrocephalus rubinus*), and the Scissor-tailed Flycatcher (*Muscivora forficata*), all species of the tyrant-flycatcher family (Tyrannidae). He coined the following terms respectively: *ʔihk'al wirin* 'black flycatcher', *cahal wirin* 'red flycatcher', and *tešereš ne wirin* 'scissor-tail flycatcher'. He thereby indicated his perception of these unfamiliar birds as kinds of the familiar category *wirin*. This name typically refers to several members of the same family that regularly occur in Tenejapa. The unfamiliar birds are not simply "similar to" *wirin*, they are new members in good standing of that taxon (see the flycatcher complex for a detailed discussion).

I have found it relatively easy to distinguish spontaneous coinages by the paralinguistic context of the naming response. Also one may ask if the informant has ever seen the animal before or if the alleged name is well known in the community.

## 6  Scientific Identifications

Ideally, a series of specimens of each species identified by informants should be collected to allow precise scientific determination and to preserve a permanent record of the data on which the ethnographic analysis is based. This ideal is more readily approximated in folk-botanical studies, since preserving and shipping plant specimens presents fewer problems than is the case with animal specimens. Birds and mammals are especially difficult (see Anderson 1965 for a detailed description of such techniques). I attempted to prepare museum skins of some mammals and birds but found the process too time-consuming and the results inadequate. The skulls of small mammals, however, are easily preserved and are often sufficient for identification purposes.

I am confident that my field identifications of over 300 species of birds seen in Chiapas are correct.* A photographic record of 60 species of birds was obtained by mist-netting and releasing specimens. A few other vertebrate species were identified by sight, but most small mammals and herptiles were collected, specimens totaling over 250. Invertebrate determinations are based on approximately 900 numbered specimens (see the Appendix for a complete listing).

* Since I identified the birds myself in the field and have no specimen documentation in most cases, I believe a brief description of my qualifications in this regard is necessary. I am not a biologist, but I am confident in my proficiency with regard to identifying species of birds and certain other animals. I have been interested in the field identification of birds since the fall of 1967. I began at that time with a field guide to North American birds (Robbins, Bruun, and Zim 1966) and a cheap pair of binoculars. I played the "life list" game, always popular among birdwatchers. One's life list is the sum total of species one has seen and identified. This game develops one's skill at bird identification. At the time of my research I had compiled a list of more than 565 of the 700-odd species of birds that regularly occur north of Mexico. I have participated in such related activities as compiling the Oakland, California, Christmas Bird Census for 1970–1971. I contribute frequently to *American Birds*, the Audubon Society journal of field observations. I was involved in the bird-banding program of the Point Reyes Bird Observatory, Bolinas, California, during 1968 and 1969. There I learned the mist-netting techniques that I put to use in Chiapas. During the summer of 1970 I traveled in Mexico and Peru, where I became acquainted with several representative tropical bird families not usually encountered in the United States. Thus the bird life of Chiapas was in large part familiar when I began my ethnographic work. My experience in identifying birds also provided a useful background for the extension of my interest to mammals, herptiles, and other forms of animal life. In short, through my avocational interests I had learned to demand high standards of critical observation and to recognize common sources of error in zoological identifications; I had also gained some understanding of scientific taxonomic principles and practice. This helped in both the ethnographic and biological aspects of the research.

The most efficient research strategy is one that is continuously guided by the incoming data, both ethnographic and biological. Ideally the ethnographer and the biologist should be one and the same individual. Failing this, ethnographer and biologist should work closely together, so that rapid feedback is possible. Since no biologist collaborated on the field portion of this research, the input of biological information was limited to the available literature and to an occasional visiting biologist.

## 7    Recording Procedures

Identifications were recorded in conjunction with specimen and sight records. The date, locality, elevation, and incidental information of biological interest were recorded for each numbered collection. Each specimen was then labeled with the corresponding number. Similar information was recorded for sight records of all but the most conspicuously common birds, the data arranged according to the bird species. Informants' initials, naming responses, and comments were noted at the same time and place. Note was taken, as well, of the circumstances of the identification if there was doubt that the informant had sufficient op-

Table 2.3
RECORDING PROCEDURES: AN EXAMPLE OF SIGHT RECORDS OF BIRDS

Species: Red-billed Azurecrown (*Amazilia cyanocephala*)

| Date | Locality, remarks | Tzeltal name | Informant |
|------|------|------|------|
| VI-17-71 | Aguacatenango | *bac'il c'unun* | AGM |
| VI-29-71 | nr. Pueblo, 2100 m | *sakil c'unun* | PVG |
| VII-13-71 | *mahosik'*, 1500 m | | no informant present |
| VIII-14-71 | nr. Teopisca, male | *bac'il c'unun honon c'unun* | JGG SMZ |
| XI-25-71 | *mahosik'*, netted | *yašal c'unun* or *sak?eal c'unun* | SMZ |
| Etc. | | | |

Table 2.4
RECORDING PROCEDURES: AN EXAMPLE OF INVERTEBRATE COLLECTION NOTES

| Collection number[a] | Locality | Date | Tzeltal name | Informant | Comment |
|---|---|---|---|---|---|
| EH 127 (EN 118104) | 40 km NE San Cris. | VII-21-71 | ʔihkʼal suʔsewal (čanul) ʔinam čab ʔihkʼal čan | SMZ JGG MMH | at collection  vague term |
| EH 128 (EN 118176) | 40 km NE San Cris. | VII-21-71 | ʔihkʼal kʼunil čan none ʔala tutin ʔus ʔakoʔ | SMZ MMH AKCʼ | descriptive no recognition descriptive |
| Etc. | | | | | |

[a]Section 1 of Chapter 5 presents an explanation of this coding system.

portunity to observe the animal adequately or if his style of response was unusual. Excerpts from these notes are cited in Tables 2.3 and 2.4. A separate notebook was kept for recording informants' responses elicited with reference to lists of terms, illustrations or tapes (see Table 2.5).

Lists of terms and probable referents were constructed from this data periodically. Constructing such preliminary lists of taxa indicated which names remained ambiguous. Special effort could then be directed toward clarifying these problem areas. The corpus of terms presented here is simply an elaborated form of the last such list prepared.

Written data obtained from literate informants include lists of edible animals, medicinal uses and recipes, artifacts made of animal products, verbal descriptions of taxa, illustrated anatomies, lists of "closest relatives" (from which covert categories may

Table 2.5
RECORDING PROCEDURES: AN EXAMPLE
OF NONIDENTIFICATION RESPONSES

| | Taxon: *toytoy* |
|---|---|
| Informant | Comments |
| AGM | Not Flammulated Owl call. |
| PVG | Knows name, has 'horns', call *ti ti ti*. |
| AGM | Includes *kʼalel toytoy* and *bacʼil toytoy*. |
| SMT | Includes *kʼalel* and *ʔahkʼubal čʼin*, first calls during day, other during night, some say *toytoy* and *turunkuc pahal* 'same'. |
| Etc. | |

sometimes be inferred), illustrated accounts of trapping techniques, and folk tales.*

## 8 The Informant Sample

Tenejapa is a large community occupying an extensive altitudinal range. One should not expect to describe the culture of such a community adequately from the statements of two or three informants. Yet a representative survey of the variety of cultural repertoires presents many difficulties. The solution to be described is practical, given time limitations, though not entirely satisfactory.

### 8.1 THE SURVEY

During November and December of 1971, I interviewed at least one informant from each of more than 25 named localities within Tenejapa (see Table 2.6). These interviews provide a geographically representative sample of Tenejapanecos. Each interview required from 5 to 8 hours of rapid ques-

* Due to the fact that I went to Chiapas at very short notice, my preparation in Tzeltal was nil. I was fortunate to have detailed linguistic materials at my disposal— much of them unpublished—and the personal assistance of researchers well versed in the language (see Acknowledgments). Thus I was able to transcribe quite accurately within a month and gained a fair understanding of the grammar before the end of my stay in the field. I never became fluent in Tzeltal. However, the specialized nature of the focus of study allowed me to obtain data of adequate quantity and quality, despite my limited knowledge of the language.

tioning. With the assistance of Santiago Mendez and José Guzman, all were conducted in Tzeltal.

Informants from particular *parajes* were solicited in the San Cristóbal market or in their home *parajes*. After a brief explanatory conversation, agreement on the payment for their services, and the recording of such basic data as sex, age, amount of schooling, and *finca* and hunting experience, the corpus of terms was presented.

Each taxon was presented as follows. *ya bal ʔana be sba X* 'are you acquainted with X?' If the informant did not know the term X, all known synonyms were then substituted. New synonyms were sought by enquiring, *ʔay šan yan sbil* 'are there other names?' Next we enquired, *ya bal shen ta Y te X-e* 'does X live in Y [*paraje*]?' This provided information about the distribution of certain animals.

Since no organisms were present during the interview, we attempted to establish the probable referential equivalence of each term for each informant indirectly. This judgment was based on a variety of cues. For example, all informants recognized the terms *šulem* and *caʔlos* and each asserted that the two were *shoyetik* 'associates'. We then enquired, *binti yilel te shole* 'what does the head look like?' The typical response specified *cahal* 'red' for *šulem* (Turkey Vulture, *Cathartes aura*) and *ʔihkʼal* 'black' for *caʔlos* (Black Vulture, *Coragyps atratus*), citing one obvious and consistent difference between these two species.

Names for animals known to have distinctive vocalizations were verified by requesting an imitation of their calls, e.g., *bi ši ya škʼopoh te X-e* 'what does X say?' The example of *šoč*, the Barn Owl, has been cited previously. Animals present seasonally were verified in part by enquiring, *bi ʔora ʔay ta skʼinal tenehapa* 'when is it present in Tenejapa?' For snakes and some insects we enquired, *ya bal štiʔwan* 'does it bite?' and to what degree.

The selection of such questions came to be an artful technique, since time was of the essence. The procedure involved evaluating

the degree to which the identity of a name was in doubt and selecting subsequent diacritical features for questioning in order to maximize a doubt-reducing factor. The sequence of questions is specifiable only as an overall strategy tailored to a particular balance of knowledge and ignorance.

Other standard survey information includes the subtypes recognized for polytypic taxa, medicinal uses and edibility of animals, and the number of each domestic species owned by the informant. Descriptive terminology was recorded verbatim in Tzeltal.

## 8.2  THE PRIMARY INFORMANTS

The survey provided a geographically representative sample of informants. However most field identifications were obtained from the following individuals.

SMZ Santiago Mendez Zapata (*hciak mentes caʔpat*),* about 40 years old, married and father of four children, resident of *mahosikʼ*. Like most Tenejapanecos of his age, his schooling was sporadic, and limited to 3 years. Yet he is an intellectual. He instituted discussions of comparative religion whenever he found the opportunity and read every Spanish-language book that came into his hands. I consider Santiago Mendez a col-

---

* Tenejapa Tzeltal names consist of three parts. First is the personal name with a prefix marking gender in referential use, *h-* for males, *š-* for females. This prefix is elided in certain phonological contexts, e.g., *ššun* is heard as *šun*. All personal names are derived forms of Spanish saint names introduced at the time of the Conquest. The second part of the name is the "clan" name derived from a Spanish surname. This defines the limits of exogamy. It is redundant, since the third part of the name, the "lineage" name (an indigenous form), implies the "clan" name. Both "clan" and "lineage" names are patrilineal. In Cancuc the redundant "clan" name may be deleted as in *htum waš* (see Table 2.6). The Ladino pattern is somewhat different. The first two parts of the name are quite comparable. However the third part is also a Spanish surname, that of the mother's family. Ladino officials in Chiapas often insist that Indians adopt this form. SMZ put one over on these officials by transforming his Tzeltal "lineage" name, *caʔpat* 'dung back', to Zapata, which passes as a valid mother's surname.

league. I was but the latest in a series of academic visitors whom he had assisted. He was familiar with folk-biological research through his association with the prior work of Berlin and Breedlove.

Though Santiago Mendez is not a "typical" Tenejapaneco, he has never abandoned the traditional subsistence activities. His discomfort in Western style pants and jacket is painful to observe. Yet he is both proud and critical of his own culture. He is skeptical of certain traditional religious and medical beliefs and chooses not to participate in the rowdier side of community fiestas. At his urging, Santiago's eldest son now attends school with Ladinos in San Cristóbal, so that he will master Spanish and thus be able to deal with Ladinos on an equal footing.

Santiago Mendez accompanied me on many trips throughout the Chiapas highlands, and I have a rather complete record of his knowledge of the local fauna. He is the source of most of the folktales collected by Katherine Branstetter and myself, and he also recorded extensive texts concerning the medicinal uses of animal products. He has illustrated some of his descriptive texts with colored pencil sketches.

JGG José Guzman Gomez (*hšoš kusman c'uhkin*), 21 years old, married and father of one child, resident of *hušal ha?*. I met José Guzman in August 1971. We began as usual by reviewing the corpus of terms. He had forgotten many of the animal terms during his 7 years in school, the last on scholarship in Tuxtla Gutiérrez. Through continued work with Santiago Mendez his memory improved, and the two formed a smoothly operating team until the completion of the work (see Figure 2.2). They traveled throughout Tenejapa collecting small mammals, buying

**Figure 2.2** Santiago (SMZ), foreground with binoculars, and José (JGG), right, pointing, on the ridge southeast of the Pueblo. [Color slide by the author.]

skulls, and recording information from a number of their fellow citizens. Their ability to work independently allowed me to work with other informants during their absence. A great deal was thus accomplished in the concluding months of field work. They returned with me to Berkeley, California, during January 1972, where they recorded further textual materials and identified birds and mammals at the Museum of Vertebrate Zoology at the University of California, Berkeley. They also inspected Joseph Copp's personal collection of Chiapas herptiles at La Jolla, California.

AGM    Alonso Gomez Mendez (*h?aluš komes ?uč'*), about 18 years old, resident of *č'ahkomah*. Alonso Gomez was a fifth-grade student when first hired as my Tzeltal tutor. He provided the majority of identifications during the first few months of field work. He is a skeptic who scoffs at any but the most certain identifications, a welcome contrast to the excesses of knowledgeability of some informants. The "Mendez" of the Spanish version of his name is his mother's patriclan name, following the Spanish pattern of family names, and an indication of his relative acculturation.

AKČ'    Antonio Guzman Ch'ihk (*h?antun kusman č'ihk*), about 30 years old, married, resident of *mahosik'*. *h?antun* knows very little Spanish. Since he has no land of his own, he hunts more than most and is particularly knowledgeable about such techniques. He did some trapping for me and provided a number of identifications during the last 2 months in the field.

AMT    Alonso Mendez Ton (*h?aluš mentes ton*), 33 years old, current president of the municipio, resident of *kul ?ak'tik*. Alonso Mendez was Dr. Berlin's primary informant during the botanical studies, but his new duties kept him occupied during my field stay. His initial illustrated list of nearly 200 animal terms commissioned by Dr. Berlin (many reproduced here) provided a significant headstart on the task.

SMT    Santiago Mendez Ton (*hciak mentes ton*), about 30 years old, originally resident of *mahosik'*, now by preference a shopkeeper in the Pueblo. He provided a number of identifications on several field trips near the Pueblo.

MMH    (*hmikel mentes holba*), about 20 years old, from *ba nabil*, AKC' (*h?aluš kusman c'uhkin*), also about 20 years old, from *san ?antonyo*, near the Pueblo; and ŠPE (*hšep peres ?elaw*); about 40 years old, from *macab*. They provided identifications of highland animals. The two last named helped in trapping and mistnetting and identified the specimens obtained.

## 8.3   THE LIST OF INFORMANTS

All informants utilized in the research are listed alphabetically by name in Table 2.6. Sex is indicated by masculine and feminine prefixes, *h-* and *š-*, respectively. *Paraje* of residence, approximate years of schooling, and role in the research are indicated when available. Distributions according to (a) place of origin, (b) "clan" affiliation, and (c) age and schooling of informants are shown in Tables 2.7, 2.8, and 2.9, respectively.

## 8.4   THE SAMPLE AS REPRESENTATIVE OF THE POPULATION

The sample adequately reflects the geographical variety within the *municipio*, and it is not significantly biased with respect to "clan," age, or amount of schooling. However it is biased by sex. Of 64 informants utilized only 3 were women, and these supplied incidental information for the most part. On the basis of this small sampling of the knowledge of Tenejapan women it seems safe to assert that their knowledge is roughly comparable to that of the men. It is restricted primarily by the fact that women are less likely to travel outside their home region. MMT, for example, knew the local fauna of *pahalton*, her home *paraje*, but was decidedly unfamiliar with lowland animals.

Table 2.6
INFORMANTS FOR THE TENEJAPA ZOOLOGICAL WORK

| Initials | Name | Paraje | Age | Schooling | Role[a] |
|---|---|---|---|---|---|
| AGM | hʔaluš komes ʔuč' | č'ahkomah | 18 | 5 | Primary informant |
| AIS | hʔaluš ʔincin sian | nabil | 50 | 0 | Survey |
| AnIS | hʔantun ʔincin sian | č'ištontik | | | |
| AKC' | hʔaluš kusman c'uhkin | san ʔantónyo | 25 | 0 | Primary informant |
| AKČ' | hʔantun kusman č'ihk | mahosik' | 30 | 1 | Primary informant |
| AKČ | šʔanton kusman čiʔ | ʔošewic | | | Survey |
| AKŠ | hʔantun kusman šilom | homal ničim | | | |
| ALC | hʔaluš lopis caʔmut | pahalton | | | Survey |
| ALČ' | hʔaluš luna č'ahkaš | balun k'anal | 45 | 2 | Survey |
| ALH | hʔaluš lopis howil c'iʔ | yehc' ʔuk'um | 30 | 0 | Survey |
| ALK | hʔaluš lopis kastil | č'ištontik | 20 | 0 | Survey |
| ALS | hʔaluš lopis setet | pokolum | 30 | 2 | Survey |
| ALSa | hʔaluš luna santis | macab | | | |
| ALW | hʔaluš lopis waskis | balun k'anal | | | |
| AMC | hʔaluš mentes caʔpat | mahosik' | 10 | 4 | |
| AMT | hʔaluš mentes ton | kul ʔak'tik | 33 | | Primary informant |
| APE | hʔaluš peres ʔelaw | č'ahkomah | 35 | 2 | Survey |
| AŠC' | hʔaluš šilom c'eh | ʔok'oč | 30 | 1 | Survey |
| AŠČ' | hʔantun šilom č'ušuw | kurus pilal | | | |
| AŠČ | hʔantun šilom čamoʔ | ʔošewic | 40 | 0 | Survey |
| AŠS | hʔaluš šilom sabin | pahalton | | | |
| CIK' | hciak ʔincin k'olin | kurus č'en | | | |
| CLL | hciak luna lopis | macab | | | Survey |
| CLT | hciak lopis tuhk'awil | winikton | 35 | 0 | Survey |
| CŠW | hciak šimnes wowo | yašanal | 42 | 0 | Survey |
| CŠWk | hciak šilom waskis | kotol teʔ | 25 | 1 | Survey |
| JGG | hšoš kusman c'uhkin | hušal haʔ | 21 | 7 | Primary informant |
| MIS | hmikel ʔincin sian | pahalton | 16 | | |
| MLC | hmikel lopis caʔmut | pahalton | | | Survey |
| MMH | hmikel mentes holba | ba nabil | 23 | 0 | Primary informant |
| MMT | šmal mentes ton | pahalton | 21 | 3 | Survey |
| MŠM | hmarkuš šilom muč | kotol teʔ | | | |
| NKČ' | hnik kusman č'ihk | mahosik' | 35 | | B. Stross's informant |
| NPK | hnik peres konte | mahosik' | | | |
| PKC' | hpetul kusman c'uhkin | šišintonil | 55 | 0 | |
| PKČ' | hpetul kusman č'ihk | mahosik' | 10 | 4 | |
| PKO | hpetul kusman ʔosil | mahosik' | | | |
| PLC | hpetul lopis caʔmut | šohleh | 42 | 3 | Survey |
| PLČ' | hpetul luna č'ahkaš | ʔamakil | 30 | 3 | Survey |
| PLK' | hpetul lopis k'ule | homal ničim | 35 | 4 | Survey |
| PLS | hpalas lopis setet | yočib | | | |
| PLT | hpetul lopis tuhk'awil | winikton | 35 | 0 | Survey |
| PMT | hpetul mentes tonil | kurus č'en | | | |
| PŠC | hpetul šilom cintaran | kurus č'en | 40 | 0 | Survey |
| PŠČ' | hpetul šilom č'uš | č'ul haʔ | 60 | 0 | Survey |
| PVG | hpetul warakis šil | sibak teʔèl | 40 | | |
| SMT | hciak mentes ton | Pueblo, mahosik' | 30 | | Primary informant |
| SMZ | hciak mentes caʔpat | mahosik' | 40 | 3 | Primary informant |
| ŠKČ' | ššun kusman č'ihk | mahosik' | 20 | | |
| ŠKČ | hšun kusman čiʔ | pakteʔton | 30 | 3 | Survey |
| ŠKK' | hšaw komes k'in | winikton | | | |
| ŠLC | hšaw lopis caʔ c'iʔ | mahosik' | 25 | 0 | |

[a]For details of the survey, see Chapter 2, Section 8.1; for detailed information about the primary informants, see Chapter 2, Section 8.2.

Table 2.6 (*Continued*)

| Initials | Name | Paraje | Age | Schooling | Role[a] |
|---|---|---|---|---|---|
| ŠLW | *hšep lopis waš* | *čilol ha?,* community of Cancuc | | | |
| ŠMT | *hšun mentes ton* | *pahalton* | | | Survey |
| ŠaMT | *hšaw mentes tonil* | *sibak te?el* | 45 | 2 | Survey |
| ŠPE | *hšep peres ?elaw* | *macab* | 40 | | Primary informant |
| ŠŠA | *hšaw šilom ?as* | *c`ahkibil hok`* | 60 | 0 | Survey |
| ŠŠS | *hšun šilom sabin* | *?amakil* | | | Survey |
| ŠŠW | *hšaw šimnes wowo* | *yašanal* | 42 | 0 | Survey |
| ŠŠW2 | *hšep šimnes wowo* | *yašanal* | | | |
| TKK' | *htin komes k`in* | *cahal č`en* | | | |
| TLH | *htin lopis howil c`i?* | *macab* | | | Survey |
| TMN | *htin meša nuhkul* | *č`ul ha?* | | | |
| TW | *htum waš* | *čilol ha?,* community of Cancuc | | | |

Table 2.7
PLACES OF ORIGIN OF THE INFORMANT SAMPLE

| Locality | Number | Locality | Number | Locality | Number |
|---|---|---|---|---|---|
| *?amakil* | 2 | *kul ?ak`tik* | 1 | Pueblo | 1 |
| *ba nabil* | 1 | *kurus č`en* | 3 | *san ?antónyo* | 1 |
| *balun k`anal* | 2 | *kurus pilal* | 1 | *sibak te?el* | 2 |
| *c`ahkibil hok`* | 1 | *macab* | 4 | *šišintonil* | 1 |
| *cahal č`en* | 1 | *mahosik`* | 9 | *šohleh* | 1 |
| *č`ahkomah* | 2 | *nabil* | 1 | *winikton* | 3 |
| *č`ištontik* | 2 | *?ok`oč* | 1 | *yaš?anal* | 3 |
| *č`ul ha?* | 2 | *?ošewic* | 2 | *yehc` ?uk`um* | 1 |
| *homal ničim* | 2 | *pahalton* | 6 | *yočib* | 1 |
| *hušal ha?* | 1 | *pakte?ton* | 1 | community of | |
| *kotol te?* | 2 | *pokolum* | 1 | Cancuc | 2 |
| | | | | Total | 64 |

Work on the *fincas* is restricted to men, though they may be accompanied by their families. Women participate in marketing,

Table 2.8
"CLAN" AFFILIATIONS OF THE INFORMANT SAMPLE[a]

| "Clan" | Number | "Clan" | Number | "Clan" | Number |
|---|---|---|---|---|---|
| *?incin* | 4 | *luna* | 4 | *šilom* | 10 |
| *komes* | 3 | *mentes* | 9 | *šimnes* | 3 |
| *kusman* | 11 | *meša* | 1 | *wereskis* | 1 |
| *lopis* | 13 | *peres* | 3 | Cancuc | 2 |
| | | | | Total | 64 |

[a] Not represented: *?ariaš, ?ernantes, ramines,* and *santis.*

as do the men, they travel to Tenango to buy pottery, and they often accompany the men to San Cristóbal. Hunting is a strictly male activity. In any case my data indicate no sex-specific patterns with respect to the naming of taxa.

No clear ranking of knowledge with respect to increasing age was evident, though most Tenejapanecos claim that older people are more knowledgeable. The two young boys in my sample (AMC, PKC') were still in the process of learning the finer distinctions of animal nomenclature. Young men who have spent several years in school

Table 2.9
AGE DISTRIBUTION AND SCHOOLING OF THE INFORMANT SAMPLE

| | *Age* | | | | | | |
|---|---|---|---|---|---|---|---|
| | *10–19* | *20–29* | *30–39* | *40–49* | *50–59* | *60–69* | *Age not given* |
| Number | 4 | 8 | 13 | 10 | 2 | 2 | 25 |

| | *Schooling* | | | | | |
|---|---|---|---|---|---|---|
| | *None* | *1–2 Yrs* | *3–4 Yrs* | *5–6 Yrs* | *7–8 Yrs* | *No information* |
| Number | 15 | 7 | 8 | 1 | 1 | 32 |

(AGM, JGG, MIS) either have forgotten or have never had the opportunity to learn some widely known terms.

Occupational or ritual specializations are minimal in **tenehapa**. I have no evidence that specialists in animal lore exist. Some Tenejapan males admit a lack of interest in and knowledge of hunting techniques, others are locally known as knowledgeable hunters who spend considerable time hunting. Such informants (AKČ', ŠPE), though quite knowledgeable, did not exhibit a larger repertoire of animal terms than several informants who rarely hunt. Curers (**hpošil**) may be found in every *paraje* (Metzger and Williams 1963). Unfortunately none of my informants was identified as such. The fact that a large number of medicinal and ritual uses of animals are widely known indicates that knowledge of the curative properties ascribed to animals is general rather than esoteric. Fabrega and Silver's detailed study of Zinacantan Tzotzil folk medicine clearly demonstrates that the identification and classification of illnesses is general knowledge (1973:Ch. 7).

In sum, differences in knowledgeability evident within the sample of informants are relatively slight and attributable to individual factors, such as curiosity and exposure, rather than to clearly defined specializations. This description of Tenejapan folk-zoological knowledge is thus attributable to an idealized Tenejapaneco of indeterminate sex and age. He is idealized to the extent that geographical and personal limitations

on knowledge are, in most instances, ignored. The corpus of zoological taxa attributed to this idealized informant is the sum of the knowledge of all informants interviewed from which apparently idiosyncratic deviations have been suppressed.

## 9 Dealing with Variability

Two techniques for reducing the complexity of the raw data of Tenejapan animal naming behavior have been described. First, correct identifications are distinguished from incorrect identifications. Second, account is taken of the restrictions on an individual's knowledge due to geographical and personal factors by defining the corpus of terms from the point of view of an "omniscient" informant (Werner 1969). Considerable variation in animal naming behavior remains. I believe this is normal when dealing with a community the size of **tenehapa**.

This variability is less confusing if the following distinctions are made. To begin, let us define the **naming ideal** as a one-to-one mapping of the corpus of names to the set of taxa such that each taxon has a unique name and each name invariably refers to a single taxon. The variability encountered is equivalent to the set of deviations from this ideal. The following five types of deviations constitute a partition of that set.

1. **Synonymy** deviates from the ideal in that a single taxon is labeled by more than one name.

2. **Homonymy** deviates in that superficially identical labels refer to more than one taxon. This deviation is distinguished from the next in that the identical names are presumed to have distinct etymologies, e.g., "red" and "read" in English, and thus to be semantically unrelated.

3. **Polysemy** deviates as above, but the varied applications of the name demonstrate some semantic relationship. Two types of polysemy may be distinguished. First, two concepts referred to by the same name may be related by set inclusion, e.g., "man$_1$," a human being, and "man$_2$," a male human being. Second, the two identically named concepts may not be so related, e.g., "father$_1$," one's father, and "father$_2$," a priest.

4. **Covert categories** deviate from the naming ideal in that a taxon demonstrably exists but is not named.

5. **Loose names** are recognized labels with neither clearly defined denotata nor defining attributes.

Synonymy, homonymy, and polysemy are typically understood to refer to deviations from the naming ideal within the repertoire of a single speaker of the language. Many such examples occur in the Tzeltal data. However it is useful to extend this typical reference to include analogous instances of microdialectal variants in complementary distribution. For example, two names may be applied to the same range of denotata but by distinct sets of individuals, so that most individuals in the community accept only one of the two names as appropriate for the taxon. This situation could be thought of as synonymy from the point of view of the ideal omniscient Tenejapaneco.

A series of examples from my data illustrates the application of this typology.

The house cat (*Felis cattus*) may be called *šawin*, *mis*, or *kátu*. Most informants recognize all three names as equivalent with respect to the denotata. *šawin* is considered the "real" name; *mis* has obscene connotations

and is used humorously; *kátu* (< Sp *gato* 'cat') is known to be a Spanish loan but may be used in some unspecified contexts. This is a typical example of synonymy.

*me? k'in ha?al* 'mother of the winter rains' is applied by most informants to the Black-headed Siskin (*Spinus notatus*). In *pahalton*, however, this term is applied to the Killdeer (*Charadrius vociferus*, see *c'u? lukum*/bird, waterbird). Since both species are most abundant in Tenejapa during the season of winter rains, the name is appropriately descriptive in both instances. This is an example of dialectal polysemy. In *pahalton* the siskin is called *bahk'al mut* 'group-of-four-hundred bird'. Thus *bahk'al mut* and *me? k'in ha?al$_1$* are dialectal synonyms, as the two names are applied to the same range of denotata by distinct sets of people. Likewise *c'u? lukum* 'worm sucker', the most widespread name for the Killdeer, and *me? k'in ha?al$_2$* are dialectal synonyms.

*čan* is a case of typical polysemy. *čan$_1$* means 'snake', *čan$_2$* refers to a rather miscellaneous category of small beetles. The semantic relationship between the uses of this term is not obvious, but there is no evidence that *čan$_1$* and *čan$_2$* are etymologically distinct.

*mut$_1$* means 'bird', *mut$_2$* means 'chicken' (*Gallus gallus*). In this example of typical polysemy, the second usage refers to a subcategory of that to which the first usage refers.

Berlin, Breedlove, and Raven (1968) describe several techniques for demonstrating the existence of covert categories. An additional technique is applied in the following example. Mice of the genus *Peromyscus* are the most commonly encountered small rodents in Tenejapa. Of the 122 such rodents (Cricetidae and Muridae) collected, 88 were assigned to this genus. Of these, 78 have been positively identified, 45 as *P. mexicanus*, 22 as *P. zarhynchus*, and 11 as *P. boylii*. Informants likewise assign these specimens to three distinct categories, *yašal č'o* 'gray mouse', *sak ?eal č'o* 'white-mouth mouse', and *k'alel č'o* 'bright mouse'. However, there appears to be a random association between the Tzeltal taxa and the biological species (see Table 5.1). Informants distinguish these taxa on the basis of pelage color alone, a characteristic that varies not only between species but also with the age of the animal. Nevertheless, these three Tzeltal names are invariably applied to mice of the genus *Peromyscus* (see Table 2.10). The five instances of other names applied to *Peromyscus* specimens are readily explained (see white-footed mouse/mammal, rat). Furthermore, informants assert that the categories to which *Peromyscus* are assigned are closely related to one another. Thus the genus *Peromyscus* is a covert Tzeltal category, which includes three or four named varieties.

The names applied to the various species of shorebirds, described in Section 3.2.1 of this chapter, are examples of "loose names." English offers many examples also, e.g., "snipe" for many English speakers refers to a nonexistent animal of some indeterminate life form and is used by practical jokers. Yet "snipe" refers to a far more concrete reality for birdwatchers and certain hunters. *š?ain* 'crocodile' might be best considered a loose name, at least for AMT. He illustrates that taxon as a whale! No doubt he had seen neither crocodile nor whale in the flesh, and knew only that *š?ain* was large and aquatic, characteristic of the whales of school primers. Loose names must play an important role in the process of linguistic diversification over time (see *?is mut*/bird, turkey).

## 10  Establishing Covert Complexes among Taxa

The definition of taxa is but one aspect of the task of accounting for the folk-biological classification system of a people. These taxa must then be organized to represent the cognitive organization imposed on the set of taxa by the folk in question.

It is immediately obvious that taxa are not simply arranged in an arbitrary (e.g., alphabetical) list in memory. Rather, two organizing principles are readily noted. First is the taxonomic relationship, X is a kind of Y. Such relationships are often though not invariably indicated by nomenclatural patterns. However, folk taxonomic structures tend to be quite shallow, often limited to a nested series of two or three named taxa (e.g., bird ⊃ duck ⊃ wood duck). If the domain in question includes several hundred named taxa (498 in the Tzeltal folk-zoological domain), the resulting taxonomic structure leaves much unsaid about the understanding of intrataxonomic relationships evident from informants' observations.

The second type of relationship among taxa is that of "horizontal" dyadic contrasts of relative similarity or relatedness. Such relationships may collectively define a class of taxa—if they are consistently mutual among a set of taxa. More often, they generate networks of perceived relationships, arranging taxa like links on a chain (as opposed to "peas in a pod"). Though these horizontal relationships may fail to generate discretely bounded higher-order taxa, they constitute an integral aspect of the texture of the fabric of folk classification. I try to describe this aspect of Tzeltal folk-zoological classification by defining covert "complexes" (cf. Berlin, Breedlove, and Raven 1974:59) and their internal structure (all such complexes are diagramed in Chapter 5, Section 2).

Complexes are abstracted from several types of data (cf. Berlin, Breedlove, and Raven 1968). Most useful in the present instance is the question frame, *binti ya shoy sba sok X* 'What is the companion of X?', where X is a named taxon. Lists were com-

**Table 2.10**
THE NAMING OF *Peromyscus* SPECIMENS

|  | Peromyscus | *Other small rodents* | *Totals* |
|---|---|---|---|
| *yašal č'o*, *sak?eal č'o*, *k'alel č'o*, or *woc č'o* | 79 | 0 | 79 |
| Other names | 5 | 38 | 43 |
| Totals | 84 | 38 | 122 |

piled from several informants substituting all known taxa in the X slot (complete lists: SMZ, JGG; partial list: AGM; spot samples: survey respondents). Informants might also be asked to sort names into groups; AMT's illustrations are so grouped. Triads test sortings were attempted, but I found it difficult to explain the desired basis for the triads test sorting (namely, overall similarity or relatedness, rather than superficial equivalences based on size, color, or some other single attribute). Nomenclatural patterns also provided valuable clues. For example, the covert hawk complex includes several generic taxa: *kok mut* 'Harpy Eagle', *likawal* 'hawk', *liklik* 'American Kestrel', *me? k'ulub* 'White-tailed Kite', and *tešereš ne* 'Swallow-tailed Kite'.

*liklik* is occasionally rendered *liklik likawal* or *sliklikil k'ulub*; *tešereš ne* may be known as *tešereš ne me? k'ulub* or *tešereš ne likawal*; *kok mut* might also be named *mamal likawal* 'grandfather hawk' or *kašlan likawal* 'Ladino hawk'. In short, synonymous usages often illuminate structural details obscured by the necessity of choosing for each taxon a "primary name" for ease of reference.

The ultimate step of translating complex skeins of pairings of this sort into the neat lines of a dendrogram is at present more art than science. What is incontrovertible is that dyadic relations of relative similarity and difference among taxa are an essential ingredient of the organization of folk-zoological knowledge.

*CHAPTER 3*

# The Framework
# of Analysis

Three analytically distinct cognitive processes interact in the definition of folk-biological systems. The first process is a basic concern of cognitive psychology, i.e., the formation and attainment of concepts (see Bruner, Goodnow, and Austin 1956). Concepts and their systematic organization constitute the process of classification. The second process is semantic, i.e., the naming of categories. The distinction between classification and naming is fundamental to the study of taxonomies. According to Kay, "the intuitive notion of taxonomy involves a taxonomic structure [of categories], a set of names [lexemes], and a mapping that relates the two [1971:879]." The third process is that by which tokens of categories are identified. It might be assumed that identification is but a trivial recapitulation of the process of concept attainment; that the features that are criterial to the definition of a category are likewise employed to evaluate the category membership of perceptual tokens. This is not necessarily the case, as I have demonstrated with respect to the identification of certain organisms (Hunn 1975b). Bruner, Goodnow, and Austin (1956:45–48) acknowledge this distinction by citing "attribute reduction" and "the development of configurational [recoded] attributes" as processes that modify the definition of a concept to reduce the time or effort required to identify exemplars. Biosystematists also note the difference between classification and identification. According to Simpson, "non-technical recognition—identification—is normally not by such separate characters [criterial attributes] but by a mental image of the whole animal [1961:12]." Furthermore, the logic of "keys," artificial systems of attributes used for identification, is quite distinct from the logic of "hierarchies," the taxonomic framework of biological classification (1961:12–16).

All three processes must be distinguished in order to achieve an adequate description of folk biosystematics, i.e., if our description is sufficient to allow a foreigner to "act appropriately" with respect to the phenomena in question as judged by the folk in question. A systematic description of identification processes, however, requires special psychological techniques and assumes the prior description of the classification and nomenclature (Hunn 1975b). Thus the present treatment is primarily restricted to the first two processes.

## 1 Lexemes: The Units of Nomenclature

Earlier, lexemes were defined, techniques for recognizing lexemes were described, and Conklin's (1962) typology was outlined in Chapter 2, Section 5. Berlin, Breedlove, and Raven (1973:217–218, 240–241) propose that Conklin's typology be modified by the addition of a fourth lexeme type. The alternative typologies are compared in Figure 3.1.

To recapitulate, the first type in both systems includes lexemes that have single root morphemes. Both systems recognize a second type, which includes lexemes composed of more than one morpheme with the proviso that no part of the name label a taxon superordinate to that labeled by the lexeme in question. Berlin's typology differs in that he recognizes a fundamental distinction between composite lexemes such as rattlesnake and planetree, on the one hand, and composite lexemes such as king cobra and black oak on the other. In both cases, part of the name labels a superordinate taxon, e.g., rattlesnakes are kinds of snakes and king cobras are kinds of cobras. However, secondary lexemes are members of a set of names, all of which are of a single type, that together labels a **partition** (i.e., an exhaustive subdivision of a set) of the superordinate taxon. For example,

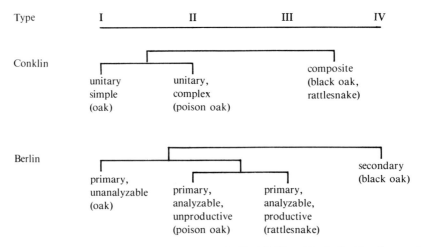

**Figure 3.1**  Types of lexemes as distinguished by Conklin (1962) and by Berlin, Breedlove, and Raven (1973).

black oak contrasts directly with other composite lexemes such as post oak, live oak, etc. Together they name all the kinds of oaks. Productive primary lexemes such as rattlesnake, however, contrast directly with unitary lexemes such as cobra and copperhead as well as with composite lexemes such as king snake and garter snake.

Given this distributional rule, Berlin's system of lexeme types may be used to make certain predictions about the system of classification from nomenclatural patterns. Berlin argues that generic and more inclusive taxa are almost always labeled by primary lexemes, while specific and less inclusive taxa are labeled by secondary lexemes.

## 2  Taxa, Taxonomic Structures, and Taxonomic Levels

A taxon is best defined as a set of real objects, in the present case, a set of animal organisms. An animal as defined in *tenehapa* is any object to which the term *čanbalam* in its most inclusive sense (see *čanbalam*₁) is applicable. In scientific terms, an animal is any organism classed in the kingdom ANIMALIA. Given the limits inherent in the Tenejapaneco's knowledge of living things, these two categories are perfectly equivalent in membership.

This is not to claim that the Tzeltal category *čanbalam* is defined or recognized on the basis of criteria identical to those definitive of the corresponding scientific taxon. Thus I reject the alternative approach to taxonomic axiomatization that would define taxa as sets of features. Such an approach is not consonant with the postulate that taxa are related to one another by set inclusion,* nor does it provide a basis for defining species as breeding populations, a basic principle of biological systematics (Simpson 1961:147). Defining taxa as sets of organisms facilitates the comparison of folk and scientific systems of classification but begs a number of relevant psychological questions.

A **taxonomic structure** is a set of taxa, one of which is the **unique beginner**, i.e., the taxon that properly includes all other taxa of the taxonomic structure. The unique beginner at level zero **immediately includes**, i.e., without intervening taxa, two or more taxa at level one, which collectively partition the unique beginner. Each taxon at level one that is further subdivided is partitioned by a set of two or more immediately included taxa, which are at level two, and so forth,

---

*If a taxon ($t$) is defined as a set of defining features ($a$, $b$, $c$), then a taxon ($t - 1$) which is immediately included in the taxon ($t$) must be defined as set of features $[a, b, c, d]$. Thus $t - 1$ cannot be a subset of $t$.

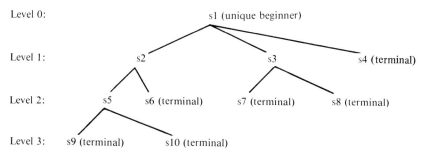

Figure 3.2   A schematic representation of a taxonomy. (Each s stands for a segregate, a named taxon.)

until the level of each taxon of the taxonomic structure is defined. Taxa that include no subordinate taxa are **terminal** at whatever level. It follows that the set of terminal taxa is also a partition of the unique beginner (from Kay 1971). The conceptual apparatus to this point entails two types of objects, taxa and names, and two relations, that of set inclusion and that of name-category correspondence (see Figure 3.2).

## 3   Categories of Taxa and the Notion of Contrast

An alternative formal treatment of taxonomies is that of Gregg (1954, 1967). His formalization differs significantly from Kay's, outlined in the previous section, since it was designed to account for biosystematic, rather than ethnographic, classification. Gregg defines sets of taxa that correspond to the biosystematist's categories (ranks): for animals, the invariant Kingdom, Phylum, Class, Order, Family, Genus, and Species, and the various optional intermediate categories. Within certain limits, taxa of the same categorical rank may be said to "contrast with" one another, since such taxa are supposed to exhibit comparable degrees of differentiation (Simpson 1961: 197–199). The specification of taxonomic ranks is necessary if monotypic genera, families, etc. are to be allowed. For example, the Limpkin (*Aramus guarauna*), a cranelike bird, is the sole living exemplar of the family Aramidae. The family includes a single genus and that genus a single species. Kay's formal-

ization does not allow of such a possibility, since all nonterminal taxa must immediately include **two** or more taxa. Yet no ornithologist would accept the classification of the Limpkin in the same genus with any other bird. Likewise, one cannot consider the Limpkin to be a family, since it is a population of organisms, i.e., a species. A taxonomy axiomatized on the basis of taxa as sets of features might better incorporate this anomaly, however, as noted earlier, at the cost of creating yet more intractable logical difficulties.

An analogous problem is readily apparent with respect to folk classification. The categories immediately included in the unique beginner, those at level 1, are quite disparate. For example, in Tzeltal, *čanbalam*$_1$ 'animal' immediately includes *mut*$_1$ 'bird', which in turn subsumes more than 100 taxa, many of which are further subdivided. Yet *čanbalam*$_1$ also immediately includes a number of categories of limited reference such as *tuluk' čan* (oil beetles, *Meloe* spp.) and *soc'* 'bat', neither of which is further subdivided.

One would like to say that *soc'* 'bat' (level 1) **contrasts with** categories such as *heš* 'jay' (level 2) in some psychologically significant sense (i.e., exhibits a comparable degree of differentiation), rather than with *mut*$_1$, which by Kay's definition belongs to the same "contrast set." In fine, taxonomic structures defined solely in terms of the relation of set inclusion cannot adequately account for the notion of contrast, which relates taxa to one another by reference to the degree of differentiation they exhibit, a notion relevant to folk as well as to scientific classification. Taxonomic ranks must be defined to account for this relation.

## 4    Berlin's System of Taxonomic Ranks

Berlin (1972) proposes a system of taxonomic ranks defined in terms of both taxonomic and linguistic criteria. He recognizes the following ranks in order of decreasing inclusiveness.

1. The **unique beginner** is that taxon which properly includes all other taxa of the domain in question. Thus the domain may define the unique beginner or vice versa. In the Berlin system, it is further assumed that the domain corresponds roughly to the kingdom level of scientific classification. Folk taxa at this level are not always named (see Berlin, Breedlove, and Raven 1968). In fact, Berlin considers the naming of the unique beginner to be a relatively recent phenomenon in the evolutionary development of taxonomic nomenclature (1972:53). Covert taxa are specifically allowed in Kay's formal definition of a taxonomy (Kay 1971:881). However it is not clear how the limits of a domain are to be unambiguously defined when no broadly inclusive taxa are named. One must either accept the most inclusive named taxon as the unique beginner regardless of its scope or allow unnamed taxa and delimit the domain of analysis in a logically arbitrary fashion.

Insisting that the unique beginner be named results, in many cases, in the definition of unique beginners such as "tree," "snake," "corn," etc., ad absurdum. On the other hand, if we accept a covert unique beginner at a level comparable to "animal" or "plant," we must be ready to accept yet more inclusive covert taxa as well. This might result in unique beginners such as "sentient being," "natural object," or "phenomenon." Such groupings tend to be vaguely defined at best. It seems preferable to accept the arbitrariness of the choice of unique beginner.

Berlin's solution is to define the unique beginner as the taxon immediately superordinate to life-form taxa, which in turn are defined as taxa immediately superordinate to generic taxa. These, as we shall see, are recognized by reference to linguistic criteria.

2. **Life-form** taxa occupy level one, as defined by Kay, i.e., they are immediately subordinate to the unique beginner. However, not all taxa at level one are life-form taxa; only those that include generic taxa in turn are so considered. Though life-form taxa are not explicitly defined by reference to the **number** of included generics, typical examples include from 20 to 200. Widespread examples of life forms are those glossed as 'tree', 'herbaceous shrub', 'vine', or 'grass' in the plant domain and 'bird', 'mammal', and 'fish'—if a sufficient number of fish species are known to the folk in question—among the animals. A common nomenclatural pattern is for the name of a life form to be identical to or a derivative of the name for a typical included generic, e.g., 'cottonwood' and 'tree' are polysemous in several Indian languages of the southwestern United States (Trager 1939). Berlin cites this pattern as evidence for the priority of generic names (1972:65–69).

3. **Intermediate** taxa are "categories of greater inclusiveness than folk generic[s] but not yet life form categories [Berlin 1972: 73]." According to Berlin, such taxa are rarely named: "Why are named intermediate taxa almost totally absent in natural ethnobiological taxonomies? The conclusion that I have tentatively come to is that such taxa are rare because they are basically unstable categories [1972:73]." A folk English example is 'duck', which is a kind of bird (the life form), but which, for hunters and birdwatchers at least, includes a number of generic taxa such as Mallard, Canvasback, scaup, etc., some of which are further subdivided.

4. **Generic** taxa form the backbone of Berlin's typology, analogous in this respect to the species of modern biosystematists. Such taxa are considered to be "psychologically basic" (Berlin 1972:54)

and "semantic primitives" (1972:55). How-ever, they are not explicitly defined in either psychological or noncircular taxonomic terms. Rather, "generic names can be seen to exhibit a readily identifiable linguistic structure [i.e., that of primary lexemes], which allows, in most cases, for their im-mediate recognition [1972:55]." And generic taxa are those labeled by generic names (1972:52).

The alleged association of a type of name, i.e., a primary lexeme, with a type of taxon, i.e., the generic, is a hypothesis requiring empirical verification. Such verification requires that independent criteria be specified for recognizing types of names and types of taxa. Berlin provides no such criteria for his taxonomic categories. Yet there is suggestive evidence that the least inclusive taxa named by primary lexemes are culturally salient, psychologically funda-mental, and historically prior.

5. **Specific** taxa are the immediate sub-divisions of generic taxa and are labeled by secondary lexemes.*

6. **Varietal** taxa are subdivisions of speci-fic taxa generated by the repeated applica-tion of the process that generates specific taxa as subdivisions of generics. They are also labeled by secondary lexemes.

The recognition of some generic and specific names is problematic, due to the fact that composite lexemes may be ab-breviated. Abbreviation depends on several factors. One expects more frequently used words to be reduced in length. Since fre-quency of use might provide a valid index of cultural salience, abbreviated second-ary lexemes might best be classed as generic names. For example, *čikinib hihte?* 'live oak', typically abbreviated as *čikinib* 'armadillo ear', is considered by Berlin to be a generic (1972:77–78), following this logic. However, abbreviation is also dependent on irrelevant factors, such as the distributional properties

of the attributive segment of the name. For example, *k'eweš hihte?* 'custard apple oak' is never abbreviated, perhaps because *k'eweš* alone refers to the custard apple (*Annona* sp.), another species of tree. Likewise, attributives such as *k'anal* 'yellow' and *muk'ul* 'large' would generate ambiguity if used alone.

In short, a typology of taxa based un-ambiguously on psychological criteria is necessary to determine the relationship between patterns of nomenclature and principles of classification.

## 5  Psychological Criteria for Ranking Taxa

Bruner, Goodnow, and Austin provide a useful starting point for this endeavor. They define an **attribute** as "any discriminable feature of an event that is susceptible of some discriminable variation from event to event [1956:26]." **Criterial** attributes may be recognized, "When such a discriminable fea-ture is used as a means of inferring the identity [i.e., the category membership] of something ... [Bruner, Goodnow, and Austin 1956:26]." Criterial attributes may be discrete, e.g., the feature is present or absent, or continuous, in which case a range of values of the attribute is considered char-acteristic of a set of events. Attributes may predict category membership with certainty or probabilistically. The determination of the criterial attributes of a category is a psychological problem. **Defining** attri-butes, on the other hand, are specified a priori according to law or convention. For example, the defining attributes of what is considered to be driving a car "too fast" is specified by law. However the criterial attri-butes of driving too fast may vary from driver to driver and may not be in accord with the legal definition.

It is assumed that most categories are not recognized in terms of a single attribute. Thus three category types are defined with reference to the logical relationship between the criterial attributes of a category. Catego-ries may be conjunctive if "defined by the **joint presence** of the appropriate value

*Bulmer (1970) defines the term "folk specific" as a terminal taxon or, more specifically, as the lowest level taxon defined in terms of multiple features. This is different from Berlin's (1972) usage.

of several attributes [Bruner, Goodnow, and Austin 1956:41]," disjunctive if the category is recognized by the presence of one set of features **or** another set of features, or relational if the criterial attributes are relations between values of other attributes. A fourth type of category is **configurational.** According to Bruner, Goodnow, and Austin (1956) such categories result when a large number of potential criterial attributes exist, and requirements of cognitive efficiency, e.g., minimizing the time required to recognize instances of a category, lead to a **recoding** of the attributes.

Such reconstruction is possible because in fact the defining features of most objects and events are redundant with respect to each other. A bird has wings and bill and feathers and characteristic legs. But ... if it has wings and feathers, the bill and legs are highly predictable. In coding or categorizing the environment, one builds up an expectancy of all of these features being present together. It is this unitary conception that has the configurational or Gestalt property of "birdness." ... When the conception is well enough established, it takes on the property of being able to serve as a discriminable and seemingly irreducible attribute of its own [p. 47].

Thus configurational categories, unlike the other category types defined, are recognized by reference to a **single** attribute rather than by reference to the concatenation of several attributes. Yet the recoding of a configurational attribute is made necessary by the recognition of manifold differences between sets of objects or events. Configurational categories are thus both more simple and more complex than categories recognized by the conscious manipulation of attribute sets. This distinction is basic to an understanding of folk classification.

This distinction may be rephrased in terms of the two fundamental logical processes, deduction and induction. Deduction generates categories a priori by the statement of a defining rule. Such categories are known by reference to a set of defining features. If an object possesses the defining features, it is a member of the category. If it lacks the features, it cannot be a member of the category. It follows that the defining features of deductive categories must be

linguistically codable in order to be communicated without direct reference to examples of the category. Defining features are thus capable of being labeled by terms of general reference. Let us call such defining criteria **abstract features**. For example, a "big truck" is a deductive category in that any truck that is relatively large must be so classified. The attributive "big" refers to an abstract feature definitive of the category. This feature is not restricted to the context of trucks but may be used to define a wide range of deductive categories. The linguistic codability of the abstract feature "big" is prerequisite for its use as a defining feature of deductive categories.

Inductive categories must be created by abstracting a **configuration** from a sample of the membership of the category. No defining rule is given. With reference to folk-biological taxa, inductive categorization is constrained by the objective discontinuities in nature. Induction tends to produce a best possible fit between natural discontinuities and a psychologically and ecologically efficient system of classification. Thus the characteristic configurations of inductive categories are entities **unique** to each category. Let us call these entities **concrete features.**

For example, the category labeled by the folk English term "raccoon" does not exist by virtue of the fact that it possesses certain features such as hair, a banded tail, and a face mask. Rather, by observing a sample of the things called raccoons an invariant perceptual pattern is induced that can only be labeled "raccoonness." This configuration is unique to those organisms that are called raccoons. "Raccoonness" is thus a concrete feature. There is no reason for labeling this feature, since it is of relevance only with respect to this category. "Raccoon" is defined by the natural boundary that exists between the raccoon pattern and the pattern of each other category of organisms.

This is not to deny that it is possible to **describe** a raccoon to a person who has never seen one. However, this description is not a definition and is necessary only in specialized communicative contexts. Prior to the rise of large-scale societies, it is likely that it was never necessary to describe a concept such as raccoon, since all members of the speech community would be directly familiar with the organisms so classified.

Only children need learn the meaning of generic labels such as "raccoon." The evidence indicates that children learn such meanings by recapitulating the inductive process (see Stross 1973). Instruction consists of pointing to exemplars of the category and correcting inappropriate creative extensions of the term. It does not normally involve verbal specification of abstract defining features. The learning process is thus analogous to that involved in learning one's native language.

Bruner, Goodnow, and Austin illustrate the process of learning a concrete feature.

The student being introduced for the first time to microscopic techniques in a course in histology is told to look for the *corpus luteum* in a cross-sectional slide of rabbit ovary. He is told with respect to its defining attributes that it is yellowish, roundish, of a certain size relative to the field of the microscope, etc. He finds it. Next time he looks, he is still "scanning the attributes." But as he becomes accustomed to the procedure and to the kind of cellular structure involved, the *corpus luteum* begins to take on something classically referred to as a *Gestalt* or configurational quality. Phenomenologically, it seems that he no longer has to go through the slow business of checking size, shape, color, texture, etc. Indeed, "corpus luteumness" appears to become a property or attribute in its own right [1956:46].

In this instance verbal cues are provided as an initial aid to learning, but the inductive process that leads to the student's ability to recognize "corpus luteumness" is not further guided by verbal instruction.

By contrast the category "female raccoon" is deductive. A female raccoon is defined by the co-occurence of the concrete feature "raccoonness" with the abstract feature labeled by the term "female." Females of whatever sort may be recognized as such regardless of the specific context. A raccoon is a female if and only if it possesses this additional defining feature. Extreme

sexual dimorphism aside, a person who has seen only male raccoons but who has had experience with females of other species should be able to correctly identify the first female raccoon he encounters given access to sufficient perceptual information.

The category "female raccoon" is not a scientific taxon. Neither is "red raccoon" or "big raccoon" or "flying animal" or "edible plant." Deductive folk categories correspond rarely with scientific taxa. On the other hand, inductive folk taxa exhibit a near perfect correspondence with scientific taxa, e.g., "raccoon," "dog," "bird," "bumblebee."

The differential relevance of inductive folk taxa, as opposed to deductive folk taxa, with reference to scientific biosystematics is not a logical necessity but an empirical fact. Yet this differential relevance also makes very good sense. Induction and deduction both generate categories of **similar** objects or events. In deduction the criteria for similarity are stated a priori and typically serve some **special purpose** (see Berlin, Breedlove, and Raven 1966; Bulmer 1970: 1084–1087). With induction, no attribute is necessarily more criterial than any other. Thus inductive categorization involves the evaluation of a potentially infinite set of attributes in order to discover which attributes are maximally informative, i.e., those that best predict the pattern of variation of all attributes among all the organisms known. This process typically produces a logically "natural" or **general purpose** classification.

Though modern biosystematics is predicated upon a special purpose, i.e., the replication of evolutionary events, it is an accepted principle that the first logical step in biological classification is the documentation of resemblances, an inductive procedure. The theory of evolution then provides deductive principles for evaluating degrees and types of resemblances. "Among a number of species some will resemble each other more than others. It is to be assumed that the resemblances, as far as homologous, reflect propinquity of descent [Simpson 1961:116]." In a restricted geographical setting and at a single point in time, resemblances provide a near perfect index of evolutionary propinquity. Thus folk-biological categories, to the extent that they are inductive, will tend to correspond with scientific taxa. Since the mutual relevance of folk and scientific classification is a basic issue in the study of folk biology (see this chapter, Section 9), the distinction between inductive and deductive categories will serve here as the primary criterion for classifying folk taxa.

Biosystematic procedures indicate two further psychological considerations relevant to the task of defining a typology of folk taxa. Given contemporaneous organisms, Simpson cites three principal criteria for the recognition of supraspecific taxa, "degrees of separation (gaps), amount of divergence [an inverse function of resemblance], and multiplicity of lower taxa [an index of diversity or heterogeneity] [1961:191]." The presence of a decided "gap" or discontinuity in terms of multiple resemblances produces a "nonarbitrary" group with respect to exclusion, i.e., with respect to what is excluded from the group. The degree to which a group is diverse or heterogeneous affects the arbitrariness of the group with respect to inclusion (Simpson 1961:115). Given that a folk taxonomy is based on the inductive recognition of resemblances, the perceived size of gaps between sets of organisms and the heterogeneity of those sets account in large measure for the observed structure of folk biotaxonomies.

A series of heuristic diagrams should clarify these distinctions. These diagrams resemble a two-dimensional profile of mountain ridges and valleys (see Figure 3.3). The "valleys" represent perceived discontinuities between groups of organisms. The wider the valley the greater the discontinuity perceived. The "ridges" represent regions of resemblance, the more narrow the ridge the more homogeneous the grouping. On the baseline, a multiplicity of variable attributes is collapsed into a single dimension, which might be glossed as overall 'similarity'. The double ridge represents a bimodal distribution of similarity, the hanging valley indicating a relative rarity but not total lack of intermediate forms.

Generic taxa typically exhibit a pattern of narrow ridges separated by wide valleys, as in Figure 3.4. A, B, and C are monotypic generic taxa and likely candidates for labeling with primary lexemes.

Specific taxa may be illustrated as in Figure 3.5. A, B, C, and D are homogeneous, inductive categories and thus nonarbitrary with respect to both inclusion and exclusion (see Simpson 1961:115). However A, B, and C are specific taxa, classed together as kinds of the polytypic generic taxon E, while D is isolated as a monotypic generic taxon. An important theoretical goal is to specify the necessary and sufficient conditions that produce this combination of polytypic generic and specific taxa. It may prove to be definable in terms of the "ratio" between the "width" of E and the width of the gap between C and D (see this chapter, Section 6[4]). Berlin defines varietal taxa simply as subdivisions of specific taxa, a quantitative rather than a qualitative contrast. Bulmer, however, suggests that a significant psychological contrast should be drawn between folk specifics (see footnote to p. 45), "definable by multiple characters," and folk varieties, "distinguished by **single** characters only [1970:1089]." Bulmer's distinction appears to be identical to that drawn here between inductive and deductive categories respectively. Following this lead varietal taxa may be illustrated, as in Figure

**Figure 3.3**   Heuristic diagram: Example.

Figure 3.4  Heuristic diagram: Typical generic taxa.

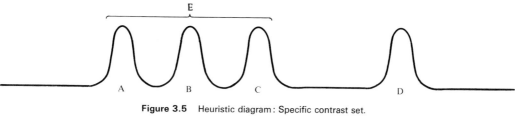

Figure 3.5  Heuristic diagram: Specific contrast set.

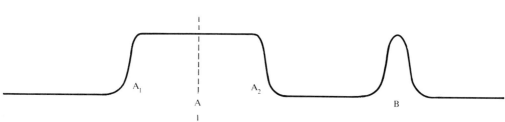

Figure 3.6  Heuristic diagram: Deductive varietal distinction.

3.6. The dotted line indicates the boundary between two varietal taxa, $A_1$ and $A_2$, which are subdivisions of the heterogeneous generic taxon A. The heterogeneity of A is perceived to be continuous. Thus the groups $A_1$ and $A_2$ must be arbitrary with respect to exclusion (see Simpson 1961: 115). They are deductive categories, since no significant discontinuity exists as a basis for distinguishing $A_1$ from $A_2$. Continuously heterogeneous categories can **only** be subdivided by a deductive rule.

Continuous heterogeneity is likely to be perceived under two conditions. First, a biological species may exhibit an exceptional range of phenotypic variability within a restricted geographical area. Such variability is characteristic of domesticated species both of plants and of animals. This helps explain the fact that polytypic generics are disproportionately common among plant species of high cultural utility as demonstrated by Berlin, Breedlove, and Raven (1966).

Second, continuous heterogeneity may be perceived as a characteristic of a bio-

logically diverse set of organisms, if the organisms are poorly known, physically small, or culturally inconsequential. For example, specific, i.e., inductive, subdivisions of **soc'** 'bat' are potentially recognizable—the vampire bat (*Desmodus rotundus*) is distinguished in Zinacantan Tzotzil (R. M. Laughlin personal communication). However in **tenehapa** only varietal distinctions are drawn, as illustrated in Figure 3.7. The dotted curves indicate the potential distinctions ignored in **tenehapa**. It is true that there are 'big bats' (**muk'ul soc'**) and 'small bats' (**č'in soc'**), but many bats are intermediate in size. These cannot be classified unambiguously by this deductive rule.

The special case of continuously variable, or **simple heterogeneous**, categories has been discussed in some detail. Discontinuously variable, or **complex heterogeneous**, categories occur with greater frequency in folkbiological taxonomies. In any case, the degree of internal heterogeneity of configurational categories is itself continuously variable. The homogeneous pole is exempli-

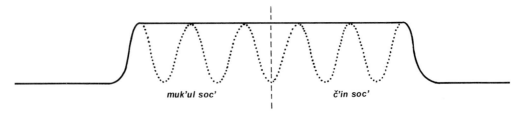

*muk'ul soc'*                    *č'in soc'*

**Figure 3.7** Heuristic diagram: Tzeltal bats.

fied by monotypic generic taxa as in Figure 3.4. The heterogeneous pole is represented by unique beginners and life-form taxa. The continuity between monotypic generic taxa and maximally heterogeneous taxa is more readily apparent when several intermediate stages are described. Figure 3.5 illustrates a discontinuously polytypic generic of the simplest type. The example illustrated in Figure 3.8 is somewhat more complex. X, Y, Z, and *čikinib* 'live oak' are all kinds of *hihte?* 'oak'. All are inductive categories distinguishable on the basis of a number of attributes. X, Y, and Z, labeled by secondary lexemes, are considered to be 'typical oaks'. *čikinib* is seen as somewhat aberrant, though still an 'oak'. It is usually referred to simply as *čikinib*, though the name *čikinib hihte?* is also acceptable to most informants. Is *čikinib* a specific taxon or a generic? If a generic, how is *hihte?* to be classified? This "difficulty" is an artifact of the discrete nature of the typology of taxa employed. The ratio of the width of X, Y, and Z to the width of the gap between *čikinib* and X is such that the distinctiveness of *čikinib* is stressed nomenclaturally, i.e., it is labeled with a primary lexeme in most cases, and is thus a generic taxon. However the width of *hihte?*, including *čikinib*, when compared to the width of the gap that isolates *hihte?*, is also such as to require nomenclatural recognition. Thus *čikinib* is a generic within a generic. Though this possibility is not allowed in Berlin's system of taxonomic categories, he arrives at a similar conclusion with respect to this example (Berlin, Breedlove, and Raven 1974:35).

Even greater heterogeneity is exhibited by the category *čan*₁ 'snake', which includes several categories comparable to *čikinib* among the 21 immediately included, inductive subdivisions. Yet the gap between snakes and nonsnakes is so apparent that the integrity of this complex group is assured. At this point it is but a small step to the larger life-form taxa such as those glossed as 'bird' and 'tree', and from those to the unique beginners. Monotypic specific and generic taxa as well as the maximally heterogeneous taxa are alike in that they are recognized by a characteristic configuration and are defined by significant discontinuities. All are nonarbitrary, inductive categories.

The significance of heterogeneity as a determinant of taxonomic structure is indicated by the fact that taxa of greater heterogeneity are far less frequent in folk taxonomic systems than less heterogeneous taxa (see Table 4.1). The frequency distribution of taxa by degree of heterogeneity—measured for example by the number of immediately included subtaxa—is linear when both variables are logarithmically transformed (Geoghegan 1973; cf. the "Willis distribution," Herdan 1960: 210–225). If the nomenclatural recognition of a category is a function of the ratio of internal heterogeneity and external gaps as suggested above, it follows that the more heterogeneous the group the less likely the existence of a sufficiently wide gap to require the naming of the group.

## 6 Proposed Modifications of Berlin's System of Taxonomic Ranks

To summarize the preceding discussion of psychological criteria relevant to a classi-

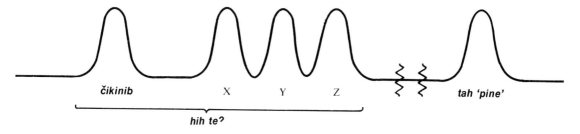

**Figure 3.8**  Heuristic diagram: Tzeltal oaks.

fication of taxa, the following modifications and reinterpretations of Berlin's system of taxonomic categories are suggested.

1. Varietal taxa should be redefined as deductive subdivisions of continuously heterogeneous inductive taxa. As such they may be immediately included in either specific or generic taxa. Subvarieties are logical possibilities and may be defined as deductive subdivisions of varietal taxa. A varietal taxon is specified by the concatenation of one or more abstract features with one or more concrete features. The concrete features are dominant, as is implied by the attribute-head structure of secondary lexemes.

2. The arbitrariness of the choice of unique beginner is made explicit, though the possibility should be investigated that unique beginners might be defined as inductive taxa of maximal heterogeneity.

3. Specific, generic, intermediate, and life-form taxa and the unique beginner, in that order, reflect a continuum of increasing heterogeneity among inductive taxa. The boundaries between adjacent taxonomic ranks are thus arbitrary.

4. The special status of generic taxa is best understood by reference to structural relationships defined in terms of two variable perceptual quantities: the width of the gaps isolating taxa and the "width," or heterogeneity, of the taxa themselves. To this end a simple symbolic notation is introduced as follows.

Let $G$ stand for the quantity "width of a gap between two taxa." Let $H$ stand for the quantity "heterogeneity of a taxon." The superscripts $x$ and $n$ may be used to distin-guish gaps in two structural positions, $G^x$ is the width of a gap external to a given taxon, $G^n$ the width of a gap separating two taxa included within a given taxon. $G_{min}$ (min = minimum) is the smallest gap of a given set of gaps, $G_{max}$ (max = maximum) the largest of a given set. Homogeneous taxa are those taxa $(t)$ for which $H(t)$ is vanishingly small. It is assumed that local populations of nondomesticated biological species, with minor exceptions, will be perceived as exhibiting such minimal heterogeneity, ignoring maturational and sexual dimorphism.

At this point a Critical Ratio $(CR)$ may be defined for any taxon $(t)$ such that $CR(t)$ increases as the minimal external gap $[G^x_{min}(t)]$ increases, and decreases as the heterogeneity $[H(t)]$ increases (see Figure 3.9). We may express this quantity as a ratio of these factors—$CR(t) = G^x_{min}(t)/H(t)$—bearing in mind that the term "ratio" is being used in a loose, metaphorical sense. The Critical Ratio is intended as an index of the relative **perceptual salience** of taxa within a domain.

Given that not all potentially recognizable groupings of organisms are named, and that the naming of potential taxa is in part a function of the perceptual salience of taxa, a naming threshold $(N)$ may be defined for each culturally defined domain such that if $CR(t)$ is greater than $N$, the taxon $(t)$ will be named, and if $CR(t)$ is less than $N$, the taxon will not be named.

A potential taxon may be defined as any inductive grouping of organisms such that $G^x_{min}$ is greater than $G^n_{mxn}$ (mxn = maxi-min). The subscript mxn refers to the largest

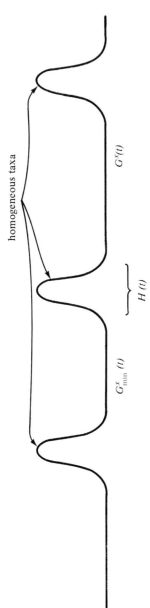

**Figure 3.9** Heuristic diagram. External gaps.

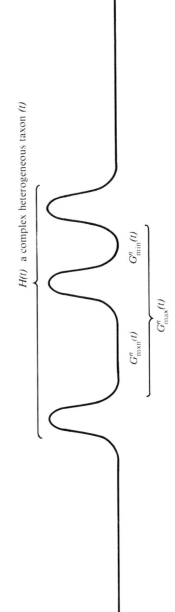

**Figure 3.10** Heuristic diagram: Internal gaps.

gap of a set that includes only the smallest gaps between each subtaxon and the remaining subtaxa of the taxon in question (see Figure 3.10) .

It is now possible to define a generic taxon as any taxon (*t*) such that $CR(t)$ is greater than or equal to $CR(t \pm n)$. The symbol $t \pm n$ indicates any taxon which either includes *t* or is included in *t*. Thus generic taxa are by definition the most perceptually salient and, by implication, are named prior to taxa of greater or lesser inclusiveness, in accord with Berlin's description (1972:54–55).

Specific taxa are simply inductive taxa, not themselves generic, that are subordinate to a generic taxon. The unique beginner, life-form, and intermediate taxa are simply inductive taxa superordinate to one or more generic taxa. Life forms are immediately included in the unique beginner, while intermediate taxa are subordinate to a life form.

The major difficulty with the above formulation is the problem of measurement. If the quantities *G* and *H* cannot be measured in some valid and reliable manner, the analytical framework proposed will remain no more than a heuristic device. I believe these quantities may be measurable, since biosystematists base their taxonomic judgments on estimates of comparable quantities (see Simpson 1961:191).

## 6.1 THE PRACTICAL EFFECTS OF THE MODIFICATIONS PROPOSED

The typology of taxa proposed here differs significantly from that of Berlin (1972) in terms of the criteria employed for defining types of taxa. However, the classification that results is not radically different. The following examples clarify the major points of divergence.

One difference involves the distinction between specific and varietal taxa as exemplified by *soc'* 'bat' (see Figure 3.7). Informants are aware that this taxon is heterogeneous with respect to the attributes of color and size. A typical subdivision recognizes two

types immediately included in the generic taxon, e.g., *muk'ul soc'* 'large bat' and *č'in soc'* 'small bat'. According to Berlin's criteria, these subdivisions are specific taxa. However, the subdivisions are deductive; each is defined by the literal application of a specific feature. By my criteria the subdivisions are varietal.

The divergence illustrated by *soc'* 'bat' is rare because deductive subdivisions of inductive taxa are not often recognized systematically in Tenejapa Tzeltal. Deductive subdivisions are not constrained by objective discontinuities, thus they may vary more freely among individuals or between cultures.

Berlin cites a few second-order subdivisions of generic taxa, i.e., "varietals," in the Tzeltal folk-botanical system (Berlin Breedlove, and Raven 1974:37). These taxa are of indeterminate status with respect to the criteria proposed here. For example, *cahal šlumil čenek'* 'red ground bean' and *ʔihk'al šlumil čenek'* 'black ground bean' are widely and consistently recognized subdivisions of the specific taxon *šlumil čenek'* (Berlin, Breedlove, and Raven 1974:474). Though the two types are distinguished primarily on the basis of a single attribute of general relevance, i.e., the color of the bean, it is unclear to what extent other criteria are also involved, e.g., taste and timing of maturity (B. Berlin personal communication). If several attributes are involved, I would consider these taxa to be inductive despite the fact that they are subdivisions of a specific taxon. Such taxa may be referred to as subspecific taxa, rather than as varietals, in order to maintain the proposed distinction between inductive specifics and deductive varietals.

The example of *čikinib* 'live oak' has been previously discussed (see Figure 3.8 and text discussion thereof). In this instance the generic taxon *čikinib* is included in a second generic taxon *hihteʔ* 'oak'. Thus generic and specific taxa (i.e., the remaining subdivisions of 'oak') occur in the same contrast set, which is contrary to Kay's formal definition of Generic Contrast (Kay 1971:884). Berlin suggests that this is an exception that by its rarity proves the rule that all taxa immediately included in a generic are specific. In the present formulation, it is readily apparent why this sort of "exception" should be rare.

No significant modification of Berlin's suprageneric ranks is proposed. Thus the two systems should agree in assigning taxa to intermediates and life forms to the extent that they agree in classifying generics. It is suggested, however, that these ranks are psychologically arbitrary because of the continuous variation of taxonomic heterogeneity ($H$). The continuity of this variation is demonstrated by the list (Table 3.1) of the most heterogeneous taxa of the Tzeltal plant and animal domains, as indicated by the number of immediately included subtaxa.

The four largest taxa are unambiguously life forms, since they include large numbers of unambiguously generic taxa. 'Beans' and 'bananas' are likewise clearly generics, despite the large number of immediately included taxa. Both are important cultigens. Thus the number of specific taxa recognized is due to their biological status as domesticated organisms and their cultural salience. The latter factor may be interpreted as lowering

the naming threshold for the distinctions within these groups. These two taxa are less heterogeneous than the number of included taxa would indicate.

The five remaining taxa exhibit some characteristics both of life-form and of generic taxa. They resemble life-form taxa in that they include a biologically diverse set of organisms and are recognized as exceptionally heterogeneous. Thus a variable but relatively large number of subdivisions are named, many of which correspond to biological taxa. The nomenclatural pattern, however, is more characteristic of generic taxa. With the exception of *ʔak'* 'vine', the great majority of the subdivisions of these taxa are named by composite lexemes, either optionally or necessarily. Furthermore, Berlin's distinction between secondary lexemes and productive primary lexemes is difficult to apply in these cases. The subdivisions of *ʔak* 'grass' with but one exception are labeled by composite lexemes (Berlin, Breedlove, and Raven 1974:400–401). Thus *ʔak* could as well be a generic taxon according to a strict interpretation of Berlin's criteria. Twelve of the 22 subdivisions of *čan₁* 'snake' are named by composite lexemes of the form **X** *čan*, where **X** is an attributive invariably present. The remaining 11 subdivisions have composite names, which may be abbreviated by the deletion of *čan*. *č'o* 'small rodent' exhibits a similar pattern, with invariably composite names applied to 9 subdivisions and optionally abbreviated forms to the remaining 4. These taxa exhibit the anomaly of *čikinib hihteʔ* (see Figure 3.8 and text discussion thereof) writ large. The optionally abbreviated names, in particular, label categories considered to be highly distinctive. Such taxa are best considered to be generics. However within the same contrast set one may find taxa such as *c'ibal čan* 'striped snake' which, while inductive, do not appear to exhibit a degree of distinctiveness characteristic of generic taxa. The possibility that a taxon such as *čan₁* might immediately include both generic and specific taxa provides one solution to this problem, and such a possibility is not

**Table 3.1**
THE MOST HETEROGENEOUS TZELTAL TAXA

| Taxon | Number of immediate subtaxa | Rank |
|---|---|---|
| *teʔ* 'tree' | 178 | life form |
| *wamal* 'herbaceous shrub' | 119 | life form |
| *mut₁* 'bird' | 106 | life form |
| *čanbalam₂* | 45, 36[a] | life form |
| *ʔak* 'grass' | 35 | life form |
| *ʔak'* 'vine' | 24 | life form |
| *čan₁* 'snake' | 23 | named complex |
| *čenek'* 'bean' | 15 | generic |
| *loʔbal* 'banana' | 12 | generic |
| *č'o* 'small rodent' | 13, 10[b] | intermediate (named complex) |
| *šuš* 'wasp' | 10 | named complex |
| *ʔeč'* 'epiphyte' | 10 | generic |
| *ʔam* 'spider' | 10 | generic |

[a] Forty-five if each generic subdivision of *č'o* 'small rodent' is counted; 36 if *č'o* is counted as one.

[b] Thirteen if each variety of *Peromyscus* is counted; 10 if the covert generic 'white-footed mouse' is counted as one.

ruled out within the modified definition of taxonomic ranks suggested here. Such a solution is not adequately motivated, however, until the problem of measuring heterogeneity and gaps is resolved. It is preferable at this point simply to note the fact that taxa such as those discussed above cannot be adequately categorized within Berlin's system.

## 7  Taxonomic Anomalies

### 7.1  COMPLEXES

A potential taxon has been defined (see Figures 3.9 and 3.10 and text discussion thereof) as a set of organisms isolated by a minimal gap which is wider than the largest gap separating a subtaxon from its closest associate, i.e., $G_{\min}^x(t)$ is greater than $G_{mxn}^n(t)$. This definition is modeled after the gap criterion that Mayr, Linsley, and Usinger (1953) suggest as the basis for recognizing genera and families of organisms (Simpson 1961: 6–117). A stricter criterion would recognize a potential taxon only if the gap isolating a cluster of percepts were greater than the diversity perceived within the taxon, i.e., if $G_{\min}^x(t)$ were greater than $H(t)$. This criterion is more stringent since $H(t)$ is always greater than $G_{mxn}^n(t)$.

It seems likely that all named inductive taxa in folk systems meet this more stringent requirement. However, "horizontal" relationships of relative similarity and difference within a contrast set are a significant feature of folk-biological classification. These relationships may generate covert complexes of minimal distinctiveness (i.e., $CR(t)$ less than 1). Such groupings may be distinguished as "chains" (see Chapter 2, Section 10).

For example, in Tenejapa Tzeltal the 'jays' (**heš**) are linked with the 'chachalaca' (**hohkot**), a bird that bears little resemblance to the 'typical jays'. These dissimilar birds are linked by the fact that the Magpie Jay (**šulub mut**) and the Brown Jay (**peya?**) are perceived as intermediate forms simultaneously related to both. The Magpie Jay (*Calocitta*

*formosa*) and the Brown Jay (*Psilorhinus morio*) are closely associated with one another in the Tenejapan view. The Magpie Jay approximates **heš** in plumage pattern, while the Brown Jay provides a link to **hohkot** in terms of plumage pattern, form, and vocalizations. Similarly, **nap'ak** 'slug' links the 'snail' complex with that of the 'worms'.

Other complexes exhibit a similar pattern. Thus relationships of similarity between pairs of taxa may be clearly apparent, but such relationships are not nomenclaturally recognized due to the absence of a "decided gap" isolating a group of associated taxa. The dictionary of zoological terms presented here is organized to reflect such covert relationships whenever possible by grouping taxa into complexes (cf. Berlin, Breedlove, and Raven 1974:59–61). Named groupings of ambiguous status such as **čan**₁ 'snake' and **c'o** 'small rodent' are treated as named complexes, since they appear to fall at the more distinctive pole of a continuum that includes covert groupings of minimal distinctiveness at the opposite pole.

### 7.2  THE "TEXTURE" OF TAXA: TYPE FORMS AND CORE VERSUS EXTENDED RANGES

The difficulty of dealing with continuous variation within a discrete system, e.g., a taxonomy, may also account for the recognition in folk systems of a "type" form or best exemplar of a heterogeneous taxon (see Berlin 1972:59–62), on the one hand, and the distinction between "true" members of a taxon, the *basic* range, and a set of peripherally associated taxa, the **extended** range (cf. Bright and Bright 1965; Berlin, Breedlove, and Raven 1974:56–58), on the other. These phenomena may occur at various taxonomic levels.

The recognition of a type form is illustrated by **toht** 'robin' (*Turdus* spp.). This generic taxon includes five specific subdivisions as in Figure 3.11. No informant knows all five subdivisions, but many recognize three or four. The two universally recognized specifics, **č'iš toht** and **k'an toht**,

Figure 3.11    The classification of robins (*Turdus*) in Tzeltal.

are common to abundant in the region. The other species are quite rare and locally distributed. *č'iš toht* may be abbreviated as *toht* by high-country informants, since it is the species they encounter daily. *k'an toht* is similarly abbreviated by low-country informants for the same reason. Both may also be known as *bac'il toht* 'true robin' in their respective regions. The type specific in this case is the most frequently encountered form.

*šanič* refers to several types of ants, in particular those of the genus *Solenopsis*. This genus may be further distinguished as *bac'il šanič* 'true ant'. This and 9 additional generic taxa form a complex that includes all true ants (Formicidae). The complex is not named, yet when required to discuss the complex in the context of ethnographic elicitation, all 10 generics may be referred to as *šaničetik* 'ants'. Furthermore, unfamiliar kinds of ants may be labeled by a descriptive phrase of the form *X šanič*. Other generic names applied to members of the complex are rarely used in this manner. *šanič* is thus the type generic of the covert complex. The term *šuš* 'wasp' plays a similar role with respect to the wasp complex. *šuš*, however, is not also a generic name, and thus may label the complex without ambiguity.

In the examples just cited, a single taxon is seen as most typical of a superordinate grouping. In other cases, however, no single type is emphasized, rather one or more taxa of a group may be considered **least** typical. *ya?al be* 'shrew' is a kind of *č'o* 'small rodent'. However informants consider it to be atypical of the complex by virtue of its carnivorous habits and dental morphology.

Most vertebrate species are unambiguously assigned to one or another named taxon.

The folk classification of invertebrates generates scientifically valid groupings in about the same proportion as among vertebrates. However many invertebrate species are simply left out of the system of named taxa or are peripherally related to named taxa, or they may be attributed to a residual category (see Section 7.3) This fact is no doubt due to the multiplicity of invertebrate species, their small size, and their cultural insignificance.

The wasp complex, for example, includes 10 generic taxa. Eight of these refer exclusively to social vespid wasps (Vespidae), some referring to a single species only, e.g., *k'ancutoh* (*Stelopolybia areata*). The ninth generic includes a social vespid wasp and a potter wasp (Eumenidae), the tenth refers to a single species of the Sphecidae (*kukai šuš* 'firefly wasp', *Larra analis*). *k'ahk'ub yat* 'fierce stinger' includes the spider wasps (Pompilidae) and is peripherally related to the wasp complex. Entomologists recognize at least a dozen families of wasps (Borror and White 1970:341) and many more related families of Hymenoptera. However only the Vespidae are typically social insects and thus notably conspicuous. Several large and distinctive solitary wasps were collected in Tenejapa to which informants responded, *ma hna be sba* 'I'm not familiar with it' or, *kol pahaluk sok šuš niwan* 'It's almost the same as a wasp perhaps' (see the wasp complex for details). By contrast almost all of the Vespidae collected were unambiguously classified. Thus the social vespid wasps (together with an occasional potter or sphecid wasp) constitute the basic range of the wasp complex. The less frequently encountered species are either not named or peripherally associated with the complex.

In sum, a taxon is not typically perceived

as an internally homogeneous entity. Taxa may have focal points or focal regions. Regions of the "classification space" may fall between taxa. Organisms in these "empty" regions may be classified only as unspecified members of the domain. This uneven contour of a classification space results from the fact that inductive classification requires a minimal data base, which may be inaccessible to or ignored by the classifier.

## 7.3  RESIDUAL CATEGORIES [R]

Residual categories are fairly common as a response to an insufficiency of data for inductive classification (see Table 4.2). A residual category is defined negatively, i.e., an organism is perceived to be a member of X but **not** a member of any distinctive kind of X. For example, a "mutt" or mongrel is any dog that is not a particular kind of dog. Residual categories such as "mutt" are sometimes considered the type of the larger category. For example, **bac'il wakaš** 'true cattle' (see **wakaš**/mammal) includes all cattle that are not of the Zebu strain (see Figure 3.12). **bac'il wakaš** 'true cattle' is nearly as heterogeneous as the generic that includes it.

The case of **pehpen** 'butterfly' demonstrates the utility of recognizing residual taxa. Unlike the folk English distinction between day-flying 'butterflies' and night-flying 'moths', the Tzeltal distinguish between butterflies and large moths, on the one hand, and a related category of very small moths (see **supul**/butterfly). This distinction roughly corresponds to the scientific distinction between Macrolepidoptera and Microlepidoptera. **pehpen** and **supul** together include all adult Lepidoptera and form a covert complex. The larvae of this order are assigned to a number of generic taxa, the facts of metamorphosis not being fully understood. Though the variation among the

Microlepidoptera is considerable from a biological point of view, all **supul** are so small that only color varietals are recognized in Tzeltal, e.g., **sakil supul** 'white mothlet'. The larger **pehpen** are more obviously varied in terms of pattern, color, shape, size, and texture. Several inductive subdivisions are consistently recognized among which the following are confidently included.

| | |
|---|---|
| **c'unun pehpen** 'hummingbird butterfly' | Sphingidae (in part) |
| **labil pehpen** 'spirit butterfly' | Brassolidae: *Caligo memnon* |
| **me? sac'** 'mother of **sac**' | Noctuidae: *Thysania agrippina* |
| **ne mut pehpen** 'birdtail butterfly' | Hesperiidae: cf. *Polythrix alcifron* |
| **tultuš pehpen** 'damselfly butterfly' | Heliconidae (in part) and Ithomiidae (in part) |

Having made these distinctions, Tenejapanecos must still deal with an extremely heterogeneous residual. The residual includes some but not all skippers (Hesperioidea), some but not all of the Heliconidae, and some but not all of the Sphingidae. It includes both moths and butterflies. It is fair to say that the residual is hardly less heterogeneous than the inclusive generic itself. How is this residual heterogeneity treated? The residual is subdivided by deduction into scientifically arbitrary classes by the application of abstract features as follows.

> **k'anal pehpen** 'yellow butterfly'
> **cahal pehpen** 'red butterfly'
> etc.
> **c'irin pehpen** 'streaked butterfly'
> **bašil pehpen** 'mottled butterfly'
> etc.
> **muk'ul pehpen** 'large butterfly'
> **k'unil pehpen** 'soft butterfly'
> etc.

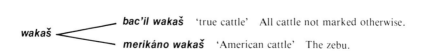

**wakaš**
— **bac'il wakaš**  'true cattle'  All cattle not marked otherwise.
— **merikáno wakaš**  'American cattle'  The zebu.

**Figure 3.12**  The classification of cattle (*Bos taurus*) in Tzeltal.

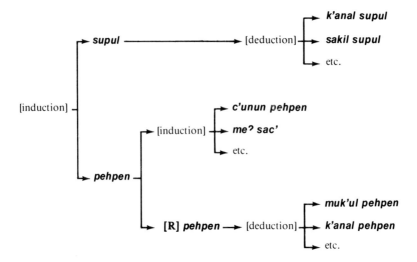

**Figure 3.13** Information-processing diagram: Adult Lepidoptera.

These terms are applied whenever descriptively appropriate, referential overlap is common, and the specific features may be combined paradigmatically. However, this naming pattern applies only to the residual, not to the otherwise distinctive subtypes of *pehpen*. The deductive rule is applied only **after** the inductive process has been exhaustively applied, as illustrated in Figure 3.13.

The temporal precedence of induction is a further indication that this process is basic to folk-biological classification.

When a generic taxon as complex as *pehpen* is subdivided by the ordered application of both inductive and deductive processes, the resulting terminal taxa may exhibit contrastive nomenclatural patterns. The deductive subdivisions are named by the association of a specific feature labeled by an adjectival form relevant to a wide variety of nominal classes, such as attributives marking color or size. When the ultimate process is inductive, however, the attribute is often a noun used adjectivally, e.g., *c'unun pehpen*, *tultuš pehpen*. Here, the modifying attribute is of very limited relevance and marks a concrete feature. The name *c'unun pehpen* indicates that the class is characterized by the concatenation of two configurational attributes, "butterflyness"

modified by the co-occurrence of "hummingbirdness," in that order. It must be stressed that this tendency is not an invariable clue to the logical status of a taxon, since, as noted for *toht* 'robin', color attributives may label inductive taxa.

## 7.4 THE INTRUSION OF DEDUCTIVE CRITERIA

The role of deductive criteria in the definition of varietal subdivisions has been discussed. In such cases, the deductive rule is only applied following the exhaustive (given the data assessed) application of induction. It was further asserted that inductive taxa exhibit a close correspondence to scientific taxa, while deductive taxa show no such tendency. The taxon *čanbalam₂* 'mammal' is presumably inductive, yet it fails to correspond to the scientific taxon MAMMALIA in several important respects. First, human beings are excluded, not only from the restricted sense of *čanbalam₂* but also from *čanbalam₁* 'animal', the unique beginner. Informants explain that men cannot be 'animals' because only men have 'souls' (*č'ulel*). Yet Tenejapanecos are not unresponsive to the **similarity** between men and other animals. This resemblance is the basis for a well-known folktale which details the relationship between men and monkeys (see the monkey complex). In antediluvian time monkeys were men but were given tails and banished to the forest for disobeying God. The exclusion of *Homo sapiens* from the category 'animal' and the resulting lack of correspondence between the scientific and the folk taxa may be attributed to the intrusion of a deductive rule, as shown in Figure 3.14.

Bats (**soc'**) and armadillos (**mayil ti?bal**) are also excluded from **čanbalam**$_2$ 'mammal'. Both are atypical with respect to basic mammalian characteristics. Bats fly, thus resembling birds, while armadillos appear to lack hair and thus resemble reptiles. Yet Tenejapanecos are competent observers, and one might expect them to recognize the basic mammalian pattern despite the superficial resemblance to other life forms. My data with respect to armadillos are insufficient to clarify this point. However, the exclusion of bats from the 'mammal' category appears due to an intrusive deductive rule comparable to the previous example. Bats cannot be 'mammals' because 'mammals' 'walk' (**ya šben**). Neither can they be 'birds' though they 'fly' (**ya šwil**), since they lack feathers (**mayuk sk'uk'umal**). Again a folktale provides clarification. Bats are transformed shrews. According to the tale, **ya?al be** 'shrew' attempts to jump across a trail (**be**). If he fails in this attempt he dies. This explains why shrews are so often found dead in the middle of the trail. If he succeeds he is transformed into a bat (**ya šk'ahta ta soc'**). Informants have also pointed out to me the striking similarity between the teeth of bats and shrews. In short 'bats' are perceptually related to 'mammals' and to 'shrews' in particular. Yet they cannot be so classified because of a deductive rule. In this case the deductive rule has a perceptual foundation. Such deductive rules result from a process of *attribute reduction* (Bruner, Goodnow, and Austin 1956:45), which reduces the cognitive effort required in utilizing categories with multiple criterial attributes. As discussed earlier (this chapter, Section 5), multiple attributes may also be recoded as a configuration. The preference for attribute reduction, as in the case of **čanbalam**, as opposed to utilizing configurational recoding, as is typical of inductive taxa, may be a function of the extreme heterogeneity of life-form taxa and unique beginners and be characteristic of such broadly inclusive taxa.

## 8 A Historical Note

The study of folk classification has a considerable history. The essential nature of categories of phenomena has been a philosophical issue since at least Plato and Aristotle. According to Durkheim and Mauss Aristotle was the first classical scholar to

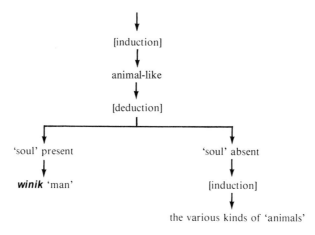

**Figure 3.14** Information-processing diagram: Men and animals.

assert that generic classes of organisms were basic and immutable (1963:4–5), an idea fundamental to Linnaeus's classification (Cain 1958). The contemporary understanding of biological evolution has but recently shifted focus to the species as the basic, though mutable, unit of biosystematics. Generic taxa as recognized by scholars from Aristotle to Linnaeus remain basic to folk systems of classification. The fundamental nature of modern biological species is purely biological, based on the isolation of breeding populations. The fundamental nature of folk genera, by contrast, is both biological and psychological. As claimed earlier, folk genera are recognized by virtue of the biological fact that discrete gaps exist between groups of organisms and the psychological fact that the cognitive process of induction naturally results in the recognition of certain of those gaps.

The degree to which folk classification corresponds to biological classification remains controversial. A related issue raised by Durkheim and Mauss in their classic *Primitive Classification* (1963) concerns the origin of the classificatory ability of human beings. Should the classification of phenomena into discrete classes hierarchically arranged be considered an innate potential of human thought or is it derivative, a product of cultural or social evolution? Durkheim and Mauss leave no doubt as to their opinion on this issue. They argue that the discreteness of human social groups, arranged increasingly in a hierarchical ordering as societies have developed from the supposed hyperprimitive, undifferentiated band, provided the model for an analogous development of man's classification of natural phenomena. They refute Frazer's opposite view (Durkheim and Mauss 1963:9, 82) that social organization is derivative of the organization perceived in nature.

Lévi-Strauss (1966) avoids both social and natural explanations of cause in favor of a psychological causality. He sees the organizational principles applied to both nature and society as reflecting innate cognitive structures. In my view, the social cause is the least convincing. However the opposing positions need qualification, since the causal nexus underlying folk classification is complex. The human mind is not free of the constraints imposed by reality, nor is the human cognitive response fully explained by that reality.

The cultural role of the objects classified is also relevant. Again this factor is but one aspect of the systemic causal network. Berlin, Breedlove, and Raven (1966) have demonstrated effects attributable to a variable dimension of cultural relevance. Yet it is clear that natural phenomena may be said to be culturally relevant simply by virtue of their existence within a human life space. Curiosity as well as hunger is a basic human drive.

Let us return to Durkheim and Mauss's argument. They clearly express an anthropological attitude toward "primitive mentality" widely held during the first half of this century and perhaps not yet obsolete. They characterize primitive thought, i.e., human thought unconditioned by experience of advanced social forms, as confused and fluid, lacking both clarity of conceptual distinctions and the perfect hierarchical organization characteristic of modern philosophical and scientific thought. They cite numerous examples of supposed confusion between human personalities and animal organisms and between social and natural groupings. "If we descend to the least evolved societies known . . . we shall find an even more general mental confusion [Durkheim and Mauss 1963:6]." In particular, "The Bororo sincerely imagines himself to be a parrot, at least, though he assumes the characteristic form only after he is dead, in this life he is to that animal what the caterpillar is to the butterfly . . . [Durkheim and Mauss:6]." Durkheim and Mauss quote from Von den Steinen, "'The Indian lacks our determination of genus, such that one does not mix with the other' [Durkheim and Mauss]."

Several modern students of folk classification have described systems of folk classification that seem predicated on organizational principles quite unrelated to the principles of science. For example, Black (1967) describes an Ojibwa classification of 'living things' based in part on a concept of life force that partially rank-orders subcategories of this global concept. The application of this principle produces named groupings of organisms that overlap in membership and thereby violate a basic principle of taxonomic structure. Such categories indeed seem to lack the clarity of boundary and the perfection of hierarchical organization that Durkheim and Mauss attribute to advanced as opposed to more primitive states of the art of classification.

These two studies are far removed in time and in basic theoretical orientation. Durkheim and Mauss sought to demonstrate the arrested development of primitive classification. Black and other ethnoscientifically oriented scholars assume the fundamental independence of cultural systems of classification. Thus both stress, though for radically different reasons, the differences between folk classification and scientific classification. Both cite data that seem to indicate a basic lack of correspondence between folk systems and scientific systems of classification.

I have claimed that the two types of systems are necessarily convergent. Bulmer (1970; with Tyler 1968) and Berlin, Breedlove, and Raven (1974:100–103) also stress the similarities between folk and scientific biosystematics, rather than the differences. This apparent contradiction results, I believe, from a contrast in emphasis. The essential fact is buried in a footnote in *Primitive Classification.* "As such they [concepts with a speculative purpose] are very clearly distinguished from what might be called **technological classifications**. It is probable that man has **always** classified, more or less clearly, the things on which he lived. . . .These distinctions are closely linked to practical concerns. . . . **It is for this reason that we have not spoken of them in this work**. . . [Durkheim and Mauss 1963:81–82; emphasis added]." In short, rabbits, raccoons, bumblebees, and oak trees have **always** been clearly distinguished one from the other. The "confusion" of classification that Durkheim and

Mauss document is at another level, a speculative or explanatory level, where categories are broadly inclusive and based on **deductive** principles of classification.

Black expresses a similar view. She quotes from Nida, " 'Cultures (and languages) differ in their manner of classifying items in hierarchical structures, and differ most of all as one ascends from the lower levels (closer to that of **perceptually distinguishable** phenomena) to the higher levels (reflecting **conceptually based** classifications). . . . Furthermore, this hierarchical structuring at the conceptual level is far more indicative of a people's world view than is the labelling of objects nearer the perceptual level' [quoted in Black 1967:123]." Black considers these higher level aspects of classification of greater ethnographic interest. Thus she refers to taxa at the lower levels only to the minimal extent necessary to discuss the higher level of organization. Nida's distinction between perceptual and conceptual aspects of classification, found respectively at the lower and higher levels of classification, seems to correspond to the distinction drawn here between inductive categories, which are directly bound to reality, and deductive categories, which are relatively free of real constraints. It should be noted, however, that both types of categories are equally conceptual.

Black shares with Durkheim and Mauss a primary interest in world view, or the folk explanation of reality. This determines their focus on the differences between various folk systems and between those and the scientific system. Bulmer, Berlin, and I share a basic interest in **descriptive** classifications, those close to the perceptual reality. This focus yields a contrary emphasis on the similarities among systems of classification, whether folk or scientific.

One's evaluation of the degree of correspondence between folk and scientific systems of classification is dependent on which aspect of classification one chooses to emphasize. I assert that folk and scientific descriptions of the basic discontinuities in the real world are basically equivalent. On the other hand, that folk and scientific **theories**, which constitute explanations of the pattern evident in the actual distribution of types of organisms, differ radically, should surprise no one. The scientific phenomenon coordinate with the classification systems described by Black and by Durkheim and Mauss is not the biological taxonomy but rather the theory of evolution. The theory of evolution is an explanatory model, deductively derived and employed to explain the perceptual regularities incorporated in the taxonomic classification. Likewise totemic classifications or the grouping of various animal species according to their "spirit masters" as described by Black are explanatory theories arrived at, once again, by deductive as opposed to inductive principles of logic.

The degree to which such explanatory models interact with the description of reality is an important subject for investigation. The theory of evolution modifies the biosystematic description of reality when, for example, the auklets (Alcidae) of northern oceans are classed in a different order than the very similar diving petrels (Pelecanoididae) of southern oceans. The similarity is attributed to convergent evolution and thus is reinterpreted. The Ojibwa classification of 'eagles' as birds, and thus of low status, conflicts with their alternate classification of eagles as 'thunderbirds' or spirits, and thus of high status. This inconsistency of assignment is due to the lack of correspondence between a descriptive system of classification based on induction, which classes 'eagles' as birds, and an explanatory system based on deduction, which classes them as 'spirits'. The modification of the basic Ojibwa description of faunal relationships is quite analogous to the modification of scientific description due to evolutionary assumptions.

In fine, descriptive classification must be clearly distinguished from explanatory classification. The two are based on radically different logical processes which, as we have seen, create a problem for folk and scientist alike of their mutual coordination. This monograph is concerned with the principles of descriptive, rather than explanatory, classification.

## 9 A Measure of the Degree of Correspondence of Folk to Scientific Biological Classification*

I propose here a technique for evaluating the degree to which any folk biotaxonomic classification agrees with the scientific classification as applied to the same set of organisms. The two types of biosystematics do not, of course, produce isomorphic, i.e., identical, classifications, neither are they totally independent of one another. I will argue, rather, that folk biotaxonomies tend to be isomorphic to a subsystem of the scientific system. That is, all the categories and their consequent relations of a folk taxonomy will, with high probability, have counterparts in the scientific system. On the other hand many of the scientific taxa and relations will have no counterpart in a given folk system. To the extent that this is true, the scientific system of biological classification may serve as an etic grid, rather than as simply a convenient language for glossing exotic lexical items. I will suggest a formula for measuring the degree to which this criterion of limited isomorphy is approximated for any given folk biological domain. To exemplify this technique I will compare the Tenejapa Tzeltal taxon *čanbalam*₂ 'mammal' point for point with the scientific class MAMMALIA.

### 9.1 TZELTAL MAMMAL CLASSIFICATION

The class MAMMALIA is represented in the Mexican state of Chiapas, of which Tenejapa is one small part, by 174 species (according to Hall and Kelson 1959). Many species are unfamiliar to the people of Tenejapa due to geographical and habitat restrictions. A reasonable estimate of the

*This section is adapted from an article of the same title that appeared in the *American Ethnologist* 2:309–327 (1975) (Hunn 1975a).

number of species of mammals which the Tenejapa Tzeltal have had some opportunity to classify is between 65 and 85.

The Tzeltal term *čanbalam* is nearly identical in extension to the scientific term MAMMALIA in one sense, but like the folk English term "animal" it can also refer to any macroscopic, actively motile living thing (see *čanbalam₁*). Thus I will distinguish between the broader reference, *čanbalam₁* 'animal', and the more restricted usage with which we are concerned here, *čanbalam₂*. As noted, *čanbalam₂* includes all known mammals except human beings, bats, and the armadillo. It includes no other organisms. There are 75 consistently named and/or well defined subcategories that are recognized (see Table 3.6), 59 (79%) of these taxa correspond exactly to some taxon of the scientific system. However let us examine a few examples of taxa that fail to correspond in this way.

The Tzeltal deny that human beings (*kirsiáno* > Sp *cristiano* 'Christian') are *čanbalam* in either sense of the term. However, they are quite cognizant of an affinity between men and monkeys, and they attribute to both a common origin (see this chapter, Section 7.4). There is no named taxon inclusive of men and monkeys; this would deny man his unique status. Bats (*soc'*) are 'animals' but not 'mammals'. Though they fly like birds, only 1 of the more than 20 informants queried considered bats to be a kind of *mut* 'bird'. Though anomalous, bats are thought to be closely related to shrews (see this chapter, Section 7.4). The armadillo (*mayil ti?bal*) is also anomalous. Though it goes 'on all fours' like 'mammals' (as do lizards and frogs, etc.) and has a nose and tail very similar to those of the opossum (*?uč*), it lacks hair, having a 'ridged' back like a turtle (*š?ahk'*).

In the Tzeltal system *č'o* 'small rodent' includes shrews (*ya?al be*) in addition to representatives of several rodent families. Shrews belong to the order Insectivora, not to the Rodentia, while several rodents, such as the Mexican porcupine (*č'iš ?uhčum*), the

paca (*halaw*), squirrels (*čuč*), and the pocket gopher (*ba*), are excluded from the category *č'o*. There is no neat correspondence between this Tzeltal taxon and any scientific taxon. However the Tzeltal recognize *ya?al be* as the most deviant subcategory of *č'o*.

The two species of peccaries (native animals related to the pig) are known as *wamal čitam* 'bush pig'. Two kinds of *wamal čitam* are widely recognized. It is clear from informants' descriptions that *niwak wamal čitam* 'large bush pig' refers to the adults of either species while *bahk'al wamal čitam* 'group-of-four-hundred bush pig' refers to the young of either species. Yet informants deny that one is a growth stage of the other. This "confusion" may be explained by reference to the fact that peccaries no longer occur near Tenejapa and by the fact that adults and young of both species often forage in separate groups (Alvarez del Toro 1952).

These examples indicate that the differences between the Tzeltal classification of mammals and that of the scientist are readily comprehensible, i.e., we have no indication that radically different principles underly the two systems. Furthermore, the similarities are striking.

## 9.2 DEFINING AN ADEQUATE MEASURE OF TAXONOMIC CORRESPONDENCE

To describe precisely how "radically different" are folk and scientific classifications of organisms, or how "striking" the "similarities" between them, requires what I propose to call a Coefficient of Dissimilarity. The specification of this coefficient involves a choice of measures. First, we want a measure that promises to be of general applicability to folk biotaxonomic systems. Second, the measure must be explicit; any two individuals analyzing the same set of data should arrive at the same result. Finally the measure should reflect as closely as possible our intuitive notions about degrees of similarity and difference.

Berlin, Breedlove, and Raven (1966) calculated the percentage of folk "specific" taxa, i.e., terminal taxa, in one-to-one correspondence with scientific species (using a sample of 200 Tzeltal botanical terms). They reported a low figure of 38% (reduced to 14% for native species). On the basis of this less than compelling figure, they concluded that there was no necessary correspondence between folk and scientific systems of botanical classification. They argued that this lack of correspondence is due to the "special purpose" nature of folk systems, as opposed to the "general purpose" nature of the scientific system.

Bulmer (1970:1072–1073) took issue with this early conclusion of Berlin, Breedlove, and Raven but provided no alternative to their method of comparison. Bulmer estimated that for the Karam of New Guinea, "only about 60% of the terminal taxa applied to vertebrates, let alone invertebrates, appear to correspond well with zoological species [1970:1075]." The percentage of correspondence in both instances did not give strong support for Bulmer's assertion that "there is a **conceptual** correspondence between the great majority of terminal taxa applied by Karam and the species recognized by zoologists [1970:1076]." In short, this method of statistical comparison does not closely reflect "intuitive notions about degrees of similarity and difference."

More recently, Berlin (1973:267–269; Berlin, Breedlove, and Raven 1974:120–122) has applied a modified version of the index cited above. The new measure avoids the most serious limitation of the earlier version by selecting "folk generic taxa" (defined in Berlin, Breedlove, and Raven 1973:216–219), rather than terminal folk taxa, as the units of comparison. Berlin then calculates the percentage of folk generic taxa that correspond in a one-to-one fashion with scientific species. Additional tabulations distinguish overdifferentiated taxa—folk generic taxa, which subdivide a scientific species—and underdifferentiated taxa of two types, those that include more than one species of a single scientific genus (type 1) and those that include species from more than one scientific genus (type 2). The substitution of generic for terminal folk taxa in the calculation raises the percentage of "basic" folk taxa in one-to-one correspondence to scientific species from 38% (for a random sample) to 61% (for the total sample, Berlin 1973:269). The revised measure thus better reflects the intuition that folk classification does not differ radically from the scientific, as in Berlin's current view: "There is at present a growing body of evidence that suggests that the fundamental taxa recognized in folk systematics correspond fairly closely with scientifically known species [Berlin 1973:267]."

However I believe Berlin's revised measure is not yet adequate in two respects. First, restricting the comparison to folk generics and scientific species ignores a significant proportion of the data, most notably (1) those folk generics that correspond perfectly with scientific taxa above the species level, as in the case of folk English "bat", and (2) those "folk specifics" that correspond in a one-to-one fashion with scientific species, such as folk English "grizzly bear." Berlin justifies this limitation as follows:

One of the difficulties in any comparison concerns the units of analysis to be considered. In the case of Western systematics, the selection of the basic unit is straight forward—it **must** be the species. In folk systematics, it now appears useful to focus on the folk genus as the primary unit. The folk genus, it will be recalled, is the smallest linguistically recognized class of organisms that is formed, as the folk zoologist Bulmer has succinctly stated, '. . . by multiple distinctions of appearance, habitat, and behavior.' These two units, then, the scientific species and the folk genus, will be those selected as the basic taxa to be examined in **any** comparison of the folk and scientific systems of classification [1973:267–268; emphasis added].

It is not the case that the scientific species **must** be selected. Scientific species are certainly the basic units of the scientific classification, due to their unique logical status vis-à-vis other taxa. However this unique status derives directly from evolutionary theory, viz., species are genetically isolated populations. Folk systematics is not predicated on such considerations. Thus, with respect to the correspondence of folk to scientific taxa, the scientific species is not necessarily the basic unit. Rather, folk taxa are directly comparable to the "arbitrary" nonspecies taxa in terms of their logical basis (see this chapter, Section 5). I will propose a measure that makes no restriction on the scientific category or rank of comparable taxa.

Second, the reliable application of Berlin's revised measure depends on the "proper" application of the distinction between folk generic taxa and other folk taxa. I have argued (this chapter, Section 4) that this distinction is not without ambiguity. Thus different investigators might arrive at varying figures for the same set of data. In addition, Berlin is not quite correct in equating Bulmer's "folk species," to which Bulmer is referring in the quotation from Berlin cited above, with his own folk genera. Berlin's folk genus is recognized primarily by reference to the type of lexeme which labels the taxon (Berlin, Breedlove, and Raven 1973:218). Bulmer's folk species is defined with reference to the multiplicity of observable differences which characterize it (Bulmer 1970:1072). These two categories of taxa broadly overlap but are not, in general, the same (cf. Tables 3.3 and 3.4). Thus it should not be assumed that one-to-one correspondence to scientific taxa is to be expected only of Berlin's folk generics. In short, Berlin's revised measure can be refined.

The numerical taxonomic literature might be expected to provide a more refined approach to the measurement problem posed here. Numerical taxonomy attempts to provide an explicit methodology for biosystematics. Rather sophisticated "measures of congruence" have been developed to evaluate alternative taxonomic approaches to the classification of a given set of OTUs (Operational Taxonomic Units). Unfortunately these measures are not appropriate for the special requirements of folk taxonomic data. Farris (1971) reviews many of these measures. All indices rely on direct or indirect comparison of "character sets." However, as argued earlier (see Chapter 1, Section 1), folk-biological taxa in general are not defined by reference to verbalizable feature contrasts. These measures are not "of general applicability to folk biotaxonomic systems."

Folk taxa are defined vis-à-vis scientific taxa by comparing the folk and the scientific names for each organism of a representative sample of familiar organisms. Small samples are quite adequate to establish the simple correspondence of a folk to a scientific taxon (see Chapter 2, Section 1). Thus the proportion of all folk taxa under consideration which correpond to scientific taxa (a folk taxon which includes, as inferred from sample data, all and only those locally occurring organisms included in a single scientific taxon is said to correspond to that scientific taxon) is a measure that is readily applied to folk-biological data. This measure avoids a significant limitation of the Berlin–Bulmer statistics, i.e., the restriction of the comparison to scientific species, on the one hand, and to folk terminal or generic taxa, on the other. There is no a priori rationale for judging the folk English taxon "raccoon" (= the species *Procyon lotor*) as corresponding more closely to the scientific system than does "bat" (= the order Chiroptera). As will be seen, these restrictions systematically lower the proportion of correspondence.

Though the proportion of all the folk taxa that correspond to scientific taxa of whatever categorical level meets the requirements of an adequate measure, it is insensitive to degrees of correspondence. For example, it would be useful to distinguish a folk taxon that includes some but not all species of a single genus from a folk taxon that groups assorted species from a variety of higher level scientific taxa, and to distinguish both from a "random" collection of organisms. (Berlin's distinction between two types of underdifferentiated taxa is a first step in this direction, but is not logically exhaustive.) Those folk taxa that fail to correspond to a scientific taxon may vary a great deal in the degree to which they approximate scientific groupings. To measure the degree of correspondence more accurately, we need to define a weighted measure. What follows is a description of a means to that end.

## 9.3   A WEIGHTED MEASURE OF TAXONOMIC DISSIMILARITY

First, we need to delimit the folk taxonomy to which the measure will apply. This is done by choosing a unique beginner. For present purposes the unique beginner may be any taxon of the folk-biological system. The folk taxonomy thus defined consists of the unique beginner and all taxa included in that unique beginner.

As noted above, the measure proposed here involves comparing a folk taxonomy with a part of the scientific taxonomy. It is necessary to pare the scientific taxonomy down to size. This is done by a series of **reduction rules**. First, one excludes all scientific taxa that have no representatives in the local flora or fauna. Such taxa are of various degrees of inclusiveness, from species to entire phyla. It is not particularly surprising that the Tzeltal do not deal with *Felis leo*, the African lion, or the COELENTERATA, a phylum composed almost entirely of marine organisms such as the jellyfish. The exclusion of a taxon from the local scientific taxonomy implies the exclusion of all of its subordinate taxa as well.

The second reduction removes from consideration all scientific taxa that contain no organisms contained in the unique beginner of the folk system under consideration. The unique beginner in this example is *čanbalam*$_2$. All organisms included in the taxon so labeled are also included in the scientific class MAMMALIA. Thus all scientific taxa not included in the class MAMMALIA are excluded. By this reduction we need no longer worry about birds, fish, or worms. At this stage we have what may be called a **truncated** and **local** scientific taxonomy, local by virtue of the first reduction and truncated by virtue of the second.

A third reduction collapses all taxa that are exactly equivalent in membership to a superordinate taxon. This follows from the specification that a minimum of two descending edges is required of all nonterminal vertices in the graphic model of a taxonomic structure. Take, for example, that section of the scientific taxonomy which includes the

two local opossum genera. The first two reduction rules leave us with the following sequence of taxa: class MAMMALIA, infraclass Metatheria, order Marsupialia, family Didelphidae, then the two genera. The third reduction rule deletes the order and the family. The family Didelphidae is the only family of marsupials found locally and is thus equivalent in extension to the order. Likewise, the order Marsupialia is the only order of the infraclass Metatheria with local representatives. The infraclass is retained because it contrasts with the infraclass Eutheria, which includes the remaining mammals. The two local opossum genera, *Didelphis* and *Philander*, are also retained since neither is equivalent to the family that includes both of them.

The final reduction eliminates all scientific taxa below the level necessary to specify the content of the terminal folk taxa. For example, the Tzeltal regularly recognize only a single kind of **ya?al be** 'shrew'. It is thus a terminal taxon. The order Insectivora is represented in southern Mexico by one family (the shrews, Soricidae) of which two genera containing several species are found locally. All these local species are classified indiscriminately as **ya?albe**. Since all and only the local representatives of the insectivores are so classified, one deletes all the scientific taxa subordinate to Insectivora. On the other hand, the several local species of the genus *Felis* (cats) are distinguished in Tzeltal. Thus no further deletion of scientific taxa is possible. What is now left of the scientific taxonomy may be described as **terminated**, **collapsed**, truncated, and local. It is the **reduced** scientific taxonomy.

We may now determine the degree to which each folk taxon fails to correspond to the scientific classification. For each folk taxon, we trace downward in the reduced scientific taxonomy, following every branch that includes some organism also included in the folk taxon. For example, "tree" in folk English includes a portion of two major botanical taxa, the cone-bearing plants and the flowering plants. It is thus necessary to follow both the cone-bearing and the flowering plant branches. We need not consider such taxa as ferns and mosses, however, since they lead to nothing that is called a tree.

We proceed downward until a taxon is reached that is a subset of the folk taxon. If a single scientific taxon is found that includes everything included in the folk taxon and nothing that is included in any other folk taxon, the corresponding scientific and folk taxa are equivalent. All such folk taxa merit a zero degree of dissimilarity. An example from Tzeltal is *čuč* 'squirrel', which both includes and is included in the family Sciuridae of the reduced scientific taxonomy.

If several scientific taxa are found that jointly partition the folk taxon, one retraces upward in the scientific taxonomic tree from each to the first taxon that includes all such scientific taxa. This taxon may be referred to as the **lowest common denominator** of the folk taxon. If we count the intervening edges of the longest path retraced, we have an index of the degree to which the folk taxon is out of correspondence with the scientific system.

The Tzeltal category *č'o* 'small rodent' provides an example (see Figure 3.15). First we trace downward from MAMMALIA. We pass the infraclass Eutheria, then continue to both Insectivora and Rodentia, since members of both orders are included in the taxon. On the rodent branch we must continue past the suborder Sciuromorpha to the family Heteromyidae (the pocket mice), since other families of that suborder are not included in *č'o*. We need not continue past the second rodent suborder, the Myomorpha, since all local representatives of the Myomorpha are included in *č'o*. We end up with three scientific taxa, which are subsets of *č'o*. Therefore we must retrace our steps until we find the lowest common denominator, which in this case is the infraclass Eutheria. A degree of three is assigned to *č'o*, since the longest retrace path involves three steps (i.e., Heteromyidae → Sciuromorpha → Rodentia → Eutheria).

A third possibility must be considered: All or part of the folk taxon may be equivalent to but a portion of a **terminal** scientific taxon, i.e., it may be impossible to find a set of scientific taxa that partition the folk taxon. The Tzeltal taxa *yašal č'o*, *sak ʔeal č'o*, and *k'alel č'o* illustrate this contingency. The lowest common denominator in each case is the genus *Peromyscus* represented locally by at least four species. Yet no species is entirely included within any one of these folk taxa (refer

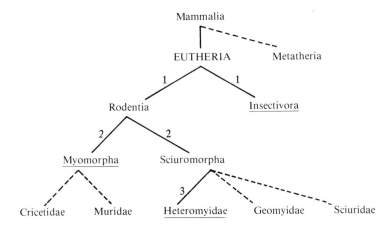

**Figure 3.15** Measuring the degree of dissimilarity of the Tzeltal taxon *č'o* 'small rodent'. (The underlined scientific names indicate the maximal subsets of *č'o*. The lowest common denominator of *č'o* is written with capital letters. Solid lines indicate edges traced in measuring this taxon. Dashed lines are not traced. The numerals beside the solid lines count the number of steps between the lowest common denominator and each maximal subset. The largest such number is the degree of dissimilarity of the taxon, in the case of *č'o*, three.)

**Table 3.2**
CALCULATION OF $D$ AND $D'$ FOR *čanbalam*$_2$
'MAMMAL'

| | | | | |
|---|---|---|---|---|
| $\#(T^0) = 59$ | | | $0 \#(T^0) = 0$ | |
| $\#(T^1) = 10$ | | | $1 \#(T^1) = 10$ | |
| $\#(T^2) = 5$ | $D = \dfrac{10 + 5 + 2}{76}$ | | $2 \#(T^2) = 10$ | $D' = \dfrac{10 + 10 + 6}{76}$ |
| $\#(T^3) = 2$ | | | $3 \#(T^3) = 6$ | |
| $\#(T) = 76$ | $= 0.22$ | | | $= 0.34$ |

to Table 5.2). We are left without scientifically recognized subsets as starting points for counting the length of the retrace paths. This dilemma is resolved by declaring that the "distance" between the subset of the species that is included in the folk taxon and the terminal scientific taxon is one. Thus these three folk taxa are all of degree two, the distance between the common genus and a proper subset of each species. In the same fashion we may count as degree one all folk taxa that are equivalent to a proper subset of a single terminal scientific taxon, e.g., *kašlan c'i?* 'Ladino dog', which is equivalent to a portion of the species *Canis familiaris*.

The unweighted Coefficient of Dissimilarity, $D$, of the entire folk taxonomy defined by the unique beginner *čanbalam*$_2$ is then calculated as the proportion of taxa of degree one or more to the total number of folk taxa in the taxonomy.

$$D = \frac{\#T^1 + \#T^2 + \cdots + \#T^n}{\#T}.$$

$\#$ indicates the cardinality, or number of members, of the set $T^k$ of all folk taxa of degree $k$, and $T$ is the set of all folk taxa of whatever degree.

The weighted Coefficient of Dissimilarity, $D'$, is derived from the unweighted measure by multiplying the number of taxa of each degree by the value of the degree itself. Thus

$$D' = \frac{1(\#T^1) + 2(\#T^2) + \cdots + n(\#T^n)}{\#T}$$

or

$$D' = \frac{\displaystyle\sum_{i=0}^{n} i(\#T^i)}{\#T}.$$

This weighting provides recognition for the

intuition that *kašlan c'i?* 'Ladino dog' (degree one) departs less from the scientific system than does *č'o* 'small rodent' (degree three). $D$ for the domain defined by *čanbalam*$_2$ is 0.22, $D'$ is 0.34, since there are 10 taxa of degree one, 5 of degree two, and 2 of degree three, of a total of 76 folk taxa (see Table 3.2).

The lowest possible value of the unweighted coefficient, $D$, is zero, indicating a perfect correspondence between the folk taxonomy and the subsystem of the scientific taxonomy generated by the reduction rules. The highest possible value is one, indicating that no folk taxon corresponds exactly to any scientific taxon. The weighted measure, $D'$, also has a minimal value of zero, again indicating a perfect fit. However a very high value of $D'$ might be in the neighborhood of 10. Such a value would be expected if organisms had been randomly assigned to taxa. The weighted measure with its wider range of values provides a more sensitive index of the degree of fit. However the upper bound of $D'$ is a function of the depth of the reduced scientific taxonomy, which varies both within and between domains. In order to gain the advantage of both a weighted and a "normalized" measure (i.e., one that varies between 0 and 1), it is necessary to recompute the degree of dissimilarity for each taxon such that it is expressed as a proportion of the maximum possible value.* This maximal value is equal to the length (i.e., number of edges) of the longest path in the reduced scientific taxonomy from the unique beginner, through the folk taxon in question, to the lowest level of the scientific taxonomy.

---

*I would like to thank Paul Kay for suggesting the idea of a normalized weighted measure.

Normalized $D'$ (i.e., $D''$) then is equal to the sum of the degrees of dissimilarity calculated in this fashion for each folk taxon, divided by the number of folk taxa. For **čanbalam$_2$**

$$D'' = 4.19/76 = 0.056$$

or barely 6% of the maximum possible dissimilarity. The values obtained in this example clearly indicate that the Tzeltal have paid close attention to the structure of "reality." The ultimate significance of these numbers depends, of course, on subsequent comparisons with coefficients calculated according to this technique for comparable domains from other cultures.

## 9.4 EVALUATION OF THE MEASURE

As noted, a measure should meet at least three criteria. How well does the present weighted measure qualify according to each criterion? First, a measure should be of wide utility. The reduction rules by which a specific subsystem of the scientific taxonomy is selected for comparison with each folk system ensures that the variations in local floras and faunas are taken into account. These same rules also minimize the effect of variations among scientific classifications due to competing schools of thought among systematists or to differential degrees of detail applied to a classification. I have performed a brief test of this factor by recomputing $D'$ using only the required taxonomic categories, i.e., class, order, family, genus, and species, ignoring the several intermediate levels, which may be poorly defined. The value of $D'$ changes only 0.02, reduced from 0.34 to 0.32. The effect of utilizing the more generalized scientific taxonomy as opposed to the finely detailed version is a slight loss of sensitivity of the measure. Thus this technique should be useful even in the absence of a fully developed scientific classification. Furthermore, the nature of the technique allows its application to biological domains of any size.

The second criterion demands an explicit procedure to ensure replicability. The procedures outlined can be precisely defined in set theoretical terms (Hunn 1975a). Thus once the folk system has been adequately described and a standard version of the scientific taxonomy agreed upon, the results are predetermined.

Finally, the measure should accurately reflect our intuitions concerning what it purports to measure. Earlier I argued (Section 9.2) that the statistic first employed by Berlin, Breedlove, and Raven (1966) and by Bulmer (1970) was deficient in this respect, systematically underestimating the degree to which folk and scientific biotaxonomic systems correspond. The summary data in Table 3.3 prove this point for the present example. Subgeneric taxa correspond rather poorly with scientific taxa in this example, but such taxa are disproportionately represented among the terminal taxa of a folk system, the basis for the first measure. It is also clear from Table 3.3 that Berlin's revised measure (1973), which is based on folk generic taxa, avoids this earlier source of bias. Thus it is not surprising that shifting from the terminal-species index to the generic-species index raises the degree of correspondence from 38% to 61% for the Tzeltal plant domain. However, avoiding selective attention to folk or scientific taxa of any particular rank, the Coefficient of Dissimilarity indicates a much higher figure than either of Berlin's

**Table 3.3**

DISTRIBUTION OF DISSIMILARITY
BY TYPE OF FOLK TAXON

| Type of taxon[a] | Degree of dissimilarity | | | | |
|---|---|---|---|---|---|
| | 0 | 1 | 2 | 3 | Totals |
| Generic | 43 | 2 | 0 | 0 | 45 |
| Subgeneric | 16 | 8 | 5 | 0 | 29 |
| Supergeneric | 0 | 0 | 0 | 2 | 2 |
| Totals | 59 | 10 | 5 | 2 | 76 |

[a]Berlin, Breedlove, and Raven (1973) define a hierarchical series of folk biotaxonomic categories as follows: varietal < specific < generic < intermediate < major life form < unique beginner. They describe procedures for deciding to which category a taxon belongs. Varietal and specific taxa are grouped here as subgeneric taxa. The remaining nongeneric taxa are supergeneric.

calculations, i.e., 93%. Does the plant taxonomy correspond less well to the scientific system than the domain treated here, or is the difference due to the contrast in measures employed? If the latter, which is the more meaningful measure? These questions require a closer examination of the data. The obvious first step is to apply Berlin's revised measure to the Tzeltal 'mammal' data (see Table 3.4). We may conclude that the Tzeltal 'mammal' taxa correspond more closely than the plant taxa to the scientific sorting (76% as opposed to 61%). The remaining difference (76% as opposed to 93%) is due to differences in the measures. Which then is the more meaningful figure? The answer depends on precisely what each purports to measure. I claim that the Coefficient of Dissimilarity is a "measure of the degree of correspondence of folk to scientific biological classification." Berlin's generic-species index is designed to demonstrate that "the fundamental taxa recognized in folk systematics correspond fairly closely with scientifically known species [1973:267]." Our goals are different, thus our measures are not the same. However I contend that the measure proposed here retains an advantage over Berlin's technique even with respect to his own stated goals.

The present measure, applied to the data at

### Table 3.4
TZELTAL 'MAMMAL' TAXA
CLASSIFIED ACCORDING TO BERLIN'S
REVISED INDEX

|  | Folk generics | Folk specifics |
|---|---|---|
| One-to-one correspondence | 34 (76%) | 14 (48%) |
| Overdifferentiated | 0 | 10 (34%) |
| Underdifferentiated | 11 (24%) | 0 |
| Type 1 | 5 (11%) | 0 |
| Type 2 | 6 (13%) | 0 |
| Not classifiable | 0 | 5 (18%)[a] |
| Totals | 45 (100%) | 29 (100%) |

[a] These five specific taxa cannot be classified because they both overdifferentiate (by splitting a species) and underdifferentiate (by combining portions of several species). Berlin does not consider this contingency.

hand, supports a key hypothesis suggested by both Bulmer and Berlin, i.e., that there is a subset of folk taxa that is psychologically fundamental in folk systems of biological classification. Berlin identifies this as the set of "generic" taxa (Berlin, Breedlove, and Raven 1973:216). Bulmer distinguishes a "hard core of lower order groupings in any [folk-biological] taxonomy," which are "multi-purpose, multi-dimensional" and logically natural groupings, from taxa "at the peripheries," which may be special purpose categories defined by a strictly limited set of attributes (1970:1087). If we examine the 'mammal' domain, we are struck by the fact that the major portion of the dissimilarity is attributable either to the most general categories or to the most specific (see Table 3.3). The 2 taxa with the highest degree of dissimilarity (3) are those that Berlin would call supergeneric, i.e., **čanbalam**$_2$ and **č'o**. Three of the 5 taxa with the next highest degree (2) are exceptional in being defined by a single attribute, fur color, and are thus what Bulmer and I call varietals. Of the 15 taxa of degree one or two, 13 have names of binomial form, according to Berlin a characteristic of specific (subgeneric), as opposed to generic, taxa. Thus there is a subset of the taxa of this domain characterized by the near-perfect correspondence of its members to scientific taxa, and this subset corresponds rather closely to the generic taxa of Berlin's system and to Bulmer's "hard core" taxa. However the tabulation indicates that, while nearly all generic taxa are fundamental in this sense (43 of 45), not all fundamental taxa are generic (43 of the 59 taxa of zero degree of dissimilarity are generic, 16 are specific, taxa). A majority of specific taxa (55%) might best be included in the "hard core" defined by Bulmer. Berlin's measure **assumes** that generic taxa are the "fundamental taxa." The present measure **demonstrates** that generic taxa exhibit the near-perfect correspondence with scientific taxa that Berlin attributes to the fundamental set of taxa, but indicates further that this property is not exclusive to the generic set.

A closer look at the data suggests an additional caution with respect to Berlin's technique. He selects the scientific species as his basis for comparison. The scientific species within a limited geographic range is the finest taxonomic distinction that can be made. Berlin's technique thus implies that folk systematists will tend to make distinctions comparable to the finest distinctions of the scientist. This ignores a significant consideration: Of the folk taxa in one-to-one correspondence, how many correspond to a scientific species that has no congeners in the local area? Correspondence to such "isolated" species provides no justification for equating this distinction with the finest distinctions of the scientist. Twenty-five of the 34 (74%) Tzeltal generic 'mammal' taxa that Berlin would describe as in one-to-one correspondence with scientific species in fact correspond to such "isolated" species, species with no close relatives known to the Tzeltal. Only 9 are actually distinguished from congeners at the species level. A more meaningful test of Berlin's contention is provided by those Tzeltal generics that apply in situations where species of a single genus might be distinguished. The Tzeltal taxa correspond to single species in only 9 of 18 (50%) of such test cases (see Table 3.5:H, I, J). It seems that Berlin's technique does not measure precisely what it purports to measure. Furthermore, our analysis indicates that since "isolated" species are more likely to correspond to folk generic taxa than nonisolated species, Berlin's index is susceptible to a gratuitous source of variation, viz., the frequency of "isolated" species in the scientific codomain. The Coefficient of Dissimilarity will not be affected in this fashion.

One final qualification is essential. The measure proposed here claims to measure the similarity of two independent classification schemes. This claim is limited by the extensional logic employed to define taxa. Taxa are defined simply as sets of organisms (see this chapter, Section 2). Obviously the mental correlate of a taxon is not a set of organisms but must be a **rule**, since human beings have no difficulty recognizing new instances of a taxon. This simplification is required by the

**Table 3.5**

CORRESPONDENCE OF TZELTAL GENERIC TAXA TO SCIENTIFIC TAXA OF VARIOUS TYPES

| Degree of correspondence | Number of taxa (percentage) |
|---|---|
| A. To no single scientific taxon | 2 (4%) |
| B. To a scientific taxon of supra-specific rank represented locally by more than one species | 9 (20%) |
| C. To an "isolated" scientific species | 25 (56%) |
| D. To a single species which is not "isolated" (i.e., more than one species of the scientific genus is known to the Tzeltal) | 9 (20%) |
| Total | 45 (100%) |
| E. One-to-one correspondence (C + D) | 34 (76%) |
| F. Underdifferentiated (A + B) | 11 (24%) |
| G. Degree of dissimilarity = 0 (B + C + D) | 43 (96%) |
| H. Situations of polytypy (B + D) | 18 |
| I. One-to-one correspondence in polytypic situations $(D/[B + D])$ | 0.50 (50% of H) |
| J. Underdifferentiation in polytypic situations $(B/[B + D])$ | 0.50 (50% of H) |

fact that most folk taxa are semantic primitives. The proposed measure does not directly compare the rules of categorization employed by folk and scientist to classify organisms. It simply compares the sortings that result. Yet it is highly unlikely that incomparable rules of categorization will produce very similar sortings repeatedly. Thus the measure proposed, if applied to an adequate comparative sample, can tell us whether or not folk and scientist employ comparable cognitive strategies in classifying living things. In addition, the method suggested here will enable students of folk biology to formulate and test specific hypotheses concerning the relationship between the categorizing activity of the human mind and a variety of conditioning factors, be they linguistic, cultural, or ecological.

Table 3.6 is a list of all the Tzeltal taxa that classify mammals. All taxa included are consistently recognized. Each is referred to by its primary name. Tzeltal taxa follow the linear order of the scientific taxa to which they correspond, except that each subordinate taxon follows its superordinate taxon. Portions of some Tzeltal names are included in parentheses. These portions are optional. The three covert taxa are bracketed. The glosses cited are English names for approximately equivalent scientific taxa. In the event that no such gloss is available, a literal translation of the Tzeltal name is cited. The taxonomic category of the lowest common denominators and maximal subsets is indicated as follows: genus names are italics and capitalized, species names are italics but not capitalized, superfamilies end in -*oidea*, families in -*idae*, subfamilies in -*inae*, all others are labeled.

## 10    Toward a Theory of Folk-Biological Classification

The ultimate goal of folk-biological research should be the generation of a theory of folk-biological classification. This theory should imply hypotheses subject to empirical verification. It should also be subject to an ultimate test, which is described here.

The ultimate test involves the prediction of the scientific denotata of all folk-biological categories nomenclaturally recognized for a particular culture resident in a specified habitat, and the subsequent and independent verification of the predictions by field investigations. This prediction would not, of course, specify the surface realization of each name, but it might specify whether the name was a primary or a secondary lexeme as defined by Berlin or by some derivative set of criteria. The taxa would be specified as to type, utilizing the scheme proposed here or some more advanced typology. Since such a prediction would involve in the neighborhood of 1000 positive assertions, the correct prediction of even 90% of all categories would be highly significant. The import of such predictive accuracy is highlighted by the fact that an assumption of absolute cultural relativity would imply an infinity of possible classificatory results. Such an assumption, of course, is untenable given the data already assembled.

The prediction would be based on the following data.

1. A natural history of the geographical area occupied by the cultural unit for which the prediction is to be made. This would specify the internal distribution and relative abundance of all groups of plants and animals in the region. This information should be accurate at the species level for vertebrates and vascular plants and at that or some higher level for invertebrates and nonvascular plants, the level to be determined by an inspection of the nature of morphological variation within such groups. Information on species occurring in the surrounding area but absent from the specified region should be available to the extent that movements of individuals from the cultural region in question, due to trade or other cultural activities, warrants.

2. An ethnographic description of subsistence and other economic, ritual, and political activities determined to be relevant to folk classification in prior studies.

3. A scientific taxonomic analysis of intergroup differences for all local groups of organisms. This analysis is to provide the basis for a preliminary rank ordering of biological groups according to the degree to which they are distinctive (i.e., a rank ordering of taxa based on an estimate of the Critical Ratio of each potential taxon).

The sufficiency of the data specified for our prediction is based on the following assumptions, which might form the basis of a theory of folk-biological classification.

1. Other things being equal, the probability that a group of organisms will be recognized and named is directly proportional to the Critical Ratio of a potential taxon as determined by scientific taxonomic analysis.

**Table 3.6**
THE TZELTAL TAXA REGARDING MAMMALS[a]

| Tzeltal name | Gloss | Lowest common denominator/ maximal subsets | d/d'' |
|---|---|---|---|
| *čanbalam*₂ | 'mammal' | MAMMALIA (class)/Metatheria (infraclass), Eutherian orders, Pilosa (infraorder), Ceboidea | 3/0.38 |
| *ʔuč* | 'Virginia opossum' | *Didelphis* | 0/0 |
| *huyum ʔuč* | 'fat opossum'[c] | *Didelphis virginiana* | 0/0 |
| *bac'il ʔuč* | 'true opossum'[c] | *Didelphis marsupialis* | 0/0 |
| *ʔuč č'o* | 'four-eyed opossum' | *Philander* | 0/0 |
| *bac'* | 'howler monkey' | *Alouatta* | 0/0 |
| *maš* | 'spider monkey' | *Ateles* | 0/0 |
| *c'uhc'uneh čab* | 'anteater' | Pilosa (infraorder) | 0/0 |
| *t'ul* | 'rabbit' | Lagomorpha (order) | 0/0 |
| *kašlan t'ul* | 'European rabbit' | *Oryctolagus* | 0/0 |
| *bac'il t'ul* | 'true rabbit'[c] | *Sylvilagus* | 0/0 |
| *čuč* | 'squirrel' | Sciuridae | 0/0 |
| *yašal čuč* | 'gray squirrel'[c] | *Sciurus aureogaster* | 0/0 |
| *c'eh (čuč)* | 'Deppe's squirrel' | *S. deppei* | 0/0 |
| *pehpen čuč* | 'flying squirrel' | *Glaucomys* | 0/0 |
| *ba* | 'pocket gopher' | Geomyidae | 0/0 |
| *č'uypat ba* | 'white-banded gopher'[c] | Geomyidae/subset of *Heterogeomys hispidus* | 1/0.20 |
| *bac'il ba* | 'true gopher'[c] | Geomyidae/subset of *H. hispidus* | 1/0.20 |
| *č'o* | 'small rodent' | Eutheria (infraclass)/ Insectivora (order), Myomorpha (suborder), Heteromyidae | 3/0.43 |
| *yaʔal be (č'o)* | 'shrew' | Insectivora (order) | 0/0 |
| *k'iwoč č'o* | 'pocket mouse' | Heteromyidae | 0/0 |
| *sabin č'o* | 'rice rat' | *Oryzomys* | 0/0 |
| *moin teʔ č'o* | 'vesper rat' | *Nyctomys* | 0/0 |
| *sin (č'o)* | 'harvest mouse' | *Reithrodontomys* | 0/0 |
| [*Peromyscus*][b] | 'white-footed mouse' | *Peromyscus* | 0/0 |
| *yašal č'o* | 'gray mouse'[c] | *Peromyscus*/subsets of *Peromyscus* spp. | 2/0.29 |
| *sak ʔeal č'o* | 'white-mouth mouse'[c] | *Peromyscus*/subsets of *Peromyscus* spp. | 2/0.29 |
| *k'alel č'o* | 'bright mouse'[c] | *Peromyscus*/subsets of *Peromyscus* spp. | 2/0.29 |
| *čitam č'o* | 'cotton rat' | *Sigmodon* | 0/0 |
| *hseʔ teʔ (č'o)* | 'tree-cutter rat'[c] | Cricetidae/*Neotoma, Tylomys* | 1/0.17 |
| *karánsa (č'o)* | 'black rat' | *Rattus* | 0/0 |
| *šlumil č'o* | 'house mouse' | *Mus* | 0/0 |
| *č'iš ʔuhčum* | 'Mexican porcupine' | Erethizontoidea | 0/0 |
| *halaw* | 'paca' | Cavioidea | 0/0 |
| *c'iʔ* | 'dog' | *Canis familiaris* | 0/0 |
| *polisía c'iʔ* | 'German shepherd' | *C. familiaris* breed | 0/0 |
| *kašlan c'iʔ* | 'Ladino dog'[c] | *C. familiaris*/subset of *C. familiaris* | 1/0.17 |
| *bac'il c'iʔ* | 'true dog'[c] | *C. familiaris*/subset of *C. familiaris* | 1/0.17 |
| *ʔok'il* | 'coyote' | *Canis latrans* | 0/0 |
| *waš* | 'gray fox' | *Urocyon* | 0/0 |

*(continued)*

[a]Taxa excluded from ***canbalam***₂ (not included in the computation):

| | | |
|---|---|---|
| ***soc'*** | 'bat' | Chiroptera (order) |
| ***kirsiáno*** | 'human being' | *Homo sapiens* |
| ***mayil tiʔbal*** | 'armadillo' | *Dasypus novemcinctus* |

[b]Covert taxon.
[c]Literal translation of the Tzeltal name.

Table 3.6 (*Continued*)

| Tzeltal name | Gloss | Lowest common denominator/ maximal subsets | d/d'' |
|---|---|---|---|
| *me?el* | 'raccoon' | *Procyon* | 0/0 |
| *kohtom* | 'coatimundi' | *Nasua* | 0/0 |
| *?uyoh* | 'kinkajou' | *Potos* | 0/0 |
| *sabin* | 'long-tailed weasel' | *Mustela* | 0/0 |
| *sak hol* | 'tayra' | *Eira* | 0/0 |
| *pay* | 'skunk' | Mephitinae | 0/0 |
| *č'in pay* | 'spotted skunk' | *Spilogale* | 0/0 |
| *?ihk'al pay* | 'hooded skunk' | *Mephitis* | 0/0 |
| *lem pat pay* | 'hog-nosed skunk' | *Conepatus* | 0/0 |
| *ha?alc'i?* | 'river otter' | *Lutra* | 0/0 |
| *balam* | 'jaguar' | *Felis onca* | 0/0 |
| *čoh* | 'cougar' | *F. concolor* | 0/0 |
| *cahal čoh̩* | 'ocelot' | *F. pardalis* | 0/0 |
| *cis balam* | 'margay' | *F. wiedii* | 0/0 |
| *?ik' sab* | 'jaguarundi' | *F. yagouaroundi* | 0/0 |
| *šawin* | 'house cat' | *F. cattus* | 0/0 |
| *cemen* | 'tapir' | Ceratomorpha (suborder) | 0/0 |
| *búro* | 'donkey' | *Equus asinus* | 0/0 |
| *kawáyu* | 'horse/mule' | *Equus/E. caballus, E. caballus* × *E. asinus* | 1/0.17 |
| $\begin{bmatrix}\text{mule}\end{bmatrix}^b$ | | *E. caballus* × *E. asinus* | 0/0 |
| $\begin{bmatrix}\text{horse}\end{bmatrix}^b$ | | *E. caballus* | 0/0 |
| *čitam* | 'pig' | Suidae | 0/0 |
| *merikáno čitam* | 'American pig'[c] | Suidae/subset of *Sus scrofa* | 1/0.20 |
| *škoen čitam* | 'low-slung pig'[c] | Suidae/subset of *S. scrofa* | 1/0.20 |
| *bac'il čitam* | 'true pig' | Suidae/subset of *S. scrofa* | 1/0.20 |
| *wamal čitam* | 'peccary' | Tayassuidae | 0/0 |
| *niwak wamal čitam* | 'large peccary'[c] | Tayassuidae/subsets of Tayassuidae spp. | 2/0.33 |
| *bahk'al wamal čitam* | 'numerous peccary'[c] | Tayassuidae/subsets of Tayassuidae spp. | 2/0.33 |
| *te?tikil čih* | 'deer' | Cervoidea | 0/0 |
| *yašal (te?tikil) čih* | 'white-tailed deer' | *Odocoileus* | 0/0 |
| *cahal (te?tikil) čih* | 'brocket' | *Mazama* | 0/0 |
| *(tunim) čih* | 'sheep' | *Ovis* | 0/0 |
| *tencun* | 'goat' | *Capra* | 0/0 |
| *wakaš* | 'cattle' | *Bos* | 0/0 |
| *merikáno wakaš* | 'zebu' | *Bos taurus* breed | 0/0 |
| *bac'il wakaš* | 'true cattle'[c] | *Bos*/subset of *B. taurus* | 1/0.17 |

2. Among the "other things" which are not equal and which therefore must be incorporated in a modification of the rank order generated by the first proposition is the relative abundance of the organisms. Other things being equal, the more abundant the group of organisms within the region the more likely that that group will be recognized and named. These data have been specified as part of the natural history data required. A related biological consideration is the size of the organisms. Other things being equal, the larger the mean size of organisms of a particular group the more likely that group will be recognized and named. Microscopic organisms regardless of how distinctive they might be are so small that the probability of their recognition, assuming a "naked-eye" state of technology, is zero.

3. Several cultural or biocultural factors must also be considered. These might be considered holistically in the construction

of a scale of cultural significance of groups of organisms. Berlin, Breedlove, and Raven (1966) have proposed one such scale and demonstrated its relevance. However, a more detailed scale along similar lines will have to be developed before it can be used to generate accurate predictions. One modification of the scale proposed by Berlin and his associates involves the assertion that all groups of organisms are of **some** cultural significance by virtue of their existence as "objects to be encountered" in the environment of the culture. Thus this factor, unlike the size of organisms, has no zero point.

4. A scheme for weighting the various relevant factors must be specified. The more empirical data on folk-biosystematics available prior to the attempt at prediction the more accurate the result. In my opinion, reasonable predictive accuracy is already a real possibility, though as yet unrecognized but significant factors remain to be discovered.

5. Finally, a cut-off point, the naming threshold, must be applied to the rank ordering of potential categorical distinctions. This threshold divides the list of potential distinctions into a named and an unnamed set. This point might be determined post hoc by the number of named taxa determined to be present in the system. A stronger test would involve the prediction of the threshold itself. I imagine a sliding scale of **attentiveness** perhaps based on an ecological factor. A **negative** correlation between "civilization" and attentiveness might be incorporated into the prediction if empirically indicated by prior research elsewhere.

In sum, a theory of folk-biological classification should specify the relative importance of the constraints imposed by objective reality, human psychology, and cultural ecology within a single system.

# CHAPTER 4

## Data Summaries

Table 4.1 summarizes essential aspects of the scope and form of the Tzeltal classification of animal life. The distribution of polytypy is given, first for all 335 generic taxa recognized in this monograph, then for the two life forms, the 106 *mut*₁ 'bird' generics and the 45 generics included in **canbalam**₂ 'mammal', and finally for the remaining 184 generic taxa that are included in neither life form. Most generic taxa include no specific subdivision, i.e., are monotypic. For example, 280 of the 335 animal generics (84%) are monotypic. Of the 55 (16%) which include specific subdivisions, 25 subsume two, 18 three, and just 12 more than three specific subdivisions. This distribution is one of uncanny regularity (Geoghegan 1973). It varies little among the three major subdivisions of the animal taxa in Table 4.1: Thirteen percent of 'bird' generics, 27% of 'mammal'

generics, and 16% of the remainder are polytypic. The inflated figure for 'mammals' is clearly due to the concentration of polytypy among taxa of domesticated organisms (cf. Geoghegan 1973:13–18). At the botton of Table 4.1 the numbers of taxa (total and covert) are given for each taxonomic rank for a grand total of 557 taxa, 498 of which are consistently named. Totals of terminal taxa are set apart. The number of terminal taxa may be obtained by adding the number of specific taxa to the number of monotypic generic taxa. The terminal taxa are the finest consistently recognized distinctions of a folk classification.

Table 4.2 lists all taxa which are residuals [R], that is, taxa which include what is left over when finer distinctions are made (see Chapter 3, Section 7.3). Such taxa may be named, as are the four residual generics and

**Table 4.1**
DISTRIBUTION OF POLYTYPY AMONG TZELTAL GENERIC ANIMAL TAXA

| Number of specific subdivisions of the generic | Total: čanbalam₁ 'animal' | Number of such generics | | |
|---|---|---|---|---|
| | | mut₁ 'bird' | čanbalam₂ 'mammal' | Other animals |
| 0 (monotypic) | **280** | 92 | 33 | 155 |
| 2 | **25** | 5 | 7 | 13 |
| 3 | **18** | 4 | 5 | 9 |
| 4 | **5** | 2 | | 3 |
| 5 | **3** | 3 | | |
| 6 | **2** | | | 2 |
| 7 | **1** | | | 1 |
| . . . | **. . .** | | | |
| 10 | **1** | | | 1 |
| ≧ 2 (polytypic) | **55** | 14 | 12 | 29 |
| **TOTAL GENERICS** (1 is covert) | **335** | 106 | 45 | 184 |
| **TOTAL SPECIFICS** (12 are covert) | **168** | 45 | 29 | 94 |
| TOTAL TERMINAL TAXA | 448 | 137 | 62 | 249 |
| **TOTAL COMPLEXES** (46 are covert) | **51** | | | |
| **TOTAL LIFE FORMS** | **2** | | | |
| **GRAND TOTAL TAXA** (59 are covert) | **557** | | | |

**Table 4.2**
SUMMARY OF OCCURRENCE OF RESIDUAL TAXA

| | | |
|---|---|---|
| Generics (4): | *su?siwal* 'bee' | Any organisms of the covert bee complex not assigned to any other generic of that complex may be placed here. |
| | *p'ilič* 'residual grasshopper' | Small individuals, whether adult or immature, of the suborder Caelifera are placed here. |
| | *čan₂* 'small beetle' | Beetles of various families not otherwise placed will be labeled **X** *čan*, where **X** is a literally appropriate attributive expression. |
| | *čup* 'caterpillar' | The caterpillars placed here share an "outlandish" quality. |
| Named specifics (6): | *č'in sik'* 'small swift' | |
| | *kašlan c'i?* 'Ladino dog' | |
| | *bac'il čitam* 'true pig' | |
| | *bac'il wakaš* 'true cattle' | |
| | *bac'il nep* 'true crab' | |
| | *bac'il puy* 'true snail' | |
| Covert residual specifics (10): | $\lceil R \rceil$ *likawal* 'residual hawk' | |
| | $\lceil R \rceil$ *mut₂* 'residual chicken' | |
| | $\lceil R \rceil$ *čuč* 'residual squirrel' | |
| | $\lceil R \rceil$ *lukum* 'residual worm' | |
| | $\lceil R \rceil$ *pehpen* 'residual moth' | |
| | $\lceil R \rceil$ *tultuš* 'residual dragonfly' | |
| | $\lceil R \rceil$ *čil* 'residual cricket' | |
| | $\lceil R \rceil$ *čanul te?* 'residual boring larva' | |
| | *syalhaul* $\lceil R \rceil$ 'residual maggot' | |
| | $\lceil R \rceil$ *?am* 'residual spider | |

Total number of residual taxa = 20

six specifics, though they are frequently not given nomenclatural recognition as such. Covert residual specifics are indicated by writing the $\lceil R \rceil$ in the place of the specific attributive expression. Residual taxa have not previously been systematically distinguished in the ethnosemantic literature though they are of considerable theoretical interest.

## 1  The Correspondence of Folk to Scientific Zoological Classification

The Tzeltal classification of animals might be cited in support of either the contention that folk and scientific classification systems are basically alike or that they are fundamentally different. Numerous examples of correspondences as well as of failures to correspond are available. The resolution of this important issue requires a workable, reliable, and meaningful measure of the **degree** of correspondence of folk to scientific classification. I have defined what I feel is such a measure (see Section 9.3 of Chapter 3). Various forms of this index of dissimilarity (i.e., $D$, $D'$, $D''$) have been calculated for 445 of the 557 taxa described in this monograph (see Table 4.3). (Excluded are 46 covert complexes and 66 generic and specific taxa not yet sufficiently well defined for a close approximation of the degree of dissimilarity $\lceil d \rceil$.)

**Table 4.3**

CORRESPONDENCE OF TZELTAL ANIMAL
TAXA TO THE SCIENTIFIC SYSTEM
MEASURED BY HUNN'S DEGREE OF
DISSIMILARITY INDEX $(D)^a$

| | $D''$ | $D'$ | $D$ |
|---|---|---|---|
| $mut_1$ 'bird' $N = 149$ (three taxa not calculable, excluded)[b] | 0.040 | 0.26 | 0.21 |
| $\check{c}anbalam_2$ 'mammal' $N = 76$ | 0.051 | 0.32 | 0.22 |
| Other vertebrates $N = 48$ (four taxa not calculable, excluded)[b] | 0.070 | $0.44\ (0.29)^c$ | 0.25 |
| Invertebrates $N = 171$ (59 taxa not calculable, excluded)[b] | 0.121 | $0.71\ (0.50)^c$ | 0.45 |
| Total taxa $\check{c}anbalam_1$ 'animal' $N = 445$ (66 taxa not calculable, excluded)[b] | 0.076 | 0.46 | 0.31 |

$^a D$ = proportion of taxa not in one-to-one correspondence with scientific taxa of any rank.
$D'$ = $D$ weighted by degree of dissimilarity.
$D''$ = $D'$ normalized by expressing degree of dissimilarity as a proportion of a maximal dissimilarity. $D''$ may be interpreted as a proportion of maximal dissimilarity.
$^b$ Taxa excluded were not sufficiently well defined. Of these, 25 are generic taxa and 41 specific taxa.
$^c$ The figures for $D'$ in parentheses are calculated without the dissimilarities due to metamorphosis.

The weighted and normalized index $(D'')$ indicates that less than 8% of the potential dissimilarity exists. This figure should be compared with the proportion of folk generics that correspond perfectly to scientific species (Berlin's index) and the proportion of terminal taxa that so correspond (Bulmer's index). Only 44% of all generic animal taxa correspond one-to-one with scientific species, and just 48% of terminal taxa so correspond (see Table 4.4). Tables 4.5 and 4.6 provide a more detailed analysis of the nature of the folk-scientific correspondence under-

lying the various indexes. Tables 4.7 and 4.8 illustrate the major ways in which folk taxa fail to correspond to scientific taxa.

A major focus of the Tzeltal folk botanical research of Berlin, Breedlove, and Raven is the correlation between the cultural utility of various plant taxa and the relative degree of correspondence of those taxa to scientific species (1966, 1974:103). They demonstrate a clear correlation. Assessing the relative cultural utility of animal taxa appears to be more difficult (Hays 1974:200). Domesticated animal species are few, and most are postconquest introductions. Goals of hunting and trapping appear determined more by the size and availability of an animal species —both factors that affect the correlation of folk and scientific taxa independently of cultural utility—than by any strictly "cultural" criteria of choice.

Rather than attempt a rank ordering of animal taxa by relative cultural utility, I have ranked them by relative "phylogenetic distance" from man. Thus birds $(D'' = 0.04)$ and mammals $(D'' = 0.05)$ are classified more "accurately" than are lower vertebrates $(D'' = 0.07)$ and these more accurately than invertebrates $(D'' = 0.12)$. Of course, this ranking is not independent of the average size of animals of the various types, which might be as good an explanation for the gross pattern as "phylogenetic proximity." Finally, the disruptive effects of metamorphosis during the maturation process has a measurable effect. The splitting of scientific species into contrasting folk taxa—whether or not these folk taxa are thought to be related by a process of 'transformation'—on the basis of the radical morphological contrasts between larval and adult forms of species that undergo metamorphic growth is confined to our "other vertebrates" (frogs, toads, and tadpoles) and "invertebrates" categories. Each such instance contributes a point to the sum of weighted dissimilarities in calculating $D'$ and $D''$. If we extract this contribution to the dissimilarity index, we reduce but do not entirely eliminate the contrast noted above. $D'$ for "other vertebrates" is reduced from 0.44 to 0.29, now less than that calculated for

**Table 4.4**

COMPARISON OF VARIOUS INDEXES OF FOLK-SCIENTIFIC SYSTEM CORRESPONDENCE

| Index used | Tzeltal animals | | | | Tzeltal plants |
|---|---|---|---|---|---|
| | Total sample | Birds | Mammals | Others | |
| Berlin's index:<br>Percentage of folk generics<br>one-to-one with scientific<br>species | 44 | 62 | 73 | 27 | 61 |
| Bulmer's index:<br>Percentage of folk terminal<br>taxa one-to-one with<br>scientific species | 48 | 72 | 68 | 26 | 38 |
| $(1 - D)$ 100:<br>Percentage of folk taxa<br>one-to-one with scientific<br>taxa | 69 | 79 | 78 | 41 | |
| $(1 - D'')100$:<br>Percentage of maximal<br>degree of system<br>correspondence | 92 | 96 | 95 | 89 | |

**Table 4.5**

DISTRIBUTION OF DEGREE OF DISSIMILARITY ($d$) OF TZELTAL ANIMAL TAXA BY TAXONOMIC RANK

| Rank<br>of folk taxa: | Degree of dissimilarity ($d$) | | | | | | Totals |
|---|---|---|---|---|---|---|---|
| | 0 | 1 | 2 | 3 | 4 | ?[b] | |
| Suprageneric[a] | 3 | 1 | 2 | 2 | | | 8 |
| Generic | 228 | 53 | 20 | 8 | 1 | 25 | 335 |
| [polytypic generic] | [25] | [16] | [7] | [4] | | | [52] |
| [terminal generic] | [203] | [37] | [13] | [4] | [1] | | [258] |
| [terminal taxa] | [280] | [68] | [29] | [7] | [1] | | [426] |
| Specific | 77 | 31 | 16 | 3 | | 41 | 168 |
| Total taxa | 308 | 85 | 38 | 13 | 1 | 66 | 511 |

[a] Only named suprageneric taxa are included here.

[b] The degree of dissimilarity ($d$) of these taxa cannot be calculated because the taxa are not adequately defined.

the 'mammals', while $D'$ for invertebrates is reduced from 0.71 to 0.50 (see Table 4.3).

In sum, though folk taxa often fail to correspond to scientific taxa—and yet more frequently fail to correspond at the species level—the "misses" tend strongly to be near misses (see Tables 4.7 and 4.8), firmly supporting Bulmer's intuition of a "conceptual correspondence" of the "hard core" of folk and scientific taxa (Bulmer 1970:1076).

## 2   Nomenclatural Patterns

Table 4.9 summarizes the occurrence of primary lexemes of three types, simple, unproductive, and productive, among the 333 named generic animal taxa (primary names only). The relative proportions of these lexeme types among animal generic terms differs notably from those found among Tzeltal plant generics (Berlin, Breedlove,

**Table 4.6**

TYPES OF ONE-TO-ONE CORRESPONDENCE OF TZELTAL ANIMAL TAXA TO SCIENTIFIC TAXA[a]

| Type of correspondence | Total: čanbalam₁ 'animal' | | | mut₁ 'bird' | | | čanbalam₂ 'mammal' | | | Other animals | | |
|---|---|---|---|---|---|---|---|---|---|---|---|---|
| | FG | FS | TT | FG | FS | TT | FG | FS | TT | FG | FS | TT |
| A. G / S (S) | 35 | 28 | 62 | 9 | 17 | 26 | 9 | 6 | 14 | 17 | 5 | 22 |
| B. F / G (G‖S) | 87 | 26 | 111 | 48 | 16 | 63 | 17 | 7 | 23 | 22 | 3 | 25 |
| C. O / F (F‖G‖S) | 27 | 7 | 32 | 9 | 1 | 10 | 7 | 0 | 5 | 11 | 6 | 17 |
| A + B + C. One-to-one correspondence to a scientific species | 149 | 61 | 205 | | | | | | | | | |
| D. F / G (G / S S) | 31 | 4 | 30 | 10 | 0 | 9 | 4 | 1 | 3 | 17 | 3 | 18 |
| E. O / F (F / G G S S) | 27 | 4 | 23 | 7 | 0 | 5 | 4 | 0 | 0 | 16 | 4 | 18 |
| F. S / V (V) | 0 | 4 | 4 | 0 | 0 | 0 | 0 | 2 | 2 | 0 | 2 | 2 |
| G. Higher level equivalences | 19 | 4 | 19 | 0 | 0 | 0 | 2 | 0 | 1 | 17 | 4 | 18 |

[a]FG = folk generic, FS = folk specific, TT = terminal taxa; V = scientific variety, S = scientific species, G = scientific genus, F = scientific family, O = scientific order. Included under V (scientific variety) are well established subspecies or breeds of domestic animals.

and Raven 1974:98–99). For example, 51% of the animal generics are labeled by simple primary lexemes; only 27% of the native generic plant names are so labeled. I have no ready explanation for this contrast. The frequency of loan words (mostly from Spanish) provides a further contrast. Eight percent of the animal generic names are loans while 19% of the plant generics are so labeled (Berlin, Breedlove, and Raven 1974:98).

Onomatopoetic terms account for 17% of all animal generic names. The distribution of such terms closely parallels the distribution of highly developed auditory signaling

**Table 4.7**

TYPES OF FAILURE TO CORRESPOND TO A SINGLE SCIENTIFIC TAXON: LUMPING[a]

| Type of lumping | Examples |
|---|---|
| Lumping:  $d = 1$ | *šluš* 'nightingale thrush' <br> *kawáyu* 'horse/mule' <br><br> *heš* 'jay' <br> *šʔiwána* 'iguana' |
| Lumping:  $d = 2$ | *peč'* 'domestic duck' <br> [R] *likawal* 'residual hawk' |
| Lumping:  $d = 3$ | *peč'ul haʔ* 'wild duck' <br> In this example the intrusion of a deductive criterion (wild–domestic) contributes to the dissimilarity. |
| Lumping: $d = 4$ | *c'uhkuton* 'salamander/gecko' |

[a] $d$ = degree of dissimilarity of a folk taxon (see Chapter 3, Section 9.3), P = scientific phylum, C = scientific class, O = scientific order, sO = scientific suborder, F = scientific family, G = scientific genus, S = scientific species.

**Table 4.8**

TYPES OF FAILURE TO CORRESPOND TO A SINGLE SCIENTIFIC TAXON: SPLITTING, LUMPING AND SPLITTING[a]

| Type of failure | | Examples |
|---|---|---|
| Splitting: $d = 1$ | (a) by morph | *č'uy pat ba* 'banded pocket gopher' (see *ba*/mammal) <br><br> *mut₁* 'chicken' The specific subdivisions of this folk generic are not known to correspond to any well defined breed. |
| | (b) by stage | *šberon* 'ranid tadpole' |
| | (c) by sex/ caste | *meʔ honon* 'mother bumblebee' (see *honon*/bee) |
| Splitting and lumping: $d = 2$ | | *sak ʔeal č'o* 'white-mouth mouse' (see white-footed mouse/mammal, rat) <br><br> *k'unil šenen* 'non-biting mosquito' (see *šenen*/fly) |
| Splitting and lumping: $d = 3$ | | [R] *pehpen* 'residual moth' |

[a] $d$ = degree of dissimilarity of a folk taxon (see Chapter 3, Section 9.3), O = scientific order, F = scientific family, G = scientific genus, S = scientific species, q = arbitrary subset of a scientific species, ad = adult, lr = larva.

behaviors among animal forms. Approximately 50% of 106 generic bird names are onomatopoetic, as are most terms for adult frogs and toads. Elsewhere we find two mammals and a few insects so named. Onomatopoeia also accounts for most of the more complex canonical forms cited in Table 4.10.

Unproductive primary lexemes are further analyzed in Table 4.11 and the relative frequency of attributive stems is summarized in Table 4.12. The semantic dimensions underlying composite terminology are analyzed in the next section.

## 2.1  THE STRUCTURE AND SEMANTICS OF COMPOSITE TERMS

Composite terms analyzed here are of three types. Those that label generic taxa are

Table 4.9

DISTRIBUTION OF TYPES OF GENERIC NAMES, LOANS, AND ONOMATOPOETIC NAMES
AMONG TZELTAL ANIMAL TAXA

| | Lexeme type | | | |
| | Simple | Unproductive | Productive | Totals |
| --- | --- | --- | --- | --- |
| **mut₁** 'bird' | | | | |
| Totals | 61 (58%) | 23 (22%) | 22 (20%) (all < **mut₁** 'bird') | 106 (100%) |
| Onomatopoetic | 37 (+6 ?) | 10 | 2 | 49 (+6 ?) |
| Loans | 6 | 0 | 2 | 8 |
| **čanbalam₂** 'mammal' | | | | |
| Totals | 26 (59%) | 13 (30%) | 5 (11%) (all < **č'o** 'rat/mouse') | 45[a] (102%) |
| Onomatopoetic | 2 | 0 | 0 | 2 |
| Loans | 4 | 0 | 0 | 4 |
| Other vertebrates | | | | |
| Totals | 21 (42%) | 13 (26%) | 16 (32%) (13 < **čan₁** 'snake', 3 < **čay** 'fish') | 50 (100%) |
| Onomatopoetic | 4 | 1 | 0 | 5 |
| Loans | 5 | 2 | 1 | 8 |
| Invertebrates | | | | |
| Totals | 63 (47%) | 39 (29%) | 31 (24%) ( 2 < **čay** 'fish', 26 < **čan₃** 'critter', 3 < **šuš** 'wasp') | 133 (100%) |
| Onomatopoetic | 2 (+4 ?) | 0 | 0 | 2 (+4 ?) |
| Loans | 1 | 3 | 2 | 6 |
| **čanbalam₁** 'animal' | | | | |
| Totals | 171 (51%) | 88 (26%) | 74 (23%) | 334[a] (100%) |
| Onomatopoetic | 45 (+10 ?) | 11 | 2 | 58 (+10 ?) |
| Loans | 16 | 5 | 5 | 26 |

[a] Includes one covert generic.

productive primary lexemes (Berlin, Breedlove, and Raven 1974:29). Those that label specific taxa are secondary lexemes. Finally, I include expressions of comparable structure that are not valid names. These may be labels for deductive varietal distinctions or spontaneous coinages. The three types may be distinguished on formal taxonomic grounds, but are syntactically equivalent.

## 2.2  STRUCTURAL TYPES

All composite terms have two segments, the head, which alone labels an animal taxon, and the attributive, which modifies the head.

In the vast majority of instances, the attributive precedes the head, e.g.,

**k'an heš** ᵃ[**k'an** 'yellow']ᵃ ʰ[**heš** 'jay']ʰ, lit. 'yellow jay'

(ᵃ = attributive, ʰ = head). In some cases however this order is reversed, a fact normally indicated by affixing a possessive prefix (pp) or relational suffix (rs) to the head segment, e.g.,

**cuhkumal cic** ʰ[**cuhkum** 'woolybear' + rs]ʰ ᵃ[**cic** 'avocado']ᵃ, lit. 'woolybear of the avocado';

**šhoč'ol čenek'** ʰ[pp + **hoč'** 'weevil' + rs]ʰ

Table 4.10
EXAMPLES OF CANONICAL FORMS OF
TZELTAL SIMPLE PRIMARY LEXEMES

| Canonical form | Examples | Gloss |
|---|---|---|
| CV | *ba* | 'pocket gopher' |
|  | *č'o* | 'rat/mouse' |
|  | *ha* | 'fly' |
| CVC | *peč'* | 'domestic duck' |
|  | *ses* | 'ant' |
|  | *ʔuč* | 'opossum' |
| CVhC | *(š)ʔahk'* | 'turtle' |
|  | *šohk* | 'chigger' |
|  | *toht* | 'robin' |
| CVVC | *sian* | 'solitaire' |
| CVCVC | *c'isim* | 'leaf-cutting ant' |
|  | *sabin* | 'weasel' |
|  | *šulem* | 'Turkey Vulture' |
| CVCVV[a] | *kukai* | 'firefly' |
| CVCCV[a] | *k'ančo* | 'speckled racer' |
| CVhCVC | *cuhkum* | 'woolybear cater-pillar' |
|  | *c'ihtil* | 'woodpecker' |
|  | *kohtom* | 'coatimundi' |
| CVCCVC | *čončiw* | 'sparrow' |
|  | *k'intun* | 'anole' |
|  | *tultuš* | 'dragonfly' |
| (CVC)₁(CVC)₂[a] | *nucnuc* | 'carpenter bee' |
|  | *ʔotʔot* | 'Yellow-billed Cacique' |
|  | *toytoy* | 'pygmy owl' |
| CVCVCVC[a] | *c'urupik* | 'earwig' |
|  | *k'oročoč* | 'Acorn Woodpecker' |
|  | *(š)purowok* | 'dovelet' |
| CVCCVCV[a] | *k'ork'owe* | 'carpenter ant' |
| (CVC)₁(CVC)₂ CV[a] | *k'ork'orʔe* | (variant of *k'ork'owe*) |
| CVhCVCVC[a] | *c'uhkuton* | 'salamander/gecko' |
|  | *čohčowit* | 'Grayish Saltator' |
| CVCVCCVC[a] | *kurunkuc* | 'screech owl' |
| CVCCVCVC[a] | *(š)ʔenkenek* | 'sheep frog' |
|  | *purkuwič* | 'whip-poor-will' |
|  | *tuncerek'* | 'Lineated Wood-pecker' |
| CVCVCVCVC[a] | *čikitoroš* | 'army ant' |
| CVCCVCVCVC[a] | *čiktawilon* | 'tinamou' |

[a]Indicates a form not cited for Tzeltal plant names (Berlin, Breedlove, and Raven 1974).

---

[a][*čenek'* 'bean']a, lit. 'weevil of the bean';

**slukumil č'uht** h[pp + **lukum** 'worm' + rs]h [a][*č'uht* 'belly']a, lit. 'worm of the belly';

**yosolil mut** h[pp + **ʔosol** 'louse' + rs]h a[**mut** 'chicken']a, lit. 'bird louse';

**pehpenul balam** h[**pehpen** 'butterfly' + rs]h a[**balam** 'jaguar']a, lit. 'butterfly of the jaguar';

**yuč' čitam** h[pp + **ʔuč'** 'louse']h a[**čitam** 'pig']a, lit. 'pig louse';

**yusil sac'** h[pp + **ʔus** 'fly' + rs]h a[**sac'** 'sphinx moth larva']a, lit. 'fly of the sphinx moth larva';

**syalhaul ʔalčaš** h[pp + **yal ha** 'maggot' + rs]h a[**ʔalčaš** 'apple']a, lit. maggot of the apple'.

The typical composite term may have a simple (single stem) attributive or a complex (multiple stem) attributive. The head segment, of course, may be single or multiple stemmed, and each stem may be a simple root or a derived form. In every case the attributive–head distinction is primary. The following examples exhibit this structural variety.

**č'in sik'** a[**č'in** 'small']a h[**sik'** 'swift']h, lit. 'small swift', simple attributive, adjectival root, simple head, nominal root;

**muk'ul bah teʔ** a[**muk'** 'large' + dd]a h[**bah teʔ** 'tree hitter']h, simple attributive, adjectival stem, complex head (dd = derivational desinence);

**nen tultuš** a[**nen** 'mirror']a h[**tultuš** 'dragon-fly']h, simple attributive, nominal root, simple head, nominal root;

**sak ʔeal č'o** a[**sak** 'white' + **ʔe** 'mouth' + rs]a h[**č'o** 'rat']h, lit. 'white-mouthed rat', complex attributive consisting of an adjectival root modifying a nominal stem, simple head;

**wak k'elum teʔtikil čih** a[**wak** 'six' + **k'elum** 'point']a h[**teʔtikil čih** 'deer']h, lit. 'six-point deer', complex attributive consisting of a numeral plus a nominal stem, complex head consisting of a nominal stem plus a nominal root.

## 2.3   COLOR

The five Tzeltal basic color terms (see Berlin and Kay 1969) figure in 217 of 586 animal naming responses of composite form recorded (see Table 4.12).

**Table 4.11**

EXAMPLES OF MAJOR TYPES OF TZELTAL UNPRODUCTIVE PRIMARY LEXEMES
WITH EXAMPLES

| | Examples | | |
|---|---|---|---|
| | *Name* | *Gloss* | *Remarks* |
| 1. Pseudospecific names | | | |
| (a) Resemblance without relationship | *bac'ul ha?* | 'damselfly larva' | not ⊂ *bac* 'howler monkey' |
| | *sbaul ?uk'um* | 'mole cricket' | not ⊂ *ba* 'pocket gopher' |
| | *muy ?am* | 'velvet ant' | not ⊂ *?am* 'spider' |
| (b) Resemblance and perceived relationship | *čimolil te?* | 'bessbug' | not quite ⊂ *čimol* 'rhinoceros beetle' |
| | *honon te?* | '*Eulaema* sp.' | not quite ⊂ *honon* 'bumblebee' |
| | *te?tikil tuluk'* | 'Crested Guan' | not quite ⊂ *tuluk'* 'turkey' |
| (c) Juxtaposition of two animal names | *k'ulub kawáyu* | 'lubber grasshopper' | [lit. 'locust' + 'horse'] |
| | *?ohkoc čan* | 'alligator lizard' | [lit. 'spiny lizard' + 'snake'] |
| | *?uč č'o* | 'four-eyed opossum' | [lit. 'opossum' + 'rat/mouse'] |
| (d) Shared head stem does not name an animal taxon | *te?tikil čih* | 'deer'/*tunim čih* 'sheep' | *čih* not used as cover term |
| | *?aha čab* | 'honey bee'/*?inam čab* 'stingless bee' | *čab* means 'honey' |
| (e) Pseudolifestage term | *yal ha* | 'maggot' | [lit. 'fly's child'], perceived relationship is transformation, not growth |
| 2. Descriptive analogy | *bak čikin* | 'mussel' | [lit. 'bone' + 'ear'] |
| | *mayil ti?bal* | 'armadillo' | [lit. 'squash' + 'meat'] |
| | *šyaš ?ič* | 'halictid bee' | [lit. 'green pepper'] |
| 3. 'Mother of ——'; indicates environmental juxtaposition or a protective relationship [a] | *me? čenek'* | 'snake: *Ninia sebae*' | [lit. 'mother of beans'] |
| | *me? k'in ha?al* | 'siskin' | [lit. 'mother of winter rains'] |
| | *me? k'ulub* | 'White-tailed Kite' | [lit. 'mother of locusts'] |
| 4. Agentive constructions [b] | *c'u? lukum* | 'Killdeer' | [lit. 'worm sucker'] |
| | *hse? te?* | 'climbing rat' | [lit. 'twig cutter'] |
| | *hti? čay* | 'heron/egret' | [lit. 'fish eater'] |
| 5. Pure descriptive constructions | *bak yat* | 'ponerine ant' | [lit. 'bone' + 'its stinger'] |
| | *sak hol* | 'tayra' | [lit. 'white head'] |
| | *tešereš ne* | 'Swallow-tailed Kite' | [lit. 'scissor-tail'] |
| 6. Onomatopoetic complexes | *či?či? bulbul* | 'house wren' | [lit. 'sweet-sweet' + 'foam-foam'] |
| | *pahal mac'* | 'Social Flycatcher' | [lit. 'sour corn gruel'] |
| | *tuhkulum pukuh* | 'Great Horned Owl' | [lit. UN + 'devil'] |

[a] But cf. *me? honon* 'bumblebee queen', labeling a specific taxon.

[b] Note also simple primary lexemes of this type:

*hohtiwaneh* 'inch worm'    [lit. < tv *hohti* 'measure it' + ag]
*likawal* 'hawk'    [lit. < tv *lik* 'lift it' + ag].

# Table 4.12
## TZELTAL ATTRIBUTIVES LISTED BY FREQUENCY OF OCCURRENCE FROM 586 ANIMAL NAMING RESPONSES OF COMPOSITE FORM

| Attributive | Gloss | Number of occurrences | Attributive | Gloss | Number of occurrences |
|---|---|---|---|---|---|
| ʔihkʼal | 'black' | 60 | bahkʼal | 'numerous' | 3 |
| bacʼ/bacʼil | 'true' | 48 | coc ʔit | 'hairy-butted' | 3 |
| mukʼul | 'large' | 47 | cʼibal | 'striped' | 3 |
| cahal | 'red' | 46 | | (+ 1 complex attributive) | |
| | (+ 3 complex attributives) | | češ kʼab | 'long-limbed' | 3 |
| čʼin | 'small' | 40 | čitam | 'pig-like' | 3 |
| kʼan/kʼanal | 'yellow' | 39 | čʼuy pat | 'band-backed' | 3 |
| yaš/yašal | 'green/gray' | 37 | huyum | 'fat' | 3 |
| | (+ 4 complex attributives) | | kʼahkʼal | 'fiery' | 3 |
| sakil | 'white' | 25 | šulub | 'horned' | 3 |
| | (+ 3 complex attributives) | | tešereš ne | 'scissor-tailed' | 3 |
| meba | 'orphan' | 13 | ʔahkʼubal | 'night-time' | 2 |
| kašlan | 'Ladino' | 12 | barsin | 'shiny' | 2 |
| cʼihtil | 'barred'? | 9 | búro | 'donkey-like' | 2 |
| bašil | 'mottled' | 7 | cʼunun | 'hummingbird-like' | 2 |
| kʼunil | 'soft' | 6 | haʔal | 'aquatic' | 2 |
| merikáno | 'American' | 6 | honon | 'bumblebee-like' | 2 |
| hlabtawaneh | 'evil omen' | 5 | škoen | 'descending' | 2 |
| teʔtikil | 'forest' | 5 | kʼahkʼet | 'fiery' | 2 |
| tiʔawal | 'biting' | 5 | mamal | 'very large' | 2 |
| čahp | 'clansman' | 4 | mutil | 'bird of' | 2 |
| meʔ | 'mother of' | 4 | pehpen | 'butterfly-like' | 2 |
| niwak | 'large (pl)' | 4 | pʼinto | 'spotted' | 2 |
| yalem | 'transitory' | 4 | pʼuhtul | 'blotched' | 2 |
| yut lumil | 'in-the-ground' | 4 | šela | 'silk' | 2 |
| | | | šik | 'grizzled' | 2 |
| | | | tan(tan) | 'ashy' | 2 |
| | | | tutin | 'tiny' | 2 |
| | | | tʼok hol | 'crest-headed' | 2 |
| | | | [Miscellaneous][a] | | 79 |

[a] Seventy-nine attributive expressions were recorded once each.

*cah* 'red'

*cahal wirin* ᵃ[*cah* 'red' + dd]ᵃ ʰ[*wirin* 'fly-catcher']ʰ;

*cahal teʔtikil čih* ᵃ[*cahal*]ᵃ ʰ[*teʔtikil čih* 'deer']ʰ;

*cahal nukʼ toht* ᵃ[*cahal* 'red' + *nukʼ* 'neck']ᵃ ʰ[*toht* 'robin']ʰ.

The simple root may occur in certain complex attributives:

*cah shol šulem* ᵃ[*cah* 'red' + *shol* 'its head']ᵃ ʰ[*šulem* 'Turkey Vulture']ʰ, lit. 'red-headed Turkey Vulture'.

*ʔihkʼ* 'black'

*ʔihkʼal cʼunun* ᵃ[*ʔihkʼ* 'black' + dd]ᵃ ʰ[*cʼunun* 'hummingbird']ʰ.

This adjective also occurs with complex heads and in complex attributives. It is not known to occur in simple root form.

*kʼan* 'yellow'

*kʼan toht* ᵃ[*kʼan* 'yellow']ᵃ ʰ[*toht* 'robin']ʰ;

*kʼanal šhočʼol ʔišim* ᵃ[*kʼanal*]ᵃ ʰ[ʰ[pp + *hočʼ* 'weevil' + rs]ʰ ᵃ[*ʔišim* 'corn']ᵃ]ʰ, lit. 'yellow corn weevil', in this case the head is a complex expression of the form head + attributive.

This adjective also occurs in complex attributives. *kʼankʼan mut* 'Squirrel Cuckoo' (*Piaya cayana*) may involve a reduplicated stem, though the dominant color of the bird is cinnamon rather than yellow.

*sak* 'white'

*sakil šanič* ᵃ[*sak* 'white' + dd]ᵃ ʰ[*šanič* 'ant']ʰ;

*sak ʔeal čʼo* ᵃ[*sak* 'white' + *ʔe* 'mouth' + rs]ᵃ ʰ[*čʼo* 'rat']ʰ;

*sakil htiʔ čay* ᵃ[*sakil*]ᵃ ʰ[ag + *tiʔ* 'eat meat' + *čay* 'fish']ʰ, lit. 'white fish-eater'.

The abbreviated form *saki na šuš* 'white nest wasp' [< *sakil na šuš*] is unique.

*yaš* 'blue/green'

*yaš heš* ᵃ[*yaš* 'blue']ᵃ ʰ[*heš* 'jay']ʰ;

*yašal čuč* ᵃ[*yaš* 'gray' + dd]ᵃ ʰ[*čuč* 'squirrel']ʰ, in this instance *yaš* is used to label a gray animal, though SMZ colored it blue in his colored pencil drawing.

This adjective, as root or as derived stem, occurs with complex heads and in complex attributives. The attributive *šyaš* [gn + *yaš* 'blue/green'] tends to imply both dark coloration and relatively large size, e.g., *šyaš nepʼ* 'large dark crab', *šyaš puy* 'large dark snail', *šyaš tuluk* 'large dark turkey'.

Other attributive expressions referring to color are rare. The term *ʔič* 'chili pepper' may refer to a scarlet color as in *ʔičil mut* 'Pink-headed Warbler' and *ʔičil čʼuht mut* ᵃ[*ʔič* 'chili pepper' + dd + *čʼuht* 'belly']ᵃ ʰ[*mut* 'bird']ʰ 'redstart'. The bright yellow eye of the Yellow-eyed Junco (*Junco phaeonotus*) is indicated by the expression *takʼin sit mut* ᵃ[*takʼin* 'gold, money' + *sit* 'eye']ᵃ ʰ[*mut* 'bird']ʰ. *yaš ʔitah čan*, lit. 'green vegetable snake', is a roundabout way of describing the color of snakes so named. Finally, *sabin čʼo*, lit. 'weasel rat', most likely refers to the reddish color of the pelage of the rice rat (*Oryzomys palustris*).

## 2.4  SIZE

More than 110 of the 586 composite naming responses summarized in Table 4.12 refer to relative size. Most such references are in terms of the following two adjectival roots.

*čʼin* 'small'

*čʼin honon* ᵃ[*čʼin* 'small']ᵃ ʰ[*honon* 'bumblebee']ʰ, both segments are simple roots;

*pʼoʔ čʼin ʔus* ᵃ[*pʼoʔ* 'animate group' + *čʼin* 'small']ᵃ ʰ[*ʔus* 'fly']ʰ, lit. 'swarming small fly'.

*mukʼ* 'large'

*mukʼul pay* ᵃ[*mukʼ* 'large' + dd]ᵃ ʰ[*pay* 'skunk'];

*mukʼul bah teʔ* ᵃ[*mukʼul* 'large']ᵃ ʰ[*bah teʔ* 'tree hitter']ʰ.

*čʼin* is not known in derived form, while *mukʼul* is not known as a simple root. Both rarely occur in complex attributives. The two following terms also mark the relative size distinction, but they appear to imply in addition that the organisms of the class occur in large groups.

*č'uhč'* 'small (pl)'

*č'uhč'ul čay* <sup>a</sup>[*č'uhč'* 'small (pl)' + dd]<sup>a</sup> <sup>h</sup>[*čay* 'fish']<sup>h</sup>, 'top minnows'.

*niwak* 'large (pl)'

*niwak wamal čitam* <sup>a</sup>[*niwak* 'large (pl)']<sup>a</sup> <sup>h</sup>[*wamal čitam* 'peccary']<sup>h</sup>.

Both minnows and peccaries are characteristically found in large groups. *č'uhč'ul* does not occur as a simple root, and *niwak* is not derived. Like *č'in* and *muk'ul*, they form a contrastive pair.

A third pair of terms used to imply relative size contrast has only been noted once.

*ʔihc'in* 'younger sibling'*

*ʔihc'inal čon čiw* <sup>a</sup>[*ʔihc'in* 'younger sibling' + dd]<sup>a</sup> <sup>h</sup>[*čon čiw* 'sparrow']<sup>h</sup>, 'Lincoln's Sparrow'.

*wiš* 'elder sister'†

*wišal čon čiw* <sup>a</sup>[*wiš* 'elder sister' + dd]<sup>a</sup> <sup>h</sup>[*čon čiw* 'sparrow']<sup>h</sup>, 'Rusty Sparrow'.

The Lincoln's Sparrow (*Melospiza lincolnii*) is the smallest member of the generic taxon *čon čiw*; the Rusty Sparrow (*Aimophila rufescens*) is the largest.

Other terms that may label the relative size contrast are not paired.

*mam* 'grandfather'‡

*mamal bašil pehpen* <sup>a</sup>[*mam* 'grandfather' + dd]<sup>a</sup> <sup>h</sup>[<sup>a</sup>[*bašil* 'mottled']<sup>a</sup> <sup>h</sup>[*pehpen* 'butterfly']<sup>h</sup>]<sup>h</sup>, lit. 'huge mottled butterfly', a descrip-

---

* *ʔihc'in* is somewhat more precisely defined as male-speaking younger brother or younger male parallel cousin and female-speaking younger sibling or younger parallel cousin.

† *wiš* is more precisely defined as elder sister, elder female parallel cousin, or father's sister.

‡ *mam* means both grandfather and male-speaking grandchild (self-reciprocal).

---

tive coinage applied to the owl butterfly (*Caligo memnon*), one of the world's largest.

*meba* 'poor, orphan'

*meba c'isim* <sup>a</sup>[*meba* 'poor, orphan']<sup>a</sup> <sup>h</sup>[*c'isim* 'leaf-cutting ant']<sup>h</sup>, lit. 'small leaf-cutting ant'.

*merikáno* 'American' [< Sp *Americano* 'North American']

*merikáno wirin* <sup>a</sup>[*merikáno* 'American']<sup>a</sup> <sup>h</sup>[*wirin* 'flycatcher']<sup>h</sup>, a term applied by SMZ to the unfamiliar, though native, Masked Tityra (*Tityra semifasciata*), a relatively large distant relative of flycatchers (Tyrannidae). In other instances, *merikáno* may refer instead to the provenience of an introduced form, e.g., *merikáno mut* 'American chicken'.

*wakaš* 'cattle' [< OSp 'cow']

*wakaš čitam* <sup>a</sup>[*wakaš* 'cow']<sup>a</sup> <sup>h</sup>[*čitam* 'pig']<sup>h</sup>, lit. 'cow-like pig', in particular notably large or cow-sized.

## 2.5   PATTERN

*barsin* [UN, cf. surface pattern of small raised bumps (Berlin, Breedlove, and Raven 1974:85)]

*barsin čan* <sup>a</sup>[*barsin* 'varicolored?']<sup>a</sup> <sup>h</sup>[*čan* 'assorted beetles']<sup>h</sup>.

*baš* [UN]

*bašil scumut* <sup>a</sup>[*baš* 'mottled' + dd]<sup>a</sup> <sup>h</sup>[*scumut* 'dove']<sup>h</sup>; this adjective appears to refer to a pattern of white on gray.

*c'ar* [UN, cf. serrated edge (Berlin, Breedlove, and Raven 1974:91)]

*c'aran k'uk* <sup>a</sup>[*c'ar* '?' + dd]<sup>a</sup> <sup>h</sup>[*k'uk* 'trogon', lit. 'feather']<sup>h</sup>; this term was used synonymously for *k'uk* 'trogon' and may refer to the shiny brilliance of these birds' plumage or to a serrated effect produced by the uneven lengths of their tail feathers.

*c'iht* [< tv *c'it* 'wipe interior clean']

*c'ihtil pehpen* <sup>a</sup>[*c'iht* 'streaked' + dd]<sup>a</sup> <sup>h</sup>[*pehpen* 'butterfly']<sup>h</sup>; streaked as the pattern left by a rough wiping action? *c'ihtil* 'small woodpecker' is an onomatopoetic homonym.

### *c'ib* 'line, mark'

*c'ibal sit c'unun* ᵃ[*c'ib* 'stripe' + dd + *sit* 'face']ᵃ ʰ[*c'unun* 'hummingbird']ʰ, lit. stripe-faced hummingbird).

### *c'ir* [UN]

*c'irin c'ihtil* ᵃ[*c'ir* 'barred?' + dd]ᵃ ʰ[*c'ihtil* 'small woodpecker']ʰ, the Ladder-backed Woodpecker (*Dendrocopos scalaris*). Other occurrences, however, might be better glossed 'streaked', e.g., *c'irin mut*.

### *čul* [UN]

*čulin mut* ᵃ[*čul* 'mottled?' + dd]ᵃ ʰ[*mut*₂ 'chicken']ʰ; the generic name *čulin* may be an onomatopoetic homonym.

### *čohk'* 'wart'

*čohk'il č'uht mut* ᵃ[*čohk'* 'wart' + dd + *č'uht* 'belly']ᵃ ʰ[*mut* 'bird']ʰ, lit. 'warty-bellied bird', referring to a spotted pattern. In other instances *čohk'il* may refer to warty texture, e.g., a toad's skin.

### *č'uy* [UN]

*č'uy pat ba* ᵃ[*č'uy* 'band?' + *pat* 'back']ᵃ ʰ[*ba* 'pocket gopher']ʰ, lit. 'banded-back gopher'. This attributive and the variant *č'uyin* refer to a wide white band around the midsection of certain pocket gophers and domestic pigs.

### *kantéla* [ < Sp *candela* 'candle']

*kantéla čan*, lit. 'candle snake', coral snakes (*Micrurus* spp.); Tenejapan ritual candles are multicolored, ringed, as are typical coral snakes.

### *kašlan* [ < OSp /kaštilyano/ 'Castilian']

*kašlan toht*, lit. 'Ladino robin'; though *kašlan* has the implication of foreign in certain contexts (Berlin, Breedlove, and Raven 1974:41), it more frequently indicates a quality of showiness when applied to animals. The robin so named is the Rufous-collared Robin (*Turdus rufitorques*), the male of which

is quite elegantly patterned in glossy black and chestnut. *kašlan t'ul* 'domestic rabbit', however, illustrates the sense of 'foreign provenience'. The femine is used in like fashion, *kaštiyána heš* 'Ladina jay', the Black-throated Jay (*Cyanolyca pumilo*).

### *ʔoal* 'necklace'

*sak ʔoal mut* ᵃ[*sak* 'white' + *ʔoal* 'necklace']ᵃ ʰ[*mut* 'bird']ʰ, lit. 'white-necklaced bird', cf. the White-collared Seedeater (*Sporophila torqueola*).

### *p'as* 'cut at a slanted angle'

*p'ahsum čan*, 'oblique-banded snake', referring to the ringed pattern of this snake's colors.

### *p'uht* [UN]

*p'uhtul pehpen* ᵃ[*p'uht* 'mottled?' + dd]ᵃ ʰ[*pehpen* 'butterfly']ʰ.

### *pínto* [ < Sp *pintojo* 'spotted']

*pínto c'iʔ*, lit. 'spotted dog', a "Dalmatian" pattern (see Figure 5.125); *píntu* is a free variant.

### *šik* [UN; cf. 'hawk' in other Tzeltal dialects]

*šik likawal* ᵃ[*šik* 'finely barred']ᵃ ʰ[*likawal* 'hawk']ʰ, appropriately descriptive of the common Roadside Hawk's (*Buteo magnirostris*) belly pattern (see Figure 5.9). Other instances of this attributive are similarly descriptive.

### *tuk* [UN]

*tukul č'uht mut* ᵃ[*tuk* 'spotted?' + dd + *č'uht* 'belly']ᵃ ʰ[*mut* 'bird'], lit. 'spotted-belly bird'.

## 2.6  TEXTURE

Textural qualities are in a sense intermediate between qualities of pattern and of shape, and at times difficult to distinguish clearly, as for example the distinction between *cocil* 'hairy' (texture) and *ʔisim* 'whisker, whiskered' (shape).

*coc* 'hair'

*coc ʔit ha* ª⌈*coc* 'hair, hairy' + *ʔit* 'abdomen'⌉ª ʰ⌈*ha* 'fly'⌉ʰ, lit. 'hairy-abdomened fly'.

*č'iš* 'spine, thorn'

*č'iš ʔuhčum* ⌈*č'iš* 'spine' + *ʔuhčum* 'opossum', archaic⌉, 'porcupine';
*č'išal pat čan*, lit. 'spiny-backed bug'.

*k'al* 'sun'

*k'alel čan* ª⌈*k'al* 'sun' + dd⌉ª ʰ⌈*čan₁* 'snake'⌉ʰ, lit. 'shiny snake', referring to the shiny, smooth scales of the lizard *Barisia moreletii*.

*k'un* 'soft, smooth'

*k'unil ʔam* ª⌈*k'un* 'soft' + dd⌉ª ʰ⌈*ʔam* 'spider'⌉, in this case apparently referring to the texture of the web of this spider. *k'unil šenen* 'soft mosquito' has a behavioral implication, i.e., nonbiting.

*mas* 'smooth'

*mas hol mut* ª⌈*mas* 'smooth' + *hol* 'head'⌉ª ʰ⌈*mut* 'bird'⌉ʰ; this usage contrasts with *t'ok hol* 'crested-head'.

*sak'al* 'itchy'

*sak'al cuhkum*, lit. 'itchy woolybear', the hairs of this caterpillar cause itching.

*tunim* 'cotton'

*tunim čih* ª⌈*tunim* 'cotton'⌉ª ʰ⌈*čih* 'deer'⌉ʰ, lit. 'cotton deer'.

*t'an* 'naked'

*t'an ʔit pewal* ª⌈*t'an* 'naked' + *ʔit* 'abdomen'⌉ª ʰ⌈*pewal* 'cockroach'⌉ʰ, lit. 'naked-abdomened roach', i.e., wingless.

## 2.7   SHAPE

References to shape may be expressed by an adjectival stem attributive, an attributive segment consisting of an adjectival stem modifying a body part name, or a metaphorical reference to another animal or object similar in shape. I will illustrate this last alternative first.

*búro tencun* ª⌈*búro* 'donkey'⌉ª ʰ⌈*tencun* 'goat'⌉ʰ; this expression was coined to refer to a large, "donkey-eared" goat.

*čan čay*, lit. 'snake fish', a generic name for an eellike fish.

*honon c'unun*, lit. 'bumblebee hummingbird', a very small hummingbird.

*koyóte c'iʔ*, lit. 'coyote dog', the German shepherd.

*láso čan*, lit. 'rope snake', ⌈< Sp *laso* 'rope'⌉; an alternate term for the vine snake (*Oxybelis aeneus*), an extremely long, thin snake.

*lukum čan*, lit. 'worm snake', an appropriate label for the blind, fossorial snakes of the genus *Leptotyphlops*.

*mansána wakaš*, lit. 'apple cattle', an alternate term for the humped zebu breed; the 'apple' reference refers to the hump.

*masan čay*, lit. 'meadow grasshopper fish', the crayfish (Decapoda: Astacidae).

*mokoč čan*, lit. 'millipede snake', applied to certain fossorial snakes (e.g., *Adelphicos veraepacis*), which due to their burrowing adaptation resemble millipedes of the most common type in spherical cross-section and in their bluntly rounded ends.

*tultuš pehpen*, lit. 'damselfly butterfly', a reference to the relatively long slender abdomens of butterflies of the Heliconidae and Ithomiidae.

Following is an alphabetical list of adjectival stems used in attributive references to shape.

*bak* 'bone'

*bak hol mut* ª⌈*bak* 'bone' + *hol* 'head'⌉ª ʰ⌈*mut* 'bird'⌉ʰ, referring to the casquelike extensions of the bills of oropendolas (Icteridae in part).

*but* 'fill it'

*butbut ʔit čan*, lit. 'full-abdomened bug', referring to the distended abdomens of antlions (Myrmeleontidae larvae).

*čaw* 'large spheroid'

**čaw hol c'isim** ᵃ[**čaw** 'spheroid' + **hol** 'head']ᵃ ʰ[**c'isim** 'leaf-cutting ant']ʰ, the largest worker caste, soldiers.

**češ** [ < **čehš** 'severed stems'? ]
**češ k'ab čan** ᵃ[**češ** 'long' + **k'ab** 'limb']ᵃ ʰ[**čan** 'critter']ʰ, lit. 'long-limbed bug', applied to water striders (Hemiptera: Gerridae).

**č'iht** [UN]
**č'ihtiba masan** ᵃ[**č'ihtib** 'broad'? + **ba** 'front']ᵃ ʰ[**masan** meadow grasshopper']ʰ, lit. 'broad-foreheaded meadow grasshopper'.

**huht** 'hole'
**ča?huht ni? čan** ᵃ[**ča?** 'two' + **huht** 'hole' + **ni?** 'nose']ᵃ ʰ[**čan**₁ 'snake']ʰ, lit. 'double nostril snake', referring to the "pits" of pit vipers (Crotalidae).

**huy** [ < tv 'bends an elastic object'? ]
**huyum ?uč** ᵃ[**huy** 'fat'? + dd]ᵃʰ[**?uč** 'opossum']ʰ, lit. 'fat opossum'.

**ko** [ < iv 'descend' ]
**škoen čitam** ᵃ[gn + **ko** 'descend' + dd]ᵃ ʰ[**čitam** 'pig']ʰ, lit. 'low-slung pig', a short-legged breed of pig. This attributive is also descriptive of behavior, cf., **koen ba** 'burrowing? pocket gropher', **škuen likawal** 'low-flying? hawk'.

**kuht** [UN]
**kuhtin karánsa**, lit. 'short-tailed black rat', perhaps the Norway rat (*Rattus norvegicus*).

**kul** [UN]
**kul ?it mut** ᵃ[**kul** '?' + **?it** 'buttocks']ᵃ ʰ[**mut** 'bird']ʰ, lit. 'tailless bird'? (see **čiktawilon**/bird, quail).

**k'oh** 'mask'
**šk'ohow čan**, lit. 'masked critter', dragonfly larvae.

**k'ol** [ < tv 'form in a ball' ]
**k'ol pat čan** ᵃ[**k'ol** 'round' + **pat** 'back']ᵃ

ʰ[**čan**₂ 'assorted beetle']ʰ, lit. 'round-backed bug'.

**leč** [ < tv 'make thin, leaflike objects' ]
**lehč šik' čan** ᵃ[**lehč** 'thin' + **šik'** 'wing']ᵃ ʰ[**čan**₂ 'assorted beetles']ʰ, lit. 'thin-winged bug'.

**naht** 'long'
**nahtil šik' čan**, lit. 'long-winged bug'.

**nol** 'round'
**nol pat čan**, lit. 'round-backed bug'.

**peč** [ < tv 'make it plane' ]
**pehč hol čan**, lit. 'flat-headed bug'.

**p'eh** 'round solid-objects'
**p'ehel nuhkul čan**, lit. 'round, solid-skinned snake'.

**p'um** 'swollen'
**p'um ni? mut**, lit. 'swollen-beaked bird', applied to the toucans (Ramphastidae).

**p'us** [UN]
**p'us pat čan** ᵃ[**p'us pat** 'hunch-backed']ᵃ ʰ[**čan**₂ 'assorted beetles']ʰ, lit. 'hunch-backed bug'.

**šal** 'many-pronged, as fingers'
**ča?šal ne c'unun** ᵃ[**ča?** 'two' + **šal** 'prong' + **ne** 'tail']ᵃ ʰ[**c'unun** 'hummingbird']ʰ, lit. 'two-pronged tail hummingbird'.

**šot** [ < tv 'coil rope' ]
**šotšot k'o?** ᵃ[**šot** 'coiled', reduplicated]ᵃ ʰ[**k'o?** 'snail']ʰ, lit. 'coiled snail'.

**tešereš** 'scissors'
**tešereš ne c'unun**, lit. 'scissor-tailed hummingbird'.

**ton** 'stone'
**tonton ni? mut** ᵃ[**ton** 'stone', redup. + **ni?** 'nose']ᵃ ʰ[**mut** 'bird']ʰ, lit. 'stone-beaked bird', applied to a grosbeak (Fringillidae in part).

*t'ok* 'crest'

*t'ok hol mut*, lit. 'crest-headed bird', the Gray Silky-Flycatcher (*Ptilogonys cinereus*).

*wol* [ < tv 'make into a ball' ]

*wol niʔ mut*, lit. 'round-beaked bird'.

Finally, distinctive shapes may be indicated by reference to some unique structural aspect.

*čikin puy* ᵃ[*čikin* 'ear']ᵃ ʰ[*puy* 'snail']ʰ, lit. 'ear snail', referring to the large ear-shaped shells of marine conchs used as trumpets.

*ʔisim čay*, lit. 'whisker fish', the catfish.

*k'iwoč č'o*, lit. 'cheek pouch rat', pocket mice (Heteromyidae).

*ne mut pehpen* ᵃ[*ne* 'tail' + *mut* 'bird']ᵃ ʰ[*pehpen* 'butterfly']ʰ, lit. 'bird-tailed butterfly', tailed skippers (Hesperiidae in part).

*šulub mut*, lit. 'horned bird', the Magpie Jay (*Calocitta formosa*).

## 2.8   ODOR

*cih* [ UN ]

*cihil čan*, lit. 'stinking bug', especially stinkbugs (Hemiptera: Pentatomidae).

*cis* 'fart'

*cis pay*, lit. 'fart skunk', a synonym for the skunk (*pay*).

*tu* 'stinking'

*tu caʔ čil* ᵃ[*tu* 'stinking' + *caʔ* 'feces']ᵃ ʰ[*čil* 'cricket']ʰ.

*tu cis čan*, lit. 'stinking-fart bug'.

The names *tu č'ič'*, lit. 'stinking-blood', orioles (Icteridae in part), and *tuh kulum pukuh* [ ON ], Great Horned Owl (*Bubo virginianus*), are probably onomatopoetic homonyms.

## 2.9   SOUND

The vast majority of animal terms that make reference to the characteristic sounds produced by an animal are not composite expressions but, rather, simple onomatopoetic forms. Occasional "hybrids" may be noted such as

*c'uhkin mut* ᵃ[*c'uhkin*, ON?]ᵃ ʰ[*mut* 'bird']ʰ.

In other instances an onomatopoetic term may masquerade as a composite name, for example,

*č'iš toht*, lit. 'spiny robin' ᵃ[*č'iš*, ON]ᵃ ʰ[*toht* 'robin', ON]ʰ.

There is nothing 'spiny' about this robin; the composite expression better mimics this robin's version of robin vocalizations.

A few expressions remain that refer to characteristic sounds less directly.

*ʔárpa* [ < Sp *arpa* 'harp' ]

*ʔárpa c'unun*, lit. 'harp hummingbird', a hummingbird that sounds like a harp.

*čitam* 'pig'

*čitam c'unun*, lit. 'pig hummingbird', a hummingbird that sounds like a pig (the Magnificent Hummingbird, *Eugenes fulgens*). The sound may be produced by the wings.

*šušubin* 'whistle'

*šušubin mut*, lit. 'whistle bird'.

## 2.10   BEHAVIOR

Summarized below are composite expressions that focus on motions or patterns of motion characteristic of the type of animal so labeled. Most numerous are straightforward descriptive attributives.

*ʔan* 'flee'

*ʔanel nep'*, lit. 'fleeing crab'.

*bahk'* 'four hundred'

*bahk'al mut* ᵃ[*bahk'* 'four hundred' + dd]ᵃ ʰ[*mut* 'bird']ʰ, lit. 'group-of-four-hundred bird', an alternate term for siskins (*Spinus* spp.).

*bahk'al wamal čitam* ᵃ[*bahk'al* 'four hundred']ᵃ ʰ[*wamal čitam* 'peccary']ʰ, lit. 'group-of-four-hundred peccary', juvenile peccaries (Tayassuidae).

Both siskins and juvenile peccaries are exceptional in their tendency to move in large groups.

**bos** [UN]

**bosbos čan**, lit. 'twitching critter' or 'swarming critter', i.e., the behavior characteristic of mosquito larvae.

**čak'** 'flea'

**čak'ul ʔit mut** ᵃ[**čak'** 'flea' + rs + **ʔit** 'buttocks']ᵃ ʰ[**mut** 'bird']ʰ, lit. 'flea-butt bird', a humorous reference to the nervous movements of wrens (Troglodytidae).

**ʔep'** 'snap'?

**ʔep' nuk' čan** ᵃ[**ʔep'** 'snap' + **nuk'** 'neck']ᵃ ʰ[**čan** 'critter']ʰ, lit. 'neck-snapping bug', click beetles (Elateridae).

**hal** 'weave it'

**hal moč ʔam** ᵃ[**hal** 'weave it' + **moč** 'basket']ᵃ ʰ[**ʔam** 'spider']ʰ, lit. 'basket-weaver spider'.

**hawal** 'lying face up'

**hawal pat nušel čan** ᵃ[**hawal** 'lying face up' + **pat** 'back' + **nušel** 'swimming']ᵃ ʰ[**čan** 'critter']ʰ, lit. 'upside-down swimming bug', backswimmers (Hemiptera: Notonectidae).

**k'al** 'sun'

**k'al čil**, lit. 'sun cricket', also known as **ba ʔay k'al čil** ᵃ[**ba** 'where' + **ʔay** 'it is' + **k'al** 'sun']ᵃ ʰ[**čil** 'cricket']ʰ, lit. 'where-the-sun-is cricket', referring to the fact that praying mantises (Mantidae) line up their bodies to the sun to minimize their shadows and thus to avoid predators.

**mah** 'hit it'

**hmah haʔ tultuš** ᵃ[ag + **mah** 'hit it' + **haʔ** 'water']ᵃ ʰ[**tultuš** 'dragonfly']ʰ, lit. 'water-striker dragonfly', referring to the way certain female dragonflies (Odonata) lay their eggs by striking the water in flight.

**mil** 'kill it'

**hmil mut čan** ᵃ[ag + **mil** 'kill it' + **mut₂**

'chicken']ᵃ ʰ[**čan** 'critter']ʰ, lit. 'chicken-killer bug', a reference to the alleged fact that certain weevils (Coleoptera: Curculionoidea) will choke a chicken if eaten.

**mo** 'ascend'

**moin teʔ č'o** ᵃ[**mo** 'ascend' + dd + **teʔ** 'tree']ᵃ ʰ[**č'o** 'rat']ʰ, lit. 'tree-climbing rat', for the arboreal vesper rat (*Nyctomys sumichrasti*).

**nap'** 'stick it to the surface'

**nap'nap' teʔ mut** ᵃ[**nap'** 'stick it to the surface', redup. + **teʔ** 'tree']ᵃ ʰ[**mut** 'bird']ʰ, lit. 'stuck-to-the-tree bird', for woodcreepers (Dendrocolaptidae).

**noc** 'cling to surface'

**nocnoc teʔ mut**, lit. 'tree-clinging bird', applied to a Black-and-White Warbler (Parulidae: *Mniotilta varia*), which feeds by clinging to the bark of tree trunks, much as do the woodcreepers of the previous example.

**nuš** 'swim'

**nušel čan**, lit. 'swimming bug', for certain aquatic insects.

**ʔoč** 'enter'

**ʔočem čak'**, lit. 'flea that entered', for chigoe fleas (Siphonaptera: Tungidae), the females of which are notorious for burrowing into people's feet to lay their eggs.

**ʔóra** [< Sp *hora* 'hour']

**ʔóra mut**, lit. 'hour bird', applied to several different types of birds referring to the alleged fact that these birds call every hour on the hour.

**pahk'** 'stuck to surface'

**špahk'in teʔ mut** ᵃ[gn + **pahk'** 'stuck to surface' + dd + **teʔ** 'tree']ᵃ ʰ[**mut** 'bird']ʰ, lit. 'stuck-to-the-tree bird', yet another way of referring to the characteristic behavior of woodcreepers (see **nap'** and **noc**).

**way** 'sleep'

**wayway čan**, lit. 'sleeping bug', for a curiously lethargic beetle (*Zopherus jourdani*), which is used to induce sleep in wakeful infants.

**wil** 'fly'

**wilel ʔam**, lit. 'flying spider', for jumping spiders (Salticidae).

Several attributives refer to the human consequences of animal behaviors.

**k'un** 'soft, smooth'

**k'unil šenen**, lit. 'soft mosquito', actually a reference to the fact that the flies so named do not bite (see **tiʔwal ʔam**).

**ʔóra** [ < Sp *hora* 'hour' ]

**ʔóra čan**, lit. 'hour snake', coral snakes (*Micrurus* spp.), unlike the use of this attributive in **ʔóra mut**, the implication here is that the snake's bite is so venomous that one dies in one hour from the bite.

**tiʔ** 'bite it'

**tiʔwal ʔam** ᵃ[ **tiʔ** 'bite it' + **ʔawal** (ag)]ᵃ ʰ[ **ʔam** 'spider' ]ʰ, lit. 'biting spider'.

**woš** 'blister'

**wošel ʔam**, lit. 'blistering spider', for a spider alleged to raise blisters if it runs across a person's skin.

Other attributives describe the results of animal behavior rather than the behavior itself.

**caʔ kawáyu (na) šuš** ᵃ[ **caʔ** 'feces' + **kawáyu** 'horse' + **na** 'nest' ]ᵃʰ[ **šuš** 'wasp' ]ʰ, lit. 'horse-dung-nest wasp', referring to the distinction drawn between wasps that construct paper nests of dark material—allegedly constructed of horse dung—and those that construct their nests of light colored material—allegedly derived from cow dung. **ʔihk'al na šuš**, lit. 'black-nest wasp', is synonymous.

**lehčel na šus** ᵃ[ **lehč** 'flat' + **na** 'house, nest' ]ᵃ ʰ[ **šuš** 'wasp' ]ʰ, lit. 'flat-nest wasp', a reference to a characteristic nest form (see **šanab šuš**/wasp and Figure 5.197).

**sakil na šuš**, lit. 'white-nest wasp', as distinct from **ʔihk'al na šuš** 'black-nest wasp'.

**šéla ʔam**, lit. 'silk spider', referring to the elaborate webs of this orb weaver (*Nephila clavipes*).

Finally, behavioral characteristics may be referred to metaphorically.

**c'unun pehpen**, lit. 'hummingbird butterfly', referring to the hummingbirdlike behavior of sphinx moths (Sphingidae).

**pehpen čuč**, lit. 'butterfly squirrel', the flying squirrel (*Glaucomys volans*).

**soldáro honon**, lit. 'soldier bumblebee', a reference to the "fierceness" of the bee (*Bombus* spp.).

## 2.11   ENVIRONMENTAL ASSOCIATIONS

### a.   Habitat or Topographical Preferences

**ʔalan** 'below'

**ʔalanil toht**, lit. 'below robin', the Clay-colored Robin (*Turdus grayi*), typically found below 1800 m.

**ʔáwa** [ < Sp *agua* 'water' ]

**ʔáwa kantil**, lit. 'water moccasin', the indigo snake (*Drymarchon corais*), an aquatic snake that superficially resembles the moccasin (*Agkistrodon bilineatus*).

**c'ahel** 'marsh'

**meʔ c'ahel**, lit. 'mother of the marsh', also known as **mutil c'ahel** 'bird of the marsh' and **čanul c'ahel** 'critter of the marsh', for rails (Rallidae).

**č'uht** 'belly'

**slukumil č'uht** ʰ[ pp + **lukum** 'worm' + rs ]ʰ ᵃ[ **č'uht** 'belly' ]ᵃ, lit. 'worm of the belly', parasitic round worms.

**haʔ** 'water'

**čanul haʔ**, lit. 'critter of the water', used polysemously for water birds in general or for a complex of aquatic insects.

**peč'ul ha?**, lit. 'water duck', to distinguish wild water fowl from the domestic varieties, also known as **peč'ul hala me?tik**, lit. 'duck of our protecting mother' or **peč'ul č'ul me?tik**, lit. 'duck of our holy mother', both references to the association of wild water fowl and Tenejapa's only "lake," dwelling place of the spirit of the 'holy mother'.*

**ha?al** 'water, rain'

**ha?al c'i?**, lit. 'water dog', the river otter (*Lutra annectens*).

**ha?al čan**, lit. 'water snake', garter snakes (*Thamnophis* spp.).

**hobel** 'San Cristóbal'

**hobelal čon čiw**, lit. 'San Cristóbal sparrow', the House Sparrow (*Passer domesticus*), a recent arrival from the north confined to the larger cities of Chiapas.

**kahal** 'above'

**kahalil toht**, lit. 'above robin', one man's choice for naming the Rufous-collared Robin (*Turdus rufitorques*), common above 1500 m in Chiapas.

**ko** 'descend'

**koen ba**, lit. 'descending pocket gopher', a reference to the burrowing habits of this rodent (Geomyidae).

**k'altik** 'milpa, Indian corn field'

**k'altik mut**, lit. 'milpa bird', an alternate name for the White-collared Seedeater (*Sporophila torqueola*), common in fields and pastures.

**lum** 'earth'

*"Certain prayers and offerings are made to particular lakes considered sacred because they are inhabited by virgins who look after the well-being of the people. The best known of these lakes is Banabil in Tenejapa. Some day during the year, a small box containing a woman's dress and all its ornaments is thrown into the water. The dress must be made by a virgin or an old woman [Villa Rojas 1969:223]." My informants asserted that this pilgrimage to the lake occurs only once in every 2 or 3 years.

**čanul lum**, lit. 'critter of the earth', for a wormlike insect larva found in soil.

**šlumil č'o** ᵃ[gn + **lum** 'earth' + rs]ᵃ ʰ[**č'o** 'mouse']ʰ, lit. 'mouse of the earth', the house mouse (*Mus musculus*).

**yut lumil mum** ᵃ[**yut** 'inside' + **lum** 'earth' + rs]ᵃ ʰ[**mum** 'wasp']ʰ, lit. 'inside-the-ground wasp', a cavity nesting social vespid wasp (*Stelopolybia panamensis*).

**te?tikil** 'forest'

**te?tikil čih**, lit. 'forest deer', to distinguish the deer from sheep, now known as **tunim čih** 'cotton deer'.

The various instances of this attributive all indicate the native, wild form of a pair of animals seen to be related (see Berlin 1972: 82–83).

**yan te?tikil likawal**, lit. 'under-forest hawk', descriptive of the habitat favored by hawks of the genus *Accipiter*.

**wamal** 'bush'

**wamal čitam**, lit. 'bush pig', the native, wild peccary (Tayassuidae), in contrast to the introduced domestic pig, **čitam** (Suidae: *Sus scrofa*).

*b. Temporal Patterns of Distribution*

**?ahk'ubal** 'nighttime'

**?ahk'ubal toytoy**, lit. 'nocturnal pygmy owl'.

**ha?al** 'water, rain'

**ha?al lukum**, lit. 'rain worm', a very large earthworm (ANNELIDA), presumably a reference to the fact that they are seen following rain.

**k'alel** 'daytime' [< **k'al** 'sun']

**k'alel toytoy**, lit. 'diurnal pygmy owl', the Ferruginous Pygmy Owl (*Glaucidium brasilianum*).

**sab** 'morning'

**sabal mut**, lit. 'morning bird', the Band-tailed Pigeon (*Columba fasciata*); the behavioral implications are unclear.

**yal** 'fall from a height'

**yalem toht**, lit. 'transitory robin', the migratory American Robin (*Turdus migratorius*).

*c.  Parasite–Host Relationships*

These expressions are without exception of the atypical form ʰ[  ]ʰ ª[  ]ª, as previously discussed (this chapter, Section 2.2). Only a few examples will be repeated here.

**čanul teʔ**, lit. 'critter of the tree', woodboring larvae.

**čupil hihteʔ**, lit. 'stinging caterpillar of the oak tree'.

**šhoč'ol ʔišim**, lit. 'corn weevil'.

**yosolil mut**, lit. 'bird mite'.

**sipul tuhkulum č'iš**, lit. 'tick of *Solanum* spp'.

**yuč' čitam**, lit. 'pig louse'.

**yusil sac'**, lit. 'fly of the sphinx moth larva'.

**syalhaul ʔahateʔ**, lit. 'maggot of the white sapote'.

*d.  Miscellaneous Behavioral Associations*

**ʔahwalil wirin**, lit. 'master flycatcher'; this alternate term for the archtypical flycatchers (*Myiarchus tuberculifer* and *Contopus pertinax*) refers to the alleged fact that a variety of smaller birds gather around these flycathers as followers.

**čihil čan**, lit. 'deer snake', for the large arboreal *Spilotes pullatus*; this reference is rather opaque, however the Nahuatl term for the boa constrictor (borrowed in Spanish as *masacuate*) also means 'deer snake'. Perhaps very large snakes are so named in recognition of their ability to take prey as large as deer.

**mutil balam**, lit. 'bird of the jaguar', also known as **mutil čoh** 'bird of the cougar'; these big cats are supposed to be close if the Mottled Owl (*Ciccaba virgata*) appears.

**mutil čan**, lit. 'bird of the snake', an infrequent synonym for the house wren (*Troglodytes* spp.), referring to the fact that this and

other small birds often noisily attack predators such as snakes.

## 2.12  MISCELLANEOUS ATTRIBUTIVE EXPRESSIONS

A few composite animal terms cite the provenance of the particular type of animal.

**ʔinsistúto** [ < Sp *Instituto Nacional Indigenista* 'National Indian Institute' (INI)]

**ʔinsistúto čitam**, lit. 'Institute pig', one way of singling out the very large breed of pig introduced by INI to improve local stock.

**kašlan** [ < OSp /*kaštilyáno*/ 'Castilian']

**kašlan t'ul**, lit. 'Castilian rabbit', the introduced domestic rabbit (*Oryctolagus cuniculus*). As noted earlier (this chapter, Section 2.5), this attributive often refers to a quality of appearance of an animal rather than to its introduced status, as intended here.

**merikáno** [ < Sp *Americano* 'North American']

**merikáno wakaš**, lit. 'North American cattle', one way to distinguish the recently introduced zebu breed. In this case 'North American' is used to mean 'foreign', with the possible added implication of relatively large size (see this chapter, Section 2.4).

**polisía** [ < Sp *policia* 'police']

**polisía c'iʔ**, lit. 'police dog', one way to distinguish the German shepherd breed.

The following attributives refer to a particular cultural significance of the animal in question.

**burúho** [ < Sp *brujo* 'witch']

**burúho mut**, lit. 'witch bird', for the Yellow-tailed Oriole (*Icterus mesomelas*). The more abundant Yellow-backed Oriole (*I. chrysater*) is also considered to be an evil omen (see next item).

**hlabtawaneh** [ < *lab* 'animal spirit companion']

**hlabtawaneh mut**  ª[ag + **labtawaneh**

'regret']ᵃ ʰ[***mut*** 'bird']ʰ, lit. 'bird of evil omen', a deductive category that includes most owls (Strigiformes), the Squirrel Cuckoo (*Piaya cayana*), and the orioles (*Icterus* spp.). Misfortune or death will come to the house visited by these birds.

***pošil*** 'medicine'

***pošil čohk***', lit. 'wart medicine', the Band-backed Wren (*Campylorhynchus zonatus*), also known as ***me? čohk***' 'mother of warts'. A person afflicted by warts may appeal to the birds to take the warts back (see this chapter, Section 4.5).

***pošil nihkel***, lit. 'malaria medicine', the Black Vulture (*Coragyps atratus*), eaten as a cure for this disease.

***pošil nušel***, lit. 'swimming medicine', ripple bugs (Veliidae); these are eaten as an aid to learning to swim.

Finally, we consider a set of terms used to indicate a variety of relationships among animal taxa.

***bac'il*** 'true'

***bac'il šanič***, lit. 'true ant', a common stinging type of ant (Formicidae: *Solenopsis* spp.).

This attributive is most commonly used to single out the most typical or characteristic example of a larger class of animals.

***čahp*** [ < ***čapomal*** 'relative with the same surname, clansman']

***čahp šmayil***, lit. 'clansman of the water-thrush', applied to the unfamiliar Ovenbird (*Seiurus aurocapillus*). ***šmayil*** 'waterthrush' proper includes the other two species of this genus (*S. motacilla*, *S. noveboracensis*).

This attributive is used to name newly encountered organisms that are seen to be "closely related" to familiar forms, though distinct.

***kawáyu*** [ < Sp *caballo* 'horse']

***k'ulub kawáyu***, lit. 'horse locust', for lubber grasshoppers (Romaleinae), cf. English "horse chestnut." The implication is that this animal is an aberrant 'locust'.

***me?*** 'mother'

***me? honon***, lit. 'mother bumblebee', queens.

***me? pewal***, lit. 'mother cockroach', large, wingless forms, may in fact be females.

This attributive is used in myriad ways, for example, to mean 'female', 'protector of', 'resident of', 'owner of', etc.

***?al*** 'child (female speaking)'

***yal ha***, lit. 'child of the fly', maggots. ***yal šuš*** 'child of the wasp' is used for wasp larvae in parallel fashion, however, ***yal ha*** has clearly assumed the status of a generic name in its own right; it is not simply a life stage term.

## 3 Animal Body Part Terminology

Tzeltal anatomical terminology is surprisingly productive. I have recorded 190 phrases used to label body parts; these are constructed of 105 stems. Five of these stems are Spanish loans. Of the remaining 100, 57 have their primary reference in the domain of human and animal anatomy. Of these 57 primarily animal anatomy stems, 19 are used metaphorically to label parts of plants (see Berlin, Breedlove, and Raven 1974:85–94). Only 10 appear to be restricted to nonhuman animal anatomical reference. Most of the 10 stems restricted to nonhuman animal anatomical reference are terms for specialized structures, such as wings (***šik'***), feathers (***k'uk'um***), crops (***čuya***), wattles (***luhub***), combs (***calub***), dewlaps (***lakam***), cheek pouches (***k'iwoč***), horns (***šulub***), etc. Analogous organs of a variety of animals are typically labeled by a single stem, e.g., a crab's claws are called its 'mouth', the abdomen of an insect is its 'buttocks', shells of turtles, snails, and eggs are all called 'backs'.

The following list includes all terms recorded. This listing is not exhaustive. An exhaustive list would require systematic elicitation with dissection of a variety of representative types of animals. The terms cited here were obtained primarily through written lists. The list is alphabetized by stem. A single asterisk before a stem indicates a primarily animal anatomy stem; a double asterisk marks those stems restricted to nonhuman animal anatomical reference. All metaphorical terminological uses to label plant parts cited by Berlin, Breedlove, and Raven (1974) are listed following the stem. All compound forms that include the stem are listed below that stem. The order of listing is alphabetical by the first letter of the first stem of the compound (ignoring the prefixes). Glosses are typically rather literal restatements of the compound form, which may then be followed by a less literal version. Further comments may follow.

The structure of the vast majority of terms is a string of units of the following form: [pp + stem (+ rs)]. The possessive prefix (pp) is manifested as [y-] before stems beginning with the glottal stop (vowel), [s-] in all other cases. The [s-] becomes [š-] before stems containing š or č. [ss-] is elided to [s-] and [šš-] becomes [š-].

## 3.1 LIST OF ALL TZELTAL ANIMAL PART TERMS RECORDED: ALPHABETICALLY BY STEM

* *ʔahč'al* 'spleen'

*yahč'al* 'its spleen'

* *ʔakan* 'leg/foot, hind limb'    (plant: trunk, basal stem)

*yakan* 'its leg'
*sba yakan* 'front of the leg', used for a toad's hind toes
*sbakel yakan* 'bones of the hind limb'
*sbakel shol yakan* 'bone of the head of the leg, kneecap'
*sbakel yit yakan* 'bone of the buttock of the leg, heel'
*sbakel snuk' yakan* 'bone of the neck of the leg, ankle'
*sbakel špahč'amil yakan* 'bone of the sole of the foot'
*sbakel steʔel yakan* 'bone of the trunk of the leg, shin'
*yehk'ečil yakan* 'hind claw, nail, or hoof'
*shol yakan* 'head of the leg, knee'

*smahk' yakan* 'cylindrical segment of the leg'
*snuk' yakan* 'neck of the leg, ankle'
*špahč'amil yakan* 'sole of the foot'
*šuhkubil yakan* 'elbow of the foot, knee' (= *shol yakan* ?)
*steʔel yakan* 'trunk of the leg, lower leg'
*st'imab ščial yakan* 'Achilles' tendon'

* *ʔak'* 'tongue'

*yak'* 'its tongue'

*ʔal* 'child, female speaking'    (plant: embryo, sprout)

*sna yal* 'house of its child', i.e., pouch of a marsupial

* *ʔat* 'penis'

*yat* 'its penis, stinger'
*yat smeʔ* 'penis of a female' (= *yusam*, see *ʔusam*)
*sbak' yat* 'seed of the penis', i.e., testicles
*ščohak'il yat* 'net bag of the penis', i.e., scrotum
*steʔel yat* 'shaft of the penis'

* *ʔaʔ* 'thigh'

*yaʔ* 'its thigh, upper portion of hind limb'
*yaʔ sk'ab* 'thigh of the forelimb'
*sbakel yaʔ* 'thigh bone, femur'
*sbak'etal yaʔ* 'flesh of the thigh, shank'
*snaktib yaʔ* 'seat of the thigh, hip joint'

*ba* 'front'

*sba yakan* 'front of the leg', used for a toad's front toes
*sba ye* 'front of the mouth', i.e., the incisors
*sba yehk'eč* 'front of the hoof:
*sba sk'ab* 'front of the arm', used for a toad's front toes
*sba sne* 'tip of the tail'
*sba šik* 'tip of the wing'
*sbakel sba šik* 'bone of the wing tip', modified "hand" bones of a bird
*stiʔba* 'forehead', lit. 'lip of the front'

* *bak* 'bone' (plant: hard central portion—xylem—of a plant stem; corn cob)

*sbakel yakan* 'bones of the hind limb'

*sbakel ya?* 'thigh bone, femur'

*sbakel sba šik'* 'bone of the wing tip'

*sbakel sc'akaba snuk'* 'bone of the joint of the neck'

*sbakel šča?am* 'bone of the molar' (= *šča?am* 'molar')

*sbakel šč'iš spat* 'bone of the spine of the back' (= *sbakel spat* 'bone of the back')

*sbakel ye* 'bone of the mouth, teeth, especially the canines', see also *sba ye* 'incisors' and *šča?am* 'molars'

*sbakel yehk'eč* 'bone of the claw, nail', the terminal bone of a digit

*sbakel shol* 'bone of the head, skull'

*sbakel shol yakan* 'bone of the head of the leg, kneecap'

*sbakel shol sk'ab* 'bone of the head of the arm, elbow'

*sbakel yit yakan* 'bone of the buttock of the leg, heel'

*sbakel yit sk'ab* 'bone of the buttock of the arm, wrist'

*sbakel skawa* 'bone of the chin or jaw'

*sbakel skub* 'bone of the hip', i.e., the upper limb bone

*sbakel sk'ab* 'bones of the forelimb'

*sbakel šmoč* 'bones of the rib cage'

*sbakel sna yo?tan* 'bones of the house of the heart', i.e., the breastbone (= *sbakel yo?tan*)

*sbakel snaktib ye* 'bone of the seat of the mouth', i.e., the jaw (= *skawa* ?, see *kawa*)

*sbakel sne* 'bones of the tail'

*sbakel snuk'* 'bones of the neck'

*sbakel snuk' yakan* 'bones of the neck of the leg, ankle'

*sbakel yo?tan* 'bone of the heart', i.e., the breastbone

*sbakel špahč'amil yakan* 'bones of the sole of the foot'

*sbakel špahč'amil sk'ab* 'bones of the palm of the hand'

*sbakel spat* 'bones of the back', i.e., vertebrae between the shoulders and the pelvis

*sbakel špéču* 'bone of the breast', of cattle, the scapula

*sbakel šik'* 'bones of the wing', of birds or bats

*sbakel sta?an* 'bone of the chest'

*sbakel ste?el yakan* 'bones of the trunk of the leg, tibia'

*sbakel sti?il šmoč* 'bone of the lip of the rib cage'

*bak'* 'pit, seed'

*sbak' yat* 'seed of the penis, testicle'

*sbak' sit* 'seed of the eye, eyeball'

*\*bak'etal* 'flesh'    (plant: softer tissues of the stem—phloem)

*sbak'etal* 'its flesh'

*sbak'etal ya?* 'flesh of the thigh, shank'

*be* 'path, road'

*sbe šcuš* 'path of the urine, urethra'

*sbe šč'ič'el yo?tan* 'path of the blood of the heart, coronary arteries'

*sbe yik'* 'path of the air' (= *stutub* 'windpipe', see *tutub*)

*sbe sim* 'path of the mucus, nostril'

*sbe ston* 'path of the egg, oviduct', especially in female birds

*sbe swe?el* 'path of the food, esophagus'

*\*bikil* 'intestines'

*sbikil* 'its intestines'

*šč'in sbikil* 'small intestine'

*smuk'ul sbikil* 'large intestine'

*šč'išil sbikil* 'thorn of the intestine'?

*\*\*calub* 'coxcomb' [< tv *cal* 'form into a a row']

*scalub* 'its coxcomb'

*\*coc* 'hair'    (plant: hairlike surface texture)

*scocil* 'its hair'

*scocil yo?tan* 'the hair of the heart', i.e., bristles under the thorax of certain insects

*scocil sit* 'hair of the eye, eyelash'

*\*con* 'pubic hair'    (plant: moss)

*scon* 'its pubic hair', also the hairlike bristles on the underside of a crab's body

*\*cukum* 'stomach'

*scukum* 'its stomach'

*šč'in scukum* 'small stomach', of cattle

*smuk'ul scukum* 'large stomach', of cattle

*c'akab* 'node' [< tv *c'ak* 'join its ends']
*sc'akaba snuk'* 'the joint of the neck (with the skull)'
*sbakel sc'akaba snuk'* 'the bone of the neck joining', i.e., the cervical vertebra adjacent to skull

*c'amal te?* 'seat'
*sc'amal te?* 'its pelvis'
*sc'amal te? yit* 'seat of the buttocks, pelvis' (= *sc'amal te?*)

*čan* 'snake, animal'
*sčanul* 'its body'
*skohtol sčanul* 'its entire body'

*ca?* 'quern, metate'
*sča?* 'its gizzard'
*sča?am* 'molars'
*sbakel sča?am* 'bones of the molars' (= *sča?am*)

*či* 'fiber'   (plant: veins in a leaf)
*sčial* 'tendon'
*st'imab sčial yakan* 'Achilles' tendon'

*\*čikin* 'ear'   (plant: lobes of a sagittate leaf)
*sčikin* 'its ear'
*sk'unil sčikin* 'the smoothness of the ear'?
*šleč šlečil sčikin* 'the flat of the ear'
*sti?il sčikin* 'the lip of the ear', i.e., the tip or edge of the ear
*yutil sčikin* 'the inside of the ear'

*\*čin* [UN]
*sčin sbak* 'brains of the bone, marrow'
*sčinam* 'its brains'

*\*čo* 'cheek'
*sčo yit* 'cheek of the buttocks, rump'
*slikab sčo yit* 'lifter of the rump', i.e., the gluteus maximus muscle?

*čohak'* 'net bag'
*sčohak'il yat* 'net bag of the penis, scrotum'

*\*čohk'* 'wart'
*sčohk'il* 'its wart', said of a toad's skin

*\*čuš* 'urine'
*sbe sčuš* 'path of the urine, urethra'
*sna sčuš* 'house of the urine, bladder'

*\*\*čuya* 'crop of a bird'
*sčuya* 'its crop'

*\*ču?* 'breast'   (plant: nipplelike tip of certain fruits, e.g., lemon)
*sču?* 'its breast, udder'
*sni? sču?* 'nose of the breast, nipple'

*č'a* 'bitter'
*sč'a* 'its gall bladder'

*\*č'ič'* 'blood'   (plant: reddish, nonsticky sap)
*sč'ič'el yo?tan* 'blood of the heart', i.e., the blood in the heart
*sbe sč'ič'el yo?tan* 'paths of the blood, blood vessels, of the heart', i.e., coronary arteries
Note: insects are not thought to have 'blood'.

*č'in* (see *bikil, cukum*)

*č'iš* 'spine, thorn'
*sč'iš spat* 'spine of a vertebrate'
*sbakel sč'iš spat* 'bones of the spine, vertebrae'
*sč'išal čan* 'spines of the snake', i.e., keeled scales?
*sč'išil sbikil* 'spines of the intestine', with reference to fish?

*č'oš* [tv 'tie tightly in the middle']
*sč'oš sč'ošil yit* 'abdominal constriction', the narrow 'waist' of a wasp where the abdomen joins the thorax

*\*č'uht* 'belly'   (plant: e.g., inferior ovary of banana flowers)
*sč'uht* 'its belly'
*sleab sč'uht* 'its underbelly'?

**\* ʔe** 'mouth'

**ye** 'its mouth'

**sba ye** 'front of the mouth', i.e., the incisors

**sbakel ye** 'bones of the mouth', i.e., teeth, especially the canines

**sbakel snaktib ye** 'bone of the seat of the mouth, jawbone'

**snaktib ye** 'seat of the mouth, jaw' (= **skawaʔ** see **kawa**)

**\* ʔehk'eč** 'claw, hoof, nail'

**yehk'eč** 'its claw, hoof, nail'

**sba yehk'eč** 'front of the hoof'

**sbakel yehk'eč** 'bone of the claw, hoof, or nail', i.e., the terminal bone of a digit

**yehk'ečil yakan** 'hind hoof'

**yehk'ečil sk'ab** 'fore hoof'

**haʔ** (see **welob**)

**\* hol** 'head'  (plant: e.g., fruit of a cabbage)

**shol** 'its head'

**sbakel shol** 'skull'

**shol yakan** 'head of the leg, knee'

**sbakel shol yakan** 'bone of the head of the leg, kneecap'

**shol sk'ab** 'head of the arm, elbow' (= **šuhkub** ?)

**sbakel shol sk'ab** 'bone of the elbow'

**ʔič'ob** [< tv **ʔič'** 'take in']

**yič'ob ʔik'** 'air intake', i.e., a fish's gills, these may also be known as **ščikin** 'its ears'

**ʔihk'** (see **mahk'**)

**ʔik'** 'air, smell'

**sbe ʔik'** 'path of the air, windpipe' (= **stutub**, see **tutub**)

**yič'ob ʔik'** 'air intake, fish gills'

**\* ʔisim** 'whisker, barbel of catfish'  (plant: roots)

**yisim** 'its whisker, barbel'

**\* ʔit** 'buttock, abdominal segment'  (plant: basal portion of leaves or fruit)

**yit** 'its buttocks'

**sc'amal teʔ yit** (= **sc'amal teʔ** 'pelvis', see **c'amal teʔ**)

**ščo yit** 'cheek of the buttock, rump'

**slikab ščo yit** 'lifter of the rump, gluteus maximus'

**šč'oš šč'ošil yit** 'abdominal constriction', "waist" of a wasp

**sk'ahk' yit** 'fire of the abdomen', i.e., venom of a stinging insect?

**stenab yit** 'flat of the buttocks', rump of a bird, toad

**yit yakan** 'buttock of the leg, heel'

**sbakel yit yakan** 'bone of the heel'

**yit sk'ab** 'buttock of the arm, elbow' (= **šuhkub** ?)

**sbakel yit sk'ab** 'bone of the elbow'

**kása** [< Sp **casa** 'house']

**škášail yoʔtan** 'house of the heart' i.e., thorax of an insect

**\* kawa** 'chin, jaw'

**skawa** 'its chin, jaw'

**sbakel skawa** 'bone of the chin, jaw'

**\* \* kohtol** [< numeral classifier **koht** 'animal']

**skohtol ščanul** 'its entire body'

**\* kub** 'hip, shoulder'

**skub** 'its hip, shoulder' (see also **nehkel**)

**sbakel skub** 'bone of the hip, shoulder' (= **sbakel yaʔ** 'bone of the thigh' + **sbakel yaʔ sk'ab** 'bone of the thigh of the arm')

**\* k'ab** 'arm/hand, forelimb'  (plant: limb, branch)

**sk'ab** 'its forelimb'

**sba sk'ab** 'front of the arm', used for a toad's foretoes

**sbakel shol sk'ab** 'bone of the head of the arm, elbow'

**sbakel yit sk'ab** 'bone of the buttock of the arm, wrist'

**sbakel sk'ab** 'bones of the arm, forelimb'

**sbakel špahč'amil sk'ab** 'bones of the palm of the hand'

**yehk'ečil sk'ab** 'fore hoof'

*shol sk'ab* 'head of the arm, elbow'
*smahk' sk'ab* 'cylindrical segment of the forelimb'
*snuk' sk'ab* 'neck of the arm, wrist'
*yok sk'ab* 'limbs'
*špahč'amil sk'ab* 'palm of the hand'
*šuhkubil sk'ab* 'elbow of the arm'
*steʔel sk'ab* 'trunk of the arm, forearm'

*k'ahk'* 'fire'
*sk'ahk' yit* 'fire of the stinger, venom?'

*k'an* 'yellow'
*sk'anal ston* 'yellow of the egg, yolk'

\*\**k'iwoč* 'cheek pouch'
*šk'iwoč* 'its cheek pouch' (cf. *k'iwoč č'o* 'pocket mouse')

\*\**k'uk'um* 'feather'    (cf. *k'uk'* 'trogon')
*sk'uk'umal* 'its feathers'
*sk'uk'umal sne* 'tail feathers'
*sk'uk'umal spat* 'back feathers'
*sk'uk'umal šik* 'wing feathers'

*k'un* 'soft, smooth'
*sk'unil sčikin* 'smoothness of the ear'?

\**lahc'ap* 'armpit'
*slahc'ap* 'its armpit'

\*\**lakam* 'dewlap, throat fan, pouch, or wattle'
*slakam* 'its dewlap', e.g., dewlap of zebu cattle, throat fan of male anole lizard (cf. *luhub*)

*lawuš* [ < Sp ? ]
*šlawuš* 'its spur', especially of a rooster; the hind toe of most birds

*leab* [ < tv *le* 'seek'? ]
*sleab šč'uht* 'underbelly'?

*leč* [ < tv 'make thin leaf-like objects ]
*šleč šlečil sčikin* 'flat of the ear'
*šleč šlečil sniʔ* 'flat of the nose', especially

of a pig, contrasts with *yošomal sniʔ* 'three-hill nose' (see *ʔosomal*)

*likab* [ < tv *lik* 'lift' ]
*slikab ščo yit* 'lifter of the rump', i.e., the gluteus maximus?

*lómo* [ < Sp 'loin' ]
*slómo* 'its loin'

\*\**luhub* 'wattle'
*sluhub* 'its wattle', especially of a male turkey

\**lut* 'back of the knee'
*slut* 'its back of the knee', especially the concave portion of a cow's limb just above the point of the heel

*mahk'* [ < tv *mak'* 'cut it horizontally' ] (plant: internodes, e.g., of bamboo)
*smahk' yakan* 'cylindrical segment of the leg', as that between hip and knee, knee and ankle, or ankle and hoof of cattle
*smahk' sk'ab* 'cylindrical segment of the forelimb'
*smahk'al mahk' sbakel spat* 'cylindrical segments of the backbone, vertebrae'
*smahk'al mahk' yihk'alum sne* 'cylindrical segments of the black of the tail', descriptive of the ringed pattern of a raccoon's tail

*méru* [ < Sp *mero* 'kind of fish' ]
*sméru* 'its scale', of a snake or a fish (= *sul*)

*moč* 'basket'
*šmoč* 'its rib cage'
*sbakel šmoč* 'bones of the rib cage, ribs'
*sbakel stiʔil šmoč* 'bone of the lip of the rib cage'

*muk'* (see *bikil, cukum, top*)

*na* 'house'
*sna yal* 'house of the child', i.e., pouch of a marsupial

*sbakel sna yoʔtan* 'bone of the house of the heart, breastbone'
*sna ščuš* 'house of the urine, bladder'
*sna yoʔtan* 'house of the heart'

*naktib* 'seat'

*snaktib yaʔ* 'seat of the thigh, pelvis'
*snaktib ye* 'seat of the mouth, jaw'
*sbakel snaktib ye* 'bone of the jaw, jawbone'
*snaktib sne* 'seat of the tail'
*snaktib snuk'* 'seat of the neck'

\*\**ne* 'tail'

*sne* 'its tail'
*sba sne* 'front of the tail, tail tip'
*sbakel sne* 'bones of the tail'
*sk'uk'umal sne* 'feathers of the tail, tail feathers'
*smahk'al mahk' yihk'alum sne* 'rings on a raccoon's tail'
*snaktib sne* 'seat of the tail'

\**nehkel* 'shoulder'

*snehkel* 'its shoulder'

\**niʔ* 'nose'      (plant: tips of leaves, flowers, fruits, etc.)

*sniʔ* 'its nose'
*šleč šlečil sniʔ* 'flat of the nose', especially of a pig
*sniʔ ščuʔ* 'nose of the breast, nipple'
*yošomal sniʔ* 'three-hilled nose', contrasting with *šleč šlečil sniʔ*
*yutil sniʔ* 'inside of the nose'

\**nuhkul* 'skin'      (plant: leathery bark or peel)

*snuhkulel* 'its skin'

\**nuk'* 'neck'      (plant: e.g., constricted "neck" of certain squash)

*snuk'* 'its neck'
*sbakel snuk'* 'bones of the neck'
*sbakel snuk' yakan* 'bones of the neck of the leg, ankle'
*sbakel sc'akaba snuk'* 'bone of the joining of the neck'

*sc'akaba snuk'* 'joining of the neck', i.e., top of the spine
*snaktib snuk'* 'seat of the neck'
*snuk' yakan* 'neck of the leg, ankle'
*snuk' sk'ab* 'neck of the forelimb, wrist'
*steʔel snuk'* 'trunk of the neck'

*ʔok* 'stem, stalk'

*yok sk'ab* 'limbs'

*ʔolil* 'center'

*yolil staʔan* 'center of the chest'

*ʔošomal* $\left[ < ʔoš \text{ 'three'} + ʔomal \text{ 'hill'} \right]$

*yošomal sniʔ* 'three hill nose', contrasts with *šleč šlečil sniʔ* 'flat of the nose', cf. *ʔomalil tiʔil* 'hill of the lip', a vertical depression in the upper lip

\**ʔoʔtan* 'heart'

*yoʔtan* 'its heart'
*sbakel yoʔtan* 'bone of the heart, breastbone'
*sbakel sna yoʔtan* 'bone of the house of the heart, breastbone'
*sbe šč'ič'el yoʔtan* 'path of the blood of the heart, coronary arteries'
*scocil yoʔtan* 'hair of the heart (thorax)', hairlike bristles on the underside of a wasp's thorax, etc.
*šč'ič'el yoʔtan* 'blood of the heart'
*škášail yoʔtan* 'house of the heart', e.g., a wasp's thorax
*sna yoʔtan* 'house of the heart'

\**pahč'am* 'palm, sole'

*špahč'amil yakan* 'sole of the foot'
*sbakel špahč'amil yakan* 'bones of the sole of the foot'
*špahč'amil sk'ab* 'palm of the hand'
*sbakel špahč'amil sk'ab* 'bones of the palm of the hand'

\**pat* 'back'      (plant: nonleathery bark, underside of leaf)

*spat* 'its back'
*sbakel šč'iš spat* 'bones of the spine of the back, vertebrae'

*sbakel spat* 'bones of the back, vertebrae'
*šč'iš spat* 'spine of the back, spine'
*sk'uk'umal spat* 'feathers of the back'
*smahk'al mahk' sbakel spat* 'cylindrical segments of the backbone', i.e., vertebra
*spat ston* 'back of the egg, eggshell'
*ste?el spat* 'trunk of the back', e.g., dorsal surface of a wasp's thorax

*\*pa?ka* 'roof of the mouth'
*spa?ka* 'its roof of the mouth'

*péču* [ < Sp *pecho* 'breast']
*špéču* 'its breast'
*sbakel špéču* 'bone of its breast', shoulder blade of cattle

*pišol* 'hat'
*špišol* 'its hat', antennae of a snail (cf. *šulub*)

*sak* 'white'     (plant: seed of a squash)
*sak ston* 'white of the egg, egg white'

*\*sehk'ub* 'liver'
*sehk'ub* 'its liver'

*\*sim* 'mucus'
*simal* 'its mucus'
*sbe sim* 'path of the mucus, nostril'

*\*sit* 'eye'     (plant: grain of wood, fruit)
*sit* 'its eye'
*sbak' sit* 'seed of the eye, eyeball'
*scocil sit* 'hair of the eye, eyelash'

*sot* 'rattle'     (plant: seed pods that rattle)
*sot* 'its rattle', of a rattlesnake

*\*sot'ot'* 'lung'
*sot'ot'* 'its lung'

*\*sul* 'fish scale'     (plant: strips of scaly bark)
*sul* 'its scale' (= *sméru* ? see *méru*)

*\*\*šik'* 'wing, fin'

*šik'* 'its wing'
*sba šik'* 'front of the wing, wing tip'
*sbakel šik'* 'bones of the wing'
*sbakel sba šik'* 'bones of the wing tip', the modified "hand" bones of the outer half of a bird's wing
*sk'uk'umal šik'* 'feathers of the wing'

*\*šuhkub* 'elbow' [ < *šuhk* 'side']
*šuhkubil yakan* 'elbow of the leg, knee' (= *shol yakan*)
*šuhkubil sk'ab* 'elbow of the forelimb, elbow' (= *shol sk'ab*)

*\*\*šulub* 'horn, crest'
*šulub* 'its horn', also antennae of insects

*\*ta?an* 'chest'
*sta?an* 'its chest'
*sbakel sta?an* 'bone of the chest'
*yolil sta?an* 'center of the chest'

*tenab* [ < tv *ten* 'flatten']
*stenab yit* 'flat of the buttocks', rump of a bird, flat portion of a toad's rump on which it sits

*te?el* 'trunk' [ < *te?* 'tree']
*ste?el yakan* 'trunk of the leg, lower leg or shin'
*sbakel ste?el yakan* 'shin bone'
*ste?el yat* 'shaft of the penis'
*ste?el šč'iš spat* 'trunk of the spine' (= *ste?el spat*)
*ste?el spat* 'trunk of the back, spine'
*ste?el sk'ab* 'trunk of the forelimb, lower arm'
*ste?el snuk'* 'trunk of the neck'

*\*ti?il* 'lip' [ < tv *ti?* 'eat meat, bite it']
*sti?ba* 'lip of the front, forehead'
*sti?il ščikin* 'lip of the ear, tip or edge of the ear'
*sti?il šmoč* 'lip of the rib cage'
*sbakel sti?il šmoč* 'bone of the lip of the rib cage'

*ton* 'stone'

**ston** 'egg' (of the bird, reptile, fish, invertebrate, etc.)

**sbe ston** 'path of the egg, oviduct'
**sk'anal ston** 'yellow of the egg, yolk'
**spat ston** 'back of the egg, shell'
**sakil ston** 'white of the egg, egg white'
**yunin ston** 'young of the egg, embryo'

**\*top** 'anus'

**stop** 'its anus'
**smuk'ul top** 'its colon'

**\*tutub** 'throat, windpipe'

**stutub** 'its windpipe' (cf. **sbe ?ik'**, **yič'ob ?ik'**)

**t'imab** [ < tv **t'im** 'string tautly']

**st'imab ščial yakan** 'taut string of the tendon of the leg', i.e., Achilles' tendon

**?unin** 'young, unripe' (plant: unripe, as of fruit)
**yunin ston** 'young of the egg, embryo'

**\*?usam** [UN]

**yusam** 'female's penis' (= **yat sme?**)

**we?el** 'food'
**sbe swe?el** 'path of the food, esophagus'

**welob** [ < tv **wel** 'fan it']
**swelob ha?** 'fan of the water, fin', pectoral fin of fish

**yut** 'inside'
**yutil ščikin** 'inside of the ear'
**yutil sni?** 'inside of the nose'

Figures 4.1–4.7 illustrate the use of some of the anatomical terminology that has been listed here.

## 4 Tzeltal Traps and Snares

Nine types of traps are distinguished: four deadfalls, three spring-pole snares, a lasso for catching nesting birds, and the unique **smahobil sik'** 'swift hitter' [ < tv **mah** 'hit it' + **sik'** 'swift']. The last named is simply a leafy

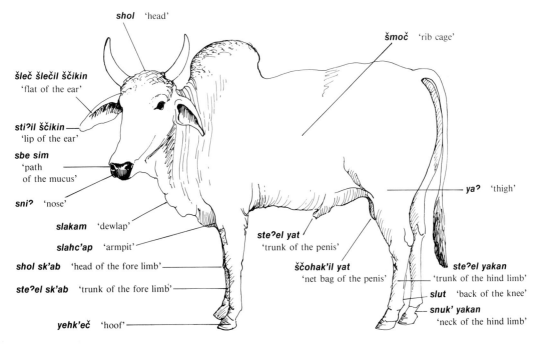

**Figure 4.1** Body parts of a bull (**stat wakaš**).

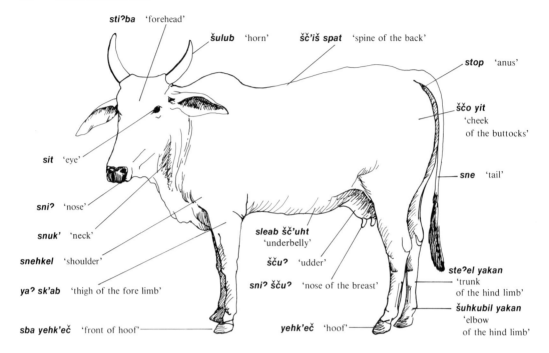

Figure 4.2    Body parts of a cow (*sme? wakaš*).

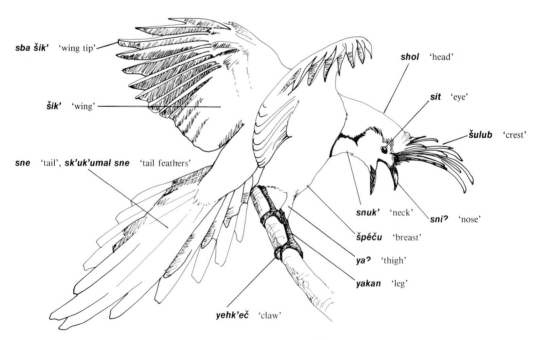

Figure 4.3    Body parts of a bird (*šulub mut*).

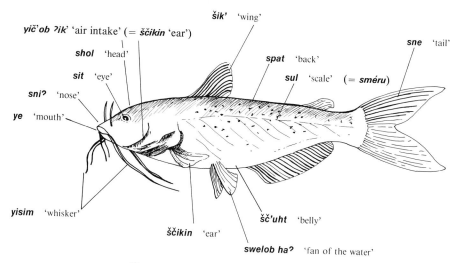

**Figure 4.4**  Body parts of a fish (*ʔisim čay*).

- *yič'ob ʔik'* 'air intake' (= *ščikin* 'ear')
- *šik'* 'wing'
- *shol* 'head'
- *spat* 'back'
- *sne* 'tail'
- *sit* 'eye'
- *sul* 'scale'  (= *sméru*)
- *sniʔ* 'nose'
- *ye* 'mouth'
- *yisim* 'whisker'
- *ščikin* 'ear'
- *šč'uht* 'belly'
- *swelob haʔ* 'fan of the water'

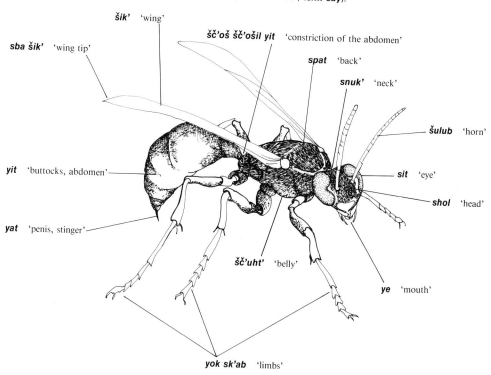

**Figure 4.5**  Body parts of a wasp (*k'an c'utoh*).

- *šik'* 'wing'
- *sba šik'* 'wing tip'
- *šč'oš šč'ošil yit* 'constriction of the abdomen'
- *spat* 'back'
- *snuk'* 'neck'
- *šulub* 'horn'
- *yit* 'buttocks, abdomen'
- *sit* 'eye'
- *shol* 'head'
- *yat* 'penis, stinger'
- *šč'uht'* 'belly'
- *ye* 'mouth'
- *yok sk'ab* 'limbs'

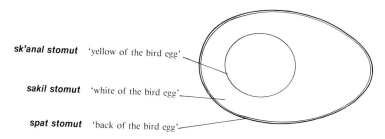

**Figure 4.6**  Parts of a bird egg (*tomut*).

- *sk'anal stomut* 'yellow of the bird egg'
- *sakil stomut* 'white of the bird egg'
- *spat stomut* 'back of the bird egg'

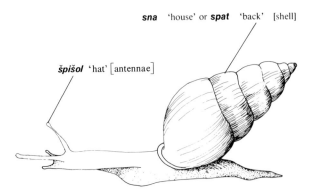

*sna* 'house' or **spat** 'back' [shell]

*špišol* 'hat' [antennae]

**Figure 4.7**  Parts of a snail (*puy*).

fence erected on certain ridge sites favored by these birds (especially the large White-collared Swift, *Streptoprocne zonaris* [Apodidae]) (see Figure 4.8). Swifts have been clocked at over 100 kph. Stunned by the collision with the fence, they may be picked up and killed for food. SMZ claimed that the *paraje* of **mahosik'** is named for this technique.

The traps may also be classified by the trigger principle employed. Three use a trip stick, which triggers the trap by releasing a tensed line tied to the trigger stick. Four use a baited line, which triggers the deadfall or snare when the prey cuts the line in taking the bait. The lasso snare, **syakobil mut** 'bird snare' [ < tv **yak** 'catch it' + **mut** 'bird'], is drawn up by hand (see Figure 4.9).

The 'log deadfall', **pehc'ul te?** [ < **pehc'** 'trap' + **te?** 'tree, log'], has a trip stick trigger (see Figure 4.10). It may be used to kill medium sized mammals such as the opossum, fox, rabbit, weasel, skunk, raccoon, coati, tayra, and paca, as well as such ground-feeding birds as the quail, roadrunner, and dove. Two parallel fences (**smakte?al**) are built of upright poles set in the ground straddling a game trail. A log (**sme? te?al** 'mother

**Figure 4.8**  *smahobil sik'* 'swift hitter'. [From an original drawing by **hšoš kusman c'uhkin** (JGG).]

**Figure 4.9** *syakobil mut* 'bird snare'. [From an original drawing by **hšoš kusman c'uhkin** (JGG).]

log') of the proper length and diameter to drop cleanly between the fences is suspended at either end by loops of vine (**yak'ul shol sme? te?al** 'vine of the head of the mother log'). These loops are supported by short sticks (**shimon te?al**) balanced in the fork of branched poles (**šheč te?al**) placed at each end of the fence. The tension line, **yak'ul sp'ilum te?al** 'vine of the trigger stick', stretches from the free end of the short stick to the trigger peg (**sp'ilum te?al**), which is hooked behind a semicircular frame set in the ground (**šotšotil sp'ilum te?al** 'coil of the trigger stick'). The trigger peg is kept in place by a rigid 'support of the trigger' (**stehk'ab sp'ilum te?al**). An animal dislodging this support in passing drops the log. This trigger mechanism has a worldwide distribution (Cooper 1949; Blom and LaFarge 1927, Vol. II:352).

The 'catbird trap' (**syakobil šč'e?**) is similar to the log deadfall, differing in its smaller dimensions, single-ended support for the deadfall log, and the use of a baited line tied to the trigger peg (see Figure 4.11). In this case the trigger peg is pulled, rather than pushed, to set the trap. Why a special trap should be designed for the catbird (*Dumetella carolinensis*)—which is neither large nor harmful and which is present only during the winter months—is unclear.

A trigger mechanism identical to that employed in the log deadfall may also be used for a spring-pole snare (**hihp'uyak**) (see Figure 4.12). A vine noose (**šohk'ail**) is suspended from a bent pole or sapling (**sme? te?al** 'mother pole') over a game runway. The pole is held taut by a tension line tied to a trigger peg hooked behind the trap 'coil' and held in place by the rigid trip stick. When this support is dislodged, the pole springs upright and the noose is jerked tight around the animal's neck. This type of trap is used for the same kinds of animals as is the log deadfall. A variant of this spring-pole snare, known as **šč'obik'** [< UN], uses a baited trigger line (see Figure 4.13). It is used to catch a variety of 'rats'.

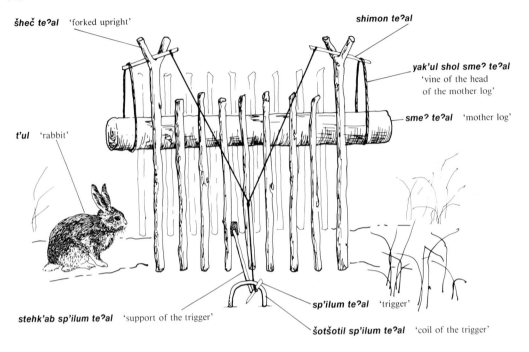

*šheč teʔal*  'forked upright'

*shimon teʔal*

*yak'ul shol smeʔ teʔal*
'vine of the head
of the mother log'

*smeʔ teʔal*  'mother log'

*t'ul*  'rabbit'

*stehk'ab sp'ilum teʔal*  'support of the trigger'

*sp'ilum teʔal*  'trigger'

*šotšotil sp'ilum teʔal*  'coil of the trigger'

**Figure 4.10**  *pehc`ul teʔ*  'log deadfall'.

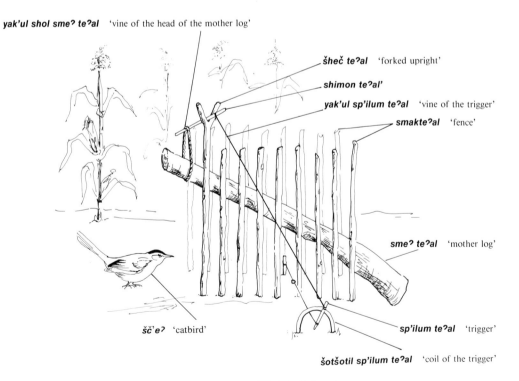

*yak'ul shol smeʔ teʔal*  'vine of the head of the mother log'

*šheč teʔal*  'forked upright'

*shimon teʔal'*

*yak'ul sp'ilum teʔal*  'vine of the trigger'

*smakteʔal*  'fence'

*smeʔ teʔal*  'mother log'

*šč`eʔ*  'catbird'

*sp'ilum teʔal*  'trigger'

*šotšotil sp'ilum teʔal*  'coil of the trigger'

**Figure 4.11**  *syakobil šč`eʔ* 'catbird trap'.

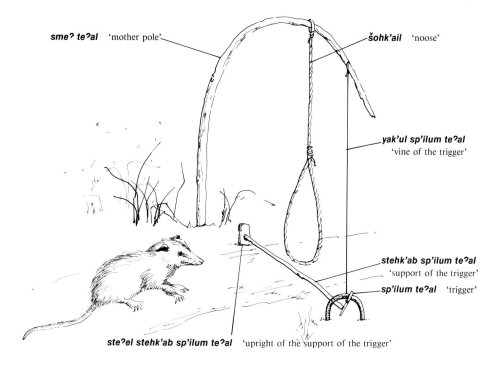

**sme⁇ te⁇al**  'mother pole'

**šohk'ail**  'noose'

**yak'ul sp'ilum te⁇al**
'vine of the trigger'

**stehk'ab sp'ilum te⁇al**
'support of the trigger'

**sp'ilum te⁇al**  'trigger'

**ste⁇el stehk'ab sp'ilum te⁇al**  'upright of the support of the trigger'

**Figure 4.12**   *hihp'uyak* 'spring-pole snare'.

**sme⁇ te⁇al**
'mother pole'

**šohk'ail**  'noose'

**yak'ul sme⁇ te⁇al**  'vine of the mother pole'

**č'o**  'rat'

**Figure 4.13**   *šč'obik'* [ <UN ].

A special pocket gopher snare (*syakobil ba*, also known as *k'ahčul č'uh te?* [< tv *kač* 'open by raising top'? + 'plank']) is quite similar to the spring-pole snare *hihp'uyak*, except that the noose is set underground in the gopher's tunnel (see Figure 4.14). It is triggered by the animal dislodging a stick to which the tension cord is directly tied or by the gopher gnawing through a baited cord.

The baited tension line trigger is employed for the 'stone deadfall' (*pehc'ul ton*) (see Figure 4.15). A large flat stone (*pehc'ul ton*) is balanced on the trigger string (*yak'ul*) itself. This is tied on a slant between an upright (*ste?el*) and a peg at the lower edge of the stone slab. The bait (*swe?el č'o* 'rat's food') is tied to the trigger string, which is cut as the animal takes the bait. This drops the stone plus the added weight of the *skahab* [< iv *kahah* 'put it above']. This trap may be used for all kinds of small rodents as well as for the four-eyed opossum and shrews.

A simple variant of the stone deadfall is the 'upside down deadfall' (*nuhlem pehc'*) (see Figure 4.16). This trap employs an old pot (*sk'a? p'in*) turned upside down over the trigger line; it is used inside the house to catch the domestic pests—the black rat and the house mouse.

It should be stressed that the knowledgeable locating of traps is of utmost importance to successful trapping. This was brought home to me after my numerous trapping efforts with commercial spring traps produced very little result. SMZ then suggested that I let him set the traps. Our success rate tripled the next night.

Table 4.13 gives estimated whole body weights of a variety of animals trapped or hunted by Tenejapanecos. Unfortunately I have no data on the frequency of capture of the various animals, so can provide no quantitative data on animal protein in the Tenejapan diet.

## 5    "Medicinal" Significance of Animals

The English term "medicine" cannot be precisely translated into Tzeltal. The closest

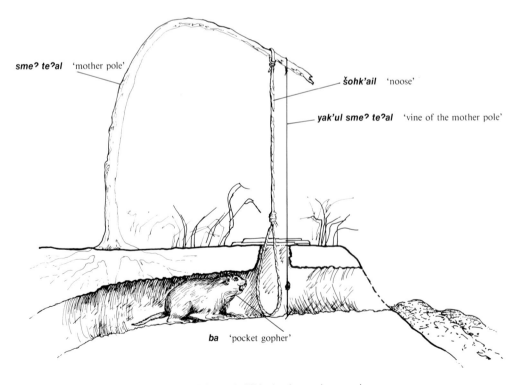

*sme? te?al* 'mother pole'

*šohk'ail* 'noose'

*yak'ul sme? te?al* 'vine of the mother pole'

*ba* 'pocket gopher'

**Figure 4.14**  *syakobil ba* 'pocket gopher snare'.

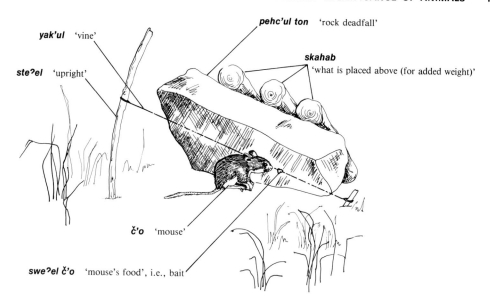

*yak'ul* 'vine'

*ste?el* 'upright'

*pehc'ul ton* 'rock deadfall'

*skahab*
'what is placed above (for added weight)'

*č'o* 'mouse'

*swe?el č'o* 'mouse's food', i.e., bait

Figure 4.15 *pehc'ul ton* 'rock deadfall'.

approximation in Tzeltal to the English concept is *pošil* [cf. *poš* 'cane liquor', tv *-pošta* 'cure someone', *hpošil* 'curer']. However, phrases of the form *špošil X* 'X's medicine' may be elicited for conditions not considered relevant to "medicinal" treatment, e.g., ridding the house of cockroaches or preventing one's hair from turning white with old age.

I have elicited an extensive but not exhaustive list of "treatments" involving animals or their products. There are 44 distinct conditions or effects considered to be subject to modification by one or more animal pro-

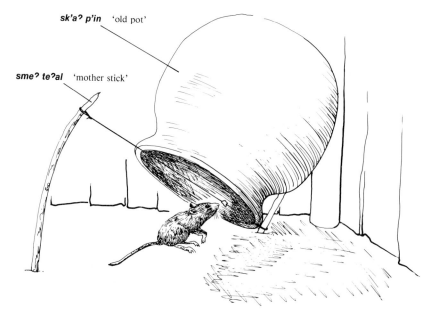

*sk'a? p'in* 'old pot'

*sme? te?al* 'mother stick'

Figure 4.16 *nuhlem pehc'* 'upside-down deadfall'.

**Table 4.13**
WHOLE BODY WEIGHTS OF CERTAIN TENEJAPAN GAME ANIMALS[a]

|  | Weight[b] |
|---|---|
| I.  Mammals |  |
|   1.  Marsupialia: opossum (*Didelphis* spp.) | 4–6 kg |
|   2.  Edentata: armadillo (*Dasypus novemcinctus*) | 3–7 kg |
|   3.  Lagomorpha: cottontail rabbit (*Sylvilagus floridanus*) | 900–1000 gm |
|   4.  Rodentia: |  |
|     (a) gray squirrel (*Sciurus aureogaster*) | 400–700 gm |
|     (b) pocket gopher (*Heterogeomys hispidus*) | 1000 gm (estimate) |
|     (c) *Peromyscus mexicanus* | 30 gm |
|     (d) paca (*Cuniculus paca*) | 10 kg (estimate) |
|   5.  Carnivora: |  |
|     (a) gray fox (*Urocyon cinereoargenteus*) | 3–6 kg |
|     (b) raccoon (*Procyon lotor*) | 5–15 kg |
|     (c) coati (*Nasua narica*) | 7–11 kg |
|     (d) weasel (*Mustela frenata*) | 200–365 gm (male) |
|  | 100–200 gm (female) |
|     (e) tayra (*Eira barbara*) | 4 kg (estimate) |
|   6.  Artiodactyla: |  |
|     (a) collared peccary (*Dicotyles tajacu*) | 14–25 kg |
|     (b) white-tailed deer (*Odocoileus virginianus*) | 36–57 kg (male) |
|  | 27–45 kg (female) |
|     (c) brocket (*Mazama americana*) | 17 + kg |
| II.  Birds |  |
|   1.  Tinamiformes: Rufescent Tinamou (*Crypturellus cinnamomeus*) | 350–500 gm |
|   2.  Galliformes: |  |
|     (a) chachalaca (*Ortalis vetula*) | 318–410 gm |
|     (b) bobwhite (*Colinus virginianus*) | 122–139 gm |
|     (c) Singing Quail (*Dactylortyx thoracicus*) | 170–266 gm |
|     (d) turkey (*Meleagris gallopavo*, wild) | 4.8–7.5 kg (male) |
|  | 2.8–4.4 kg (female) |
|   3.  Columbiformes: |  |
|     (a) Band-tailed Pigeon (*Columba fasciata*) | 280–350 gm |
|     (b) White-fronted Dove (*Leptotila verreauxi*) | 145–205 gm |
|   4.  Cuculiformes: roadrunner (*Geococcyx velox*) | 125 gm (estimate) |

[a] Adapted from Leopold (1972) and Burt and Grossenheider (1964).
[b] Note gm = grams and kg = kilograms.

ducts. Many of these modifications may also be achieved by use of plant products or by ritual means or by some combination of approaches. Fifty-five generic animal taxa are cited as having some "medicinal" effect. This is approximately 15% of the total inventory of generic animal taxa. We may compare this figure with the more than 50% percent of Hanunóo terminal plant taxa for which some "medicinal" use is cited (Conklin 1954:248–249, 257). However, Conklin's summary statement that "animals and animal products seldom feature in Hanunóo medicine [p. 249]" would be an overstatement if applied to the Tzeltal. Nevertheless, the relative unimportance of animals in folk medicine is clear for Tenejapa. This is seen more clearly in Table 4.14 where conditions treated with animal products are classified by type. Few of the total treatable conditions are virulent, and many might best be described as "cosmetic." Table 4.15 lists the Tzeltal animal taxa that were cited for "medicinal" use (***pošil***).

Table 4.14
A TYPOLOGY OF CONDITIONS SUBJECT TO TREATMENT WITH ANIMAL PRODUCTS

| *Condition/desired effect* | *Animal/animal part used in treatment* |
|---|---|
| A. Acute pathological states | |
| 1. Systemic | |
| *nihkel* 'malaria' | *pokok* 'toad': |
| | *ʔečeh* 'basilisk lizard' |
| | *caʔlos* 'Black Vulture' |
| | *ba* 'pocket gopher' |
| *sihtʼubel* 'swelling' | *caʔlos* 'Black Vulture' |
| | *ba* 'pocket gopher' |
| | *tunim čih* 'sheep' |
| *suhtem čamel* 'measles' | *pay* 'skunk' (odor) |
| 2. Respiratory | |
| *ʔobal* 'cough' | *šberon* 'large tadpole' |
| | *pay* 'skunk' (odor) |
| *hikʼhikʼ ʔobal* 'whooping cough' | *pewal* 'cockroach' |
| | *čʼuhčʼul čay* 'top minnow' |
| | *pay* 'skunk' (odor) |
| 3. Intestinal | |
| *čʼičʼ* 'dysentery' | *mayil tiʔbal* 'armadillo' |
| | *čitam* 'pig' |
| unspecified | *ʔahaw čan* 'rattlesnake' |
| 4. Urinogenital | |
| *cu ʔat* 'hernia'? | *cʼuhkuton* 'salamander' |
| | *cʼunun* 'hummingbird' (eggs) |
| *kʼuš čušil* 'painful urination' | *ščʼučʼ* 'true frog' |
| 5. Skin | |
| *čahil* '?' | *šanič* 'fire ant' (bite) |
| *čakal* 'tumor' | *yérwa* 'tarantula' (bite) |
| *čohkʼ* 'wart' | *pošil nušel* 'ripple bug' |
| | *tulukʼ čan* 'oil beetle' (secretion) |
| | *coʔkoy* 'Band-backed Wren' |
| *hataw* 'split foot' | *meʔ toyiw* 'Diptera larva' |
| | *wakaš* 'cattle' (gall bladder) |
| *ya šhat ʔakʼan yuʔun* 'causes split foot' | *kawáyu* 'horse/mule' (urine) |
| *ʔunin kʼabal* '?' | *cuhkum* 'woolybear caterpillar' |
| *wahba* 'acne' | *mut₂* 'chicken' (egg white) |
| 6. Supernatural | |
| *komel* 'soul loss' | *tulukʼ* 'turkey' |
| 7. Mental | |
| *howil wayel* 'nightmare' | *kawáyu* 'horse/mule' (bucking) |
| B. Chronic pathological conditions | |
| *cacal* 'impotence' | *puy* 'snail' |
| | *yat naab* 'snail' |
| | *kʼohčin teʔ* 'snail' |
| | *kohtom* 'coati' (penis) |
| *kohkobel* 'deafness' | *bak čikin* 'mussel' |
| *sikil winik sok ʔanc* 'sterility' | *mut₂* 'chicken' (young male) |
| C. Modifying natural functions | |
| *ma šʔalah ʔanc yuʔun* 'contraception' | *kawáyu* 'horse/mule' (hoof of female mule) |

*(continued)*

**Table 4.14** (*Continued*)

| Condition/desired effect | Animal/animal part used in treatment |
|---|---|
| *ya šk'išna* 'heating (woman's belly following childbirth)' | *mut₂* 'chicken' (large rooster) |
| *ya štohk ʔalal* 'ease childbirth' | *mut₂* 'chicken' (eggs) |
| | *ʔuč* 'opossum' (tail) |
| | *teʔtikil čih* 'deer' (horn) |
| | *tunim čih* 'sheep' (horn) |
| *yaʔlel ščuʔ ʔanc* 'increase flow of breast milk' | *nep'* 'crab' |

D.  Modifying personality or behavior

| | |
|---|---|
| *halabil yuʔun ʔanc* 'improve weaving skill' | *šela ʔam* 'orb weaver' (web) |
| *lom k'opoh ʔalal* 'ensure effective speech in child' | *čikitin* 'cicada' |
| | *períko* 'parrot' |
| *ʔip* 'give strength' | *mut₂* 'chicken' (first egg laid) |
| | *wakaš* 'cattle' (blood) |
| | *kawáyu* 'horse/mule' (young mule's blood) |
| *ya sk'unil yip* 'counteracts strength' | *ses* 'ant' |
| *ma šʔok' niʔtik ta wayel* 'stops snoring' | *k'intun* 'anole' (place in nose) |
| | *ʔohkoc* 'spiny lizard' (place in nose) |
| *nušel* 'helps learn to swim' | *pošil nušel* 'ripple bug/water strider' |
| *wayel* 'helps baby sleep' | *wayway čan* '*Zopherus jourdani*' |
| *ya šbolob winik yuʔun* 'makes a fierce man tame' | *nap'ak* 'slug' |
| | *k'oʔ* 'snail' |
| | *mokoč* 'millipede' |
| | *k̦'olom* 'grub' |
| *ya šk'ahk'ub winik yuʔun* 'makes a man fierce' | *k'ahk'ub yat* 'spider wasp' |
| | *c'ibon* 'vespid wasp' |
| | *honon* 'bumblebee' |
| 'improves tortilla making'[a] | *ba* 'pocket gopher' (rub belly of gopher) |

E.  Modifying appearance

| | |
|---|---|
| *ya snit yat* 'stretch penis' | *búro* 'donkey' (calls of a male) |
| 'the opposite effect'[a] | *búro* 'donkey' (calls of a female) |
| *ya šmuk'ub ščuʔ ʔanc* 'enlarge a woman's breasts' | *butbut ʔit čan* 'antlion' (bite) |
| *ya šmuk'ub yat winik* 'enlarge a man's penis' | *wakaš* 'cattle' (horns) |
| *ya sakub holol yuʔun* 'whiten a man's hair' | *ʔuč* 'opossum' (touch) |
| *ma sakub holol yuʔun* 'prevent hair turning white' | *hoh* 'raven' (blood) |
| 'prevent growth of beard'[a] | *soc'* 'bat' (blood) |

F.  Modifying immediate environment

| | |
|---|---|
| *c'isim* 'eliminate leaf-cutting ants' | *c'iʔ* 'dog' (dead) |
| *pewal* 'eliminate roaches' | *peskáro* 'market fish' (bones) |

[a]Tzeltal term not available.

**Table 4.15**
TZELTAL ANIMAL TAXA CITED FOR MEDICINAL USE (*pošil*)

| Animal taxon | Scientific name | 'Medicine'/ 'treatment' name | Comments |
|---|---|---|---|
| 1. (a) *puy* 'snail' | MOLLUSCA: *Pachychilus* sp. | *špošil cacal* | *cacal* refers to a male condition which is best glossed as 'impotence'. Men suffering from this condition have no sexual interest in their wives (or other women, presumably). According to one account, the cure must be performed surreptitiously by a curer with the necessary power. The cure involves giving the afflicted man corn gruel to drink in which the snail is hidden. All the snails cited have high conical shells, suggesting a phallus. *yat kohtom* 'coati's penis' is also cited as 'medicine' for this condition (see No. 41). |
| (b) *yat naab* 'snail' | MOLLUSCA: Physidae | | |
| (c) *k'ohčin teʔ* 'snail' | MOLLUSCA: Oleacinidae | | |
| 2. (a) *nap'ak* 'slug' | MOLLUSCA: Limacidae | *špošil ya šbolob winik yuʔun* | *bol* means 'stupid' or 'dull', thus eating these animals (as well as *mokoč* 'millipede' or *k'olom* 'scarab beetle larva', see below) is thought to make a 'fierce man' (*k'ahk'al winik*) less of an insufferable tyrant. A woman whose husband beats her too frequently is apt to slip these 'medicinal' items into her husband's dinner. |
| (b) *k'oʔ* 'snail' | MOLLUSCA: *Lysinoe ghiesbreghti* | | |
| 3. *bak čikin* 'mussel' | MOLLUSCA: Unionidae | *špošil kohkobel* | *kohkobel* 'deafness' may be treated by grinding the shell of the pearl-button mussel and mixing it in hot water. This mixture is then put into the ear daily for a month or two. This is thought to "open" the ear. This shell is shaped much like an ear. |
| 4. *yérwa* 'tarantula' | ARACHNIDA: Mygalomorpha | *špošil čakal* | *čakal* may be glossed as 'tumor', 'carbuncle', or 'boil'. The treatment involves using the bite of the 'tarantula' to lance the head of the boil. |
| 5. *šela ʔam* 'orb weaver' | ARACHNIDA: *Nephila clavipes* | *špošil halobil yuʔun ʔancetik* | This treatment illustrates the range of reference of the term *pošil* 'medicine'. Women (*ancetik*) wishing to learn to weave proficiently seek out this spider and wrap its web around their hands. *halobil* means 'loom'. |

*(continued)*

Table 4.15 (*Continued*)

| Animal taxon | Scientific name | *'Medicine'/ 'treatment' name* | Comments |
|---|---|---|---|
| 6. **nep'** 'crab' | CRUSTACEA: Pota-monidae | **špošil ya?lel šču? ?ancetik** | Nursing women desiring a more ample supply of breast milk (**ya?lel šču?**) cook and eat a crab in a chili pepper broth. |
| 7. **mokoč** 'millipede' | DIPLOPODA | **špošil ya šbolob winik yu?un** | 'Medicine' to make a fierce man weak and dull (see No. 2 **nap'ak** 'slug', and **k'o?** 'snail', and No. 14, **k'olom** 'grub'). |
| 8. **pewal** 'cockroach' | INSECTA: Blattidae | **špošil hik'hik' ?obal** | Roasted, ground up, and drunk to cure 'whooping cough' (see also **č'uhč'ul čay** 'min-now', No. 20). |
| 9. **pošil nušel** 'ripple bug' | INSECTA: Veliidae, Gerridae | **špošil nušel, špošil čohk'** | The ripple bugs and the water striders (Gerridae: which also may be included as **pošil nušel**) are eaten by those wanting to learn to swim (< iv **-nuš** 'swim'). They do double duty as one of several treatments for 'warts' (**čohk'**, see also **tuluk' čan** 'oil beetle', No. 12, and **co?koy** 'Band-backed Wren', No. 35). |
| 10. **čikitin** 'cicada' | INSECTA: Cicadidae | **špošil lom k'opoh ?alal** | To encourage a child (**?alal**) to speak a lot (**lom k'opoh**), one collects 13 (the magic number) cicadas, bakes them, and gives them to the child to eat (see also **períko** 'parrot', No. 32). |
| 11. **butbut ?it čan** 'antlion' | INSECTA: Myrmeleon-tidae (larva) | **špošil ya šmuk'ub šču? ?anc** | The antlion larva is caught at the bottom of its conical sand trap and induced to bite the woman's breast (**šču? ?anc**). This is said to ensure that in a few years her breasts will be large (**ya šmuk'ub**). The logic behind this treatment would appear to be sympathetic magic, since the larva's ab-domen is swollen and/or since the sand trap made by this creature is shaped like an inverted breast. |
| 12. **tuluk' čan** 'oil beetle' | INSECTA: Coleoptera: *Meloe* spp. | **špošil čohk'** | These "are called oil beetles be-cause they exude an oily sub-stance from the joints of the legs when disturbed; this substance can raise blisters on one's skin [Borror and White 1970:184]." The substance con-tains the active ingredient |

(*continued*)

Table 4.15 (*Continued*)

| Animal taxon | Scientific name | 'Medicine'/ 'treatment' name | Comments |
|---|---|---|---|
| | | | cantharidin, extracted for modern medicinal uses. The people of Tenejapa prick the surface of the offending wart (*čohk'*) and then apply the oil exuded from this insect's leg joints to the surface (for other 'wart' cures see *pošil nušel* 'ripple bug', No. 9, and *co?koy* 'Band-backed Wren', No. 35). |
| 13. *wayway čan* [lit. sleep-bug'] | INSECTA: Coleoptera: *Zopherus jourdani* | *špošil wayel* | 'Sleeping (*wayel*) medicine'; if a woman is driven to distraction by the cries of her infant, she will seek out this beetle and tie it so that it hangs down her child's back. It should then sleep peacefully. This is a curious beetle somewhat reminiscent of a turtle; when disturbed it draws its legs up under its extremely hard dorsum and lies motionless, often for long periods. This characteristic behavior no doubt suggests its name. |
| 14. *k'olom* 'grub' | INSECTA: Coleoptera: Scarabaeidae (larva) | *špošil ya šbolob winik yu?un* | Another creature useful for 'taming' (*ya šbolob*) a 'fierce man' (*k'ahk'al winik*); see also *mokoč* 'millipede', No. 7, *k'o?* 'snail', and *nap'ak* 'slug', No. 2. |
| 15. *cuhkum* 'woolybear caterpillar' | INSECTA: Lepidoptera (larva) | *špošil ?unin k'abal* | *?unin k'abal* [lit. 'unripe arm'] is an as yet undefined illness. The pupal case (*sna cuhkum*) of this larva is used in the cure. |
| 16. *me? toyiw* [lit. 'mother of ice'] | INSECTA: Diptera? (larva) | *špošil hataw* | *hataw* [< tv 'tear vertically in halves'] is a debilitating foot condition common in the high country in winter. The cold causes splitting of the skin on the soles and heels of the feet. Stepping on horse or mule urine on the trail is also thought to cause this condition. One cure involves rubbing the sore foot in a mass of this swarming larva when a swarm is found on the trail. The 'black' variety (*?ihk'al me? toyiw*) is the most effective. |

(*continued*)

**Table 4.15** (*Continued*)

| Animal taxon | Scientific name | 'Medicine'/ 'treatment' name | Comments |
|---|---|---|---|
| 17. **ses** 'ant' | INSECTA: Formicidae: *Pheidole* spp. | **špošil ya šk'unub yip** | This is a common ant in houses. If it gets into one's food and is inadvertently eaten, it is thought to weaken (**ya šk'unub**) one's strength (**yip**). |
| 18. **šanič** 'fire ant' | INSECTA: Formicidae: *Solenopsis* spp. | **špošil čahil** | **čahil** is some sort of skin affliction. The 'cure' involves putting the affected arm or leg on this ant's hill, allowing the ants to bite. The very painful bites counteract the illness. |
| 19. (a) **k'ahk'ub yat** 'spider wasp' (b) **c'ibon** 'social vespid wasp' (c) **honon** 'bumblebee' | INSECTA: Pompilidae  INSECTA: Vespidae: *Epipona tatua* INSECTA: Apidae: *Bombus* spp. | **špošil ya šk'ahk'ub winik yuʔun** | If a man wishes to be 'fierce' (**k'ahk'al**), to fear nothing and no one, he must catch and eat 13 live spider wasps. This is an obvious test of courage as spider wasps have a powerful sting. Alternatively he might settle for 13 **c'ibon** a social vespid wasp or 13 bumblebees (**honon**). |
| 20. **č'uhč'ul čay** 'top minnow' | PISCES: Poeciliidae | **špošil hik'hik' ʔobal** | These small native fish are eaten as a cure for 'whooping cough' (**hik'hik' ʔobal**), see also **pewal** 'cockroach', No. 8. |
| 21. **peskáro** 'market fish' | PISCES | **špošil pewal** | An unidentified type of market fish (**šulem čay** 'Turkey Vulture fish') is purchased in San Cristóbal, the flesh eaten, and the bones burned in the house. The 'bitter' smoke kills the roaches which infest the thatch of the roof. Thus the term **pošil** 'medicine' is not restricted to treatments of psycho–physical conditions, but is applied as well to "environmental cures." |
| 22. **c'uhkuton** 'salamander' | AMPHIBIA: Plethodontidae | **špošil cu ʔat** | **cu ʔat** [lit. 'gourd penis'] is an affliction of the male genital region, possibly hernia. This animal is ground up and applied to the affected area as a salve. Some salamanders do secrete a poisonous substance from glands in the skin, so there may exist a physiological justification for this treatment. Alternatively one might cite the swollen tails typical of these animals as an indication |

**Table 4.15** (*Continued*)

| Animal taxon | Scientific name | 'Medicine'/ 'treatment' name | Comments |
|---|---|---|---|
| | | | that this treatment involves sympathetic magic. See also *c'unun* 'hummingbird', No. 33. |
| 23. *pokok* 'toad' | AMPHIBIA: Bufonidae | *špošil nihkel* | This is one of several treatments for 'malaria' (*nihkel*, lit. 'earthquake'). Some informants state that the toad's flesh is eaten in this cure, though the toad is otherwise considered inedible. Another informant describes the cure as follows: "You take to hitting it [the toad] on the flat part of its buttocks.... He says to it, 'take away the malaria, toad, take away this song, toad, take it away to the river, toad,' he admonishes it. In this way, in a week there is no more malaria." |
| 24. *šč'uč'* 'leopard frog' | AMPHIBIA: Ranidae | *špošil k'uš čušil* | The frog is cooked with 13 green peppers, the broth is drunk, and the entire animal including the bones is eaten as a cure for 'painful urination' (*k'uš čušil*). |
| 25. *šberon* 'large tadpole' | AMPHIBIA: Ranidae (larva) | *špošil ʔobal* | These are eaten to treat 'cough' (*ʔobal*). |
| 26. (a) *k'intun* 'anole'<br><br>(b) *ʔohkoc* 'spiny lizard' | REPTILIA: Lacertilia: *Anolis* spp.<br>REPTILIA: Lacertilia: *Sceloporus* spp. | *špošil ma šʔok' niʔtik ta wayel* | Both of these lizards are alleged to be effective as a 'cure' for 'snoring' (*ʔok' niʔtik ta wayel*, lit. 'noses wail in sleeping'). The lizard is inserted in the offending nostril! |
| 27. *ʔečeh* 'basilisk lizard' | REPTILIA: Lacertilia: *Basiliscus vittatus* | *špošil nihkel* | The sufferer from 'malaria' (*nihkel*) must catch one of these swift lizards. It is then baked on the fire and eaten without peppers or tortillas (see also *ba* 'pocket gopher', No. 39). |
| 28. *ʔahaw čan* 'master snake' | REPTILIA: Ophidia: *Crotalus durissus*, *Pituophis lineaticollis* | n.a. | Both the rattlesnake and the local gopher snake are included here. The flesh is said to have medicinal value for an unspecified intestinal affliction. |
| 29. *caʔlos* 'Black Vulture' | AVES: Cathartidae: *Coragyps atratus* | *špošil nihkel*, *špošil siht'ubel* | Vultures are not normally considered edible. However the flesh is eaten in treating both 'malaria' (*nihkel*) and a serious disease called 'swelling' (*siht'ubel*). In the latter instance the afflicted person either |

(*continued*)

**Table 4.15** (*Continued*)

| Animal taxon | Scientific name | 'Medicine'/ 'treatment' name | Comments |
|---|---|---|---|
| | | | shoots the vulture where it is feeding on a carcass or buys one for 5 pesos (ca. U.S. $0.40). It is then cooked very thoroughly with lots of chili peppers. The patient drinks the broth and eats the flesh in the morning, then, carefully covered against any chill, goes to sleep before the house patio cross. Alternative cures use *tunim čih* 'domestic sheep' see No. 44, or certain parts of cattle (*wakaš*), see No. 45. |
| 30. *mut₂* 'domestic chicken' | AVES: Phasianidae: *Gallus gallus* | *špošil sikil winik sok ʔanc* *špošil ya stohk ʔalal* *špošil ya yicʼ yip* *špošil wahba* | A young male chicken (*čʼiom tat mut*) is eaten with lots of chili peppers and the body washed with the foam of the broth by a man who has failed to conceive children (*špošil sikil winik sok ʔanc*, lit. 'medicine of a cold [i.e., sterile] man and woman'). A larger rooster (*mamal tat mut*) is killed following child-birth. The new mother drinks the broth and the meat is divided between the curer and certain relatives. This is to 'warm' (*ya škʼišna*) the woman's stomach. Chicken eggs (*ton mut = tomut*) are eaten to aid delivery of a child (*špošil ya štohk ʔalal*). The first eggs of a growing hen (*sbabi ston sčʼiom ʔancil mut*) are eagerly sought by Tenejapanecos. They are eaten raw for the extra strength they are thought to give (*špošil ya yičʼ yip*). Egg whites (*sakil tomut*) are applied with salt to the face by one suffering from *wahba* ('acne'). |
| 31. *tulukʼ* 'domestic turkey' | AVES: *Meleagris gallopavo* | *špošil komel* | Turkeys are sacrificed as part of the cure for 'soul loss' (*komel*), see Chapter 5 for details. |
| 32. *periko* 'parrot' | AVES: Psittacidae in part | *špošil ya škʼopoh ʔalal* | To ensure that a child (*ʔalal*) will speak well (*ya škʼopoh*), one must borrow a parrot from a Ladino (Tenejapanecos do not keep parrots) and have the bird tear off pieces of a tortilla with its beak, which are then |

(*continued*)

**Table 4.15** (*Continued*)

| Animal taxon | Scientific name | 'Medicine'/ 'treatment' name | Comments |
|---|---|---|---|
| | | | fed to the child. See also **čikitin** 'cicada', No. 10. |
| 33. **c'unun** 'hummingbird' | AVES: Trochilidae | **špošil cu ʔat** | Hummingbird's eggs (**ston c'unun**) are cited as a cure for **cu ʔat** [lit. 'gourd' + 'penis']. The egg is broken over the swollen part. This cure suggests that the swollen part may be the scrotum rather than the penis. The informant concludes, "I don't know if this is effective, because there are a lot of 'gourd testicles' in Tenejapa." See also **c'uhkuton** 'salamander', No. 22. |
| 34. **hoh** 'raven' | AVES: *Corvus corax* | **špošil ma sakub holol** | Raven's blood (**šč'ič'el hoh**) is used to keep one's hair (**holol**) from turning white (**sakub**). One shoots the raven, then applies its blood to one's hair. The raven's blood is said to be dark red, its skin blackish, and its feathers, of course, are pure black. Thus as an old man one's hair remains dark. |
| 35. **coʔkoy** 'Band-backed Wren' | AVES: *Campylorhynchus zonatus* | **špošil čohk'** | This is one of several cures for warts (**čohk'**), see also **pošil nušel** 'ripple bug', No. 9, and **tuluk' čan** 'oil beetle, No. 12. This wren is also known as **meʔ čohk'** 'mother of the wart'. Thus one who is afflicted seeks out a flock of these birds; he dances and sings to them, "Put the disease on your leg, put the wart on your leg, **coʔkoyi coʔkoy**." Thus little by little the warts vanish. |
| 36. **ʔuč** 'opossum' | MAMMALIA: *Didelphis* spp. | **špošil ya štohk ʔalal** | The opossum's tail (**sne ʔuč**) is roasted, ground up, mixed with hot water, and drunk to ensure an easy delivery in childbirth (**ya štohk ʔalal**). A similar role is cited for chicken's eggs, see **mut₂** 'chicken', No. 30, and the horns of sheep or deer, see **tunim čih** 'sheep' and **teʔtikil čih** 'deer', No. 44. |
| | | **špošil ya sakub holol yuʔun** | The opossum's hair (**scocil ʔuč**) may cause ones hair to turn white like that of this animal. So if an opossum is caught in the log deadfall (**pehc'ul teʔ**), the person who picks it up |

(*continued*)

**Table 4.15** (*Continued*)

| Animal taxon | Scientific name | *'Medicine'/ 'treatment' name* | Comments |
|---|---|---|---|
| | | | must not touch his hair. If his head itches, he must wash his hand well with black ashes before he can safely scratch it. |
| 37. *soc'* 'bat' | MAMMALIA: Chiroptera | n.a. | Bat's blood (*šč'ič'el soc'*) is used to prevent the growth of a beard, which is considered unsightly. |
| 38. *mayil ti?bal* 'armadillo' | MAMMALIA: *Dasypus novemcinctus* | *špošil č'ič'* | The flesh is prescribed to cure 'dysentery' (*č'ič'*, lit. 'blood'). The flesh is considered to be *sik* 'cold', as is that of the pig (*čitam*), another cure for this illness, see No. 43. |
| 39. *ba* 'pocket gopher' | MAMMALIA: Geomyidae | *špošil siht'ubel špošil nihkel* | A soup made by cooking the flesh of a pocket gopher is drunk in treating 'swelling' (*siht'ubel*) and 'malaria' (*nihkel*), see also *pokok* 'toad', No. 23, *?ečeh* 'basilisk lizard', No. 27, and *ca?los* 'Black Vulture', No. 29. In addition, a woman may improve her tortilla-making skills by rubbing the belly of a pocket gopher. |
| 40. *c'i?* 'domestic dog' | MAMMALIA: *Canis familiaris* | *špošil c'isim* | Dead dogs (*čamen c'i?*) are placed on the nests of leaf-cutting ants (*c'isim*) in order to drive them out. |
| 41. *kohtom* 'coati' | MAMMALIA: *Nasua narica* | *špošil cacal* | The coati's penis (*yat kohtom*) is considered effective against impotence (*cacal*), see also *puy* 'snail', *yat naab* 'snail', and *k'ohčin te?* 'snail', No. 1. |
| 42. *pay* 'skunk' | MAMMALIA: Mephitinae | | One may kill a skunk and hang it up at the back of the house to protect the occupants against the ravages of serious epidemic diseases such as 'cough' (*?obal*), 'whooping cough' (*hik'hik' ?obal*), or measles (*suhtem čamel*). The odor of the skunk is believed to counteract the disease. |
| 43. *čitam* 'pig' | MAMMALIA: *Sus scrofa* | *špošil č'ič'* | The flesh is used to treat 'dysentery' (*č'ič'*, lit. 'blood'), see also *mayil ti?bal* 'armadillo', No. 38. |
| 44. (a) *te?tikil čih* 'deer' | MAMMALIA: Cervidae | *špošil ya štohk ?alal* | The horns (*šulub*) of deer or sheep are burnt, ground, mixed |
| (b) *tunim čih* 'sheep' | MAMMALIA: *Ovis aries* | *špošil ya štohk ?alal* | with hot water, and drunk to ease childbirth (*ya štohk ?alal*), |

(*continued*)

**Table 4.15** (*Continued*)

| Animal taxon | Scientific name | 'Medicine'/ 'treatment' name | Comments |
|---|---|---|---|
| | | *špošil siht'ubel* | see also *mut₂* 'chicken', No. 30, and *ʔuč* 'opossum', No. 36. The flesh of Chamula sheep (Tenejapanecos do not keep sheep), may be substituted for the flesh of the Black Vulture (*caʔlos*) in the treatment of 'swelling' (*siht'ubel*) (see No. 29). |
| 45. *wakaš* 'cattle' | MAMMALIA: *Bos taurus* | *špošil ʔip* *špošil hataw* *špošil ya smuk'ub yat winik yuʔun* | Cattle's blood (*č'ič'el wakaš*) is believed to strengthen (*ʔip*) a person as also does mule's blood (see No. 49). The gall bladder (*č'a wakaš*) is applied to heal a 'split' heel and sole of the foot (*hataw*). The horns (*šulub*) of young cattle (*č'in wakaš*) help make a boy's penis (*yat winik*) grow larger (*ya smuk'ub*). |
| 46. *búro* 'donkey' | MAMMALIA: *Equus asinus* | *špošil ya snit yat* | Hearing a male donkey cry (*ya šʔok' kelem búro*) is alleged to 'pull' (*ya snit*) a man's penis (*yat*), thus lengthening it. The female donkey's cry has the opposite effect. |
| 47. *kawáyu* 'horse/mule' | MAMMALIA: *Equus caballus, E. asinus × E. caballus* | *špošil howil wayel* | An aberrant mental condition called *howil wayel* [lit. 'rabid sleeping', or 'nightmare'] is treated as follows: the sufferer must seek out a group of these animals when they are 'bucking'? (*ya šbalbal cahka*). He must join with them and 'buck' as they do. He must do this several times until his 'madness' passes over to the animals. |
| | | *špošil hataw* | It is considered dangerous to step on the urine of horse or mule on the trail, as this is thought to cause 'splitting' of the foot (see *meʔ toyiw*, No. 16). |
| | | *špošil ʔip* | The young mule's blood (*č'ič'el č'iom múla*) is thought to strengthen a person. |
| | | *špošil ma šʔalah ʔanc yuʔun* | The female mule's hoof (*yehk'eč múla*), burnt, ground up, mixed with water, and drunk, is thought to prevent conception. A fern (*Ophioglossum* spp.) referred to as *yehk'eč múla* 'mule's hoof' is also used as a contraceptive [Berlin, Breedlove, and Raven 1974:371]. |

# CHAPTER 5

# The Fauna

## 1 Key to the Arrangement of the Chapter

Unique beginner, life-form, complex, and subcomplex headings include a descriptive title or Tzeltal name. The entries include a brief resume of the data that establish the existence of the category and a description of the organisms included by reference to scientific taxa. A type generic taxon is defined for some complexes (see Chapter 3, Section 7.2). Incidental information relevant to the category as a whole may be included as well.

Entries for generic and specific taxa include the Tzeltal name followed by a brief linguistic characterization, then a definition in terms of corresponding scientific taxa. For birds, the initial reference to a scientific taxon within a generic heading includes both English and Latin names (genus and species). (English names for birds are standard and thus capitalized. Other common names are not capitalized.) Subsequent references are in English. This convention is followed also with any scientific taxon for which a generally accepted English equivalent exists. Otherwise Latin names are cited in each reference to the taxon. The authors of Latin names are not cited. Latin names for suprageneric taxa are cited whenever useful to place a species name in a broader context. Since family names have a standard Latin suffix (-idae), as do subfamily names (-inae), no reference to their category level is made. Such additional Latin names immediately follow the species designation in a descending order, e.g., *Mecistogaster ornata* (suborder Zygoptera: Pseudostigmatidae). Only genus and species names are italicized. When no confusion is possible, the genus name is abbreviated to the initial letter in successive references to one or more species of a single genus.

A list of specimens is cited in conjunction with the scientific denotatum of a Tzeltal name whenever specimens have been so named by informants and identified scientifically. Such specimens are coded as follows: EH, author's collection number; CAS, California Academy of Sciences, San Francisco, California; EN, entomological collection, Division of Entomology, University of California, Berkeley, California; MVZ, Museum of Vertebrate Zoology, University of California, Berkeley, California. The type specific of a generic may be noted (see Chapter 3, Section 7.2).

Then follows a brief descriptive account of the organisms involved, their morphology, behavior, and distribution. Attributes of relevance to informants, as evidenced by etymologies of their own devising or native descriptions, are discussed. The following terms are used to indicate relative abundance for birds; all assume appropriate season and elevation.

| | |
|---|---|
| "abundant": | Large numbers are usually encountered. |
| "common": | Often encountered, not necessarily in large numbers. |
| "uncommon": | Encountered infrequently or irregularly. |
| "rare": | Encountered on but a few occasions. |
| "local": | Occurs in a very restricted area within the region; applied also to species restricted to a habitat type of limited distribution in the region. |

The abundance of species of nocturnal or secretive habits will tend to be underestimated. Since many other animals are rarely seen, though they may be abundant, the above terms are based in such cases on informants' statements or on relative frequency of capture.

The distinction between 'highland' and 'lowland' sectors of the *municipio* is referred to repeatedly. This distinction is fundamental in Tenejapan thought. In Tzeltal **sikil k'inal** 'cold country' refers to that part of the *municipio* above about 1800 m. **k'išin k'inal** 'hot country' refers to land below 1500 m. No basic term corresponding to the Spanish *tierra templada* 'temperate land' is used. However, land between 1500 and 1800 m elevation is sometimes characterized as **k'išin htebuk** 'a bit hot'. "Highland" and "lowland" are used here synonymously for 'cold country' and 'hot country' respectively. It should be noted that this is a local usage quite distinct from the usual Mexican Spanish usage, i.e., *tierra caliente* 'hot land' is below 800 m; *tierra templada* is that between 800 and 1600 m; and *tierra fría* 'cold land' lies above 1600 (Palerm 1967:28).

The occurrence of migratory birds is determined by the northern temperate seasonal cycle. Thus the terms summer, winter, spring, and fall should be understood in those terms. The tropical cycle of rainy season (June to December) and dry season (January to May) affects the behavior of some resident species.

All recorded alternate names are listed. The "primary name" is that used first and is used in all cross-indexing. This name is in most instances that most widely used by my sample of informants. If no clearly dominant usage is apparent, I have applied the following ordered criteria to determine the primary name. First, preference is given to an established form (i.e., not idiosyncratic) that is morphologically simple. The scale is that of Berlin, Breedlove, and Raven (1973), from simple to complex: (a) unanalyzable primary lexemes, (b) unproductive primary lexemes, (c) productive primary lexemes, (d) secondary lexemes, (e) polylexemic forms. For example, the giant toad (*Bufo marinus*) may be called either **henhen** or **muk'ul pokok** 'large toad'. Preference is given to the first form, and thus this taxon is treated as a generic rather than as a specific subdivision of the generic **pokok**. In this case **henhen** is also clearly the preferred form. Among alternative terms of equal complexity, preference is given to that term

deemed most appropriately descriptive by the author or according to some other essentially arbitrary criterion. The primary names are not assumed to have any special cognitive status in Tenejapan thought. If such is the case, however, that fact will be noted, e.g., **šulem** (bird, vulture).

Secondary names include the following types (see Chapter 2, Section 9):

1. **Variants** are semantically equivalent forms that differ only in phonemic detail (e.g., the presence or absence of an affix), alternate onomatopoetic renditions, or secondary lexemes that differ only in the attributive used.
2. **Synonyms** are semantically equivalent forms that are etymologically distinct, e.g., the domestic cat (*Felis cattus*) may be known as **šawin**, **čoh**, or **mis**. True synonyms are alternate forms known by a single speaker, as in the previous example. Synonyms may also exist in complementary distribution, e.g., the highland and lowland names for **ʔus ʔakoʔ** (wasp). Variants are typically in complementary distribution.
3. **Alternate classifications** are often implied by alternate nomenclatural usages, as in the case of the giant toad cited earlier (see **henhen**/frog-toad). Such cases are discussed in detail.

The phrase "also known as" is used to indicate both variants and synonyms. The Tzeltal phrase **kol pahaluk sok** 'almost the same as' is often used by informants to indicate that a particular organism is related to some named category. Many unfamiliar forms are so treated. This phrase is abbreviated **kps**.

Additional data of ethnographic interest may be included in the description of a taxon. Edibility is treated differently, depending on the type of animal. Most birds are considered edible, thus the few exceptions are noted. Most snakes, on the other hand, are considered to be inedible. Thus the few exceptions noted refer to edibility. This information may be noted only in the life-form or complex heading if a general pattern exists.

Most edible forms are classified by Tenejapanecos as either *k'išin* 'hot' or **sikil** 'cold'. This distinction, which has nothing to do with heat, is widespread throughout Latin America. It is believed to be derived from the Hippocratic concept of body humors (Adams and Rubel 1967:342), though a comparable preconquest distinction may have existed (Redfield and Villa Rojas 1934: 372). Health consists in a certain balance of 'hot' and 'cold' in the body. Many pathological conditions are attributed to specific imbalances of these qualities. If one's body is too 'hot', 'cold' foods are prescribed and vice versa. It is not clear to what extent this distinction is significant in **tenehapa** today, however informants can readily classify most foods. Some disagreement does exist, and not all informants can classify all food products. In particular, certain edible insect larvae were left unclassified by SMZ and JGG. Classification may also depend on mode of preparation. I have not yet been able to determine if perceptual attributes are relevant to this distinction.

The term "medicine" or "medicinal use" is used in a specialized sense, i.e., as a gloss of the Tzeltal term **pošil** (see Chapter 4, Section 5). Though some cited 'medicinal' applications may in fact have the desired physiological effect (e.g., the use of a secretion of a meloid beetle to cure warts, see **tuluk'čan**/beetle-bug), other cures could be classified as sympathetic magic (e.g., the use of antlion larvae to make a woman's breast swell, see **butbut ʔit čan**).

English and Latin names for birds follow Roger T. Peterson and Edward L. Chalif 1973: *A Field Guide to Mexican Birds*, except as amended by the American Ornithologists' Union (1973). English and Latin names for mammals follow E. Raymond Hall and Keith R. Kelson 1959: *The Mammals of North America*, unless otherwise noted. Latin names for reptiles follow Miguel Alvarez del Toro 1973: *Los Reptiles de Chiapas*, except for revisions suggested by Joseph Copp (personal communication). Amphibian nomenclature follows L. C. Stuart 1963: *A Checklist of the Herpetofauna of Guatemala*, whenever possible. The basic source for higher order insect taxa is Donald J. Borror and Richard E. White 1970: *A Field Guide to the Insects of America North of Mexico*. Noninsect invertebrate groups follow Richard A. Pimentel 1967: *Invertebrate Identification Manual*. Departures from these sources and invertebrate names below the family level are as cited by the specialists who identified each group of specimens (see Acknowledgments). Butterfly (Lepidoptera: Papilionoidea) families and genera follow H. L. Lewis 1973: *Butterflies of the World*, which was used by the author to identify specimens.

The lineal ordering of taxa is constrained by the following ordered considerations. First, all hierarchical relationships are maintained such that all taxa immediately included in a superordinate taxon immediately follow that taxon. This is true at all taxonomic levels. Second, whenever possible, adjacent taxa are those perceived to resemble one another most closely (i.e., most likely to be considered **shoyetik** 'associates'). Since these paired comparisons are generally based on multiple attributes, the linear format does not reflect the full complexity of these relationships.

These cognitive constraints, however, do not fully determine the order. To that extent the order is arbitrary from the Tenejapan point of view. Biosystematic considerations were applied to determine fully the sequence, i.e., the lineal ordering of the scientific taxa used to define the Tzeltal taxa is maintained whenever cognitive considerations provide no clue. I do not claim that the ordering applied is necessarily the best, given the limits of the data, but it does relatively little violence to the cognitively relevant data as I interpret them.

A few examples will illustrate the ordering technique. The 110 generic taxa included in the life form **mut**$_1$ 'bird' immediately follow the life-form heading. Succeeding generic taxa are not included in that life form. The five generic taxa included in the covert waterbird complex immediately follow that heading. However, the fact that the waterbird complex precedes the other bird taxa is cognitively arbitrary. It simply provides the closest fit to the biosystematic ordering of birds in which grebes (Podicipedidae, *špeč'ul ha?* in part) and ducks (Anatidae, *peč'* and *špeč'ul ha?* in part) precede most other groups of birds. *peya?* (Brown Jay, *Psilo-rhinus morio*) immediately follows **hohkot** (Plain Chachalaca, *Ortalis vetula*) because it is considered **shoy** 'associate' by several informants. This order is applied despite the fact that they are not included in a complex and despite the fact that ornithologists place them in distinct orders.

## 2  The *tenehapa* Tzeltal Animal Taxa

## UNIQUE BEGINNER: *čanbalam*₁ 'ANIMAL'

The taxon *čanbalam*₁ 'animal' may be defined as all known species of the Kingdom ANIMALIA with the exception of *Homo sapiens*. The following phyla are included here on the basis of specimens: PLATYHELMINTHES (see *lukum*, *?ohcel*), ASCHELMINTHES (see *lukum*; *cocil holol čan*), MOLLUSCA (see *nap'ak*; 'snail' complex), ANNELIDA (see *lukum*; *?ohcel*), ARTHROPODA, and CHORDATA. The 17 remaining phyla cited by Pimentel (1967) include mainly marine organisms. Some of the remaining phyla (e.g., COELENTERATA) may be represented in the region, however I neither observed nor collected any such specimens. Thus the question of their inclusion remains moot. No plant organisms or inanimate objects were included.

The name *čanbalam* is morphologically complex. *balam* is the name applied to the jaguar (*Felis onca*), while *čan* may be interpreted in several ways. Two, perhaps three, polysemous uses of the term *čan* are distinguished. *čan*₁ is the name applied to the 'snake' complex. *čan*₂, sometimes distinguished as *č'uhč'ul čan* 'small (pl.) bug', refers to a residual category of beetles. In addition, practically any animal may be referred to in certain contexts as *čan*, e.g., *čanul ha?*₁ names a complex that includes several orders of aquatic insects, while *čanul ha?*₂ is occasionally used to refer to certain types of waterbirds. *k'alel čan* is a species of lizard and is not considered to be a snake (i.e., *čan*₁). *cocil holol čan* refers to a worm of the phylum ASCHELMINTHES. *čanul ?ako?*, *čanul ?aha čab*, etc., are variant forms of names for a type of wasp and the honey bee respectively. Thus the morpheme *čan* is distributed among names for a wide variety of animals. Furthermore, the form *ščanul* [pp + *čan* + rs] can be glossed as 'its body' in reference to a variety of animals.

*čanbalam* structurally resembles the form *te?ak'* [lit. 'tree-vine'] used to name the unique beginner 'plant' by some Tenejapan informants (Berlin 1972:80). My assistant SMZ suggested an alternative etymology, that *čan-* is the root of the number four and refers to the fact that *čanbalam* have four legs. However, no precedent for such a morphological construction is known from Tzeltal. Number stems in Tzeltal are bound morphemes and must have a numeral classifier suffixed. *balam* is not such a suffix (see Berlin 1968). It appears that SMZ created a rationale to support his preference for a more restricted application of the term *čanbalam* (see *čanbalam*₂).

Two polysemous uses of the term *čanbalam* are cited here, i.e., *čanbalam*₁ 'animal' and *čanbalam*₂ 'mammal'. They are not clearly distinguished by informants. Rather, the term refers unambiguously to a core designatum, all mammals—with the exception of human beings, bats, and armadillos—about which all informants agree, but it may be extended to varying degrees up to and including all animals except *Homo sapiens.* Twenty-three informants were surveyed on this point with the following distribution of included forms resulting:

core

| | | | |
|---|---|---|---|
| mammals 23/23 | all vertebrates | 16/23 |
| plus legged | plus certain | |
| herptiles 21/23 | invertebrates | 13/23 |
| plus snakes 18/23 | | |
| | all animals | |
| plus birds 17/23 | except man | 8/23 |

I contend that a distinct polysemous use does not exist for each opinion expressed. Rather, some types of animals are simply more **typical** of *čanbalam* than are others. The cut-off point in a given case will depend on the momentary perception of the balance between the core and the extended range of the term. For simplicity's sake I define these poles as two distinct polysemous taxa.

Given the ambiguity associated with this term, what other evidence exists that the unique beginner is recognized? First, the transitive verb *-ti?* 'eat meat' is used in reference to eating any and all kinds of edible animal tissue (Berlin 1967). It is also used to refer to the eating of mushrooms and chili peppers. However, none of the informants

surveyed considered mushrooms (*t'onkos, čehčew,* etc.) or chili peppers (*?ič*) to be kinds of *čanbalam.* Second, the numeral classifier *-koht* is used for counting all animals with the sole exception of human beings, for which the classifier *-tul* is appropriate. Third, a number of body-part terms may be applied to a wide variety of animals. However, many of these terms may also be used to name human body parts, plant parts, and parts of inanimate objects, e.g., *ni?* 'nose' is applied to people's noses, birds' beaks, tree tops, and roof tops. Finally, in response to the question *bi yu?un la sbilin čanbalam* 'Why is it called animal?', I received the following definition from JGG. "They are called animals because they don't speak like people, and because they live in the forest; they have no souls." This response focuses on the distinction between animals and men. Plants (*te?ak'*) are distinguished by the fact that they 'don't move' (*ma šnihik*) (Berlin, Breedlove, and Raven 1974:30).

The evidence cited is sufficient to establish the existence of a concept 'animal' as defined above. The question remains as to the logical status of the concept, i.e., is it inductive or deductive? As argued earlier (Chapter 3, Section 7.4), it appears to be constructed by the prior application of induction modified by a deductive, or a priori, rule. The deductive rule excludes human beings because they have 'souls' (*č'ulel*).

## Life Form: *mut*₁ 'Bird'

This taxon includes all birds species (class AVES) known to Tenejapanecos. Nothing else is included. The following definition was provided by SMZ in response to the question, *bi yu?un la sbilin mut* 'Why is it called bird?' "They are called birds because they have feathers, two wings, two legs, and they fly on their two wings." Since Tenejapanecos have no experience of flightless birds, it is difficult to determine if the category is inductive or deductive. The explicit rule stated by

SMZ unambiguously delimits the category. However there is no evidence that this category is not also defined by a configurational feature. The point is moot. Bats (*soc'*) "fly on two wings" but lack feathers. All informants but one denied that *soc'* 'bat' is a kind of *mut.*

The polysemous term *mut*₂ 'chicken' is clearly distinguished by all informants. In potentially ambiguous contexts the life form may be labeled *te?tikil mut* ['forest' + 'bird']. Some informants express uncertainty about the propriety of including the Turkey Vulture (*šulem*/vulture) and certain other large, distinctive bird taxa in the life form. No informant denies the fact that **mut** can be applied to all birds, however this hesitation indicates an element of ambiguity comparable to that in the application of *čanbalam*. This same ambiguity occurs in English as well. If asked outright if any particular kind of bird is a bird, the response will be affirmative. Yet English speakers often distinguish eagles, swans, and vultures from the mass of "real birds."

With the exception of 'birds of evil omen' (*hlabtawaneh mut*), hummingbirds (*c'unun*), which are 'messengers' of the gods, and vultures, all birds are edible. One special trapping technique for capturing birds was recorded (see Chapter 4, Section 4). Domestic turkeys (*tuluk'*/turkey) and chickens (*mut₂*) are important in ritual and in the diet.

## WATERBIRD COMPLEX
(See Figure 5.1)

The following taxa are considered *shoyetik* 'associates' [< tv **-hoy** 'to accompany'] by

SMZ, JGG, and AKC : *peč'* and *peč' ul ha?* grouped by AGM, and *c'u? lukum*, *me? c'ahel*, and *hti? čay*, grouped by AMT (see Figure 5.1). None are commonly encountered, because of the scarcity of suitable habitat in the *municipio*, though many species occur sporadically at San Cristóbal and Aguacatenango. Examples of *peč'ul ha?*, *c'u? lukum*, and *me? c'ahel* may breed in the *colonia* of *banabil*, Tenejapa. The general term *čanul ha?₂* 'water critter' is sometimes used to refer to this complex or a residual subset not otherwise named. A distinctly different use, *čanul ha?₁* refers to certain aquatic invertebrates.

*peč'* [UN] (see Figure 5.2): Domestic forms of the Mallard (*Anas platyrhynchos*) and Muscovy (*Cairina moschata*)

Since species of this family freely hybridize in captivity, it is not possible to define many individuals specifically. Of these forms only the Muscovy breeds in Chiapas, and it may have been the original referent of the term. Wild mallards winter infrequently to Chiapas and beyond. A domestic goose (*Anser* sp.)

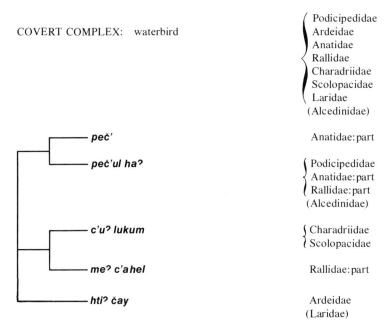

Figure 5.1  The waterbird complex.

Figure 5.2  *peč'* domestic duck: (a) *tat peč'* 'male duck'; (b) *me? peč'* 'female duck'. [Drawings by AMT.]

was observed on one occasion and was assigned to this category. The few wild species of the Anatidae observed at Aguacatenango were assigned to the following category, *peč'ul ha?*.

*peč'* is commonly though optionally subdivided into varietal taxa by reference to the attributes of color, pattern, and size as follows:

*muk'ul peč'* 'large duck'. This varietal includes domestic ducks of large size of both Muscovy and mallard stock. The goose mentioned earlier was also called *muk'ul peč'*.

*č'in peč'* 'small duck'. One informant (SMZ) asserted that this varietal is also white, referring in particular to an albino mallard breed.

*sakil peč'* 'white duck': Albino forms.

*yašal peč'* 'green duck': One informant (AGM) restricted this varietal to normal plumage Muscovy breeds, also modified as *muk'ul yašal peč'* 'big green duck'.

*bašil peč'* 'mottled duck': One informant, in reference to a female domestic mallard.

*?ihk'al peč'* 'black duck' and *k'anal peč'* 'yellow duck' were also elicited, though the referents were not determined.

Varietal distinctions within this category

are of low salience perhaps due to the fact that Tenejapanecos rarely keep waterfowl. Sex distinctions may be recognized. The flesh is considered edible and categorized as *sikil* 'cold'.

*peč'ul ha?* ['duck' + rs + 'water']: Grebes (Podicipedidae), wild ducks (Anatidae), and the American Coot, *Fulica americana* (Rallidae)

The focal referent is the Least Grebe (*Podiceps dominicus*) (see Figure 5.3), the only

Figure 5.3  *peč'ul ha?* Least Grebe (*Podiceps dominicus*). [From Emmet Reid Blake, *Birds of Mexico: A Guide for Field Identification*. Copyright 1953 by The University of Chicago Press.]

species known to breed in the immediate environs of Tenejapa (young observed at San Cristóbal, June 1971; possibly breeds in **banabil**, Tenejapa). That the Least Grebe is the type species is further indicated by the fact that one informant (MMH) identified it by call. The calls of the various species included in the range of this term are quite distinct. The following species constitute the full observed range of denotata:

> Least Grebe, *Podiceps dominicus* (Podicipedidae), breeds San Cristóbal.
>
> Pied-billed Grebe, *Podilymbus podiceps* (Podicipedidae), breeds Aguacatenango.
>
> Black-bellied Tree-Duck, *Dendrocygna autumnalis* (Anatidae), breeds lowland Chiapas.
>
> Blue-winged Teal (female), *Anas discors* (Anatidae), winter visitor.
>
> Ruddy Duck, *Oxyura jamaicensis* (Anatidae), breeds Chiapas.
>
> American Coot, *Fulica americana* (Rallidae), breeds Chiapas.

Two other species observed at a distance were considered **kps peč'ul ha?** 'almost the same as **peč'ul ha?**':

> Northern Pintail, *Anas acuta* (Anatidae), winter visitor.
>
> American Wigeon, *A. americana* (Anatidae), winter visitor.

Using Berlin's distinction between the core referent of a term and its *extended range*, **peč'ul ha?** is properly equivalent to the locally breeding Least Grebe, while other grebes, all wild ducks, and the coot are included in the extended range of the species.

One informant called the Belted Kingfisher, *Ceryle alcyon* (Alcedinidae), **peč'**. The several species of kingfishers are unfamiliar to most Tenejapanecos. Three species (*Ceryle torquata, C. alcyon, Chloroceryle amazona*) observed with SMZ and JGG were called **hcak čay** 'fish catcher', after long thought and admission of their unfamiliarity, in an effort to distinguish them from the heron category, **hti? čay** 'fish eater'. The first usage, lacking even the distinction between **peč'** proper and **peč'ul ha?**, which is almost universal, indicates that **peč'** may occasionally be used to refer to waterbirds in general.

No subcategories of **peč'ul ha?** are consistently recognized though the taxon is perceived as heterogeneous.

A number of lexical variants and synonyms are widely recognized in naming this taxon as below:

> **peč'ul ha?** may be abbreviated to **peč' ha?**. Both variants may be modified by prefixing **š-** as follows **špeč'ul ha?, špeč' ha?**.
>
> **č'ul me?tik** 'holy mother' or **hala me?tik** 'protecting mother' may be substituted in place of **ha?**. Both refer to the lake in the *colonia* of **banabil** and the legend associated with that lake.* Thus we have **peč' č'ul me?tik** or **špeč' č'ul me?tik** and **peč' hala me?tik** or **špeč' hala me?tik**.
>
> **yalak'** [pp + 'domestic animal'] may be substituted for **peč'** or **špeč'**.

No particular distributional pattern is evident with respect to these variants; they coexist within the competence of most individuals.

**c'u? lukum** 'Worm Sucker' (see Figure 5.4a): Shorebirds (suborder Charadrii)

The focal species is the Killdeer (*Charadrius vociferus*), a fairly common winter visitor in the region, recognizable by call. Though no shorebirds were observed in Tenejapa, I have seen Killdeer near the Tenejapa border at Las Ollas, Chamula, and rather regularly at San Cristóbal. Other shorebirds observed at San Cristóbal and Aguacatenango that were assigned to the extended range of this category include the following:

> Spotted Sandpiper, *Actitis macularia*.
>
> Solitary Sandpiper, *Tringa solitaria*.

---

*See the footnote on p. 97.

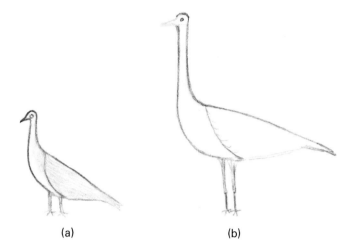

**Figure 5.4** (a) *c'uʔ lukum* 'shore-bird'; (b) *htiʔ čay* Great Egret (*Egretta alba*). [Drawings by AMT.]

(a)

(b)

Least Sandpiper, *Calidris minutilla*.

Pectoral Sandpiper, *C. melanotos*.

Several other shorebird species might also occur in similar habitat, in particular the Semipalmated Plover (*Charadrius semipalmatus*), and are probably referable to this category. Though these species do not eat worms, their feeding habits suggest the name.

One informant (AGM) called the Pectoral Sandpiper *čanul haʔ* 'water critter', which may be synonymous usage, a general term for this and certain related categories (see the waterbird complex), or a more specific usage to contrast with *c'uʔ lukum* proper, i.e., the Killdeer. Too few instances were observed to define this term clearly as coordinate with other waterbird terms.

A second informant (SMZ) called the Spotted Sandpiper *htiʔ čanul haʔ* 'waterbug eater'. Yet this same informant used the term *c'uʔ lukum* for the same species on other occasions. Since shorebirds are sporadically encountered, because of habitat restrictions, the heterogeneity of the category is inconsistently recognized nomenclaturally. The category *c'uʔ lukum* is recognized as heterogeneous.

The primary name may be reduplicated as *c'uʔc'uʔ lukum*. This suggests an alternate etymology, since the call is described as *c'uʔ c'uʔ c'uʔ*.

A geographical variant recorded in the *paraje* of **pahalton** is **meʔ k'in haʔal** 'mother of the winter rains', accurately accounts for the seasonality of the distribution of these birds. However **meʔ k'in haʔal** (see the siskin–seedeater complex) is usually applied to species of siskin, *Spinus* spp. (Fringillidae). In **pahalton** such birds are known instead as **bahk'al mut** 'groups-of-four-hundred birds'.

**meʔ c'ahel** 'mother of the marsh': Identification not determined, but, as this type is described as hiding in marsh vegetation, perhaps rails (Rallidae in part)

The Virginia Rail (*Rallus limicola*) is known to breed at San Cristóbal (L. Binford personal communication), and the Sora (*Porzana carolina*) was observed in the same locality. Though my assistant (SMZ) was familiar with this taxon only by name, other informants clearly distinguished it from other taxa of this complex, in particular by choice of habitat.

A high country variant is **meʔ ʔahč'al** 'mother of mud' cognate with the Zinacantan-Tzotzil term applied to the Killdeer (Laughlin n.d.). It is also known as **čanul c'ahel** 'critter of the marsh' and **mutil c'ahel** 'bird of the marsh'.

**htiʔ čay** 'fish eater': Herons (family Ardeidae)

The focal species is the Great Egret (*Egretta alba*) since it is typically described as 'white' and illustrated (by AMT; see Figure 5.4b) as having a yellow bill. These specifications eliminate other local species. The taxon also properly includes the following species observed in the region with informants:

Great Blue Heron, *Ardea herodias*.
Green Heron, *Butorides virescens*.
Little Blue Heron, *Florida caerulea*.
Snowy Egret, *Egretta thula*.

Several additional species occur in Chiapas and are probably attributable to the extended range of this taxon. The Black-crowned Night-Heron (*Nycticorax nycticorax*) observed with SMZ and JGG in Oakland, California, was excluded from the category and assigned, by virtue of its call, to the taxon **wáko mut**, a term that may refer to the Laughing Falcon (*Herpetotheres cachinnans*, see "Hypothetical List: Birds." No ibises, spoonbills (Threskiornithidae), or bitterns (Ardeidae, in part) were observed. It seems safe to conclude that Tenejapanecos are unfamiliar with these related species.

**hti? čay** is perceived as heterogeneous and is subdivided optionally by the recognition of varietals based on color, as follows:

**sakil hti? čay** 'white heron': Great Egret, Snowy Egret.

**yašal hti? čay** 'green–blue–grey heron': Great Blue Heron, Green Heron, Little Blue Heron (adult).

The following alternate terms were recorded:

**hcak čay** 'fish eater': Apparently idiosyncratic; used to distinguish kingfishers from herons by SMZ and JGG. Other informants (e.g., AGM) asserted that the terms are synonymous.

**nahtil nuk' mut** 'long-necked bird'.

**muk'ul čanul ha?** 'large-water critter'.

**čanul nabil** 'critter of the lake'.

**hti? peskáro** 'eater of fish' [ < Sp *pescado* 'fish']. **peskáro** is used in Tzeltal to refer to a vague, broadly inclusive subcategory of the complex **čay** 'fish'. One informant

(SMZ) applied this term to the Laughing Gull, *Larus atricilla* (Laridae), encountered once at Aguacatenango, stressing the uniqueness of the bird. His usage is apparently idiosyncratic as he admitted never having seen the bird before. Furthermore, we observed flocks of terns (*Sterna forsteri*, *Thalasseus elegans*, both also Laridae) at Salina Cruz, Oaxaca. These he called **kps hti? čay**. Birds of the Laridae, probably rarely seen by Tenejapanecos, are best considered an unnamed grouping related to the herons.

**kársa** [ < Sp *garza* 'heron']. This Spanish loan is used synonymously.

**yaš ?ičil** 'green pepper' is also cited as a synonym. A similar term is used to refer to certain species of bees (see **šyaš ?ič**/bee). Its usage in this context is inexplicable.

VULTURE COMPLEX (See Figure 5.5)

This complex is clearly recognized though not named. It includes two common and one rare species. One informant used the term **hos** to refer to the two common species, a potential general term for the complex. **hos** is commonly encountered in several dialects of Tzeltal and Tzotzil in reference to the Black Vulture and is reconstructed as the proto-Mayan term for that category (Kaufman 1964). It is considered a humorous synonym in Tenejapan Tzeltal for either of the two common species. Vultures are protected, i.e., according to SMZ the *municipio* officials punish those who kill such animals, since they play an essential role as scavengers. All three taxa of this complex are homogeneous. The complex includes all local species of the Cathartidae.

**?usel** [ < ?us 'fly'?]: King Vulture *Sarcoramphus papa* (see Figure 5.6)

This species is rare in southern Mexico and was not observed. However, the name is rather widely known, and the identity is inferred from verbal descriptions, i.e., a large, white-winged relative of the common

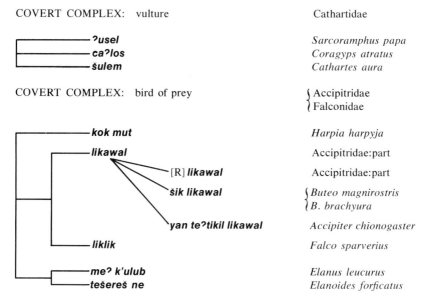

COVERT COMPLEX:    vulture                                Cathartidae

*?usel*                              *Sarcoramphus papa*
*ca?los*                             *Coragyps atratus*
*šulem*                              *Cathartes aura*

COVERT COMPLEX:    bird of prey                    { Accipitridae
                                                   { Falconidae

*kok mut*                            *Harpia harpyja*

*likawal*                            Accipitridae:part

[R] *likawal*                        Accipitridae:part

*šik likawal*                        { *Buteo magnirostris*
                                     { *B. brachyura*

*yan te?tikil likawal*               *Accipiter chionogaster*

*liklik*                             *Falco sparverius*

*me? k'ulub*                         *Elanus leucurus*
*tešereš ne*                         *Elanoides forficatus*

**Figure 5.5**    The vulture and bird of prey complexes.

**Figure 5.6** *?usel* King Vulture (*Sarcoramphus papa*). [From Emmet Reid Blake, *Birds of Mexico: A Guide for Field Identification*. Copyright 1953 by The University of Chicago Press.]

species of vulture. It is also known as **sbankil ca?los** 'Black Vulture's elder brother' and **k'ahk'al mut**, 'fierce bird', a term applied to the other vulture species as well.

**ca?los** [ < **ca?al** 'excrement' + **hos** 'Black Vulture' (archaic) ]: The Black Vulture (*Coragyps atratus*) (see Figure 5.7a)

This species is less widespread than the following one, but it is common around towns and throughout the countryside below 2300 m. **macab** informants (at 2400 m.) assert that it does not occur in that *paraje*. **ca?los** is eaten (the meat is first dried and powdered) as a cure for **nihkel**, a serious disease sometimes glossed as 'malaria', as well as for **siht'ubel** 'swelling'. Vulture flesh is not otherwise considered edible.

Many synonyms are in use, as follows:

**?ihk'al mut** 'black bird'.

**?ihk'al šulem** 'black Turkey Vulture'. This usage demonstrates the close relationship recognized between this and the following category. In Zinacantan Tzotzil the two common species of vultures are treated as subclasses of the cognate **šulem** (see fol-

(a)                                    (b)

**Figure 5.7**   (a) *ca?los* Black Vulture (*Coragyps atratus*); (b) *šulem* Turkey Vulture (*Cathartes aura*). [Drawings by AMT.]

lowing category). The usage is occasionally recorded in Tenejapa.

***k'ahk'al mut*** 'fierce bird', ***k'ahk'al šulem*** 'fierce Turkey Vulture'.

***sak šik' mut*** 'white-wing bird', ***sak šik' šulem*** 'white-wing Turkey Vulture', presumably referring to the white primary bases, a distinguishing feature of this species.

***sak sba šik'*** 'white wing tip', as above.

***hos***, see word derivation of the taxon.

***human*** or ***homen***, derivation uncertain.

***pošil nihkel*** 'malaria medicine', see opening paragraph of this category.

***šulem*** [UN]: Turkey Vulture (*Cathartes aura*) (see Figure 5.7b)

This species is common throughout Tenejapa. No medicinal use is recorded, though this taxon figures in a favorite folk tale. In that tale a lazy man, envious of the Turkey Vulture's easy life (i.e., scavenging), trades places with the vulture. The vulture instructs the man to follow clouds of smoke to locate his food. The man attempts this and is destroyed by fire. The vulture, despite his offensive odor, eventually wins acceptance as husband to the man's wife by dint of diligent labor in the man's fields (Berlin 1962b).

The recognition of the vulture's essential ecological role as scavenger, as noted earlier and alluded to in the story, demonstrates that Tenejapanecos are aware of the value of otherwise "useless" species.

The following synonyms were recorded:

***?ihk'al mut*** 'black bird', ***?ihk'al šulem*** 'black Turkey Vulture'. These synonyms are applied rather indiscriminately, though rarely, to this or the preceding taxon.

***cahal šulem*** 'red Turkey Vulture', referring to the red head of this species.

***cah shol šulem*** 'red-headed Turkey Vulture'.

***human***, see previous taxon.

***hos***, see previous taxon.

***kičan***, ***kičantik*** 'my mother's brother', a humorous usage.

***niwak kawílto*** 'great *cabildo*' [< Sp *cabildo* 'town hall, council'], also humorous.

In the case of ***ca?los*** and ***šulem***, the synonyms recorded are decidedly secondary, never replacing the primary name.

## BIRD OF PREY COMPLEX

This complex is not named but is defined by the statements ***kol pahaluk sok likawal*** 'almost the same as ***likawal***' or ***shoy sba sok likawal*** 'associate of ***likawal***'. ***likawal*** is the type generic and may be utilized as part of the name of some related taxa (see ***kok mut, lik lik***, and ***tešereš ne***). All locally recorded species of the Accipitridae and Falconidae are included here.

***kok mut*** [UN + 'bird']: Harpy Eagle, *Harpia harpyja* (Accipitridae) (see Figure 5.8a)

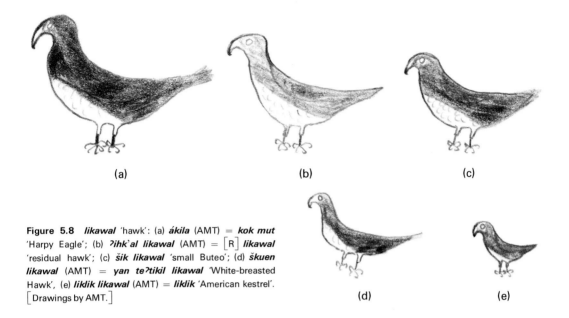

Figure 5.8 *likawal* 'hawk': (a) *ákila* (AMT) = *kok mut* 'Harpy Eagle'; (b) *ʔihkʼal likawal* (AMT) = [R] *likawal* 'residual hawk'; (c) *šik likawal* 'small Buteo'; (d) *škuen likawal* (AMT) = *yan teʔtikil likawal* 'White-breasted Hawk', (e) *liklik likawal* (AMT) = *liklik* 'American kestrel'. [Drawings by AMT.]

This huge and powerful bird of prey is very rare in virgin forest regions of southern Mexico. A speciman caged at the Tuxtla Gutiérrez zoo was so named by several informants. The taxon is widely recognized, though few Tenejapanecos claim to have actually seen the bird in the wild. It is known by hearsay as a huge hawklike bird. It is also known as *meʔ takʼin* 'mother of gold', referring to its role in legend. If one prays on certain mountains, this bird may bring money to the supplicant. A similar legend recorded from Zinacantan attributes this role to the King Vulture (Acheson 1966).

Possible synonyms include:

*mamal likawal* 'grandfather hawk'. *mamal* is often used to indicate exceptional size.

*kašlan likawal* 'Ladino hawk'. This term was recorded by Berlin as equivalent to Spanish *águila* or eagle.

*ʔákila* [< Sp *águila* 'eagle'] is also listed by some informants. Others aver, however, that *ʔákila* and *kok mut* are not the same. *ʔákila*, they say, is the bird pictured on the Mexican flag, presumably the Golden Eagle, *Aquila chrysaetos* (Accipitridae), *águila* to the Mexicans though not known south of central Mexico. This exemplifies

the difficulties involved in utilizing contact language glosses as data.

*likawal* [< tv -*lik* 'raise up', as a hawk with its prey?] 'hawk'

A residual category that includes all species of the Accipitridae and Falconidae not otherwise isolated as named taxa. All are said to prey on domestic fowl. The type species is the ubiquitous though uncommon Red-tailed Hawk, *Buteo jamaicensis* (Accipitridae). Two inductive subtypes are clearly distinguished from the residual core. The situation is complicated by the fact that the many species of hawks and falcons resident or transient in the region are rarely encountered. Furthermore, hawks and falcons are difficult to identify due to polymorphism within many species. Immature and adult plumages as well as color phases are distributed with no apparent geographical consistency. Notable sexual dimorphism occurs in a few species.

The four species recorded within Tenejapa were classified as follows:

a. [R] *likawal* (see Figure 5.8b): Within this residual, color attributives are commonly and literally applied. *cahal likawal* 'red hawk' was applied several times to Red-tailed Hawks, *Buteo jamaicensis* (Accipitridae). This large hawk is more common above 1800 m. However, a dark phase bird was labeled *ʔihkʼal likawal* 'black hawk'.

The following terms were also used for Red-tailed Hawks: *kʼanal likawal* 'yellow hawk' and *mukʼul likawal* 'large hawk'. *yašal likawal* 'grey hawk' was applied to an immature Red-tailed Hawk in company with adult hawks. The adults were called *cahal likawal*. The immature Red-tailed Hawk is heavily streaked below and lacks the red tail to which the term *cahal* of *cahal likawal* apparently refers. *ʔošom* [UN] is sometimes considered synonymous with the generic and replaces that term in other dialects (cf. Hopkins 1970), while *ʔošom likawal* may be used to label this subdivision of *likawal*.

*ʔihkʼal likawal* 'black hawk' could refer to the Zone-tailed Hawk (*Buteo albonotatus*), the Great Black Hawk (*Buteogallus urubitinga*), the Common Black Hawk (*B. anthracinus*), or perhaps the Solitary Eagle (*Harpyhaliaetus solitarius*), all of the Accipitridae. None were observed. As noted earlier, this term was applied once to a dark phase of the Red-tailed Hawk, which might prove to be the most common referent of the term.

*sakil likawal* 'white hawk' might apply to the White-tailed Hawk (*Buteo albicaudatus*), which I observed once near Tuxtla Gutiérrez, or to the White Hawk (*Leucopternis albicollis*), which also occurs in Chiapas. Both are of the Accipitridae. *tantan likawal* ['ash' redup + 'hawk'] is a synonym referring to the plumage color.

b. *šik likawal* 'grizzled hawk': The Roadside Hawk, *Buteo magnirostris* (Accipitridae) (see Figures 5.8c, 5.9) and the Short-tailed Hawk (*B. brachyurus*). Both are small buteos. The first is common near Ocosingo and widespread below 1200 m. The second is rare and locally distributed in Mexico. It is resident in Tenejapa as I observed it on several occasions in *mahosikʼ* and *čʼištontik*. *šik* is a dialectal synonym of *likawal*, replacing it in Cancuc

Figure 5.9 *šik likawal* Roadside Hawk (*Buteo magnirostris*). [From Emmet Reid Blake, *Birds of Mexico: A Guide for Field Identification*. Copyright 1953 by The University of Chicago Press.]

(TMN). The term is used adjectivally in Tenejapa to label a grizzled-grey plumage pattern (cf. *šik mut* 'grizzled chicken', see *mut₂*/bird, and *šik pehpen* 'grizzled butterfly', see *pehpen*/butterfly-moth). It is clearly distinguished from *šikʼ* 'wing'.

c. *yan teʔtikil likawal* 'under-forest hawk': The White-breasted Hawk, *Accipiter chionogaster* (Accipitridae). This small hawk was twice observed in Tenejapa at elevations near 2100 m, but never in company of an informant. Verbal descriptions, i.e., small size, white belly, and forest habitat, are most appropriate for this species. The Short-tailed Hawk (see previous paragraph) is similarly patterned but more like the Roadside Hawk in shape, size, and behavior. The rarity of these species makes their identification uncertain. *škoen likawal* (< iv 'descend' + 'hawk'), a type illustrated by AMT (see

Figure 5.8d) may be this type. He clearly shows the white underparts and relatively long tail of this species.

***liklik*** [ON]: the American Kestrel, *Falco sparverius* (Falconidae)

This falcon feeds primarily on mice and insects. It is the most common bird of prey in the region. One race (*F. s. tropicalis*) breeds in the highlands of Chiapas, and other races are common throughout in winter.

One informant (AMT) treated ***liklik*** as a subtype of ***likawal*** by labeling it ***liklik likawal*** (see Figure 5.8e). Other informants agree that the two taxa are closely related but distinct. Some informants assert that two varieties exist, *č'in liklik* 'small kestrel' and *muk'ul liklik* 'large kestrel'. Others assert that this is but a sexual difference, which is in fact the case. Informants of the latter opinion mistakenly considered the larger to be the male, an error based on the more typical pattern of sexual dimorphism among bird species.

***sliklikil k'ulub*** [pp + 'kestrel' + rs + 'locust'] is a synonym reflecting an accurate assessment of the bird's diet (see following taxon).

***me? k'ulub*** ['mother' + 'locust'] (see Figure 5.10a): The White-tailed Kite, *Elanus leucurus* (Accipitridae)

This species was observed on several occasions near Tenejapa. It is probable that the term traditionally referred to some other species of kite, since the White-tailed Kite is a recent arrival in the region (Eisenmann 1971). The Mississippi Kite (*Ictinia misisippiensis*) in winter and the Plumbeous Kite (*I. plumbea*) in summer are possible referents, though neither was observed. Both are of the Accipitridae.

The name refers to the fact that large flocks of these birds appear coincident with locust plagues. Such occurrences are rare. One informant asserted that no such visitation had occurred in over a decade. Thus the category is known to many Tenejapanecos by hearsay only. It is also known as ***mutil k'ulub*** 'bird of the locust'.

***tešereš ne*** 'scissor-tail': The Swallow-tailed Kite, *Elanoides forficatus* (Accipitridae) (see Figures 5.10b and 5.11)

I never had the fortune to see this bird. However, the name almost certainly refers to this species and no other. It is described as a large, white-bellied relative of ***likawal***, with a long, forked tail. It may also be referred to as ***tešereš ne likawal*** or ***tešereš ne me? k'ulub***, indicating that it is thought to be closely related to other members of this complex. Some informants see this bird as related also to the swift-swallow complex. It is also

(a)

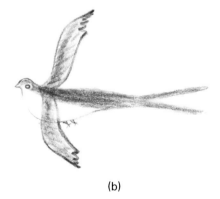

(b)

**Figure 5.10**  (a) ***me?k'ulub*** kite sp.; (b) ***tešereš ne*** Swallow-tailed Kite (*Elanoides forficatus*). [Drawings by AMT.]

**Figure 5.11** *tešereš ne* Swallow-tailed Kite *Elanoides forficatus.* [From Emmet Reid Blake, *Birds of Mexico: A Guide for Field Identification.* Copyright 1953 by The University of Chicago Press.]

known as *tešereš mut* 'scissor bird'. D. Breedlove reports seeing several Swallow-tailed Kites at Lagos de Montebello in Chiapas near the Guatemalan border in the company of AKČ' and other Tenejapanecos. This is the term they used (personal communication).

Two alternative referents were excluded. When the Great Swallow-tailed Swift, *Panyptila sanctihieronymi* (Apodidae), and the Scissor-tailed Flycatcher, *Muscivora forficata* (Tyrannidae), were observed, informants present denied that they were *tešereš ne*.

Many additional species of hawks, eagles, kites, falcons, and the Osprey, *Pandion haliaetus* (Pandionidae), occur in Chiapas but are apparently unknown.

## TURKEY COMPLEX (See Figure 5.12)

AMT and SMZ grouped the following taxa

as *shoyetik* 'associates'. All locally occurring species of the Cracidae and the Meleagrididae are included. This complex is linked by a chaining process to the jays (Corvidae in part), as will be described subsequently.

*tuluk'* [UN]: The domestic Wild Turkey, *Meleagris gallopavo* (Meleagrididae) (see Figure 5.13)

Turkeys are kept by most Tenejapan families (see Table 1.2). Though not regularly eaten, they serve an essential medicinal and ritual function. Turkeys are sacrificed to avert 'soul loss' (*hilel, komel*), a condition especially dangerous for children (whose 'souls' are but tenuously established) brought on by a fall or any sort of frightening experience. This condition is recognized throughout Mexico by the term *espanto* [< Sp *espantarse* 'to be frightened'] (Adams and Rubel 1967:335). A male turkey (*koc*) is sacrificed if the patient is male, a female (*me? tuluk'*) if the patient is female. In Zinacantan, black chickens are used for this and other ritual purposes (Vogt 1969a:67). In Tenejapa the color of the bird is irrelevant.

The domestic turkeys now kept in Tenejapa are not native but were domesticated at an early date in central Mexico. A related species, the Ocellated Turkey (*Agriocharis ocellata*), with peacocklike tail feathers, is still common in the Petén, Guatemala, and in the Yucatán. The local Maya refer to the male as "cutz" (Bowes and Castillo Perez 1964:xix). The feathers of the Peacock, *Pavo cristatus* (Phasianidae), used by Zinacantecos for their *alferez* costume, are perhaps recent replacements for the similar tail feathers of the native turkey.

The use of a primary lexeme for the male turkey (*koc* or *hkoc*) is evidence of the importance of the Ocellated Turkey in aboriginal Maya culture. This nomenclatural pattern is not otherwise found in Tenejapan Tzeltal with the exception of the introduced horse and mule (see *kawáyu*/horse). In fact, obligatory sex distinctions are suppressed in reference to cattle, the Spanish term for cow, *vaca*,

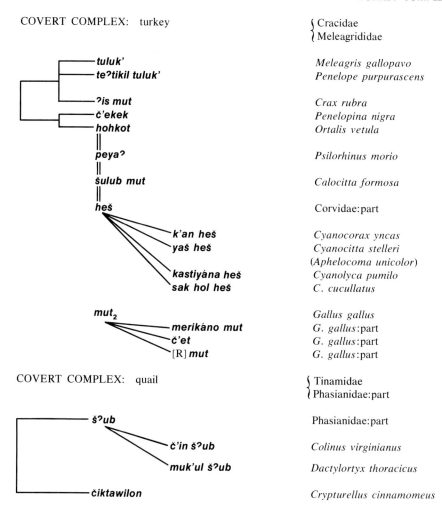

COVERT COMPLEX:   turkey

{ Cracidae
{ Meleagrididae

**tuluk'**  ·  *Meleagris gallopavo*
**te?tikil tuluk'**  ·  *Penelope purpurascens*

**?is mut**  ·  *Crax rubra*
**č'ekek**  ·  *Penelopina nigra*
**hohkot**  ·  *Ortalis vetula*

**peya?**  ·  *Psilorhinus morio*

**šulub mut**  ·  *Calocitta formosa*

**heš**  ·  Corvidae:part

**k'an heš**  ·  *Cyanocorax yncas*
**yaš heš**  ·  *Cyanocitta stelleri*
  (*Aphelocoma unicolor*)
**kastiyána heš**  ·  *Cyanolyca pumilo*
**sak hol heš**  ·  *C. cucullatus*

**mut₂**  ·  *Gallus gallus*
**merikáno mut**  ·  *G. gallus*:part
**č'et**  ·  *G. gallus*:part
**[R] mut**  ·  *G. gallus*:part

COVERT COMPLEX:   quail

{ Tinamidae
{ Phasianidae:part

**š?ub**  ·  Phasianidae:part

**č'in š?ub**  ·  *Colinus virginianus*

**muk'ul š?ub**  ·  *Dactylortyx thoracicus*

**čiktawilon**  ·  *Crypturellus cinnamomeus*

**Figure 5.12**   The turkey and quail complexes and associated generics.

(a)                              (b)

**Figure 5.13**   *tuluk'* domestic turkey *Meleagris gallopavo*: (a) **koc** (AMT) = **stat tuluk'** 'male turkey';
(b) **me? tuluk'** 'female turkey'. [Drawings by AMT.]

in borrowed form (**wakaš**), being used without regard to the sex of the animal. Due to
pattern pressure, the male turkey may also be
known as **tat tuluk'** 'father turkey'.

Despite the cultural significance of turkeys,
no great number of varietal distinctions are
recognized. The following were commonly
recognized:

> **puyum tuluk'** 'fat turkey'; known synony-
> mously as **bašil tuluk'** 'mottled turkey'
> according to some informants.

> **sakil tuluk'** 'white turkey'. Albinism is quite
> common among the domestic turkeys in
> Tenejapa. This varietal is literally defined
> as any turkey more white than not.

> **šyaš tuluk'** [gn + 'green' + 'turkey']. The
> attributive **šyaš** occurs in several other
> instances, e.g., **šyaš nep'**, a large grey-
> green crab, and **šyaš te?**, the silk cotton
> tree, *Ceiba pentandra* (Berlin, Breedlove,
> and Raven 1974:304–305). The distribu-
> tion of this attributive variant indicates
> that it implies large size as well as color.
> **šyaš tuluk'** is both large and slate grey, a
> color more usually referred to as **?ihk'al**
> 'black'.

Turkeys also belong to the disjunctive class
**yalak'** [pp + 'domestic animal']. The flesh
and eggs (**ston tuluk'**) are considered **sik**
'cold'.

> **te?tikil tuluk'** 'forest turkey': Either the Great
> Curassow, *Crax rubra* (Cracidae), or the Crested
> Guan, *Penelope purpurascens* (Cracidae)

The former is implied by AMT's illustration (see Figure 5.14), the latter accords with
SMZ's identification at the Tuxtla Gutiérrez
zoo. Neither species is found in Tenejapa.
They prefer heavy forest cover at low elevations. As most Tenejapanecos know these
species only from hearsay, they are uncertain
as to the labels appropriate to each species.
This confusion is heightened by the strong
sexual dimorphism of the curassow. This or
the following taxon or both are also known as
**paisáno** [< Sp. *faisán* 'Great Curassow'] and
**páwa** or **páša** [< Sp *pava* 'Crested Guan'].
It is possible that local Ladinos use these con-

Figure 5.14  *(tat) te?tikil tuluk*  (male) Great Curassow
(*Crax rubra*). [ Drawing by AMT. ]

trasting terms loosely, further confusing the
situation.

> **?is mut** [ archaic 'sweet potato' + 'bird' ]: The
> Great Curassow, *Crax rubra* (Cracidae)

SMZ preferred this term for the curassow
to the preceding one. A Tzeltal-speaking resident of the *municipio* of Huitiupan* used a
cognate term, **me? ?is** 'mother of sweet
potato', in response to a verbal description of
the black, curly-crowned male curassow.
This suggests that the original Tzeltal term
for the curassow involved the morpheme **?is**.
**te?tikil tuluk'** appears to be a recent coinage,
perhaps replacing the original term in areas
where the curassow is no longer seen locally.

The case just cited illustrates the effect of
relative rarity on nomenclatural distinctions.
Names may remain without clear referential
content, while new names are coined for old
categories rediscovered. And loan words may
be incorporated into the repertoire with no
clear idea as to their denotata vis-à-vis the
native terms or their precise referents in the
contact language.

Possible synonyms for **?is mut** include a
reduplicated form, **?is?is mut**, and a phonological variant, **?ik' mut** [ 'air' + 'bird' ].

---

* Most maps of the distribution of Tzeltal and Tzotzil
in the Chiapas highlands cite Huitiupan as a Tzotzil-
speaking *municipio* (Vogt 1969b:136). However, during a
visit there in September of 1971, we met a young man
who spoke Tzeltal. He conversed readily with SMZ and
JGG and claimed that the local language was Tzeltal.

*te ?tikil tuluk'* may also be known as ***tuluk' mut*** 'turkey bird'.

***?is mut*** and ***te ?tikil tuluk'*** are listed separately, since some informants at least distinguish two generic taxa within this referential range. Neither is confused with the taxon that follows.

*č'ekek* [ UN ]: The Black Penelopina, *Penelopina nigra* (Cracidae) (see Figure 5.15)

**Figure 5.15** *č'ekek* Black Penelopina *Penelopina nigra*. [From A. Starker Leopold, *Wildlife of Mexico*, 1959. Originally published by the University of California Press; reprinted by permission of The Regents of the University of California.]

In contrast to the preceding, this species occurs in highland cloud forest, a habitat found sparingly in and near Tenejapa. Informants from ***macab***, near the cloud forest in ***?ač' lum***, and from ***pahalton***, near similar habitat on ***con te? wic*** 'tree-moss mountain', provide the clearest descriptions of this rare bird. It is the size of ***hohkot*** (see next taxon), but black with a red 'throat pouch' (***lak am***), an adequate characterization of the penelopina. *č'ekek* is hunted on occasion in these areas.

In other parts of Tenejapa confusion exists between *č'ekek* and the next taxon, some informants asserting (incorrectly according to the zoogeographical data) that both species are found at all elevations throughout the region. This confusion is again attributable to the scarcity of these birds in Tenejapa today. The Black Penelopina was not observed. The Plain Chachalaca (*Ortalis vetula*) was observed once near Yajalón at 700 m.

*hohkot* [ ON ]: The Plain Chachalaca, *Ortalis vetula* (Cracidae) (see Figure 5.16)

The raucous dueting of this cracid is well known to Tenejapanecos, though it can hardly be considered common in the *municipio*. According to informants, it occurs to fairly high elevations (over 1500 m) in heavily wooded areas. The fact that it is a favorite wild food item might explain its scarcity.

*peya?* [ON]: The Brown Jay, *Psilorhinus morio* (Corvidae)

**Figure 5.16** *hohkot* Plain Chachalaca (*Ortalis vetula*). [From Emmet Reid Blake, *Birds of Mexico: A Guide for Field Identification.* Copyright 1953 by The University of Chicago Press.]

This bird is fairly common at lower elevations in Tenejapa. In size, color, long tail, flocking behavior, and raucous voice this species resembles the Plain Chachalaca (see preceding taxon). It was observed with informants on several occasions.

***šulub mut*** 'horned bird': The Magpie Jay, *Calocitta formosa* (Corvidae) (see Figure 5.17)

This species replaces the Brown Jay in the semiarid valley of the Upper Grijalva and in the Pacific coastal lowlands. These two species are geographically isolated by the fact that they rarely occur above 1200 m. ***šulub mut*** is known to those with *finca* experience. Its vocal repertoire is similar to that of the Brown Jay to the extent that SMZ misidenti-

**Figure 5.17** ***šulub mut*** Magpie Jay (*Calocitta formosa*). [From Emmet Reid Blake, *Birds of Mexico: A Guide for Field Identification*. Copyright 1953 by The University of Chicago Press.]

fied as ***peya?*** a Magpie Jay heard near Villa las Rosas. When the birds were seen, he quickly corrected his error. Though this species is similar to the Brown Jay in size, shape, behavior, and call, its blue and white plumage links it readily to the 'typical jays' (***heš***, see next taxon). Thus a chain is established through the Plain Chachalaca and the Brown Jay, linking the quite dissimilar Cracidae with the Corvidae (see Chapter 3, Section 7.1).

***heš*** [ON]: The smaller jays of several genera and species (all Corvidae)

The name may be reduplicated as ***hešheš***. This taxon includes several specific subdivisions as follows:

a. ***k'an heš*** 'yellow jay': The Green Jay (*Cyanocorax yncas*) (see Figure 5.18a).  This jay is yellow below but green above. It is common and conspicuous below 1500 m and occurs with the Steller's Jay (*Cyanocitta stelleri*) between 1500 and 1800 m. A Green Jay that was mist-netted was happily consumed by informants. The name may be abbreviated in casual reference as ***heš*** in the lowlands or specified more formally as ***k'anal heš***, though ***k'an heš*** is preferred.

b. ***yaš heš*** 'blue jay': The Steller's Jay (*Cyanocitta stelleri*) (see Figure 5.18b).  This jay is abundant in pine–oak forests above 1500 m, though not nearly as tame as its North American relatives; no doubt it is frequently hunted. It may be referred to as ***yašal heš*** or abbreviated to ***heš*** in casual contexts by highland informants, for whom it is also known as ***bac'il heš*** 'true jay'. A Unicolored Jay (*Aphelocoma unicolor*) observed once on ***conte?wic*** was included here, though its rarity and superficial similarity to the Steller's Jay, coupled with the fact that the informant in that instance was from ***mahosik'***, a low country *paraje*, leave open the possibility that this species is distinguished by Tenejapanecos who know both species well. This possibility is strengthened by the following instance.

**Figure 5.18**  (a) *kʼan heš* Green Jay (*Cyanocorax yncas*); (b) *yaš heš* Steller's Jay (*Cyanocitta stelleri*). [Drawings by AMT.]

c. ***kastiyána heš*** 'Ladina Jay': The Black-throated Jay (*Cyanolyca pumilo*).  This rare jay was observed once and netted on another occasion. At that time, with both Black-throated and Steller's Jays at hand simultaneously, the local informant (AKZ) supplied this name, not otherwise elicited. It is perhaps the referent implied by a second informant who distinguished between ***mukʼul yašal heš*** 'big blue jay', presumably the Steller's Jay, and ***čʼin yašal heš*** 'little blue jay', possibly this species.

d. ***sakhol heš*** 'white-headed jay': The Azure-hooded Jay (*Cyanolyca cucullata*).  Several lowland informants described this jay, which is known to occur nearby at Ocosingo. It is the sole remaining species known to occur in Chiapas and is very distinctly marked. A museum skin at the Museum of Vertebrate Zoology, Berkeley, California, was so identified by SMZ.

These four subdivisions of ***heš*** are specific taxa, rather than varietals, since several dimensions of difference among them are recognized. Though similar in size, shape, behavior, and vocalizations to a point, they differ in color, pattern, presence or absence of a crest, habitat preference, etc. ***yašal*** may be glossed as 'green' as well as 'blue', but this attributive is never applied to what is known in English as the Green Jay. This clearly indicates that the color attributives are not purely descriptive.

One additional corvid occurs in the area,

the Common Raven (*Corvus corax*, see ***hoh***/ black bird). It is seen as more closely related to a biologically heterogeneous group of black birds and will be treated in that context.

The following taxon is associated to some extent with both the turkey complex and the quail complex.

***mut₂*** [UN, ***mut₁*** 'bird' is polysemous]: The domestic chicken, *Gallus gallus* (Phasianidae) (see Figure 5.19)

This bird is a postconquest introduction kept by all Tenejapan families (median number per family sampled is 18 birds, counting all ages; see Table 1.2). Chickens are eaten as a luxury item and on special occasions. Their eggs (***tomut*** [< 'stone' + 'bird']) are eaten in similar contexts. Both eggs and birds are sold at the various markets for cash. The flesh and eggs are considered 'somewhat hot' (***kʼišin htebuk***).

The recent introduction of this species implies the priority of ***mut₁***, the inclusive sense. ***bacʼil mut*** 'true bird' is occasionally used to distinguish the restricted sense of the term from ***teʔtikil mut*** 'forest bird', the inclusive sense minus the chicken, in ambiguous contexts. Distinctions of sex and maturity are optional, for example:

***tat mut*** 'male chicken'.

***meʔ mut*** 'female chicken'.

***kelem mut*** 'boy chicken', for immature males.

***ʔancil mut*** 'girl chicken', for immature females.

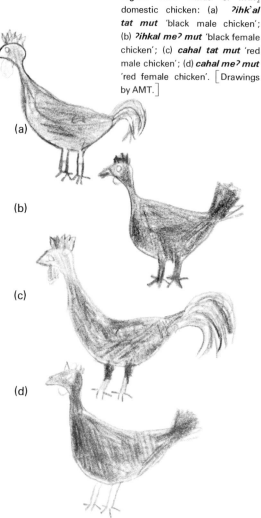

Figure 5.19 Kinds of *mut*₂ domestic chicken: (a) *ʔihkʼal tat mut* 'black male chicken'; (b) *ʔihkal meʔ mut* 'black female chicken'; (c) *cahal tat mut* 'red male chicken'; (d) *cahal meʔ mut* 'red female chicken'. [Drawings by AMT.]

(a)

(b)

(c)

(d)

*čʼin mut* 'small chicken', or *tutin mut*, likewise referring to chicks.

*čʼuhčʼul mut* 'small (pl) chicken', as above.

*yal mut* 'female's child chicken', as above.

*čʼiom tat mut* 'grown male chicken', a stage between *kelem mut* and *tat mut*, is used to make a soup effective against sterility in men and women (*špošil sikil winik sok ʔanc*). Birds that do not yet know how to crow are selected. Their flesh is *kʼišin* 'hot'.

Two specific subdivisions are regularly recognized, in contrast with a third, residual, subdivision:

a. *merikáno mut* 'American chicken': An especially large, reddish breed introduced by Protestant missionaries. The Rhode Island Red?

b. *čʼet* [ < tv 'make heaps'?]: Also known as *kašlan mut* 'Ladino chicken', referent unclear.

c. [R] *mut*: This residual includes all chickens not attributable to (a) or (b). Varietal distinctions are made within this residual as follows:

*bašil mut* 'mottled chicken'.

*cahal mut* 'red chicken', not to be confused with the homonymous usage (see *ʔičil mut*/wood-warbler, *kaptan mut*/bird).

*coc ʔakan mut* 'hairy-legged chicken', referring to chickens with heavily feathered legs.

*cuk sit mut* 'eyebrowed chicken'.

*čulin mut* 'mottled chicken' (but see *čulin*/mockingbird).

*kʼanal mut* 'yellow chicken'.

*pehkʼeč mut* 'short-legged chicken' [UN + chicken'].

*pohčʼ nukʼ mut* 'peeled-neck chicken', referring to chickens suffering from a condition that causes them to lose feathers about the head and neck.

*sakil mut* 'white chicken', not to be confused with two homonymous usages (see *palomaš*/dove and *htiʔ cuhkum*/mockingbird).

*šik mut* 'grizzled chicken'.

*mut*₂ is included in the domestic animal category, *yalakʼ*.

## QUAIL COMPLEX

AMT and SMZ consider the following taxa to be *shoyetik* 'associates'. The species included in this complex together with the domestic chicken account for all species of the Phasianidae known to occur locally. The Thicket Tinamou, *Crypturellus cinnamomeus* (Tinamidae), is also included.

*šʔub* [gn + UN]: Quail (Phasianidae in part)

Two specific subdivisions are widely recognized; the first is the type specific, to which the unmodified generic name is commonly applied.

a. *č'in š?ub* 'small quail': The Common Bobwhite (*Colinus virginianus*) (see Figure 5.20). This species is common throughout Tenejapa in fields and brushy areas. It is trapped and eaten. Tenejapanecos readily recognize tape-recorded versions of its typical "bobwhite" call. It is commonly abbreviated as *š?ub*.

Figure 5.21 *muk'ul š?ub* Singing Quail (*Dactylortyx thoracicus*). [From A. Starker Leopold, *Wildlife of Mexico*, 1959. Originally published by the University of California Press; reprinted by permission of The Regents of the University of California.]

Figure 5.20 *č'in š?ub* Common Bobwhite (*Colinus virginianus*). [From A. Starker Leopold, *Wildlife of Mexico*, 1959. Originally published by the University of California Press; reprinted by permission of The Regents of the University of California.]

b. *muk'ul š?ub* 'large quail': Probably the Singing Quail (*Dactylortyx thoracicus*) (see Figure 5.21). The Spotted Wood-Quail (*Odontophorus guttatus*) and the Ocellated Quail (*Cyrtonyx ocellatus*) are other possibilities. However neither is widely known in Chiapas. The Spotted Wood-Quail is a rare denizen of virgin rain forest (Leopold 1972), while the Ocellated Quail is known only from a few locations in Western Chiapas (Alvarez del Toro 1971). The Singing Quail, on the other hand, has a wide altitudinal distribution. Descriptions of the call of *muk'ul š?ub* approximate that of the Singing Quail (Davis

1972:31), and it is somewhat larger than the bobwhite. None of these birds was observed.

A number of synonyms and phonological variants have been recorded. Most are onomatopoeic, imitative of the bobwhite, the focal species.

*haš pik'* or *huš pik'* [ON].

*koe šč'in, koen šč'in, kore šč'in, koren šč'in, kurun šč'in, ?uen šč'in,* or *koin šč'en* [all ON].

*kul?it mut* [UN + 'buttock' + 'bird'] referring to its short tail, equally characteristic of (a) and (b).

*š?ub* is unique in that it can take either prefix, i.e., *h?ub* has also been recorded.

*čiktawilon* [ON]: Probably the Thicket Tinamou, *Crypturellus cinnamomeus* (Tinamidae) (see Figure 5.22)

This species had red legs, a feature commonly attributed to *čiktawilon*, and is considerably larger than the bobwhite. This tinamou is reported at all elevations up to 2000 m. Finally, the vocalizations of the tinamou as described by Davis (1972:3–4) are similar to those reported for *čiktawilon*. In fact, "tawi-

Figure 5.22 *čiktawilon* Thicket Tinamou (*Crypturellus cinnamomeus*). [From Emmet Reid Blake, *Birds of Mexico: A Guide for Field Identification.* Copyright 1953 by The University of Chicago Press.]

lon" and "tinamou" are both onomatopoetic and sufficiently similar to suggest their correspondence here. Other tinamous reported from Mexico are more strictly lowland birds and/or do not have red legs.

*kulʔit mut* (see also previous taxon) is also recorded as a synonym for *čiktawilon*, which implies that the bird in question is short-tailed, quite appropriate for the tinamou.

Other synonyms recorded are phonological variants:

*čiktawil, čiktulub, čištulub, čiktulum, čištulum* [all ON].

*pokowéla* was used synonymously by a single informant, AMT (but see *burúho mut*/oriole).

*šʔuman* [gn + ON?]: The Lesser Roadrunner, *Geococcyx velox* (Cuculidae) (see Figures 5.23 and 5.24).

Figure 5.23 *šʔuman* Lesser Roadrunner (*Geococcyx velox*). [Drawing by AMT.]

This taxon is sometimes associated with the quail complex. They are roughly comparable in size and in terrestrial habits. Some informants recognize a relationship with

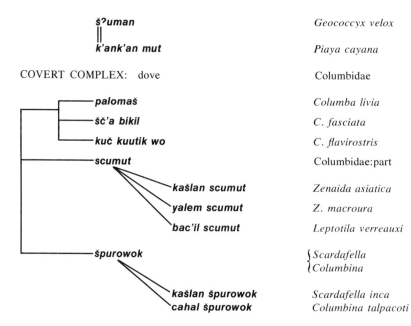

Figure 5.24   Some cuckoos and the dove complex.

the Squirrel Cuckoo (*Piaya cayana*, see following taxon) as well. The roadrunner is fairly common throughout Tenejapa below 2100 m. It is trapped and eaten.

*ʔuman* is a common variant. *k'uš hol* 'headache' is a rare highland synonym cognate with the Zinacantan Tzotzil name for this species (R. Laughlin personal communication). This synonym refers to its moaning call.

*k'ank'an mut* ['yellow'? reduplicated + 'bird']: The Squirrel Cuckoo, *Piaya cayana* (Cuculidae) (see Figure 5.25)

This bird was not observed in Tenejapa, but I have seen it throughout Chiapas below 1200 m. It may range to somewhat higher elevations but prefers dense cover, uncommon habitat in the *municipio*. It is considered a harbinger of ill-fortune and thus a member of the disjunctive category, *hlabtawaneh mut*. The phonological variant *k'ank'al mut* occurs.

## DOVE–PIGEON COMPLEX

The following five generic taxa are considered to be closely related (AMT, SMZ). AGM grouped *palomaš* with *šč'a bikil*, and *scumut* with *špurowok*. *scumut* is the type generic, as evidenced by the occasional use of that stem in naming the related taxa. The species included here account for all locally occurring forms of the Columbidae.

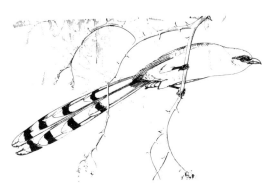

**Figure 5.25** *k'ank'an mut* Squirrel Cuckoo (*Piaya cayana*). [From Emmet Reid Blake, *Birds of Mexico: A Guide for Field Identification.* Copyright 1953 by The University of Chicago Press.]

**Figure 5.26** *šč'a bikil* Band-tailed Pigeon (*Columba fasciata*). [From A. Starker Leopold, *Wildlife of Mexico*, 1959. Originally published by the University of California Press; reprinted by permission of The Regents of the University of California.]

*palomaš* [< OSp *palomas* 'dove']: The Rock Dove or domestic pigeon (*Columba livia*)

This species is found about most Chiapas towns, though it is rarely kept by Tenejapanecos. It was apparently introduced shortly after the conquest, as the name is an early loan. The relationship with its native congeners (see following taxa) is clearly recognized. The more recent Spanish loan, *palóma*, is also heard, but is considered less appropriate by many informants. It is also known occasionally as *sakil mut₁* 'white bird', though this term may be restricted to albino forms.

*šč'a bikil* 'gall bladder': The Band-tailed Pigeon (*Columba fasciata*) (see Figure 5.26)

This species is fairly common in highland areas. It is also known as *sabal mut* 'morning bird'. I am uncertain about the rationale for these names. Informants may apply these terms also to the Red-billed Pigeon (*C. flavirostris*) of the lowlands, if ignorant of the following term.

**kuč kuutik wo** [ON]: The Red-billed Pigeon (*Columba flavirostris*) (see Figure 5.27)

Figure 5.27 *kuč kuutik wo* Red-billed Pigeon (*Columba flavirostris*). [From A. Starker Leopold, *Wildlife of Mexico*, 1959. Originally published by the University of California Press; reprinted by permission of The Regents of the University of California.]

This species is rather rare in Tenejapa. I observed it on two occasions nearby. In the first instance, the informant present (SMZ) called it **yašal scumut** 'grey dove' (see following taxon). This informant was not familiar with the onomatopoetic name, nor had he seen the bird before. This indicates that a relationship is perceived to exist with the following taxon. JGG correctly identified a recording of its call as **kuč kuutik wo**. An onomatopoetic variant is **ʔuč kʼišin haʔ** ['opossum' + 'hot' + 'water'].

**scumut** [ON]: Most appropriate name for the focal species, the White-tipped Dove (*Leptotila verreauxi*)

The White-tipped Dove is a common and conspicuous resident to at least 2100 m. This and several less common species are distributed among the following three specific subdivisions:

a. **kašlan scumut** 'Ladino dove': The White-winged Dove (*Zenaida asiatica*) (see Figure 5.28). This species is restricted to more arid regions and probably does not occur in Tenejapa, though it was observed at Zinacantan and Aguacatenango. It is also known as **bašil scumut** 'mottled dove' (SMZ), referring to the pattern of white on the wings.

Figure 5.28 *kašlan scumut* White-winged Dove (*Zenaida asiatica*). [From A. Starker Leopold, *Wildlife of Mexico*, 1959. Originally published by the University of California Press; reprinted by permission of The Regents of the University of California.]

b. **yalem scumut** 'temporary dove': The Mourning Dove (*Zenaida macroura*) (see Figure 5.29). This species occurs at San Cristóbal in the winter and should also occur in Tenejapa. The term is descriptive of the seasonal pattern of this species' occurrence. The term **kašlan scumut** (see previous subdivision) is also applied to this species by some informants. Neither this nor the White-winged Dove is of regular occurrence, and thus they are poorly known.

c. **bac'il scumut** 'true dove': The White-tipped Dove (see Figure 5.30). This name is commonly elicited for this species in response to the query **bi scumutil** 'which dove?' It may also be distinguished as **muk'ul scumut** 'large dove', as it is larger than either of the two preceding species.

**Figure 5.30** **bac'il scumut** White-tipped Dove (*Leptotila verreauxi*). [From A. Starker Leopold, *Wildlife of Mexico*, 1959. Originally published by the University of California Press; reprinted by permission of The Regents of the University of California.]

A few informants cite another subdivision, **cahal scumut** 'red dove', to which the White-faced Quail-Dove (*Geotrygon albifacies*) might be assigned. However this cloud forest species was not observed.

**špurowok** [gn + ON]: Several species of small doves

The name is appropriately descriptive of the call of the Ruddy Ground-Dove (*Columbina talpacoti*), which occurs in Tenejapa below 1500 m. The Inca Dove (*Scardafella inca*), the call of which is quite different, is more widespread, occurring up to 2400 m. Common Ground-Doves (*Columbina passerina*) are not known to occur in Tenejapa. However those seen at Aguacatenango were placed here. The Plain-breasted Ground-Dove (*C. minuta*) of lowland regions of the Gulf slope might also occur near or in Tenejapa. In that case it should also be included, as all three species of *Columbina* are very similar. The following specific subdivisions were recorded with some regularity.

**Figure 5.29** **yalem scumut** Mourning Dove (*Zenaida macroura*). [From A. Starker Leopold, *Wildlife of Mexico*, 1959. Originally published by the University of California Press; reprinted by permission of The Regents of the University of California.]

a. **kašlan špurowok** 'Ladino dovelet': The Inca Dove, distinguished by white in the tail. Several informants recognized this subdivision from a tape recording of its call. It is sometimes distinguished as **č'in scumut** 'little dove', further evidence for the inclusion of **špurowok** in this complex.

b. **cahal špurowok** 'red dovelet': The Ruddy Ground-Dove.   The males of this species are notably ruddy.

Since the two remaining species are probably extralimital, there is no need to define a residual to include them. Nor is there a type specific. Though the Inca Dove is more common, the name best describes the Ruddy Ground-Dove's call. Several other species of doves and pigeons occur in Chiapas. However, habitat and altitudinal restrictions indicate that they are not a part of the Tenejapan fauna.

A number of phonological variants exist.

The prefix **š-** may or may not occur in each case:

**puruwok, porowok, puruwuk** [all ON].

**špuruk mut** [gn + ON + 'bird'].

This alternation between **u** and **o** is a common feature of what Stross (n.d.) labels irregular phonological variation in Tenejapa Tzeltal. Note, however, the apparent rule that **u** precedes **o**. This pattern applies with few exceptions throughout the Tenejapan vocabulary.

OWL  COMPLEX  (See Figure 5.31)

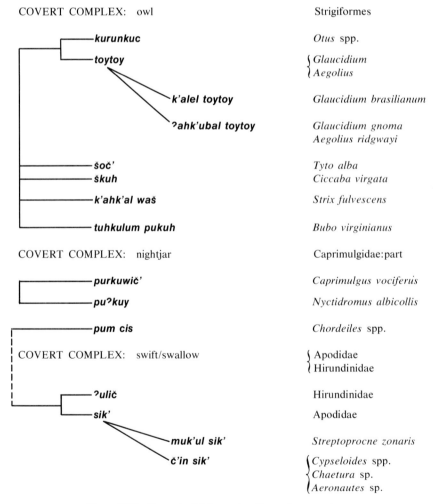

**Figure 5.31**   The owl, nightjar, and swift–swallow complexes.

This complex includes every locally occurring species of the order Strigiformes and nothing else. All taxa of this complex are also classified as **hlabtawaneh mut** 'harbinger-of-evil bird'. AMT uses this term to label the complex. However, **hlabtawaneh mut** also refers to several taxa unrelated to this complex (see **k'ank'an mut**; the woodpecker complex; **tu č'ič'**/oriole). None of the owls is considered edible.

**kurunkuc** [ON]: The screech-owls (*Otus* spp.) (see Figure 5.32), in particular the Whiskered Screech-Owl (*O. trichopsis*) common in the highlands

**Figure 5.32** *kurunkuc* screech-owl (*Otus* spp.). [From Emmet Reid Blake, *Birds of Mexico: A Guide for Field Identification*. Copyright 1953 by The University of Chicago Press.]

This species was heard at the Pueblo of Tenejapa and mist-netted above San Cristóbal. Several informants identified it from a tape-recorded call. Two other screech-owls also occur in the region. The Bearded Screech-Owl (*O. barbarus*) and the Vermiculated Screech-Owl (*O. guatemalae*) are found at lower elevations (Davis 1972:59). A good imitation of the call of *O. guatemalae* was given by SMZ, a lowland informant. All three are very similar in appearance. However the name best describes the call of *O. trichopsis*.

Alternate renditions include the following:

**kurumkuc, turukuc, turunkuc, kurunkuckuc** [all ON]

Though considered an evil omen, informants exhibited no fear of the captured screech-owl.

**toytoy** [ON]: Other small owls (*Glaucidium* spp. and *Aegolius ridgwayi*)

Two specific subdivisions are commonly recognized:

a. **k'alel toytoy** 'daytime pygmy-owl': The Ferruginous Pygmy-Owl (*G. brasilianum*), the most diurnal of local owls. Several informants recognized this species from tape-recorded calls. Informants assert that **k'alel toytoy** is found in the lowlands, **ʔahk'ubal toytoy** in the highlands, which is quite accurate. **k'alel toytoy** is not always considered an evil omen. **kawkaw mut** [ON + 'bird'] is synonymous.

b. **ʔahk'ubal toytoy** 'nighttime pygmy-owl': The Northern Pygmy-Owl (*G. gnoma*) (see Figure 5.33) for most informants; the Unspotted Saw-whet Owl (*A. ridgwayi*) for others. The former species was heard once near San Cristóbal. The latter, heretofore unknown in the region, was netted twice, in **macab** at 2500 m and at **san ʔantónyo**, 2150 m (Hunn 1973). Local informants in both cases referred to the saw-whet owl as **toytoy**. They were not familiar with and did not distinguish a diurnal, lowland form. The voice of the saw-whet owl is quite similar to that of the pygmy-owl, though in body size it more closely approximates the screech-owls. In coloration and in the absence of "horns" it is also more like the pygmy-owls.

This taxon may also be distinguished as **bac'il toytoy** 'true pygmy-owl' or **hlabtawaneh toytoy** 'harbinger-of-evil pygmy-owl', for

Figure 5.33 *ʔahk'ubal toytoy* Northern Pygmy-Owl (*Glaucidium gnoma*). [From Emmet Reid Blake, *Birds of Mexico: A Guide for Field Identification*. Copyright 1953 by The University of Chicago Press.]

Figure 5.34 *šoč'* Barn Owl (*Tyto alba*). [From Emmet Reid Blake, *Birds of Mexico: A Guide for Field Identification*. Copyright 1953 by The University of Chicago Press.]

those who do not consider *k'alel toytoy* to be an evil omen.

*toytoy* is sometimes applied, when *kurunkuc* (see preceding taxon) is absent from the repertoire, to refer to screech-owls as well.

*šoč'* [ON]: The Barn Owl (*Tyto alba*) (see Figure 5.34)

Though this species was not observed, every informant without exception described its call as *šššt*, quite appropriate for this species. It is accurately described as 'white' or 'yellow'.

*škuh* [ON]: Probably the Mottled Owl (*Ciccaba virgata*) (see Figure 5.35)

This species was not observed, and I had no recording of its call. However voice descriptions in Davis (1972:62), i.e., "hut hut," seem similar to informants' descriptions. This species is the only common, widespread

(to 2400 m), large "hornless" owl known from the region. The Crested Owl (*Lophostrix cristata*), Spectacled Owl (*Pulsatrix perspicillata*), Black-and-white Owl (*Ciccaba nigrolineata*), Striped Owl (*Rhinoptynx clamator*), and Stygian Owl (*Asio stygius*) are restricted to lowland forests, or are "horned," or are exceedingly rare, and they may thus be eliminated from consideration. This leaves the Fulvous Owl (*Strix fulvescens*), which is tentatively assigned to the following taxon.

*škuh* is also known as *mutil balam* ['bird' + rs + 'jaguar'], or *mutil čoh* 'bird of the cougar'. Local lore asserts that when this bird appears these animals are close behind.

*k'ahk'al waš* 'fierce fox': Probably the Fulvous Owl (*Strix fulvescens*)

This highland owl is congeneric with the Spotted Owl (*S. occidentalis*) and the Barred Owl (*S. varia*) of the United States. The

**Figure 5.35** *škuh* Mottled Owl (*Ciccaba virgata*). ⌊From Emmet Reid Blake, *Birds of Mexico: A Guide for Field Identification.* Copyright 1953 by The University of Chicago Press.⌋

Spotted Owl characteristically "barks," a sound attributed also to *k'ahk'al waš*. This may also explain the nomenclatural reference to 'fox'. It is described as a large, dark, earless owl encountered rarely in the high country. This prescription eliminates all other possibilities. However most informants know the animal from hearsay only. All agree that it is **not** a fox but rather a bird of this complex.

*tuhkulum pukuh* ⌈ON, UN + 'devil'⌉: The Great Horned Owl (*Bubo virginianus*)

This owl is rare in the highlands of Chiapas. SMZ identified it from a tape-recorded call. Its characteristic call does sound very much like the name. Most Tenejapanecos know it from hearsay only. Variants include the following:

*tuhkulum mut, tuhkulum muk*, and *mukmuk mut* ⌈all ON⌉

The term *ʔičin*, applied to this species in Zinacantan Tzotzil (Laughlin n.d.), is apparently unknown in Tenejapa.

## NIGHTJAR COMPLEX

Most caprimulgids are lowland birds. The Whip-poor-will (*Caprimulgus vociferus*) and the nighthawks (*Chordeiles* spp.) are the exceptions. Of the lowland species the Pauraque (*Nyctidromus albicollis*) is apparently the only species known to Tenejapanecos. The Buff-collared Nightjar (*Caprimulgus ridgwayi*), known to Zinacantecos (R. Laughlin personal communication), is restricted to the drier south slope of the central highlands. The Tawny-collared Nightjar (*C. salvini*) apparently does not reach Tenejapa from the Gulf coastal lowlands. The Chuck-will's-widow (*C. carolinensis*) winters in the region but is silent at that time. No other likely possibilities exist. The nighthawks are not included in this complex (see *pum cis*).

*purkuwič'* ⌈ON⌉: The Whip-poor-will (*Caprimulgus vociferus*) (see Figure 5.36a)

This species is common throughout the central highlands. Both English and Tzeltal names closely approximate the rhythm of this species' call. Unlike the next taxon, *purkuwič'* is not an evil omen (*hlabtawaneh mut*). Alternate renditions include the following:

*purkowič'* and *purpurwič'* ⌈both ON⌉.

*puʔkuy* ⌈ON⌉: The Pauraque (*Nyctidromus albicollis*) (see Figures 5.36b and 5.37)

Though not observed in Tenejapa, one killed by a car near Ixtapa was identified as

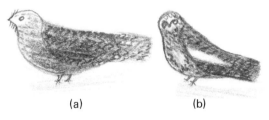

(a)                    (b)

**Figure 5.36**  (a) *purkuwic'* Whip-poor-will (Caprimulgus vociferus); (b) *puʔkuy* Pauraque (Nyctidromus albicollis). ⌈Drawings by AMT.⌉

**Figure 5.37** *pu?kuy* Pauraque (*Nyctidromus albicollis*). [From Emmet Reid Blake, *Birds of Mexico: A Guide for Field Identification*. Copyright 1953 by The University of Chicago Press.]

*pu?kuy* by JGG and SMZ. AMT's illustration clearly indicates the distinctive white wing-patch of this species. SMZ and JGG also identified its tape-recorded call. It is classified as *hlabtawaneh mut* 'harbinger-of-evil bird'. The prefix *š-* is optionally affixed.

*pum cis* [ON, lit. tv 'hit, causing to resound' + 'fart']: Common and Lesser Nighthawks, *Chordeiles minor* and *C. acutipennis* (Caprimulgidae) (see Figure 5.38)

JGG reports this bird as resident near *yočib*, Tenejapa. This would be the resident race of the Common Nighthawk described from Chiapas by Alvarez del Toro (1971). Migratory Lesser Nighthawks observed over San

**Figure 5.38** *pum cis* Lesser Nighthawk (*Chordeiles acutipennis*). [From Emmet Reid Blake, *Birds of Mexico: A Guide for Field Identification*. Copyright 1953 by The University of Chicago Press.]

Cristóbal were called *pum cis* by JGG. The name is most appropriate for the Common Nighthawk, which is also known in English as the "booming nighthawk." This taxon is not widely known. A probable synonym is *?ahk'ubal sik'* 'nighttime swift' (SMZ), indicating some relationship perceived with the following complex.

SWIFT–SWALLOW COMPLEX

These two unrelated families are considered to be *shoyetik* 'associates' (AGM, AMT, JGG, SMZ). One informant misidentified a Barn Swallow (*Hirundo rustica*) as *sik'* 'swift'. Members of these two families are superficially similar due to convergent adaptations to an aerial existence. The recognition of some relationship between swifts and both nighthawks (see preceding taxon) and hummingbirds (*c'unun*) accords better with the biological ordering. Several informants also associate the kites (Accipitridae in part, see the bird of prey complex) with this complex.

*?ulič* [ON]: All swallows (Passeriformes: Hirundinidae)

This taxon is perceived to be heterogeneous, but no subdivisions are consistently recognized. The following species were positively identified as *?ulič*:

Cliff Swallow (*Petrochelidon pyrrhonota*) (see Figures 5.39), transient.

Cave Swallow (*P. fulva*), common resident in towns.

Barn Swallow (*Hirundo rustica*), transient.

Rough-winged Swallow (*Stelgidopteryx ruficollis*), resident.

Black-capped Swallow (*Notiochelidon pileata*), common resident of the highlands.

Bank Swallow (*Riparia riparia*), transient.

Tree Swallow (*Tachycineta bicolor*), transient.

Mangrove Swallow (*T. albilinea*), resident on lowland rivers.

**Figure 5.39**  *ʔulič* Cliff Swallow (*Petrochelidon pyrrhonota*). [From Emmet Reid Blake, *Birds of Mexico: A Guide for Field Identification*. Copyright 1953 by The University of Chicago Press.]

I also observed the Violet-green Swallow (*T. thalassina*), a transient, but without informants. It certainly falls within the range of variation already established for this taxon.

The Gray-breasted Martins (*Progne chalybea*) observed at Ocosingo, where they nest, were unfamiliar to SMZ. He appropriately coined a name for them, **muk'ul ʔulič** 'large swallow'. A few other informants claimed to know the term. However there is no indication that these martins normally occur in Tenejapa, and most informants make no distinctions within this taxon.

Another informant listed **tešereš ne ʔulič** 'scissor-tailed swallow' as a variety. This most likely refers to the Barn Swallow. In any case, the heterogeneity of this taxon is clearly recognized and gives rise occasionally to named subdivisions. However the aerial habits of these species make the consistent recognition of the numerous species difficult.

**sik'** [ON?]: All swifts (Apodiformes: Apodidae)

The focal species is clearly the large, abundant White-collared Swift (*Streptoprocne zonaris*). AMT's illustration of this taxon is recognizable as this species only (see Figure 5.40b). Several informants clearly distinguish between the type specific and the residual as follows:

a. **muk'ul sik'** 'large swift': The White-collared Swift. The White-naped Swift (*Streptoprocne semicollaris*), which has been recorded from Chiapas, would no doubt also be included here. The White-collared Swift roosts in large numbers in *sumideros* at the Pueblo of Tenejapa and at **yočib**. During feeding, it ranges throughout.

b. **č'in sik'** 'small swift': All other species of the family. The following have been identified as of this type:

Vaux's Swift (*Chaetura vauxi*) (see Figure 5.41), observed at lower elevations near Ocosingo.

Chestnut-collared Swift (*Cypseloides rutilus*), common at the Pueblo and at **yočib**.

Black Swift (*C. niger*), observed at the Pueblo.

White-throated Swift (*Aeronautes saxatalis*), observed near the Pueblo and in **mahosik'**.

The Great Swallow-tailed Swift (*Panyptila sanctihieronymi*) was observed once near Ocosingo. The informants present did not see it however. It is quite rare and in flight appears quite similar to the other species.

The *paraje* **mahosik'** [< tv 'hit' + ag + 'swift'] owes its name to a technique for

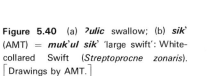

**Figure 5.40**  (a) *ʔulič* swallow; (b) **sik'** (AMT) = **muk'ul sik'** 'large swift': White-collared Swift (*Streptoprocne zonaris*). [Drawings by AMT.]

(a)                                                    (b)

Figure 5.41  *č'in sik'* Vaux's Swift (*Chaetura vauxi*). [From Emmet Reid Blake, *Birds of Mexico: A Guide for Field Identification*. Copyright 1953 by The University of Chicago Press.]

capturing swifts employed there (see Figure 4.8). Fences are constructed on ridges favored by swifts. They pass at such speed (some have been clocked at near 200 kph) that they are unable to avoid the fence. Stunned by the collision they are easily captured. The amount of meat involved, however, is small.

This taxon may also be referred to as *sik'il* or *silik'*. Informants generally consider their personal variant to be the only correct form. The distributional basis for these variants is unclear.

*c'unun* [ON]: All hummingbirds (Trochilidae)

These tiny birds exhibit a wide range of variation. In addition to more than 15 species occurring in the local area, sex and age differences are often striking, immature and female forms of several species often defy field identification. They are difficult to observe at close hand because of their diminutive size and rapid flight. These factors have created a rather intractable nomenclatural confusion. The taxon is occasionally left undivided or is subdivided deductively. Most Tenejapanecos, however, recognize several specific subdivisions. Following is my best approximation to the facts.

a. *c'ibal sit c'unun* 'stripe-faced hummingbird': The White-eared Hummingbird (*Hylocharis leucotis*) (see Figure 5.42) common throughout the year in a variety of habitats above 1200 m. The name adequately characterizes this species. The term *yašal c'unun* 'green hummingbird' is a commonly used synonym. For example, AMT's illustration of *yašal c'unun* clearly shows the face marking of this species, though the attributive 'green' is appropriate for the great majority of hummingbirds. This species may also be known as *cahal ni? c'unun* 'red-billed hummingbird', descriptive of a characteristic of this as well as several other species.

Figure 5.42  *c'ibal sit c'unun* White-eared Hummingbird (*Hylocharis leucotis*). [From Emmet Reid Blake, *Birds of Mexico: A Guide for Field Identification*. Copyright 1953 by The University of Chicago Press. Head only.]

b. *kašlan c'unun* 'Ladino hummingbird': For most, a large vari-colored hummingbird, in particular the Green Violet-ear (*Colibri thalassinus*) (see Figure 5.43). This species is abundant in *milpas* when the beans are in flower, an association recognized by informants. SMZ identified this species by its chirping call. The Magnificent Hummingbird (*Eugenes fulgens*), uncommon in the highlands, is sometimes included here, though it is also known as *?ihk'al c'unun* 'black hummingbird' (see folk species (d)).

Figure 5.43  *kašlan c'unun* Green Violet-ear (*Colibri thalassinus*). [From Emmet Reid Blake, *Birds of Mexico: A Guide for Field Identification*. Copyright 1953 by The University of Chicago Press. Head only.]

Other terms applied to the Green Violet-ear are as follows:

*c'uhkin c'unun* [ON + 'hummingbird'].

*muk'ul c'unun* 'large hummingbird'.

*muk'ul yašal c'unun* 'large green hummingbird'.

Several informants (e.g., AGM) consider *kašlan c'unun* to be a small hummingbird, rather than a large one. For these informants the Fork-tailed Emerald (*Chlorostilbon canivetii*), fairly common below 1800 m, is the proper referent of the term. An informant from a lowland *paraje* called the emerald *yašal c'unun* 'green hummingbird'.

    c. *tešereš ne c'unun* 'scissor-tailed hummingbird': The Slender Sheartail (*Doricha enicura*). This tiny long-tailed species is locally distributed in Chiapas between 900 and 2100 m. It was observed at two localities in Tenejapa where local informants identified it as of this type. *ča?šal ne c'unun* 'two-tailed hummingbird' is a synonym sometimes applied, though less appropriately, to the Fork-tailed Emerald as well.

    d. *?ihk'al c'unun* 'black hummingbird': This is described as a large, black-breasted hummingbird, in particular the Amethyst-throated Hummingbird (*Lampornis amethystinus*). SMZ so named a mist-netted male of this species. The name is equally appropriate for the Magnificent Hummingbird (see folk species (b)) and the Garnet-throated Hummingbird (*Lamprolaima rhami*). All three are large hummingbirds with dark underparts. The Amethyst-throated is spottily distributed in highland areas but is definitely known from Tenejapa. The Garnet-throated is less common, though it was observed in the *municipio* on one occasion (at 2200 m).

    e. *sakil c'unun* 'white hummingbird': The Red-billed Azurecrown (*Amazilia cyanocephala*). Though females and immatures of several species are some shade of white below, this name is typically restricted to the Red-billed Azurecrown, a large hummingbird, brilliant white ventrally, which is rather common at moderate elevations (900–2100 m). A Plain-capped Star-throat (*Heliomaster constantii*), which is whitish below, was called *muk'ul c'unun* 'large hummingbird' by SMZ and AGM. This species is restricted to more arid regions outside of Tenejapa. The fact that the star-throat and females of the Broad-tailed Hummingbird (*Selasphorus platycercus*) and Ruby-throated Hummingbird (*Archilochus colubris*), all of which are whitish below, are not considered to be *sakil c'unun* indicates that the attributive is not applied literally.

Synonymous forms may include the following:

*čitam c'unun* 'pig hummingbird', referring to a pig-like noise attributed to the azurecrown by JGG.

*bac'il c'unun* 'true hummingbird', used by AGM to refer to this species. However he also applied this term to the Berylline Hummingbird (*Amazilia beryllina*), which shows no white. AGM tends to recognize fewer distinctions throughout the corpus. His use of *bac'il c'unun* may thus refer to a residual category of "typical hummingbirds."

The remaining terms elicited occurred sporadically and could not be established with certainty.

*?árpa c'unun* [< Sp *arpa* 'harp' + 'hummingbird'], referring to a sound produced by what SMZ describes as a small red hummingbird, perhaps female hummingbirds of the genus *Calothorax*, which were observed at moderate elevations in and near Tenejapa on several occasions.

*cahal c'unun* 'red hummingbird', appropriately descriptive of several species, e.g., female *Calothorax* spp., the Garnet-throated Hummingbird (see folk species (d)), or the Rufous Sabrewing (*Campylopterus rufus*). The latter has been reported to occur on **con te? wic**.

**č'in c'unun** 'small hummingbird', even less restricted as potentially appropriate than the preceding variant.

**honon c'unun** 'bumblebee hummingbird', alleged to be a small hummingbird that sounds and acts like that insect. In my experience, the female Slender Sheartail would be an ideal referent. However, this form was not observed with informants. The diminutive Wine-throated Hummingbird (*Atthis ellioti*), observed on **con te? wic**, is very similar to a species sometimes called the "bumblebee hummingbird" (*A. heloisa*) in English.

**sak ?oal c'unun** 'white-necklace hummingbird': the male Ruby-throated Hummingbird, a common winter visitor, according to SMZ.

**šéla c'unun** [<OSp/*seda*/'silk, ribbon' + 'hummingbird'], the Fork-tailed Emerald (see folk species (b)), according to two informants.

The following names were also elicited but could not be determined:

**korion c'unun** [< Sp *acordeón* 'accordion' + 'hummingbird'], referring to the sound produced.

**k'anal c'unun** 'yellow hummingbird', might also be appropriate for most hummingbirds described as 'red', since these are typically buffy or rust-colored.

**paharíto c'unun** [< Sp *pajarito* 'little bird' + 'hummingbird'].

**pehpen c'unun** 'butterfly hummingbird'.

**sabal c'unun** 'dawn hummingbird'.

The great diversity of local hummingbird species, their small size, rapid flight, and the local occurrence of many species produces a situation in which the heterogeneity may be treated at various levels. The number of terms elicited is most likely due to the fact that many independent solutions have arisen for dealing with this heterogeneity. The subdivisions recognized are relatively widespread among informants in the sample and appear to be based on the recognition of manifold distinctions. Further study is needed and should indicate that some individuals, at least, recognize a considerable number of biologically appropriate specific subdivisions.

**ničničimal čenek'** ['flower' reduplicated + rs + 'bean'] is synonymous, for some informants, with the generic name. Thus the association of hummingbirds with flowers is recognized.

Informants state that one should not kill hummingbirds as they are messengers of the 'spirits' (**labil**). Most are considered 'good', though an animal known variously as **?ahk'ubal c'unun** 'nighttime hummingbird', **pále? c'unun** [< Sp *padre* 'priest' + 'hummingbird'], or **hlabtawaneh c'unun** 'harbinger-of-evil hummingbird' is feared as portending death. The actual identity of this animal is a puzzle. Hummingbirds are not known to feed at night. Most informants claim only to have heard this animal and assert that it sounds like a hummingbird. One informant described one which had entered his house at night as feathered and a 'hummingbird'. However JGG claims to have seen it as well. He asserts that it looks like **pehpen** 'butterfly' thus it is perhaps a sphinx moth (order Lepidoptera: Sphingidae: see also **pehpen**/butterfly–moth).

## PARROT COMPLEX (See Figure 5.44)

If any parrots (Psittacidae) occur in Tenejapa, they are of sporadic and local occurrence. None were observed in the *municipio*, though several species are common on the drier south slope of the central highlands and in the valley of the upper Grijalva River. At least one other species is common at Ocosingo and Huitiupán in the lower montane forest regions to the north. Various species are also kept by Ladinos, but Tenejapanecos

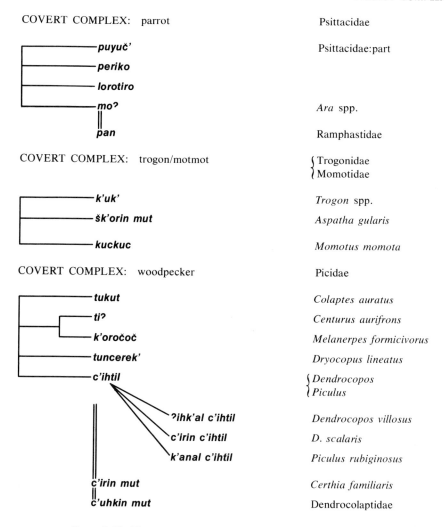

COVERT COMPLEX:   parrot                                    Psittacidae

    *puyuč'*                                         Psittacidae:part

    *periko*

    *lorotiro*

    *mo?*                                           *Ara* spp.

    *pan*                                           Ramphastidae

COVERT COMPLEX:   trogon/motmot                             {Trogonidae  
                                                             {Momotidae

    *k'uk'*                                         *Trogon* spp.

    *šk'orin mut*                                   *Aspatha gularis*

    *kuckuc*                                        *Momotus momota*

COVERT COMPLEX:   woodpecker                                Picidae

    *tukut*                                         *Colaptes auratus*

    *ti?*                                           *Centurus aurifrons*

    *k'oročoč*                                      *Melanerpes formicivorus*

    *tuncerek'*                                     *Dryocopus lineatus*

    *c'ihtil*                                       {*Dendrocopos*  
                                                             {*Piculus*

    *?ihk'al c'ihtil*                               *Dendrocopos villosus*

    *c'irin c'ihtil*                                *D. scalaris*

    *k'anal c'ihtil*                                *Piculus rubiginosus*

    *c'irin mut*                                    *Certhia familiaris*

    *c'uhkin mut*                                   Dendrocolaptidae

**Figure 5.44**   The parrot, trogon–motmot, and woodpecker complexes.

do not keep them as pets. Nevertheless, several generic categories are widely recognized in Tenejapan Tzeltal. All are considered **shoyetik** 'associates' (AMT, SMZ). All known species of the Psittacidae are included in this complex.

### *puyuč'* [UN]: Small parrots

This term was first elicited from a Tzeltal-speaking informant in the *municipio* of Huitiupán, for a medium-sized, short-tailed parrot common at that locality. This species is most likely either the White-crowned

Parrot (*Pionus senilis*) or the White-fronted Parrot (*Amazona albifrons*). SMZ, who was also present, called this parrot **periko** (see following taxon), not having heard the native Tzeltal term. It was later discovered that many Tenejapanecos know this term and associate it with this complex. I was unable to determine further the range of referents properly so called. One highland informant asserted that **puyuč'** occurred near his home. If correct, he was most likely referring to the Barred Parakeet (*Bolborhynchus lineola*), a rare cloud-forest species not otherwise known to occur near Tenejapa.

**períko** [ < Sp *perico* 'parrot spp.'] : Medium-sized parrots not included in **puyuč'** or **lorotíro**, in particular the Yellow-headed Parrot (*Amazona ochrocephala*), a common cage bird (see Figure 5.45)

SMZ also applied this name to the Orange-fronted Parakeet (*Aratinga canicularis*), which is common near Chiapa de Corzo, and the Green Parakeet (*A. holochlora*), seen near Villa las Rosas. AGM, however, considered the former species to be **lorotíro** (see following taxon).

Other Spanish loans are used synonymously:

**kotóro, kotoríta** [ < Sp *cotorra, cotorrita* 'parrot spp.', 'small parrot spp.'].

**lóro** [ < Sp *loro* 'parrot spp.'].

No difference in referent is recognized among these terms by Tenejapanecos, though distinctions may be drawn by Ladinos. For some reason most Tenejapanecos consider **períko** to be the **bac'il sbil** 'true name'.

Figure 5.46  *lorotíro* Orange-fronted Parakeet (*Aratinga canicularis*). [From Emmet Reid Blake, *Birds of Mexico : A Guide for Field Identification.* Copyright 1953 by The University of Chicago Press.]

Figure 5.45 *períko* 'parrot' (*Amazona* sp.) [Drawing by AMT.]

**lorotíro** [ < Sp *loro* 'parrot spp.' + UN]: Small parrots, especially the Orange-fronted Parakeet (*Aratinga canicularis*) of the upper Grijalva valley (see Figure 5.46, see also preceding taxon)

The Orange-chinned Parakeet (*Brotogeris jugularis*) of the Pacific coastal lowlands is also a likely referent for informants with *finca* experience. **períko** and **lorotíro** are distinguished in this presentation from **puyuč'**, since no two are clearly synonymous. Infor-

mants who recognized **puyuč'** contrasted it with **períko**, while informants who contrasted **lorotíro** and **períko** were not familiar with **puyuč'**. However it is not certain that **puyuč'** and **lorotíro** refer to the same range of denotata. As used in Huitiupán **puyuč'** refers to a species that SMZ called **períko**. The absence of parrots from the Tenejapan fauna confuses both informants and ethnographer.

**mo?** [UN]: Macaws (*Ara* spp.) (see Figure 5.47).

Informants who claim to have seen this bird describe it as 'red', thus the Scarlet Macaw (*Ara macao*) is implied. This species is more likely in the Gulf coast drainage than is the primarily green Military Macaw (*A. militaris*); it is thus more likely to be encountered by Tzeltal speakers on the whole. Most informants know this taxon from hearsay only.

A cognate term with the same meaning is reported for Yucatec Maya (Bowes and

Figure 5.47  *wakamáyo* (AMT) = *moʔ* macaw (*Ara* sp.). [Drawing by AMT.]

Castillo Perez 1964:xix) and Zinacantan Tzotzil (R. Laughlin personal communication). The Spanish loan, **wakamáyo** [< Sp. *guacamayo* 'macaw'], is sometimes used synonymously, as in AMT's heading on Fig. 5.47.

The following taxon is considered related to both the parrot complex and the trogon–motmot complex, and provides a link between those two complexes. Like the parrot, trogon, and motmot, it is a large, long-tailed, large-billed and showy bird.

**pan** [UN]: Toucans (Ramphastidae)

Three species of this family occur in Chiapas, though none occurs regularly in Tenejapa.

Emerald Toucanet (*Aulacorhynchus prasinus*).

Collared Araçari (*Pteroglossus torquatus*) (see Figure 5.48).

Keel-billed Toucan (*Ramphastos sulfuratus*).

All three were identified as **pan** at the Tuxtla Gutiérrez zoo (AGM, JGG, SMZ). The araçari was also seen by JGG and SMZ at Huitiupán and so labeled. Many informants have never seen these birds. Synonyms include **pan mut** 'toucan bird' and **pum niʔ mut** 'swollen-beaked bird'. Some recognize heterogeneity within this taxon, but no consistently named varietals were recorded.

# TROGON – MOTMOT COMPLEX

This complex includes all species of trogons (Trogonidae) and motmots (Momotidae) known to the Tenejapa Tzeltal. This complex is linked to the preceding parrot complex through the generic **pan** 'toucan'.

**k'uk'** 'feather': Trogons (Trogonidae), in particular the Mountain Trogon (*Trogon mexicanus*) (see Figure 5.49)

The Mountain Trogon is common in highland pine forests; it may be recognized by call. Sexual dimorphism is correctly interpreted. The yellow-bellied Violaceous Trogon (*T. violaceus*) seen at Huitiupán was included here (JGG, SMZ). However most verbal descriptions specify a 'red' belly.

Cognate terms are widely reported throughout the Mayan area and are invariably

Figure 5.48  *pan* Collared Araçari (*Pteroglossus torquatus*). [From Emmet Reid Blake, *Birds of Mexico: A Guide for Field Identification.* Copyright 1953 by The University of Chicago Press.]

**Figure 5.49** *k'uk'* Mountain Trogon (*Trogon mexicanus*).
[From Emmet Reid Blake, *Birds of Mexico: A Guide for Field Identification.* Copyright 1953 by The University of Chicago Press.]

glossed as 'quetzal'. The Resplendent Quetzal (*Pharomachrus mocinno*) is a trogon, but to the best of my knowledge presently occurs no closer to Tenejapa than the virgin montane rain forest near Pueblo Nuevo Solistahuacán (D. Breedlove personal communication). None of my informants seemed familar with that species.

The association of trogons with the term for 'feather' is explicable in terms of the historical importance of quetzal feathers in classic Mayan culture. In Tenejapa this etymological relationship is not clearly recognized. Rather, the name is alleged to be onomatopoetic.

Alternate forms recorded include the following:

*šk'uk'* [pp + 'feather'].

*c'aran k'uk'* 'shining feather'.

No subdivisions are consistently recognized.

*šk'orin mut* [gn + ON + 'bird']: The Blue-throated Motmot (*Aspatha gularis*)

This beautiful but secretive bird is fairly common in the highland pine forests of Tenejapa. I netted individuals on two occasions, which were so named by SMZ. Other lowland informants present were unfamiliar with both the name and the bird. Informants most likely to know the bird, i.e., highland residents, were not available on those occasions, though several such informants did recognize the name. Others responded to a verbal description of this motmot but were unfamiliar with the term *šk'orin mut* and unable to supply an alternative. It is difficult to understand why this taxon is poorly known. SMT misidentified this bird's call as that of *toytoy* (see the owl complex), while AGM denied that its call was that of an 'owl' but could recall no appropriate name.

A possible synonym is *kulinpe mut* [UN + 'bird']. Other motmots are treated in the following taxon.

*kuckuc* [ON]: The Blue-crowned Motmot (*Momotus momota*) (see Figure 5.50)

This large, racket-tailed species occurs at lower elevations to the north (e.g., Yajalón, 700 m, and Huitiupán, 300 m). According to lowland Tenejapanecos it occurs occasionally in the *municipio*. JGG recognized it by call. Variants include *kuckuc mut* and *kučkuč mut* [both, ON + 'bird'].

The Russet-crowned Motmot (*M. mexicanus*) is common and conspicuous near Chiapa de Corzo in the upper Grijalva valley. AGM, JGG, and SMZ all asserted that it was a strange bird they had never seen before, though perhaps related to *kuckuc*. They did not consider it a kind of any known generic category.

## WOODPECKER COMPLEX

This complex includes all locally occurring species of woodpeckers (Picidae). The complex is occasionally referred to by the mor-

**Figure 5.50** *kuckuc* motmot [Drawing by AMT.]

phologically complex term **hut te? mut** [ < tv 'pierce' + 'tree' + 'bird'] or **toh te? mut** ['straight' + 'tree' + 'bird'], descriptive of the characteristic habits of these birds. These terms are not widely recognized and are polylexemic. The type genus of the complex is **ti?** (see second taxon in this complex), and that term may be used to refer to all members of the complex with the exception of **tukut** 'flicker' (see first taxon in this complex), the least woodpeckerlike of the woodpeckers.

**tukut** [ON]: The Common Flicker (*Colaptes auratus*) (see Figure 5.51a)

This species is a common resident throughout Tenejapa, especially in the highlands, and is known to everyone. One, shot with a slingshot (**tirerol**) by two young informants, was eaten. It is considered to be related to the other members of the complex though its ground-feeding behavior is remarked upon. It is also known as **tuktuk mut** [ON + 'bird'], possibly a loan from Tzotzil (R. Laughlin personal communication).

**ti?** [ON]: The Golden-fronted Woodpecker (*Centurus aurifrons*) (see Figure 5.51b)

This species, common below 1800 m, is also known as **k'anal ti?** 'yellow woodpecker'. SMZ, however, insisted that **ti?** is properly applied to the Acorn Woodpecker (*Melanerpes formicivorus*). SMZ has apparently reversed this term with the next, since his opinion is out-voted. **ti?** is considered to be **hlabtawaneh mut** 'harbinger-of-evil bird'.

**k'oročoč** [ON]: The Acorn Woodpecker (*Melanerpes formicivorus*) (see Figures 5.51c, 5.52)

This species is common throughout. The

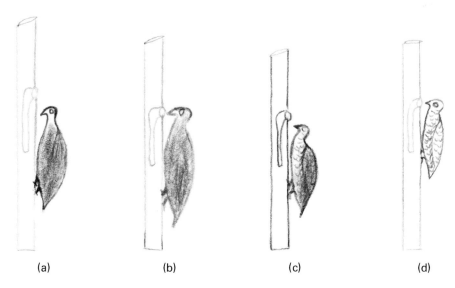

(a)        (b)        (c)        (d)

**Figure 5.51** *hut te? mutetik* 'woodpeckers': (a) *tukut* 'flicker'; (b) *ti?* 'Golden-fronted Woodpecker'; (c) *k'oročoč* 'Acorn Woodpecker'; (d) *c'ihtil* 'small woodpecker'. [Drawings by AMT.]

Figure 5.52 *k'oročoč* Acorn Woodpecker (*Melanerpes formicivorus*). [From Emmet Reid Blake, *Birds of Mexico: A Guide for Field Identification*. Copyright 1953 by The University of Chicago Press.]

name is particularly appropriate for the call of this species (but see *ti?*).

**tuncerek'** [ON]: The Lineated Woodpecker (*Dryocopus lineatus*) (see Figure 5.53)

This species was observed at Ocosingo (900 m). The less common Pale-billed Woodpecker (*Campephilus guatemalensis*) would

Figure 5.53 *tuncerek'* Lineated Woodpecker (*Dryocopus lineatus*). [From Emmet Reid Blake, *Birds of Mexico: A Guide for Field Identification*. Copyright 1953 by The University of Chicago Press.]

no doubt also be included. Both rarely occur above 1200 m and are thus not well known. Some informants consider **tuncerek'** to be synonymous with either **ti?** (see earlier taxon) or **c'ihtil** (see next taxon). One informant identified pictures of the Lineated and Pale-billed Woodpeckers as **t'ok hol ti?** 'crest-headed woodpecker', another as **muk'ul ti?** 'large woodpecker'. Both terms are descriptively appropriate and indicate the relationships perceived within the complex. Only the largest of the local woodpeckers are known as *carpintero* in local Spanish. Some tenejapanecos also apply **karpintéro** to this category. Phonological variants include the following:

**tumcerek'**, **tunčerek'** [both ON].

**tunčerek' mut** [ON + 'bird'].

**c'ihtil** [ON]: The smaller woodpeckers, in particular the widespread Hairy Woodpecker (*Dendrocopos villosus*) (see Figure 5.51d)

The following subdivisions may be recognized (SMZ):

a. *?ihk'al c'ihtil* 'black woodpecker': The Hairy Woodpecker.

b. *c'irin c'ihtil* 'streaked woodpecker': The Ladder-backed Woodpecker (*D. scalaris*). This species is resident locally, as at Ocosingo, though not seen in Tenejapa. It is also known as *p'uhtul c'ihtil* 'blotched woodpecker'.

c. *k'anal c'ihtil* 'yellow woodpecker': The Golden-olive Woodpecker (*Piculus rubiginosus*) (see Figure 5.54). This species is uncommon in Tenejapa below 1800 m.

One informant considered **tuncerek'** (see preceding taxon) synonymous with this taxon. **c'ihtil** is considered to be **hlabtawaneh mut** 'harbinger-of-evil bird'. **c'ihtil** is used as a pattern-descriptive adjective, in naming certain other animal taxa (e.g., **pehpen** /butterfly-moth).

**c'irin mut** 'streaked bird': The Brown Creeper, *Certhia familiaris* (Certhiidae) (see Figure 5.55)

Figure 5.54 *kʼanal cʼihtil* Golden-olive Woodpecker (*Piculus rubiginosus*). [From Emmet Reid Blake, *Birds of Mexico: A Guide for Field Identification*. Copyright 1953 by The University of Chicago Press.]

Figure 5.55 *cʼirin mut* Brown Creeper (*Certhia familiaris*). [From Emmet Reid Blake, *Birds of Mexico: A Guide for Field Identification*. Copyright 1953 by The University of Chicago Press.]

This uncommon highland species is not related to either woodpeckers (Picidae) or woodcreepers (Dendrocolaptidae), though it is similarly adapted to feeding on insects found in the bark of trees. Though smaller than most woodcreepers, this species is quite similar even as to its voice. SMZ, the only informant with whom I saw both, distinguished this species from the woodcreepers. However SMZ used the term **tutin cʼihtil** 'baby woodpecker' (see *cʼihtil*/woodpecker) for the Brown Creeper, by which he meant to suggest only that it was related to that category, not that it was a developmental stage of *cʼihtil*. Neither **tutin cʼihtil** nor *cʼirin mut* is widely recognized. The bird is readily overlooked, since it is small, inconspicuous, and uncommon. For an alternate application of this name see **cob nič ʔak**/siskin-seedeater.

**cʼuhkin mut** [ON + 'bird']: Woodcreepers (Dendrocolaptidae) (see Figure 5.56), in particular the Spot-crowned Woodcreeper (*Lepidocolaptes affinis*)

Figure 5.56 *pakʼin teʔ mut* (AMT) = *cʼuhkin mut* woodcreepers (Dendrocolaptidae). [Drawing by AMT.]

This species is widespread, though like all species of the family, it is secretive and rarely encountered. This name was supplied by AKCʼ for a bird mist-netted in **san ʔantónyo**. Other local informants verified the name. JGG and SMZ prefer the term **špahkʼin teʔ mut** [< tv 'paste to surface' + 'tree' + 'bird'], for this and the Ivory-billed Woodcreeper (*Xiphorhynchus flavigaster*) and are not familiar with the primary name. Several other related species might occur in the region, in particular the Strong-billed Wood-creeper (*Xiphocolaptes promeropirhynchus*), which was observed once near San Cristóbal. I have no evidence, however, that this category is perceived to be heterogeneous.

Other variants include the following:

**špak'in teʔ mut**, **špahkʾ teʔ mut**. These two variants, with or without the prefix **š-**, are essentially equivalent.

**nap'nap' teʔ mut** [ < tv 'stick to the surface' reduplicated + 'tree' + 'bird'] is similarly descriptive.

**c'uhkin** is also the name of a lineage of the **kusman** "clan".

## FLYCATCHER COMPLEX
(See Figure 5.57)

This complex includes all locally occurring species of the Tyrannidae, the tyrant fly-catchers. Besides being commonly described as *shoyetik* 'associates', evidence from newly coined names supports this grouping. The type genus is **wirin** (see first taxon of this complex) since that term is used when unfamiliar species of this family are encountered.

**wirin** [ON] (see Figure 5.58): Two species in particular constitute the core range, the Dusky-capped Flycatcher (*Myiarchus tuber-*

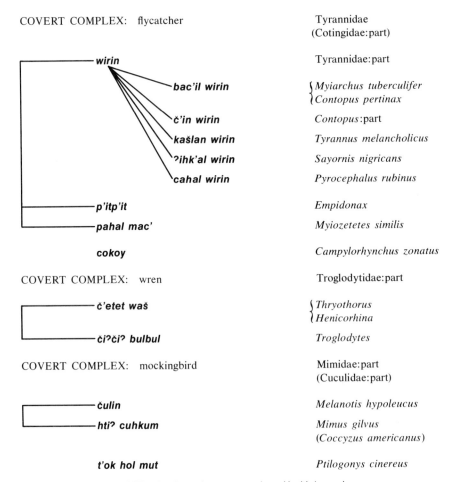

| COVERT COMPLEX: flycatcher | Tyrannidae (Cotingidae:part) |
|---|---|
| wirin | Tyrannidae:part |
| bac'il wirin | { *Myiarchus tuberculifer* / *Contopus pertinax* |
| č'in wirin | *Contopus*:part |
| kašlan wirin | *Tyrannus melancholicus* |
| ʔihk'al wirin | *Sayornis nigricans* |
| cahal wirin | *Pyrocephalus rubinus* |
| p'itp'it | *Empidonax* |
| pahal mac' | *Myiozetetes similis* |
| cokoy | *Campylorhynchus zonatus* |
| COVERT COMPLEX: wren | Troglodytidae:part |
| č'etet waš | { *Thryothorus* / *Henicorhina* |
| čiʔčiʔ bulbul | *Troglodytes* |
| COVERT COMPLEX: mockingbird | Mimidae:part (Cuculidae:part) |
| čulin | *Melanotis hypoleucus* |
| htiʔ cuhkum | *Mimus gilvus* (*Coccyzus americanus*) |
| t'ok hol mut | *Ptilogonys cinereus* |

**Figure 5.57** The flycatcher, wren, and mockingbird complexes.

**Figure 5.58** *wirin* flycatcher. [Drawing by AMT.]

*culifer*) and the Greater Pewee (*Contopus pertinax*)

Both are medium-sized flycatchers common throughout Tenejapa. Several less common species are included in the following widely recognized specific subdivisions.

a. **bac'il wirin** 'true flycatcher'. As above. Both species are also referred to as **muk'ul wirin** 'large flycatcher' or **ʔahwalil wirin** 'boss flycatcher'. This latter term refers to the alleged fact that other small birds 'gather around' these species as subordinates around a leader. A third synonym is **t'ok hol wirin** 'crest-headed flycatcher', quite descriptive, at least of the Greater Pewee. Other synonyms include:

**butbut mut** [ON + 'bird'].

**hmak ʔus** 'flycatcher' (MMH).

**htiʔ čikitin** 'cicada eater'.

**htiʔ ʔus** 'fly eater'.

**t'ukt'uk** [ON].

**wirwin** [ON].

Several of these synonyms indicate a correct assessment of the birds' feeding habits.

b. **č'in wirin** 'small flycatcher': The smaller pewees.  Definitely recorded for the Western Wood-Pewee (*Contopus sordidulus*) found breeding near Soyatitán, and the Tropical Pewee (*Contopus cinereus*), singing in June near Ocosingo. A possible Eastern Wood-Pewee (*Contopus virens*) heard in migration in Tenejapa was called **parantun** by DMT, a name not otherwise recorded. These species are all very similar in appearance.

A synonym for the specific name is **mashol wirin** 'smooth-headed flycatcher', since they lack the crest of their larger congener, the Greater Pewee (see the previous folk species). *Empidonax* flycatchers are included here by some informants though distinguished by others (see **p'ltp'it** and **pahal mac'**).

c. **kašlan wirin** 'Ladino flycatcher': Kingbirds, in particular the resident Tropical Kingbird (*Tyrannus melancholicus*). This species, found below 1500 m, is also called **yašal wirin** 'green flycatcher'. Informants did not seem very familiar with this species or with the Cassin's Kingbird (*Tyrannus vociferans*), which was observed in migration in drier areas to the south. I observed the Eastern Kingbird (*Tyrannus tyrannus*) once at San Cristóbal. However, there is no evidence that it would be included here.

d. **ʔihk'al wirin** 'black flycatcher': The Black Phoebe (*Sayornis nigricans*).  This species is a rare resident in Tenejapa along the rivers. SMZ and JGG were not familiar with it. They considered this name appropriate, and several other informants seemed familiar with the term.

e. **cahal wirin** 'red flycatcher': Either the Vermilion Flycatcher (*Pyrocephalus rubinus*) or the Tufted Flycatcher (*Mitrephanes phaeocercus*).  The former species is common at San Cristóbal but not definitely known from Tenejapa (where its meadow habitat is scarce); the latter, common in pine forests throughout, was also called **t'ok hol wirin** 'crest-headed flycatcher' (but see first taxon in this complex) and **p'itp'it** [ON] by other informants. In any case Tenejapanecos correctly place these species in this complex.

Other subdivisions recorded are clearly inventions. These coinages demonstrate, however, that the extended range of **wirin** embraces the entire family and perhaps certain of the Cotingidae as well.

**k'anal wirin** 'yellow flycatcher' was applied to the following unfamiliar species by SMZ:

Great Kiskadee (*Pitangus sulphuratus*).

Boat-billed Flycatcher (*Megarynchus pitangua*).

Social Flycatcher (*Myiozetetes similis*), but see **pahal mac'**, this complex.

Sulphur-bellied Flycatcher (*Myiodynastes luteiventris*).

These four species are restricted by altitude such that only the Social Flycatcher was recorded in Tenejapa.

**cahp wirin** 'clansman of the flycatcher': This attributive is often used to indicate a relationship between an unfamiliar species and a familiar taxon. In this instance AGM was referring to the Tropical Kingbird.

**merikáno wirin** 'American flycatcher': SMZ related how his father had described such a category. He first stated that it was 'red' but then applied the term to the Masked Tityra, *Tityra semifasciata* (Cotingidae), modifying it to **sakil merikáno wirin** 'white American flycatcher'. It is clear that SMZ has no personal knowledge of this alleged taxon, nor had he seen the tityra before. However, his placement of the tityra in **wirin** is instructive, as the cotingas are closely related to the tyrant flycatchers. The 'red' species originally described might apply to several large reddish cotingas, in particular the Rufous Mourner (*Rhytipterna holerythra*), though none of these species was observed. All are rare, tropical forest species. Why the attributive **merikáno** is selected can only be guessed. In other contexts it suggests large size and thus is appropriate to the tityra and mourner.

**tešereš ne wirin** 'scissor-tail flycatcher': For the Scissor-tailed Flycatcher (*Muscivora forficata*) seen near Chiapa de Corzo.

**p'itp'it** [ON]: *Empidonax* flycatchers (see Figure 5.59)

**Figure 5.59**  *p'itp'it* flycatchers (*Empidonax* spp.). [From Emmet Reid Blake, *Birds of Mexico: A Guide for Field Identification*. Copyright 1953 by The University of Chicago Press. *E. difficilis*.]

Applied by SMZ to the Buff-breasted Flycatcher (*E. fulvifrons*) and the White-throated Flycatcher (*E. albigularis*). The first species is fairly common in the drier woodland near San Cristóbal. It was considered somewhat atypical by SMZ. Perhaps a related species occurs in his home *paraje*. Edwards (1972: 155) describes the call note of the Buff-breasted Flycatcher as "pit," however other species of this genus have similar call notes. The White-throated Flycatcher is rare and local, especially attracted to marshy areas as in **banabil**, where one was observed. Though SMZ called that bird **p'itp'it**, the local informant (MMH) called it **kuikui sit** [ON]. A second variant is **loslos mut** [ON + 'mut'] applied to the Buff-breasted Flycatcher by AGM. Other variants include **pi?pi? mut** and **wikwik mut** both of which are onomatopoetic.

SMZ also assigned a Tufted Flycatcher (*Mitrephanes phaeocercus*), which was mistnetted, to this taxon (but see (e) of the previous taxon). He was unable, however, to recognize its song from a tape recording.

Yellowish Flycatchers (*Empidonax flavescens*) were captured on two occasions. In the first instance several informants (including AMT) did not recognize the species. One informant called it *šušubin mut* [ < iv 'whistle' + 'bird']. *šušub mut* is a variant of this. The second specimen was called *pihwač* [ON], a term elicited on several occasions. It appears that a great deal of variation exists in the naming or failure to name these small flycatchers. The low salience of the taxon allows it to be named differently in different areas of the *municipio*. The Yellowish Flycatcher does, however, breed in Tenejapa, as a nest under construction was observed near the Pueblo of Tenejapa.

A Pine Flycatcher (*Empidonax affinis*) netted near San Cristóbal also generated disagreement. Some thought it was *p'itp'it*, others considered it to be *č'in wirin* (see (b) of the previous taxon). The Greater Pewee (*Contopus pertinax*, see previous taxon) was called *muk'ul p'itp'it* 'large empidonax' on one occasion in response to its call note. This evidence indicates that *p'itp'it* and *wirin* are associated categories. In migration and during winter, many northern species of *Empidonax*, which are indistinguishable in the field, also occur. Thus a range of continuous variation is created, which makes clear distinctions among the various resident species difficult to perceive. It seems best to treat all these names as variants for a single taxon.

**pahal mac'** [ON, lit. 'sour' + 'corn gruel']: The Social Flycatcher (*Myiozetetes similis*)

This species occurs sparingly in Tenejapa below 1500 m. The same term is applied to the similar, though extralimital, Great Kiskadee (*Pitangus sulphuratus*) and possibly would be extended also to include the Boat-billed Flycatcher (*Megarhynchus pitangua*). This term is widely distributed; identical or similar forms, with identical or related meanings, are reported from Huitiupán Tzeltal (for the Great Kiskadee) and from Zinacantan Tzotzil (R. Laughlin personal communication).

SMZ called these species *k'anal wirin* 'yellow flycatcher' (see **wirin**) in the un-familiar setting of Ocosingo, but recognized the Social Flycatcher as **pahal mac'** when observed in his home *paraje*. This indicates the relationship perceived between this taxon and the type generic. Variants include *k'anal č'uht mut* 'yellow-bellied bird' (but see Hypothetical List: Birds) and *ʔak' yihkac teʔ* ['vine'? + 'mistletoe']. A variant of the latter term is typically applied to the Rufous-browed Peppershrike, *Cyclarhis gujanensis* (Cyclarhidae, see **yihkac teʔ**/bird).

**coʔkoy** [ON]: The Band-backed Wren, *Campylorhynchus zonatus* (Troglodytidae) (see Figure 5.60)

This bird is common and conspicuous throughout Tenejapa. Informants readily recognize it by its voice.

Alternate names indicate the association of this bird with warts (*čohk'*), i.e., *meʔ čohk'* 'mother of the wart' and *pošil čohk'* 'wart medicine'. The first cure for an outbreak of warts is to seek out these birds, sing and dance in imitation of them, and pray that the bird will take away the warts. If this fails other remedies are applied. The rationale for this association is unclear.

When SMZ first encountered the Red-throated Ant-Tanager, *Habia fuscicauda* (Thraupidae), he coined the term *cahal coʔkoy* 'red Band-backed Wren'. The ant-tanager produces similar raucous calls, but it is restricted to elevations below 1200 m and probably does not occur in Tenejapa.

**Figure 5.60** *coʔkoy* Band-backed Wren (*Campylorhynchus zonatus*). [Color slide by author.]

## WREN COMPLEX

Two categories of small wrens are recognized as **shoyetik** 'associates'. The association of **coʔkoy** with this complex is not recognized. These three taxa include all the local species of wrens (Troglodytidae).

**č'etet waš** [ON, lit. UN + 'fox']: The Plain Wren (*Thryothorus modestus*) (see Figure 5.61a) and the Grey-breasted Wood-Wren (*Henicorhina leucophrys*)

The former species was so named by lowland informants (below 1800 m); the latter, by highland informants. These two species were not found together in Tenejapa. Though not closely related, both are clearly distinguished from the following taxon, which includes a widely distributed species. The Plain Wren is abundant in brushy growth. It produces a great variety of song. I found myself asking **bi mutil ya šk'ahin** 'what is the bird that is singing?' repeatedly for what seemed to be several species of birds. The inevitable response was **č'etet waš**, and in every case it proved to be this wren. My informants were not misled by the vocal variation. The woodwren is less common, usually keeping to heavy forest cover. It was identified from a captured specimen.

The Spot-breasted Wren (*Thryothorus maculipectus*) and the Banded Wren (*T. pleurostictus*), both found at lower elevations in the region, were assigned to this taxon on the basis of voice and superficial observation. The category remains homogeneous, however, since the variety of referents is explicable in zoogeographical terms.

**Figure 5.61**  (a) *č'et č'et waš* (AMT) = *č'etet waš* Plain Wren (*Thryothorus modestus*), (b) *čiʔčiʔ bulbul* Southern House-Wren (*Troglodytes musculus*). [Drawings by AMT.]

Alternative names include the following:

**č'etč'et waš, č'itč'it waš,** and **č'ikč'ik waš** [all ON].

**č'akulʔit mut** ['flea' + rs + 'buttocks' + 'bird']. a humorous reference to the bird's rapid flitting within the vegetation.

**ʔóra mut₂** 'hour bird', a term usually applied to **ʔotʔot** (see the black bird complex). It is claimed that these birds mark the hour with their singing (see also **sian/** thrush).

A Canyon Wren (*Catherpes mexicanus*) observed near Chiapa de Corzo was unfamiliar to SMZ and AGM. However they considered it to be **kol pahaluk sok č'etet waš** 'almost the same as the house-wren'.

**čiʔčiʔ bulbul** [ON]: The Southern House-Wren (*Troglodytes musculus*) (see Figures 5.61b, 5.62)

**Figure 5.62**  *čiʔčiʔ bulbul* Southern House-Wren (*Troglodytes musculus*). [From Emmet Reid Blake, *Birds of Mexico: A Guide for Field Identification.* Copyright 1953 by The University of Chicago Press.]

This species is abundant throughout Tenejapa. A few informants fail to distinguish between this and the preceding category, considering the terms to be synonymous. The majority, however, recognize both. The similar Rufous-browed Wren (*Troglodytes rufo-ciliatus*) is uncommon in damp forest at higher elevations (above 2100 m). It is probably included here without the perception of heterogeneity.

*mutil čan* 'snake bird', is a synonym. This refers to an association noted between this wren and snakes. A factual basis exists for this, as small birds often flock together to harass predators. While observing an excited house-wren once at *yočib*, I noticed that a small snake was the cause of his excitement.

## MOCKINGBIRD COMPLEX

The first species is well known to all Tenejapanecos. The second is poorly known but clearly recognized as related, despite no obvious similarity in plumage. These two species are the only local resident forms of the Mimidae (but see *sč'e?*/bird).

*čulin* [ON]: The Blue-and-white Mockingbird (*Melanotis hypoleucus*) (see Figure 5.63)

**Figure 5.63**   *čulin* Blue-and-white Mockingbird (*Melanotis hypoleucus*). [Drawing by AMT.]

This species is fairly common throughout but keeps to thick cover. The only element of confusion with respect to this taxon involves the recognition by several informants of varietal subdivisions, *yašal čulin* 'blue mockingbird' and *?ihk'al čulin* 'black mockingbird'. I know of no obvious explanation for this distinction. Perhaps the immatures, which lack the white belly, are distinguished from the adults. However 'black' seems inappropriate in either case.

*čulin mut* is a variety of domestic chicken

(see *mut₂*). No direct connection seems to exist between these homonymous usages.

*hti? cuhkum* 'woolybear caterpillar eater': The Tropical Mockingbird (*Mimus gilvus*)

This species rarely occurs in Tenejapa, (e.g., *macab*), since it is restricted to a short-grass habitat. It is common, however, in the valley of San Cristóbal. No single term is widely used for this taxon, though quite a few informants recognize and name the category.

Alternate names include the following:

*sak mut*, *sakil mut* 'white bird' (see also *mut₂* and *palomaš*/dove).

*sakil čulin* 'white mockingbird'.

*kašlan čulin* 'Ladino mockingbird'.

The latter two terms specify the relationship between this taxon and *čulin* proper.

AGM included the migratory Yellow-billed Cuckoo, *Coccyzus americanus* (Cuculidae), as *hti? cuhkum* also, appropriately descriptive of a preferred food of this cuckoo. Other informants were unfamiliar with this cuckoo and no further evidence concerning it was collected. It is not uncommon throughout the central highlands in migration. An informant from Cancuc (TMN) seemed to know the bird well and called it *yalem mut* 'transitory bird'. This term is polylexemic in Tenejapan usage.

## THRUSH COMPLEX (See Figure 5.64)

The following four taxa are clearly associated. All well-known thrushes (Turdidae) are included with the exception of the bluebird (*Sialia sialis*, see *yaš mut*). The genus *Seiurus* of the wood-warbler family (Parulidae) is also included. It is noteworthy that the most common species of this genus are known in English as "waterthrushes."

*toht* [ON]: Robins, *Turdus* spp. (Turdidae)

The unmodified use of this term may refer specifically to the Rufous-collared Robin (*T. rufitorques*) in high country, or to the Clay-colored Robin (*T. grayi*) in low country. The

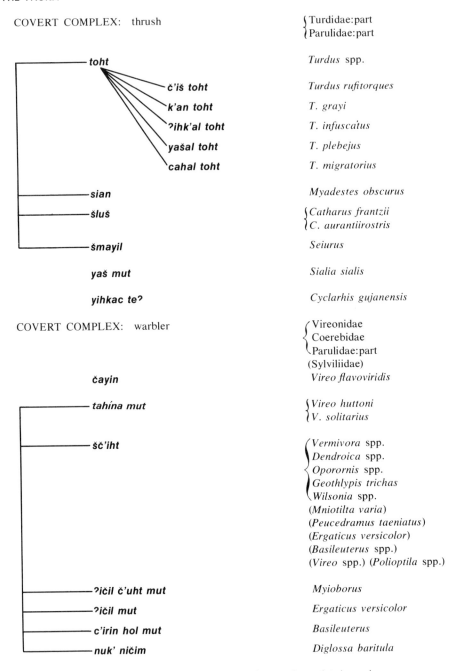

COVERT COMPLEX:   thrush                 Turdidae:part
                                          Parulidae:part

— toht                                    *Turdus* spp.

    č'iš toht                             *Turdus rufitorques*

    k'an toht                            *T. grayi*

    ʔihk'al toht                         *T. infuscatus*

    yašal toht                           *T. plebejus*

    cahal toht                           *T. migratorius*

— sian                                    *Myadestes obscurus*

— šluš                                    *Catharus frantzii*
                                          *C. aurantiirostris*

— šmayil                                  *Seiurus*

yaš mut                                   *Sialia sialis*

yihkac teʔ                                *Cyclarhis gujanensis*

COVERT COMPLEX:   warbler                 Vireonidae
                                          Coerebidae
                                          Parulidae:part
                                          (Sylviliidae)

čayin                                     *Vireo flavoviridis*

— tahína mut                              *Vireo huttoni*
                                          *V. solitarius*

— šč'iht                                   *Vermivora* spp.
                                          *Dendroica* spp.
                                          *Oporornis* spp.
                                          *Geothlypis trichas*
                                          *Wilsonia* spp.
                                          (*Mniotilta varia*)
                                          (*Peucedramus taeniatus*)
                                          (*Ergaticus versicolor*)
                                          (*Basileuterus* spp.)
                                          (*Vireo* spp.) (*Polioptila* spp.)

— ʔičil č'uht mut                         *Myioborus*

— ʔičil mut                               *Ergaticus versicolor*

— c'irin hol mut                          *Basileuterus*

— nuk' ničim                             *Diglossa baritula*

**Figure 5.64**   The thrush and warbler complexes and associated generics.

following inductive subdivisions are clearly recognized:

a. *č'iš toht* [ON, lit. 'thorn' + 'robin']: The Rufous-collared Robin (*T. rufitorques*) (see Figures 5.65a, 5.65b). This species is common and conspicuous above 1500 m. Sexual differences are accurately assessed by all informants questioned on this point. Many synonyms have been recorded as follows:

**kašlan toht** 'Ladino robin' (AMT), the attributive refers to the relatively colorful

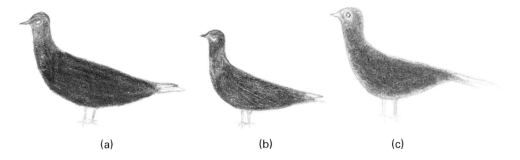

(a)                    (b)                    (c)

Figure 5.65 (a) *tat kašlan toht* (AMT) = *tat č'is toht* 'male Rufous-collared Robin: (b) *me?
kašlan toht* (AMT) = *me? č'is toht* 'female Rufous-collared Robin'; (c) *bac'il toht* (AMT) = *k'an toht*
'Clay-colored Robin'. [Drawings by AMT.]

plumage of this species. The choice of attributive was explained by one informant as due to the fact that "it is very fine looking" (*Es muy fino*). He was chagrined by the implication (see also *c'unun*/bird). This attributive may imply foreignness in other contexts (Berlin, Breedlove, and Raven 1974:43).

*bac'il toht* 'true robin', for highland informants (see (b)).

*cahal nuk' toht* 'red-necked robin', and *k'anal nuk' toht* 'yellow-necked robin'. Both names are adequately descriptive of the "rufous" collar.

*kahalil toht* 'highland robin', citing the distributional fact.

*ha?malil toht* 'jungle robin', *te?tikil toht* 'forest robin'. It is not clear with what this contrasts. Perhaps the following species is somewhat less partial to forested areas?

b. *k'an toht* 'yellow robin': The Clay-colored Robin (*T. grayi*) (see Figure 5.65c). This bird is abundant below 1800 m, where it eventually replaces the preceding species. It is also known as *bac'il toht* 'true robin', to contrast with *kašlan toht* 'Ladino robin'. This variant is reported from *kulak'tik* where the Clay-colored Robin predominates. Also known as *?alanil toht* 'lowland robin' to contrast with *kahalil toht* (see (a)). In both cases, the salient contrast is binary, between the Rufous-collared and Clay-colored robins. The three other species known to occur in the environs of Tenejapa are rare and not so widely recognized.

c. *?ihk'al toht* 'black robin': The Black Robin (*T. infuscatus*). I do not know if the sexual dimorphism of this rare highland robin is recognized. The male, however, was identified as the referent of this term from verbal descriptions and colored illustrations by several informants, as well as from museum specimens by JGG and SMZ. It is described as having a yellow bill, thus color is not the sole attribute noted.

An alternative classification was suggested by one informant (PKC'). He recognizes three types of robins organized as in the following diagram:

This suggests that Black and Rufous-collared robins are more closely associated than either is to the Clay-colored Robin. Superficially this is true.

d. *yašal toht* 'gray robin': The Mountain Robin (*T. plebejus*) (see Figure 5.66). This is the rarest resident species. Two were netted in the *paraje* of *macab*, Tenejapa. The local informant knew this species well and named it without hesitation. The term was not otherwise elicited. It is possible that this species is restricted to this very limited area of Tenejapa.

e. *cahal toht* 'red robin': Probably the American Robin (*T. migratorius*). This species was

Figure 5.66  *yašal toht* Mountain Robin (*Turdus plebejus*). [Color slide by author.]

also *č'etet waš*/wren and *ʔot ʔot*/black bird), as with Zinacantan Tzotzil usage (R. Laughlin personal communication). *sian* is also a lineage name of the *ʔincin* 'clan'.

*šluš* [ON]: Nightingale-thrushes, in particular the Ruddy-capped Nightingale-Thrush, *Catharus frantzii* (Turdidae)

This species is common above 1800 m in Tenejapa. The name imitates the call note. The Orange-billed Nightingale-Thrush (*C. aurantiirostris*) is found in drier areas at lower elevations, such as at *yočib*. SMZ considered the latter species to be atypical, though the local informant (SLL) called it *šluš*. As in the case of *č'etet waš* (see the wren complex) similar allopatric species may be considered typical in different regions. It is also known as *šluš mut*, *slus* or *slus mut*. *slus* is a personal name derivative of Spanish *Lucia*.

not observed in Tenejapa, though it occurs at San Cristóbal in the winter (D. Breedlove personal communication). Several informants considered this term synonymous with *yalem toht* 'transitory robin' and stated that it occurred only during the winter months. However SMZ denied that an American Robin seen near Mexico City was of this category. Yet I can imagine no other species that both fits SMZ's own description of this category and that might occur in Tenejapa. Despite his denial, I consider the American Robin the probable referent of this term.

A few informants also described a bird called *sakil toht* 'white robin'. I was unable to determine the referent of this term. It does not seem appropriate for the sixth species of the genus reported from Chiapas, the White-throated Robin (*T. assimilis*), a rather dark-gray robin of the lowlands, which was never observed.

*sian* [ON]: The Brown-backed Solitaire, *Myadestes obscurus* (Turdidae) (see Figure 5.67)

The beautiful voice of this bird is heard throughout Tenejapa above 1500 m, though it is not often seen. The Slate-colored Solitaire (*M. unicolor*) may also occur, at lower elevations, but it was not observed. The name is sometimes pronounced *san* or *sirin*. It may also be known as *ʔóra mut₃* 'hour bird' (see

Figure 5.67  *sian* Brown-backed Solitaire (*Myadestes obscurus*). [Color slide by author.]

*šmayil* [gn + 'squash']: The Louisiana Waterthrush, *Seiurus motacilla*, and the Northern Waterthrush, *S. noveboracensis* (both Parulidae) (see Figure 5.68)

The reference to *mayil* 'squash' (*Cucurbita ficifolia*) is apparently descriptive of the spotted underparts of these species, a pattern like that of this squash. Both species are common visitors throughout, especially near water. This taxon is widely recognized and may be identified by call note alone. The congeneric Ovenbird (*Seiurus aurocapillus*) was encoun-

**Figure 5.68** *šmayil* Northern Waterthrush (*Seiurus nove-boracensis*). [From Emmet Reid Blake, *Birds of Mexico: A Guide for Field Identification*. Copyright 1953 by The University of Chicago Press.]

tered on one occasion. AGM called it **čahp šmayil** 'clansman of the waterthrush', thus clearly recognizing the distinctiveness of the genus. **mayil mut** 'squash bird' is a variant.

**yaš mut** 'blue bird': The Eastern Bluebird, *Sialia sialis* (Turdidae).

This species is fairly common in the highlands and may occasionally be found below 1500 m in Tenejapa. Variants include the following:

**yašal mut, yašal pat mut** 'blue-backed bird'.

**yaš haʔwil** 'blue year'.

**ʔulič haʔwil** 'swallow year', indicating a relationship with swallows (**ʔulič**)? It is also considered to be an 'associate' of **šluš** (see earlier taxon in this complex).

**t'ok hol mut** 'crest-headed bird': The Gray Silky-flycatcher. *Ptilogonys cinereus* (Ptilogonatidae) (see Figure 5.69)

This species, rather conspicuous in treetop flocks above 1800 m, is not a true flycatcher. It is also known by the following synonyms:

**hloʔ čičoteʔ, hloʔ čičoteʔ mut** [< tv 'eat' + 'cherry' + 'bird'], referring to a typical food.

**t'ukul toht** [UN + 'robin'], suggesting a relationship with the robins.

**Figure 5.69** *t'ok hol mut* Gray Silky-flycatcher (*Ptilogonys cinereus*). [From Emmet Reid Blake, *Birds of Mexico: A Guide for Field Identification*. Copyright 1953 by The University of Chicago Press.]

**č'utub** [ON].

**wisánte** [<Sp?], perhaps idiosyncratic (AMT).

**yihkac teʔ** 'mistletoe': The Rufous-browed Peppershrike, *Cyclarhis gujanensis* (Cyclarhidae) (see Figure 5.70)

**Figure 5.70** *yihkac teʔ* Rufous-browed Peppershrike (*Cyclarhis gujanensis*). [Color slide by author.]

Fairly common throughout to at least 2100 m. More often heard than seen. The rationale for the name is unclear. A synonym is *ʔalkawéta* which is alleged to be onomatopoetic, though it has Spanish stress. AGM names this taxon *ʔalkawéta* and applies a variant of the primary name, i.e., *ʔak' yihkac te ʔ* ['vine' + 'mistletoe'] to refer to what is usually called *pahal mac'* (see the flycatcher complex). *ʔalkawéta mut* is a variant.

## WOOD-WARBLER COMPLEX

This group comprises all the taxa that include vireos (Vireonidae), wood-warblers (Parulidae), and honey creepers (Coerebidae) with the sole exception of the waterthrushes, *Seiurus* spp. (Parulidae). The wood-warblers constitute the bulk of the species considered. The majority of these are migratory. All are small, often brightly colored, but difficult to see since they prefer thick vegetation cover. They are too small to be considered worth eating but are not otherwise considered inedible. The type generic is *šč'iht* (third taxon in this complex), since species not readily named are most often assigned to the extended range of this taxon. Several of the taxa of this complex are of low salience, as attested to by the fact that many informants are unfamiliar with them. For these informants, all but the best-known species, e.g., Wilson's Warbler (*Wilsonia pusilla*), Slate-throated Redstart (*Myioborus miniatus*), and the Cinnamon Flower-piercer (*Diglossa baritula*), are considered either *kps šč'iht* or X *mut*, where X is a literally descriptive adjective.

*čayin* [UN]: Term used by SMZ for the Yellow-green Vireo, *Vireo flavoviridis* (Vireonidae)

He considered the highland Hutton's Vireo (*V. huttoni*) to be *kps čayin* (but see following taxon). The Yellow-green Vireo is at best rare in Tenejapa. It was observed only at lower elevations outside the *municipio*. This taxon, also labeled *šayin*, is not widely known.

*tahína mut* [< iv 'play'? + 'bird']: The Hutton's Vireo, *Vireo huttoni* (Vireonidae), and the transient Solitary Vireo (*V. solitarius*) (see Figure 5.71)

Both were mist-netted in *san ʔantónyo*, Tenejapa (AKC'). This term is not known to lowland informants. The similar White-eyed (*V. griseus*) and Warbling Vireos (*V. gilvus)* were referred to as *kps šč'iht* (see below) by lowland informants. Thus a relationship between vireos (Vireonidae) and wood-warblers (Parulidae) is implied.

Figure 5.71  *tahína mut* Solitary vireo (*Vireo solitarius*). [Color slide by author.]

*šč'iht* [gn + ON]: A residual category usually restricted to the wood-warblers (Parulidae), in particular those of primarily yellow plumage.

The most abundant species, which is invariably assigned here, is the migratory Wilson's Warbler (*Wilsonia pusilla*). Other species usually included are as follows:

Nashville Warbler (*Vermivora ruficapilla*), common visitor.

Crescent-chested Warbler (*V. superciliosa*), highland resident (see Figure 5.72).

Yellow Warbler (*Dendroica petechia*), common visitor.

Magnolia Warbler (*D. magnolia*), common visitor.

Yellow-rumped Warbler (*D. coronata*), common visitor.

**Figure 5.72**  Crescent-chested Warbler (*Vermivora super-ciliosa*). [From Emmet Reid Blake, *Birds of Mexico: A Guide for Field Identification.* Copyright 1953 by The University of Chicago Press.]

Townsend's Warbler (*D. townsendi*), common visitor.

Black-throated Green Warbler (*D. virens*), common visitor.

Golden-cheeked Warbler (*D. chrysoparia*), rare visitor.

Hermit Warbler (*D. occidentalis*), common visitor in pine forest.

MacGillivray's Warbler (*Oporornis tolmiei*), common visitor.

Common Yellowthroat (*Geothlypis trichas*), common visitor to riverine scrub.

Canada Warbler (*Wilsonia canadensis*), common visitor.

Several other parulids occur in the area but were not identified by informants. The following, however, would most likely be considered *šč'iht* also.

Orange-crowned Warbler (*Vermivora celata*), rare visitor.

Tropical Parula (*Parula pitiayumi*), resident below 4000 feet.

Yellow-throated Warbler (*Dendroica dominica*), rare visitor.

Grace's Warbler (*D. graciae*), rare highland resident.

Chestnut-sided Warbler (*D. pensylvanica*), uncommon visitor.

Mourning Warbler (*Oporornis philadelphia*), rare visitor.

A few informants recognize varietal distinctions within this taxon. These informants distinguish typical *šč'iht* as *k'anal šč'iht* 'yellow warbler' or *bac'il šč'iht* 'true warbler'. Other varietals recorded include:

*yašal šč'iht* 'blue warbler': The Tennessee Warbler (*Vermivora peregrina*), an uncommon visitor, and the Black-throated Blue Warbler (*Dendroica caerulescens*), an extremely rare visitor.

*cahal šč'iht* 'red warbler': The Pink-headed Warbler (*Ergaticus versicolor*), a highland resident usually distinguished as *ʔičil mut* (see later taxon in this complex).

*bašil šč'iht* 'mottled warbler': For some informants the Townsend's (*Dendroica townsendi*) and Hermit Warblers (*D. occidentalis*), the attributive referring especially to the black and white pattern of the wings of these species, and the Black-and-white Warbler (*Mniotilta varia*), a common visitor (but see *nocnoc teʔ mut*, Hypothetical list: Birds).

*cahal hol šč'iht* 'red-headed warbler': The Rufous-capped Warbler (*Basileuterus rufifrons*), a common resident throughout, also known as *č'irin hol mut* 'stripe-headed bird' (see later taxon in this complex).

Other species referred to as *kps šč'iht* include the Olive Warbler (*Peucedramus taeniatus*), an uncommon highland resident, and the Warbling Vireo, *Vireo gilvus* (Vireonidae), and White-eyed Vireo (*V. griseus*) (but see *tahína mut*).

Phonological variants of the onomatopoetic *šč'iht* include:

*č'iht, č'iht mut.*

*šč'ihk* or *č'ihk* (the prefix *š-* is optional).

*č'ipč'ip, č'ipč'ip mut.*

*č'eʔč'eʔ mut, č'ebč'eb mut.*

*č'ikč'ik mut.*

*c'ikc'ik* or *c'ikc'ik mut* (but see Hypothetical List: Birds).

All are reasonably accurate imitations of the typical wood-warbler call note, characteristic of most of the species treated above. The related taxon *šmayil* (see fourth taxon in the thrush complex), which is restricted to wood-warblers of the genus *Seiurus* is distinguished from this taxon partly on the basis of their louder, sharper call notes, a rather subtle distinction. The role played by sound in identification is illustrated by the fact that SMZ on one occasion misidentified the Mac-Gillivray's Warbler (*Oporornis tolmiei*) on the basis of its call note as *šmayil*. When this yellow-bellied bird was seen, however, he corrected his identification to *šč'iht*. The MacGillivray's Warbler does in fact have a rather heavy note compared to most war-blers, thus approximating the notes of water-thrushes (*Seiurus* spp.).

One informant (AGM) distinguished *šč'iht* (identification uncertain in this case but des-cribed as 'yellow') from *koen mut* [< iv 'descend'? + 'bird']. He included the follow-ing species in the latter category: Crescent-chested Warbler (*Vermivora superciliosa*), Olive Warbler (*Peucedramus taeniatus*), Black-throated Green Warbler (*Dendroica virens*), and Blackburnian Warbler (*D. fusca*), a common visitor.

Thus some informants may distinguish a residual category of typical wood-warblers (*koen mut*) from the core meaning of *šč'iht*, possibly restricted to the Wilson's Warbler in this case.

In Tzeltal plant terminology *č'iht* refers to a varied collection of plants similar to the genus *Eugenia* of the myrtle family (Berlin, Breedlove, and Raven 1974:272–274). No semantic association between wood-warblers and these plants is known, however.

*ʔičil č'uht mut* 'pepper-bellied bird': The Painted Redstart (*Myioborus picta*) and the Slate-throated Redstart (*Myioborus miniatus*) (see Figure 5.73)

These wood-warblers are common resi-dents, especially in the highland pine-oak forests. One informant (AMT) included the Blackburnian Warbler (*Dendroica fusca*), establishing a link with the preceding taxon. Variant names include *cahal č'uht mut* 'red-

**Figure 5.73** *ʔičil č'uht mut* Slate-throated Redstart (*Myioborus miniatus*). [From Emmet Reid Blake, *Birds of Mexico: A Guide for Field Identification.* Copyright 1953 by The University of Chicago Press.]

bellied bird' and *cahal ʔotan mut* 'red-heart bird'. Some informants fail to distinguish this taxon from the following one, applying the terms *cahal mut* 'red bird' or *ʔičil mut* 'pepper bird' to both.

*ʔičil mut* 'pepper bird': The Pink-Headed Warbler (*Ergaticus versicolor*)

Lowland informants (e.g., SMZ) who are unfamiliar with this species may refer to it as *cahal šč'iht* 'red warbler' or simply *cahal mut* 'red bird'. The monolexemic status of the latter term is not clearly established.

*c'irin hol mut* 'stripe-headed bird': The Rufous-capped Warbler (*Basileuterus rufifrons*) (see Figure 5.74) and probably the Golden-browed Warbler (*B. belli*)

The latter is an uncommon highland resi-dent. Several informants (AGM, SLL) clear-ly distinguish these resident birds from the migratory *šč'iht*. However, other informants fail to maintain this distinction, referring to them as *cahal hol šč'iht* 'red-headed warbler' (SMZ) or *k'anal c'ikc'ik mut* 'yellow warbler'. (In this instance *c'ikc'ik mut* is used synonymously with *šč'iht*. See also Hypothetical List: Birds.) *c'irin sit mut* is a variant.

The low salience of the preceding three taxa is clearly evident. The difficulty of establishing consistent names, frequent inclusion of these taxa within the widely re-cognized *šč'iht*, and the admission of un-

Figure 5.74 *c'irin hol mut* Rufous-capped Warbler (*Basileuterus rufifrons*). ⌈Color slide by author.⌉

familiarity by some informants of even common resident species, which are available for close inspection, define the limits of the typical Tenejapanecos' concern. The small size and confusing heterogeneity exhibited by the many species discussed above help explain the nomenclatural confusion.

*nuk' ničim* 'flower sucker': The Cinnamon Flower-piercer, *Diglossa baritula* (see Figure 5.75) (Coerebidae)

The name accurately describes the distinctive feeding behavior of this species which is a common highland resident. This taxon is widely recognized.

Figure 5.75 *nuk' ničim* Cinnamon Flower-piercer (*Diglossa baritula*). ⌈From Emmet Reid Blake, *Birds of Mexico: A Guide for Field Identification.* Copyright 1953 by The University of Chicago Press. Head only.⌉

## SISKIN–SEEDEATER COMPLEX
(See Figure 5.76)

The following two taxa include the smallest finches (Fringillidae). They are considered *shoyetik* 'associates' (SMZ). Some relationship is also recognized with the flower-piercer (*nuk' ničim*, preceding) on the one hand, and the sparrow complex on the other.

*me? k'in ha?al* 'mother of the winter rains': All species of the genus *Spinus* (Fringillidae), in particular the Black-headed Siskin (*S. notatus*), the focal species (see Figure 5.77)

These species gather in flocks after breeding. Thus they are especially conspicuous from August through the winter. This movement coincides with the onset of the *nortes* or soft winter rains. Also included in this taxon are the following:

Black-capped Siskin (*Spinus atriceps*), fairly common above 2100 m.

Pine Siskin (*S. pinus*), rare highland resident.

Dark-backed Goldfinch (*S. psaltria*), common throughout.

The heterogeneity within this taxon is recognized, but no varietals are distinguished. On one occasion the streaked Pine Siskin was alleged to be an immature form of *me? k'in ha?al*, recognizable from AMT's illustration as the Black-headed Siskin. This assessment, though incorrect in this instance, is not unfounded, as immatures of all species are less clearly patterned than the adults. That the Black-capped Siskin, rather than the equally common and conspicuous Dark-backed Goldfinch, is the focal species is indicated by the fact that SMZ considered the latter species atypical of this taxon and coined the term *?ihk'al me? k'in ha?al* 'black mother-of-the-winter-rains' to describe it.

Variant names include the following:

*me? ha?al* 'mother of rain' (see following variant).

*bahk'al mut* ⌈< 'four hundred' + 'bird'⌉: descriptive of the flocking behavior of these species. This variant is utilized in the *paraje* of *pahalton* where *me? k'in ha?al* is applied instead to a waterbird taxon (see *c'u? lukum*). Other informants are aware of this term but unsure as to its meaning. SMZ thought it might refer to the Olive Warbler, *Peucedramus taeniatus* (Parulidae: see *šč'iht*/wood-warbler), a highland species with which

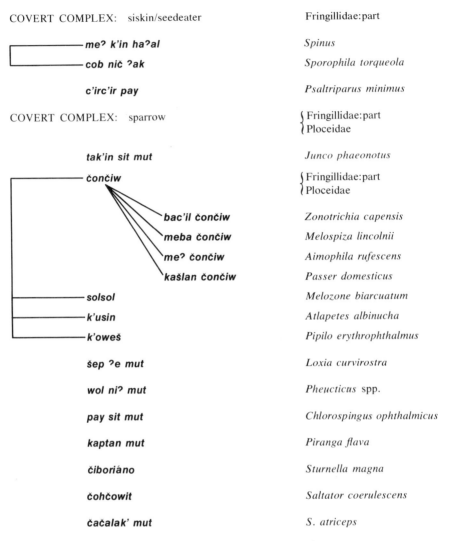

| | |
|---|---|
| COVERT COMPLEX:  siskin/seedeater | Fringillidae:part |
| *me? k'in ha?al* | *Spinus* |
| *cob nič ?ak* | *Sporophila torqueola* |
| *c'irc'ir pay* | *Psaltriparus minimus* |
| COVERT COMPLEX:   sparrow | { Fringillidae:part <br> { Ploceidae |
| *tak'in sit mut* | *Junco phaeonotus* |
| *čončiw* | { Fringillidae:part <br> { Ploceidae |
| *bac'il čončiw* | *Zonotrichia capensis* |
| *meba čončiw* | *Melospiza lincolnii* |
| *me? čončiw* | *Aimophila rufescens* |
| *kašlan čončiw* | *Passer domesticus* |
| *solsol* | *Melozone biarcuatum* |
| *k'usin* | *Atlapetes albinucha* |
| *k'oweš* | *Pipilo erythrophthalmus* |
| *šep ?e mut* | *Loxia curvirostra* |
| *wol ni? mut* | *Pheucticus* spp. |
| *pay sit mut* | *Chlorospingus ophthalmicus* |
| *kaptan mut* | *Piranga flava* |
| *čiboriáno* | *Sturnella magna* |
| *čohčowit* | *Saltator coerulescens* |
| *čačalak' mut* | *S. atriceps* |

**Figure 5.76**   The siskin–seedeater and sparrow complexes, etc.

he was not familiar but which is superficially similar to the siskins in coloration, breeding habitat and voice.

***hsonowil mut*** 'musician bird'.

***cob nič ?ak*** 'gatherer of grass flowers': The White-collared Seedeater, *Sporophila torqueola* (Fringillidae) (see Figure 5.78)

This species is common and conspicuous throughout Tenejapa below 2300 m. It feeds in *milpa*, as do the siskins, and thus is more frequently encountered than warblers and other woodland birds. Sexual dimorphism within this species is correctly noted by most informants. Variant names include the following:

***bašil lip' nič ?ak*** ['mottled' + UN + 'flower' + 'grass'].

***cob nič ?ak mut***, ***nič ?ak mut***, and ***nič ?ak***.

***sak?oal mut*** 'white-necklaced bird'.

***c'irin mut*** 'streaked bird' (but see ***c'irin mut***).

Two other species of similar size and habits are common in the region:

The Yellow-faced Grassquit, *Tiaris oliva-*

**Figure 5.77**  *me ʔ k`in ha ʔal* Black-headed Siskin (*Spinus notatus*). [From Emmet Reid Blake, *Birds of Mexico: A Guide for Field Identification*. Copyright 1953 by The University of Chicago Press.]

**Figure 5.78** *cob nič ʔak* White-collared Seedeater (*Sporophila torqueola*). [From Emmet Reid Blake, *Birds of Mexico: A Guide for Field Identification*. Copyright 1953 by The University of Chicago Press.]

*cea* (Fringillidae). This species is found up to 2300 m and is included within the extended range of this taxon by some informants. However, it may be distinguished as *c`ulul mut* (see Hypothetical List: Birds).

The Blue-black Grassquit, *Volatinia jacarina* (Fringillidae). This species is common below 1500 m. It was named *č`in šče ʔ* 'little catbird' (see *šč'e ʔ*) by SMZ and JGG, though they seemed unfamiliar with the species. Another informant (AGM) called it *ʔihk`al mut* 'black bird', though he claimed that another more appropriate name existed that he was unable to recall.

*c`irc`ir pay* [ON + 'skunk']: The Bushtit, *Psaltriparus minimus* (Paridae) (see Figure 5.79)

This species is common above 1800 m. It is widely recognized by highland informants, though several lowland informants could not supply a name when this bird was seen. It is considered to be unaffiliated, **mayuk shoy** 'there are no relatives'. Alternate names are phonological variants:

**Figure 5.79** *c`irc`ir pay* Bushtit (*Psaltriparus minimus*). [From Emmet Reid Blake, *Birds of Mexico: A Guide for Field Identification*. Copyright 1953 by The University of Chicago Press. Head only.]

**cilcil pay** [ON + 'skunk'].
**cilcil ʔuhč'** [ON, lit. a plant, *Litsea* spp., Berlin, Breedlove, and Raven 1974:269].
**calcal mut** [ON + 'bird'].

A cognate form, **cicil ʔul**, is recorded from Zinacantan Tzotzil as applying to the Yellow-eyed Junco, *Junco phaeonotus* (Fringillidae) (see first taxon in the sparrow complex). The Bushtit has no close relatives in Chiapas.

## SPARROW COMPLEX

All sparrows, including the House Sparrow (Ploceidae), ground-sparrows, brush-finches, towhees, and juncos (Fringillidae in part) are included here. The boundaries of this complex are not clearly defined, though dyadic associations and larger groupings among these taxa are often cited by informants. The type generic is *čončiw* (see second taxon in the complex).

*tak'in sit mut* 'gold-eyed bird': The Yellow-eyed Junco (*Junco phaeonotus*) (see Figure 5.80)

This fairly common highland resident is known to highland informants only. The name is quite accurately descriptive.

Figure 5.80    *tak'in sit mut* Yellow-eyed Junco (*Junco phaeonotus*). [Color slide by author.]

*čončiw* [ON]: The Rufous-collared Sparrow (*Zonotrichia capensis*) (see Figure 5.81)

The taxon is universally known in reference to this, the focal species, which is abundant in the highlands about fields and towns and is found sparingly down to 1200 m. *čončiw* may be used without modifying attributives to denote this species. Several specific subdivisions are widely recognized as follows:

a. *bac'il čončiw* 'true sparrow': The Rufous-collared Sparrow.

Figure 5.81    *bac'il čončiw* Rufous-collared Sparrow (*Zonotrichia capensis*). [From Emmet Reid Blake, *Birds of Mexico: A Guide for Field Identification*. Copyright 1953 by The University of Chicago Press.]

b. *meba čončiw* 'orphan sparrow': The Lincoln's Sparrow (*Melospiza lincolnii*), a common winter visitor. The attributive *meba* 'orphan' is used rather frequently in animal terminology to indicate the smaller of a set of contrasting specific taxa. Variant names for this subdivision include *ʔihc'inal čončiw* ['younger sibling' + rs + 'sparrow']* and *c'irin čončiw* 'streaked sparrow'.

c. *meʔ čončiw* 'mother sparrow': The Rusty Sparrow (*Aimophila rufescens*) (see Figure 5.82). This common and widespread species is larger than the Rufous-collared Sparrow, hence the name. It is also called *wišal čončiw* ['elder sister' + rs + 'sparrow'].* Alternatively the Rusty Sparrow is classified as a kind of *solsol* (see next taxon in this complex), by lowland informants in particular.

d. *kašlan čončiw* 'Ladino sparrow': The House Sparrow, *Passer domesticus* (Ploceidae). This introduced species first arrived in San Cristóbal during the 1960s (Alvarez del Toro

*ʔihc'in* is somewhat more precisely defined as male-speaking younger brother or younger male parallel cousin and female-speaking younger sibling or younger parallel cousin.

*wiš* is more precisely defined as elder sister, elder female parallel cousin, or father's sister.

Figure 5.82 *me? čončiw* Rusty sparrow (*Aimophila rufescens*). [Color slide by author.]

1971). It is now common in San Cristóbal but does not occur in Tenejapa. Many informants recognize a verbal description of the species but do not name it other than by citing its relationship to this generic, i.e., *kps čončiw* or *čahp čončiw* 'clansman of the sparrow'. An alternate name is *hobelal čončiw* 'San Cristóbal sparrow'.

*solsol* [ON]: The White-faced Ground-Sparrow (*Melozone biarcuatum*)

The term and the species are restricted to areas below 1800 m. The Rusty Sparrow (*Aimophila rufescens*) is sometimes included as *cahal solsol* 'red ground-sparrow' or *muk'ul solsol* 'large ground-sparrow' (but see also *k'usin*, following); this pattern appears to be typical of lowland informants.

The Rusty Sparrow is a kind of *čončiw* for highland informants, where the Rufous-collared Sparrow (*Zonotrichia capensis*) is most conspicuous, and as a kind of *solsol* in the lowlands, where the White-faced Ground-Sparrow is the dominant form. It is curious that the Rusty Sparrow is not labeled independently, since it is clearly perceived as different and is widely known. The only explanation at hand is the secretiveness of the Rusty Sparrow. Like most of its congeners it keeps within thick vegetative cover and is difficult to see.

Variant names include *solsol mut* [ON + 'bird'] and *colcol* [ON].

*k'usin* [ON]: The White-naped Brush-Finch (*Atlapetes albinucha*) (see Figure 5.83)

This universally recognized species is common throughout Tenejapa. It is also referred to by the following variants:

*kusin, k'usi, k'usik, k'usit* [all ON].

*k'usiw mut, k'usk'us mut* [both ON + 'bird'].

One informant asserted that two types exist, *bac'il k'usin* 'true brush-finch', also known as *?ihk'al k'usin* 'black brush-finch', which is this species, and *te?tikil k'usin* 'forest brush-finch' or *cahal k'usin* 'red brush-finch'. This latter set of alternate terms may be yet another way of referring to the Rusty Sparrow (*Aimophila rufescens*, see *čončiw* and *solsol*, preceding).

Figure 5.83 *kusin* (AMT) = *k'usin* White-naped Brush Finch (*Atlapetes albinucha*). [Drawing by AMT.]

*k'oweš* [ON]: The Rufous-sided Towhee (*Pipilo erythrophthalmus*) (see Figure 5.84)

This universally recognized species is found practically throughout the *municipio*. It is readily recognized by call alone. It is interesting to note that, in Zinacantan Tzotzil, *k'oviš*, a cognate term, includes both this species and the White-naped Brush-Finch (*Atlapetes albinucha*, see *k'usin*, preceding). In Zinacantan the towhee is distinguished as

Figure 5.84 *k'oweš* Rufous-sided Towhee (*Pipilo erythrophthalmus*). [Drawing by AMT.]

*ʔikʼal kʼoviš* 'black towhee', the brush-finch as *kʼanal kʼoviš* 'yellow towhee' (R. Laughlin personal communication). In Tenejapa the two species are also thought to be related.

***šep ʔe mut*** [ < tv 'cut'? + 'mouth' + 'bird' ]: The Red Crossbill (*Loxia curvirostra*) (see Figure 5.85)

This fringillid is rare in Chiapas. A flock was observed once near San Cristóbal, but no informants were present at the time, and no term was elicited in response to pictures or verbal descriptions. However SMZ used this term for a museum specimen of this species (MVZ) and asserted that he had seen the bird in life. He state that it was also known as *kurus niʔ mut* 'cross-billed bird'.

Figure 5.85   *sep ʔe mut* Red Crossbill (*Loxia curvirostra*). [ From Emmet Reid Blake, *Birds of Mexico: A Guide for Field Identification*. Copyright 1953 by The University of Chicago Press. Head only. ]

***wol niʔ mut*** 'round-billed bird': Probably the Rose-breasted Grosbeak, *Pheucticus ludovicianus* (Fringillidae) (see Figure 5.86)

This species is a fairly common visitor. The Yellow Grosbeak (*P. chrysopeplus*), resident in Chiapas below 1200 m, might also be included here. However, the informants (SMZ, JGG, AKČ') who saw an individual of this species mist-netted at Villa las Rosas were familiar neither with the bird nor with this name or its probable synonyms. It is certain only that this taxon is distinguished by several informants; it is described as a large-billed bird, approximately the size of this species, and is present only during the winter months. Several other names elicited are possible synonyms:

Figure 5.86   *hloʔ karanato mut* (AMT) = *wol niʔ mut* grosbeak? [ Drawing by AMT. ]

***bakʼ niʔ mut*** 'seed-billed bird'.

***hloʔ karanáto mut*** 'passion fruit eater bird'.

***ton ʔe mut*** 'stone-mouthed bird'.

***tonton niʔ mut*** [ 'stone' reduplicated + 'bill' + 'bird' ].

***pay sit mut*** 'skunk-faced bird': The Common Bush-Tanager, *Chlorospingus ophthalmicus* (Thraupidae) (see Figure 5.87)

This species is found only above 2300 m and is thus unknown to lowland informants. This name was applied to a freshly killed bird. A more widely known term is *sak ʔisim* 'white whisker' and its variants, *sak ʔisim mut* 'white whisker bird' and *sak yisim* [ 'white' + pp + 'whisker' ]. *sak ʔisim* was specifically rejected as applying to this species by one highland informant (AKC'), but he was unable to recall its true name. Verbal

Figure 5.87   *pay sit mut* Common Bush-Tanager (*Chlorospingus ophthalmicus*). [ From Emmet Reid Blake, *Birds of Mexico: A Guide for Field Identification*. Copyright 1953 by The University of Chicago Press. ]

descriptions of **sak ʔisim** and of its habitat, however, strongly suggest that it refers to this species. No other readily apparent possibility exists.

**kaptan mut** [ < Sp **capitan** 'captain' + 'bird']: The Hepatic Tanager, *Piranga flava* (Thraupidae)

This taxon is widely recognized. The species is fairly common in pine forests throughout, though somewhat more so at higher elevations. Sexual dimorphism is correctly assessed. In winter the similar Summer Tanager (*P. rubra*) is present, and it is probably also included here. **cahal mut** 'red bird' may be used synonymously (but see **mut₂** and **ʔičil mut**/wood-warbler).

A Ladino informant from Bachajón used the cognate Spanish term *capitan* to refer to the Crimson-collared Tanager, *Phlogothraupis sanguinolenta* (Thraupidae), which is found near Ocosingo. This clarifies the origin of the primary name. SMZ called the Crimson-collared Tanager **cahal č'ič'hol mut** 'red blood-headed bird' (see Hypothetical List: Birds), reserving **kaptan** for the more familiar Hepatic Tanager.

**čiboriáno** [ON, < Sp ?]: The Eastern Meadowlark, *Sturnella magna* (Icteridae)

Though this species is common near San Cristóbal, it occurs in Tenejapa only in **banabil**, where suitable pastureland is found. The name is similarly restricted, elicited only from a single informant (MMH) of that **paraje**.

**čohčowit** [ON]: The Grayish Saltator, *Saltator coerulescens* (Fringillidae) (see Figure 5.88)

This species is common below 1500 m. The taxon is unknown to many highland informants but well known elsewhere. It is also known by the following variants:

**čočowiš**, **čohčohwit** [all ON].

**ti? čotawaič** [ON].

**čočob mut** [ON + 'bird'].

**Figure 5.88** *čohčowit* Grayish Saltator (*Saltator coerulescens*). [From Emmet Reid Blake, *Birds of Mexico: A Guide for Field Identification*. Copyright 1953 by The University of Chicago Press. Head only.]

**waskis mut** [ON + 'bird'].

**hlo? ni? kulul** [ < tv 'eat' + 'tip' + UN].

**petul mut** [ < Sp 'Peter' + 'bird'].

The following taxon is not considered a close relative, though it includes another species of the same genus. In my experience, the voices of the two species are radically different.

**čačalak' mut** [ON + 'bird']: The Black-headed Saltator, *Saltator atriceps* (Fringillidae) (see Figure 5.89)

This larger species is less common in Tenejapa and is not found above 1200 m. Its distinctive, cacophonus repertoire of vocalizations is readily recognized by informants. The superficial resemblance of the name to the Spanish *chachalaca*, *Ortalis* spp. (Cracidae), is purely coincidental, as the bird known as *chachalaca* in Spanish is called **hohkot** (see the turkey complex) in Tzeltal.

**Figure 5.89** *čačalak' mut* Black-headed Saltator (*Saltator atriceps*). [From Emmet Reid Blake, *Birds of Mexico: A Guide for Field Identification*. Copyright 1953 by The University of Chicago Press. Head only.]

Informants have assured me that ***čačalak' mut*** is not synonymous with ***hohkot***. Variant names include the following:

***čačaláko, čačaláko mut*** [both ON].
***kakate?, kakate? mut*** [both ON].
***lutul kac'al mut*** [ON + 'bird'].
***hlo? ?alčaš mut*** 'orange eater bird'.

## ORIOLE COMPLEX (See Figure 5.90a)

All species of orioles, *Icterus* spp. (Icteridae), that occur in the region are included in these two taxa. The first is the type generic of the complex; the second is considered to be ***shoy*** 'its associate' (AMT, SMZ). A more

tenuous relationship is recognized with a variety of other taxa, e.g., for AGM ***wol ni? mut***, for SMZ ***hti? cuhkum, yihkac te?*** and ***čačalak' mut***. All orioles are considered to be ***hlabtawaneh mut*** 'harbinger-of-evil bird'.

***tu č'ič*** [ON, lit. 'stinking' + 'blood']: Most orioles, but in particular the common, resident Yellow-backed Oriole (*Icterus chrysater*) (see Figure 5.90b), which is the focal species ***tu č'ič*** may be used unmodified to refer to this species. The following specific subdivisions are widely recognized:

a. ***bac'il tu č'ič*** 'true oriole': The Yellow-backed Oriole, also known as ***k'anal tu č'ič*** 'yellow oriole'.

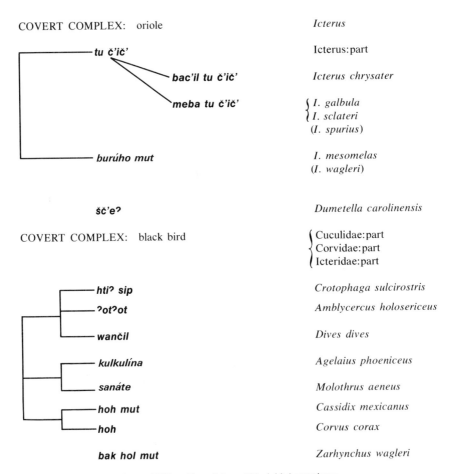

Figure 5.90a   The oriole and black bird complexes.

Figure 5.90b *tu č'ič'* Yellow-backed Oriole (*Icterus chrysater*). [Drawing by AMT.]

b. *meba tu č'ič'* 'orphan oriole': This appears to be a residual to which most orioles (i.e., those that are neither the Yellow-backed nor the Yellow-tailed Oriole, *I. mesomelas*, see next taxon) may be assigned.   In this case, all such orioles are smaller than the Yellow-backed Oriole. The Northern Oriole (*I. galbula*), a common winter visitor, is included here. The Streak-backed Oriole (*I. sclateri*) of the drier lowlands to the south, while clearly unfamiliar to informants, was attributed to this subtype. *kašlan tu č'ič'* 'Ladino oriole' is a preferred synonym for the Streak-backed Oriole in AGM's opinion.

The Yellow Grosbeak, *Pheucticus chrysopeplus* (Fringillidae) (see *wol niʔ mut*), was treated as *kps tu č'ič'* by SMZ. *tu č'ič'* was further modified as follows:

*cahal tu č'ič'* 'red oriole', not identified.
*c'irin tu č'ič'* 'streaked oriole', applied to the Streak-backed Oriole, lexemic status uncertain.
*muk'ul tu č'ič'* 'large oriole', not identified.
*ʔihk'al tu č'ič'* 'black oriole', not identified.

In short, the heterogeneity of this taxon is clearly recognized, since modifying attributives are applied by most informants. However only the common resident species is clearly distinguished; the remainder are classed in the residuum and named by the selection of an appropriately descriptive attributive.

The male Orchard Oriole (*I. spurius*), which is both exceptionally small and atypically colored (i.e., brick red), was considered to be *kps tu č'ič'*, rather than an example of the residual category.

*burúho mut* [< Sp *brujo* 'witch' + 'bird']: the Yellow-tailed Oriole, *Icterus mesomelas* (Icteridae)

This is a resident oriole found in Tenejapa below 1200 m. The taxon is regularly recognized by lowland informants only. The attributive *burúho* refers to the fact that this species, like *tu č'ič'*, is an evil omen. The relationship of these two taxa is further attested to by the fact that this taxon may also be called *merikáno tu č'ič'* 'American oriole'. The choice of this attributive is atypical, as the Yellow-tailed Oriole is no larger than the Yellow-backed (the focal species of *tu č'ič'*). Other alternative names include the following:

*k'orol mut* [UN + 'bird'].
*pokowéla* [< Sp?] (see also *č'ekek*/ turkey).

The Black-vented Oriole (*I. wagleri*) of the drier south slope of the highlands was also included here on the basis of a rather brief glimpse (SMZ).

*šč'eʔ* [ON]: The Gray Catbird, *Dumetella carolinensis* (Mimidae) (see Figure 5.91)

This common winter visitor in known to every Tenejapaneco. A few informants distinguish two subdivisions, *yašal šč'eʔ* 'gray catbird', which is this species, and *k'anal šč'eʔ* 'yellow catbird', also known as *k'an č'uht šč'eʔ* 'yellow-bellied catbird'. This latter variety might refer to the Yellow-breasted Chat, *Icteria virens* (Parulidae), an atypical wood-warbler which resembles the catbird somewhat in voice and behavior.

Figure 5.91 *šč'eʔ* Gray Catbird (*Dumetella carolinensis*). [Drawing by AMT.]

However, I have no direct evidence on this conjecture.

The Blue-black Grassquit, *Volatinia jacarina* (Fringillidae), was called *č'inšč'e?* 'small catbird' by SMZ and JGG. However, they did not consider the grassquit to be a kind of *šč'e?*, much as *hoh mut* is not a kind of *hoh* (see the black bird complex following). This usage was not encountered among other informants. Thus *šč'e?* is typically homogeneous.

## BLACK BIRD COMPLEX

These birds are considered *shoyetik* 'associates' (AGM, AMT, JGG, SMZ), though they represent three distinct families (Cuculidae, *hti? sip*; Icteridae, *?ot?ot*, *wančil*, *sanáte*, *kulkulína*, and *hoh mut*; Corvidae, *hoh*). All are rather large, conspicuous, primarily black birds.

*hti? sip* 'tick eater': The Groove-billed Ani, *Crotophaga sulcirostris* (Cuculidae) (see Figures 5.92 and 5.93).

This species is common below 1800 m but known to many highland informants as well. Some highland informants, however, consider this term to be synonymous with *sanáte* (see fifth taxon in this complex). The ani does in fact eat ticks and is often found on and about cattle. The name may also be onomatopoetic, as its call was so

Figure 5.93 *hti? sip* Groove-billed Ani (*Crotophaga sulcirostris*). [Drawing by AMT.]

described by one informant; a *double entendre*.

*?ot?ot* [ON]: The Yellow-billed Cacique, *Amblycercus holosericeus* (Icteridae) (see Figure 5.94)

This rather secretive species is quite common below 1800 m. It is known to all but a few highland informants. All describe it accurately as 'black' with a 'yellow' or 'white' bill. It is also the bird most commonly referred to as *?óra mut* [< Sp *hora*

Figure 5.94 *?ot?ot* Yellow-billed Cacique (*Amblycercus holosericeus*). [Drawing by AMT.]

'hour' + 'bird'] (see also *č'etet waš*/wren and *sian*/thrush), as it allegedly calls every hour on the hour. Alternative names include the following:

*?ot'?ot'* [ON].

*hlo? kanélo mut* 'sugar eater bird'.

*šušub mut* 'whistle bird' (see also *p'it-p'it*/flycatcher.

*wančil* [ON]: The Melodious Blackbird (*Dives dives*) (see Figure 5.95)

This icterid is abundant below 1800 m and is well known to all Tenejapanecos. Some informants were able to identify this

Figure 5.92 *hti? sip* Groove-billed Ani (*Crotophaga sulcirostris*). [From Emmet Reid Blake, *Birds of Mexico: A Guide for Field Identification*. Copyright 1953 by The University of Chicago Press.]

**Figure 5.95** *wančil* Melodious Blackbird (*Dives dives*). [From Emmet Reid Blake, *Birds of Mexico: A Guide for Field Identification*. Copyright 1953 by The University of Chicago Press.]

species correctly from a brief series of its tape-recorded calls.

***kulkulína*** [ON, < Sp?]: The Red-winged Blackbird, *Agelaius phoeniceus* (Icteridae)

This species has a distribution similar to that of the meadowlark (see *čiboriáno*/bird). It is known only from the reed marsh in **banabil**, where a local informant (MMH) supplied this name. Other informants were unfamiliar with both the bird and the name, despite the fact that it is common near San Cristóbal. SMZ considered the bird to be **kps sanáte** (see next taxon), an accurate assessment of familial resemblance, and **kps čanul c'ahel** (see the waterbird complex) on the basis of habitat. But he had never noticed the bird before.

***sanáte*** [< Sp **sanate** 'grackle']: The Bronzed Cowbird, *Molothrus aeneus* (Icteridae) (see Figure 5.96)

This species is common throughout the region in towns and fields and is universally

**Figure 5.96** *sanáte* Bronzed Cowbird (*Molothrus aeneus*). [Drawing by AMT.]

known. The name is borrowed from the Spanish term for a different though related species (see next taxon)—a further illustration of the pitfalls of contact-language translations. Indigenous names also exist but are considered secondary synonyms, as **ʔakot mut** 'dancing bird', cited by several informants. An alternative Spanish loan cited by JGG is **satanas** [< OSp 'satan'?). Some highland informants also considered **htiʔ sip** (see first taxon of this complex) synonymous. This is the basis for the occasional assertion that **htiʔ sip**, the ani, is found in **sikil k'inal** 'cold country'.

***hoh mut*** 'raven bird': The Great-tailed Grackle, *Cassidix mexicanus* (Icteridae) (see Figure 5.97a)

This bird is abundant throughout in fields and second growth, and is known to all informants. Some were able to recognize tape-recorded vocalizations. The grackle is considered to be related to but not included in the taxon **hoh** (see next taxon). This usage occurs sporadically elsewhere. **lóro mut** and **palóma mut** are names coined to refer to birds distinct from both **lóro** (see **períko**/ parrot) and **palóma** (see **palomaš**/dove) but resembling them in some way.

***hoh*** [ON]: The Common Raven, *Corvus corax* (Corvidae) (see Figure 5.97b)

This bird is an uncommon resident in isolated areas throughout the region and is known to all informants. It is also considered to be related to **šulem** (vulture complex), the Turkey Vulture, *Cathartes aura* (Cathartidae), as in size and feeding habits it resembles that species.

***bak hol mut*** 'bone-headed bird': The oropendolas, in particular the Chestnut-headed Oropendola, *Zarhynchus wagleri* (Icteridae) (see Figure 5.98)

I observed this species once near Yajalón (700 m). SMZ states that this species, identified from a museum specimen (MVZ), occurs occasionally at the lower boundary of the *municipio* and is known by this name. The

Figure 5.97    (a) *tat hoh mut* (AMT) 'male grackle' (left) and *me? hoh mut* (AMT) 'female grackle' (right): (both) Great-tailed Grackle (*Cassidix mexicanus*); (b) *hoh* 'raven': Common Raven (*Corvus corax*). [Drawings by AMT.]

taxon is included on that basis alone, since the species involved are not to be confused with any others.

*Hypothetical List: Birds*

*cahal č'ič'hol mut* 'red blood-headed bird'. Applied by SMZ to the Crimson-collared Tanager, *Phlogothraupis sanguinolenta* (Thraupidae).

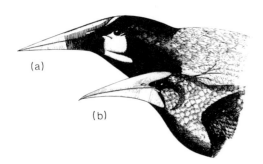

Fig 5.98    *bak hol mut* oropendolas: (a) *Zarhynchus wagleri*; (b) *Gymnostinops montezuma*. [From Emmet Reid Blake, *Birds of Mexico: A Guide for Field Identification*. Copyright 1953 by The University of Chicago Press. Heads only.]

*c'ikc'ik mut* [ON + 'bird']. Possibly refers to a category of wood-warblers (Parulidae) distinct from those cited in the wood-warbler complex.

*c'ulul mut* [ON + 'bird']. Possibly refers to the Yellow-faced Grassquit, *Tiaris olivacea* (Fringillidae), as that species is fairly common in Tenejapa below 2300 m and is not otherwise named (see *cob nič ?ak*/siskin-seedeater). Possibly synonymous forms include: *c'ururik mut* and *c'urin mut* [both ON + 'bird'].

*čiwčiw mut* [ON + 'bird']. Alleged to be distinct from *čončiw* (sparrow complex).

*čočob mut* [UN + 'bird']. Possibly refers to the Long-billed Gnatwren, *Ramphocaenus rufiventris* (Sylviidae), which may occur rarely at lower elevations in or near Tenejapa (see also *čohčowit*/bird).

*č'ič' nuk' mut* 'blood-necked bird'. Possibly refers to the Rose-throated Becard, *Platypsaris aglaiae* (Cotingidae), which was observed near the Pueblo of Tenejapa and is not otherwise accounted for.

*č'ipč'ip mut* [ON + 'bird']. Applied by SMZ to the Blue-gray Gnatcatcher, *Polioptila caerulea* (Sylviidae), and the White-lored Gnatcatcher (*P. albiloris*). The Blue-gray Gnatcatcher occurs in Tenejapa, where a second informant referred to it by this same term. However this informant applied *č'ipč'ip mut* to a variety of the wood-warblers (Parulidae) as well (see *šč'iht*/wood-warbler). SMZ asserted that this term and the gnatcatcher also are distinct from *šč'iht*.

*himhim k'abal* [ON]. Not determined, possibly an owl (Strigiformes), potoo (Nyctibiidae), or nightjar (Caprimulgidae). This name is ascribed to a large hawklike animal which calls out its name while flying overhead at night. It is widely known, but only as a sound or a glimpse in the night. It is said to be encountered frequently on ridges in high country. It is classified as *hlabtawaneh mut* 'harbinger-of-evil bird'.

*húryo* [UN]. Illustrated by AMT (see Figure 5.99a) but not otherwise known. He shows a small bird, possibly some kind of tyrant flycatcher (Tyrannidae). *húlyo* is a variant.

*hkastilána mut* [pp + Sp 'Ladina' + 'bird']. Illustrated by AMT (see Figure 5.99b) but not otherwise known.

*škuen* [pp + UN] (see Figure 5.99c). Verbal descriptions suggest that this term might refer to the American Dipper, *Cinclus mexicanus* (Cinclidae). This species has been reported from the Chiapas highlands (R. Laughlin personal communication) and is like no other. Variant forms of this name include the following: *kuen*, *škoen*, *koen*, *koen mut*, and *škoin*.

*k'an č'uht mut* 'yellow-bellied bird'. Applied by TNM to the Grey-crowned Yellow-throat, *Geothlypis poliocephala* (Parulidae), a common resident below 1800 m, and by JGG to the Dark-backed Goldfinch, *Spinus psaltria* (Fringillidae, see also *me? k'in ha?al*/ siskin-seedeater).

*k'ušk'uš ?eal* ['painful' reduplicated + 'mouth', or ON?]. Possibly synonymous with *t'ost'os* (Hypothetical List: Birds). *k'uš ?eal* is a variant.

*masaklan* [< Sp *Mazatlán*?]. This term is widely known but I was never able to learn to what it might refer. It is probably a Spanish loan, perhaps from Mazatlán, a seacoast

(a)          (b)                    (c)              (d)

(e)              (f)                    (g)

**Figure 5.99**   Hypothetical birds: (a) *huryo*; (b) *hkastilána mut*; (c) *škuen*; (d) *ti?e mut*; (e) *hti? šuš mut*; (f) *st'ost'os*; (g) *?utin* [Drawings by AMT.]

town in northern Mexico. No recognizably cognate form is cited by Land (1970), Edwards (1972), or Alvarez del Toro (1971). From informants' descriptions it may refer to the Magnificent Frigatebird, *Fregata magnificens* (Fregatidae), a strikingly distinctive bird of ocean shores.

***moin te? mut*** 'tree-climbing bird'. Possibly refers to the Rufous-breasted Spinetail, *Synallaxis erythrothorax* (Furnariidae), a name supplied by SMZ to my description of a bird of this species seen near Ocosingo.

***nocnoc te?*** [< tv 'cling to surface' reduplicated + 'tree']. Possibly used to distinguish the Black-and-white Warbler, *Mniotilta varia* (Parulidae), from the majority of wood-warblers (see *šč'iht*/wood-warbler), though several informants referred to this species as *šč'iht* or some modification thereof. This term was also applied to an illustration of the Barred Antshrike, *Thamnophilus doliatus* (Formicariidae), a species of distinctive appearance observed near Tenejapa. ***nocnoc te? mut*** 'tree-clinging bird' is a variant.

***ti?e mut*** [< tv 'eat meat' + 'mouth' + 'bird'?]. Illustrated by AMT (see Figure 5.99d) but not otherwise known.

***hti? šuš mut*** 'wasp eater bird'. Illustrated by AMT (see Figure 5.99e) but not otherwise known.

***tukul č'uht mut*** 'spot-bellied bird'. Possibly refers to the Wood Thrush, *Hylocichla mustelina* (Turdidae), an uncommon winter visitor to the region. The similar Swainson's Thrush, *Catharus ustulatus* (Turdidae), was netted on one occasion, but was referred to simply as ***kps šmayil*** (see *šmayil*/thrush). Alternative names include the following: *c'irin č'uht mut* 'streak-bellied bird', *čohk'il č'uht mut* 'wart-bellied bird', and ***bik' karawánco mut*** [< tv 'swallow' + 'garbanzo bean' + 'bird'].

***t'ost'os*** [ON]. Possibly the Yellow-winged Tanager, *Thraupis abbas* (Thraupidae), which is found sparingly in Tenejapa below 1200 m. One bird of this species was observed in ***habenal***. A local informant called it by this term. SMZ as emphatically disagreed. According to SMZ's description, the bird properly so called is 'yellow' and similar to ***tu č'ič'*** (oriole complex). He did not recognize this species except as ***kps kaptan*** (see ***kaptan mut***), which accurately assesses the familial resemblance. AMT's illustration (see Figure 5.99f) shows a red bird. The Yellow-winged Tanager is basically blue-gray. In any case, although the term is widely recognized, there is obviously little consistency in the associated concept. It is also pronounced ***st'ost'os***, a sound it supposedly makes with its wings.

***?utin*** [UN]. Illustrated by AMT (see Figure 5.99g) and recognized by JGG. AMT shows a small, sparrow-like bird.

***wáko mut*** [< Sp *guaco* (ON) 'Laughing Falcon' + 'bird']. May refer to the Laughing Falcon, *Herpetotheres cachinnans* (Falconidae). This bird is restricted to the tropical lowlands. I observed one on the Pacific coast. Some informants report seeing this species in the *fincas*.

***wilon mut*** [< iv 'fly'? + 'bird']. Not identified.

\* \* \* \* \*

***soc'*** [UN]: Bats (MAMMALIA: Chiroptera) (see Figure 5.100)

Sixty-two species representing eight families [according to Hall and Kelson (1959)] are known from the vicinity of Chiapas. Since bats may cover considerable distances, it is not possible to reduce this figure significantly for Tenejapa on zoogeographical grounds. In any case, this great biological diversity is not significant to Tenejapanecos.

Bats are not considered to be ***čanbalam*** in the restrictive sense described later (see

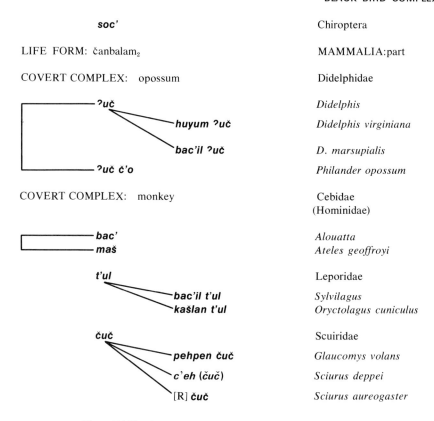

| | |
|---|---|
| **soc'** | Chiroptera |
| LIFE FORM: čanbalam₂ | MAMMALIA:part |
| COVERT COMPLEX:  opossum | Didelphidae |
| ʔuč | *Didelphis* |
| huyum ʔuč | *Didelphis virginiana* |
| bac'il ʔuč | *D. marsupialis* |
| ʔuč č'o | *Philander opossum* |
| COVERT COMPLEX:  monkey | Cebidae |
| | (Hominidae) |
| bac' | *Alouatta* |
| maš | *Ateles geoffroyi* |
| t'ul | Leporidae |
| bac'il t'ul | *Sylvilagus* |
| kašlan t'ul | *Oryctolagus cuniculus* |
| čuč | Scuiridae |
| pehpen čuč | *Glaucomys volans* |
| c'eh (čuč) | *Sciurus deppei* |
| [R] čuč | *Sciurus aureogaster* |

Figure 5.100    Bats, opossums, monkeys, rabbits, and squirrels.

life form *čanbalam₂*). Some relationship to birds is recognized (one informant considered **soc'** to be a kind of ***mut₁***), though the closest tie is clearly with the shrews (Soricidae, see ***yaʔal be***/rat complex), a kind of ***čanbalam₂***.

Bats are considered to be inedible, a characteristic extended to shrews because of the presumed relationship between these animals (see ***ya ʔal be*** for details). All bats are alleged to be blood-eaters, though this is in fact true of the two species of the Desmodontidae only. The vampire bat (*Desmodus rotundus*), however, was one of the most commonly captured species. A story is told to the effect that bats suck the blood of Indians in order to sell it to Ladinos, an allegory of Ladino–Indian relations in Chiapas. Informants report that people are rarely bitten, only when they sleep in the open while traveling (an unusual situation). Rather, domestic animals

are the usual victims. Bat's blood (*šč'ič'el* **soc'**) is smeared on one's face to prevent the growth of beard (since bat's wings are bare?) which, according to informants, improves a young man's chances of obtaining a wife.

The heterogeneity of this taxon is optionally marked by the recognition of varietals as follows:

*ʔihk'al* **soc'** 'black bat' and ***cahal soc'*** 'red bat' (AMT's version)

or

***muk'ul soc'*** 'large bat' and ***č'in soc'*** 'small bat' (SMZ's version).

These distinctions are literal, and many individual bats are considered to be intermediate. SMZ utilized the following paradigm (after exposure to AMT's version) to name the six species collected:

*muk'ul soc'* 'large bat:
vampire bat (*Desmodus rotundus*)
Jamaican fruit-eating bat (*Artibeus jamaicensis*)

*č'in ʔihk' al soc'* 'small black bat':
Anthony's bat (*Sturnira ludovici*)

Seba's short-tailed bat (*Carollia perspicillata*)
Geoffroy's tailless bat (*Anoura geoffroyi*)

*č'in cahal soc'* 'small red bat':
black myotis (*Myotis nigricans*)

## Life Form: *čanbalam₂* ['Snake' + 'Jaguar']

This taxon (see Chapter 3, Section 7.4 for a discussion of its logical status) includes all mammals (class MAMMALIA) with the exception of human beings, bats (*soc'*, preceding), and perhaps the armadillo (see *mayil tiʔbal*/following mammal). Human beings have 'souls' (*č'ulel*) and thus, by deduction, are neither 'animals' (*čanbalam₁*) nor 'mammals' (*čanbalam₂*). A comparable intrusion of deductive logic may explain the exclusion of bats and the armadillo (see *mayil tiʔbal*). The majority of animals included in this life form are considered to be edible. Exceptions are discussed as they arise.

### OPOSSUM COMPLEX

The two generic taxa included here account for the three species of opossum (Didelphidae) known in Tenejapa. Species of the genera *Caluromys* and *Marmosa* known to occur in southern Mexico are apparently restricted to lower elevations. The smaller of the known species (see *ʔuč č'o*) is also considered to be related to the rat complex *č'o*, though the stronger link is with the taxon *ʔuč* which is the type generic of this complex.

*ʔuč* [UN]: Opossums of the genus *Didelphis*

According to informants these animals are fairly common throughout Tenejapa. Three skulls obtained in the *municipio* provide positive records of the occurrence of *D. virginiana* (MVZ Nos. 141220, 141700, 141701). The very similar *D. marsupialis* was not definitely recorded in the region.

Opossums are trapped and eaten with some regularity. Two 'medicinal' uses are reported. The tail (*sne ʔuč*) is used to aid childbirth (*špošil ya stohk ʔalal*). The hair

(*cocil ʔuč*) is feared because of its whitening effect on a man's hair (*špošil ya sakub holol yuʔun*).

Two forms of this opossum are widely recognized, distinguished by size, color, pattern, and behavior. Several of these criteria correspond to the most obvious distinguishing characters cited by Gardner (1973) in his revision of the genus as distinguishing *D. virginiana* from *D. marsupialis* in the Chiapas area.

a. *huyum ʔuč* 'fat opossum': The Virginia opossum (*D. virginiana*) (see Figure 5.101a). All specimens collected were attributed to this subdivision. And all are of this species.

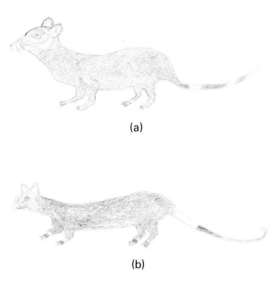

(a)

(b)

**Figure 5.101** (a) *huyum ʔuč* Virginia opossum (*Didelphis virginiana*); (b) *bac'ilʔuč* Mexican opossum (*D. marsupialis*). [Drawings by SMZ.]

This type is considered the larger and darker of the two and is supposed to be a more solitary animal. The flesh is *k'išin* 'hot'. Synonyms include *yaš ʔuč* 'grey opossum' and *muk'ul ʔuč* 'large opossum'. An illustration by SMZ clearly indicates the distinctive pale face markings and the more extensive black at the base of the tail of the widespread *D. virginiana*.

b. *bac'il ʔuč* 'true opossum': The Mexican opossum (*D. marsupialis*) (see Figure 5.101b). No specimens of this type were collected perhaps because this species is a lowland forest dweller. It is described as smaller, paler, and more social than *huyum ʔuč*, being encountered in small family groups. The flesh, by contrast, is *sikil* 'cold'. Alternate names include *sakil ʔuč* 'white opossum' and *cail ʔuč* 'small opossum'.

*ʔuč č'o* [ 'opossum' + 'small rodent' ]: The four-eyed opossum (*Philander opossum*) (Figure 5.102a).

No specimens of this species were collected. The identification is based on verbal descriptions, i.e., it has a pouch, is somewhat larger than a black rat, *Rattus rattus*, (Rodentia: Muridae), and has white spots above the eyes. SMZ and JGG also identi-

**Figure 5.102a** *ʔuč č'o* four-eyed opossum (*Philander opossum*). [From E. Raymond Hall and Keith R. Kelson, *The Mammals of North America*. Copyright 1959 The Ronald Press Company, New York.]

fied this species at MVZ. The flesh is *k'išin* 'hot'. Despite the name, most informants stress its relationship to the preceding category, *ʔuč*, rather than its resemblance to *č'o* 'small rodent'. Similar naming behavior is illustrated by *k'ulub kawáyu* [ 'locust' + 'horse' ], which is a kind of grasshopper (see grasshopper complex). In these instances the attributivizing morpheme follows rather than precedes the head term.

## MONKEY COMPLEX

Three species of native primates are found in Chiapas. All have retreated to isolated tracts of tropical forest and are known to Tenejapanecos only indirectly, i.e., through verbal descriptions, schoolbook illustrations, and captive animals. Thus the distinctions among these taxa are not too well defined.

Men and monkeys are believed to have had a common origin. Both shared an antediluvian paradise, so runs the tale. But the men, following God's advice, built an ark to ride out the flood. Those who rejected God's advice, who retreated instead to the forested mountain tops, were punished by having to have tails. And they live to this day in the forest. Despite the recognition of a relationship between men and monkeys (expressed also in triad-test sorting tasks* in which men and monkeys are paired in opposition to birds or reptiles), monkeys are *čanbalam* while men are not. The edibility of monkey flesh is a moot point, though several informants questioned considered the possibility to be incongruous.

*Among 75 animal name triads that I presented to SMZ were the following: *kirsiáno* 'human being', *maš* 'spider monkey', *caʔlos* 'black vulture'; *winik* 'man', *maš* 'spider monkey', *c'iʔ* 'dog'. In the first instance, 'black vulture' was singled out as the most different. "It flies, it's a bird," was the reason given. In the second the 'dog' was singled out, because, "It has four legs." I had some difficulty getting the idea across to SMZ that overall resemblance was the important consideration. In other instances unsatisfactory— to my way of thinking—choices were made simply on the basis of size or some other simple attribute. The technique has promise (see Berlin, Breedlove, and Raven 1966).

***bac'*** [ < 'true'? ]: The howler monkey (*Alouatta* spp. (see Figure 5.102b)

Neither species of this genus known from Chiapas occurs in Tenejapa. Most informants describe this type as larger than the following one, which is true. It is also less likely to be known than the following type, as the howler is particularly dependent upon virgin rain forest habitat—habitat no longer present near Tenejapa.

Figure 5.103 *maš* spider monkey (*Ateles geoffroyi*). [From A. Starker Leopold, *Wildlife of Mexico*, 1959. Originally published by the University of California Press; reprinted by permission of The Regents of the University of California.]

Figure 5.102b *bac'* howler monkey (*Alouatta villosa*). [From A. Starker Leopold, *Wildlife of Mexico*, 1959. Originally published by the University of California Press; reprinted by permission of The Regents of the University of California.]

***maš*** [UN]: Geoffroy's spider monkey (*Ateles geoffroyi*) (see Figure 5.103)

This species was identified at the Tuxtla Gutiérrez zoo as ***maš*** by several informants (AGM, JGG, SMZ).

***t'ul*** [UN]: Rabbits (Lagomorpha: Leporidae)

Two specific subdivisions are universally recognised.

a. ***bac'il t'ul*** 'true rabbit': The eastern cottontail (*Sylvilagus floridanus*) (see Figure 5.104). The occurrence of this species in Tenejapa is based on two specimens (MVZ Nos. 141220,

141706) and several sight records. A few informants also cited the existence of a ***cahal t'ul*** 'red rabbit' alleged to occur at lower elevations to the north. This may refer to the forest rabbit (*S. brasiliensis*), which is not otherwise known to occur near Tenejapa. The forest rabbit is a denizen of tropical

Figure 5.104 *bac'il t'ul* eastern cottontail (*Sylvilagus floridanus*). [From A. Starker Leopold, *Wildlife of Mexico*, 1959. Originally published by the University of California Press; reprinted by permission of The Regents of the University of California.]

forest habitat not found in the *municipio*. Eastern cottontails are eaten quite often, as evidenced by the high proportion of rabbit skulls among those observed in the possession of Tenejapanecos. The flesh is *k'išin* 'hot'. The term *te?tikil t'ul* 'forest rabbit' is synoymous.

b. *kašlan t'ul* 'Ladino rabbit': The introduced domestic European rabbit (*Oryctolagus cuniculus*). This species is rarely kept by Tenejapanecos. Informants cite the difficulty of maintaining them. They are kept by Ladinos in towns. They are considered to be edible and the flesh is *k'išin* 'hot'.

*čuč* [UN]: Squirrels (Rodentia: Sciuridae) This family is represented in Tenejapa by three distinct types. The most distinct is the southern flying squirrel (*Glaucomys volans*). The remaining species known from the region are all classed in the genus *Sciurus*. Deppe's squirrel (*S. deppei*) is considerably smaller than the gray squirrels (*S. aureogaster*). Several closely related species were recognized by Hall and Kelson (1959) among the gray squirrels: the red-bellied squirrel (*S. aureogaster*) found at lower elevations on the north slope of the central highlands, the Guatemalan grey squirrel (*S. griseoflavus*) of the central highlands, and the sociable squirrel (*S. socialis*) of the drier lowlands to the south. However, a recent taxonomic treatment reduces all three of these forms to two subspecies within an expanded *S. aureogaster* (Musser 1968). These two subspecies, *S. a. aureogaster* and *S. a. socialis* (> *S. griseoflavus sensu lato*) intergrade throughout the region. The Tenejapan Tzeltal classification corresponds closely to this latter treatment.

a. *pehpen čuč* 'butterfly squirrel': The southern flying squirrel (*Glaucomys volans*) (see Figure 5.105). This species is found in highland pine–oak forests. It is well known only among informants from such highland *parajes* as *macab* and *kurus č'en.* Though

Figure 5.105  *pehpen čuč* southern flying squirrel (*Glaucomys volans*). [From E. Raymond Hall and Keith R. Kelson, *The Mammals of North America*. Copyright 1959 by The Ronald Press Company, New York.]

no specimens were collected, the descriptions supplied by informants leave no doubt as to the identity of this taxon. It is also known as *mutil čuč* 'bird squirrel'.

b. *c'eh* [ON]: Deppe's squirrel (*Sciurus deppei*) (see Figure 5.106). No specimens were collected, however a squirrel of this species was seen in Tenejapa at 2300 m. It is alleged to occur throughout and is distinguished on the basis of small size relative to its congeners, reddish coloration, and distinctive vocalizations, as imitated by the primary name. It is also known as *c'eh čuč*

Figure 5.106  *c'eh* Deppe's squirrel (*Sciurus deppei*). [From A. Starker Leopold, *Wildlife of Mexico*, 1959. Originally published by the University of California Press; reprinted by permission of The Regents of the University of California.]

[ON + 'squirrel'] and **cahal čuč** 'red squirrel'. However this latter term is more often
applied to a variety of the residual category
(see later).

c. [gray squirrel]: This grouping is typically
named according to the dominant color of the
individual encountered, thus the varietal names
**yašal čuč** 'grey squirrel' (MVZ No. 141707),
**muk'ul cahal čuč** 'large red squirrel' (see also
above) or simply **cahal čuč** 'red squirrel, and
**ʔihk'al čuč** 'black squirrel'.    This last term is
not widely known, since melanistic forms of
the species in Tenejapa are rare. Melanistic
forms however, are commonly reported from
the Gulf coast lowlands. A melanistic Deppe's
squirrel kept in the Tuxtla Gutiérrez zoo was
called *ʔihk'al c'eh* by SMZ. Thus the color
varietals mentioned above are restricted to
the large squirrels of the *S. aureogaster*
complex (see Figure 5.107).

Squirrels of all types are eaten, and the
flesh is considered **k'išin** 'hot'.

**Figure 5.107**  [R] *čuč* gray squirrel (*Sciurus aureogaster*).
[From A. Starker Leopold, *Wildlife of Mexico*, 1959.
Originally published by the University of California Press;
reprinted by permission of The Regents of the University of
California.]

**ba**: The hispid pocket gopher, *Heterogeomys
hispidus* (Rodentia: Geomyidae), MVZ Nos.
141219, 141708, 141709 (see Figures 5.108
and 5.109)

This is the only species of the family known
from the central highlands. It has several
times the bulk of the pocket gophers found in
the United States and thus provides a fair
meal. The flesh is considered **sik** 'cold'. Two
medicinal uses are recorded. A soup made by
cooking the flesh is consumed to combat **sih-
t'ubel** 'swelling' and **nihkel** 'malaria'. Women
may also improve their tortilla making by
rubbing the belly of a pocket gopher. Presumably the body of the gopher has a certain
resemblance to the balls of corn batter from
which tortillas are made. A humorous
synonym for this taxon is **mentes** 'Mendez',
the name of a Tenejapan 'clan'. The correspondence of an animal name with personal or
family names occurs elsewhere (e.g., **k'intun**
and **ʔohkoc** of the lizard complex). It is also
known as **koen ba** [< iv 'to descend' +
'gopher'], a reference to its burrowing habits.

Two inductive subdivisions of **ba** are
widely recognized, though the zoological
basis of the distinction remains a mystery:

*a. bac'il ba* 'true pocket gopher'.    One specimen, of which the skin was seen, is typical of
the hispid pocket gopher as described in Hall
and Kelson (1959). Some informants recognize color varieties within this type, i.e.,
**ʔihk'al ba** 'black pocket gopher', **k'anal ba**
'yellow pocket gopher', or **cahal ba** 'red
pocket gopher'.

*b. č'uy pat ba*: [UN + 'back' + 'pocket
gopher']. A gopher distinguished by its
larger size and the presence of a wide white
band encircling the body just behind the fore-
legs. The attributive *č'uy pat* is also used to
distinguish a variety of domestic pig (see
*čitam*/mammal) with similar markings. Two
skulls purchased in Tenejapa were ascribed
to this type. Both, however, are indistinguishable from typical *Heterogeomys hispidus*.
Curiously Underwood's pocket gopher
(*Macrogeomys underwoodi*) of Costa Rica is
identically patterned. *č'uy pat ba*, however, is
most probably a well-marked form of the
local species, as well-marked local populations are common in this family. The final
determination of the identity of this taxon
awaits the collection of skin as well as skull.

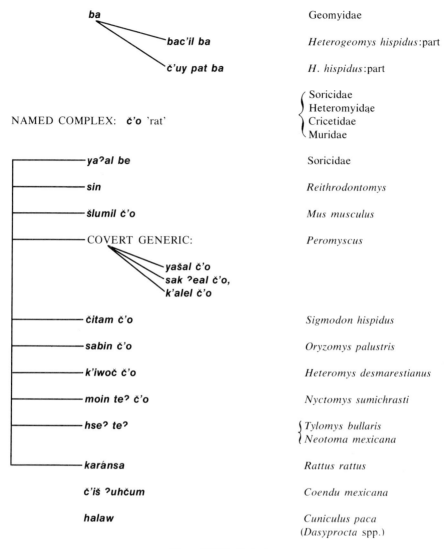

| | |
|---|---|
| ba | Geomyidae |
| bac'il ba | Heterogeomys hispidus:part |
| č'uy pat ba | H. hispidus:part |
| | ⎧ Soricidae |
| | ⎨ Heteromyidae |
| NAMED COMPLEX:  č'o 'rat' | ⎨ Cricetidae |
| | ⎩ Muridae |
| ya²al be | Soricidae |
| sin | Reithrodontomys |
| šlumil č'o | Mus musculus |
| COVERT GENERIC: | Peromyscus |
| yašal č'o |
| sak ²eal č'o, |
| k'alel č'o |
| čitam č'o | Sigmodon hispidus |
| sabin č'o | Oryzomys palustris |
| k'iwoč č'o | Heteromys desmarestianus |
| moin te² č'o | Nyctomys sumichrasti |
| hse² te² | ⎰ Tylomys bullaris |
| | ⎱ Neotoma mexicana |
| karánsa | Rattus rattus |
| č'iš ²uhčum | Coendu mexicana |
| halaw | Cuniculus paca |
| | (Dasyprocta spp.) |

Figure 5.108    Rodents.

This type is also known as **č'uyin ba** [UN + 'pocket gopher'] and **yalem ba** 'transitory pocket gopher', referring to the fact that it cannot be found during most months of the year.

Some relationship between **ba** 'pocket gopher' and **k'iwoč č'o** 'pocket mouse' (Rodentia: Heteromyidae) of the following complex is noted.

## č'o 'RAT' COMPLEX  (See Figure 5.110)

This named grouping is treated as a complex rather than as a generic because it includes several taxa that are clearly generic

in their own right (**ya²al be, sin, hse² te², karánsa**). The following rodent families are included here in their entirety: the Heteromyidae, of the suborder Sciuromorpha (to

(a)                         (b)

Figure 5.109    (a) **²ihk'al ba** (AMT) = **bac'il ba** 'true pocket gopher' and (b) **č'uy pat ba** 'white-banded gopher': (both) hispid pocket gopher (Heterogeomys hispidus). [Drawings by AMT.]

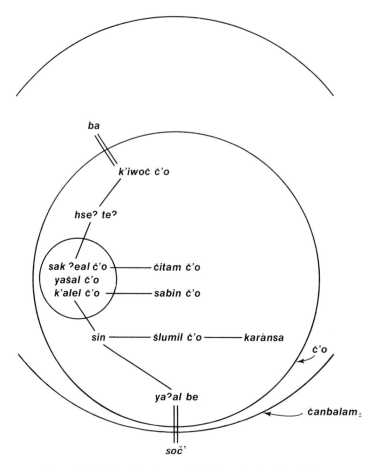

**Figure 5.110**  Heuristic diagram: Tzeltal 'small rodents' and allies.

which squirrels and pocket gophers also belong), and the Cricetidae and Muridae, of the suborder Myomorpha. The suborder Hystrichomorpha, to which the porcupine and paca belong, is treated elsewhere. The taxon considered to be the most divergent of the group by Tenejapanecos is *ya ʔal be* 'shrew' (Soricidae), of the order Insectivora.

All members of this complex are considered edible, with the exception of the murid rodents and the shrews. The latter are rejected because of their association with *soc'* 'bats'. The flesh of the edible forms is considered *k'išin* 'hot' in each case.

*ya ʔal be* ['weakness' + 'trail']: The shrews (Insectivora: Soricidae) (see Figure 5.111)

All four specimens collected in Tenejapa are Guatemalan small-eared shrews (*Cryptotis micrura*). Several other species of this genus or of the genus *Sorex* might also occur. No other insectivores (e.g., moles, Talpidae) occur in Chiapas. Some informants distinguish two varieties, *č'in ya ʔalbe* 'small shrew' and *muk'ul ya ʔalbe* 'large shrew'. The four specimens were all considered *č'in* 'small'. *Cryptotis micrura* is in fact the smallest shrew known from this region of Chiapas.

The shrew's name relates to a story known to all Tenejapanecos. Shrews are transformed into bats (*ya šk'ahta ta soc'*). A shrew attempts to jump across a trail. If he is successful he becomes a bat, if unsuccessful

Figure 5.111 *ya ʔal be* shrew (*Soricidae*). [From E. Raymond Hall and Keith R. Kelson, *The Mammals of North America*. Copyright 1959 by The Ronald Press Company, New York. *Cryptotis parva.*]

he dies. This explains the fact that dead shrews are often found lying in the trails (*be*), thus the name. This association of shrews with bats, while fanciful, reflects an accurate assessment of the morphological resemblances between the two orders. This association is given as the reason *ya ʔal be* are considered inedible. The fact that the flesh of insectivores is sometimes poisonous (Dennis Paulson personal communication) provides further justification and explains, as well, the frequency with which dead shrews are found in the trails, i.e., predators kill them but do not eat them.

The carnivorous habits of shrews is recognized by Tenejapanecos and cited as one feature distinguishing them from the remainder of the taxa included in *č'o*. Though *ya ʔalbe č'o* is an acceptable synonym to most informants, one informant insisted that *ya ʔal be* was quite distinct from *č'o*.

*sin* [ON]: Harvest mice, *Reithrodontomys* spp. (Cricetidae) (see Figure 5.112)

Figure 5.112 *sin* harvest mouse (*Reithrodontomys* spp.). [From E. Raymond Hall and Keith R. Kelson, *The Mammals of North America*. Copyright 1959 by The Ronald Press Company, New York. *R. fulvescens.*]

Two species of this genus are common in Tenejapa. Specimens assigned here are as follows: *Reithrodontomys megalotis*, MVZ Nos. 141787–147192, 141794, 141795–141799; and *Reithrodontomys mexicanus*, MVZ Nos. 141215, 141793.

One informant (who consistently demonstrated his lack of knowledge of animal names) referred to two specimens of *Peromyscus* (*P. boylii*, MVZ No. 141719, and *P. mexicanus*, MVZ No. 141731) as *muk'ul sin* 'big harvest mouse'. Other informants (JGG, SMZ) considered his classification to be erroneous. SMZ called two specimens of the house mouse (*Mus musculus*, MVZ Nos. 141206 and 141207) *yašal sin* 'grey harvest mouse' but admitted to an unfamiliarity with *šlumil č'o*, the name applied to these same specimens by other informants (AGM and his father). Thus this taxon is in near perfect correspondence with the genus *Reithrodontomys*.

Two varieties are recognized by many informants, *yašal sin* 'grey harvest mouse' and *cahal sin* 'red harvest mouse'. There is a tendency for the first variety to correspond with *R. megalotis* and the second with *R. mexicanus*. The two specimens of *R. mexicanus* were called *cahal sin*, but several specimens of *R. megalotis* (i.e., MVZ Nos. 141791, 141796, 141798, 141799) were also distinguished as 'red'. Pelage color, however, is not a perfectly reliable feature, since it varies within species due to seasonal and maturational factors.

*šlumil č'o* 'ground mouse': The house mouse, *Mus musculus* (Muridae) (see Figure 5.113)

House mice are rare in the rural areas of Tenejapa, though they are found in the Pueblo and commonly in San Cristóbal, where both specimens were collected (MVZ Nos. 141206, 141207). House mice are superficially very similar to harvest mice (*Reithrodontomys*), though they belong to a different family. According to Tenejapan belief they arrived with Venustiano Carranza's army. Thus the black rat (*Rattus rattus*) is called *karánsa*. Neither of the Muridae are considered

**Figure 5.113**  *šlumil č'o* house mouse (*Mus musculus*). [From E. Raymond Hall and Keith R. Kelson, *The Mammals of North America.* Copyright 1959 The Ronald Press Company, New York.]

edible, since they are believed to be the 'souls' of the revolutionary army soldiers.

Since this species is not often encountered by Tenejapanecos, errors of identification are common. The two specimens referred to above were called *yašal sin* 'grey harvest mouse' by SMZ, although AGM and his father correctly identified MVZ No. 141207 as *šlumil č'o*. AKČ' sent me two skulls labeled *šlumil č'o*, which he had trapped in *mahosik'*. They proved to be immature mice of the genus *Peromyscus*. It is noteworthy that he did not confuse these immature mice with the better known category *sin*. Despite these misidentifications, it is certain that *šlumil č'o* properly refers only to the house mouse, since it is invariably described as restricted to the vicinity of houses and towns. And of course it is known to be an introduced species.

In Zinacantan Tzotzil the cognate term *lumtikil č'o* refers without distinction to both *Mus* and *Reithrodontomys* (R. Laughlin personal communication). *yut lumil č'o* 'inside the ground mouse' is also heard in Tenejapa as a synonym.

[covert] 'white-footed mouse': The genus *Peromyscus* (Cricetidae)

This taxon is defined on the basis of the fact that mice of this abundant genus, with very few exceptions, are called *yašal č'o* 'grey mouse' (see Figure 5.114a), *sak ʔeal č'o* 'white-mouthed mouse' (see Figure 5.114b), or *k'alel č'o* 'bright mouse' (see Figure 5.114c). The distinction between these three types is based on a simple feature, the color

of the pelage, a feature of limited taxonomic relevance within the genus. These varietal distinctions are drawn only within the boundary of the covert taxon. Thus it is not a residual rodent category. *Peromyscus* that are basically grey on back and sides are called *yašal č'o*, those that are reddish on back and sides are *k'alel č'o*. Intermediates, i.e., with grey back and reddish sides, are *sak ʔeal č'o*. Table 5.1 shows the naming pattern. Each unit represents one specimen identified by one informant. The total number of units is thus greater than the total number of specimens (see Table 5.2), as a few were identified by more than one informant.

As can be seen, the majority of exceptions

**Table 5.1**
NAMING PATTERNS OF *PEROMYSCUS*[a]

|  | yašal č'o | sak ʔeal č'o | k'alel č'o | Total | Other names |
|---|---|---|---|---|---|
| *P. boylii* | 3 | 5 | 0 | 11[b] | 0 |
| *P. mexicanus* | 20 | 19 | 5 | 44 | 1 |
| *P. zarhynchus* | 7 | 6 | 7 | 20 | 2 |
| *Peromyscus* sp. | 1 | 1[c] | 2 | 4 | 2 |
| Total *Peromyscus* | 31 | 31 | 14 | 79[b] | 5 |
| Other genera (< *č'o*) | 0 | 0 | 0 | 0 | 38 |

[a]$\chi^2 = 8.003$, $P > .05$ ($N = 72$, *Peromyscus* sp. excluded, identifications as *woc č'o* excluded).
[b]Three identifications of *P. boylii* as *woc č'o* were recorded.
[c]This specimen is perhaps *P. oaxacensis*.

**Table 5.2**
*PEROMYSCUS* SPECIMENS

*P. boylii* (8), MVZ Nos. 141208–141210, 141718(?), 141719–141722.

*P. mexicanus* (43), MVZ Nos. 141211, 141212, 141723–141763.

*P. zarhynchus* (20), MVZ Nos. 141765, 141767–141776, 141777(?), 141778–141785.

*Peromyscus* sp. (6), MVZ Nos. 141712–141717.

*Peromyscus* total (77)[a]

[a]Some specimens were not identified while others were identified by more than one informant. Thus this total does not equal the total of *Peromyscus* identifications in Table 5.1.

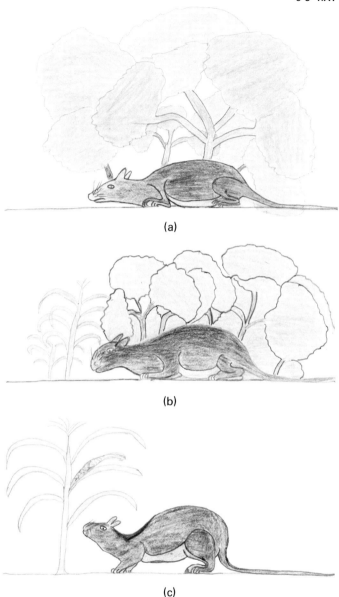

(a)

(b)

(c)

**Figure 5.114**    (a) *yašal č'o*, (b) *sak ʔeal č'o*, and (c) *k'alel č'o*: (all) 'white-footed mice' (*Peromyscus* spp.). [Drawings by SMZ.]

involve either forms of indeterminate species (some of which are immature), or *Peromyscus zarhynchus*. Some *P. zarhynchus* are nearly as large as wood rats (*Neotoma*, see **hseʔ teʔ**) and black rats (*Rattus rattus*, see **karánsa**) and thus are atypical. The two exceptions noted were in fact erroneously classed as **hseʔ teʔ** and **karánsa**.

**woc č'o** 'bushy-tailed mouse' is a rare highland name. It might properly refer to *Peromyscus lophurus*, the crested-tailed mouse, known to occur near San Cristóbal. The three specimen assignments noted for **woc č'o** in Table 5.1 were by a single informant. Other informants called the same specimens **sak ʔeal č'o**.

Synonyms include **yaš pat č'o** 'grey-backed mouse', for **yašal č'o**, and **sak č'uht č'o** 'white-bellied mouse', for **sak ʔeal č'o**.

**čitam č'o** 'pig rat': The hispid cotton rat, *Sigmodon hispidus* (Cricetidae) (see Figure 5.115)

This is a fairly common lowland resident in Tenejapa. The identifications are given in Table 5.3.

One identification each of *Peromyscus mexicanus* (MVZ No. 141731) and *Rattus rattus* (MVZ No. 141814) were incorrectly assigned here. The *R. rattus* specimen was an immature. An immature example of *Sigmodon* was classed as **sin** (see second taxon in the **č'o** complex).

Figure 5.116 *sabin č'o* Coues's rice rat (*Oryzomys palustris*). [From E. Raymond Hall and Keith R. Kelson, *The Mammals of North America*. Copyright 1959 The Ronald Press Company, New York.]

Figure 5.115 *čitam č'o* hispid cotton rat (*Sigmodon hispidus*). [From E. Raymond Hall and Keith R. Kelson, *The Mammals of North America*. Copyright 1959 by The Ronald Press Company, New York.]

**Table 5.3**
THE MAPPING OF *ČITAM Č'O* TO *SIGMODON HISPIDUS*

|  | *čitam č'o* | *Other names* |
|---|---|---|
| *Sigmodon hispidus saturatus* | 9 | 1 |
| Other species (⊂ *č'o*) | 2 | 110 |

**sabin č'o** 'weasel rat': The rice rats, in particular the marsh rice rat, *Oryzomys palustris* (Cricetidae), MVZ Nos. 141800–141802 (see Figure 5.116)

This genus is rare in Tenejapa. The specimens were collected near Ocosingo and no informant present at the time (SMZ, JGG, AKČ') had seen the type before. They agreed however that the name **sabin č'o**, current in Tenejapa, was the most appropriate. At a later time other informants cited the existence of a **čan č'o** 'snake rat' or **haʔal č'o** 'water rat', which names are most likely synonyms. Rice rats exhibit a preference for living near water.

**k'iwoč č'o** 'cheek-pocket mouse': The only animals appropriately so-called are mice of the Heteromyidae

Of these, only a single species is known from the central highland region of Chiapas, Desmarest's spiny pocket mouse (*Heteromys desmarestianus*) (see Figure 5.117). Informants describe it as a rock dweller nearly the size of **hseʔ teʔ** (Cricetidae: *Tylomys*) but with cheek pouches similar to those of the pocket gopher (see **ba**). It is local and rather rare, and I was not able to obtain a specimen. Some informants give **kuhtin č'o** 'short-tailed mouse' as a synonym, though this species does not have a notably short tail.

**moin teʔ č'o** 'tree-climbing rat': Possibly the vesper rat, *Nyctomys sumichrasti* (Cricetidae)

No specimens were collected, but the vesper rat is a likely candidate for the "vacant slot" occupied by this distinct form. It is described as medium-sized, arboreal, and of

**Figure 5.117**   *k'iwoč č'o* Desmarest's spiny pocket mouse
(*Heteromys desmarestianus*): ⌈Drawing by SMZ.⌉

bright, reddish coloration, thus the synonym *cahal č'o* 'red rat'. All these features are quite characteristic of the vesper rat (Hall and Kelson 1959:577–578).

*hse? te?* 'twig-cutter': climbing rats (*Tylomys* sp.) and/or wood rats (*Neotoma* sp.) (see Figure 5.118)

A single specimen of the Chiapas climbing rat, *Tylomys bullaris* (Cricetidae), MVZ No. 141786, was named *yašal hse? te?* 'grey twig-cutter'. However the Mexican wood rat, *Neotoma mexicana* (Cricetidae), is probably also included here. No specimens of this species were obtained; however informants pointed out trails and nests which probably belong to this species as being those of *hse? te?*. If the local race of wood rat is one of the red forms (see Hall and Kelson 1959:695), then *cahal hse? te?* 'red twig-cutter' might distinguish the wood rat from *yašal hse? te?* 'grey twig-cutter', the climbing rat. A third

**Figure 5.118**   *hse? te?* climbing rat or wood rat (*Tylomys* or *Neotoma*). ⌈Drawing by SMZ.⌉

alternative is possible and it is described here as an alternative system.

Several informants, notably AMT, recognize three types of *hse? te?* as follows:

*yašal hse? te?* 'grey twig-cutter'.

*cahal hse? te?* 'red twig-cutter'.

*čin?ak' hse? te?* ['vine sp.' + 'twig-cutter'].

The first two may refer to color variations within the Mexican wood rat (*Neotoma mexicana*) and would thus be varietal subdivisions within a residual specific taxon contrasting with *čin?ak' hse? te?*, the climbing rat (*Tylomys* spp.). This subtype is usually described as having a bare, vinelike tail (hence the name), dark at the base and light at the tip, which exactly defines the climbing rat. The term *čučil č'o* 'squirrel rat' might be synonymous with *čin?ak' hse? te?*.

*karánsa* [< Sp Venustiano Carranza, president of Mexico, 1914–1920]: The black rat, *Rattus rattus* (Muridae) (see Figure 5.119)

Three of four specimens collected (MVZ Nos. 141766, 141813, 141815) were assigned here. An immature (MVZ No. 141814) was called *čitam č'o* (see earlier taxon in this complex). This rat is considered inedible. A story that is current recounts how house cats (*šawin*) were first created of corn dough

(*wah*) by the mother of the house in order to defend her stores of corn from the ravages of *karánsa*.

Black rats are rather common in the homes of Tenejapanecos and must take a certain toll of the food supply. I have no evidence, however, concerning the presence or absence of the Norway rat (*Rattus norvegicus*) in the region. It may occur in San Cristóbal. This is tentatively suggested by the fact that a few informants distinguish two varieties of *karánsa*. *bac'il karánsa* 'true house rat', also known as *yašal karánsa* 'grey house rat', i.e., the black rat. This is contrasted with *kuhtin karánsa* 'short-tailed house rat' or *sakil karánsa* 'white house rat', which fits the Norway rat, which is paler and has a shorter tail than the black rat. However, a specimen identified by SMZ as *sakil karánsa* proved to be the white-bellied phase of the common black rat (i.e., *R.r. frugivorus*).

*č'iš ?uhčum* ['spiny' + 'opossum' archaic]: The Mexican porcupine, *Coendou mexicanus* (Rodentia: Erethizontidae) (see Figure 5.120)

Some informants, at least, consider this animal to be edible. No specimens were obtained, but a dead porcupine examined on the road near Chiapa de Corzo was identified as being of this species. Several informants also identified the porcupine in the Tuxtla

Figure 5.119    *karánsa* black rat (*Rattus rattus*). [Drawing by SMZ.]

**Figure 5.120** *č'iš ʔuhčum* Mexican porcupine (*Coendou mexicanus*). [From A. Starker Leopold, *Wildlife of Mexico*, 1959. Originally published by the University of California Press; reprinted by permission of The Regents of the University of California.]

Gutiérrez zoo, and AMT's illustration of *č'iš ʔuhčum* (not included here) is unmistakable. No other similar species occur in Chiapas.

**halaw** [UN]: The paca, *Cuniculus paca* (Rodentia: Dasyproctidae) MVZ Nos. 141217, 141710, 141711 (see Figure 5.121)

This large rodent is still fairly common in Tenejapa up to 1800 m. Though none were observed, several skulls of animals killed

**Figure 5.121** *halaw* paca (*Cuniculus paca*). [From A. Starker Leopold, *Wildlife of Mexico*, 1959. Originally published by the University of California Press; reprinted by permission of The Regents of the University of California.]

in the *municipio* were obtained. The closely related agoutis (*Dasyprocta* spp.) do not occur near Tenejapa. However several are kept in the Tuxtla Gutiérrez zoo. Informants referred to the paca as **bac'il halaw** 'true paca', and coined the term **ʔihk'al halaw** 'black paca' for the agouti, demonstrating that they recognize a relationship.

Several varieties were elicited, but with little consistency. **bak č'oh halaw** 'bone-cheek paca' refers to the shape of the skull of mature specimens. **cahal halaw** 'red paca' was applied to the immature specimen. Immatures are reddish. **huyum halaw** 'fat paca' is apparently descriptive of healthy adults.

## DOG COMPLEX (See Figures 5.122, 5.123)

This complex includes two species of the genus *Canis* as well as a mustelid, the river otter. None are eaten because of the relationship assumed to exist with the domestic dog, which is not eaten because it is a pet.

**ʔok'il₁** [< iv 'cry']: The coyote, *Canis latrans* (Canidae) (see Figure 5.124)

This species is now rare in Tenejapa, though it still occurs in the more heavily forested areas. It is known humorously as **te ʔtikil c'i ʔ** 'forest dog', and **koyóte** [<Sp *coyote*]. **ʔok'il** is considered the most appropriate term by most informants. It occasionally takes domestic chickens. See **ʔok'il₂**/ grasshopper for a polysemous usage.

**c'i ʔ** [UN]: The domestic dog, *Canis familiaris* (Canidae) (see Figure 5.125)

Most families keep one or more dogs about their houses (see Table 1.2). They are fed tortilla scraps and are enjoyed as pets. No special hunting breeds exist, though some men train their dogs to help hunt such animals as raccoons and pacas. One story with no clear moral recounts the adventures of a hunter and his dog. Dead dogs are used as **pošil c'isim** 'leaf-cutting ant medicine', i.e., to discourage the ravages of these ants.

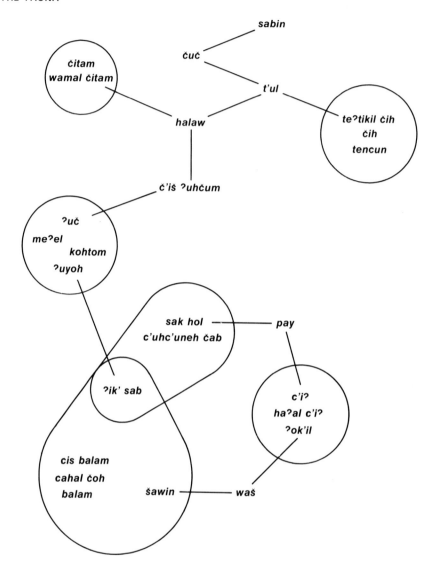

**Figure 5.122** Heuristic diagram: Perceived relations among certain Tzeltal mammal taxa.

Several specific subdivisions are widely recognized:

a. **bac'il c'iʔ** 'true dog': The indigenous breed of short-haired dogs, usually tan-colored. This type may also be referred to by the unmodified generic name, illustrating type specific polysemy (Berlin 1973:265).

b. **kašlan c'iʔ** 'Ladino dog': Most long-haired dogs (breed uncertain) are included here. They are not kept by Indians but may be found in towns. Many varieties may be named, as this taxon is residual, e.g., AMT cites the following:

**cahal poh čikin kašlan c'iʔ** 'red earless Ladino dog'.

**ʔik' woc'an tek' čikin kašlan c'iʔ** [ < tv 'beckon' + <tv 'knead corn dough'(?) + 'raised-eared Ladino dog'].

**píntu pehkeč kašlan c'iʔ** 'spotted short-legged Ladino dog'.

COVERT COMPLEX:   dog

{ Canidae:part
{ Mustelidae:part

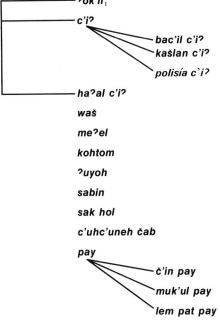

| | |
|---|---|
| ʔok'il₁ | *Canis latrans* |
| c'iʔ | *C. familiaris* |
| bac'il c'iʔ | *C. familiaris*:part |
| kašlan c'iʔ | *C. familiaris*:part |
| polisía c'iʔ | *C. familiaris*:part |
| haʔal c'iʔ | *Lutra annectens* |
| waš | *Urocyon cinereoargenteus* |
| meʔel | *Procyon lotor* |
| kohtom | *Nasua narica* |
| ʔuyoh | *Potos flavus* |
| sabin | *Mustela frenata* |
| sak hol | *Eira barbara* |
| c'uhc'uneh čab | *Tamandua tetradactyla* |
| pay | Mephitinae |
| č'in pay | *Spilogale angustifrons* |
| muk'ul pay | *Mephitis macroura* |
| lem pat pay | *Conepatus mesoleucus* |
| ʔik' sab | *Felis yagouaroundi* |

COVERT COMPLEX:   cat

*Felis*:part

| | |
|---|---|
| balam | *Felis onca* |
| čoh | *F. concolor* |
| cahal čoh | *F. pardalis* |
| cis balam | *F. wiedii* |
| šawin | *F. cattus* |

**Figure 5.123**   Carnivores.

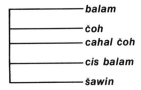

*yašal pač ʔit kašlan c'iʔ* 'gray hairy(?)-buttocked Ladino dog'.

c. *polisía c'iʔ* [ < Sp *policia* 'police' + 'dog' ]: The German shepherd. Also known as *koyóte c'iʔ* [ < Sp *coyote* 'coyote' + 'dog' ].   This type

**Figure 5.124** *ʔok'il* coyote (*Canis latrans*). [ From A. Starker Leopold, *Wildlife of Mexico*, 1959. Originally published by the University of California Press; reprinted by permission of The Regents of the University of California. ]

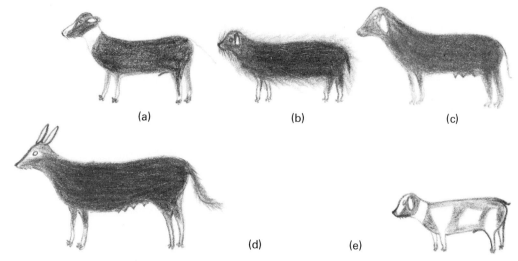

(a)        (b)        (c)

(d)        (e)

**Figure 5.125** Types of *c'i?* domestic dog (*Canis familiaris*): (a) *?ihk'al sak?oal kelem c'i?* ['black' + 'white-necklace' + 'male' + 'dog'], an example of *bac'il c'i?* 'true-dog'; (b) *yašal pac?it me? kašlan c'i?* ['gray' + 'hairy(?)-buttock' + 'female' + 'Ladino' + 'dog'], an example of *kašlan c'i?* 'Ladino dog'; (c) *cahal pohčikin me? kašlan c'i?* ['red' + '? — ear' + 'female' + 'Ladino' + 'dog'], an example of *kašlan c'i?* 'Ladino dog'; (d) *?ik'woc'an tek'čikin me? kašlan c'i?* ['beckon-?' + 'standing-ear' + 'female' + 'Ladino' + 'dog'], an example of *kašlan c'i?* 'Ladino dog'; (e) *píntu pehkeč kelem kašlan c'i?* ['spotted' + 'short-legged'? + 'male' + 'Ladino' + 'dog'], an example of *kašlan c'i?* 'Ladino dog'. [Drawings by AMT.]

is also not kept by Indians. SMZ's illustration, however, suggests a Dalmation.

Some breeds are not included in any of these categories, e.g., the Weimaraner and Saint Bernard, although they are recognized as *c'i?*.

*ha?al c'i?* 'rain dog': The southern river otter, *Lutra annectens* (Mustelidae) (see Figure 5.126)

Despite the name, this species is not considered to be a dog. It is rather rare in the rivers on the northern and eastern edges of the *municipio*. Though not observed in the *municipio*, a skin in a San Cristóbal shop was so identified by AKČ'. No other local animal fits the description given by informants.

*waš* [UN]: The gray fox, *Urocyon cinereoargenteus* (Canidae), MVZ No. 141702 (see Figure 5.127)

This species is fairly common in Tenejapa and is the only fox found in Chiapas. The

flesh is eaten and is considered to be *k'išin* 'hot'. Some informants recognize two varieties, *yašal waš* 'grey fox' and *cahal waš* 'red fox'. This variation could be accounted for

**Figure 5.126** *ha?al c'i?* Southern river otter (*Lutra* sp.). [From A. Starker Leopold, *Wildlife of Mexico*, 1959. Originally published by the University of California Press; reprinted by permission of The Regents of the University of California. *L. canadensis.*]

Figure 5.127 *waš* gray fox (*Urocyon cinereoargenteus*). [From A. Starker Leopold, *Wildlife of Mexico*, 1959. Originally published by the University of California Press; reprinted by permission of The Regents of the University of California.]

by intraspecific variation. However it is also suggested that the 'red' variety is an animal spirit (*lab*). Thus the red variety may be legendary. *wet* is a rare synonym, which is probably a loan from Tzotzil, as the fox is known as *vet* in Zinacantan (as in proto-Mayan, see Kaufman 1964). Fox skins are used as 'toys' (*ʔištobil*) during *Carnivál* (*loil k'in*).

*meʔel* 'old lady': The raccoon, *Procyon lotor* (Procyonidae), MVZ Nos. 141221, 141703 (see Figure 5.128)

This animal is fairly common in Tenejapa; it is eaten and the flesh is *k'išin* 'hot'. It is

Figure 5.128 *meʔel* raccoon (*Procyon lotor*). [From A. Starker Leopold, *Wildlife of Mexico*, 1959. Originally published by the University of California Press; reprinted by permission of The Regents of the University of California.]

also known as *meʔčuntik* 'grandmother'. The skin (*snuhkulel meʔel*) is used for making bags (*woša*) for carrying bullets on hunting trips.

*kohtom* [UN]: The coatimundi, *Nasua narica* (Procyonidae) (see Figure 5.129)

Though not observed, informants assert that it is found in Tenejapa. Several informants identified it at the Tuxtla Gutiérrez zoo. It is eaten, and the flesh is *k'išin* 'hot'.

Figure 5.129 *kohtom* coatimundi (*Nasua narica*). [From A. Starker Leopold, *Wildlife of Mexico*, 1959. Originally published by the University of California Press; reprinted by permission of The Regents of the University of California.]

The coatimundi's penis (*yat kohtom*) is considered to be *pošil cacal*, or a medicine for sexual weakness in men. The penis is also used for carrying a tobacco mixture (*bankilal*). Some informants recognize two varieties, *bac'il kohtom* 'true coati' and *bahk'al kohtom* 'groups-of-four-hundred coati'. This destinction perhaps reflects the contrast between the solitary old males and the more typical mixed bands (Leopold 1972: 435).

*ʔuyoh* [UN]: The kinkajou, *Potos flavus* (Procyonidae) (see Figure 5.130)

Figure 5.130 *ʔuyoh* kinkajou (*Potos flavus*). [From A. Starker Leopold, *Wildlife of Mexico*, 1959. Originally published by the University of California Press; reprinted by permission of The Regents of the University of California.]

Figure 5.131 *sabin* long-tailed weasel (*Mustela frenata*). [From A. Starker Leopold, *Wildlife of Mexico*, 1959. Originally published by the University of California Press; reprinted by permission of The Regents of the University of California.]

This species was identified in the Tuxtla Gutiérrez zoo and from skins on sale in San Cristóbal. It is eaten, and the flesh is *k'išin* 'hot'. The term *č'in ʔuyoh* 'little kinkajou' was coined to name a mounted species of the two-toed anteater, *Cyclopes didactylus* (Myrmecophagidae), which is otherwise unknown to Tenejapanecos. The name is superficially appropriate (J. Patton personal communication).

**sabin** [UN]: The long-tailed weasel, *Mustela frenata* (Mustelidae), MVZ No. 141704 (see Figure 5.131)

This animal is quite common in Tenejapa and one observed near San Cristóbal was identified as **sabin** by MMH. Several varieties may be recognized: ***huyum sabin*** 'fat weasel',

***cahal sabin*** 'red weasel', ***ʔihk'al sabin*** 'black weasel'. These types probably describe intraspecific variation. An apochryphal animal called ***herínka sabin*** 'syringe weasel' is known from folklore accounts. It allegedly crawls into the anus of cattle, which are then consumed from within. My informants considered this story quite amusing. See also ***herínka lukum*** 'syringe worm'.

***sak hol*** 'white head': The tayra, *Eira barbara* (Mustelidae) (see Figure 5.132)

This species is found throughout Tenejapa according to informants. Positive identification was obtained at the Tuxtla Gutiérrez zoo from several informants. It is eaten, and the flesh is *k'išin* 'hot'. In highland *parajes* this animal may be called ***c'uhc'uneh čab*** 'honey

**Figure 5.132** *sak hol* tayra (*Eira barbara*). ⌈From A. Starker Leopold, *Wildlife of Mexico*, 1959. Originally published by the University of California Press; reprinted by permission of The Regents of the University of California.⌉

**Figure 5.133** *c'uhc'uneh čab* tamandua (*Tamandua tetradactyla*). ⌈From A. Starker Leopold, *Wildlife of Mexico*, 1959. Originally published by the University of California Press; reprinted by permission of The Regents of the University of California.⌉

licker' by informants unfamiliar with the tamandua (see next taxon).

*c'uhc'uneh čab* 'honey licker': The tamandua (*Tamandua tetradactyla*) (see Figure 5.133)

This is the only anteater (Myrmecophagidae) known to Tenejapanecos. It is apparently found sparingly in lowland Tenejapa. The name may be applied to the tayra, *Eira barbara* (Mustelidae, see previous taxon), by highland informants not familiar with the tamandua. The name is based on the assumption that the animal eats honey, when the bees are its actual prey. The flesh is considered *k'išin* 'hot'. The name is also rendered as *c'uhc'un čab*. The two-toed anteater (*Cyclopes didactylus*) is apparently unknown. A mounted specimen of this species was called *č'in ʔuyoh* 'small kinkajou' (see *ʔuyoh*).

*pay* ⌈UN⌉: Skunks (Mustelidae: Mephitinae), also known as *cis pay* 'fart skunk'

Three types are recognized which correspond well to the three species occurring in Tenejapa, though most informants recognize only two types, presumably due to distribu-

tional limitations. The composite picture is as follows:

a. *č'in pay* 'small skunk': The southern spotted skunk (*Spilogale angustifrons*) (see Figure 5.134). It is also known as *c'ibal pay* 'striped skunk'. This species was identified from verbal descriptions and, by SMZ and JGG, from museum skins (MVZ).

b. *muk'ul pay* 'large skunk': The hooded skunk (*Mephitis macroura*) (see Figure 5.135). It is also known as *ʔihk'al pay* 'black skunk'.

**Figure 5.134** *č'in pay* spotted skunk (*Spilogale* sp.). ⌈From E. Raymond Hall and Keith R. Kelson, *The Mammals of North America*. Copyright 1959 by The Ronald Press Company, New York. *S. putorius.*⌉

Identified by SMZ and JGG from museum skins (MVZ).

c. **lem pat pay** 'shining-back skunk': The hog-nosed skunk (*Conepatus mesoleucus*) (see Figure 5.136). It is also known as **sakil pat pay** 'white-backed skunk' and **č'uypat pay** (see **ba** for an analysis of this attributive), also identified at MVZ.

All species are considered to be edible, and the flesh is **k'išin** 'hot', though the odor deters most informants. During epidemics (e.g., **ʔobal** 'cough', **hik'hik' ʔobal** 'whooping cough') dead skunks may be placed to the rear of the house in an effort to protect one's family from the disease. The odor is alleged to have the deterrent effect.

**ʔik' sab** [< tv 'beckon'? + 'dawn']: The jaguarundi (*Felis yagouaroundi*) (see Figure 5.137)

This is the only wild cat still regularly encountered in Tenejapa. It was identified at the zoo in Tuxtla Gutiérrez by several informants. It is eaten and the flesh is **k'išin** 'hot'. A degree of relationship is perceived with the tayra (Mustelidae: *Eira barbara*, see **sakhol**), the tamandua (Myrmecophagidae: *Tamandua tetradactyla*, see **c'uhc'uneh čab**), and the kinkajou (Mustelidae: *Potos flavus*, see **ʔuyoh**).

## CAT COMPLEX

All local species of the genus *Felis* (Felidae) are grouped here with the exception of the jaguarundi (*Felis yagouaroundi*), which links the cats with several other groups (see former taxon). The boundaries of this complex are further confused as house cats (**šawin**, see fifth taxon in this complex) are associated with foxes (**waš**). However, the internal relationships are strongly perceived. The large wild cats are all extremely rare at present and thus poorly known, with a resulting nomenclatural confusion.

**balam** [UN]: The jaguar (*Felis onca*) (see Figure 5.138)

Figure 5.138 *balam* jaguar (*Felis onca*). [From A. Starker Leopold, *Wildlife of Mexico*, 1959. Originally published by the University of California Press; reprinted by permission of The Regents of the University of California.]

It is also known as *muk'ul balam* 'large jaguar'. The flesh is considered *k'išin* 'hot', though contemporary Tenejapanecos have no direct experience with this endangered species. One was identified at the Tuxtla Gutiérrez zoo by several informants. The Mottled Owl (*škuh* or *mutil balam*, *Ciccaba virgata*) is alleged to anticipate the appearance of this big cat.

*čoh* [UN]: The cougar (*Felis concolor*) (see Figure 5.139)

This is certainly the aboriginal meaning of this term, though most Tenejapanecos today consider it an abbreviation of *cahal čoh* 'red cougar', by which the ocelot is usually known. However SMZ correctly describes the large size and unspotted coat of this species. They have apparently been extirpated in the region for some time. The term is applied jokingly to the house cat (*šawin*, see later taxon in this complex).

*cahal čoh* 'red cougar': The ocelot (*Felis pardalis*) (see Figure 5.140)

Most informants describe three spotted cats; the largest is *balam* (see first taxon in this complex), the smallest is *cis balam* (following taxon), and *cahal čoh* is medium-sized. It must therefore refer to this species. The rarity of these animals precludes any more exact proof at present. An alternate classificatory system is that of SMZ, who reserves the term *čoh* for the cougar, with *cahal čoh* but a variety of that species. He thus recognizes two subdivisions of *cis balam*. The ocelot, in this system, is *muk'ul cis balam* 'large fart-jaguar'; the margay (see following

Figure 5.139 *čoh* cougar (*Felis concolor*). [From A. Starker Leopold, *Wildlife of Mexico*, 1959. Originally published by the University of California Press; reprinted by permission of The Regents of the University of California.]

Figure 5.140 *cahal čoh* ocelot (*Felis pardalis*). [From A. Starker Leopold, *Wildlife of Mexico*, 1959. Originally published by the University of California Press; reprinted by permission of The Regents of the University of California.]

taxon) is *č'in cis balam* 'small fart-jaguar'. He identified the ocelot and the margay in the Tuxtla Gutiérrez zoo as such. The flesh is *k'išin* 'hot'.

*cis balam* 'fart-jaguar': The margay (*Felis wiedii*) (see Figure 5.141)

This is the smallest spotted cat. For most Tenejapanecos it is a generic taxon. For SMZ it is *č'in cis balam* 'little fart-jaguar', a specific taxon. The "true" nomenclatural system must remain unknown, since the animals are

Figure 5.142 *šawin* domestic cat (*Felis cattus*). *yašal kelem čoh* (= *šawin*) 'gray male cat' (AMT). [Drawing by AMT.]

Figure 5.141 *cis balam* margay (*Felis wiedii*). [From A. Starker Leopold, *Wildlife of Mexico*, 1959. Originally published by the University of California Press; reprinted by permission of The Regents of the University of Californa.]

now known by hearsay only. The rationale for the term 'fart-jaguar' is obscure, as these cats produce no musk to my knowledge. Despite the name, it is not considered to be a kind of jaguar. The flesh is *k'išin* 'hot'.

*šawin* ['Sebastian' + diminutive]: The domestic cat (*Felis cattus*) (see Figure 5.142)

The name cited here is universally known in Tenejapa but has not been recorded for other dialects of Tzeltal or Tzotzil. *šaw* is an Old Spanish loan, and the species is not native, thus no truly aboriginal term exists. A widespread synonym is obscene, i.e., *mis*, possibly a Nahuatl loan meaning 'female genitalia' (Kaufman 1964). Other joking synonyms include *čoh* 'cougar' and, occa-

sionally, *balam* 'jaguar'. House cats are not often kept in Tenejapa (see Table 1.2) though their presence is legitimized in folklore (see *karánsa*/rat). Many varieties may be described but no types are consistently elicited (e.g., *ʔihk'al šawin* 'black cat', *yašal šawin* 'grey cat', etc.). The flesh is *k'išin* 'hot'. However, supernatural sanctions are alleged to apply to those who kill house cats.

*cemen* [UN]: Baird's tapir, *Tapirus bairdii* (Perissodactyla: Tapiridae) (see Figure 5.143)

This animal is all but extirpated in Mexico. A few remain in isolated lowland areas

Figure 5.143 *cemen* Baird's tapir (*Tapirus bairdii*). [From A. Starker Leopold, *Wildlife of Mexico*, 1959. Originally published by the University of California Press; reprinted by permission of The Regents of the University of California.]

(Leopold 1972:490). For Tenejapanecos they are as little known as the elephants, *Elephas* spp. (Proboscidea: Elephantidae), occasionally seen in traveling circuses. Thus the following alternative classification is understandable: *č'in cemen* 'small tapir', the tapir, and *muk'ul cemen* 'large tapir', the elephant. Their flesh is considered *sik* 'cold', though none are available for consumption.

## PIG COMPLEX (See Figure 5.144)

The native peccaries (Artiodactyla: Tayassuidae) were *čitam* originally. The name today, in unmodified form, applies to the closely related domestic pig (same infraorder, Suiformes, but Suidae) introduced after the conquest. The peccaries have now come to be called *wamal čitam* 'bush peccary'. (See Berlin 1972:82–83, for an analysis of this diachronic process.)

*čitam* [UN]: The domestic pig, *Sus scrofa* (Artiodactyla : Suidae)

These animals are now kept fairly commonly by Tenejapanecos. The flesh is eaten or sold to Ladinos for cash. The flesh is *sik* 'cold' and is eaten as a cure for 'dysentery' (*špošil č'ič'*). The several widely recognized specific subdivisions are as follows:

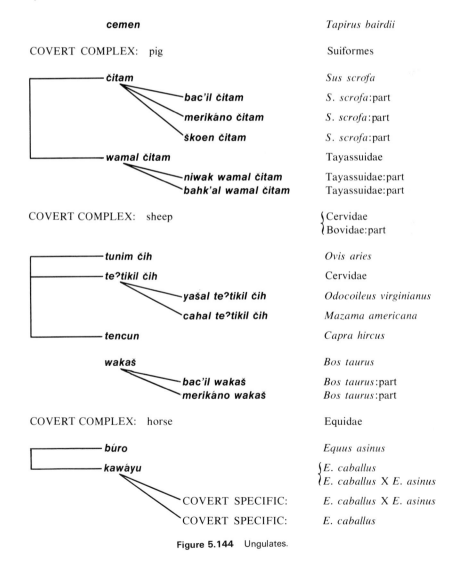

| | |
|---|---|
| **cemen** | *Tapirus bairdii* |
| COVERT COMPLEX: pig | Suiformes |
| **čitam** | *Sus scrofa* |
| **bac'il čitam** | *S. scrofa*:part |
| **merikáno čitam** | *S. scrofa*:part |
| **škoen čitam** | *S. scrofa*:part |
| **wamal čitam** | Tayassuidae |
| **niwak wamal čitam** | Tayassuidae:part |
| **bahk'al wamal čitam** | Tayassuidae:part |
| COVERT COMPLEX: sheep | {Cervidae / Bovidae:part |
| **tunim čih** | *Ovis aries* |
| **te?tikil čih** | Cervidae |
| **yašal te?tikil čih** | *Odocoileus virginianus* |
| **cahal te?tikil čih** | *Mazama americana* |
| **tencun** | *Capra hircus* |
| **wakaš** | *Bos taurus* |
| **bac'il wakaš** | *Bos taurus*:part |
| **merikáno wakaš** | *Bos taurus*:part |
| COVERT COMPLEX: horse | Equidae |
| **búro** | *Equus asinus* |
| **kawáyu** | {*E. caballus* / *E. caballus* X *E. asinus* |
| COVERT SPECIFIC: | *E. caballus* X *E. asinus* |
| COVERT SPECIFIC: | *E. caballus* |

**Figure 5.144**  Ungulates.

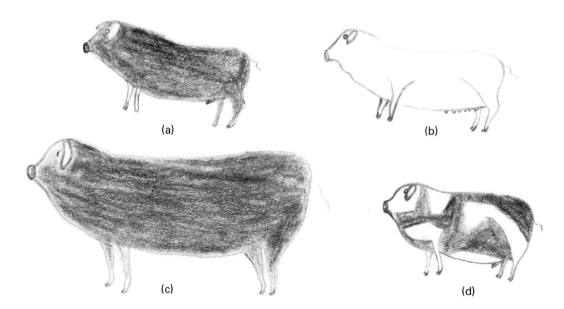

(a)

(b)

(c)

(d)

Figure 5.145   Kinds of *čitam* domestic pig (*Sus scrofa*): (a) *bac'il ʔihk'al čitam* (AMT) and (b) *bac'il sakil čitam*; (both *bac'il čitam* 'true pig'); (c) *cahal wakaš čitam* (AMT) cf. *merikáno čitam* 'American pig'; (d) *píntu škuin čitam* (AMT) cf. *škuen čitam* 'low-slung pig'. [Drawings by AMT.]

a. ***bac'il čitam*** 'true pig' (see Figures 5.145a, 5.145b): Apparently a residual category of quite varied appearance, which includes most examples of this species. Varietals are recognized within this residual, e.g., *č'uy pat čitam* (see *ba* 'pocket gopher', for an analysis of this attributive), which is black with a wide white band around the body behind the fore-legs; ***bac'il ʔihk'al čitam*** 'true black pig'; ***bac'il sakil čitam*** 'true white pig'.

b. ***merikáno čitam*** 'American pig' (see Figure 5.145c): This is a recently introduced, exceptionally large breed also known as ***insistúto čitam***, referring to the Instituto Nacional Indigenista (National Indian Institute), which has been attempting to improve local stock. This type is also notably clean, hardly a taxonomic character however. Also known as ***wakaš čitam*** 'cow pig' because of its large size

c. ***škoen čitam*** [< iv 'descend'? + 'pig'] (see Figure 5.145d): The attributive refers in this instance to the short legs and squat appearance

of this type (see ***likawal*** 'hawk' and ***ba*** 'pocket gopher' for other instances of this attributive). ***škuin čitam*** is a variant.

***wamal čitam*** 'bush pig': The peccaries, the white-lipped, *Tayassu pecari*, and the collared, *Dicotyles tajacu* (Artiodactyla: Tayassuidae) (see Figure 5.146)

These animals are no longer found in Tenejapa but are still alleged to exist nearby in Guaquítepec. They are thus poorly known, and the types listed below are not well defined. Examples of both species were identified at the Tuxtla Gutiérrez zoo as ***wamal čitam***.

a. ***niwak wamal čitam*** 'large (pl) bush pig': Adult peccaries. The only discriminating features noted by informants are the animal's large size and a somewhat lesser tendency to move in large groups.

b. ***bahk'al wamal čitam*** 'groups-of-four-hundred bush pig': Probably juvenile peccaries. This type is alleged to be smaller and to be

(a)                                                (b)

Figure 5.146 *wamal čitam* peccary: (a) white-lipped peccary (*Tayassu pecari*); (b) collared peccary (*Pecari tajacu*). [From A. Starker Leopold, *Wildlife of Mexico*, 1959. Originally published by the University of California Press; reprinted by permission of The Regents of the University of California. *Dicotyles tajacu* = *Pecari tajacu*.]

found in larger groups than the preceding, thus the name. The larger species, the white-lipped peccary (*T. pecari*), forms large bands. However it is unlikely that this type is known to Tenejapanecos, since it is an animal of dense tropical forests (Leopold 1972:498). The most sensible explanation is that *niwak wamal čitam* 'large bush pig' refers to the adults (of either species, though the collared peccary (*Dicotyles tajacu*) is the more widespread and common form), while *bahk'al wamal čitam* refers to the subadults, since juvenile peccaries of both species typically move in large groups in advance of the adults.

The issue is further confused by the fact that a few informants recognize three or even four subdivisions within *wamal čitam*. *cahal wamal čitam* 'red bush pig' is described as relatively small. This term may refer to the juvenile white-lipped peccary, as it alone among the peccaries is distinctly reddish (Leopold 1972:500). Alvarez del Toro (1952) notes that Ladinos in Chiapas recognize three types of peccaries, one of which is described as small and red, which he pre-

sumes refers to juvenile white-lipped peccaries. *čik čitam* ['red' + 'pig'] is synonymous.

Consistent with this pattern is a fourth category elicited in Tzeltal, *skem wamal čitam* [< tv 'dig in the earth' + 'bush pig'], a reference to typical peccary behavior. This last category is described as the smallest of the four (by the one informant who recognized four types). The term *k'ayob wamal čitam* 'drummer bush pig' obviously refers to the juveniles of one or the other species of peccary. These peccaries precede the main pack as the drummers precede fiesta processions, precisely as reported for juvenile peccaries. If these animals were better known, four categories, corresponding to the adults and juveniles of the two species, might be more widely recognized. In any case the flesh is considered *sik* 'cold'.

## SHEEP COMPLEX

The native deer (Artiodactyla: Cervidae) and the introduced domestic sheep, *Ovis aries* (Artiodactyla: Bovidae), are named in a fashion parallel to that described for peccaries and pigs. The aboriginal term for deer (*čih*) has come to be applied to the introduced sheep, while the deer are now known as *teʔtikil čih* 'forest sheep' (Berlin 1972: 82–83). The introduced domestic goat, *Capra hircus* (Bovidae), is included in this complex, since it is considered to be an 'associate' (*shoy*) of the sheep.

*tunim čih* 'cotton sheep': The domestic sheep (*Ovis aries*)

These animals are not kept by Tenejapanecos. They are considered the appropriate property of the Indians of Chamula. Some are kept in the Pueblo of Tenejapa by Ladinos. The name is usually abbreviated as *čih*. Sheep in Chamula and Zinacantan provide wool, which is woven locally. Chamulas make the woolen *chamarras* worn by all Tenejapan males. Tenejapanecos do not weave woolen garments themselves (Branstetter 1974). Color varieties are sometimes noted, e.g., *sakil* 'white' and *ʔihk'al* 'black'. The flesh is eaten and is *k'išin* 'hot'. Two medicinal uses were elicited. The flesh is *špošil siht'ubel* 'medicine for swelling' and the horn (*šulub tunim čih*) is reduced to ash and drunk by women to ease childbirth (*špošil ya stohk ʔalal*).

*teʔtikil čih* 'forest sheep': Deer (Cervidae)

Two types are universally recognized and they correspond to the two local species:

a. *yašal teʔtikil čih* 'grey forest sheep': The white-tailed deer (*Odocoileus virginianus*) (see Figure 5.147). It is also known simply as *yašal čih* 'grey deer'. In folk English we have "six-point buck," etc. In Tzeltal males are commonly described as *wak k'elum čih* 'six-point deer' or *wašak k'elum čih* 'eight-point deer'. It is recognized that only males have antlers. None were seen in Tenejapa, but specimens were identified at the Tuxtla Gutiérrez zoo.

b. *cahal teʔtikil čih* 'red forest sheep': The red brocket, *Mazama americana* (Cervidae) (see Figure 5.148). One skull of this small tropi-

Figure 5.147   *yašal teʔtikil čih* white-tailed deer (*Odocoileus virginianus*). [From A. Starker Leopold, *Wildlife of Mexico*, 1959. Originally published by the University of California Press; reprinted by permission of The Regents of the University of California.]

cal deer was obtained (MVZ No. 141705). It was killed in Cancuc near Tenejapa. A skin of another brocket was examined in *hušal haʔ*, Tenejapa, which was also taken in Cancuc. Thus it is likely that a few deer of both species still occur in or near Tenejapa. However they are too rare to provide any meat to the average Tenejapan family. The flesh of both species is *k'išin* 'hot'. A rare highland syn-

Figure 5.148   *cahal teʔtikil čih* red brocket (*Mazama americana*). [From A. Starker Leopold, *Wildlife of Mexico*, 1959. Originally published by the University of California Press; reprinted by permission of The Regents of the University of California.]

onym for this second type is **hul bak**, cognate with the current term for this species in Zinacantan Tzotzil (R. Laughlin personal communication) and probably a Tzotzil loan.

**tencun** [UN]: The domestic goat (*Capra hircus*)

This species is not usually kept by Tenejapanecos, though one exception has come to my attention (K. Branstetter personal communication). It is eaten, and the flesh is **k'išin** 'hot'. The name poses a mystery in that the animal is a postconquest introduction and no local species could have supplied the name. Furthermore, the animal is referred to by the Spanish loan **čívo** in Zinacantan Tzotzil. However R. Laughlin reports that **tencun** is used in Zinacantan to refer to a spirit alleged to resemble the goat. Such a spirit, known as **ʔahk'ubal tencun** 'night-time goat', is widely recognized in Tenejapa and Cancuc. It is alleged to be the 'spirit' (**labil**) of a dead man which, in the form of a goat, enters people's houses at night. **hlabtawaneh tencun** 'harbinger-of-evil goat' is synonymous. Perhaps an aboriginal term referring to a spirit has come to be assocated with the goat throughout the highlands.*

Varieties may be named, e.g., **ʔihk'al tencun** 'black goat' and **cahal tencun** 'red goat'. SMZ invented the term **búro tencun** 'donkey goat' for a large, long-eared specimen in the Tuxtla Gutiérrez zoo.

**wakaš** [< OSp/vacas/'cow']: Domestic cattle, *Bos taurus* (Bovidae) (see Figure 5.149)

The obligatory sex distinctions in Spanish have been suppressed. Cows are **smeʔ wakaš** 'female cattle' and bulls are **stat wakaš** 'male cattle'. My impression is that cattle are raised by Tenejapanecos with increasing frequency. The typical procedure is to buy a young bull, fatten it for a year or two, and then sell it in the Pueblo for the cash profit. Occasionally

such bulls will be slaughtered, a portion eaten, and the remainder sold locally. The flesh is **k'išin** 'hot'.

A wide assortment of uses are reported. The skin is used in the following artifacts:

**tiʔ čohak'** net bag straps.

**tespatil** [UN + 'back' + rs], a flat rectangular piece used to protect the back while carrying loads.

**lehčel tepil** [< 'flat' + UN], a cover to protect objects from dust while traveling.

**warač'il** [< Sp *huarache* 'sandal'].

**pehk'** [UN] tump-line for carrying large loads, as firewood.

**č'ahan** cords for carrying large loads.

**syawartaul kawáyu** [pp + UN + rs + 'horse'], a covering to protect the backs of loaded mules.

**woša**, a bag, especially for carrying bullets in hunting.

**k'ayub**, the drum-head.

Several medicinal uses are also recorded:

**šulub wakaš** 'cattle horn', to make a man's penis grow larger (**špošil ya smuk'ub yat winik yuʔun**).

**č'ič'el wakaš** 'cattle blood', to strengthen a person (**špošil ʔip**).

**č'a wakaš** 'cattle gall bladder', medicine for chopped and split skin of feet and lips (**špošil hataw**).

The following inductive types are widely recognized:

a. **bac'il wakaš** 'true cattle': A residual category of "typical cattle." The variety within this residual is recognized in descriptive phrases, e.g., **píntu wakaš** 'spotted cattle', **barsin wakaš** [UN + 'cattle'], and in color terms.

b. **merikáno wakaš** 'American cattle': The zebu breed (largely grey, humped, and with dewlap). Some of this breed are now kept by Tenejapanecos. Many synonyms are current: **čahp wakaš** 'clansman of the cattle'; **kučpat**

---

*An alternative explanation is suggested by Allan Burns (personal communication). The Yucatec Maya recognize a dangerous spirit known by the Spanish loan, *tentación*. It travels about at night. The resemblance between **tencun** and *tentación* is at least suggestive.

(a)                                              (b)

**Figure 5.149**   Kinds of **wakaš** cattle (*Bos taurus*): (a) **píntu meʔ wakaš** 'spotted cow'; (b) **yašal tat búro wakaš** 'gray zebu bull'. [Drawings by AMT.]

**wakaš** [ < tv 'carry it' + 'back' + 'cattle']; **mansána wakaš** 'apple cattle', referring to the hump; **maléta wakaš** [ < Sp *maleta* ?]; **búro wakaš** 'donkey cattle' (but see following paragraph); **p'us wakaš** 'bent cattle'.

Some informants assert that **búro wakaš** 'donkey cattle' is distinct from the above type, being grey but without a hump. Zebu cattle with notably long ears are called **merikáno búro wakaš** 'American donkey cattle', or **mansána búro wakaš** 'apple donkey cattle', etc. These "hybrids" are noted as exceptional.

## HORSE COMPLEX

This complex includes all known animals of the genus *Equus* (Artiodactyla: Equidae). None of these animals are considered edible.

**búro** [ < Sp *buro* 'donkey']: The domestic donkey (*Equus asinus*)

Donkeys are not kept by Tenejapanecos; they are considered too weak for hauling loads, for which purpose mules are preferred. The role of male donkeys in producing the sterile mule is well understood, though mules are not bred locally. One medicinal use is noted: Hearing the male donkey cry (**ya šʔok' kelem búro**) is alleged to 'pull' (**ya snit**) a man's penis, thus lengthening it. The cry of a female donkey (**ʔancil búro**) has an opposite effect. Color varieties are occasionally recognized, e.g., **sakil búro** 'white donkey' (see Figure 5.150a).

**kawáyu** [ < Sp *caballo* 'horse']: Typically includes both the horse (*Equus caballus*) and the mule (*E. caballus* × *E. asinus*)

SMZ explains that in response to an inquiry such as **hay koht kawáyuetik ʔay ʔawuʔun**, 'how many horses do you have?', the number given will be inclusive of horses and mules. However AMT considers **kawáyu** 'horse' to contrast with **múla** 'mule'. Two normally unnamed specific subdivisions are recognized.

a. [covert]: The mule (see Figure 5.150b). The sex distinction is obligatory as in Spanish:

**múla** [ < Sp *mula* 'female mule'] the female mule. The hoof of this animal (**yehk'eč múla**) is used medicinally to prevent con-

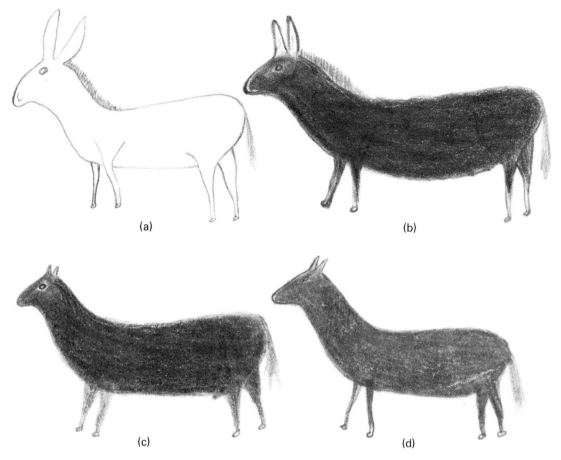

(a)　(b)

(c)　(d)

**Figure 5.150** Horse complex (*Equus* spp.): (a) ***sakil búro*** 'white donkey' (*E. asinus*); (b) ***ʔihkʼal mula*** 'black mule' (*E. caballus* × *E. asinus*); (c) ***cahal tat kawáyu*** 'red male horse' (*E. caballus*); (d) ***kʼanal meʔ kawáyu*** 'yellow female horse' (*E. caballus*). ⌈Drawings by AMT.⌉

ception in women (***špošil ma šʔalah ʔanc yuʔun***), perhaps due to the sterility of the mule. The blood of a half-grown mule (***ščʼičʼel čʼiom múla***) is considered to have the power to give strength (***špošil ʔip***).

***máču*** [ < Sp *macho* 'male mule'] the male mule.

b. [covert]: The horse (see Figures 5.150c, 5.150d). The sex distribution is obligatory:

***yewaš*** [ < OSp/*yevas*/ 'mare'], the female horse.

***bacʼ kawáyu*** 'true horse', the male horse.

Two medicinal uses are attributed to ***kawáyu*** in general: A 'dead' horse (***čamen kawáyu***) is believed to protect the home from mad dogs (***howil cʼiʔ***). 'Horse urine' (***čuš kawáyu***) is thought to cause a 'torn foot' (***špošil ya šhat ʔakanil yuʔun***) if stepped on. Color attributives are applied to distinguish intraspecific variation.

\* \* \* \* \*

The armadillo (see following taxon) is considered to be related to turtles (***šʔahkʼ***) and snakes, in particular ***ʔahaw čan*** (see snake complex). This presumed connection is due to the hard outer covering shared by armadillos and turtles. Both are occasionally included within the restricted sense of *čan-balam* (see *čanbalam₂* 'mammal').

***mayil ti?bal*** [ < 'squash sp.' + 'meat']: The nine-banded armadillo, *Dasypus novemcinctus* (Dasypodidae) (see Figures 5.151 and 5.152)

This species occurs throughout Tenejapa. The identification is based on verbal descriptions, AMT's illustration (not shown here), and one specimen (MVZ No. 141222). Purses (***woša***) are made from the shell, and it is also used to carry seed during the sowing of the *milpa*. The flesh is eaten and is considered *sik* 'cold'. The flesh is considered effective against 'dysentery' (***špošil č'ič***). The term ***col ti?bal*** 'round meat', current in Cancuc, is known by some Tenejapanecos but is not considered to be the true name. The proto-Mayan term *?ib* still current in Aguacate-nango (Kaufman 1964) is unknown in Tenejapa, though the morpheme is found in the plant term *čikinib* 'live oak' (*Quercus* spp.) (Berlin, Breedlove, and Raven 1974:276) as an unproductive form.

### *š?ahk'* 'turtle'

The only species of this order (Testudinata) likely to be found in Tenejapa are primarily aquatic and thus strictly limited to the low-

**Figure 5.151** *mayil ti?bal* nine-banded armadillo (*Dasypus novemcinctus*). [From A. Starker Leopold, *Wildlife of Mexico*, 1959. Originally published by the University of California Press; reprinted by permission of The Regents of the University of California.]

land rivers that border Tenejapa on the north and northeast and to a few marshy areas in the same general region. According to the *banabil* informant (MMH), they do not occur in the highland aquatic habitat in that *paraje*. Two varieties are consistently recognized: *č'in š?ahk'* 'small turtle' and *muk'ul š?ahk'* 'large turtle'. The mud turtle, *Kinosternon cruentatum* (Kinosternidae) (see Figure 5.153), collected near Bachajón was assigned to the former category. It is among the smallest of the turtles known from Chiapas, and the most widespread. A very similar species (*K. leucostomum*) might also occur. The remaining possibilities are quite limited. A larger kinosternid (*Staurotypus triporcatus*) occurs in northern Chiapas, as does the pond slider (*Chrysemys scripta*) of the family Testudinidae. Either is a likely candidate for the term *muk'ul š?ahk'*.

The flesh and the eggs (*ston š?ahk'*) are considered edible and are *sik* 'cold'. The prefix *š-* is occasionally omitted.

### *š?ain* 'crocodile'

Three species of this order (Crocodilia) occur in Chiapas, though it is doubtful if any reach Tenejapa. Some informants claim that small individuals may be found at the northeastern corner of Tenejapa in the Tanaté River. If so, the species most likely is the black crocodile (*Crocodylus moreletii*, Crocodylidae) (see Figure 5.154), the smaller of the two crocodile species. The yellow crocodile (*C. acutus*) is also found in the rivers of northern Chiapas, but the caiman (*Caiman crocodilus*, Alligatoridae) is restricted to the Pacific coast. Examples of all three species at the zoo in Tuxtla Gutiérrez were referred to without distinction as *š?ain*. The prefix *š-* is often omitted.

### LIZARD COMPLEX

The third order of reptiles found in Chiapas (Squamata) includes both lizards and snakes. The Tenejapanecos clearly isolate the snakes (suborder Ophidia) as a named complex (*čan₁*). The lizards (suborder Lacertilia), with

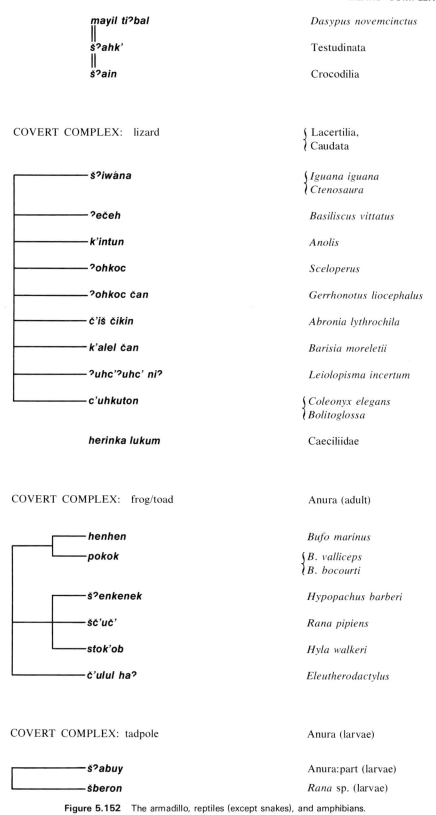

| | |
|---|---|
| **mayil ti?bal** | *Dasypus novemcinctus* |
| ‖ | |
| **š?ahk'** | Testudinata |
| ‖ | |
| **š?ain** | Crocodilia |

COVERT COMPLEX:   lizard { Lacertilia, Caudata

**š?iwána** { *Iguana iguana* *Ctenosaura*

**?eČeh** *Basiliscus vittatus*

**k'intun** *Anolis*

**?ohkoc** *Sceloperus*

**?ohkoc Čan** *Gerrhonotus liocephalus*

**Č'iš Čikin** *Abronia lythrochila*

**k'alel Čan** *Barisia moreletii*

**?uhc'?uhc' ni?** *Leiolopisma incertum*

**c'uhkuton** { *Coleonyx elegans* *Bolitoglossa*

**herinka lukum** Caeciliidae

COVERT COMPLEX:   frog/toad                    Anura (adult)

**henhen** *Bufo marinus*

**pokok** { *B. valliceps* *B. bocourti*

**š?enkenek** *Hypopachus barberi*

**šČ'uČ'** *Rana pipiens*

**stok'ob** *Hyla walkeri*

**Č'ulul ha?** *Eleutherodactylus*

COVERT COMPLEX:   tadpole                    Anura (larvae)

**š?abuy** Anura:part (larvae)

**šberon** *Rana* sp. (larvae)

**Figure 5.152**   The armadillo, reptiles (except snakes), and amphibians.

**Figure 5.153** *š?ahk'* turtle (*Kinosternon cruentatum*). [Color photo by J. H. Tashjian; No. 74–24–8.]

the salamanders of the class AMPHIBIA, form another well-defined but unnamed complex with links to the crocodiles (see preceding taxon), turtles (*š?ahk'*), frogs and toads (the frog-toad complex), the armadillo (*mayil ti?bal*) and the fish (*čay* 'fish' complex).

*š?iwána* [gn + < Sp *iguana* 'iguana']

Two genera of large iguanid lizards are isolated here. None occur in Tenejapa, though all three species may be encountered in the *fincas* or in lowland markets. The largest and least aggressive, *Iguana iguana* (see Figure 5.155), is found on the Pacific coast. Two ctenosaurs also occur, *Ctenosaura similis* of the coasts and *C. pectinata* of the upper

**Figure 5.154** *š?ain* crocodile (*Crocodylus moreletii*). [Slide, KU No. 1512. Photo courtesy of Museum of Natural History, University of Kansas.]

Grijalva valley. All are referred to as *iguanas* in local Spanish (Alvarez del Toro 1973). A varietal distinction is sometimes drawn between **merikáno š?iwána** 'American iguana', which is described as the larger, and **bac'il š?iwána** 'true iguana'. However, verbal descriptions of these types are inconsistent, and it is not possible to define them unambiguously. The confusion is no doubt due to the fact that these animals are poorly known in the *municipio*. The use of a Spanish loan is a further indication of their extralimital status, though the use of the prefix *š-* indicates that the loan is not recent. In Zinacantan Tzotzil a native term is applied (*?inatab*). However the Zinacantan life space overlaps the range of *Ctenosaura pectinata*. The large, venomous beaded lizard (*Heloderma horridum*) of the upper Grijalva valley is distinguished from the iguanas by Zinacantecos (R. Laughlin n.d.) but is apparently unknown in Tenejapa. The flesh of the iguanas is considered edible and *sik* 'cold'.

**Figure 5.155** *š?iwána* iguana (*Iguana iguana*). [Slide, KU No. 378. Photo courtesy of Museum of Natural History, University of Kansas.]

*?ečeh* 'axe': The basilisk lizard (*Basiliscus vittatus*) (see Figure 5.156)

This fairly large iguanid species is common below 1500 m throughout the region. The name presumably refers to the axe-shaped crest especially evident on the head of the male. This species is not usually eaten,

Figure 5.156 *ʔečeh* basilisk lizard (*Basiliscus vittatus*). [Color slide by author.]

though, like the Black Vulture, it may be consumed as medicine for 'malaria' (*špošil nihkel*). The flesh is considered *k'išin* 'hot'. Two varieties are occasionally recognized. *bac'il ʔečeh* 'true axe' is the adult of this species, while *meba ʔečeh* 'orphan axe' most likely refers to the young. However informants who make this distinction maintain that the small type is a fully developed form. The prefix *h-* is sometimes added.

*k'intun* [UN]: Lizards of the genus *Anolis* (Iguanidae)

Two common highland species are *Anolis anisolepis* and *A. crassulus* (MVZ Nos. 99539–99541) (see Figure 5.157). However numerous very similar species are known to occur in lowland areas of Tenejapa, e.g., *A. sericeus* and *A. tropidonotus*. Males of these small iguanids are readily distinguished by their colorful throat fans (*lakam*), a feature considered criterial by informants. Small speci-

Figure 5.157 *k'intun* anole (*Anolis crassulus*). [Slide, KU No. 2464. Photo courtesy of Museum of Natural History, University of Kansas.]

mens of *Sceloporus teapensis* (of lowland Tenejapa) and *S. variabilis* (observed near Aguacatenago) may also be called *k'intun* (see following taxon). Such cases are misindentifications, since informants expect the throat fan to be present when it is not. These animals are protected because of their 'medicinal' value, i.e., to prevent snoring they are inserted in the offending nostril (*špošil ma š ʔok' ni ʔtik ta wayel*). An alternative explanation might involve their association with persons named *h ʔantun*, which is also cited as a synonym for *ʔohkoc* (see following taxon). The prefix *h-* may also be applied to the primary name *k'intun*.

Some informants recognize two types, *bac'il k'intun* 'true anole' and *meba k'intun* 'orphan anole', referring to the smaller size of this type. This distinction may apply to adults and immatures as in the case of *ʔečeh* (see preceding taxon), or the second type may refer to one or more smaller species. In any case size appears to be the only criterion for distinguishing these varietals and the distinction is thus deductive.

*ʔohkoc* [UN]: Iguanid lizards of the genus *Sceloporus*, in particular the common and widespread *S. malachiticus* (see Figure 5.158a)

Typical descriptions of *ʔohkoc* cite its bright 'green' color, characteristic of this species. However large specimens of *S. teapensis* (see Figure 5.158b), which is found below 1500 m in Tenejapa, are also assigned here. In nearby Aguacatenango two other species are found, both of which were called *ʔohkoc* by Tenejapan informants. The large reddish *S. serrifer* was referred to as *muk'ul cahal ʔohkoc* 'large red spiny lizard' while large specimens of *S. variabilis* were called *c'irin ʔohkoc* 'streaked spiny lizard', referring to the whitish stripes on the back of this species. Small specimens of both *S. variabilis* and the very similar *S. teapensis* of the Gulf slope were often misidentified as *k'intun* (see preceding taxon) probably due to their small size, obscure coloration, and the smoothness of their scales. These always lack the

(a)                                              (b)

Figure 5.158  *ʔohkoc* spiny lizard: (a) *Sceloporus malachiticus*); (b) *S. teapensis*. ⌈Slides, KU
Nos. 1559, 1180. Photo courtesy of Museum of Natural History, University of Kansas.⌉

colorful throat fans ascribed to *k'intun*. However, female *Anolis* lizards also lack the
brightly colored fans considered so distinctive of *k'intun*. The two types are considered
especially close relatives, and their names
are typically adjacent in elicited lists.

Most informants recognize two or three
varieties. The most typical form is *yašal
ʔohkoc* 'green spiny lizard', the brightly
colored *S. malachiticus*. This species, however, is able to change color, chamaeleon-
like, from brilliant green, blue and orange to
black. The dark condition of this species is
called *ʔihk'al ʔohkoc* 'black spiny lizard'.
Informants, however, assert that the two are
distinct forms. These varieties as well as
*c'irin ʔohkoc* 'streaked spiny lizard' described
above, are best considered deductive varietal
distinctions.

As with *k'intun* (preceding taxon), *ʔohkoc*
may also be referred to as *hʔohkoc* or *hʔantun*.
They are not eaten but may be used to
counteract snoring.

*ʔohkoc čan* 'spiny lizard snake': The local
species of alligator lizard, *Gerrhonotus liocephalus* (Anguidae)

According to informants, this species is
rare but occurs near lowland streams in
Tenejapa. It was identified as such by SMZ
from specimens preserved in alcohol at the
Museo de Historia Natural in Tuxtla Gutié-
rez and by JGG and SMZ from specimens in

the Copp collection. The name indicates a
close relationship with *ʔohkoc* (see preceding
taxon), though this species is a member of the
Anguidae rather than the Iguanidae. The *čan*
'snake' segment of the name refers to this
species' exceptionally long tail. No subtypes
are recognized. It is not eaten.

*č'iš čikin* 'spiny ear': *Abronia lythrochila*
(Anguidae)

This is a lizard with enlarged spiny scales
above the ears. I photographed a specimen
found dead on the trail in *balun k'anal*, Tenejapa, which was identified as this species by
M. Alvarez del Toro. It is a rare, arboreal
highland lizard only recently described. No
subtypes are recognized. It is considered
most closely related to *ʔohkoc* but is feared as
an evil omen (*ya slabtawan*). It is considered
inedible.

*k'alel čan* 'shiny snake': *Barisia moreleti*
(Anguidae) (see Figure 5.159)

This species is common in the highland
areas of Tenejapa but might also be found in

Figure 5.159  *k'alel čan Barisia moreleti*. ⌈Slide, KU
No. 1580. Photo courtesy of Museum of Natural History,
University of Kansas.⌉

the lowlands. The name is derived from the noun *k'aal* 'sun' and refers to the reddish coloration and shiny texture of the scales of this species. Despite the name, it is not considered to be a kind of *čan* 'snake', as it has legs (*?ay yak'an yu?un*). The variant *k'alawil čan* is of similar derivation. No subtypes are consistently recognized. It is considered inedible.

Lizards of the genera *Ameiva* and *Cnemidophorus* (both Teiidae) found in the drier regions to the south were also assigned here on the basis of alcoholic specimens examined. However neither genus is known to occur in Tenejapa, though *A. undulata* should occur nearby.

*?uhc'?uhc' ni?* 'sniffer': Skinks (Scincidae), in particular *Leiolopisma incertum* (see Figure 5.160)

Figure 5.160   *?uhc'?uhc' ni?* skink (*Leiolopisma incertum*). [Slide, KU No. 1568. Photo courtesy of Museum of Natural History, University of Kansas.]

A specimen of this rare lizard was collected in *banabil*, Tenejapa, at 2400 m. No subtypes are recognized. This animal is considered inedible. A close relationship is perceived with the salamanders (see the following taxon).

*c'uhkuton* [UN]: Salamanders and presumably the gecko *Coleonyx elegans* (REPTILIA: Squamata: Gekkonidae) (see Figure 5.161a)

The great majority of salamanders found in Chiapas are of the genus *Bolitoglossa* (AMPHIBIA: Caudata: Plethodontidae). Two varieties are recognized, *cahal c'uhkuton* 'red salamander' and *?ihk'al c'uhkuton* 'black slamander'. These types are appropriately descriptive of the following species of salamanders known to occur in the *municipio*.

a. *cahal c'uhkuton* 'red salamander':

*Bolitoglossa mexicana* (1500 m) (see Figure 5.161a).

*B resplendens* (2400 m).

b. *?ihk'al c'uhkuton* 'black salamander':

*B. hartwegi* (2400 m)

*B. rostrata* (2400 m)

The three highland species were found at the edge of cloud forest after diligent searching. It is thus likely that salamanders are rarely encountered.

Informants assert that *c'uhkuton* is the source of a particular squeaking noise often heard in forested areas. Salamanders are not known to be capable of vocalization. However, the superficially similar geckoes make a squeaking sound like that attributed to *c'uhkuton*. Though no geckos were seen, *Coleonyx elegans* (see Figure 5.161 b) should occur. It resembles local salamanders in size, shape of tail and head, skin texture, slowness, and habitat. Geckoes and salamanders are both objects of fear for local Ladinos (Alvarez del Toro 1973).

The animal is ground up to make an ointment to cure 'swollen penis' (*špošil cuat*). Since many salamanders produce irritating

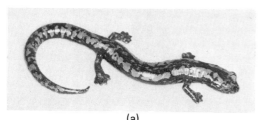

(a)                                        (b)

Figure 5.161   *c'uhkuton*: (a) salamander (*Bolitoglossa mexicana*); (b) gecko (*Coleonyx elegans*). [Slides, KU Nos. 1218, 674. Photo courtesy of Museum of Natural History, University of Kansas.]

secretions through skin glands, there may be some physiological justification for this treatment.

## *čan*₁ 'SNAKE' COMPLEX
(see Figure 5.162)

All true snakes (suborder Ophidia) are included here. Due to the great variety of snakes and the rarity with which they are encountered, it has not been possible to define all the snake names elicited. Thus a hypothetical list is appended which treats those names that are not clearly distinct. Snakes in general are not eaten, though an exception will be described. Their flesh is *sik* 'cold'. Deadly venomous snakes are recognized as such, though a degree of venomousness is attributed to many harmless species as well. The typical attitude is fearful, and many species are killed on sight. However, certain species are considered beneficial and are not killed (see *masakwáto* and *me? čenek'*). Several apochryphal species, which play a role in folklore, are described in the hypothetical list.

*masakwáto* [< Sp *masaguate* 'boa'], originally Nahuatl 'deersnake': The boa constrictor, *Boa constrictor* (Boidae) (see Figure 5.163)

NAMED COMPLEX: *čan*₁ 'snake'    Ophidia

| | |
|---|---|
| masakwáto | *Boa constrictor* |
| ?ahaw čan | *Crotalus durissus* / *Pituophis lineaticollis* |
| kantil | *Agkistrodon bilineatus* |
| ?áwa kantil | *Drymarchon corais* |
| c'in te? čan | *Bothrops godmani* |
| ?ik'os čan | *B. nummifer* |
| kantéla čan | *Micrurus* spp. |
| me? c'isim | *Lampropeltis triangulum* |
| k'ančo | *Drymobius margaritiferus* |
| ha?al čan | *Thamnophis* spp. |
| me? čenek' | *Ninia sebae* |
| pacan sihk' | *N. diademata* |
| me? ?išim | *Rhadinaea hempsteadae* |
| me? k'apal | *Coniophanes imperialis* |
| c'ibal čan | *C. schmidti* |
| mokoč čan | *Adelphicos veraepacis* |
| p'ahsum čan | *Tropidodipsas fischeri* |
| šč'oš čan | *Oxybelis aeneus* |
| yaš ?itah čan | *O. fulgidus* / *Leptophis* spp. |
| p'ehel nuhkul čan | *Leptodeira septentrionalis* |
| čihil čan | *Spilotes pullatus* |
| lukum čan | *Leptotyphlops phenops* |

Figure 5.162    The snake complex.

Figure 5.163 *masakwáto Boa constrictor.* [Color photo by J. H. Tasjian, No. 66–99–6.]

This largest Chiapan snake is not definitely known to occur in Tenejapa. A story is told relating how a Tenejapaneco working in the *fincas* was saved by a boa from an attack by a moccasin (*kantil*, see later taxon). For this reason, boas are considered friendly to man and are protected, as they are believed to give protection from snake bite. This taxon was identified from verbal descriptions. Variants include *masakwáto čan, masaʔwáto,* and *masaʔwáte.* The Spanish term is an earlier Nahuatl loan (Antonio Castro 1965:62),

which may be analyzed as 'deer' + 'snake' (cf. *čihil čan* snake).

*ʔahaw čan* 'the master snake': *Pituophis lineaticollis* (Colubridae) (see Figure 5.164a)

This species is congeneric with the gopher, pine and bull snakes of the United States and is the typical referent of this category. The Neotropical rattlesnake, *Crotalus durissus* (Crotalidae) (see Figure 5.164b) is also included here, though it is at best very rare in the *municipio.* Gopher snakes, however, are notably adept at imitating rattlesnakes to the point of flattening their heads, hissing, and rattling their tails against foliage and fallen leaves. The fear associated with this animal suggests that the rattlesnake, though rarely encountered, is the focal referent of this category. The nonvenomous gopher snake is, thus, considered a kind of rattlesnake. It is thought to be the male, since it lacks the rattles (*sot*) presumed to be characteristic of the female *ʔahaw čan.* Some informants recognize two subtypes rather than this sexual distinction:

*sot čan* 'rattlesnake': The Neotropical rattlesnake.

*bak ne čan* 'bone-tailed snake': *Pituophis lineaticollis.*

Both, however, are *ʔahaw čan.* The situation is confused by the fact that other informants

(a)

(b)

Figure 5.164 *ʔahaw čan* (a) gopher snake (*Pituophis lineaticollis*); (b) tropical rattlesnake (*Crotalus durissus*). [Slides, KU Nos. 1163, 1643. Photo courtesy of Museum of Natural History, University of Kansas.]

consider **bak ne čan** (see **ʔikˈos čan**/snake) to be distinct.

An individual of *Pituophis lineaticollis* was killed and eaten by AGM on one occasion. However most informants do not consider this or any other snake edible. AGM asserted that the intestines (**bikil**) of this snake have medicinal value. AGM also said the snake has two hearts, and that one must not say the snake's name in its presence or one would be fatally bitten. The flesh is **sik** 'cold'.

**kantil** [< Sp *cantil* 'moccasin', originally Quiché?]: The moccasin, *Agkistrodon bilineatus* (Crotalidae) (see Figure 5.165)

This species is not known to occur in Tenejapa, though it is reported from the *fincas*. It is properly recognized as deadly. The identification in this case rests solely on verbal descriptions and the fact that the cognate Spanish term refers to this species. Variants include **kantil čan**, **kantin**, and **kantin čan**.

**ʔáwa kantil** [< Sp *agua* 'water' + 'moccasin']: The indigo snake, *Drymarchon corais* (Colubridae)

This is one of the largest snakes found in Chiapas. Its size, aggressiveness, and dark coloration suggest the relationship with the moccasin though the indigo snake is not venomous. Its preference for the edges of streams and rivers (Alvarez del Toro 1973) explains the attributive. An alcoholic specimen was identified as this taxon by one infor-

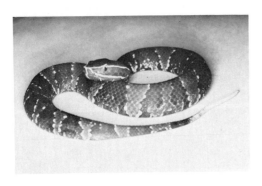

Figure 5.165 **kantil** moccasin (*Agkistrodon bilineatus*). [Slide, KU No. 793. Photo courtesy of Museum of Natural History, University of Kansas.]

mant though SMZ called it simply **kantil**. It is known only from the *fincas*. A probable synonym is **be haʔul čan** 'river bed snake' or **ʔikˈan čan** [UN + 'snake'].

**cˈin teʔ čan** 'manioc snake': *Bothrops godmani* (Crotalidae) (see Figure 5.166a)

This is a small but deadly highland relative of the fer-de-lance (*B. asper*). An individual of this species encountered in **banabil** was so named. Its bite is appropriately feared. Informants assert that the bite kills in 3 minutes. The cure involves sucking the venom while chanting a series of color terms. One informant who was bitten, however, was taken to Oxchuc for modern medical assistance. The name presumably refers to the short, thick bodies of these snakes which bear a resemblance to manioc roots. That this term is restricted to this species is further suggested by the frequent assertion that the animal is restricted to the highlands (**sikil kˈinal**). Some informants use the term **bacˈil čan** 'true snake' synonymously (see also **haʔal čan** 'rain-snake').

**ʔikˈos čan** [UN + 'snake']: Probably *Bothrops nummifer* (see Figure 5.166b)

This species is found at moderate altitudes in northern Chiapas and is thus the most likely possibility. No positive record exists for the *municipio*, however. It is considered deadly.

**čan huht niʔ** 'four-holed nose' is a common synonym. This name refers to the nostrils and nostrillike pits characteristics of all pit vipers (Crotalidae), e.g., rattlesnakes, moccasins, and the genus *Bothrops*. Variants include **čan huht niʔ čan** and **ča huht niʔ** 'two-holed nose', referring to one side of the head rather than both. A small specimen of the fer-de-lance (*B. asper*) in J. Copp's collection was identified as this species. **bak ne čan** 'bone-tailed snake' (see **ʔahaw čan**/snake) might apply to the fer-de-lance, as it is known colloquially as 'bone tail' because of its short, pointed tail.

(a)                                    (b)

**Figure 5.166**  (a) *c'in te? čan Bothrops godmani*; (b) *?ik'os čan B. nummifer.* [Color photos by J. H. Tashjian; Nos. 74–22–7, 74–22–2.]

**kantéla čan** [< Sp *candela* 'candle' + 'snake']: Coral snakes, *Micrurus* spp. (Elapidae)

One individual photographed in **mahosik'** (1500 m) was identified by M. Alvarez del Toro as *Micrurus elegans*, an atypically patterned species. More typical is *Micrurus diastema* (see Figure 5.167) which may also occur at lower elevations in the *municipio*. It is accurately described as venomous. One synonym, *?óra čan* 'hour snake', allegedly alludes to the fact that the venom acts rapidly. **kantéra čan** is a variant. The reference to candles refers to a special type of candle used ritually which consists of concentric rings of color, similar to the typical coral snake pattern. **koral čan** [> Sp 'coral snake' + 'snake'.] May be synonymous with **kantéla čan** for some informants, but is more often considered synonymous with the following term.

**me? c'isim** 'mother of leaf-cutting ants': Probably a kingsnake, *Lampropeltis triangulum* (Colubridae) (see Figure 5.168)

This identification is based on verbal descriptions. **me? c'isim** is appropriately described as similar in coloration to the coral snake, though with the yellow replaced by white, and about twice as large. **koral čan** [< Sp 'coral snake' + 'snake'] is usually considered synonymous with **me? c'isim** (but see above, preceding taxon). This kingsnake is in fact often mistaken for the coral snake in the United States and Mexico (see Alvarez del Toro 1973), where it is known as the "false coral." The primary name alludes to

**Figure 5.167 kantéla čan** coral snake (*Micrurus diastema*). [Slide, KU No. 597. Photo courtesy of Museum of Natural History, University of Kansas.]

Figure 5.168 *me? c'isim* king snake (*Lampropeltis triangulum*). [Drawing by AMT.]

the assertion that this snake makes its home in the nest of the leaf-cutting ant. To eliminate the insect pest, one must dig until one finds the snake and then kill it. It is also known as **mak te? čan** 'fence snake'.

**k'ančo** [UN]: The speckled racer (*Drymobius margaritiferus*) (see Figure 5.169)

This species was identified by several informants from dead specimens. It is common and widespread in the area. It is also known as **k'ančo čan**. The term **hcak šč'uč' čan** 'frog catcher snake' is considered to be synonymous. Frogs, in fact, are this snake's preferred food (Alvarez del Toro 1973:123).

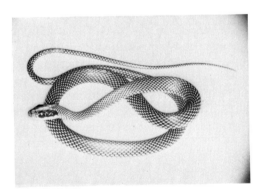

Figure 5.169 *k'ančo* speckled racer (*Drymobius margaritiferus*). Slide, KU No. 1155. Photo courtesy of Museum of Natural History, University of Kansas.]

**ha?al čan** 'rain snake': The garter snakes (*Thamnophis* spp.)

The common highland species are the western ribbon snake (*T. proximus*) (see Figure 5.170) and the black-necked garter snake (*T. cyrtopsis*: MVZ No. 99542). Both were identified by highland informants as of this taxon. Garter snakes are notably aquatic, thus the name is appropriate (see **ha?al c'i?** mammal for a similarly named aquatic animal). This taxon is not well known to low-

land informants. Some informants consider this term synonymous with **bac'il čan** 'true snake' (but see **c'in te? čan** snake).

Figure 5.170 *ha?al čan* garter snake (*Thamnophis proximus*). [Slide by D. E. Breedlove.]

**me? čenek'** 'mother-of-beans': *Ninia sebae* (see Figure 5.171)

This small, colorful species was photographed in **mahosik'**. It was subsequently identified as this species by M. Alvarez del Toro. According to informants, one should never kill this snake; if you do your bean crop will fail, hence the name. It is possible that several similar small snakes might also be included here, since many informants recognized two or more color varieties. However the congeneric *Ninia diademata* is clearly distinguished (see **pacan sihk'**, following taxon). Furthermore, a distinctive feature of this category is its ring-necked pattern (**č'okowil snuk'**). This is appropriate only

Figure 5.171 *me? čenek'* *Ninia sebae*. [Slide, KU No. 1612. Photo courtesy of Museum of Natural History, University of Kansas.]

for *Ninia* and the black-headed snakes (*Tantilla*). However *Tantilla* is not known from the Gulf slope of Chiapas (Alvarez del Toro 1973:171). *Ninia sebae* is variable in color pattern, and the varieties might be descriptive of this intraspecific variation. The following were elicited, though no single informant recognized more than three: *cahal me? čenek'* 'red mother-of-beans', *?ihk'al* 'black', *k'anal* 'yellow', *sakil* 'white', and *yašal me? čenek'* 'green mother-of-beans'. *me? čenek' čan* is a variant.

**pacan sihk'** [UN + UN]: *Ninia diademata* (see Figure 5.172)

This name was first elicited for a live specimen collected near San Cristóbal. The name proved to be widely known. No confusion was evident between this and its congener *N. sebae* (see *me? čenek'* 'mother-of-beans', preceding taxon). Two color varieties were cited by SMZ; the specimen observed was considered *yašal* 'grey' rather than *?ihk'al* 'black'. Also known as *pacan sihk' čan*.

Figure 5.172  *pacan sihk'* *Ninia diademata*. [Slide by D. E. Breedlove.]

**me? ?išim** 'mother-of-corn': *Rhadinaea hempsteadae* (see Figure 5.173)

A specimen of *R. hempsteadae* collected near San Cristóbal was called *sbankil me? ?išim* 'big brother of mother-of-corn' by SMZ and JGG. However, neither knew this highland category with assurance. A process of elimination utilizing verbal descriptions (i.e., a small, yellow-bellied, snake without stripes or rings found in the highland *milpas*) strongly suggests the above interpretation. Also known as *me? ?išim čan* and *k'anal č'uht čan* 'yellow-bellied snake'.

Figure 5.173  *me? ?išim* *Rhadinaea* sp. [Slide by D. E. Breedlove.]

**me? k'apal** 'mother-of-refuse': The black-striped snake (*Coniophanes imperialis*) (see Figure 5.174)

A badly decomposed specimen of this genus (MVZ No. 99543) found in *banabil*, Tenejapa (2400 m), was referred to as *cahal č'uht čan* 'red-bellied snake' by AKČ. This term is considered synonymous with *me? k'apal* by many informants and is appropriately descriptive of this species. The species noted is the most likely of the genus to occur in the central highlands of Chiapas (see also *c'ibal čan* 'striped snake', *C. schmidti*). According to M. Alvarez del Toro (1973) this snake is often found "en los montones de basura," in mounds of refuse. Thus the primary name is appropriate. It may also be known as *me? k'apal čan*.

**mokoč čan** 'millipede snake': *Adelphicos veraepacis*

This highland species was identified by

Figure 5.174  *me? k'apal* black-striped snake (*Coniophanes imperialis*). [Slide, KU No. 732. Photo courtesy of Museum of Natural History, University of Kansas.]

SMZ and JGG as of this category. It is adapted for burrowing, being rather short and stout-bodied (Alvarez del Toro 1973), and thus resembles a common type of millipede (see **mokoč** millipede). *Stenorrhina freminvillii* is similar in size, color, and shape, and preserved specimens of this species were called **mokoč čan** by several informants. However this latter species is restricted to lower elevations, while **mokoč čan**, according to informants, occurs only in the highlands. Species of *Ficimia* and *Geophis*, though not observed, might be included here. Both genera are represented in the region and are fossorial snakes of similar form.

### c'ibal čan 'striped snake'

A preserved specimen of *Conophis vittatus* (J. Copp collection) was referred to by this name by SMZ, who asserted that it is well known in Tenejapa. However, *Conophis* is known only from the central depression and the Pacific coast. Thus the name more likely refers to *Coniophanes schmidti*, a specimen of which (J. Copp collection) was collected in **habenal** (900 m). This specimen was considered **kps c'ibal čan**.

### p'ahsum čan [ < tv 'cut at slanted angle' + 'snake']: *Tropidodipsas fischeri* (see Figure 5.175)

The name refers to the pattern of white rings on a black body described for this species by informants. A preserved specimen (J. Copp collection) of *T. fischeri* collected near the Pueblo of Tenejapa was identified as of this taxon by SMZ.

**Figure 5.175** *p'ahsum čan Tropidodipsas fischeri.* [Slide, KU No. 1629. Photo courtesy of Museum of Natural History, University of Kansas.]

### šč'oš čan [ < tv 'tie tightly in the middle'? + 'snake']: The vine snake (*Oxybelis aeneus*) (see Figure 5.176)

This species was identified as such by several informants from specimens in the collections of D. Breedlove and J. Copp. Most informants consider this term to be synonymous with **čil č'ahan čan** [UN + 'cord' + 'snake'] and **láso čan** [ < Sp *laso* 'rope' + 'snake']. Both of these terms are descriptive of the long thin body of this species. Less common synonyms include **behúko čan** [ < Sp *bejuco* 'vine'] and **behukíya čan** [ < Sp *bejuquilla* 'little vine'], and **čin ʔak' čan** ['morning glory vine' + 'snake'].

**Figure 5.176** *šč'oš čan* vine snake (*Oxybelis aeneus*). [Color photo by J. H. Tashjian; No. 66–87–12.]

### yaš ʔitah čan 'green vegetable snake': The green vine snake (*Oxybelis fulgidus*)

This bright green snake is similar in shape and habits to the preceding, and both are widespread in the lowlands. SMZ identified this species at the zoo in Tuxtla Gutiérrez and claimed to have seen it in the *fincas*. The similar green rat snake (*Elaphe triaspis*) was considered **kps yaš ʔitah čan** by SMZ and JGG (specimen, J. Copp collection). The bright green *Bothrops nigroviridis* (Crotalidae) in the J. Copp collection was referred to this taxon also. Thus *Leptophis modestus* and *L. ahaetulla* might also be included. The former is known from highlands of the region; the latter, from nearby lowlands. Any slim, bright green snake might be assigned here. The green vine snake, however, epitomizes the criterial features cited by informants (i.e., bright green, very long and thin, like a piece of rope). *yašal čan* 'green snake' is a widespread synonym.

*p'ehel nuhkul čan* ['round, solid'? + 'skin' + 'snake']: Probably the cat-eyed snake (*Leptodeira septentrionalis*) (see Figure 5.177)

This species is the most likely possibility, though no specimens were examined. Specimens of the lyre snake (*Trimorphodon biscutatus*) of lowland regions is similarly patterned and specimens (D. Breedlove and J. Copp collections) were referred to by this or a synonymous term by several informants. SMZ considered the lyre snake to be *kps p'ehel nuhkul*. Since this animal is allegedly found in the highlands (AKS) and obviously resembles the lyre snake, I believe the most likely possibility is the cateyed snake. Another possibility is the similarly patterned *Xenodon rabdocephalus* of lower elevations in the region. *čikóte čan* [ < sp *chicote* 'whip' + 'snake'] is widely recognized as a synonym, as is the variant *čikotéra čan* [ < *chicotera* 'whipper' + 'snake'].

Figure 5.177  *p'ehel nuhkul čan* cat-eyed snake (*Leptodeira septentrionalis*). [Slide, KU No. 765. Photo courtesy of Museum of Natural History, University of Kansas.]

*čihil čan* ['deer' + rs + 'snake']

SMZ identified a preserved specimen of the Mexican rat snake (*Spilotes pullatus*) (see Figure 5.178) as of this taxon. The snake cited is described as very large, distinctively

Figure 5.178  *čihil čan* *Spilotes pullatus*. [Slide, KU No. 784. Photo courtesy of Museum of Natural History, University of Kansas.]

marked black and yellow, arboreal, and widespread in lowland areas–all characteristic of this species. Despite the fact that the Nahuatl name for the boa constrictor also means 'deer snake', *čihil čan* is not so used (see earlier taxon, *masakwáto*). *latonéra* [ < Sp *ratonera* 'rat catcher'] is often cited by informants as synonymous with *čihil čan*, an appropriate if somewhat indefinite usage. AKS describes a very large, blotched (*p'uhtultik*), arboreal snake which he names *čičikwúya*, a term widely used for *Spilotes* in Chiapas (Alvarez del Toro 1973).

*lukum čan* 'worm snake': A slender blind snake, *Leptotyphlops goudotii* (Leptotyphlopidae) (see Figure 5.179)

A preserved specimen of the very similar *L. humilis* (J. Copp collection) was so identified by SMZ and JGG. Verbal descriptions from many informants, though not entirely consistent, allow of no other possibility. It is widespread in lowland areas of Chiapas.

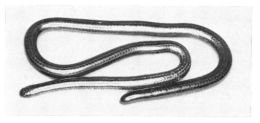

Figure 5.179  *lukum čan* slender blind snake (*Leptotyphlops phenops*). [Slide, KU No. 1152. Photo courtesy of Museum of Natural History, University of Kansas.]

*Hypothetical List: Snakes*

**cahal čan** 'red snake'.   It is possibly synonymous with **kantéla čan** snake.

**cek čan** 'scorpion snake'.   Attributed to coral snakes by local Ladinos (Alvarez del Toro 1973); thus see **kantéla čan** snake. It stings with its tail. This name might also be appropriate for the slender blind snake (Leptotyphlopidae, see **lukum čan** 'worm snake'), since these burrowers have a tail-spine used for leverage in burrowing.

**c'irin čan** 'streaked snake'.   Perhaps a descriptive phrase or synonymous with **ha?al čan**.

**čitam čan** 'pig snake'.   It may be apochryphal or refer to the fer-de-lance (*Bothrops asper*). Known only from hearsay. This snake is said to be large and deadly and to grunt like a pig; if you see one count to thirteen before running or suffer a fatal bite. (No informant interviewed had ever seen one.)

**čuhkil holol čan** 'belt-necked snake'.   Appropriately descriptive of **kantéla čan** and **me? čenek'**.

**hač'obil čan** 'comb snake'.   A patch-nosed snake, *Salvadora lemniscata* (J. Copp collection), according to SMZ, but the species is restricted to drier areas south of the central highlands. The name was not otherwise elicited.

**hoč'obel čan** [ < tv 'clean out by scraping'? + 'snake']. *Loxocemus bicolor* (J. Copp collection) according to SMZ, but not otherwise elicited. This small member of the Boidae is rare in eastern Chiapas and not likely to be known to Tenejapanecos.

**?ihk'al čan** 'black snake'.   Probably a descriptive phrase.

**mak'um čan** 'blackberry snake'.   *Lampro-*

*peltis triangulum* (J. Copp collection) according to SMZ, though he also considered **me? c'isim** (snake complex) an appropriate name for the specimen. Not otherwise elicited. Possibly a variant of **mak te? čan** (see **me? c'isim**/snake.

**moin te? čan** 'tree-climbing snake'.   Appropriately descriptive of many kinds of snakes.

**pohpal čan** ['straw mat' + 'snake']. Apochryphal. According to legend this monumental snake once plugged up a *sumidero* in Cancuc. Only the patron saint (**san ciak**) of Tenejapa was able to open the *sumidero* again and prevent a disastrous flood. A similar Spanish term, *petatilla* 'straw mat,' is applied to *Drymobius margaritiferus* (see **k'ančo**/snake) referring to the color pattern of its scales.

**sakil č'uht čan** 'white-bellied snake'.   Appropriately descriptive of many kinds of snakes.

**šulub čan** 'horned snake'.   Apochryphal. This huge snake has horns like a bull, eyes like the headlights of a truck, and in times past made the underground passages for the rivers by smashing through the rock.

**?uč čan** 'opossum snake'.   Suggested as synonymous with **mokoč čan** 'millipede snake'.

**yut ?uk'umil čan** 'inside-the-river snake'. Also supposedly synonymous with **mokoč čan**, though the implication of the name is inexplicable.

Though I have attempted to account for most species of snakes likely to be known to Tenejapanecos, the following should prove to be recognized nomenclaturally if further study were undertaken:

*Dryadophis melanolomus.* Known from near Comitán, terrestrial.

*Pliocercus elapoides.* Northern Chiapas at all altitudes, terrestrial.

\*\*\*\*\*

**herínka lukum** [< sp *jeringa* 'syringe' + 'worm']: Caecilians (see Figure 5.180).

These wormlike amphibians (Gymnophiona) are known to local Ladinos by the term *tapaculo* 'anus-plugger'. They allegedly enter a person's anus while he is relieving himself and consume him from within (cf. **herínka sabin**, **sabin**/mammal). These animals are restricted to the tropical Pacific slope of Chiapas and are known to Tenejapanecos only by virtue of the verbal descriptions of residents (Ladinos) of those areas. The name alludes to this borrowed belief.

Figure 5.180 **herínka lukum** caecilian (*Dermophis mexicanus*). [Slide, KU No. 1145. Photo courtesy of Museum of Natural History, University of Kansas.]

## FROG–TOAD COMPLEX

All adult anurans are included here. The relationship of tadpoles to the adult frogs and toads is recognized as one of transformation [<iv *-k'ahta*]. Thus tadpoles are not considered to be kinds of frogs and toads, unlike the young of other animals for which the resemblance of young to adult forms is more obvious. Similarly, eggs are related to birds, and shrews to bats, by the transformation process. This same distinction between development and transformation is obvious in folk English concepts. Caterpillars and eggs are of a different order than colts and other adolescents, i.e., entities in their own right rather than stages of a single entity. Vocalizations play an essential role in the Tenejapan recognition and naming of anuran categories, which accords well with recent scientific taxonomic practice with respect to this group of organisms.

**henhen** [ON]: The giant toad, *Bufo marinus* (Bufonidae) (see Figure 5.181)

Figure 5.181 **henhen** giant toad (*Bufo marinus*). [Slide, KU No. 839. Photo courtesy of Museum of Natural History, University of Kansas.]

This species was heard and photographed near Ocosingo and Yajalón, to the north of Tenejapa. The name is an accurate rendition of the animal's call. According to informants it occurs also in lowland Tenejapa. Subadults of this species (J. Copp collection) were, however, misidentified as **pokok** (see following taxon). Thus the species is recognized primarily by size and voice. The prefix *š-* is optional. **muk'ul pokok** 'large toad' is an occasional synonym, a further indication that the generic relationship is recognized. This species is considered inedible.

**pokok** [ON]: A residual category of toads (*Bufo* spp.) not otherwise distinguished

The common highland species is *B. bocourti* (MVZ No. 99524) (see Figure 5.182a) which is replaced below 1800 m by *B. valliceps* (MVZ Nos. 99521–99523) (see Figure 5.182b). Normally considered inedible, it may be consumed as a cure for 'malaria' (**špošil nihkel**). Subtypes are recognized in a reduced nomenclatural system as follows:

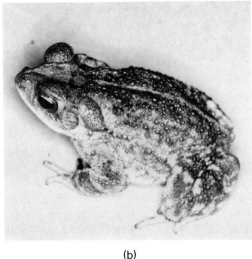

(a)                                        (b)

Figure 5.182  *pokok* toad: (a) *Bufo bocourti*; (b) *B. valliceps.* [Slides, KU Nos. 1257, 1130. Photo courtesy of Museum of Natural History, University of Kansas.]

*muk'ul pokok* 'large toad' equals *henhen*.

*bac'il pokok* 'true toad' equals *pokok.*

*č'in pokok* 'small toad' may equal *š?en-kenek* (see next taxon).

Color varieties are occasionally recognized, e.g., *k'anal pokok* 'yellow toad'. *špokok* is sometimes heard. The smaller tadpoles (*š?abuy*) are believed to transform into animals of this taxon. According to Tenejapan belief one should not kill these animals.

*š?enkenek* [ON]: The sheep frog, *Hypopachus barberi* (Microhylidae), MVZ Nos. 99534–99535

This species is well known only in the highland *parajes* of Tenejapa. For some highland informants unfamiliar with the giant toad of the lowlands (see *henhen*/frog-toad), the name *henhen* or *henhen čan* is applied to the sheep frog. This explains why some informants describe *henhen* as 'small'. *sk'o* appears to be synonymous also, as it was used to name this species by JGG. It is also likely that the sheep frog is sometimes known as *č'in pokok* 'small toad' (see *pokok*) or as *pek'pek'* (see *stok'ob*). A tiny adult toad (*Bufo* sp., MVZ No. 99536) was mistakenly identified as of this taxon by SMZ. Sheep frogs are considered inedible.

*šč'uč'* 'frog': True frogs, Ranidae

The common and perhaps sole representative of this family in Tenejapa is the leopard frog (*Rana pipiens*, MVZ Nos. 99529–99533) (see Figure 5.183). It is considered edible, and the flesh is *k'išin* 'hot'. It is considered medicinally effective against 'painful urination' (*špošil k'uš čušil*). The larger tadpoles (*šberon*/tadpole) are believed to transform into this kind of animal, a quite accurate assessment. *kurus hol* 'cross head' and *kurus hol šč'uč'* are synonyms that allude to a marking on the back of this species. Robber frogs, Leptodactylidae: *Eleutherodactylus* spp. (*č'ulul ha?*/frog-toad), are sometimes misidentified as *tutin šč'uč'* 'baby frog'.

Figure 5.183  *šč'uč* leopard frog (*Rana pipiens*). [Slide, KU No. 935. Photo courtesy of Museum of Natural History, University of Kansas.]

Color varieties may occasionally be recognized.

**stok'ob** [ON]: Tree frogs of the genus *Hyla*, in particular *H. walkeri* (Hylidae) MVZ Nos. 99526-99527, the common highland species (see Figure 5.184)

Two other species of this family collected near Simojovel were considered unfamiliar though **kps stok'ob** (*H. microcephala*, MVZ No. 99528, and *Smilisca baudini*, MVZ No. 99525), as their vocalizations were not typical of **stok'ob**. A larger hylid (D. Breedlove collection) from the Sierra Madre region was recognized as **stok'ob**, despite the fact that it was as large as a typical ranid. The recognition is based apparently on the toe discs and the body shape typical of this genus. An example of *Hyla regilla*, common in California, was also recognized without hesitation as representative of **stok'ob**, though it was not green. Thus the category properly includes most if not all species of the genus. **stok'oy** and **tok'oy** ['willow'?] are variants. **pek'pek'** is considered synonymous by most informants. AKČ' named a specimen of *H. walkeri* **pek'pek'**. It remains possible that some informants recognize two classes of tree frogs, as some aver that **pek'pek'** and **stok'ob** are distinct. Further study is needed here, as the small frogs of the Hylidae and Leptodactylidae are not completely known for the region. Tree frogs are considered inedible.

**Figure 5.184** **stok'ob** tree frog (*Hyla walkeri*). [Slide, KU No. 1392. Photo courtesy of Museum of Natural History, University of Kansas.]

**č'ulul ha?** [ON, 'smooth'? + 'water']: Robber frogs, *Eleutherodactylus* spp. (Leptodactylidae) (see Figure 5.185)

Two specimens of this genus were collected in lowland Tenejapa (MVZ Nos. 99537, 99538). The taxon is not widely known and is confined to lowland areas. For some informants these frogs are simply **tutin šč'uč'** 'baby frogs' (see **šč'uč'**). These specimens are the only representatives of the Leptodactylidae collected. I have no indication that

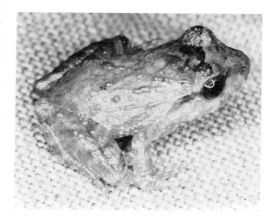

**Figure 5.185** **č'ulul ha?** robber frog (*Eleutherodactylus rugulosus*). [Slide, KU No. 861. Photo courtesy of Museum of Natural History, University of Kansas.]

Tenejapanecos are familiar with the second major genus of the family, *Leptodactylus*.

## TADPOLE COMPLEX

These taxa are considered biological entities in their own right rather than "kinds of" or "stages of" frogs and toads though the facts of metamorphosis are known.

**š?abuy** [gn + UN]: Small, blackish tadpoles

Specimens assigned to this taxon are referable to the genera *Hyla* (EH No. 125), *Hypopachus* (EH No. 144), and *Rana* (EH Nos. 137, 138, 151?). The ranid tadpoles are in an early stage of development and have not yet attained the size considered distinctive of the following category. No tadpoles of *Bufo* were collected, though they would no doubt be classed here as they are typically small and black to the point of transformation. **š?abuy** is believed to transform into either **pokok** or **stok'ob** depending on one's informant. These are not eaten. **č'in š?abuy** 'little tadpole' is an occasional synonym (see later).

**šberon** [gn + UN]: Large, pale tadpoles (*Rana* spp.)

One specimen of this genus (EH No. 124) was classed here. Tadpoles of this sort are typically ranids. Thus the Tenejapan belief that **šberon** transforms into **šč'uč'** (*Rana* spp., see the frog–toad complex) is quite accurate. Synonyms include **š?onkolan** [gn + UN] and **šrána** [gn + < Sp *rana* 'frog']. They are eaten as medicine for coughing (**špošil ?obal**) and are considered **k'išin** 'hot'.

### **čay** 'FISH' COMPLEX (See Figure 5.186)

Included here are native fish, market fish, and two types of aquatic crustaceans, the native crayfish and the market shrimp. The two latter categories are included because **čay** is typically part of the names applied to the categories, but more importantly because they are readily elicited in response to the enquiry **binti sbil huhuten čayetik**, 'what are the names of all the kinds of fish?' However when informants draw pictures of **čay** they draw a typical fish complete with fins and scales, features which the crustaceans lack. Furthermore the two crustacean categories clearly form a sub-complex as they are considered to be closely related to one another as opposed to the remaining members of the complex. Thus I will recognize two sub-complexes in this instance. All members of this complex are edible and **k'išin** 'hot'.

### *True Fish Subcomplex*

I have not been able satisfactorily to identify most of the taxa included here. I have collections for one (**č'uhč'ul čay**) and have observed examples of a second (**?isim čay**) near Ocosingo. A third category (**čan čay**) is rather obvious from verbal descriptions. The fourth native category (**škokoy**) remains un-

identified. Several examples of market fish were tentatively identified by a fisheries biology student, Geza Telekie, from fresh market specimens. In any case, fish are a relatively unimportant aspect of the native fauna, as suitable aquatic habitat is severly restricted. Tenejapanecos who live near the small rivers bordering lowland Tenejapa on the north and east do fish. The preferred technique is poisoning, for which lime (**tan**)* is used, or several local plant varieties as follows; **bak te?**, *Tephrosia sinapou* (Papilionaceae); **ca? tuluk'**, *Diospyros dignya* (Ebenaceae); **?ičil ?ak'**, *Clematis* spp. (Ranunculaceae); **tom ?ak'**, *Brunellia mexicana* (Brunelliaceae); **bac'il hihte?**, *Quercus peduncularis* (Fagaceae); **tohp'os te?**, *Cupania dentata* (Sapindaceae). This technique is applicable only during the height of the dry season, in April and May, when the streams are reduced to quiet pools. This season had passed before I began serious collecting, and I was thus unable to observe these techniques. Fishing by hook (**šluhkuč tak'inal čay**) and line is also employed, but it is secondary to poisoning. Certain fish (**peskáro**, this subcomplex) have been stocked in ponds constructed in the highland *paraje* of **macab** and are consumed locally. Dried fish have also been distributed by INI (the National Indian Institute), but this type of fish is not locally named. Both fresh and dried fish are sometimes purchased by Tenejapanecos in the San Cristóbal market. However, nomenclature for these market fish, most of which originate in the Pacific Ocean at Salina Cruz, Oaxaca, is extremely variable. The less wellknown names for market fish are treated in an appended hypothetical list.

**č'uhč'ul čay** 'little (pl) fish': Top minnows (Poeciliidae)

Two collections (EH Nos. 151, 183) of this

---

*It is possible that the "lime water" cited as a fish poison is actually mixed with the plant preparations to heighten their effectiveness. It is well known that lime is widely mixed with tobacco, coca, betel nut, etc., and that it acts as a releaser of effective alkaloids.

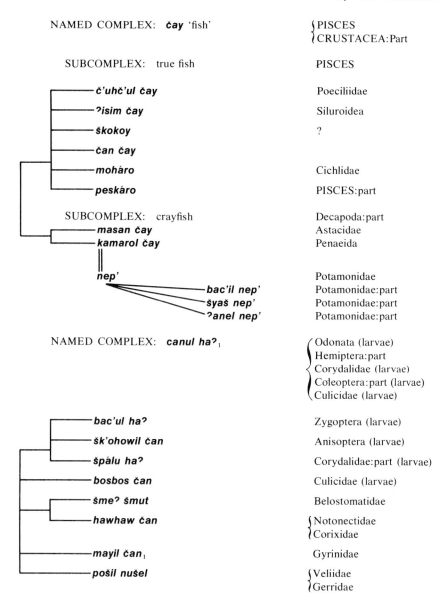

NAMED COMPLEX:  **čay** 'fish'

{ PISCES
{ CRUSTACEA:Part

SUBCOMPLEX:  true fish — PISCES

- **č'uhč'ul čay** — Poeciliidae
- **ʔisim čay** — Siluroidea
- **škokoy** — ?
- **čan čay**
- **moháro** — Cichlidae
- **peskáro** — PISCES:part

SUBCOMPLEX:  crayfish — Decapoda:part

- **masan čay** — Astacidae
- **kamarol čay** — Penaeida

- **nep'** — Potamonidae
  - **bac'il nep'** — Potamonidae:part
  - **ṡyaṡ nep'** — Potamonidae:part
  - **ʔanel nep'** — Potamonidae:part

NAMED COMPLEX:  **canul haʔ**₁

{ Odonata (larvae)
{ Hemiptera:part
{ Corydalidae (larvae)
{ Coleoptera:part (larvae)
{ Culicidae (larvae)

- **bac'ul haʔ** — Zygoptera (larvae)
- **šk'ohowil čan** — Anisoptera (larvae)
- **špálu haʔ** — Corydalidae:part (larvae)
- **bosbos čan** — Culicidae (larvae)
- **šmeʔ šmut** — Belostomatidae
- **hawhaw čan** — { Notonectidae { Corixidae
- **mayil čan**₁ — Gyrinidae
- **pošil nušel** — { Veliidae { Gerridae

**Figure 5.186**  The fish complex and the **čanul haʔ** (water bug) complex.

category were made which were tentatively identified as of this family by J. Lynch (MVZ). This family constitutes a large portion of the native fish fauna of highland Chiapas streams (Stuart 1964:334). Though the attributive *č'uhč'ul* may be employed to indicate a developmental stage, in this instance it names a valid taxonomic category, as informants assert that these fish do not develop or transform into any other. Furthermore, a specific medicinal value as a cure for whooping cough (**špošil hik'hik' ʔobal**) is ascribed to this taxon. It is not certain, however, that similarly sized fry of other types of fish would be distinguished.

**ʔisim čay** 'whisker fish': Catfish (order Suriformes), most likely the genus *Rhamdia* of the Pimeiodidae

This category is native and is distinguished

in particular by the whiskerlike barbels characteristic of the type. Some were observed in the Río Virgen near Ocosingo, and an example purchased in San Cristóbal was also so identified. This term is used by a few informants to name the native crayfish (see *masan čay*/aquatic crustacean).

**škokoy** [gn + UN]: (see Figure 5.187a)

An unidentified, native fish averaging 15 cm in length. Illustrated by AMT. May be referred to as *masan čay*, a usage distinct from *masan čay* of the aquatic crustacean subcomplex.

**čan čay** 'snake fish': Eels (Anguillidae) or other eellike fish (see Figure 5.187b)

Verbal descriptions indicate that this native taxon is distinguished by its long, slender shape.

**muháro** [< Sp *mojarra* 'cichlid']: (see Figure 5.187c)

The Spanish term properly applies to an important freshwater food fish (Cichlidae: *Cichlasoma*, Stuart 1964:335) of the region. It is not known to occur in Tenejapa, and it is not certain that the Tzeltal usage corresponds to the proper Spanish usage. For those informants who use the term *peskáro* (see following taxon) for all nonnative fish, this type is known as *č'in peskáro* 'little fish'. *moháro* is a variant.

**perskáro** [< Sp *pescado* 'fish']: (see Figure 5.187d)

A residual category of nonnative fish. Several alternative classifications of market fish exist. Most commonly, at least two categories are distinguished, *moháro*, which is the smaller of the two, and *peskáro*. Some informants class all nonnative fish as *peskáro* and recognize size varietals, i.e., *č'in peskáro* 'little fish' (equals *muháro*?), *bac'il peskáro* 'true fish', or simply *peskáro* and *muk'ul peskáro* 'large fish' (may equal *šulem čay*, see Hypothetical List: Fish). A third alternative ignores this term in favor of the recognition of several named varieties (see Hypothetical List: Fish). This name is sometimes rendered without modification as *peskádo*, more or less as pronounced in Spanish. A medicinal use is cited. The fish is burned in the hearth, for the smoke is believed to kill cockroaches (*špošil pewal*). Artifical ponds in *macab*, Tenejapa, have been stocked with fish attributed to this category, which are eaten locally.

*Hypothetical List: Fish*

**pehpen čay** 'butterfly fish'.    It may be a flying fish (Exocoetidae) or a ray of some sort (class CHONDRICHTHYES, order Rajiformes), as it is alleged to fly. SMZ has heard descriptions of this Pacific Ocean fish.

**pum ca? čay** 'feces-hitter fish'.    A market fish

**sakil č'uht čay** 'white-bellied fish'.    An example so named was tentatively identified as a tuna (Scombridae) from a market specimen.

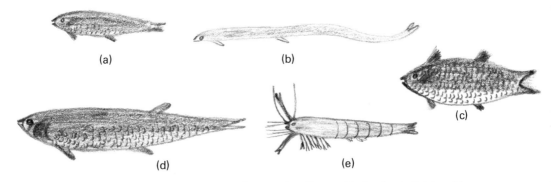

(a)          (b)

(c)

(d)          (e)

Figure **5.187** *čayetik* 'fish': (a) *masan čay* (AMT) = *škokoy*; (b) *čan čay* 'eel'; (c) *muháro*; (d) *peskáro*; (e) *kamarol čay* 'shrimp'. [Drawings by AMT.]

**sartines** [< Sp *sardinas* 'sardines']. Sardines. Canned sardines are sold in many Indian-owned shops throughout Tenejapa. They are recognized as kinds of *čay*.

**šulem čay** 'Turkey Vulture fish'. A large market fish sometimes called *muk'ul peskáro* 'large fish'.

**tam pat čay** [derivation uncertain]. A market fish, possibly a tuna.

**tešereš ne čay** 'scissor-tailed fish'. A market fish with a noticeably forked tail.

**yašal čay** 'blue–green–grey fish'. A market fish.

*Aquatic Crustacean Subcomplex*

These two taxa are considered to be kinds of *čay* 'fish' but form a closely related subgrouping within that complex. Crabs (*nep'*) are not included here though they are crustaceans (class CRUSTACEA).

**masan čay** 'meadow grasshopper fish': Fresh water crayfish (order Decapoda, Astacidae: CAS, EH No. 433)

One specimen was collected near Bachajón and others were seen in the Tanaté River in *habenal*, Tenejapa. *ʔisim čay* 'whisker fish' is used synonymously by a few informants (but see *ʔisim čay*/true fish). *šun čay* 'Joan fish' is also synonymous (AKČ'). It is considered edible and is *k'išin* 'hot'. The primary name refers to a resemblance perceived between this taxon and *masan* ('meadow grasshopper', see grasshopper complex).

**kamarol čay** [< Sp *camarón* 'shrimp' + 'fish']: Shrimp (Decapoda, section Penaeida: CAS, EH No. 176) (see Figure 5.187e)

These are encountered by Tenejapanecos in the San Cristóbal market. *cahal čay* is a variant. *čay* is optionally present in conjunction with the Spanish loan.

**nep'** 'crab': Crabs (Decapoda, section Brachyura) (see Figure 5.188a)

All specimens collected are of the family Potamonidae (=Pseudothelphusidae). These native crustaceans are considered to be related to the shrimp and crayfish, though they are not included in the *čay* 'fish' complex. They are edible and the flesh is *k'išin* 'hot'. Crab flesh is eaten with lots of pepper (*ʔič*) to increase the flow of breast milk for nursing mothers (*špošil yaʔlel ščuʔ ʔancetik*). The following inductive subtypes are widely recognized.

a. **bac'il nep'** 'true crab'. Small, pale-colored crabs (CAS, EH Nos. 723, 730) found by turning stones in stream beds. This taxon is probably a residual category.

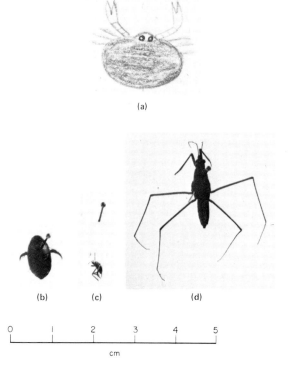

**Figure 5.188** (a) *nep'* 'crab'. [Drawing by AMT.] (b) *haw haw čan* or *hawal pat nušel čan* Coleoptera, Dytiscidae: EN No. 118073; (c) *pošil nušel* Hemiptera, Veliidae: EN No. 117984; (d) *čes k'ab čanul haʔ* Hemiptera, Gerridae: EN No. 117985. [Photos by author.]

b. **šyaš nep'** 'large dark crab'.   Large, dark colored crabs (CAS, EH Nos. 596, 721) found in fresh water. A large market crab was also included here, which may be a marine form. Though the attributive is derived from **yaš** 'blue–green–grey', in the present form, i.e., **šyaš**, it implies large size (see Chapter 4, Section 2.3).

c. **ʔanel nep'** 'fleeing crab': Land crabs. These are typically found in the fields where they "flee" when approached, hence the name. Babies are not allowed to eat this type of crab or they will flee from the house. A variant is **hʔanel nep'**.

## čanul haʔ₁ 'WATER BUG' COMPLEX

This complex is defined in part by habitat and is thus deductive. Aquatic larvae of several insect orders (Odonata, Neuroptera, and Diptera) as well as the nymphs and adults of the aquatic Hemiptera and Coleoptera comprise the complex. Though some shorebirds may be referred to as **čanul haʔ₂**, they are not included here as that use of the term is clearly polysemous (see the shorebird complex). Aquatic vertebrates as well as crustaceans, mollusks, and worms are also excluded. Thus body form obviously plays a role in defining this complex in conjunction with considerations of habitat. None of the included taxa are considered inedible, and several are the object of collecting trips during the low-water season.

**bac'ul haʔ** 'howler monkey of the water'?: Damselfly larvae (Odonata: superfamily Zygoptera; EN Nos. 1002297, 1002298, 1002302, 1002342)

According to informants, these are collected for food. **bac'** is a variant. What relation is thought to exist between these animals and the howler monkey (**bac'**/monkey) is not clear. Tenejapanecos are not aware of the facts of metamorphosis in this case.

**šk'ohowil čan** 'masked bug': Dragonfly larvae (Odonata: superfamily Anisoptera; EN Nos. 1002371, 1002378)

They are collected for food by turning stones at the water's edge. Variants include **šk'ohow čan** and **šk'ohowil čanul haʔ** 'masked water bug'. The prefix **š-**is optional. The name refers to the shape of the heads of these larvae. The facts of metamorphosis in this case are not known.

**špálu haʔ** [gn + < Sp *palo* 'stick'? + 'water']: Hellgrammites (larval Corydalidae in part; EN Nos. 1002391, 1003258)

This animal is one of two representatives of the order Neuroptera recognized nomenclaturally (see **but but ʔit čan**). They are collected for food and are common beneath streamside stones. **špálo haʔ** is a variant. It is not known to metamorphosize.

**bosbos čan** [< iv 'twitch' reduplicated + 'bug']: Mosquito pupae (Diptera: Culicidae)

No specimens were collected, but this name was applied to the masses of twitching pupae seen on several occasions in stagnant pools. The name refers to the characteristic movement of a mass of these animals (see also **bosbos lukum, lukum**/worm. Synonyms include **čanul ʔahč'al** 'mud critter' and **cahal čan** 'red bug'. The facts of metamorphosis are unknown in this case.

**šmeʔ šmut** [gn + 'mother' + gn + 'bird']: In particular giant water bugs (Hemiptera: Belostomatidae; EN No 1002379, nymph 1003256), but also including creeping water bugs (Hemiptera: Naucoridae; EN No. 1002379)

Nymphs and adults are not distinguished. The eggs carried on the back of certain species are recognized as such (**ston šmeʔ šmut**). These animals are collected for food by searching under streamside stones. The prefix **š-** is optional in either or both positions.

**hawhaw čan** 'on-the-back bug': The backswimmers (Hemiptera: Notonectidae; EN Nos. 1002285, nymphs 1002286, 1002294, 1002295) in particular, but also including water boatmen (Hemiptera: Corixidae; EN No. 1002293) and predaceous diving beetles (Coleoptera: Dytiscidae; EN Nos. 118073, 1002287, 1002310) (see Figure 5.188b)

Dytiscids may also be called **šme? šmut** (EN No. 1002295) by some informants or be unnamed (EN No. 118072). **hawal pat nušel čan** 'on-the-back swimming bug' is a variant. These names refer to the characteristic behavior of the Notonectidae. Nymphs are not distinguished from adults.

**mayil čan**₁ ['squash sp.' + 'bug']: The whirligig beetles (Coleoptera: Gyrinidae; EN Nos. 1002288, 1002290, 1002292, 1002315) in particular, but also including water scavenger beetles (Coleoptera: Hydrophilidae; EN No. 1002291)

**nuhpat čan**₁ 'round-backed bug' is synonymous. Both terms may be applied polysemously to sowbugs and pill-bugs (Isopoda in part, see **škoen čan**) but these are not **čanul ha?**₁ 'water bug'.

**pošil nušel** 'swimming medicine': Ripple bugs (Hemiptera: Veliidae *sensu lato*; EN Nos. 117984, 1002283, 1003289, 1003316) (see Figure 5.188c) and water striders (Hemiptera: Gerridae; EN Nos. 117985–117987, 1002289, 1002316) (see Figure 5.188c,d)

The name refers to the belief that eating these bugs helps a person learn to swim. A synonym **pošil čohk'** 'wart medicine' refers to a second medicinal use attributed to these animals. **baba ha? čan** 'top-of-the-water bug' is also synonymous. Water striders (Hemiptera: Gerridae) are distinguished as **češ k'ab nušel čan** 'long-legged swimming bug' by some informants.

*Hypothetical List: čanul ha?*₁

Several informants distinguish two additional taxa, but no examples were collected.

**k'ohk'oč ton** [UN + 'stone']. An animal similar to **šk'ohowil čan** (water bug complex) which is found under streamside stones.

**mokoč čan** 'millipede bug'. This is neither the millipede (**mokoč**) nor the snake (**mokoč čan**/snake) of the same name. An aquatic arthropod of some kind.

*Snail Complex (See Figure 5.189)*

All shelled mollusks (phylum MOLLUSCA in part) are included here. Slugs (MOLLUSCA in part, see **nap'ak**) are seen as linking this complex with the worm complex following. Since mollusks are primarily aquatic, this phylum is represented by but six taxa. All taxa refer to the class GASTROPODA unless otherwise noted. One taxon (**puy** is considered edible, and medicinal applications are noted for that and one other taxon (**yat naab**). A bivalve arthropod (a clam shrimp, CRUSTACEA: Conchostraca) is included with the freshwater bivalves (MOLLUSCA: PELECYPODA) in **bak čikin** 'bone ear'.

**puy** [UN]: Aquatic and terrestial snails with conical shells (see Figure 5.190a)

They are larger than the similarly shaped **yat naab** (this complex). The focal type appears to be the genus *Pachychilus* (Thiaridae: CAS, EH Nos. 724, 725), a genus of snails reported as being eaten by the Indians of Vera Paz, Guatemala (Von Martens 1890: 152). One specimen of a related family (Cyclophoridae: *Neocyclotus* cf. *N. dysoni*; CAS, EH No. 522) was also included. The shell (**spat puy**), according to a current tale, can cure sexual impotence in men (**šposil cacal**). Young people are warned not to blow on the shell (as a trumpet) or their teeth will fall out. The flesh is **sik** 'cold' because it is cooked with the plant **kulantu** (*Coriandrum sativum*), which is also **sik** 'cold'. The following specific subdivisions are widely recognized, though the small specimen sample precludes a biological definition, if such is possible, of the subdivision.

a. **bac'il puy** 'true conical snail'. "Typical" **puy** not otherwise distinguished. The follow-

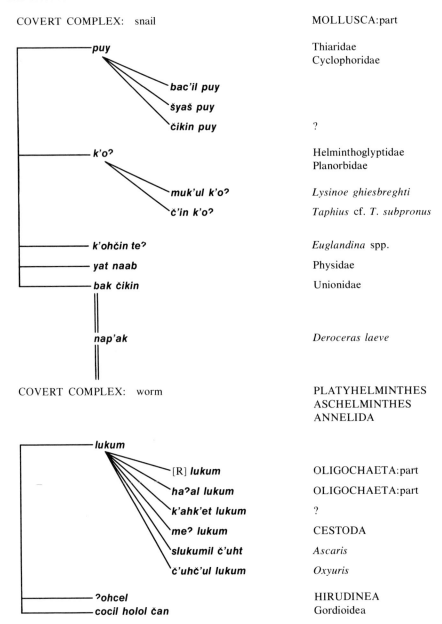

Figure 5.189 Mollusks and worms.

ing specimens are of this type: CAS, EH Nos. 522, 725.

b. **šyaš puy** 'large dark conical snail'. Larger, dark-colored, conical-shelled snails (CAS, EH No. 724). Also known as **ʔihkʼal puy** 'black conical snail'. As described previously (see **tulukʼ**/turkey) the attributive **yaš** in this form (i.e., **š** + **yaš**) implies large size and dark coloration.

c. **čikin puy** 'ear conical snail'. Very large, marine snails. This category is not native. They can be used as trumpets (**yokʼesan**). Also known as **bak puy** 'bone conical snail', or **meʔ puy** 'mother conical snail'.

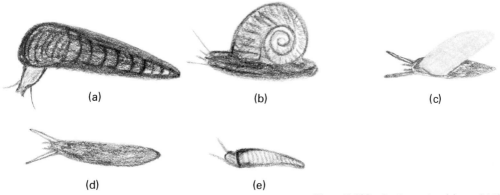

(a)          (b)                              (c)

(d)          (e)

**Figure 5.190**   Snail complex: (a) *puy*; (b) *k'o?*; (c) *k'ohčin te?*;   (d) *yat naab*; (e) *nap'ak* 'slug'. [Drawing by AMT.]

***k'o?*** [UN]: Cylindrical-shelled snails, either aquatic or terrestrial (see Figure 5.190b)

Two specific subdivisions are often distinguished. The first is the type specific.

a. ***muk'ul k'o?*** 'large cylindrical snail'.   In particular the large terrestrial species *Lysinoe ghiesbreghti* (Helminthoglyptidae; CAS, EH Nos. 523b, 524, 901). ***šotšot k'o*** [UN + 'cylindrical snail'] is synonymous. Though used as food by some Guatemalan Indians (von Martens 1890:152), informants did not list it as an edible species.

b. ***č'in k'o?*** 'small cylindrical snail'.   The one specimen so distinguished is *Taphius* cf. *T. subpronus* (Planorbidae; CAS, EH No. 465) collected at San Cristóbal.

***k'ohčin te?*** [UN + 'tree']: Conical-shelled terrestrial snails (Oleacinidae: *Euglandina* spp.) (see Figure 5.190c)

This animal is possibly distinguished from *puy* (this complex) by the elongated mouth of the shell. The three specimens positively referred to this taxon represent several species of the genus *Euglandina* (*E. sowerbyana*, EH No. 529; *Euglandina* sp., EH No. 546; cf. *E. monolifera*, EH No. 771), a genus of carnivorous snails. Informants did not indicate any awareness of this peculiar habit. Variants include ***k'ohčin puy***, ***k'ohčin puy te?***, and ***k'ohčin te? puy***.

***yat naab*** 'penis of the lake': Tiny, conical-shelled freshwater snails (see Figure 5.190d)

Three collections were made at San Cristóbal (all Physidae). Two are of the genus *Aplexa* (CAS, EH Nos. 467, 549), the third is *Physa* cf. *P. berendti* (CAS, EH No. 467a). Also known as ***mol puy*** or ***č'in puy***, suggesting an alternative classification as a kind of *puy* (this complex). Like *puy* these are considered "medicine" for sexual impotence (***špošil cacal***).

***bak čikin*** 'bone ear': Pearl-button mussels (PELECYPODA: Unionidae)

The one collection is *Elliptio* (= *Nephronaias*), cf. *E. calamitarum* (CAS, EH No. 786). Also included here is a bivalve arthropod, the clam shrimp (phylum ARTHROPODA: CRUSTACEA: Conchostraca; CAS, EH Nos. 469, 470, 549), which, however, is considered atypically small.

***nap'ak*** [UN]: Slugs (MOLLUSCA: GASTROPODA in part) (see Figure 5.190e)

All collections are the species *Deroceras laeve* (Limacidae; CAS, EH Nos. 161, 451, 575). ***?abak*** is a variant. Varieties based on size are sometimes recognized, for instance, ***č'in nap'ak*** 'small slug' and ***muk'ul nap'ak*** 'large slug'. Slugs are considered inedible and the distaste mixed with fear attached to all wormlike animals is typical of this taxon also. A jumping bristletail (ARTHROPODA:

INSECTA: Thysanura: Machilidae; EH No. 118258) was considered *kps nap'ak*. *nap'ak* is considered to be associated both with *k'ohčin te'* of the snail complex and *'ohcel* of the following worm complex, thus linking the two complexes.

## WORM COMPLEX

This complex includes species of several lower phyla, i.e., ANNELIDA (*lukum* in part, *'ohcel*), ASCHELMINTHES (*lukum* in part, *cocil holol čan*), and PLATYHELMINTHES (*lukum* in part). Both parasitic and free-living forms are included.

*lukum* [UN] (see Figure 5.191a)

Several inductive subdivisions are widely recognized. The focal species of this taxon are the earthworms (ANNELIDA: OLIGOCHAETA), most of which are included in a covert residual.

a. [R]*lukum*. Earthworms, with the exception of very large species (CAS, EH Nos. 103, 161, 328, 445, 451, 541, 575, 591, 592). Two color varieties are recognized, *cahal lukum* 'red worm' and *sakil lukum* 'white worm'.

b. *ha'al lukum* 'rain worm'. A giant earthworm (ANNELIDA: OLIGOCHAETA in part; CAS, EH No. 581). These are greatly feared as evil omens (*yašlabtawan*) and are killed on sight. The name refers to the fact that these worms surface after rains. Also known as *muk'ul lukum* 'large worm'. The individual collected is approximately 25 cm long and 12 mm in diameter.

c. *k'ahk'et lukum* 'fiery worm': An uni-

dentified worm described as varicolored and subterranean. *k'ahk'al lukum* 'fierce worm' is a variant.

d. *me' lukum* 'mother worm': tapeworms (PLATYHELMINTHES: CESTODA; probably *Taenia*). The term is not widely known, but by inference from verbal descriptions probably refers to this animal.

e. *slukumil č'uht* 'intestine worm': Parasitic round worms (ASCHELMINTHES: NEMATODA, probably *Ascaris*) (see Figure 5.191b). This worm was identified tentatively from verbal descriptions. *slukumil ca'* 'worm of feces' is synonymous.

f. *č'uhč'ul lukum* 'small (pl) worm': Parasitic round worms, most likely pinworms (ASCHELMINTHES: NEMATODA; *Oxyuris* spp.), on the basis of verbal descriptions. *bosbos lukum* 'twitching worm' is synonymous.

*'ohcel* [UN]: Leeches (ANNELIDA: HIRUDINEA; CAS, EH Nos. 544, 597, 598, 715) (see Figure 5.191c)

These are also greatly feared. *'ohcel lukum* is synonymous and indicates the close relationship perceived between this taxon and the preceding. A free-living planarian PLATYHELMINTHES: TURBELLARIA: Tricladia: CAS, EH No. 789) was considered to be *kps 'ohcel*.

*cocil holol čan* 'hair-of-the-head critter': Horse-hair worms (ASCHELMINTHES: NEMATOMORPHA: Gordioidea; CAS, EN NO. 573)

Despite the fact that these animals appear to be inanimate on first glance, their "animal-

(a)

(b)

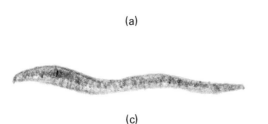

(c)

Figure 5.191 Worm complex: (a) *lukum* 'earthworm'; (b) *slukumil č'uht* 'intestine worm'; (c) *'ohcel* 'leech'. [Drawings by AMT.]

ness" is clearly recognized. *č'ahan lukum* 'string worm', *č'ušub čan* 'thread critter', and *lukum čan* 'worm critter' are synonyms and indicate the relationship with the category *lukum* (this complex).

## ANT COMPLEX (see Figure 5.192)

All true ants (Hymenoptera: Formicidae) are included in this complex. Very few mis-identifications occurred. A strange hirsute ant of the genus *Camponotus* found outside the *municipio* was classed as *muy ʔam* ('velvet ant', Hymenoptera: Mutillidae). A winged ponerid (Formicidae) was thought to be *kps ʔus ʔako* (see *ʔus ʔakoʔ*/wasp). Winged forms of various ant species are considered to be female (*smeʔ*). This is partly correct, since

queens as well as males may be winged. Workers are considered to be male (*stat*). The fine detail applied to ant classification by Tenejapanecos is most readily explicable in terms of the fact that these insects often bite, sting, or attack cultivated plants. *šanič* (see following taxon) is the type generic, and that term is occasionally used to refer to the complex. Termites [INSECTA: Isoptera] are inexplicably unfamiliar to most informants. They are considered to be related to ants (see *šanič* following).

*šanič* [UN]: Myrmecine ants (Myrmecinae) with the exception of *Atta* (*c'isim*, see later taxon)

Termites (INSECTA: Isoptera, EN Nos.

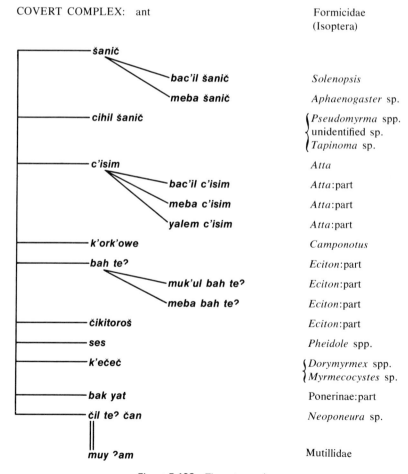

| COVERT COMPLEX: ant | | Formicidae (Isoptera) |
|---|---|---|
| šanič | | |
| | bac'il šanič | *Solenopsis* |
| | meba šanič | *Aphaenogaster* sp. |
| cihil šanič | | { *Pseudomyrma* spp.<br>unidentified sp.<br>*Tapinoma* sp. |
| c'isim | | *Atta* |
| | bac'il c'isim | *Atta*:part |
| | meba c'isim | *Atta*:part |
| | yalem c'isim | *Atta*:part |
| k'ork'owe | | *Camponotus* |
| bah teʔ | | *Eciton*:part |
| | muk'ul bah teʔ | *Eciton*:part |
| | meba bah teʔ | *Eciton*:part |
| čikitoroš | | *Eciton*:part |
| ses | | *Pheidole* spp. |
| k'ečeč | | { *Dorymyrmex* spp.<br>*Myrmecocystes* sp. |
| bak yat | | Ponerinae:part |
| čil teʔ čan | | *Neoponeura* sp. |
| muy ʔam | | Mutillidae |

**Figure 5.192**   The ant complex.

1002319, 1003254) are sometimes referred to as **sakil šanič** 'white ant' or **yut lumil šanič** 'inside-the-ground ant' though this usage is not definitely established. Two specific subdivisions are clearly recognized.

a. **bac'il šanič** 'true ant': Fire ants (*Solenopsis* spp.). These stinging ants (**ya šti ʔwan ta yit** 'they bite with their tails') are abundant throughout Tenejapa and cause discomfort to Tenejapanecos working in their fields. Three varieties are known. **ʔihk'al šanič** 'black ant' (EN Nos. 118224, 1002306), **cahal šanič** 'red ant' (EN Nos. 118225, 1002304, 1002336, 1003250) (see Figure 5.193a), and a third, bicolored type (**ča ʔ sbonil**).

b. **meba šanič** 'orphan ant': A small myrmecine ant (*Aphaenogaster*, EN No. 1002274) (see Figure 5.194a). These are too small to inflict a noticeable bite and are considered innocuous (**mayuk smul**). They are distinguished from other superficially similar ants (e.g., **ses** and **k'eček**) apparently on the basis of the fact that their nesting behavior is typical of **šanič**.

**cihil šanič** 'stinking ant': *Pseudomyrma* spp. (Pseudomyrmecinae) (see Figure 5.194b)

A single specimen (EN No. 1002282) collected on the host plant (*Acacia* spp.) is of this genus. Several other specimens of an as yet unidentified genus (EN Nos. 118230, 1002284, 1002328) (see Figure 5.193b) were

**Figure 5.193** Specimens in the ant complex HYMENOPTERA, FORMICIDAE: (a) **cahal šanič** Myrmecinae, *Solenopsis* sp.: EN No. 118225; (b) **cihil šanič** Formicinae, genus?: EN No. 118230; (c) **c'isim** Myrmecinae, *Atta* sp.: EN No. 118212; (d) **čaw hol c'isim** Myrmecinae, *Atta* sp.: EN No. 118211; (e) **k'ork'owe** Formicinae, *Camponotus* sp.: EN No. 118219; (f) **sme ʔ k'ork'owe** Formicinae, *Camponotus* sp.: EN No. 118219; (g) **meba bah te ʔ** Dorylinae, *Eciton* sp.: EN No. 118216; (h) **bak yat** Ponerinae, *Odontomachus* sp.: EN No. 118234. HYMENOPTERA, MUTILLIDAE: (i) **muy ʔam** Mutillidae: EN No. 118138.

**Figure 5.194**  Ants and their nests: (a) **_meba šanič_** 'orphan ant'; (b) **_cihil šanič_** 'stinking ant'; (c) **_bac`il c`isim_** 'true leaf-cutting ant'; (d) **_čaw hol c`isim_** 'big-headed leaf-cutting ant'; (e) **_me?_ _c`isim_** 'mother leaf-cutting ant'; (f) **_meba c`isim_** 'orphan leaf-cutting ant'; (g) **_muk`ul bah te?_** 'large army ant'; (h) **_k`ečeč_**. [Color pencil originals by JGG.]

referred to this taxon by informants, though one other specimen of that genus (EN No. 118223) was classed elsewhere (see *k'ork'owe*). According to informants, this ant typically nests in plants of this type, stings, and has a distinctive odor, all features characteristic of *Pseudomyrma* (Wilson 1971:48–55). The unidentified genus may or may not fit this verbal description. The single specimen of *Tapinoma* (Dolichoderinae) was also classed here. It has a distinctive odor and may, like many dolichoderines, nest in trees.

*c'isim* [UN]: The leaf-cutting ants, *Atta* spp. (Myrmecinae) (see Figure 5.193c)

This distinctive genus of tropical ants abounds in lowland Tenejapa. These ants often destroy growing crops. Several specific subdivisions are recognized within this genus.

a. *bac'il c'isim* 'true leaf-cutting ant': *Atta* spp., workers (see Figure 5.194c). The ravages of these ants are combated by digging up the nests in search of *me? c'isim* 'mother-of-the-leaf-cutting ant (see *me? c'isim*/ snake), a snake believed to control the colony. If the snake is killed the ants will also die. Dead dogs are placed on the ants' nest also, as it is believed that the odor drives them away. The following specimens are attributed to this type: EN Nos. 118212, 118213, 1002327, 1003249, 1003251. The major soldier caste found in the nests of this type are distinguished as *čaw hol c'isim* 'large-headed parasol ant' (see Figures 5.193d and 5.194d) or *me? c'isim* 'mother leaf-cutting ant' (see Figure 5.194e) (EN Nos. 118211, 1002317). These are induced to leave the nest by whistling at a nest opening, an effective procedure, which I witnessed.

b. *meba c'isim* 'orphan leaf-cutting ant': A smaller type of *Atta* (EN Nos. 1002320, 1002330) (see Figure 5.194f). It constructs a small nest with a single entrance (observed in the case of No. 1002320).

c. *yalem c'isim* 'transitory leaf-cutting ant': *Atta* queens. These are considered to be a

distinct type; they are winged and solitary. This is the only type of ant that is eaten. They are found only during the month of *?uč* ('May'). None were collected. *me? k'is* ['mother' + UN] is a synonym.

*k'ork'owe* [UN]: Formicine ants of the genus *Camponotus* (see Figure 5.193e)

These do not sting but flee (*ya/š?an*) underground when their nests are disturbed. They are common throughout and well known. Winged males (EN No. 118218) are distinguished as *sme? k'ork'owe* 'female *Camponotus*' (see Figure 5.193f), while the workers (EN Nos. 118219, 118220, 1002273, 1002327, 1002335, 1002338, 1002346, 1003252) are known as *stat* 'male'. Many variants are current as follows: *k'ork'or?e, k'ork'orwet, k'ork'orwéra, k'ork'oč, k'ork'oš, k'ork'ow, k'ork'oy*.

*bah te?* 'tree striker': Most army ants, *Eciton* spp. (Dorylinae)

These ants are recognized in part by their swarming behavior, crossing trails on a wide front—behavior described as characteristic of *E. burchelli* within this genus (Wilson 1971:58). They 'bite with the mouth'. (*ya šti?wan ta ye*), and the bite is considered to be very painful. They are known to eat other insects and to invade wasp and bee nests. One collection was taken from a column attacking a nest of the wasp *?us ?ako?* (EN No. 1002333). They are commonly found only during the rainy season and forage both day and night— accurate natural history notes supplied by informants. Two specific subdivisions are recognized:

a. *muk'ul bah te?* 'large army ant'. The following specimens of *Eciton* are of this type: EN Nos. 1002333, 1002350, 1003253 (see Figure 5.194g). Both 'black' (*?ihk'al*) and 'red' (*cahal*) varieties are known, though all specimens are of the black variety. *niwak bah te?* 'large (pl) army ant' is a variant.

b. *meba bah te?* 'orphan army ant'. A small, black type of *Eciton* (EN Nos. 118216, 118217,

1002332, 1002351, 1002352) (see Figure 193g). Also known as *č'in bah te?* 'small army ant'.

***čikitoroš*** [UN]: A small, red army ant (*Eciton* sp., EN No. 1002353)

The single specimen was collected from a foraging column at night. Their stinging bite is considered very painful, equal to that of *bah te?* (see preceding taxon). This category may differ from *bah te?* in foraging behavior, foraging in columns rather than in swarms (Wilson 1971: 58). A specimen of *Camponotus* (EN No. 1002329) and another of *Solenopsis* (EN No. 1002315) were assigned here. The latter identification was by a highland informant of a red, stinging species. JGG disagreed with that identification, calling it *cahal šanič* (see *šanič*, this complex). *Camponotus* does not sting or bite. Thus *Eciton* is the correct referent. *čikitološ* is a variant.

***ses*** [UN]: Small, black, nonstinging ants, *Pheidole* (Myrmicinae; EN No. 1002275)

It is the typical ant found in houses, quite characteristic of the feeding habits of this genus (E. I. Schlinger personal communication). However, further collections might involve other genera. It is believed to make no nest. The name is sometimes rendered as *seys*.

***k'ečeč*** [UN]: Small, nonstinging ants, *Dorymyrmex* (Dolichoderinae; EN Nos. 1002311, 1002326) (see Figure 5.194)

A third specimen assigned here was a honey ant, *Myrmecocystus* (Formicinae: EN No. 1002331). The nest is characteristic; a single entrance surrounded by a symmetrical crater about 5 cm in diameter (noted for EN Nos. 1002326, 1002331). 'Red' and 'black' varieties are known. *k'erečeč* is a variant.

***bak yat*** 'bone-stinger': Most Ponerinae, a subfamily of minimally colonial ants

Most are large and black with a long abdomen and a powerful sting. Two common genera are included without distinction (*Odontomachus*: EN Nos. 118233, 118234, 1002352 [see Figure 5.193h]; *Pachycondyla*: EN Nos. 1002277, 1002278, 1002318). Two other genera of this subfamily are considered somewhat atypical, but are referred here nonetheless (*Leptogenys*: EN No. 118226; *Neoponeura*: EN No. 118214). Variants include *bakre ?at*, *bakéro yat*, and *bakariš yat*.

***čil te? čan*** ['elderberry' (i.e., *Sambucus mexicana*) + 'bug']: The specimens are male ponerines of the genus *Neoponeura* (EN No. 1002349)

This taxon is not widely known, and it is not clear on what basis it is distinguished from *bak yat*, nor is the implication of the name clear.

***muy ?am*** 'chewing spider': Velvet ants (Hymenoptera: Mutillidae) (see Figure 5.193i)

Despite the name, these are not considered to be a kind of *?am* 'spider' but, rather, are thought to be related to ants and wasps though not a member of either complex. All four specimens of this family (EN Nos. 118136–118139) were placed here. Two specimens of an extralimital species of *Camponotus* (Hymenoptera: Formicidae: EN Nos. 118209, 118210) were also attributed to this taxon. This attribution is erroneous since ants of the genus *Camponotus* do not sting, while an extremely powerful sting is considered characteristic of *muy ?am*, which is accurate for the velvet ants.

## šuš 'WASP' COMPLEX
(See Figure 5.195a)

This named complex includes the vespid, eumenid, and sphecid wasps, however the greatest differentiation applies to the social vespid wasps (Vespidae: Polistinae). The spider wasps (Pompilidae) are included in the complex by a few Tenejapanecos. I exclude them here following the opinion of the majority of informants. The form and location of the nests (*sna šuš*) of the social species is an important taxonomic criterion

NAMED COMPLEX: **šuš** 'wasp'

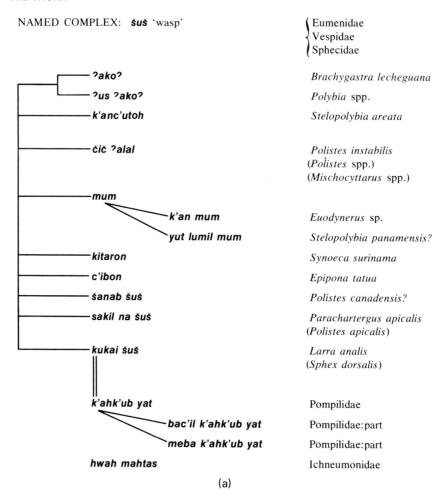

{ Eumenidae
Vespidae
Sphecidae

**ʔakoʔ** — *Brachygastra lecheguana*

**ʔus ʔakoʔ** — *Polybia* spp.

**k'anc'utoh** — *Stelopolybia areata*

**čič ʔalal** — *Polistes instabilis*
(*Polistes* spp.)
(*Mischocyttarus* spp.)

**mum**

**k'an mum** — *Euodynerus* sp.

**yut lumil mum** — *Stelopolybia panamensis?*

**kitaron** — *Synoeca surinama*

**c'ibon** — *Epipona tatua*

**šanab šuš** — *Polistes canadensis?*

**sakil na šuš** — *Parachartergus apicalis*
(*Polistes apicalis*)

**kukai šuš** — *Larra analis*
(*Sphex dorsalis*)

**k'ahk'ub yat** — Pompilidae

**bac'il k'ahk'ub yat** — Pompilidae:part

**meba k'ahk'ub yat** — Pompilidae:part

**hwah mahtas** — Ichneumonidae

(a)

**Figure 5.195a**    The *šuš* 'wasp' complex.

for both Tenejapanecos and entomologists (Wilson 1971) and provides the basis for several identifications. This provides a good example of the convergence of folk and scientific classification. Size, shape, and color of nests are noted. Colors are described as falling on a continuum from dark to light. Dark nests are alleged to be made of 'horse dung', while light nests are of 'cow dung'. Nests of an intermediate shade are assumed to have been constructed of a mixture of these materials. The color of the nests is no doubt due in part to the construction materials, which are typically vegetable matter but may include dung.

Social vespid wasps are common and conspicuous, their larvae (**yal šuš**) are considered edible, and they sting (**ya štiʔwan ta yit**). These facts help explain the detail applied to the recognition of categories within this single subfamily. Solitary wasps are less often encountered and are never encountered in large numbers. This may explain the fact that large and distinctive solitary wasps such as some scoliids (EN Nos. 118148, 118149, 118241) (see Figure 5.195b), a pelicinid (EN No. 118153) (see Figures 5.195c) and a thread-waisted wasp, *Sceliphron assimile* (Sphecidae; EN No. 118152)—some of which were collected within a hundred yards of informants' houses—were considered entirely strange and were not included in any named category.

Two classificatory systems exist in Tenejapa, the lowland system is the basis for the following account. The highland system is

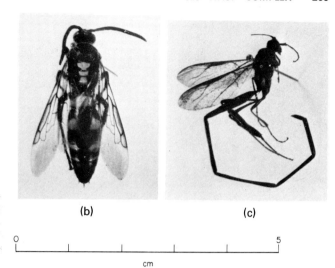

**Figure 5.195b,c** Assorted wasps. HYMENOPTERA: (b) not known, Scoliidae: EN No. 118241; (c) not known, *kps tultus* Pelicinidae: EN No. 118153. ("Not Known" indicates that informants were unfamiliar with the specimen.)

(b)                    (c)

restricted by the fact that the variety of wasps found above 1800 m is considerably reduced. This restricted highland system will be described in the taxonomic account as synonyms.

Though the names for the taxa of this complex fall into two groups—one obligatorily including *šuš*, another for which this morpheme is optionally included—there is no evidence that the first group is taxonomic.

*ʔakoʔ* [UN]: A social vespid wasp (*Brachygastra lecheguana*; EN No. 118172) (see Figure 5.196a)

These wasps are distinguished as medium-sized, short-bodied, and dark-colored, with yellow transverse bands on the tip of the abdomen. They construct large, closed, spherical nests of a mixture of 'cow dung' (*caʔ wakaš*) and 'horse dung' (*caʔ kawáyu*) (see Figure 5.197a), thus the nest is intermediate in color between the 'white' of a nest of pure 'cow dung' and the 'black' (actually dark grey) of a nest constructed of 'horse dung'. *ʔakoʔ* is a lowland species and the taxon is unknown to many highland informants. Variants include *ʔakoʔ šuš*, *čanul ʔakoʔ*. The specimens assigned here are actually a superficially similar but diverse assortment that includes the proper referent, a potter wasp (Eumenidae: *Stenodynerus* sp.: EN No. 118169) (see Figure 5.196b), a digger wasp (Sphecidae: *Hoplisoides vespoides*: EN

No. 118173), and even a fly (Diptera: Stratiomyiidae: EN No. 118398) that very ably mimics the wasp. Two other potter wasp (*Euodynerus*) specimens were assigned here by a minority of informants; the majority, however, considered them to be *kʼan mum* (see this complex). This species of wasp is "kept" in a semidomesticated state by some Mexican communities for the honey it stores (Richards and Richards 1951:26). However this practice is not known in Tenejapa.

*ʔus ʔakoʔ* 'fly wasp': Social vespid wasps of the genus *Polybia* (*Polybia occidentalis*: EN No. 118182 [see Figure 5.196c]; *P. parvulina*: EN Nos. 118175, 118177; *P. pygmaea*: EN Nos. 118178, 118179, 118183 [see Figure 5.196d])

They are distinguished by small size, elongated form, and dark coloration broken only by pale edges to the abdominal segments. This feature is incorporated in the highland synonym *cʼibal ʔit šuš* 'striped-abdomen wasp'. It is also known in the highlands as *čʼin šuš* 'small wasp'. The nest (see Figure 5.197b) is closed, spherical, and allegedly constructed of a mixture of cow and horse dung (see complex heading for a discussion of this point); it is about one-half of the diameter of the nests of *ʔakoʔ*. I observed several nests of this species that were 15 to 20 cm in diameter, suspended from the crossbars of telephone poles. Two specimens were collected

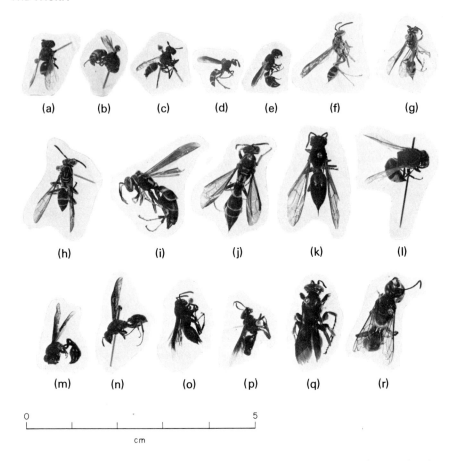

0                              5

cm

**Figure 5.196** Specimens in the wasp complex. HYMENOPTERA, VESPIDAE (unless otherwise noted): (a) *ʔakoʔ Brachygastra lecheguana*: EN No. 118172; (b) *ʔakoʔ* (*sic.*) Eumenidae, *Stenodynerus* sp.: EN No. 118169; (c) *ʔus ʔakoʔ Polybia occidentalis*: EN No. 118182; (d) *ʔus ʔakoʔ Polybia pygmaea*: EN No. 118178; (e) *ʔus ʔakoʔ* (*sic.*) Eumenidae, *Hypalastoroides* sp.: EN No. 118187; (f) *k'an c'utoh Stelopolybia areata*: EN No. 118190; (g) *k'an c'utoh Stelopolybia areata*: EN No. 118198; (h) *k'an c'utoh* (*sic.*) *Mischocyttarus cubensis*: EN No. 118143; (i) *čič ʔalal Polistes instabilis*: EN No. 118140; (j) *čič ʔalal Polistes instabilis*: EN No. 118142; (k) *yut lumil mum Stelopolybia panamensis*: EN No. 118159; (l) *k'an mum* Eumenidae, Euodynerus sp.: EN No. 118170; (m) *c'ibon Epipona tatua*: EN No. 118165; (n) *c'ibon Stelopolybia* sp.: EN No. 118163; (o) *sakil na šuš Parachartergus apicalis*: EN No. 118167; (p) *sakil na šuš* Trigonalidae, *Trigonalys* sp.: EN No. 118168; (q) Sphecidae, Larrinae, *Larra analis*: EN No. 118150; (r) *kukai šuš* Sphecidae, Sphecinae, *Sphex dorsalis*: EN No. 118151. ("*sic.*" indicates misidentifications [see text for discussion].)

at the nest (*Polybia pygmaea*: EN Nos. 118178, 118179). In addition, two specimens of *Mischocyttarus pallidipectus* (Vespidae: EN Nos. 118184, 118185) and two potter wasps (*Eumenidae: Parancistrocerus* n. sp. nr. *productus:* EN No. 118180; and *Hypalastoroides* sp.: EN No. 118187 [see Figure 5.196e]) were placed here, erroneously in view of the nest form criterion. A solitary tiphiid wasp (EN No. 118186) was considered *kps ʔus ʔakoʔ*.

One informant (JGG) asserted that two varieties exist, *ʔihk'al ʔus ʔakoʔ* 'black fly wasp', which is the typical form, and *cahal ʔus ʔakoʔ* 'red fly wasp', distinguished by color and by its more powerful sting. No specimens of this second type were collected, however. *ʔus ʔakoʔ šuš* 'fly wasp', and *čanul ʔus ʔakoʔ* are variants. *ʔus ʔit* may be a microdialectal variant.

*k'an c'utoh* ['yellow' + 'cornflower']: A

Sna ʔakoʔ, lom muk'sna yuʔun yanTik
šušetik; haʔsnaine ɣaʔ wakaš.

(a)

Sna Tus ʔakoʔ, haʔ snaine
ɣaʔ wakaš. lom čink šɔanul

(b)

kàn č̓utoh: ʔay sna ta homol yok teʔ
spisil ʔoʔa sok ta homol čin.
haʔ ya spas snain ɣaʔ wakaš.

(c)

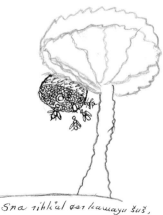

sna čič ʔalal; č̓in lečel
spisil ʔoʔa ʔay ta yanil yabenal
lɔbal sok ta yanil yabenal teʔ.
    ya
haʔ spas snain ɣaʔ wakaš sok ɣaʔ kawayu.

(d)

Sna kitaron: lom niwak šɔanul
napʼal ta č̓uh teʔ
haʔ snaine ɣaʔ kawayu.

(e)

Sna ʔihk'al ɣaʔ kawayu šuš,
te sna ʔihk'al ɣaʔ kawayu; ha snaine
puro ɣaʔ kawayu.
te sna ɣahal č̓ibon ya skap snain
ɣaʔ kawayu sok ɣaʔ wakaš sok
lom toyol ta muk'ul teʔ ya spas sna.

(f)

Lehčel na šuš / šanab šuš:
Lehčel na šuš spisil ʔoʔa
ʔay ta yabenal teʔ sok ta
yabenal ʔak.
haʔ ya spas snain ɣaʔ kawayu

(g)

Sakil na šuš, "haʔ snaine ɣaʔ
wakaš"; pero lomsak sposoh

(h)

**Figure 5.197** Wasps and their nests: (a) *sna ʔako ʔakoʔ*'s nest'; (b) *sna ʔus ʔakoʔ* 'fly-*ʔakoʔ*'s nest'; (c) *sna k̓an c̓utoh* 'yellow-corn-flower's nest'; (d) *sna čič ʔalal* 'nest of the 'mother's-brother's-wife''; (e) *sna kitaron* 'guitaron's nest'; (f) *sna c̓ibon* 'c̓ibon's nest'; (g) *sna šanab šuš* 'nest of the sandal wasp'; (h) *sna sakil na šuš* 'nest of the white nest wasp'. [Color pencil drawings by SMZ.]

social vespid wasp (*Stelopolybia areata* : EN Nos. 118188–118196, 118198, 118199) (see Figure 5.196f, g)

These are small to medium-sized, slim-bodied, primarily yellow wasps which nest in hollow trees. EN No. 118188 was collected at a nest in the base of a live tree, as is typical of the species and as illustrated by SMZ (see Figure 5.197c). Like *ʔihk'al ʔus ʔakoʔ* (see preceding taxon), the sting is not powerful (*ma ba lom k'uš ya šti ʔwan*). This taxon is known to both highland and lowland informants. *čanul k'an c'utoh* and *k'an c'utoh šuš* are variants.

A male of the species *Mischocyttarus basimacula* (EN No. 118197) was assigned here by some informants, as were two typical specimens (i.e., females) of *M. cubensis mexicanus* (EN Nos. 118143, 118144) (see Figure 5.196h). However this genus constructs nests of the *čič ʔalal* type (see following taxon).

*čič ʔalal* ['mother's-brother's-wife' + 'child'] : Social vespid wasps, in particular the widespread and common *Polistes instabilis* (EN Nos. 118140–118142) (see Figure 5.196 i, j)

This species was considered to be *bac'il čič ʔalal* 'true mother's-brother's-wife's child' or *cahal čič ʔalal* 'red mother's-brother's-wife's child'. It is medium to large, slim-bodied, and dark red patterned with black. It is known at all elevations in the region. *ʔihk'al čič ʔalal* 'black mother's-brother's-wife's child' is a variety recognized by several informants. One specimen of the species *Polistes canadensis* (EN No. 118145) was so named by two informants. A specimen of the species *Polistes dorsalis* (a male, EN No. 118146) was also assigned here, though distinguished by the descriptive qualification *k'anal* 'yellow'. The very large species *Polistes carnifex* (EN No. 118147), was unknown to most informants. Such informants, however, described it either as *kps kitaron* (see this complex) or as *muk'ul čič ʔalal* 'large mother's-brother's-wife's child'. In size it resembles *kitaron*, but the pattern is reminiscent of *čič ʔalal*. A specimen of the species *Mischocyttarus cubensis*

(EN No. 118143) was referred to as *č'in čič ʔalal*, 'small mother's-brother's-wife's child'. In fact, only the genera *Polistes* and *Mischocyttarus* are known to construct nests of the type considered by Tenejapanecos to be typical of *čič ʔalal*, i.e., an open comb suspended by thin stalks from the undersides of leaves (see Figure 5.197d). Thus the extended range of *čič ʔalal* is equivalent to these two genera. *ʔihk'al čič ʔalal* may be synonymous with *šanab šuš* (see this complex) for some informants. Variants include *čanul čič ʔalal* and *čič ʔalal šuš*.

*mum* [UN]: Hole-nesting wasps (Vespoidea in part)

Informants could not agree as to the identity of many mounted specimens and it remains unclear on what perceptible basis, if any, these wasps are distinguished. *čanul mum* and *mum šuš* are variants. This taxon is unknown to many highland informants. Two specific subdivisions are widely recognized:

a. *yut lumil mum* 'inside-the-ground hole-nesting wasp': *Stelopolybia panamensis* (Vespidae) (see Figure 5.196k). This wasp is medium to large, slender bodied, and entirely black. The name refers to the fact that it constructs its nest (of 'horse dung') in the ground. It is thus a "paper wasp", but a hole nester (i.e., *Stelopolybia* sp.) Its sting is powerful while that of the following type is not. *ʔihk'al mum* 'black hole-nesting wasp' and *bac'il mum* 'true hole-nesting wasp' are synonymous. Most specimens of the species *Stelopolybia panamensis* (Vespidae: Polistinae; EN Nos. 118154, 118156–118158, 118237, 118238) were assigned to this form by one or another informant. The first four specimens were also classed as *šanab šuš* (see this complex).

b. *k'an mum* 'yellow potter wasp': A potter wasp (Eumenidae: *Euodynerus* sp.; EN Nos. 118170, 118171) (see Figure 5.196e). It nests in the 'deep center' (*puhul yolil*) of trees and caves. It is similar in appearance to

ʔako ʔ (see this complex). The sting is not as powerful as that of **yut lumil mum** (see preceeding taxon). When mounted specimens are identified, this category, **ʔako ʔ**, and **k'an c'utoh** are often confused.

***kitaron*** [< Sp *guitaron* 'bass guitar']: The social vespid wasp *Synoeca surinama*

This is a large, black, slender-bodied wasp whose sting is greatly feared. This reputation, in fact, extends as far as Panama (Rau 1933). I observed one nest that was attached to a vertical tree trunk 12 m above the ground, about 50 cm long by 25 cm wide and with the characteristic corrugated surface of the nests of this species (see Figure 5.197e). I was unable to collect a specimen however. The name refers to the unique 'drumming' produced by these wasps inside the nest as a means of defense (Evans and Eberhard 1970: 179–180). It is also known as **kitaron šuš**. It is restricted to the lowlands but is known to some highland informants. A large yellow wasp (*Polistes carnifex*: EN No. 118147) was considered **kps kitaron** by several informants because of its large size (see also **čič ʔalal**, this complex).

***c'ibon*** [UN]: *Epipona tatua* (Vespidae), EN Nos. 118165–118166 (see Figure 5.196m)

The typical form (for both specimens) is black, i.e., **ʔihk'al c'ibon** 'black *c'ibon*' (*Stelopolybia* sp.: EN Nos. 118163, 118164) (see Figure 5.196n). **cahal c'ibon** 'red *c'ibon*' recognized by some informants, is considered to have a more painful sting than the typical form. This type is said to build its nest higher in trees than **ʔihk'al c'ibon** 'black *c'ibon*' and to use a mixture of 'cow' and 'horse dung' to construct its nest. In contrast **ʔihk'al c'ibon** constructs a nest of pure 'horse dung' and is thus known synonymously as **ca ʔ kawáyu na šuš** 'horse-dung house wasp' or **ca ʔ kawáyu šuš** 'horse-dung wasp'. In highland areas this taxon is known as **bac'il šuš** 'true wasp' or **ʔihk'al šuš** 'black wasp', and the term **c'ibon** is unknown. The nest is described as closed and spherical (see Figure 5.197f). Thus the attribution of two

specimens of a species of *Stelopolybia* (EN Nos. 118163, 118164) here is probably a misidentification, as this genus typically constructs a nest inside a natural opening lacking an "envelope."

***šanab šuš*** 'high-backed sandal wasp': A social vespid wasp (probably *Polistes canadensis*; EN No. 118145)

A medium to large wasp, black, with a slender body. Two types of nest have been attributed to this taxon. One which I observed in **ʔošewic**, Tenejapa, was similar to that of **kitaron**, i.e., attached to a vertical tree trunk. However it lacked the corrugated exterior, was shaped as in Figure 5.198, i.e., like the high-backed sandal (**šanab**) of formal Tenejapan attire, and was smaller than that of **kitaron**. However, I was unable to obtain a specimen from this nest. The nest of this taxon pictured by JGG (see Figure 5.197g) was an open comb suspended by a stalk beneath a leaf, exactly as is that of **čič ʔalal**. Such a nest is appropriate for *Polistes canadensis*. In this latter case **šanab šuš** is probably synonymous with **ʔihk'al čič ʔalal** (see **čič ʔalal**, this complex). The situation is further confused by the fact that a few informants assigned specimens of *Stelopolybia panamensis* to this taxon (properly **yut lumil mum**, see **mum**). However, this wasp's nest is unlike either of these described above. One halictid bee, a male (EN No. 118174), was also placed here.

Synonyms include **lehčel na šuš** 'flat-house wasp' and **ʔihk'al na šuš** 'black-house wasp', the latter in contrast to **sakil na šuš** 'white-house wasp' (see next taxon).

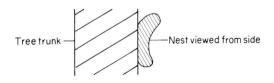

**Figure 5.198** One type of nest attributed to **šanab šuš** 'sandal wasp'.

***sakil na šuš*** 'white-house wasp': A social vespid wasp (*Parachartergus apicalis*: EN Nos. 118161, 118162, 118167) (see Figure 5.196o)

This is a medium-sized, slender-bodied, black wasp, with pale wing tips. The nest (see Figure 5.197h) is closed, roughly spherical (similar to that of *ʔus ʔakoʔ*, this complex), and said to be made of 'cow dung', thus the white color. ***saki na šuš*** is a variant. It is not known in high country.

SMZ distinguished a second taxon, ***sak šikʼ šuš*** 'white-winged wasp', from this. He assigned EN Nos. 118161 and 118162, which are slightly smaller and were collected in ***mahosikʼ***, to the former, and 118167, collected at Soyatitán, to the latter. No other informant made this distinction. EN No. 118161 was collected at the nest: a spherical, closed, pale-colored paper nest attached to the branches of a small tree about 2.5 m above the ground. One specimen of the species *Polistes apicalis* (EN No. 118155), collected at Aguacatenango, was also assigned here, since it is black with pale wing tips. However this genus characteristically constructs nests of the *čič ʔalal* type (see *čič ʔalal*, this complex). A solitary wasp (Trigonalidae: *Trigonalys* sp.: EN No. 118168) (see Figure 5.196p) was also placed here.

***kukai šuš*** 'firefly wasp': A sand-loving wasp (Sphecidae: *Larra analis*; EN No. 118150) (see Figure 5.196q)

Most informants claim that the nest of this type is unknown, which accords with its solitary character. It is medium-sized, with a clear, red-orange abdomen and is found near lowland rivers, which accords with its choice of sand as a nesting site. A second specimen (Sphecidae: *Sphex dorsalis*; EN No. 118151) (see Figure 5.196r) was considered ***kps kukai šuš***.

Two informants considered a large, yellow social vespid wasp (*Polistes carnifex*: EN No. 118147, see also *čič ʔalal* and ***kitaron***), captured near Chiapa de Corzo, to be this type, and they ascribed a paper nest to this taxon. It is possible that two distinct concepts are associated with this name.

***kʼahkʼub yat*** 'fierce stinger': Spider wasps (Hymenoptera: Pompilidae)

These wasps are common in the region at all altitudes. The sting is considered to be very painful. Thus this wasp is eaten by men who wish to be ***kʼahkʼal*** 'fierce'. Thirteen wasps and 13 chili peppers (***yaš ʔič***) are cooked and eaten in this treatment (***špošil ya škʼahkʼub winik yuʔun***). Two specific subdivisions are widely recognized:

a. ***bacʼil kʼahkʼub yat*** 'true fierce stinger': Large species (EN Nos. 118128, 118134, 118135) (see Figure 5.199a).   Some wasps of the family Scoliidae (EN Nos. 118135, 118239) (see Figure 5.199b) were considered to be ***kps kʼahkʼub yat***.

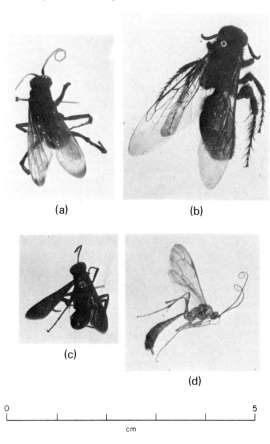

(a)                         (b)

(c)

(d)

0                                                     5

cm

**Figure 5.199**  Assorted wasps. HYMENOPTERA: (a) ***bacʼil kʼahkʼub yat*** Pompilidae: EN No. 118134; (b) not known, ***kps kʼahkʼub yat*** Scoliidae: EN No. 118239; (c) ***meba kʼahkʼub yat*** Pompilidae: EN No. 118129; (d) ***hwah mahtas*** Ichneumonidae: EN No. 118203. ("Not known" indicates that informants were unfamiliar with the specimen.)

b. *meba k'ahk'ub yat* 'orphan fierce stinger': Small species (EN Nos. 118129, 118131) (see Figure 5.199c).    Also known as *č'in k'ahk'ub yat* 'small fierce stinger'.

*k'ahk' yat* 'fire stinger' is a variant. *slab h?ihk'al* 'spirit of the black devil', and *slab nuruč'*, with the same meaning, are synonyms, though perhaps restricted by some informants to the largest species as a contrasting form. Spider wasps are considered to be marginally related to the *šuš* complex.

*hwah mahtas* [ag + tv 'sow' + 'plant sp.' (i.e., *Bidens* spp.)]: Ichneumonidae (order Hymenoptera)

This is a family of wasplike insects that parasitize wood-boring larvae by depositing their eggs into the burrows of the larvae. The name refers to this behavior, which is similar to planting with a digging stick. The following ichneumonid specimens were assigned here: EN Nos. 118202–118207, 118236 (see Figure 5.199d). A fly mimic (Diptera: Micropezidae: Taeniapterinae; EN No. 118208) was also attributed to this category. Synonyms include *hc'um mahtas*, of uncertain derivation but with the same implication as the primary name, and *yalese mahtas* [< tv 'lower it' + '*Bidens* sp.'] again descriptive of the ovipositing behavior of the Ichneumonidae. This taxon is considered intermediate between the wasp and the fly complexes. For a few informants this taxon may include some crane flies as well (Diptera: Tipulidae, but see *la lum*/fly).

## BEE COMPLEX (See Figure 5.200)

This complex includes all bees (Hymenoptera: Apoidea) and a category of flower flies (Diptera: Syrphidae; *šut*) that resemble certain bees and are commonly found feeding on pollen. This category provides a link to the fly complex, which follows. The honey (*čab*) of many kinds of bees is considered edible, though only one type of bee is commonly

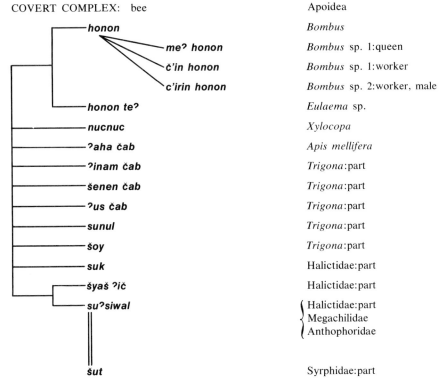

| COVERT COMPLEX: bee | Apoidea |
|---|---|
| honon | *Bombus* |
| me? honon | *Bombus* sp. 1:queen |
| č'in honon | *Bombus* sp. 1:worker |
| c'irin honon | *Bombus* sp. 2:worker, male |
| honon te? | *Eulaema* sp. |
| nucnuc | *Xylocopa* |
| ?aha čab | *Apis mellifera* |
| ?inam čab | *Trigona*:part |
| šenen čab | *Trigona*:part |
| ?us čab | *Trigona*:part |
| sunul | *Trigona*:part |
| šoy | *Trigona*:part |
| suk | Halictidae:part |
| šyaš ?ič | Halictidae:part |
| su?siwal | Halictidae:part / Megachilidae / Anthophoridae |
| šut | Syrphidae:part |

**Figure 5.200**    The bee complex.

kept (**sunul**), a stingless bee of the genus *Trigona*. Hives (**sna** 'its house') of other types may be raided for honey.

**honon** [ON]: Bumblebees, *Bombus* spp. (Apidae: Bombinae)

Several inductive subdivisions are widely recognized:

a. **me? honon** 'mother bumblebee': Bumblebee queens (*Bombus* sp. A: EN No. 118076, a queen or worker; No. 118077, a worker; No. 118083, a queen [see Figure 5.201a]). This distinction is based primarily on the large size of this type, and the correspondence is not perfect. The name implies some knowledge of the role of the queen caste. **niwak honon** 'large (pl) bumblebee' and **muk'ul honon** 'large bumblebee' are synonyms.

b. **č'in honon** 'small bumblebee': *Bombus* sp. A, workers (EN Nos. 118075, 118081, 118082) (see Figure 5.201b). The only exception is EN No. 118077, attributed to the preceding subdivision.

c. **c'irin honon** 'striped bumblebee': *Bombus* sp. B, workers (EN Nos. 118079, 118084) (see Figure 5.201c) and a male (EN No. 118090). This subtype is distinguished from the previous folk species by pattern. No queens of this species were collected.

Several other species of *Bombus* no doubt occur in the region, however it is quite likely that the two species represented by collections are the dominant ones.

**honon te?** 'bumblebee of the tree': *Eulaema* sp., (Apidae: Euglossinae; EN No. 118078) (see Figure 5.201d)

Typical bumblebees are known to nest in the ground. This genus is said to nest in trees, thus the name.

**nucnuc** [< iv 'hunt animals' redup.]: large carpenter bees, *Xylocopa* spp. (Anthophoridae)

The name refers to a behavioral trait.

According to informants, this bee follows flying objects such as other insects or even rocks thrown at the bees as a diversion. The typical form is 'black' **?ihk'al nucnuc**, however only specimens of the smaller **k'anal nucnuc** 'yellow carpenter bee' (EN Nos. 118090–118093) (see Figure 5.201e) were collected. The specimens represent at least two species. **nucnuc honon** 'carpenter bee bumblebee', and **nucnuc ?us** 'carpenter bee fly' are synonyms indicating relationships perceived to exist with bumblebees and flies, respectively. A flower fly (Diptera: Syrphidae) of the genus *Volucella* (EN No. 118458) was placed here also. It is an able mimic.

**?aha čab** 'master of honey': The honey bee, *Apis mellifera* (Apidae: Apinae; EN Nos. 118085–118087, 118089, all workers) (see Figure 5.201f)

This introduced species is not kept by Tenejapanecos, though some local Ladinos keep them in wooden hives (**sna ?aha čab**). Some informants assert that two types exist, one that stings **ti?wal ?aha čab** 'stinging honey master', **ti?wal čab** 'stinging honey', or **séra čab** [< Sp. *cera* 'wax' + 'honey'], and one that does not (**bac'il ?aha čab** 'true honey master'). This distinction may refer to that between workers (which sting) and drones (which do not) or to varieties of the species that are more or less aggressive. Included here is a queen of the genus *Melissodes* (Anthophoridae; tribe Eucerini; EN No. 118088) (see Figure 5.201g), a ground-nesting, solitary bee superficially similar to the honey bee. Also included are three flower flies (Diptera: Syrphidae: *Eristalis* sp.; EN Nos. 118450–118452), which ably mimic the bee. **?aha čab honon** 'honey master bumblebee' is synonymous, indicating a close relationship perceived with the bumblebees (see first taxon in this complex). **čanul ?aha čab** is a variant.

**?inam čab** 'wife of honey': Stingless bees, *Trigona* spp. (Apidae)

This small bee (slightly smaller than

*sunul* and *šoy*) is distinguished by its red-orange, triangular abdomen. It is not kept, but the honey is considered edible. This category is apparently very similar to the following one (*šenen čab*), as there was dis-agreement among informants as to which category was appropriate for several specimens (EN Nos. 118114, 118115, 118118, 118123, 118124) (see Figure 5.201h). Number 118105 involved no such disagreement; how-

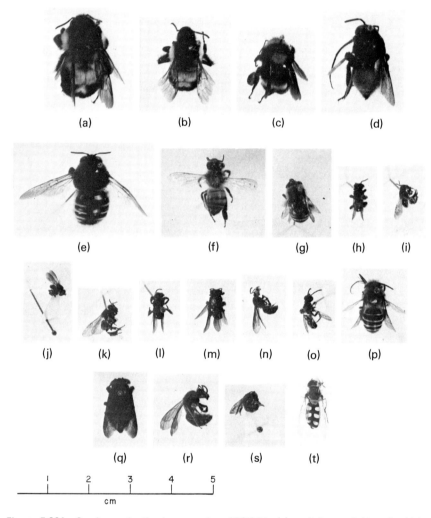

**Figure 5.201** Specimens in the bee complex. APOIDEA: (a) *meʔ honon* Apidae, Bombini, *Bombus* sp. A, queen: EN No. 118083; (b) *č'in honon* Apidae, Bombini, *Bombus* sp. A, worker: EN No. 118081; (c) *c'irin honon* Apidae, Bombini, *Bombus* sp. B, worker: EN No. 118084; (d) *honon teʔ* Apidae, Euglossinae, *Eulaema* sp.: EN No. 118078; (e) *nucnuc* Anthophoridae, Xylocopinae, *Xylocopa* sp.: EN No. 118093; (f) *ʔaha čab* Apidae, *Apis mellifera*, worker: EN No. 118085; (g) *ʔaha čab* (*sic.*) Anthophoridae, Eucerini, *Mellisodes* sp.: EN No. 118088; (h) *ʔinam čab* Apidae, *Trigona* sp.: EN No. 118115; (i) *šenen čab* Apidae, *Trigona* sp.: EN No. 118103; (j) *ʔus čab* Apidae, *Trigona* sp.: EN No. 118122; (k) *cahal sunul* Apidae, *Trigona* sp.: EN No. 118108; (l) *sunul* Apidae, *Trigona* sp.: EN No. 118110; (m) *šoy* Apidae, *Trigona* sp.: EN No. 118116; (n) *suk* Halictidae, Augochlorini, genus?: EN No. 118117; (o) *šyaš ʔič* Halictidae, Augochlorini, genus?: EN No. 118009; (p) *suʔsiwal* Anthophoridae, Anthophorinae, *Anthophora* sp.: EN No. 118094; (q) *suʔsiwal* Megachilidae, *Megachile* sp.: EN No. 118096; (r) *suʔsiwal* Halictidae, *Pseudaugochloropsis* sp.: EN No. 118097; (s) *suʔsiwal* Halictidae, *Augochloropsis* sp.: EN No. 118098; (t) *sut* Syrphidae, *Syrphus* sp. ("*Sic.*" indicates misidentifications [see text for discussion].)

ever, in the case of No. 118104 there was disagreement between *ʔinam čab* and *suʔsi-wal* (this complex). In any case, *šenen čab* and *suʔsiwal* are said to sting, while species of *Trigona*, with the exception noted under the next taxon, do not. *hʔinam čab* and *ʔancil čab* 'woman-of-honey' are variants, as is *čanul ʔinam čab*.

*šenen čab* 'mosquito honey': Possibly *Trigona tataira*, which though stingless, excretes an extremely irritating liquid as a defensive measure (Schwarz 1948)

This interpretation accords with the typical coloration of this species, i.e., a red abdomen, which characterized both this and the preceding taxon. EN No. 118103 (*Trigona* sp.) (see Figure 5.201i), collected at the nest (in a hollow at the base of a tree, with a projecting wax tube entranceway) was assigned here. There was disagreement between *šenen čab* and *ʔinam čab* for the following specimens: EN Nos. 118114, 118115, 118118, 118123, and 118124. For a few informants this taxon is known as *mukʻul šenen čab* 'large mosquito honey', in contrast with the following taxon.

*ʔus čab* 'fly honey': Tiny, stingless bees (*Trigona*: subgenus *Hypotrigona*?: EN Nos. 118121, 118122) (see Figure 5.201j)

Also known as *ʔusam čab*, *ʔusum čab*, and *čʻin šenen čab* 'small mosquito honey' (see preceding taxon). The honey is edible, though this type of bee is not kept.

*sunul* [UN]: Medium-sized, stingless bees (*Trigona spp.*)

This is the type commonly kept by Tenejapanecos. The ground nests are dug up and installed in pottery shards or hollow logs under the eaves of a house. I would estimate that no more than 10% of Tenejapan households keep bees, since I encountered them on only two occasions. It is possible that refined sugar (*sakil ʔaskal*) is replacing this traditional source. Schwarz (1948) gives a detailed summary of the role of stingless bees as a

source of sugar on the American continent. These bees provided the only source of sugar in pre-Columbian times, and techniques of apiculture were well known to both the Maya and the Aztecs. Two collections were made at the hives in Tenejapa, EN Nos. 1002358 and 1002359, the former is an example of the 'red' or 'yellow' variety, *cahal* or *kʻanal sunul*. Other specimens attributed here include EN Nos. 118102, 118106–118112 (see Figure 5.201k,l), and 118119. Disagreement existed for No. 118105 between *sunul* and *ʔinam čab*, and for No. 118113 between *sunul* and *šoy* (see following taxon). *čanul sunul* is a variant.

*šoy* [UN]: Medium-sized, tree-nesting, stingless bees (*Trigona* spp.)

These are very similar to *sunul* but nest in tree cavities rather than in the ground. They are not kept, though the honey is edible. EN No. 118116 (*Trigona* sp.) (see Figure 5.20m) was captured at the nest; No. 118113 (*Trigona* sp.) was thought to be *šoy* by one informant but *sunul* by others. *čanul šoy* is a variant.

*suk* [UN]: Sweat bees (Halictidae: Halictinae: Augochlorini: genus uncertain; EN No. 118117) (see Figure 5.201n)

This taxon is superficially very similar to the preceding one (*šoy*), but with a sting. *čanul suk* is a variant. Most species of this tribe do not resemble bees of the genus *Trigona* but by contrast are metallic blue or green. These more typical forms are treated below.

*šyaš ʔič* 'green pepper': Metallic blue or green sweat bees (Halictidae: Halictinae: Augochlorini in part)

This taxon is not widely recognized and may be included as a variety of *yašal suʔsiwal* 'blue–green digger bee' (see following taxon). EN No. 118099 (Augochlorini: genus uncertain, male) (see Figure 5.201o) and No. 118100 (Halictidae: Halictinae: *Augochloropsis* sp., male) were assigned here by some informants, though both were also referred to as **yašal su?siwal**.

**su?siwal** [UN]: A residual category of solitary bees

It may include digger bees (Anthophoridae: *Anthophora* spp., male; EN No. 118094) (see Figure 5.201p). A second example of this genus (male; EN No. 118095) was considered **kps ?aha čab** or **kps honon**. It is known to nest in the ground (**ya yak' sna ta lumilal**). Also included here is a single specimen of the leaf-cutting bees (Megachilidae: *Megachile* sp., queen; EN No. 118096) (see Figure 5.201q), distinguished as **?ihk'al su?siwal** 'black **su?siwal**', and two sweat bees (Halictidae: *Pseudaugochloropsis* sp.; EN No. 118097 [see Figure 5.201r]; and *Augochloropsis* sp., queen; EN No. 118098 [see Figure 5.201s]) known as **yašal su?siwal** 'blue–green digger bee'. **su?sewal** is a variant.

Three distinct classificatory uses of this term exist in Tenejapa. The most restricted has been described above. A second has been alluded to, i.e., the inclusion of **šyaš ?ič** as a variety of **su?siwal**. The most inclusive usage distinguishes **ti?wal su?siwal** 'stinging digger bee', equivalent to the second usage, from **k'unil su?siwal** 'soft digger bee', an assortment of beelike flies usually distinguished as **šut** (see following taxon). **šut** provides a link between the bee and the fly complexes.

**šut** [UN]: Flower and hover flies (Diptera: Syrphidae in part)

These flies are common about flowers, feeding on pollen. Many syrphid species are mimics of various species of bees and wasps, even to the point of buzzing. As discussed under the preceding taxon, they are sometimes included as a subtype of **su?siwal**, known as **k'unil su?siwal** 'soft digger bee', a reference to the fact that they do not sting. They are also considered to be related, depending on the species, to various categories of flies such as **?us**, **šenen** and **škač**.

The following specimens were clearly placed here:

Diptera: Syrphidae: *Syrphus* sp.: EN Nos. 118469, 118470 (see Figure 5.201t)

Diptera: Syrphidae: unidentified genera: EN Nos. 118462, 118464–118468

Diptera: Bibionidea: unidentified genus: EN No. 118430

Diptera: Otitidae: unidentified genus: EN No. 118482

Psocoptera: unidentified genus: EN No. 118494

A tachinid fly (Diptera: Tachinidae; EN No. 118442) was ambiguous between **šut** and **?us**. A crane fly (Diptera: Tipulidae; EN No. 118473) and an ichneumonid (Hymenoptera: Ichneumonidae; EN No. 118480) were ambiguous between **šut** and **šenen**.

FLY COMPLEX (See Figure 5.202)

All adult flies (order Diptera), with the exception of those included as **šut** (see last taxon of bee complex), are included here, as are some Braconidae (order Hymenoptera, see **yusil sac'**, see **?us**, type [g]). The relationship of larval to adult forms is explicitly recognized only in the case of **yaš ton ha** (see **ha**, type [a]). None are considered edible, and no medicinal uses are recorded. The unity of this complex is further indicated by the fact that the major categories have overlapping ranges in synonymous usages. Several flies which mimic wasps and bees are not recognized as flies, e.g., a stilt-legged fly (Micropezidae: Taeniapterinae) confused with ichneumonids, Stratiomyidae confused with the wasp **?ako?**, a syrphid fly of the genus *Eristalis* confused with the honey bee (*Apis mellifera*, see **?aha čab** bee).

**ha** [UN]: Large muscoid flies (Diptera: Calliphoridae, Tachinidae in part)

Two subtypes are widely recognized. The occasional inclusion here of the house flies (Muscidae) and flesh flies (Sarcophagidae) as a third subtype labeled either **bac'il ha** 'true

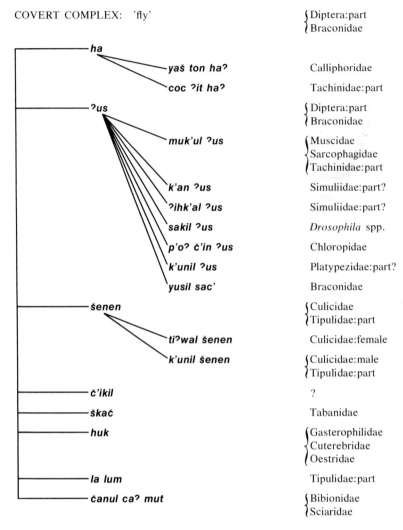

COVERT COMPLEX: 'fly'

| | |
|---|---|
| **ha** | { Diptera:part<br>{ Braconidae |
| yaš ton haʔ | Calliphoridae |
| coc ʔit haʔ | Tachinidae:part |
| **ʔus** | { Diptera:part<br>{ Braconidae |
| muk'ul ʔus | ( Muscidae<br>{ Sarcophagidae<br>( Tachinidae:part |
| k'an ʔus | Simuliidae:part? |
| ʔihk'al ʔus | Simuliidae:part? |
| sakil ʔus | *Drosophila* spp. |
| p'oʔ č'in ʔus | Chloropidae |
| k'unil ʔus | Platypezidae:part? |
| yusil sac' | Braconidae |
| **šenen** | { Culicidae<br>{ Tipulidae:part |
| tiʔwal šenen | Culicidae:female |
| k'unil šenen | { Culicidae:male<br>{ Tipulidae:part |
| **č'ikil** | ? |
| **škač** | Tabanidae |
| **huk** | ( Gasterophilidae<br>{ Cuterebridae<br>( Oestridae |
| **la lum** | Tipulidae:part |
| **čanul caʔ mut** | { Bibionidae<br>{ Sciaridae |

**Figure 5.202**    The fly complex.

fly' or **bol ha** 'stupid fly' provides a link with the following taxon, **ʔus**.

a. **yaš ton ha** ['green' + 'stone' + 'fly']: Blow flies (Calliphoridae: EN Nos. 118433–118434, 118441) (see Figure 5.203a,b). This name is relatively opaque, though the morph **yaš** clearly refers to the characteristic metallic blue or green abdomens of these flies. Also known as **yaš tun ha**.

**yal ha** 'child (female speaking) of the fly' (maggots, Diptera larvae in part, see **yal ha**) are correctly believed to transform (**ya šk'ahta**) into this type of fly. A tachinid fly

(Diptera: Tachinidae; EN No. 118435) with a metallic blue abdomen was placed here by three informants, though a fourth placed it in the following specific taxon (**coc ʔit ha**). Two syrphid flies (Diptera: Syrphidae; EN Nos. 118457, 118458, see **šut**) were placed here by several informants. Such flies mimic many other insects, e.g., carpenter bees (see **nucnuc** /bee) and honey bees (see **ʔaha čab**/bee).

b. **coc ʔit ha** 'hairy-abdomened fly': Tachinid flies (Diptera: Tachinidae; especially EN Nos. 118440, 118447) (see Figure 5.203c,d). The name refers to the long bristles covering the

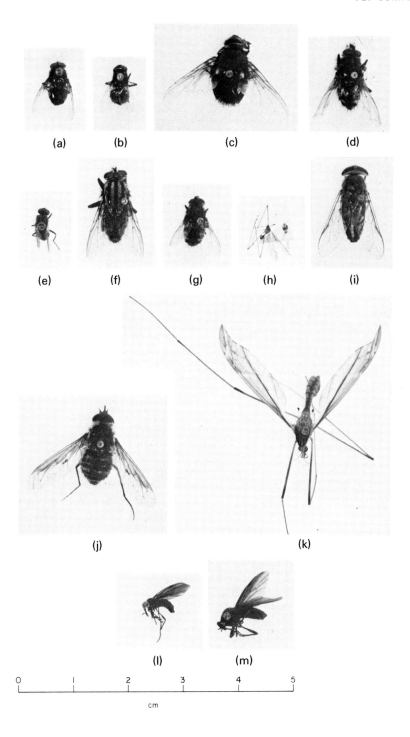

**Figure 5.203** Specimens in the fly complex. DIPTERA: (a) *yaš ton ha* Calliphoridae, genus No. 1; (b) *yaš ton ha* Calliphoridae, genus No. 2; (c) *coc ʔit ha* Tachinidae; (d) *coc ʔit ha* Tachinidae; (e) *mukʼul ʔus* Muscidae; (f) *mukʼul ʔus* Sarcophagidae; (g) *mukʼul ʔus* Tachinidae; (h) *kʼunil šenen* Tipulidae; (i) *škač* Tabanidae; (j) *škač* Bombyliidae; (k) *la lum* Tipulidae; (l) *čanul caʔ mut* Bibionidae; (m) *čanul caʔ mut* Bibionidae.

abdomens of most such flies. This type may be included as a kind of *ʔus* (see following taxon), then known as *coc ʔit ʔus. ton ha* 'stone fly' is another synonym. Most tachinid specimens were not distinguished from the muscid flies, but were treated simply as *muk'ul ʔus* 'large fly' (e.g., EN Nos. 118442–118444, 118446). EN Nos. 118432, 118436, and 118445 (Diptera: Tachinidae) were classed alternately as *coc ʔit ha* or *muk'ulʔus*.

*ʔus* [UN]: A residual category of small and medium-sized flies (Diptera in part)

Numerous subdivisions are recognized. However, the number of distinct categories recognized is quite variable, and considerable confusion is generated by varied uses of the same terms. The following appear to deserve specific status:

a. *muk'ul ʔus* 'large fly': the house fly (Muscidae: *Musca domestica*; EN No. 118431) (see Figure 5.203e), other muscid flies (EN Nos. 118437–118438), a flesh fly (Sarcophagidae; EN No. 118439) (see Figure 5.203f), and a tachinid fly (see Figure 5.203g). Synonyms include *niwak ʔus* 'large (pl) fly' and *čitam ʔus* 'pig fly' as well as *bac'il ha* 'true fly' and *bol ha* 'stupid fly'. These two latter synonyms illustrate an alternate classification of this type as a kind of *ha*. Most parasitic tachinid flies (Tachinidae) were placed here by at least some informants (EN Nos. 118442–118444, 118446) (see Figure 5.203h), other tachinid flies were either included here or treated as *coc ʔit ha* 'hairy-abdomened fly' (see preceding taxon).

b. *k'an ʔus* 'yellow fly': The single specimen attributed to this taxon is a leaf-miner fly (Agromyzidae; EN No. 118484). This is best treated as a misidentification, since leaf-miner flies do not bite, while *k'an ʔus* is said to be a vicious biter (*ya šti ʔwan bayel*). The proper referent is probably a type of black fly (Simuliidae). These may resemble the specimen in question in general form and size.

*k'an ʔus* is not common in Tenejapa, as it is confined to lowland regions. It is also known as *k'anal ʔus* and *k'anal šenen* 'yellow mosquito'.

c. *ʔihk'al ʔus* 'black fly': Perhaps also properly referring to the Simuliidae in part. However the single specimen alleged to be this type of biting fly (see [b]) is a milichiid fly (Milichiidae; EN No. 118490). These may be attracted to people's faces, but they do not bite. Also known as *ʔihk'al šenen* 'black mosquito', stressing the fact that it bites.

d. *sakil ʔus* 'white fly': A pomace fly (Drosophilidae: *Drosophila* sp.; EN No. 1002309). This type is not known to bite. It may also be known as *č'in ʔus* 'small fly' (but see [e]).

e. *p'o ʔ čin ʔus* 'swarming small fly': Frit flies (Chloropidae; EN Nos. 118485–118487, 118492). These flies swarm about open wounds. Some informants consider this and *sakil ʔus* (see [d]) to be synonymous. Also known as *č'in ʔus* 'small fly' or *č'uhč'ul ʔus* 'small (pl) fly'.

f. *k'unil ʔus* 'soft fly': Perhaps some flat-footed flies (Platypezidae in part) as "adults of some species are attracted to smoke [Borror and White 1970:280]." No specimens were collected, but verbal descriptions—this tiny, nonbiting fly is attracted by the smoke created when new fields are cleared by burning—suggest this type of fly. Also known as *tan ʔus* 'ash fly' and *meba ʔus* 'orphan fly'. Some informants assert that these flies are generated by the smoke.

g. *yusil sac'* 'fly of the hawk-moth larva': No specimens were collected, but this 'fly' is described as parasitic on the caterpillar known as *sac'* (Lepidoptera: Sphingidae, larvae, see caterpillar complex). This is characteristic of some braconids (Hymenoptera: Braconidae), most of which are appropriately small. A few informants consider this term synonymous with *č'ikil* (this complex).

Some informants describe a type of fly called *kašlan ?us* 'Ladino fly', a small, swarming fly alleged to smell like soap, thus the name. *yusil kawáyu* 'fly of the horse' may be synonymous. No examples were encountered.

*šenen* [UN]: Mosquitoes (Diptera: Culicidae) in particular

However, the name may be extended to include various related families of small, long-legged flies or, alternatively, various small biting flies (*k'an ?us*, see *?us*[b], *?ihk'al ?us*, see *?us*[c], and *č'ikil*, see next taxon). Thus the most salient features of the core referent, long legs and blood-sucking habits, may be extended to nonbiting, long-legged flies, on the one hand, and biting, short-legged flies on the other. Two types are widely recognized.

a. *ti?wal šenen* 'biting mosquito': Female mosquitoes (Culicidae in part? EH No. 109). Also known by the Spanish loans *sankúro* [< Sp *zancudo* 'mosquito'] or *sánkre* [< Sp *sangre* 'blood'].

b. *k'unil šenen* 'soft mosquito': Small crane flies (Tipulidae in part; EN Nos. 118475–118477) and, most likely, male mosquitoes (Culicidae in part) (see Figure 5.203i). One female mosquito—the sex that "bites"—was erroneously placed here.

A further extension of *šenen* is implied by the use of the term *muk'ul šenen* for large crane flies (see *la lum*, this complex) and *škač šenen* for horse flies (see *škač*, this complex). A long-legged fly (Dolichopodidae; EN No. 118488) was called *yašal šenen* 'green mosquito' but was considered to be unfamiliar.

*č'ikil* [UN] The single alleged specimen of this taxon is a long-legged fly (Dolichopodidae; EN No. 118481), not known to bite

However, *č'ikil* is considered among the worst of biters. Thus the proper referent remains unknown. Synonyms include *?untik* [UN], *?untik šenen*, and *č'ikil ?us*.

*škač* [UN]: Horse flies (Diptera: Tabanidae: two species; EN Nos. 118453, 118454) (see Figure 5.203j)

These flies are described as pests of cattle, and the specimens cited were collected from the leg of a cow. Some bee flies (Diptera: Bombyliidae; EN Nos. 118455, 118456, 118460, 118461) (See Figure 5.203k) were misidentified as *škač*, due to superficial resemblances, as was a flower fly (Syrphidae: EN No. 118459). Synonyms include *škač šenen* and *škač ?us*, which indicate the relationships perceived among these categories. One robber fly (Diptera: Asilidae; EN No. 118463) was referred to as *č'in škač* 'small horse fly' by one informant.

*huk* [UN] Adult bot flies (Diptera: Gasterophilidae, Cuterebridae, and Oestridae)

These parasitic flies lay their eggs on the bodies of various hosts, mammals for the most part. The larvae develop in the intestines (Gasterophilidae), but, more appropriate in terms of the defining attributes of this taxon, they may also develop just beneath the skin of the host animal (Cuterebridae, Oestridae). The adult fly was described as similar to a louse fly (Diptera: Hippoboscidae; EN No. 118489) collected from a dead bird. The larvae are widely known as *hukulub* (see parasite complex) and are reported to develop beneath the skin of *t'ul* 'rabbits' and *hse? te?* 'wood rats' (these must be the Cuterebridae) or of cattle (the Oestridae). The lack of familiarity with the present taxon, i.e., the adult flies, is understandable, since adults are rarely encountered (cf. Borror and White 1970:304). No specimens were collected.

*la lum* [< tv 'copulate' + 'earth']: Large crane flies (Diptera: Tipulidae in part; EN Nos. 118471–118474) (see Figure 5.203e)

These large, long-legged flies are not well known, despite the fact that they are relatively common both in houses and out-side. Many informants appeared to use des-criptive terminology coined on the spot to name them. Synonyms include *češ k'ab čan* 'long-legged critter', *češ k'ab ʔus* 'long-legged fly', *muk'ul šenen* 'large mosquito', and *čanul la lum*. The primary name is descriptive of the females laying eggs. Some informants class these flies as *hwah mahtas* (Hymenoptera: Ichneumonidae).

*čanul caʔ mut* 'critter of chicken feces': March flies (Diptera: Bibionidae; EN Nos. 118423, 118424, 118427) (see Figure 5.203l,m)

These black-winged flies are abundant in open areas throughout Tenejapa during the rainy season. Most informants recognize this category, but it is rare to find more than two who agree on the proper name. Synonyms include *yusil caʔ mut* 'fly of chicken feces', *hoh mut* (an extension from the name for the Great-tailed Grackle, *Cassidix mexicanus*, see *hoh mut*/bird, blackbird), *hoh ʔus* 'raven fly' and *ʔihk'al čan* 'black critter'. The last three names refer to the color of this fly. Also included here are dark-winged fungus gnats (Diptera: Sciaridae; EN Nos. 118428, 118429), which mimic march flies. This taxon is seen to be associated with *supul* 'mothlet', providing a link with the following complex.

## BUTTERFLY COMPLEX
(See Figure 5.204)

All adult Lepidoptera are included here. The larval forms are assigned to a wide variety of named groups, and relationships of metamorphosis are only sporadically re-cognized. The fact that considerably finer detail is applied to the classification of larvae than to the adults is an example of the effect of cultural relevance. Adult Lepidoptera, in general, are neither pests nor directly utilized for food or medicine. The larvae, however, often consume growing crops, sting power-fully, and a few types are eaten.

The distinction drawn between *pehpen* and *supul* does not correspond to the folk English distinction between butterflies and moths. Though this distinction seems ob-vious and salient to us, it is totally ignored in the Tenejapan system. *supul* are tiny moths, generally white, tan, or dark grey, with 'soft wings' (*k'unil šik*) that are folded horizontally at rest but not spread. Other cues may be important as well. In any case the distinction is roughly comparable to the scientific distinction between Macrolepidop-tera and Microlepidoptera, the two divisions of the frenate Lepidoptera (suborder Fre-natae; the Jugatae are few and relatively rare), as demonstrated in Table 5.4. In short, there is a very high probability that a Micro-

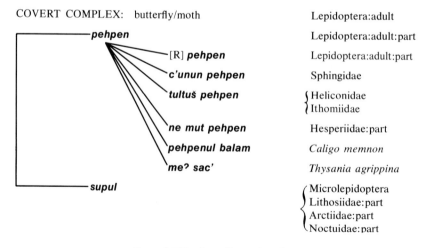

**Figure 5.204**   Butterflies and moths.

lepidoptera will be called **supul**, and a fairly high probability that a Macrolepidoptera will be **pehpen**. However, since Microlepidoptera are relatively scarce, it is impossible to predict the scientific affiliation of a random specimen of **supul**.

**Table 5.4**
NAMING PATTERNS OF ADULT LEPIDOPTERA

|  | Microlepidoptera | Macrolepidoptera | Total |
|---|---|---|---|
| *pehpen* | 0 | 40 | 40 |
| *pehpen* or |  |  |  |
| *supul* | 1 | 10 | 11 |
| *supul* | 6 | 6 | 12 |
| Totals | 7 | 56 | 63 |

**pehpen** [UN]: Macrolepidoptera

Several thousand species belonging to more than two dozen families may be included here (R. Wind personal communication). The size range varies from the blues (Lycaenidae in part), with wing spans under 25 mm, to the giant moth, *Thysania agrippina* (Noctuidae: EH No. 787), which has as large a wing span as any lepidopteran in the world (20 cm). Color, pattern, shape, and behavior are also extremely variable. The nomenclatural system is confused, since this extreme heterogeneity is recognized by a plethora of varietal labels. Most informants distinguish in addition up to half-a-dozen specific subdivisions from the residual.

a. [R] **pehpen**: The unnamed residual to which color and pattern terminology is applied.

The following attributives are quite literally applied:

Size:  **č'in pehpen** 'small butterfly'
       **muk'ul pehpen** 'large butterfly'
       **mamal pehpen** 'grandfather butterfly', implying extra large size
       **tutin pehpen** 'baby butterfly', implying small size

Color:  **cahal pehpen** 'red butterfly'
        **ʔihk'al pehpen** 'black butterfly'
        **k'anal pehpen** 'yellow butterfly',

especially the sulphurs (Pieridae: *Colias, Phoebis, Eurema*)
**sakil pehpen** 'white butterfly', especially the whites (Pieridae: *Pieris, Synchloe*)
**yašal pehpen** 'grey/blue/green butterfly', especially the morphos (Morphidae, no specimens)

Patterns:  **bašil pehpen** 'mottled butterfly'
           **c'ibal pehpen** 'striped butterfly'
           **c'ihtil pehpen** 'streaked butterfly'
           **c'irin pehpen** 'streaked butterfly'
           **lučul pehpen** [ < 'to weave' + 'butterfly'], referring to a bold red, black, and white pattern, typical of Tenejapan weaving (K. Branstetter personal communication), Papilionidae: *Parides iphidamas*
           **pínto pehpen** [ < Sp *pinto* 'blotched' + 'butterfly']
           **p'uhtul pehpen** 'barred? butterfly'
           **šik pehpen** 'grizzled butterfly'

Texture:  **cocʔit pehpen** 'hairy-abdomened butterfly'
          **k'unil pehpen** 'soft butterfly'
          **tunim pehpen** 'cotton butterfly'

Two or more attributives may be applied in sequence. The typical result is that two informants rarely apply the same "name" to the same specimen.

The use of an animal term as attributive is also common, though this usage tends to be more consistently applied to inductive subdivisions (see **c'unun pehpen, tultuš pehpen**). The following combinations appear to be idiosyncratic:

**ʔakoʔ pehpen** 'wasp butterfly' for EN No. 118360 (Noctuidae).

**čič ʔalal pehpen** 'wasp butterfly' for EN No. 118344 (Papilionidae: *Papilio polyxenes*).

**čikitin pehpen** 'cicada butterfly' for EN No. 118383 (Arctiidae).

*kukai pehpen* 'firefly butterfly' for EN No. 118372 (Ctenuchidae).

*k'ahk'ub yat pehpen* 'spider wasp butterfly' for EN No. 118346 (Papilionidae: *Parides iphidamas*).

*spehpenul ca? mut* 'butterfly of bird feces' for EN no. 118359 (Ctenuchidae), the name patterned on *čanul ca? mut* (see the fly complex).

*šanič pehpen* 'ant butterfly' for EN No. 118372 (Ctenuchidae).

*šenen pehpen* 'mosquito butterfly' for EN No. 118344 (Papilionidae: *Papilio polyxenes*).

*šoč' pehpen* 'Barn Owl butterfly' for EN No. 118340 (Nymphalidae: *Hamadryas feronia*).

*šuš pehpen* 'wasp butterfly' for EN No. 118338 (Nymphalidae: *Prepona laertes*).

*?us pehpen* 'fly butterfly' for several small butterflies and moths.

*yaš ton ha pehpen* 'blow fly butterfly' for EN No. 118358 (Ctenuchidae).

The principle in all cases is the same. The attributive refers to a characteristic shared by the butterfly specimen and the associated animal, especially when the shared feature is not readily named by single adjectival forms. In most of the above cases, however, more typical attributives (as listed previously) were used alternatively by other informants for the same specimens. It is clear that this residual is *no less* heterogeneous than the superordinate *pehpen*.

The following specimens were included in this residual category and named varietally:

Butterflies (superfamily Papilionoidea):

Swallowtails: Papilionidae (*Papilio polyxenes*: EN No. 118344; *Parides iphidamas*: EN No. 118346 [see Figure 5.205a]) Pieridae: whites (*Pieris* sp.: EN No. 118321); sulphurs (*Colias* sp.: EN No. 118322 [see Figure 5.205b]; *Eurema lisa*: EN No. 118324); other pierids (*Synchloe callidice*: EN No. 118323; *Phoebis eubule*: EN No. 118326)

Lycaenidae: blues (Plebiinae: EN No. 118327); hairstreaks (Theclinae: EN No. 118328) (see Figure 5.205c)
Owl butterflies (Brassolidae: *Caligo memnon*, see *pehpenul balam*)
Nymphalidae:
  Mourning cloak (*Nymphalis antiopia*: EN No. 118336)
  Lady (*Vanessa carye*.: EN No. 118331)
  Gulf fritillary (*Dione vanillae*: EN No. 118332)
  Sister (*Anartia fatima*: EN No. 118333)
  Checkerspot (*Euphydryas* sp.: EN No. 118334)
  Buckeye (*Junonia lavinia*: EN No. 118335)
  Other nymphalids: EN Nos. 118338–118340, 118345
Satyridae: satyrs (*Taygetis* sp.: EN No. 118347)
Heliconidae (see *tultuš pehpen*)
Danaidae: monarch (*Danaus plexippus*: EN No. 118348
Skippers (Hesperiidae: EN Nos. 118329, 118353 [see Figure 5.205d]; see also *ne mut pehpen*)

Marco-moths:

Sphinx moths (Sphingidae: see *c'unun pehpen*)

---

**Figure 5.205** Specimens in the butterfly–moth complex. LEPIDOPTERA: (a) e.g., *cahal šik' pehpen* or *?ihk'al c'irin pehpen* Papilionidae, cf. *Parides iphidamas*: EN No. 118346; (b) *k'anal pehpen* Pieridae, cf. *Colias philodice*: EN No. 118322; (c) e.g., *č'in yašal pehpen* Lycaenidae: EN No. 118328; (d) *č'in pehpen* or *muk'ul supul* Hesperiidae: EN No. 118353; (e) e.g., *cahal pehpen* or *coc ?it pehpen* Saturniidae: EN No. 118391; (f) e.g., *?ihk'al pehpen* or *spehpenul ca? mut* Ctenuchidae: EN No. 118359; (g) *sakil supul* Arctiidae: EN No. 118376; (h) e.g., *čikitin pehpen* or *muk'ul supul* Arctiidae: EN No. 118383; (i) *c'unun pehpen* Sphingidae: EN No. 118357; (j) *tultuš pehpen* Heliconidae, cf. *Heliconias ismenius*: EN No. 118341; (k) *ne mut pehpen* Hesperiidae, cf. *Polythrix alcitron*: EN No. 118350; (l) *pehpenul balam* Brassolidae, *Caligo memnon*: EN No. 118337; (m) *me? sac'* (*pehpen*) Noctuidae, *Thysania agrippina*: EH No. 787; (n) *supul* Pyralidae: EN No. 118377; (o) *supul* Pyralidae: EN No. 118388; (p) *k'anal supul* Lithosiidae: EN No. 118368; (q) *pehpen* or *supul* Hesperiidae: EN No. 118352. ("E.g." indicates that the Tzeltal terms cited are *examples* of variable nomenclatural responses, not stable "names.")

(a)

(b)

(c)

(d)

(e)

(f)

(g)

(h)

(i)

(j)

(k)

(l)

(n)

(o)

(p)

(q)

(m)

0       5
cm

Giant silkworm moths (Saturniidae: EN Nos. 118389–118392) (see Figure 5.205e)
Ctenuchidae: EN Nos. 118358, 118359, 118366, 118369, 118372 (see Figure 5.205f)
Tiger moths (Arctiidae: *Utethesia*: EN No. 118361, see also *supul*)
Other arctiids: EN Nos. 118362, 118367, 118376, 118378, 118379, 118381–118383, 118386, 118387 (see Figure 5.205g, h) (see also *supul*)
Lithosiidae (see *supul*)
Noctuidae: *Thysania agrippina* (see *me? sac'*/caterpillar)
Other noctuids: EN Nos. 118360, 118364, 118380, 118394 (see also *supul*)
Pericopidae: EN No. 118393

Microlepidoptera:
Pyralidae (see *supul*)
Other microlepidoptera (see *supul*)

b. *c'unun pehpen* 'hummingbird butterfly': Sphinx moths (Sphingidae in part: EN No. 118357) (see Figure 5.205i). The specimen is a day-flying species and appeared to be a hummingbird when first noted feeding at flowers. Thus the name is appropriate in a complex way. *honon pehpen* 'bumblebee butterfly' is probably synonymous. Both terms were also applied by a few informants to a ctenuchid moth (EN No. 118358) closely resembling the sphinx moths.

c. *tultuš pehpen* 'dragonfly butterfly': Heliconians (Heliconidae: *Heliconius ismenius*; EN No. 118341 (see Figure 5.205j); unidentified genus, EN No. 118342; and the similar ithomiids (Ithomiidae: *Ithomia patilla*; EN No. 118330). This type is unknown in the highlands. *hayal pehpen* 'thin butterfly' is a descriptive synonym.

d. *ne mut pehpen* 'bird-tail butterfly': Tailed skippers, *Polythri̧x* spp., cf. *P. alcifron* (Hesperiidae: EN Nos. 118349–118351) (see Figure 5.205k). This term is never applied to swallowtails (Papilionidae), which are treated

as residual 'butterflies' by the Tzeltal. Synonyms include *tut sne pehpen* 'little tail butterfly' and *tešereš ne pehpen* 'scissor-tail butterfly'.

e. *pehpenul balam* 'butterfly of the jaguar': Owl butterflies (Brassolidae: *Caligo memnon*, EN No. 118337) (see Figure 5.205l). Also known as *balamil pehpen* and *labil pehpen* 'animal spirit butterfly'. This type is distinguished by only a few informants but is treated here since it is a large conspicuous type, though restricted to lower elevations. Informants unfamiliar with this type may refer to it as *mamal pehpen* 'grandfather butterfly' or *muk'ul bašil pehpen* 'large mottled butterfly' or by another such descriptive phrase.

f. *me? sac'* 'mother of the sphinx moth larva': *Thysania agrippina* (Noctuidae: EH No. 787) (see Figure 5.205m), one of the largest moths known. It is apparently rather common at all elevations. The association with *sac'* (see the caterpillar complex) is inaccurate in detail, though it demonstrates that Tenejapanecos are aware of some connection between larval and adult Lepidoptera. Noctuid larvae are wood borers and are known as *bac'il čanul te?* (see *čanul te?*). These may in fact be the larva of this moth. *sac'* is one of the largest larvae and that is most likely the basis for the misassociation. *me? sac' pehpen* and *pehpenul sac'* 'butterfly of the sphinx moth larva' are variants. *yašib senyóra* 'Lady's umbrella', *yašib senyóra pehpen*, and *paráwa pehpen* [< Sp *paraguas* 'umbrella' + 'butterfly'] all refer to the large wings of this species.

One informant (AKČ') classified several butterflies on the basis of their presumed relationship to various categories of larvae as follows: *cuhkum pehpen* 'wooly-bear butterfly', EN No. 118389, which is of the Saturniidae and thus inappropriately named (see *cuhkum*/caterpillar)—most such larvae are of the Arctiidae; *wah čan pehpen* 'corndough critter' (see *wah čan*/caterpillar: EN

No. 118321, Pieridae *Pieris* sp.), which may be appropriate; *čup pehpen* (see *čup*/caterpillar: EN No. 118390, Saturniidae), which may also be appropriate.

#### *supul* [UN]: Microlepidoptera

As described under the complex heading, this distinction is not perfect (see Table 5.4). Specimens unambiguously included are as follows:

Microlepidoptera:
> Pyralidae: EN Nos. 118363, 118373, 118375, 118377, 118388 (see Figure 5.205n, o) (EN No. 118385 of this family was ambiguous.)
> Other Microlepidoptera: EN No. 118371

Macrolepidoptera:
> Lithosiidae: EN Nos. 118368, 118374 (see Figure 5.205p)
> Arctiidae: EN Nos. 118376, 118378, 118382
> Noctuidae: EN No. 118364

The Macrolepidoptera so classified are all small and dull colored. Specimens classified as *supul* by some but not all informants include:

Microlepidoptera:
> Pyralidae: EN No. 118385

Macrolepidoptera:
> Lycaenidae, Plebeinae: EN No. 118327
> Hesperiidae: EN Nos. 118352, 118353, 118356 (see Figure 5.205q)
> Ctenuchidae: EN No. 118372
> Noctuidae: EN Nos. 118360, 118380
> Arctiidae, *Utethesia*: EN No. 118361
> Other genera: EN Nos. 118367, 118383

According to SMZ, among the definitive criteria of this taxon, as opposed to *pehpen*, are small size (wing spread less than 25 mm), dull coloration, and 'soft' or hair-fringed wings that are folded back and horizontally (not spread) at rest. Though Microlepidoptera is a valid scientific category, no obvious criterial features exist for distinguishing this taxon from the Macrolepidoptera. Thus it is not surprising that the correspondence of *supul* is not perfect.

Distinctions within this taxon are varietal: e.g., *ʔihk'al supul* 'black mothlet', *k'anal supul* 'yellow mothlet', *sakil supul* 'white mothlet', and *c'irin supul* 'streaked mothlet' have been recorded.

#### *tultuš* [UN]: Dragonflies and damselflies (INSECTA: Odonata) (see Figure 5.206)

This diverse group is dealt with in much the same way as the adult Lepidoptera, i.e., a few distinctive types are isolated, while varietal distinctions are recognized within the unnamed residual. Specimens representing 7 of the 11 North American families were collected. In addition, a pelecinid (Hymenoptera: Pelicinidae; EN No. 118153) collected in *mahosik'*, Tenejapa, was considered *kps tultuš*. Dragonflies are not eaten, nor are medicinal uses recorded. This may explain the relative lack of detailed distinctions recognized here. Larvae (see *bac'ul ha'*, *šk'ohowil čan*/water bug) are not recognized as such.

a. [R] *tultuš*: A residual category of 'typical' dragonflies. Attributives are applied quite literally in naming members of this category, as below:

*č'in tultuš* 'small dragonfly' (see also *meba tultuš*): EN Nos. 118410, 118413, 118415, 118418, 118420.

*muk'ul tultuš* 'large dragonfly': EN No. 118421 (see Figure 5.207a).

*cahal tultuš* 'red dragonfly': EN Nos. 118412, 118414, 118416 (see Figure 5.207b).

*ʔihk'al tultuš* 'black dragonfly': EN Nos. 118411, 118414, 118421.

*k'anal tultuš* 'yellow dragonfly': EN No. 118416 (see Figure 5.207c).

*muk'ul k'anal tultuš* 'large yellow dragonfly'; (see also *nen tultuš* below): EN No. 118419.

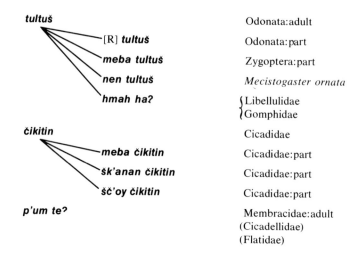

| | |
|---|---|
| ***tultuš*** | Odonata:adult |
| [R] ***tultuš*** | Odonata:part |
| ***meba tultuš*** | Zygoptera:part |
| ***nen tultuš*** | *Mecistogaster ornata* |
| ***hmah ha?*** | { Libellulidae<br>{ Gomphidae |
| ***čikitin*** | Cicadidae |
| ***meba čikitin*** | Cicadidae:part |
| ***šk'anan čikitin*** | Cicadidae:part |
| ***šč'oy čikitin*** | Cicadidae:part |
| ***p'um te?*** | Membracidae:adult<br>(Cicadellidae)<br>(Flatidae) |

**Figure 5.206**    Dragonflies and assorted Homopterans.

*yašal tultuš* 'green–blue dragonfly': EN Nos. 118410, 118411, 118415 (see Figure 5.207 d).

*c'ibal tultuš* 'striped dragonfly' (see also *cahal tultuš*, above): EN No. 118414.

Little agreement is evident in this descriptive naming, as informants are free to emphasize either size, pattern or, within limits, a variety of colors—all of which are descriptively appropriate.

The residual is quite diverse and may include any odonata specimen, depending on informants.

b. *meba tultuš* 'orphan dragonfly': Most damselflies (suborder Zygoptera in part). Four of five narrow-winged damselflies (Coenagrionidae) were so classified (EN Nos. 118410, 118413, 118418, 118420) (see Figure 5.207 e). The other was considered 'typical' (EN No. 118411). A spread-winged damselfly (Lestidae: EN No. 118417) (see Figure 5.207 f) was placed here by all informants. Most informants considered the relatively large ruby-spot (Calopterygidae: *Hetaerina* sp.; EN No. 118414) to be 'typical' (see [a]). One dragonfly specimen (Anisoptera: Gomphidae: EN No. 118415) was also placed here by several informants. *č'in tultuš* 'little dragonfly' and *k'unil tultuš* 'soft dragonfly' are synonymous.

c. *nen tultuš* 'mirror dragonfly': *Mecistogaster ornata* of the tropical family Pseudostigmatidae (EN No. 118419) (see Figure 5.207 g). These forest damselflies with extremely long abdomens are rare in lowland Tenejapa. The name refers to the wing-tip pattern, which flashes like a mirror in the sunlight. Synonyms include *hkil te? tultuš* 'wood-carrier dragonfly', which refers to the long slender abdomen as does *nahtil tultuš* 'long dragonfly'.

d. *hmah ha?* 'water-hitter'. The name refers to the behavioral trait of depositing eggs by striking the water in flight. This is characteristic of all female skimmers (Anisoptera: Libellulidae) and clubtails (Anisoptera: (Gomphidae). Thus the assignment by some

**Figure 5.207** The dragonflies. ODONATA: (a) *hmah ha?* or *muk'ul tultuš* Anisoptera, Aeshnidae: EN No. 118421; (b) e.g., *cahal tultuš* or *c'ibal tultuš* Zygoptera, Calopterygidae, *Hetaerina* sp.: EN No. 118414; (c) e.g., *k'anal tultuš* Anisoptera, Libellulidae: EN No. 118416; (d) e.g., *yašal tultuš* Anisoptera, Gomphidae: EN No. 118415; (e) *meba tultuš* Zygoptera, Coenagrionidae: EN No. 118420; (f) *meba tultuš* Zygoptera, Lestidae: EN No. 118417; (g) *nen tultuš* Zygoptera, Pseudostigmatidae, *Mecistogaster ornata*: EN No. 118419. ("E.g." indicates that the Tzeltal terms cited are *examples* of variable nomenclatural responses, not stable "names.")

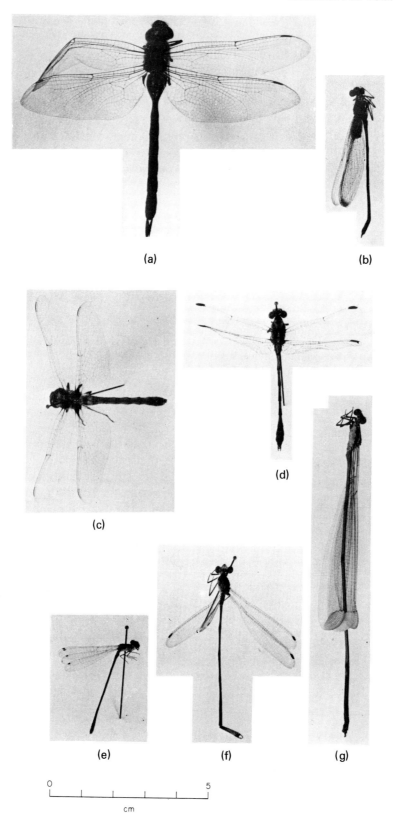

(a)

(b)

(c)

(d)

(e)

(f)

(g)

0       5

cm

informants of a clubtail (EN No. 118415, see also *meba tultuš*, above) and two skimmers (EN Nos. 118412, 118416) to this taxon is descriptively appropriate. However, some informants attributed this name as well to a darner (Anisoptera: Aeshnidae; EN No. 118421) and even to a damselfly (Zygoptera: Calopterygidae; EN No. 118414). Though the behavioral trait noted is taxonomically significant, most informants identify specimens on the basis of size, the largest odonata being assigned here. Thus identification procedures are not in accord with classificatory principles.

*mah haʔ*, *mah haʔ tultuš* are variants. Informants who do not recognize the existence of this taxon describe these specimens as deductive subtypes of *tultuš* modified by reference to size or color. *tultuš* is not considered to have close associates.

*čikitin* [ON]: Cicadas (Homoptera: Cicadidae)

Baked cicadas are fed to children who talk too much in order to cure them of this trait (*špošil lom k'opoh ʔalal*). This use is sympathetic, the insect and the child both making loud and incessant noise. Cicadas are not known to have close relatives. Three specific subdivisions are widely recognized:

a. *meba čikitin* 'orphan cicada': Small species (EN No. 118399) (see Figure 5.208a). This type calls year round at lower elevations. *bac'il čikitin* 'true cicada' is synonymous.

b. *šk'anan čikitin* [ON + 'cicada']: A larger type of cicada.  It calls during the dry season (March).

c. *šč'oy čikitin* [ON + 'cicada']: Another large type of cicada.  It calls during the dry season. *šč'oš čikitin* is synonymous.

*p'um teʔ* 'tree chewer': Treehoppers in partic-

ular (Homoptera: Membracidae; EN Nos. 118404, 118406, 1002356) (see Figure 5.208b)

Leafhoppers (Homoptera: Cicadellidae) were considered to be *kps p'um teʔ* (EN No. 118400) or were descriptively named (EN Nos. 118402, 118403, 118405). A planthopper (Homoptera: Flatidae; EN No. 118401) was considered *kps p'um teʔ* by one informant, *p'um teʔul may* 'tree-chewer of tobacco' by another. Variants include *p'umul teʔ* and *šp'um teʔ*.

Two other categories of the Homoptera are recognized in Tenejapa but are treated separately, mealy bugs (see *ʔosol* [c]/parasite) and *sipul tuh kulum č'iš* (parasite complex).

## GRASSHOPPER COMPLEX
(See Figure 5.209)

This complex corresponds closely to the order Orthoptera, excluding only the cockroaches (Blattidae), which are more closely associated with the earwigs (order Dermaptera) and the parasite complex. Most of the included categories are clearly defined and scientifically relevant; however, *p'ilič* and the residual subdivision of *čil* are 'dumping grounds' for a variety of immature and smaller forms. The detail applied to the classification of orthopterans may be explained in terms of the cultural significance of these insects. Many are considered edible, and a few are pestiferous. Wingless nymphal stages of several taxa are recognized as such. Alternatively, they may be placed in the residual categories mentioned earlier.

*p'ilič* [UN]: Small (typically less than 25 mm long) short-horned grasshoppers (Acrididae in part)

This residual category is apparently recognized on the basis of small size in conjunction with a 'family resemblance' shared by *šk'ah* (this complex) and *k'ulub* (this complex). Medium-sized specimens of this family create considerable disagreement between the alternative classifications as *muk'ul p'ilič* 'large residual grasshopper', *č'in šk'ah* 'small grasshopper', or *č'in k'ulub* 'small locust'. Varietal distinctions are indicated as follows:

*yašal p'ilič* 'green residual grasshopper'.

*k'anal p'ilič* 'yellow residual grasshopper'.

*muk'ul p'ilič* 'large residual grasshopper'.

*č'in p'ilič* 'small residual grasshopper'.

Wingless forms (often indicative of immaturity) may be known as *ʔunin p'ilič* 'baby residual grasshopper' or *t'anpat p'ilič* 'naked-backed residual grasshopper'.

The following specimens of the Acrididae were considered to be *p'ilič* by a majority of informants:

Acrididae sp., immature: EN Nos. 118291–118292.

Acridinae: EN Nos. 118278, 118279 (see Figure 5.210a).

Cyrtacanthacridinae: EN Nos. 118271, 118277, 118280.

Oedipodinae: EN Nos. 118270, 118272, 118274–118276, 118290 (see Figure 5.210b, c).

Pyrgomorphinae: *Spenarium* sp. 2: EN Nos. 118265–118266.

The latter two specimens were thought to be quite strange—they were collected at some

distance from the *municipio* (see also *masan*, this complex).

*šk'ah* [UN]: Medium to large short-horned grasshoppers (Acrididae)

It is not clear on what basis this taxon is distinguished from *p'ilič* (see preceding taxon) or *k'ulub* (see following taxon). Examples of *p'ilič* are relatively small, while those of *šk'ah* and *k'ulub* are relatively large (see Figure 5.210d). However, many medium-sized specimens are ambiguous. The distinction between *šk'ah* and *k'ulub* is yet more difficult to discern (see Figure 5.210e). It may hinge on the behavioral contrast within certain of the Cyrtacanthacridinae between a normal and a swarming state (see later discussion). Table 5.5 illustrates the assignment of specimens of the suborder Caelifera to Tzeltal taxa. Despite informants' uncertainty about the assignment of some specimens, they are unanimous in asserting that *šk'ah* and *k'ulub* are distinct. *šk'ah k'ulub* and *šk'ahben* are variants. These animals are considered to be edible.

*k'ulub* [UN]: Large spur-throated grasshoppers (Acrididae: Cyrtacanthacridinae)

See the preceding taxon and Table 5.5 for further discussion and specimen data. Several specific subdivisions are recognized:

a. *bac'il k'ulub* 'true locust': All specimens are of this type.

b. *meba k'ulub* 'orphan locust': The attributive indicates small size. None of this type were collected.

c. *c'unun k'ulub* 'hummingbird locust': The largest type. No specimens were collected.

According to informants, *k'ulub* was more common in the past, when large swarms would periodically occur. No such swarms are reported to have occurred during the last few years. Curiously, none stressed the destructiveness usually associated with locust swarms. It is possible that all the specimens

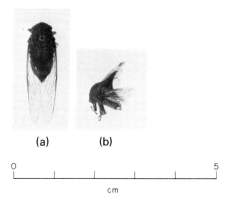

(a)          (b)

0 |___|___|___|___|___| 5

cm

**Figure 5.208**  Cicadas and tree hoppers. HOMOPTERA: (a) *meba čikitin* Cicadidae: EN No. 118399; (b) *p'um teʔ* Membracidae: EN No. 118404.

**Table 5.5**

THE ASSIGNMENT OF SPECIMENS OF THE SUBORDER CAELIFERA TO TZELTAL TAXA [a]

| Caelifera | (a)<br>p'ilič | (a) or (b) | (b)<br>šk'ah | (b) or (c) | (c)<br>k'ulub | Other |
|---|---|---|---|---|---|---|
| Acrididae sp.<br>(immature) | 118291–<br>118292 | | | | | |
| Acridinae | 118278–<br>118279 | | | | | |
| Cyrtacanthacridinae<br>sp. (immature) | 118277 | | | | | |
| (adult) | 118271,<br>118280 | | 118281 | 118282 | 118285–<br>118289 | |
| Oedipodinae<br>(immature) | | 118270 | | | | |
| (adult) | 118272,<br>118274,<br>118276,<br>118290 | 118275 | | | 118283 | |
| Pyrgomorphinae:<br>Spenarium<br>sp. 1 | | | | | | **masan**<br>118264,<br>118267–118268 |
| sp. 2 | 118265–<br>118266 | | | | | |
| Romaleinae: Taeniopoda<br>sp. 1 (immature) | 118262 | | | | | |
| sp. 2 | | | | | | **k'ulub kawáyu**<br>118259–118261,<br>118263 |
| Eumastacidae | 118273 | | | | | |

[a]Numbers in columns refer to the EN numbers of the specimens.

collected are actually examples of **šk'ah** and that **k'ulub** properly refers to these species only when swarming, as with the English "grasshopper" and "locust". All subtypes are considered to be edible.

**k'ulub kawáyu** 'locust horse': Lubber grasshoppers (Acrididae: Romaleinae: *Taeniopoda* sp. 1: EN Nos. 118259–118261, 118263) (see Figure 5.210f)

These large, thick-bodied grasshoppers are fairly common in season (e.g., November and December, at least). They are not considered to be destructive (**mayuk smul**). They are not eaten.

**čil** [UN]

Three specific subdivisions are widely recognized:

a. [R] **čil**: The unnamed residual of small (typically less than 25 mm long) and immature long-horned grasshoppers (Tettigonidae). Varietal distinctions are labeled, such as **č'in čil** 'small cricket', **yašal čil** 'green cricket', **k'anal čil** 'yellow cricket'. Immature wingless forms may be known as **ʔunin čil** 'baby cricket' or **t'an pat čil** 'naked-backed cricket' (see also **p'ilič**, first taxon in this complex). The following specimens of the Tettigonidae were placed here:

Phaneropterinae: EN Nos. 118294, 118295, 118305.

Pseudophyllinae: EN No. 118299 (see Figure 5.210g).

Specimens of other orthopterans (mostly immatures) were included here by a few informants (note overlap with **p'ilič**, see this complex):

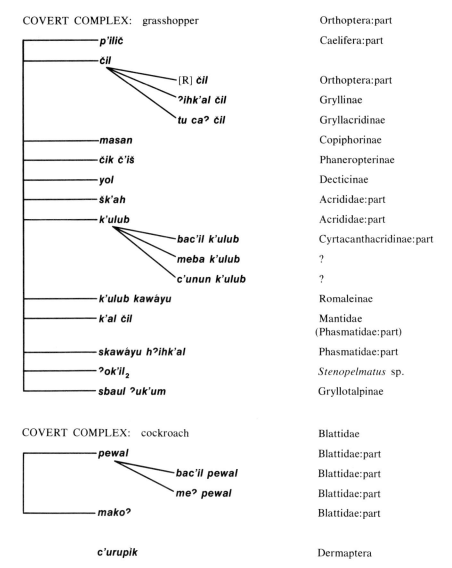

| COVERT COMPLEX:   grasshopper | | Orthoptera:part |
| --- | --- | --- |
| **p'ilič** | | Caelifera:part |
| **čil** | | |
| | [R] **čil** | Orthoptera:part |
| | **ʔihk'al čil** | Gryllinae |
| | **tu caʔ čil** | Gryllacridinae |
| **masan** | | Copiphorinae |
| **čik č'iš** | | Phaneropterinae |
| **yol** | | Decticinae |
| **šk'ah** | | Acrididae:part |
| **k'ulub** | | Acrididae:part |
| | **bac'il k'ulub** | Cyrtacanthacridinae:part |
| | **meba k'ulub** | ? |
| | **c'unun k'ulub** | ? |
| **k'ulub kawáyu** | | Romaleinae |
| **k'al čil** | | Mantidae (Phasmatidae:part) |
| **skawáyu hʔihk'al** | | Phasmatidae:part |
| **ʔok'il₂** | | *Stenopelmatus* sp. |
| **sbaul ʔuk'um** | | Gryllotalpinae |

| COVERT COMPLEX:   cockroach | | Blattidae |
| --- | --- | --- |
| **pewal** | | Blattidae:part |
| | **bac'il pewal** | Blattidae:part |
| | **meʔ pewal** | Blattidae:part |
| **makoʔ** | | Blattidae:part |

| **c'urupik** | Dermaptera |
| --- | --- |

**Figure 5.209**   The grasshopper and cockroach complexes.

Acrididae sp., immature: EN Nos. 118291–118292.

Acrididae: Oedipodinae, immature: EN No. 118270.

Acrididae: Romaleinae: *Taeniopoda*, immature: EN No. 118262.

Eumastacidae: EN No. 118273.

A very small immature walking stick (Phasmatidae: EN No. 118242) was considered **kps čil**.

b. **ʔihk'al čil** 'black cricket': Field crickets (Gryllidae: Gryllinae; EN Nos. 118313, 118315–118318) (see Figure 5.210h). The consistency with which this name is applied is in sharp contrast to the variation evident with respect to the varietals such as **yašal čil** 'green cricket' and **k'anal čil** 'yellow cricket'. Thus this taxon is inductive. Some informants also placed here my only ground cricket specimen (Gryllidae: Nemobiinae; EN No. 118311), also classed as **p'ilič** (see first taxon in this complex).

c. **tu caʔ čil** 'stinking feces cricket': My single specimen of a leaf-rolling cricket (Gryllacrididae:

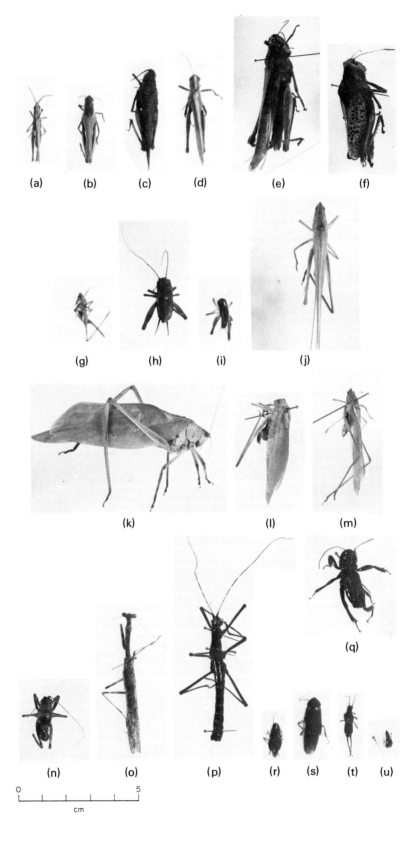

(a)    (b)    (c)    (d)    (e)    (f)

(g)    (h)    (i)    (j)

(k)    (l)    (m)

(n)    (o)    (p)    (r)    (s)    (t)    (u)

(q)

0                    5

cm

Gryllacridinae; EN No. 118319) (see Figure 5.210i) was considered to exemplify this taxon. Two other specimens were classed here by an occasional informant: EN No. 118294 (Tettigoniidae: Phaneropterinae, immature) and EN No. 118313 (Gryllidae: Gryllinae). These are probably misidentifications, as most informants place these elsewhere.

Synonyms include *tu cis čil* 'stinking-fart cricket'; *ʔon caʔ čil* 'avacado feces cricket', referring to the odor; and *p'uskin čil* 'bass guitar cricket', which is descriptive of the shape; *yut lumil čil* 'inside-the-ground cricket' describes the habitat ascribed to this type, which, however, is not characteristic of the Gryllacridinae. Camel crickets (Gryllacrididae: Rhaphidophorinae) are possible referents, however no specimens of this subfamily were collected. This type is not considered to be edible.

*masan* [UN]: Meadow grasshoppers (Tettigonidae: Copiphorinae; EN Nos. 118301–118303, 118307–118310) (see Figure 5.210j)

---

Figure 5.210  Specimens in the grasshopper, cockroach, and earwig complexes. ORTHOPTERA: (a) e.g., *yašyaštik p'ilič* Acrididae, Acridinae: EN No. 118279; (b) e.g., *yašal p'ilič* Acrididae, Oedipodinae: EN No. 118276; (c) *p'ilič* or *šk'ah* Acrididae, Oedipodinae: EN No. 118275; (d) e.g., *c'in šk'ah* Acrididae, Cyrtacanthacridinae: EN No. 118281; (e) *k'ulub* or *šk'ah* Acrididae, Cyrtacanthacridinae: EN No. 118282; (f) *k'ulub kawa' yu* Acrididae, Romaleinae, *Taeniopoda* sp. 1: EN No. 118260; (g) e.g., *yašal čil* Tettigonidae, Pseudophyllinae: EN No. 118299; (h) *ʔihk'al čil* Gryllidae, Gryllinae: EN No. 118317; (i) *tuh caʔ čil* Gryllacrididae: EN No. 118319; (j) *masan* (= *stel hol*) Tettigonidae, Copiphorinae: EN No. 118301; (k) *čik č'is* Tettigonidae, Phaeneropterinae: EN No. 118293; (l) *čik č'iš* Tettigonidae, Phaeneropterinae: EN No. 118298; (m) *čik č'iš* Tettigonidae, Phaenopterinae: EN No. 118306; (n) *yol* Tettigonidae, Decticinae: EN No. 118269; (o) *k'al čil* Mantidae: EN No. 118243; (p) *skawáyu hʔihk'al* Phasmidae: EN No. 118246; (q) *ʔok'il* Gryllacrididae, Stenopelmatinae, *Stenopelmatus* sp.: EN No. 118248; (r) *bac'il pewal* Blattidae, *Blatella germanica*: EN No. 118249; (s) *makoʔ* Blattidae, *Pseudomops* sp.: EN No. 118253; (t) *c'urupik* DERMAPTERA, Forficulidae, *Neolobophora ruficeps*: EN: No. 118256; (u) not known, *kps c'urupik* COLEOPTERA, Staphylinidae: EN No. 118396. ("E.g." indicates that the Tzeltal terms cited are *examples* of variable nomenclatural responses, not stable "names." "Not known" indicates that informants were unfamiliar with the specimens.)

Also assigned here were three specimens of a species of *Spenarium* (Acrididae: Pyrgomorphinae; EN Nos. 118264, 118267–118268). Another species of this genus was called *p'ilič* (see first taxon in this complex). Synonyms include *stel hol* 'pointed head', descriptive of the head shape of meadow grasshoppers; *rawel čil* 'fiddle cricket', referring either to the animal's shape or the sound it produces; *šorman* and its variants *šorob* and *solóba*, perhaps onomatopoetic; *sirsir* [ON]; and the variants *masian* and *masan k'ulub*. The appearance of the roots *čil* and *k'ulub*—which are the generic names for the two focal taxa of this covert complex—among the synonyms for this and related taxa helps verify the existence of the covert complex.

Some informants cite an alternate classificatory system in which this taxon is distinguished from *č'ihtiba masan* 'broad-headed meadow grasshopper', a term more appropriate for the round-headed katydids (Tettigonidae: Phaneropterinae in part). All specimens of that subfamily, however, were considered to be *čik č'iš* (see following taxon). *masan* is considered edible. *yašal masan* 'green meadow grasshopper' or *yašal stel hol* 'green pointed head', and *k'anal masan* 'yellow meadow grasshopper' or *k'anal stel hol* 'yellow pointed head' are cited as varietals.

*čik č'iš* [lit. 'red spine', the tree *Mimosa albida*]: Bush and round-headed katydids (Tettigonidae: Phaneropterinae; EN Nos. 118293, 118296, 118298, 118300, 118304, 118306) (see Figures 5.210k–5.210m), in particular the angular-winged katydids, *Microcentrum* spp., which are considered most typical

The wings of this katydid are shaped like the ovate, asymmetrical leaves of the plant after which it is named (cf. Berlin, Breedlove, and Raven 1974:Figure 7.54). *čik č'iš k'ulub* is a variant. Synonyms include *yabenal teʔ* 'tree leaf' (katydids imitate foliage to evade predators) and *meʔ bohč* 'mother of the gourd'. This latter synonym may be reserved for very large specimens, however there is not sufficient evidence at present to define *meʔ*

*bohč* as distinct. These insects are considered to be edible. Varieties include **yašal čik č'iš** 'green katydid' and **k'anal čik č'iš** 'yellow katydid'. Some informants consider this an evil omen (**ya šlabtawan**) and may refer to it as **hlabtawaneh čil, bal ?ahk'ubal čil** 'rolled-up-at-night cricket?', or **sérka čil** [< Sp *cerca* 'near' + 'cricket'].

**yol** [UN]: Camel crickets (Tettigonidae: Decticinae: EN Nos. 118269, 1003305) (see Figure 5.210n)

Synonyms include **pum ca? yol** 'feces-hitting camel cricket' and **koncal yol** [UN + 'camel cricket']. **yol** is considered to be edible.

**k'al čil** 'sun cricket': The praying mantis (Mantidae: EN Nos. 118243–118245) (see Figure 5.210o), including also most walking sticks (Phasmatidae)

The name is most appropriate, however, for the mantis, i.e., it indicates the position of the sun with its enlarged forelegs. This may be true, as it would cast a minimal shadow in that position, an advantage in evading predators. **ba?ay k'al čil** is a more obvious variant meaning 'where-the-sun-is cricket'. **?óra čil** 'hour cricket' is also synonymous. They are not eaten.

**skawáyu h?ihk'al** 'the black devil's horse': A large black, thick-bodied walking stick (Phasmatidae in part: EN Nos. 118246, 1003240) (see Figure 5.210p)

It is restricted to the highlands. It is also known as **yat pukuh** 'devil's penis'. It is considered to be an evil omen (**ya šlabtawan**) and is not eaten.

**?ok'il₂** 'coyote': The Jerusalem cricket (Gryllacrididae: Stenopelmatinae: *Stenopelmatus* sp.: EN Nos. 118247, 118248, 1003245) (see Figure 5.210q)

These are evil omens (**ya šlabtawan**) and are considered to be inedible. The association with the coyote (**?ok'il₁**/mammal, dog) is not readily explicable.

**sbaul ?uk'um** 'gopher of the river': Mole crickets (Gryllidae: Gryllotalpinae: EN No. 1002355)

These burrow in the sand on the banks of rivers on the lowland fringe of Tenejapa and are not widely known. Local informants consider them edible. Capture is effected by tracing with a finger the molelike mounds left by these insects until one is encountered. Synonyms include **ba** 'pocket gropher' (see **ba**/mammal) and **mentes čil** 'Mendez cricket'. This latter term is an extension of the wordplay associating pocket gophers with the **mentes** 'clan'.

## COCKROACH COMPLEX

All the Blattidae are included here. No relationship is recognized with the remaining Orthoptera included in the preceding complex. Earwigs (order Dermaptera, see **c'urupik**) are the only insects with which association is recognized.

**pewal** [UN]: Most cockroaches (Blattidae in part)

All household roaches and the smaller of those found in decaying wood are included here. Two subtypes are widely recognized:

a. **bac'il pewal** 'true roach': Winged roaches found in houses. Specimens included here are EN Nos. 118249 (*Blattella germanica*) (see Figure 5.210r), 118251 (*Pseudomops* sp.), and 118252. Though not normally eaten, roaches of this type are roasted, ground to powder, and drunk with water as a cure for 'whooping cough' (**šposil hik'hik' ?obal**). Dead fish (**peskáro**/fish) are used to drive roaches from one's house. The odor is believed to be effective. These are common household pests in Tenejapa and the use of insecticides is now common in preference to the traditional deterrent.

b. **me? pewal** 'mother roach': Wingless roaches (Blattidae in part: EN Nos. 118250, 1002257) (see Figure 5.210s). Synonyms include *t'an pat pewal* 'naked-backed roach' and *te?tikil pewal* 'forest roach'.

**mako?** [UN]: Large, winged forest cockroaches (Blattidae in part: EN Nos. 118253, 1002357) (see Figure 5.210t)

This is the preferred sense, though a few informants considered this taxon equivalent to *me? pewal* (see earlier).

**c'urupik** [UN]: Earwigs (order Dermaptera)

Both specimens are common earwigs, *Neolobophora ruficeps* (Forficulidae: EN Nos. 118255, 118256) (see Figure 5.210u). It remains uncertain whether two types deserve recognition or not. One informant asserted that *cek c'urupik* 'scorpion earwig' was distinct from *bac'il c'urupik* 'true earwig'. The former would then be distinguished by relatively long abdominal cerci, perhaps a male characteristic. In addition one informant classed a small beetle (Staphylinidae: EN Nos. 118395, 118396) (see Figure 5.210v) as *c'urupik*. However most informants considered those specimens to be unfamiliar.

## BEETLE–BUG COMPLEX
(See Figure 5.211)

This complex is not well defined, in that the binary relationships recognized between taxa of this complex become gradually less well established. Several additional taxa (e.g., *čan₂*, *hoč'*) might also be included as links in a chain of binary relationship; however, the resulting complex would include too heterogeneous a collection of organisms. Many but not all beetles (order Coleoptera) are included, as well as most types of bugs (order Hemiptera).

**kuhtum ca?** 'elbower of dung': Dung beetles (Scarabaeidae: Scarabaeinae: EN Nos. 118017, 118018, 118021, 118027) (see Figure 5.212a,b), earth-boring dung beetles (Scarabaeidae: Geotrupinae: EN Nos. 118016, 118022) (see Figure 5.212c), and flower beetles

(Scarabaeidae: Cetoniinae: EN No. 118026) (see Figure 5.212d)

Synonyms include *muk ca?* 'dung burier', *kuč ca?* 'dung carrier', *c'elkuneh ca?* [UN + 'dung'], *balkuneh ca?* [< tv 'to roll up'? + 'dung']. Varieties include *yašal kuhtum ca?* 'blue dung beetle', *?ihk'al kuhtum ca?* 'black dung beetle', *cahal kuhtum ca?* 'red dung beetle'. Horned forms (males) are called *stat kuhtum ca?* 'male dung beetle' or *šulub kuhtum ca?* 'horned dung beetle'. Those without horns may be known as *sme? kuhtum ca?* 'female dung beetle'. These are not to be killed, since their scavenging role is considered essential. Because of their association with dung, they are not considered edible.

**čimol** [UN]: Rhinoceros beetles (Scarabaeidae: Dynastinae: EN Nos. 118019, 118020, 118024, 118025) (see Figure 5.212e,f)

EN No. 118023 (Rutelinae, see Figure 5.212g) was placed here by two informants, though considered to be *?umoh* or *kuhtum ca?* by others. Horned males are recognized as such and are referred to as *stat čimol* 'male rhinoceros beetle' or *šulub čimol* 'horned rhinoceros beetle'. The remainder are considered to be *sme?* 'female'. Color varieties may be recognized, e.g., *?ihk'al čimol* 'black rhinoceros beetle', *yašal čimol* 'blue–green rhinoceros beetle', and *cahal čimol* 'red rhinoceros beetle'. These are edible, in contrast to the preceding taxon.

**čimolil te?** 'tree rhinoceros beetle': Bessbugs (Coleoptera: Passalidae: EN Nos. 117950–117954) (see Figure 5.212h)

Synonyms include *čimolil k'a?al te?* 'rotten tree rhinoceros beetle', referring to the fact that bessbugs are typically found under fallen logs. One informant referred to these specimens as *kps wayway čan* (see this complex).

**?umoh** [UN]: June beetles and relatives (Scarabaeidae: Melolonthinae: EN Nos. 118007, 118047) (see Figure 5.212i) and

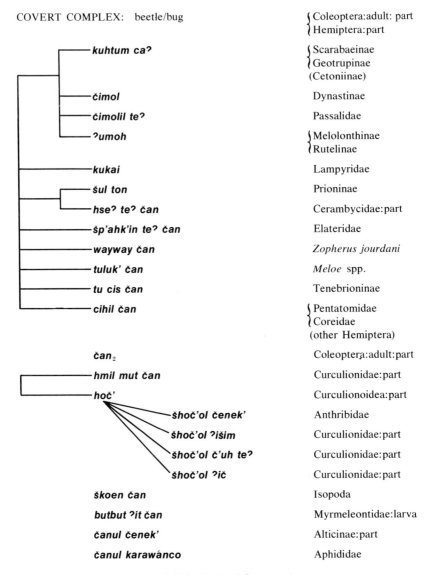

| COVERT COMPLEX:   beetle/bug | { Coleoptera:adult: part<br>{ Hemiptera:part |
|---|---|
| **kuhtum ca?** | { Scarabaeinae<br>{ Geotrupinae<br>(Cetoniinae) |
| **čimol** | Dynastinae |
| **čimolil te?** | Passalidae |
| **?umoh** | { Melolonthinae<br>{ Rutelinae |
| **kukai** | Lampyridae |
| **šul ton** | Prioninae |
| **hse? te? čan** | Cerambycidae:part |
| **šp'ahk'in te? čan** | Elateridae |
| **wayway čan** | *Zopherus jourdani* |
| **tuluk' čan** | *Meloe* spp. |
| **tu cis čan** | Tenebrioninae |
| **cihil čan** | { Pentatomidae<br>{ Coreidae<br>(other Hemiptera) |
| **čan₂** | Coleoptera:adult:part |
| **hmil mut čan** | Curculionidae:part |
| **hoč'** | Curculionoidea:part |
| **šhoč'ol čenek'** | Anthribidae |
| **šhoč'ol ?išim** | Curculionidae:part |
| **šhoč'ol č'uh te?** | Curculionidae:part |
| **šhoč'ol ?ič** | Curculionidae:part |
| **škoen čan** | Isopoda |
| **butbut ?it čan** | Myrmeleontidae:larva |
| **čanul čenek'** | Alticinae:part |
| **čanul karawánco** | Aphididae |

**Figure 5.211**   The beetle/bug complex.

shining leaf chafers (Scarabaeidae: Rutelinae: EN Nos. 118008–118010, 118023 [See Figure 5.212j]; see also *čimol*)

Variants include *?umuh* and *?omoh*. These are considered edible. Varieties include *?ihk'al ?umoh* 'black June beetles' and *k'anal ?umoh* 'yellow June beetles'.

***kukai*** [UN]: Fireflies (Coleoptera: Lampyridae: EN Nos. 117997–117999) (see Figure 5.212k)

*kokai* is a variant. According to informants fireflies shine at night (*ya stil ta ?ahk'ubal*).

***šulton*** 'horned stone': Large long-horned beetles (Cerambycidae: Prioninae: EN Nos. 118028, 118029) (see Figure 5.212l)

Variants include *šulub ton* 'horned stone', *šurub ton*, and *harak čan* [UN + 'bug']. These are edible.

***hse? te? čan*** 'tree-cutter bug': Small long-horned beetles (Cerambycidae in part)

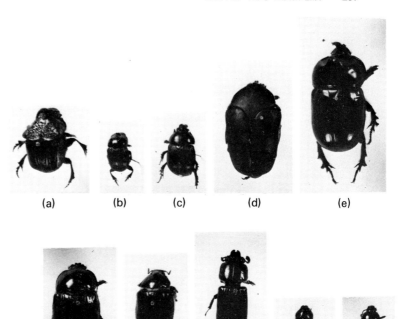

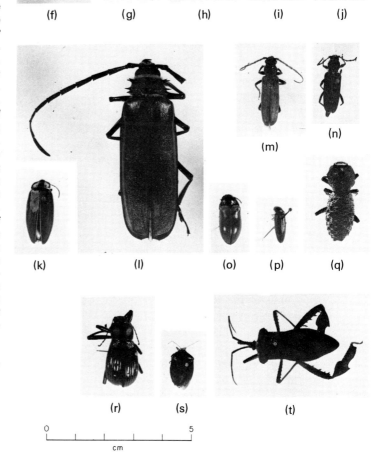

**Figure 5.212** Specimens in the beetle complex. COLEOPTERA (unless otherwise noted by an asterisk): (a) *kuhtum caʔ* Scarabaeidae, Scarabaeinae: EN No. 118017; (b) *kuhtum caʔ* Scarabaeidae, Scarabaeinae: EN No. 118021; (c) *kuhtum caʔ* Scarabaeidae, Geotrupinae: EN No. 118022; (d) *kuhtum caʔ* Scarabaeidae, Cetoninae: EN No. 118026; (e) *čimol* Scarabaeidae, Dynastinae: EN No. 118025; (f) *čimol* Scarabaeidae, Dynastinae: EN No. 118019; (g) *čimol, kuhtum caʔ*, or *ʔumoh* Scarabaeidae, Rutelinae: EN No. 118023; (h) *čimolil teʔ* Passalidae: EN No. 117950; (i) *ʔumoh* Scarabaeidae, Melolonthinae: EN No. 118007; (j) *ʔumoh* Scarabaeidae, Rutelinae: EN No. 118008; (k) *kukai* Lampyridae: EN No. 117999; (l) *šulton* Cerambycidae, Prioninae: EN No. 118028; (m) *hseʔ teʔ čan* Cerambycidae, Aseminae: EN No. 117989; (n) *hseʔ teʔ čan* Cerambycidae, Clytinae: EN No. 117991; (o) *špˋahkˋin teʔ čan* or e.g., *cahal čan* Elateridae: EN No. 118000; (p) e.g., *peč hol čan, kˋanal čan* Elateridae: EN No. 118002; (q) *wayway čan* Zopheridae, *Zopherus jourdani*: EN No. 117992; (r) *tu cis čan* Tenebrionidae, *Eleodes* sp.: EN No. 118070; (s) *cihil čan* *HEMIPTERA, Pentatomatidae: EN No. 117961; (t) *cihil čan* *HEMIPTERA, Coreidae: EN No. 117958. ("E.g." indicates that the Tzeltal terms cited are examples of variable nomenclatural responses, not stable "names.")

Two subfamilies are represented by specimens: Aseminae (EN No. 117989) (see Figure 5.212m) and Clytinae (EN Nos. 117988, 117990, 117991) (see Figure 5.212n). This and the preceding category are considered to be closely related. Synonyms include *hk'uš te? čan* 'tree-eater bug' and *sererol* [< Sp '?'] or *sererol čan*.

*šp'ahk'in te? čan* [< 'sound of footfalls' + 'tree' + 'bug']: Click beetles (Elateridae: EN Nos. 118000, 118001) (see Figure 5.212o)

Two smaller click beetles (EN Nos. 118002, 118045) (see Figure 5.212p) were thought to be *kps kukai* (see *kukai*). However the specimens were mounted, and the characteristic behavior could not be observed. Synonyms inlcude *k'ohčin te? čan* ['carnivorous snail' + 'bug'] and *?ep' nuk' čan* 'neck-snapper bug'.

*wayway čan* 'sleep-sleep bug': A slow moving, very hard-bodied beetle (Zopheridae: *Zopherus jourdani*: EN Nos. 117992, 117993) (see Figure 5.212q)

Other members of the genus and family might be included, but specimens are lacking. These beetles are placed near a child to aid sleep (*šposil wayel*). Synonyms include *way čan* and *wayel čan*. One informant placed the bessbugs here (but see *čimolil te?*).

*tuluk' čan* 'turkey bug': Oil beetles (Meloidae: *Meloe nebulosus*: EN No. 1002256; *Meloe laevis*: EN No. 1003231)

A smaller beetle of this family was not recognized (EN No. 118056). Members of the genus *Meloe* "exude an oily substance from the joints of the legs when disturbed; this substance can raise blisters on one's skin [Borror and White 1970:184]." Thus the belief that this exudant is effective against warts (*šposil čohk'*) may be correct. This beetle is known by various names in various parts of Tenejapa: *liméte čan* and *limeton čan* [both < Sp 'bottle' + 'bug'], *burin čan* [< Sp 'barrel' + 'bug'], *pále? čan* [< Sp

*padre*, 'priest' + 'bug'], *loktor čan* [< Sp *doctor*, 'doctor' + 'bug'], and *šposil čohk'* 'wart medicine'. The beetles are shaped like small bottles.

*tu cis čan* 'stinking-fart bug': A darkling beetle (Tenebrionidae: Tenebrioninae: *Eleodes*: EN No. 118070) (see Figure 5.212r)

Another species of this family (Tentyriinae: EN No. 118053) was considered to be *kps kukai* (see *kukai*). The first specimen is similar to darkling beetles known colloquially in the United States as "stink bugs."

*cihil čan* 'stink bug': Stinkbugs (order Hemiptera: Pentatomidae: EN Nos. 117959–117962) (see Figure 5.212s) and the leaf-footed bugs (Hemiptera: Coreidae: EN Nos. 117955–117958, 117982) (see Figure 5.212t)

Both in fact have a strong odor. Synonyms include *tuil čan* 'stink bug' and *cih yik' čan* 'stink-odor bug'. The extended range of this taxon may include a variety of Hemiptera families: assassin bugs (Reduviidae: EN Nos. 117963, 117966), ash-grey leaf bugs (Piesmatidae: EN Nos 117967, 117970, 117980), seed bugs (Lygaeidae: EN Nos. 117969, 117972), red bugs or stainers (Pyrrhocoridae: EN Nos. 117975–117976), and toad bugs (Gelastocoridae: EN No 117983). In fact this extended usage is practically equivalent to terrestrial bugs, despite the fact that most have no odor. In addition, net-winged beetles (Coleoptera: Lycidae: EN Nos. 117994–117996) are often included in the extended range.

The following taxa include animals that are typically smaller than those included in the beetle complex, to which they are marginally related in the Tenejapan system. At this point it is often difficult to distinguish between well-defined taxa and a large, heterogeneous residual, which serves as a "catch-all" for specimens not assigned to the well-defined taxa. These animals are descriptively named by the conjunction of *čan* 'bug' or 'critter' and a literally descriptive adjective.

*čan₂* 'bug': Assorted, non-affiliated beetles (Coleoptera in part)

The included animals are named as varietals. The following adjectives are typical of those used to name the variety of organisms dealt with in this context: Color adjectives: *cahal* 'red', *ʔihkʼal* 'black', *kʼanal* 'yellow', *sakil* 'white', and *yašal* 'blue/grey', *saksaktik* 'whitish', and *kʼankʼantik* 'yellowish'. Pattern adjectives: *cʼirin* 'streaked', *cʼihtil* 'barred', *pínto* 'blotched', *barsin* 'varicolored', *tilel* 'shiny'. Shape-texture adjectives: *norin* 'round', *čʼišal* 'thorny', *kʼunil* 'soft'.

Adjectives in combination with body parts: *cahal pat* 'red-backed', *ʔihkʼal pat* 'black-backed', *yašal pat* 'blue–green-backed', *cʼirin pat* 'streak-backed', *pʼus pat* 'hunch-backed', *lehč pat* 'thin-backed', *čʼišal pat* 'spiny-backed', *čʼuš pat* 'tendon-backed', *noh pat* 'full-backed', *nol pat* 'round-backed', *nor pat* 'round-backed', *nuh pat* 'covered-backed', *peč pat* 'braided-backed', *wol pat* 'spherical-backed', *lehč šikʼ* 'thin-winged', *nahtil šikʼ* 'long-winged', *čʼuš nukʼ* 'tendon-necked', *kʼan snukʼ* 'yellow-necked', *kʼan yit* 'yellow-abdomened', *pehč hol* 'flat-headed', *ʔoškah* 'three-pronged'.

Additional descriptive terminology utilizes yet more complex combinations, i.e., *cʼirin nol pat čan* 'streaked, round-backed bug', or *yašal pat cʼirin čan* 'green-backed streaked bug', etc.

The preceding list is not exhaustive but represents a rather complete accounting of this type of naming response. It should be noted that structurally similar names are not necessarily varietals of this residual; for example, *mayil čan* (see *škoen čan*) are isopod crustaceans; *wah čan* (see the caterpillar complex) is a type of caterpillar; *češ kʼab čan* (see *la lum*/fly) is a category of flies; *čil teʔ čan* (see the ant complex) is a category of ants; *yašal čan* (see *čanul čenekʼ*) may refer to a well-defined category of small beetles, etc.

The primary criterion for distinguishing a variety of this residual from an inductive taxon is consistency of application of the name to a single morphological type.

The scientific taxa characteristically treated in this context are as follows (all are Coleoptera):

Ground beetles (Carabidae: EN Nos. 118030–118033, 118036, 118037) (see Figure 5.213a).

Net-winged beetles (Lycidae: EN Nos. 117994–117996) (see Figure 5.213b).

Soft-winged flower beetles (Melyridae: EN No. 118057).

Checkered beetles (Cleridae: EN No. 118066).

Pleasing fungus beetles (Erotylidae: EN Nos. 118011, 118012, 118044, 118062, 118067, 118068) (see Figure 5.213c,d).

Handsome fungus beetles (Endomychidae: EN No. 118049) (see Figure 5.213e).

Ladybird beetles (Coccinellidae: EN Nos. 118046, 118058, 118065) (see Figure 5.213f).

Leaf beetles (Chrysomelidae: EN Nos. 118013, 118015, 118048, 118052, 118054, 118055, 118059–118061, 118063, 118064; see *čanul čenekʼ* (see Figure 5.213g,h).

*čan* is polysemous. *čan₁* means 'snake' (see the snake complex), *čan₂* means 'assorted beetles'. This latter meaning may be distinguished as *čʼuhčʼul čan* 'small (pl) bug'. The term appears in other contexts as well (for discussion see Chapter 4, Section 2.4).

## COVERT COMPLEX: WEEVIL

*hmil mut čan* 'chicken-killer bug': Large snout beetles (Curculionidae in part: EN Nos. 118038, 118040, 118042) (see Figure 5.213i)

According to informants, when chickens eat these beetles, the beetles become lodged in their throats and choke them. Informants

**Figure 5.213** Assorted small beetles and isopods. COLEOPTERA: (a) e.g., *čanul k`aʔal teʔ*, *čimolil k`aʔal teʔ* Carabidae, Oryptini: EN No. 118032; (b) e.g., *lehč šik` čan, lehč pat čan* Lycidae: EN No. 117994; (c) e.g., *barsin čan, c`irin čan* Eroltylidae: EN No. 118044; (d) e.g., *nol pat čan* Erotylidae: EN No. 118067; (e) e.g., *k`anal čan, c`irin čan* Endomychidae: EN No. 118049; (f) e.g., *nol pat čan, k`anal c`irin čan* Coccinellidae: EN No. 118065; (g) e.g., *yašal pat c`irin čan, kps ʔumoh* Chrysomelidae, Galerucinae: EN No. 118013; (h) e.g., *k`anal c`irin nol pat čan* Chrysomelidae, Alticinae: EN No. 118063; (i) *hmil mut čan* Curculionidae: EN No. 118038; (j) *šhoč`ol ʔišim* or *muk`ul hoč`* Curculionidae: EN No. 118041; (k) *šhoč`ol č`uhteʔ* or *muk`ul hoč`* Curculionidae: EN No. 118040; (l) *šhoč`olil ʔič* Curculionidae: EN No. 118043; (m) *škoen čan* Isopoda, Porcellionidae; EN No. 118497; (n) *škoen čan* Isopoda, Armadillididae: EN No. 118496; (o) *čanul čenek`* Chrysomelidae, Alticinae: EN No. 118051. ("E.g." indicates that the Tzeltal terms cited are *examples* of variable nomenclatural responses, not stable "names.")

who do not recognize this taxon class these specimens as *hoč`* (see following taxon).

***hoč`*** [UN]: Weevils (Coleoptera: Curculionoidea) with the exception of those placed above

Specific subdivisions are recognized by reference to the host plant:

a. ***šhoč`ol čenek`*** 'bean weevil': A small, black weevil.   The specimen is a fungus weevil

(Anthribidae: EN No. 1002303). This type is also known as *šhoč'olil čenek'* or *šhoč'ol škantéra čenek'*. *škantéra čenek'* refers to the bean *Vigna sinensis*.

b. *šhoč'ol ʔišim* 'corn weevil': Some snout beetles (Curculionidae in part: EN Nos. 118039, 118041 [see Figure 5.213j], 118042; see *hmil mut čan*, preceding taxon). These are larger than type (a) and may be either *ʔihk'al* 'black' or *k'anal* 'yellow'. *muk'ul hoč'* 'large weevil' is synonymous.

c. *šhoč'ol č'uh teʔ* 'plank weevil': Some snout beetles (Curculionidae in part: EN No. 118040 [see Figure 5.213k]; see also *hmil mut čan*). These are found in boards used to form the walls of houses.

d. *šhoč'ol ʔič* 'pepper weevil': Some snout beetles (Curculionidae in part: EN No. 118043) (see Figure 5.213l). This specimen was found on a pepper. It is doubtful that this type would be recognized as such in the absence of that information. *šhoč'olil ʔič* is a variant.

Some individuals do not recognize the subdivisions listed above, utilizing varietal distinctions instead: e.g., *ʔihk'al hoč'* 'black weevil', *č'in hoč'* 'small weevil', *muk'ul hoč'* 'large weevil', etc.

*škoen čan* [< iv 'descend' + 'bug'] i.e., 'burrowing bug': Sowbugs (CRUSTACEA: Isopoda: Porcellionidae: EN Nos. 118497, 1002272, 1002276) (see Figure 5.213m) and pillbugs (order Isopoda: Armadillididae: EN No. 118496) (see Figure 5.213n)

This taxon is recognized by most informants, but a variety of names are utilized, some purely descriptive: *mayil čan₂* 'squash sp. bug' (see also *čan₂*), *mayil ʔak'* 'squash vine sp.', *k'ol pat čan* 'round-backed bug', *nuh pat čan* 'covered-back bug', and *sul pat čan* [UN + 'back' + 'bug'].

*butbut ʔit čan* [UN + 'buttocks' + 'bug']:

Antlion larvae (Neuroptera: Myrmeleontidae: EN No. 1002280)

These are found at the apex of their craterlike ant traps in sandy soil. Women desiring larger breasts collect these and induce them to bite their nipples (*sniʔ čuʔ*). This ensures that in a few years their breasts will enlarge (*špošil ya šmuk'ub ščuʔ ʔanc*), in imitation of the round abdomens of these larvae.

*čanul čenek'* 'bean bug': A flea beetle (Coleoptera: Chrysomelidae: Alticinae: EN Nos. 118050, 118051) (see Figure 5.213o)

This tiny red and blue beetle is a well-known pest of beans. It eats the leaves, leaving a lacy pattern. Various other small beetles may be considered *kps čanul čenek'*, i.e., pleasing fungus beetles (Erotylidae) and ladybird beetles (Coccinellidae). However these are most likely to be treated as varieties of *čan₂*. *yašal čan* 'blue bug' is a well-defined synonym.

*čanul karawánco* 'pea bug': Aphids (Homoptera: Aphididae: EN No. 1002339).

Since aphids may be found on a variety of plants other than peas (*Pisum sativum*), it is not certain if this name is limited to a particular variety of aphid or is of general reference.

*čanul yabenal nahk* 'alder-leaf critter': A leaf beetle larva (Cucujoidea: Chrysomelidae?: EN No. 1002301)

A small caterpillarlike organism. No association with the adult form is recognized. This larva is found on alder leaves (*Alnus* spp.).

*čanul hi* 'green-corn critter': Unidentified

It is probably a larva that attacks green ears of corn.

*čanul sakil bok* ['critter' + rs + 'herb sp.']: An unidentified larva

It attacks the plant *Brassica campestris*.

*čanul te?* 'tree critter': Wood-boring larvae (orders Coleoptera, Lepidoptera, Diptera, etc.)

Most individuals are named according to the host plant, e.g., *čanul hihte?* 'oak critter'. Two specific subdivisions are recognized:

a. *bac'il čanul te?* 'true tree critter' (see Figure 5.215a): A large (to 7.5 cm) brown larva with yellow bands (order Lepidoptera). This may prove to be the larva of the giant noctuid moth (*Thysania agrippina*, see *pehpen*[f], butterfly-moth), known incorrectly as *me? sac* 'mother of the sphinx moth larva'. This type is found in a variety of trees, to which the following varietal names refer:

*čanul hihte?* 'oak critter'.

*čanul munis te?* ['critter' + rs + '*Lippia hypoleia*'].

*čanul nahk* 'alder critter'.

*čanul pišonič* ['critter' + rs + '*Lippia* spp.'].

*čanul sak bah te?* ['critter' + rs + '*Buddleia* spp.'].

The fact that all these terms are thought to label a single type of animal suggests that such naming by host is varietal (but see *čanul čenek'*, *čanul karawánco*, etc., for generic names of this form). This animal is considered to be edible. To locate the larvae, one searches for the hole made by the larva upon entering the wood, then cuts down through the wood with a machete to the larva inside.

b. [residual]: All other wood-boring larvae. These are of various colors: *sakil* 'white' and *k'anal* 'yellow' are considered to be edible; *?ihk'al* 'black' is inedible since it is too 'spicy' (*ya šti?wan*). Individual specimens may be named according to their dominant color, or more typically according to the host plant. The following list may not be exhaustive:

*čanul bahkalel ?išim* 'dead cornstalk critter'; two types are known, 'small' and 'large', though informants disagree as to their respective colors.

*čanul ca?mut te?* 'critter of *Miconia* spp.', 'white'.

*čanul č'opak* 'critter of *Ricinis communis*', though many informants deny that such exists.

*čanul ?išim* 'corn critter', which includes *čanul bahkalel ?išim* and *čanul te?el ?išim*.

*čanul kašlan čenek'* 'peanut critter', though many informants deny that such exists.

*čanul k'an te?* 'critter of *Diphysa* sp., *Pistacia* sp., *Eysenhardtia* sp.'.

*čanul mes te?* 'critter of *Baccharis* spp.'.

*čanul ?on* 'avocado critter', 'white'.

*čanul pikac* 'critter of an unidentified plant', 'white'.

*čanul šašib* 'critter of *Leucaena* spp., *Acacia* spp., *Calliandra* spp., *Lysiloma* spp.', 'white' or 'blackish'.

*čanul tah* 'pine critter', 'white', also known as *čanul tahal te?*. A single specimen of this type is a larval crane fly (order Diptera: Tipulidae; EN No. 1002382).

*čanul te?el ?išim* 'growing cornstalk critter', 'yellowish'.

*čanul wale* 'sugar cane critter' 'blackish'.

Other specimens were classed simply as *čanul te?* and the host plant is not known: e.g., a larval beetle (Cerambycidae: EN. No. 1003244). All *čanul te?* are wood- or stalk-boring larvae. Larvae that feed externally, e.g., *čanul yabenal nahk*, or those that bore into fruit (see *yalha*) or seeds (see *čanul hi*) are specifically excluded.

*k'olom* [UN]: Scarab beetle larvae (see Figure 5.215b) (Coleoptera: Scarabaeidae: EN Nos. 1002259, 1003236, 1003237)

These large white grubs are pests, in that they eat the roots of cultivated plants. Some informants recognize two types, treated here as varieties since further information is lacking: *muk'ul k'olom* 'large grub' and *č'in k'olom* 'small grub'. These grubs are not considered to be edible. If eaten, they make a fierce man stupid (*špošil ya šbolob k'ahk'al winik yu?un*). Informants assert that *k'olom* 'transforms' (*ya šk'ahta*) into *?umoh* (June beetles and chafers, see the beetle–bug complex) and *čimol* (rhinoceros beetles, see the beetle–bug complex), which is quite accurate, since these beetles are scarabs.

## CATERPILLAR COMPLEX (See Figure 5.214)

Included here are most Lepidoptera larvae (excluding the wood-boring types) and a few larval flies (order Diptera). *k'olom* (see the preceding taxon) and the worm complex are marginally associated. The detail lacking

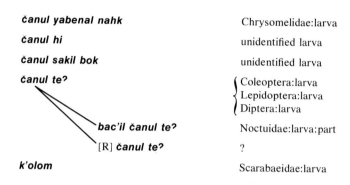

| | |
|---|---|
| *čanul yabenal nahk* | Chrysomelidae:larva |
| *čanul hi* | unidentified larva |
| *čanul sakil bok* | unidentified larva |
| *čanul te?* | { Coleoptera:larva<br>Lepidoptera:larva<br>Diptera:larva |
| *bac'il čanul te?* | Noctuidae:larva:part |
| [R] *čanul te?* | ? |
| *k'olom* | Scarabaeidae:larva |

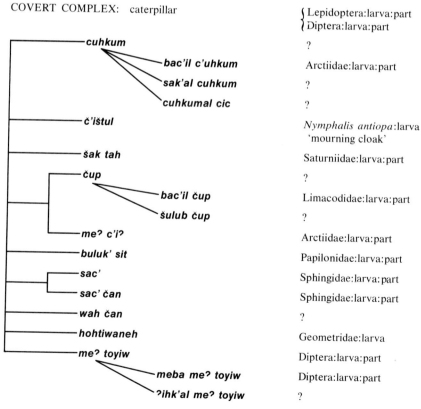

| | |
|---|---|
| COVERT COMPLEX: caterpillar | { Lepidoptera:larva:part<br>Diptera:larva:part |
| *cuhkum* | ? |
| *bac'il c'uhkum* | Arctiidae:larva:part |
| *sak'al cuhkum* | ? |
| *cuhkumal cic* | ? |
| *č'ištul* | *Nymphalis antiopa*:larva 'mourning cloak' |
| *šak tah* | Saturniidae:larva:part |
| *čup* | ? |
| *bac'il čup* | Limacodidae:larva:part |
| *šulub čup* | ? |
| *me? c'i?* | Arctiidae:larva:part |
| *buluk' sit* | Papilonidae:larva:part |
| *sac'* | Sphingidae:larva:part |
| *sac' čan* | Sphingidae:larva:part |
| *wah čan* | ? |
| *hohtiwaneh* | Geometridae:larva |
| *me? toyiw* | Diptera:larva:part |
| *meba me? toyiw* | Diptera:larva:part |
| *?ihk'al me? toyiw* | ? |

Figure 5.214   Caterpillars and assorted larvae.

in the classification of adult Lepidoptera is not lacking with respect to the larvae. The explanation is the cultural relevance of the larvae, many of which sting or are pestiferous, devouring cultivated plants. Only one category is eaten (*sac'*). Relationships between these larvae and the adult forms is partially and imperfectly recognized. Most larvae remain to be determined, thus identifications are tentative, at best.

***cuhkum*** [UN]: "Woolybear" caterpillars (order Lepidoptera in part) (see Figure 5.215c)

Some tiger moth larvae (Arctiidae) are of this type, however the limits of this taxon cannot be defined more precisely at present. Pupal cases (***sna cuhkum***) are considered to have medicinal value for a condition known as 'unripe arm' (***špošil ʔunin k'abal***). Several specific subdivisions are recognized:

a. ***bac'il cuhkum*** 'true woolybear': Hairy nonstinging caterpillars. Color varieties are named, i.e., ***ʔihk'al cuhkum*** 'black woolybear', ***k'anal cuhkum*** 'yellow woolybear', ***cahal cuhkum*** 'red woolybear'.

b. ***sak'al cuhkum*** 'itchy woolybear'. These are distinguished from [a] by their longer, softer but itch-causing hairs. ***k'unil cuhkum*** 'soft woolybear' is apparently synonymous.

c. ***cukumal cic*** 'avocado woolybear'. No collections of this type were obtained. It is typically found on the tree known as ***cic***, an avocado (*Persea americana* var. *drymifolia*).

***č'ištul*** ['spine' + UN]: Stinging caterpillars (see Figure 5.215d) (Lepidoptera: especially Nymphalidae)

These have simple spines restricted to transverse rows on each abdominal segment. A caterpillar so named was raised. It proved to be the familiar mourning cloak (*Nymphalis antiopa*: EN No. 118339). The chrysalis (EN No. 1003316) was referred to as ***sna č'ištul*** 'house of the spiny caterpillar'.

Many nymphalid larvae are of this type. Most are dark colored and thus described as ***ʔihk'al č'ištul*** 'black spiny caterpillar'. A 'red' variety is also reported, ***cahal č'ištul***.

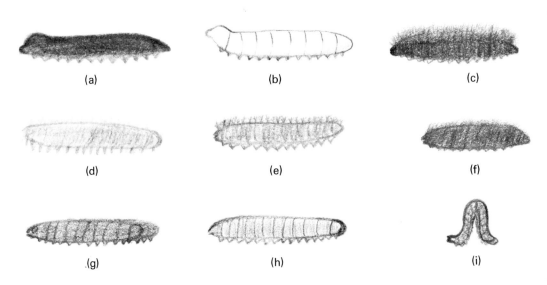

(a)        (b)        (c)

(d)        (e)        (f)

(g)        (h)        (i)

**Figure 5.215**   Insect larvae: (a) ***bac'il čanul teʔ*** 'tree boring larva'; (b) ***k'olom*** 'scarab beetle larva'; (c) ***cuhkum*** 'wooly bear'; (d) ***č'ištul*** 'stinging caterpillar'; (e) ***šakitah*** 'stinging caterpillar'; (f) ***čup*** 'stinging caterpillar'; (g) ***buluk' sit*** 'eyed caterpillar'; (h) ***sac'*** sphinx moth larva'; (i) ***hohtiwaneh*** 'looper'. [Drawings by AMT.]

*šaktah* 'pine needle' : Stinging caterpillars (see Figure 5.215e) (Lepidoptera in part)

They have many-branched spines, and many are brightly colored. One individual of the 'black' variety (*ʔihkʼal šaktah*), identified from a photograph, is a larval giant silkworm mouth (Saturniidae). Other color varieties include *cahal šaktah* 'red needle caterpillar', *kʼanal šaktah* 'yellow needle caterpillar', *sakil šaktah* 'white needle caterpillar', and *yašal· šaktah* 'blue–green needle caterpillar'. *šakitah* is a variant.

*čup* [UN]: Hairy, stinging caterpillars (see Figure 5.215f) (Lepidoptera in part) of various, often bizarre, types

Specific subdivisions are recognized (the first, (a), is a residual specific taxon):

a. *bacʼil čup* 'true bizarre caterpillar'. One example is a slug caterpillar (Microlepidoptera: Limacodidae); it is small and green with stinging hairs. *mutil čup* 'bird bizarre caterpillar' was given as a synonym for the individual cited. The following variants may be synonymous: *mer pat čup*, *mereš pat čup*, *méru pat čup* [< Sp *mero, -a* 'naked' + 'back' + 'bizarre caterpillar']. Color varieties may also be distinguished, e.g., *cahal* 'red', *ʔihkʼal* 'black', *kʼanal* 'yellow', and *sakil* 'white'.

b. *šulub čup* 'horned bizarre caterpillar'. One example seen was covered with very long, dark, stinging hairs. It had no "horns," however.

The following taxon (*meʔ cʼiʔ*) is considered a subdivision of *čup* by some informants. It may then be distinguished as *kʼanal čup* 'yellow bizarre caterpillar' or *čupil hihteʔ* 'oak bizarre caterpillar'.

*meʔ cʼiʔ* 'mother of dog': A tiger moth larva (Lepidoptera: Arctiidae in part)

This large, stinging caterpillar is covered with very long, flowing golden-buff hairs. Also known as *čupil hihteʔ* 'bizarre caterpillar of oak', as it is typically found on oaks

(*Quercus* spp.). *kʼanal čup* 'yellow stinging caterpillar' is a synonym for some informants (but see preceding paragraph).

*bulukʼ sit* [UN + 'eye']: Some swallowtail butterfly larvae (see Figure 5.215g) (Papilionidae)

These are hairless and marked with prominent eye-spots, to which the name refers. Color varieties are recognized as follows: *ʔihkʼal bulukʼ sit* 'black eyed caterpillar', *kʼanal bulukʼ sit* 'yellow eyed caterpillar', *yašal bulukʼ sit* 'blue-green eyed caterpillar'. *bulukʼ sit* is feared as an evil omen (*ya šlabtawan*). Women who see this caterpillar will not bear children.

*sacʼ* [UN]: Large sphinx moth larvae (see Figure 5.215h) (Sphingidae in part)

These large, swarming caterpillars are dark colored, without hairs, and they protrude a hornlike osmaterium when disturbed. These larvae are considered to be edible and a delicacy, but a trip to lower areas to the north is required, as they do not commonly occur in Tenejapa. *sacʼ* is believed to transform (*ya škʼahta*) into the giant noctuid moth known as *meʔ sacʼ* 'mother of the swarming caterpillar' (*Thysania agrippina*, see *pehpen*/butterfly–moth). This is apparently incorrect.

*sacʼ čan* 'swarming caterpillar critter' : Smaller sphinx moth larvae (Sphingidae in part)

Similar to *sacʼ* but smaller. This type may be subsumed under *wah čan* (the following taxon) by some informants.

*wah čan* 'corn dough critter': Hairless caterpillars (Lepidoptera in part)

They are considered pestiferous, since they destroy growing crops. Color varieties are recognized: *ʔihkʼal wah čan* 'black corn dough critter', *kʼanal wah čan* 'yellow corn dough critter', *cʼirin wah čan* 'streaked corn dough critter'. *wahwah čan* is a variant.

*hohtiwaneh* [< tv 'measure between index finger and thumb + ag]: Loopers or inch worms (see Figure 5.215i) (Lepidoptera: Geometridae; possibly related families as well)

Hairless caterpillars that move by looping. Varieties include *ʔihkʼal hohtiwaneh* 'black inch worm', **yašal hohtiwaneh** 'green inch worm'. They are considered innocuous (**mayuk smul**).

**meʔ toyiw** 'mother of ice': Small, swarming larvae (probably Diptera in part)

The name refers to the fact that these appear in cold country during the rainy season (June–December). Two distinct types are recognized.

a. **meba meʔ toyiw** 'orphan mother-of-ice'. These are smaller than *ʔihkʼal meʔ toyiw* 'black mother-of-ice' (see [b]) and pale colored, thus also known as *čʼin meʔ toyiw* 'small mother-of-ice', or **sakil meʔ toyiw** 'white mother-of-ice'. One specimen is a larval fly (order Diptera: EN No. 1002296).

b. **ʔihkʼal meʔ toyiw** 'black mother-of-ice': Larger and darker than the first subtype.   This type is the most effective in treating **hataw**, a painful and debilitating cracking of the soles of the feet in cold weather.

**yal ha** 'fly's child': Small, whitish larvae

Two distinct types are recognized.

a. **bacʼil yal ha** 'true fly's child': Maggot (Diptera in part: EN No. 1002393).   This is the familiar maggot of decaying flesh. **syalhaul čahem wakaš** 'maggot of dead cattle' is synonymous. As the name indicates, this type is believed to transform (**ya škʼahta**) into blow flies (Calliphoridae, see **ha[a]/fly**), an accurate assessment.

b. [residual]: Larva found in fruit, etc.   Individual specimens are typically named by reference to the fruit in which they are found. Color varieties vary from **sakil** 'white' to **kʼanal** 'yellow'. The following list may not be exhaustive:
**syalhaul ʼahete'** 'maggot of ʼahete' (*Casimiroa edulis*)'.

**syalhaul ʔalčaš** 'maggot of oranges', EN No. 1002322.

**syalhaul čehčew** 'maggot of mushroom sp.'.

**syalhaul čʼiš teʔ** 'maggot of hawthorne' (*Crataegus pubescens*), EN No. 1002321.

**syalhaul ʔelemoneš** 'maggot of limes'.

**syalhaul kʼeweš** 'maggot of custard apple' (*Annona* sp.).

**syalhaul mansána** 'maggot of apples'.

**syalhaul páta** 'maggot of guava' (*Psidium* sp.).

**syalhaul tulésna** 'maggot of peach' (*Prunus persica*).

Another specimen (EN No. 1002373), found near a stream, was called **syalhaul haʔ** 'maggot of water'.

**yal šuš** 'wasp's child' are wasp larvae (see **šuš**/wasp complex). However, patherns of use indicate that **yal šuš** is not a taxon but rather a growth stage term. This may be due to the more obvious physical association of wasps and their larvae in comparison to flies and their larvae.

PARASITE COMPLEX
(See Figure 5.216)

An assortment of arthropods; typically, it is the tiny human parasites that are included here. It is not clear to what extent this complex is defined in terms of morphological as opposed to behavioral criteria.

**čʼak** [UN]: Fleas (INSECTA: Siphonaptera)

Two specific subdivisions are recognized:

a. **bacʼil čʼak** 'true flea'.   Included here are the common fleas found on dogs (Siphonaptera: Pulicidae). The one specimen (EN No. 118422) was collected from a dog and alternatively referred to as **ščʼakul cʼiʔ** 'flea of the dog'. **mukʼul čʼak** 'large flea' and **čʼin čʼak** 'small flea' varieties are recognized.

b. **ʔočʼem čʼak** 'flea that entered': Chigoe

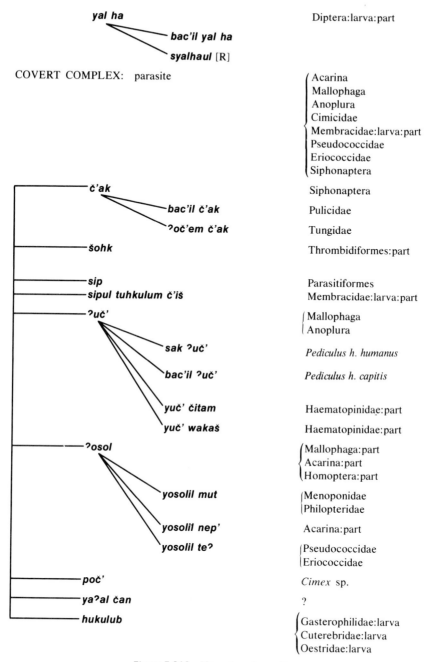

**Figure 5.216**   Maggots and parasites.

fleas (Siphonaptera: Tungidae). The females of these tiny fleas burrow into people's feet, especially under the toenails, where they lay their eggs. As the eggs develop they produce an intolerable itching and considerable danger of infection. According to legend, the original Pueblo of Tenejapa was moved from the lowland *paraje* of **pokolum** (literally 'old town') to its present site at 2200 m to escape these fleas. For some reason they are no longer common even in lowland Tenejapa. This identification is based on detailed verbal descriptions that eliminate all other possibilities.

*šohk* [UN]: Chiggers (ARACHNIDA: Acarina: Thrombidiformes in part)

The identification is based on verbal descriptions, i.e., minute, red animals that cause itching about the waist, etc.

*sip* [UN]: Ticks (ARACHNIDA: Acarina: Parasitiformes; EN Nos. 118495 and 118495b are of the Ixodidae)

*muk'ul sip* 'large tick' and *č'in sip* 'small tick' varieties are recognized. Both specimens are considered to be 'small'. The Spanish loan *karapáta* is occasionally heard. A bat fly (INSECTA: Diptera: Streblidae: EN No. 1002314), collected from a bat, was called *sipul soc'* 'bat tick'. However it is not clear that this insect is consistently recognized as such.

*sipul tuhkulum č'iš* 'tick of nightshade': Treehopper nymphs (INSECTA: Homoptera: Membracidae: EN No. 1002348).

They are so named because they suck plant juices and swell up like ticks. The specimen was collected on the plant so named (*Solanum* spp.). Also known as *čanul tuhkulum č'iš* 'critter of nightshade'.

*ʔuč'* [UN]: Lice (INSECTA: Mallophaga and Anoplura)

Several distinct varieties are recognized:

a. *sak ʔuč'* 'white louse': The body louse (Anoplura: Pediculidae: *Pediculus humanus humanus*). Found on humans, restricted to the body and clothing of human beings.

b. *bac'il ʔuč'* 'true louse': The head louse (*Pediculus humanus capitis*). Restricted to the heads of humans. *ʔihk'al ʔuč'* 'black louse' is synonymous.

c. *yuč' čitam* 'pig louse': Most likely a mammal-sucking louse (Anoplura: Haematopinidae).

d. *yuč' wakaš* 'cattle louse': Probably also a mammal-sucking louse (Haematopinidae).

Some informants assert that a type of *ʔuč'* is found also on dogs (*yuč' c'iʔ*) and chickens (*yuč' mut*). Others deny this. If it is true, the dog louse might either be a species of the Haematopinidae or a mammal-chewing louse (Mallophaga: Trichodectidae). It is not clear if the bird louse is distinct from the following category (*ʔosol*).

*ʔosol* [UN]: A variety of minute parasitic arthropods

Types are distinguished according to the host animal or plant:

a. *yosolil mut* 'chicken louse': Bird louse (INSECTA: Mallophaga: Menoponidae or Philopteridae). The lice found on turkeys are not considered distinct. Thus *yosolil tuluk'* 'turkey louse' is synonymous.

b. *yosolil nep'* 'crab louse': Probably a mite (ARACHNIDA: Acarina in part). A red mite on a lizard (*k'alel čan* lizard) was called *yosolil k'alel čan*, but this type is not regularly recognized.

c. *yosolil teʔ* 'tree louse': Mealy bugs (INSECTA: Homoptera: Pseudococcidae or Eriococcidae: EN No. 1003273). Some informants also cite the existence of *yosolil con teʔ* 'tree moss louse', a similar organism found on spanish moss, and *yosolil lum* 'ground louse', an unidentified organism found in soil.

*poč'* [UN]: Bedbugs (INSECTA: Hemiptera: Cimicidae)

These pests are not common in Tenejapa. Curiously, bed bugs, lice, and the dog are the domestic animals first introduced to the North American continent. Domestic, because the species found in human habitations (*Cimex* spp.) are found nowhere else. Introduced, because the wild forms ancestral to these species are native to Asia.

*yaʔal čan* 'weak bug': A virus?

Cankersores are allegedly caused by a minute animal known by this name. Some informants claim to have seen this animal.

It is unclear what this term refers to. However, it is widely cited.

**hukulub** 'becomes the botfly': Botfly larvae (INSECTA: Diptera: Gasterophilidae, Cuterebridae, and/or Oestridae)

Some, i.e., the robust botflies (Cuterebridae), are found beneath the skin of rabbits (*t'ul*/mammal) and wood rats (*hse? te?*/ mammal, rat). Others, i.e., the Oestridae, parasitize cattle. The identification is based on inferences from verbal descriptions. See **huk** (the fly complex).

## MILLIPEDE COMPLEX
(See Figure 5.217)

The following two taxa together comprise the MYRIAPODA. Alternate naming patterns clearly indicate their close mutual association for the Tzeltal.

**mokoč** [UN]: Millipedes (class DIPLOPODA)

Varietal distinctions are recognized as follows: **cahal mokoč** 'red millipedes', **?ihk'al mokoč** 'black millipedes', and **sakil mokoč** 'white millipedes'. It is possible that an inductive distinction is recognized by some informants between **pehč pehč mokoč** 'flat-flat millipede', the flat-backed millipedes (order Polydesmida), and those described as 'round backed' (**nolol spat**), millipedes of the orders Spirostreptida and Spirobolida. However this distinction is not consistently recognized. Specimens include EN Nos. 118498, 1002260, 1002263 (Polydesmida); 1002368, 1003238 (Spirostreptida); 1002262 (Spirobolida); and 1002261, 1003267 (not identified as to order). Centipedes (class CHILOPODA) are included in the extended range of this taxon by a few informants and may be known as **ti?wal mokoč** 'biting milli-

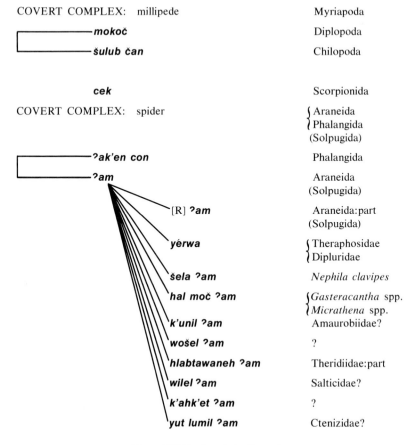

Figure 5.217   Assorted arthropods.

pede' (but see following taxon). Millipedes, if eaten, are believed to make a man stupid (**šposil ya šbolob k'ahk'al winik yuʔun**).

**šulub čan** 'horned bug': Centipedes (class CHILOPODA)

Many informants are unfamiliar with this taxon, naming it descriptively as **cahal čan** 'red bug' or **pehč hol čan** 'flat-headed bug'. Others include it within the extended range of the preceding taxon as **kps mokoč** or **tiʔwal mokoč** 'biting millipede'. The latter term refers to the fact that centipedes possess stinging fangs on the first pair of legs. Specimens include EN Nos. 1002341 and 1002367 (order Scolopendromorpha); 1002366 (order Lithobiomorpha); and 118074 (not identified as to order).

**cek** [UN]: Scorpions (ARACHNIDA: Scorpionida: EN Nos. 118499 [see Figure 5.218a], 1002370, 1003235, all belonging to the Buthidae; and EH No. 598)

Color varieties are recognized, e.g., **ʔihk'al cek** 'black scorpion'. Their sting is feared.

## SPIDER COMPLEX

The following two generic taxa are considered to be closely related. Note in particular the alternate usage, **ʔak'en con ʔam** 'harvestman spider' for **ʔak'en con**.

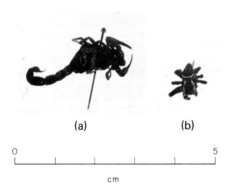

(a)                          (b)

0                                              5

cm

Figure 5.218  Assorted arthropods: (a) **cek** Scorpionida, Buthidae: EN No. 118499; (b) **bac'il ʔam** Araneida, Salticidae: EN No. 118505.

**ʔak'en con** 'plank moss': Harvestmen (ARACHNIDA: Phalangida: EN Nos. 118501–118503)

**ʔak'en con ʔam** 'harvestman spider' is a variant and indicates a close relationship perceived with the following taxon.

**ʔam** [UN]: Spiders (ARACHNIDA: Araneida)

All spiders are included here, as well as the related order Solpugida (Ammotrechidae: EN Nos. 1002268, 1002313). The web is known as **sna ʔam** 'spider's house'. Several specific subdivisions are recognized:

a. **bac'il ʔam** 'true spider'. This residual category includes all spiders not specifically distinguished, as well as the Solpugida. Varietal distinctions are cited as follows:

**ʔam** 'spider' (Thomisidae: EN No. 1002300).

**bac'il ʔam** 'true spider' (Lycosidae: *Pardosa* sp.: EN No. 1002365; *Lycosa* sp.: EN No. 1002369).

**češ k'ab ʔam** 'long-legged spider', also known as **posk'ab ʔam** [UN + 'leg' + 'spider'] (Pisauridae: EN No. 1002362).

**č'in ʔam** 'small spider' (Clubionidae: EN No. 118504; Thomisidae: EN No. 1002265), see also **muk'ul ʔam**.

**č'išpat ʔam** 'spiny-backed spider' (Araneidae: *Verrucosa arenata*: EN Nos. 1003259, 1003260).

**ʔihk'al ʔam** 'black spider' (Salticidae: EN No. 118505) (see Figure 5.218b).

**muk'ul ʔam** 'large spider', same as **č'in ʔam** (see above). This indicates that there is little agreement about the size of the "typical" spider.

**sakil ʔam** 'white spider' (Linyphiidae: EN No. 1002299).

**wol ʔit ʔam** 'round-tailed spider' (Lycosidae: *Pardosa* sp.: EN No. 1003265).

**wol ʔit ʔihk'al ʔam** 'round-tailed black spider', (Salticidae: EN No. 1003266).

b. **yérwa** [< Sp 'tarantula']: Tarantulas (suborder Mygalomorphae).  Specimens represent two families; the true tarantulas (Theraphosidae: EN No. 1003233, EH No. 240) and the funnel-web tarantulas (Dipluridae: EN No. 1003232). Tarantulas are used as a cure for 'tumors' (*špošil čakal*). The cure involves inducing the spider to bite the surface of the 'tumor', drawing blood. *ti ̓wal ̓am* 'biting spider' may be synonymous as the one specimen so named is a theraphosid.

c. *šela ̓am* [ < OSp/*seda*/ 'silk, ribbon' + spider']: Some orb weavers (Araneidae in part), in particular the golden silk spider (*Nephila clavipes*: EN No. 1003239). A second specimen included here has been identified only as of this family (EN No. 1002308). The females of this species are large, with brightly patterned, elongated abdomens. The web consists of an irregular set of criss-crossing strands with a partial orb at the center. According to folklore, women wishing to learn to weave better must wrap the web of this spider around their hands (*špošil halabil yu ̓un ̓ancetik*).

d. *hal moč ̓am* 'basket-weaver spider': Some orb weavers (Araneidae in part). Specimens assigned to this taxon are brightly colored, with spiny abdomens, and construct perfect orb webs (*Gasteracantha* sp.: EN No. 1002267; *Micrathena* sp.: EN No. 1002360). Also known as *moč ̓am* 'basket spider'.

e. *k ̓unil ̓am* 'soft spider': Probably the Amaurobiidae (EN No. 1002361). Their webs are described as 'soft', thus the name, and are funnels built about a crevice in a rock or other such retreat. A wolf spider, *Lycosa* sp. (Lycosidae), was also placed here, though such spiders do not build nests as described. Three other wolf spider specimens were treated as *bac ̓il ̓am* (see above).

f. *wošel ̓am* 'blister spider': An unidentified type of spider that allegedly raises blisters when it runs across one's body. *beel ̓am* 'walking spider' is synonymous.

g. *hlabtawaneh ̓am* 'harbinger-of-evil spider': A small, red cobweb spider (Theridiidae: EN No. 1002363). This type is not widely recognized.

h. *wilel ̓am* 'flying spider': Perhaps jumping spiders (Salticidae). The one specimen of this family identified by informants was treated as a variety of *bac ̓il ̓am* (see above).

i. *k ̓ahk ̓et ̓am* 'fiery spider'. This spider allegedly kills orange trees by covering them with its webs. *hmil ̓alčaš ̓am* 'orange-killer spider' is a synonym.

j. *yut lumil ̓am* 'inside-the-ground spider': Perhaps trapdoor spiders (Ctenizidae), though I have no specimens.

# SYSTEMATIC LIST OF ANIMAL TAXA CITED, CATALOG OF SPECIMENS AND OBSERVATIONS, INDEXED TO CLOSEST RELEVANT TZELTAL ANIMAL CLASS*

PLATYHELMINTHES
  TURBELLARIA
    Tricladia                 *?ohcel*                 CAS–EH 789
  CESTODA
    *Taenia*                 *me? lukum*
ASCHELMINTHES
  NEMATOMORPHA
    Gordioidea            *cocil holol čan*       CAS–EH 573
  NEMATODA
    *Ascaris*                *slukumil č'uht*
    *Oxyuris*                *bosbos lukum*
MOLLUSCA
  GASTROPODA
    Cyclophoridae
      *Neocyclotus* cf *N. dysoni*    *puy*            CAS–EH 522
    Thiaridae
      *Pachychilus* sp.          *puy*            CAS–EH 724–725

*Abbreviations used in this appendix:

| | |
|---|---|
| cf | Indicates a species similar to that which follows. |
| sp. | An unspecified or unidentified species (spp. is plural). |
| CAS | Specimen deposited at the California Academy of Sciences. |
| EH | E. Hunn collection number. |
| EN | Entomology Museum number, University of California, Berkeley. |
| MVZ | Museum of Vertebrate Zoology catalog number. |
| HLB | Hypothetical List: Birds. |
| HLS | Hypothetical List: Snakes. |
| [R] | Indicates a residual subset of the taxon cited. |
| P | Exemplars identified substantiated by photographs. |
| S | Identification based on sight records of exemplars. |
| Z | Identification of live specimens in a zoological collection. |
| Sp | Specimen identified by informants; initials following indicate location of specimen: |
| JFC | Joseph F. Copp herpetological collection |
| MAT | Miguel Alvarez del Toro collection, Tuxtla Gutiérrez, Chiapas, Mexico |
| MVZ | Museum of Vertebrate Zoology, University of California, Berkeley, California |

Planorbidae
    *Taphius* cf *T. subpronus*      *č'in k'oʔ*      CAS–EH 465
Physidae
    *Aplexa* sp.      *yat naab*      CAS–EH 467, 549
    *Physa* cf. *P. berendti*      *yat naab*      CAS–EH 467a
Limacidae
    *Deroceras laeve*      *nap'ak*      CAS–EH 161, 451, 575
Oleacinidae
    *Euglandina sowerbyana*      *k'ohčin teʔ*      CAS–EH 529
    *Euglandina* cf. *E. monolifera*      *k'ohčin teʔ*      CAS–EH 771
    *Euglandina* sp.      *k'ohčin teʔ*      CAS–EH 546
Helminthoglyptidae
    *Lysinoe ghiesbreghti*      *k'oʔ*      CAS–EH 523b, 524, 901
PELECYPODA
  Unionidae
    *Elliptio* cf *E. calamitarum*      *bak čikin*      CAS–EH 786
ANNELIDA
  OLIGOCHAETA
    (large sp.)      *haʔal lukum*      CAS–EH 581
    (other spp.)      [R] *lukum*      CAS–EH 103, 161, 328, 445, 451, 541, 575, 591–592

  HIRUDINEA spp.      *ʔohcel*      CAS–EH 544, 597–598, 715
ARTHROPODA
  ARACHNIDA
    Scorpionida
      Buthidae      *cek*      EN 118499, 1002370, 1003235; EH 598

    Acarina
      Thrombidiformes      *šohk, yosolil nep'*
      Parasitiformes
        Oxididae      *sip*      EN 118495, 118495b
    Phalangida spp.      *ʔak'en con*      EN 118501–118503
    Solpugida
      Ammotrechidae sp.      [R] *ʔam*      EN 1002268, 1002313
    Araneida
      Theraphosidae      *yérwa ʔam*      EN 1003233; EH 240
      Ctenizidae      *yut lumil ʔam*
      Dipluridae      *yérwa ʔam*      EN 1003232
      Therididae      *hlabtawaneh ʔam*      EN 1002363
      Linyphiidae      [R] *ʔam*      EN 1002299
      Araneidae
        sp.      *šela ʔam*      EN 1002308
        *Gasteracantha* sp.      *hal moč ʔam*      EN 1002267
        *Micrathena* sp.      *hal moč ʔam*      EN 1002360
        *Nephila clavipes*      *šela ʔam*      EN 1003239
        *Verrucosa arenata*      [R] *ʔam*      EN 1003259–1003260
      Pisauridae      [R] *ʔam*      EN 1002362
      Lycosidae
        *Lycosa* sp.      [R] *ʔam*      EN 1002369
        *Pardosa* sp.      [R] *ʔam*      EN 1002365, 1003265
      Clubionidae      [R] *ʔam*      EN 118504
      Thomisidae      [R] *ʔam*      EN 1002265, 1002300
      Salticidae      *wilel ʔam*      EN 1003266
      Amaurobiidae      *k'unil ʔam*      EN 1002361
CRUSTACEA
  Conchostraca      *bak čikin*      CAS–EH 469–470, 549
  Isopoda
    Porcellionidae      *škoen čan*      EN 118497, 1002272, 1002276
    Armadillididae      *škoen čan*      EN 118496

| | | |
|---|---|---|
| Decapoda | | |
| Penaeida | *kamarol čay* | CAS–EH 176 |
| Reptantia | | |
| Astacidae | *masan čay* | CAS–EH 433 |
| Brachyura | | |
| Potamonidae | *nep'* | CAS–EH 596, 721, 723, 730 |
| MYRIAPODA | | |
| DIPLOPODA | | |
| sp. | *mokoč* | EN 1002261, 1003267 |
| Polydesmida | *mokoč* | EN 118498, 1002260, 1002263 |
| Spirobolida | *mokoč* | EN 1002262 |
| Spirostreptida | *mokoč* | EN 1002368, 1003238 |
| CHILOPODA | | |
| sp. | *šulub čan* | EN 118074 |
| Lithobiomorpha | *šulub čan* | EN 1002366 |
| Scolopendromorpha | *šulub čan* | EN 1002341, 1002367 |
| INSECTA | | |
| Thysanura | | |
| Machilidae | *nap'ak* | EN 118258 |
| Ephemeroptera sp. | | EN 118409 |
| Odonata | | |
| Anisoptera | | |
| spp. (larvae) | *šk'ohowil čan* | EN 1002371, 1002378 |
| Gomphidae | [R] *tultuš, hmah ha?* | EN 118415 |
| Aeshnidae | [R] *tultuš, hmah ha?* | EN 118421 |
| Libellulidae | [R] *tultuš* | EN 118412, 118416 |
| Zygoptera | | |
| spp. (larvae) | *bac'ul ha?* | EN 1002297–1002298, 1002302, 1002342 |
| Calopterygidae | | |
| *Hetaerina* sp. | [R] *tultuš* | EN 118414 |
| Lestidae | *meba tultuš* | EN 118417 |
| Coenagrionidae | *meba tultuš* | EN 118410–118411, 118413, 118418, 118420 |
| Pseudostigmatidae | | |
| *Mecistogaster ornata* | *nen tultuš* | EN 118419 |
| Orthoptera | | |
| Caelifera | | |
| Acrididae | | |
| sp. (immature) | *p'ilič* | EN 118291–118292 |
| Cyrtacanthacridinae | *k'ulub, p'ilič* | EN 118271, 118277, 118280–118282, 118284–118289 |
| Acridinae | *p'ilič* | EN 118278–118279 |
| Oedipodinae | *p'ilič, šk'ah* | EN 118270, 118272, 118274–118276, 118283, 118290 |
| Pyrgomorphinae | | |
| *Spenarium* sp. 1 | *masan* | EN 118264, 118267–118268 |
| *Spenarium* sp. 2 | *p'ilič* | EN 118265–118266 |
| Romaleinae | | |
| *Taeniopoda* sp. 1 | *k'ulub kawáyu* | EN 118259–118261, 118263 |
| *Taeniopoda* sp. 2 (immature) | *p'ilič* | EN 118262 |
| Eumastacidae | *p'ilič* | EN 118273 |
| Ensifera | | |
| Tettigonidae | | |
| sp. (immature) | [R] *čil* | EN 118320 |
| Phaneropterinae | *čik č'iš,* [R] *čil* | EN 118293–118298, 118300, 118304–118306 |
| *Microcentrum* sp. | *čik č'iš* | |
| Pseudophyllinae | [R] *čil* | EN 118299 |

| | | |
|---|---|---|
| Copiphorinae | *masan* | EN 118301–118303, 118307–118310 |
| Decticinae | *yol* | EN 118269, 1003305 |
| Gryllacrididae | | |
| Rhaphidophorinae | *tu ca? čil* | |
| Gryllacridinae | *tu ca? čil* | EN 118319 |
| Stenopelmatinae | | |
|   *Stenopelmatus* sp. | *?ok'il₂* | EN 118247–118248, 1003245 |
| Gryllidae | | |
| Gryllotalpinae | *sbaul ?uk'um* | EN 1002355 |
| Nemobiinae | *?ihk'al čil, p'ilič* | EN 118311 |
| Gryllinae | *?ihk'al čil* | EN 118313–118318 |
| Mantodea | | |
| Mantidae | *k'al čil* | EN 118243–118245 |
| Phasmatodea | | |
| Phasmatidae | | |
|   sp. (immature) | [R] *čil* | EN 118242 |
|   (large, black sp.) | *skawáyu h?ihk'al* | EN 118246, 1003240 |
| Blattodea | | |
| Blattidae | | |
|   spp. | *pewal, mako?* | EN 118250, 118253–118254, 1002257, 1002357 |
|   *Blattela germanica* | *pewal* | EN 118251 |
|   *Pseudomops* sp. | *pewal* | EN 118249 |
| Isoptera | *šanič* | EN 1003254 |
| Plecoptera | | |
| Perlidae | | EN 118407 |
| Dermaptera | | |
| Forficulidae | | |
|   *Neolobophora ruficeps* | *c'urupik* | EN 118255–118256 |
| Psocoptera | *šut* | EN 118494 |
| Mallophaga | | |
| Menoponidae | *yosolil mut* | |
| Philopteridae | *yosolil mut* | |
| Trichodectidae | *?uč'* | |
| Anoplura | | |
| Haematopinidae | *?uč'* | |
| Pediculidae | | |
|   *Pediculus humanus capitis* | *bac'il ?uč'* | |
|   *P. h. humanus* | *sak ?uč'* | |
| Hemiptera | | |
| Corixidae | *hawhaw čan* | EN 1002293 |
| Notonectidae | *hawhaw čan* | EN 1002285–1002286, 1002294–1002295 |
| Belostomatidae | *šme? šmut* | EN 1002379, 1003256 |
| Naucoridae | *šme? šmut* | EN 1002379 |
| Gelastocoridae | *cihil čan* | EN 117983 |
| Gerridae | *pošil nušel* | EN 117985–117987, 1002289, 1002316 |
| Veliidae | *pošil nušel* | EN 117984, 1002283, 1003289, 1003316 |
| Cimicidae | | |
|   *Cimex* sp. | *poč'* | |
| Reduviidae | | |
|   *Pothea* sp. | *cihil čan* | EN 117966 |
|   *Pselliopus* sp. | *cihil čan* | EN 117965 |
|   *Repipta* sp. | *cihil čan* | EN 117964 |
|   *Zelus* sp. | *cihil čan* | EN 117963 |
| Piesmatidae | *cihil čan* | EN 117967, 117970–117971, 117980 |
| Lygaeidae | *cihil čan* | EN 117969, 117972 |

| | | |
|---|---|---|
| Pyrrhocoridae | *cihil čan* | EN 117975–117977, 117979 |
| Coreidae | *cihil čan* | EN 117955–117958, 117974, 117982 |
| Corizidae | | EN 117973 |
| Aradidae | | EN 118034–118035 |
| Pentatomidae | *cihil čan* | EN 117959–117962 |
| Homoptera | | |
| Auchenorrhyncha | | |
| Cicadidae | *čikitin* | EN 118399 |
| Membracidae | | |
| sp. (larva) | *sipul tuhkulum č'iš* | EN 1002348 |
| sp. (adults) | *p'um te ʔ* | EN 118404, 118406, 1002356 |
| Cercopidae | *p'um te ʔ* | EN 118014, |
| Cicadellidae | *p'um te ʔ* | EN 118400, 118402–118403, 118405 |
| Flatidae | *p'um te ʔ* | EN 118401 |
| Sternorrhyncha | | |
| Aphididae | *čanul karawánco* | EN 1002339 |
| Pseudococcidae, Eriococcidae | *yosolil te ʔ* | EN 1003273 |
| Neuroptera | | |
| Corydalidae (larvae) | *špálu ha ʔ* | EN 1002391, 1003258 |
| Dilaridae | | EN 118408 |
| Myrmeleontidae (larva) | *butbut ʔit čan* | EN 1002280 |
| Coleoptera | | |
| Carabidae | | |
| Harpalini | *čan₂* | EN 118030–118031 |
| Oryptini | *čan₂* | EN 118032, 118036 |
| Pterostichini | *čan₂* | EN 118033, 118037 |
| Dytiscidae | *hawhaw čan, šme ʔ šmut* | EN 118072–118073, 1002287, 1002295, 1002310 |
| Gyrinidae | *mayil čan₁* | EN 1002288, 1002290, 1002292, 1002315 |
| Hydrophilidae | *mayil čan₁* | EN 1002291 |
| Staphylinidae | *c'urupik* | EN 118003–118006, 118074, 118395–118396 |
| Lampyridae | *kukai* | EN 117997–117999 |
| Lycidae | *čan₂* | EN 117994–117996 |
| Melyridae | *čan₂* | EN 118057 |
| Cleridae | *čan₂* | EN 118066 |
| Elateridae | *šp'ahk'in te ʔ čan* | EN 118000–118002, 118045, 118069 |
| Erotylidae | *čan₂* | EN 118011–118012, 118044, 118062, 118067–118068 |
| Endomychidae | *čan₂* | EN 118049 |
| Coccinellidae | *čan₂* | EN 118046, 118058, 118065 |
| Meloidae | | |
| sp. | *kukai* | EN 118056 |
| *Meloe laevis* | *tuluk' čan* | EN 1002256 |
| *M. nebulosus* | *tuluk' čan* | EN 1003231 |
| Tenebrionidae | | |
| Tenebrioninae | | |
| *Eleodes* sp. | *tu cis čan* | EN 118070 |
| Tentyriinae | *kukai* | EN 118053 |
| Zopheridae | | |
| *Zopherus jourdani* | *wayway čan* | EN 117992–117993 |
| Passalidae | *čimolil te ʔ* | EN 117950–117954 |
| Scarabaeidae | | |
| Cetoniinae | *kuhtum ca ʔ* | EN 118026 |
| Dynastinae | *čimol* | EN 118019–118020, 118024–118025 |
| Geotrupinae | *kuhtum ca ʔ* | EN 118016, 118022 |

| | | |
|---|---|---|
| Melolonthinae | *ʔumoh* | EN 118007, 118047 |
| Rutelinae | *čimol, ʔumoh* | EN 118008–118010, 118023 |
| Scarabaeinae | *kuhtum caʔ* | EN 118017–118018, 118021, 118027 |
| Cerambycidae | | |
| Aseminae | *hseʔ teʔ čan* | EN 117989 |
| Clytinae | *hseʔ teʔ čan* | EN 117988, 117990–117991 |
| Prioninae | *šulton* | EN 118028–118029 |
| Chrysomelidae | | |
| sp. | *čan₂* | EN 118054 |
| Alticinae | | |
| (bean parasite) | *čanul čenek'* | EN 118050–118051 |
| (other spp.) | *čan₂* | EN 118055, 118060–118061, 118063–118064 |
| Cryptocephalinae | *čan₂* | EN 118048 |
| Eumolpinae | *čan₂* | EN 118052 |
| Galerucinae | *čan₂* | EN 118013, 118015 |
| Anthribidae | *hoč'* | EN 1002303 |
| Curculionidae | *hoč', hmil mut čan* | EN 118038–118043 |
| Trichoptera | | |
| Leptoceridae | | EN 118397 |
| Lepidoptera | | |
| Frenatae: Macrolepidoptera | | |
| Papilionidae | | |
| cf *Papilio polyxenes* | [R] *pehpen* | EN 118344 |
| cf *Parides iphidamas* | [R] *pehpen* | EN 118346 |
| Morphidae | [R] *pehpen* | S |
| Brassolidae | | |
| *Caligo memnon* | *pehpenul balam* | EN 118337 |
| Nymphalidae | | |
| sp. | [R] *pehpen* | EN 118345 |
| cf *Anartia fatima* | [R] *pehpen* | EN 118333 |
| cf *Diaethria anna* | [R] *pehpen* | EN 118343 |
| cf *Dynamine* sp. | [R] *pehpen* | EN 118325 |
| cf *Euphydryas* sp. | [R] *pehpen* | EN 118334 |
| cf *Hamadryas feronia* | [R] *pehpen* | EN 118340 |
| cf *Junonia lavinia* | [R] *pehpen* | EN 118335 |
| *Nymphalis antiopa* (adult) | [R] *pehpen* | EN 118336 |
| (larva) | *č'ištul* | EN 1003316 |
| cf *Prepona laertes* | [R] *pehpen* | EN 118338 |
| cf *Vanessa carye* | [R] *pehpen* | EN 118331 |
| Heliconidae | | |
| sp. | *tultuš pehpen* | EN 118342 |
| cf *Dione vanillae* | [R] *pehpen* | EN 118332 |
| cf *Heleconius ismenius* | *tultuš pehpen* | EN 118341 |
| Ithomiidae | | |
| cf *Ithomia patilla* | *tultuš pehpen* | EN 118330 |
| Danaidae | | |
| *Danaus plexippus* | [R] *pehpen* | EN 118348 |
| Pieridae | | |
| *Colias* sp. | [R] *pehpen* | EN 118322 |
| cf *Eurema lisa* | [R] *pehpen* | EN 118324 |
| cf *Phoebis eubule* | [R] *pehpen* | EN 118326 |
| *Pieris* sp. | [R] *pehpen* | EN 118321 |
| cf *Synchloe callidice* | [R] *pehpen* | EN 118323 |
| Satyridae | | |
| cf *Taygetis* sp. | [R] *pehpen* | EN 118347 |
| Lycaenidae | | |
| Plebiinae | [R] *pehpen, supul* | EN 118327 |
| Theclinae | [R] *pehpen* | EN 118328 |

Nemeobiidae
   cf *Lymnas alena* — [R] *pehpen* — EN 118339
Hesperiidae
   spp. — [R] *pehpen, supul* — EN 118329, 118352–118356
   cf *Polythrix alcifron* — *nemut pehpen* — EN 118349–118351
Sphingidae (adult) — *c'unun pehpen* — EN 118357
   (larvae) — *sac', sac' čan* — EN 1002396, 1003226
Saturniidae — [R] *pehpen* — EN 118389–118392
Geometridae (larvae) — *hohtiwaneh*
Ctenuchidae — [R] *pehpen, supul* — EN 118358–118359, 118366, 118369, 118372
Lithosiidae — [R] *pehpen, supul* — EN 118368, 118370, 118374
Arctiidae
   spp. — [R] *pehpen, supul* — EN 118362, 118367, 118376, 118378–118379, 118381–118383, 118386–118387
   *Utethesia* sp. — [R] *pehpen, supul* — EN 118361
Noctuidae
   spp. — [R] *pehpen, supul* — EN 118360, 118364, 118380, 118394
   *Thysania agrippina* — *me? sac' (pehpen)* — EH 787
Pericopidae — [R] *pehpen* — EN 118393
Frenatae: Microlepidoptera
   sp. — *supul* — EN 118371
Limacodidae (larva) — *bac'il čup*
Pyralidae — *supul* — EN 118363, 118365, 118373, 118375, 118377, 118385, 118388

Diptera
   Tipulidae — *lalum, šenen* — EN 118471–118477
   Culicidae — *šenen* — EN 118478–118479;
   (pupae) — *bosbos čan* — EH 109
   Simuliidae — *k'an ?us, ?ihk'al ?us*
   Bibionidae — *čanul ca? mut* — EN 118423–118427, 118430
   Sciaridae — *čanul ca? mut* — EN 118428–118429
   Stratiomyidae — *?ako?* — EN 118398
   Tabanidae — *škač* — EN 118453–118454
   Asilidae — *škač* — EN 118463
   Bombyliidae — *škač* — EN 118455–118456, 118460–118461
   Dolichopodidae — *č'ikil, šenen* — EN 118481, 118488, 118493
   Platypezidae — *k'unil ?us*
   Syrphidae
     spp. — *šut, škač, yaš ton ha* — EN 118449, 118457, 118459, 118462, 118464–118468
     *Eristalis* sp. — *?aha čab* — EN 118450–118452
     *Syrphus* sp. — *šut* — EN 118469–118470
     *Volucella* sp. — *nucnuc* — EN 118458
   Micropezidae
     Taeniapterinae — *hwah mahtas* — EN 118208
   Otitidae — *šut* — EN 118482–118483
   Lonchaeidae — *yaš ton ha* — EN 118491
   Chloropidae — *p'o? č'in ?us* — EN 118485–118487, 118492
   Agromyzidae — *k'an ?us* — EN 118484
   Milichiidae — *?ihk'al ?us* — EN 118490
   Drosophilidae
     *Drosophila* sp. — *sakil ?us* — EN 1002309
   Hippoboscidae — EN 118489
   Streblidae — *sip* — EN 1002314
   Gasterophilidae,

Cuterebridae,
Oestridae
   (adults)                  *huk*
   (larvae)              *hukulub*
Muscidae
   spp.                    *muk'ul ?us*            EN 118437–118438
   *Musca domestica*     *muk'ul ?us*            EN 118431
   Tachinidae         *muk'ul ?us, coc ?it ha*     EN 118432, 118435–118436,
                                                   118440, 118442–118448

   Calliphoridae (adult)    *yaš ton ha*         EN 118433–118434, 118441
   (larva)                *yal ha*               EN 1002393
   Sarcophagidae       *muk'ul ?us*            EN 118439
Siphonaptera
   Pulicidae          *bac'il č'ak*          EN 118422
   Tungidae           *?oč'em č'ak*
Hymenoptera
  Chalcidoidea
   Chalcididae                             EN 118200
  Ichneumonoidea
   Braconidae         *yusil sac'*
   Ichneumonidae      *hwah mahtas*       EN 118202–118207, 118236,
                                                 118480

  Pelecinoidea
   Pelecinidae         *tultuš*               EN 118153
  Bethyloidea
   Trigonalidae        *?us ?ako?*           EN 118168
  Scolioidea
   Tiphiidae          *?us ?ako?*           EN 118181, 118186
   Scoliidae          *šuš* complex, *k'ahk'ub yat*    EN 118135, 118148–118149,
                                                  118239–118241

   Mutillidae         *muy ?am*            EN 118136–118139
   Formicidae
    Myrmicinae
     *Aphaenogaster* sp.   *meba šanič*        EN 1002274
     *Atta* spp.           *c'isim*             EN 118211–118215, 1002315,
                                                  1002317, 1002320, 1002325,
                                                  1002330, 1002337, 1003249,
                                                  1003251

     *Crytocerus* sp.     ant complex        EN 118232
     *Pheidole* spp.      *ses*                EN 1002275, 1002334
     *Solenopsis* spp.    *bac'il šanič*         EN 118224–118225, 1002304,
                                                  1002306, 1002311, 1002326,
                                                  1002331, 1002336, 1003250

    *Pseudomyrmecinae*
     *Pseudomyrma* spp.   *cihil šanič*         EN 118235, 1002282
    Formicinae
     (unidentified sp.)   *cihil šanič*         EN 118223, 118229–118231,
                                                  1002284, 1002328
     *Camponotus* spp.   *k'ork'owe*         EN 118209–118210, 118218–
                                                  118222, 1002273, 1002327,
                                                  1002329, 1002335, 1002338,
                                                  1002346, 1003252

     *Myrmecocystus* sp.   *k'ečeč*           EN 1002331
    Dolichoderinae
     *Dorymyrmex* spp.   *k'ečeč*           EN 1002311, 1002326
     *Tapinoma* sp.      *cihil šanič*         EN 1002337
    Dorylinae
     *Eciton* spp.        *bah te?, čikitoroš*     EN 118216–118217, 1002332–
                                                  1002333, 1002350–1002351,

|  |  | 1002353–1002354, 1002391, 1003253 |
|---|---|---|
| Ponerinae |  |  |
| *Leptogenys* sp. | **bak yat** | EN 118226 |
| *Neoponeura* spp. | **čil teʔ čan, bak yat** | EN 118176, 118214, 1002349 |
| *Odontomachus* spp. | **bak yat** | EN 118233–118234, 1002352 |
| *Pachycondyla* spp. | **bak yat** | EN 118227, 1002277–1002278, 1002318 |
| Vespoidea |  |  |
| Pompilidae | **kʼahkʼub yat** | EN 118128–118134, 118201 |
| Eumenidae |  |  |
| *Euodynerus* sp. | **kʼan mum** | EN 118170–118171 |
| *Hypalastoroides* sp. | **ʔus ʔakoʔ** | EN 118187 |
| *Parancistrocerus* n. sp. nr. *dorsalis* | **ʔus ʔakoʔ** | EN 118180 |
| *Stenodynerus* sp. | **ʔakoʔ** | EN 118169 |
| Vespidae |  |  |
| *Brachygastra lecheguana* | **ʔakoʔ** | EN 118172 |
| *Epipona tatua* | **cʼibon** | EN 118165–118166 |
| *Mischocyttarus basimacula* (♂) | **kʼan cʼutoh** | EN 118197 |
| *M. cubensis mexicanus* | **čič ʔalal** | EN 118143–118144 |
| *M. pallidipectus* (♂, ♀) | **ʔus ʔakoʔ** | EN 118184–118185 |
| *Parachartergus apicalis* | **sakil na šuš** | EN 118161–118162, 118167 |
| *Polistes apicalis* | **sakil na šuš** | EN 118155 |
| *P. canadensis* | **čič ʔalal, šanab šuš** | EN 118145 |
| *P. carnifex* | **čič ʔalal** | EN 118147 |
| *P. dorsalis* (♂) | **čič ʔalal** | EN 118146 |
| *P. instabilis* | **čič ʔalal** | EN 118140–118142 |
| *Polybia occidentalis* | **ʔus ʔakoʔ** | EN 118182 |
| *P. parvulina* | **ʔus ʔakoʔ** | EN 118175, 118177 |
| *P. pygmaea* | **ʔus ʔakoʔ** | EN 118178–118179, 118183 |
| *Stelopolybia areata* | **kʼan cʼutoh** | EN 118188–118196, 118198–118199 |
| *S. panamensis* | **šanab šuš, yut lumil mum** | EN 118154, 118156–118160, 118237–118238 |
| *Stelopolybia* sp. | **cʼibon** | EN 118163–118164 |
| *Synoeca surinama* | **kitaron** |  |
| Sphecoidea |  |  |
| Sphecidae |  |  |
| *Hoplisoides vespoides* | **ʔakoʔ** | EN 118173 |
| *Larra analis* | **kukai šuš** | EN 118150 |
| *Sceliphron assimile* | **šuš** complex | EN 118152 |
| *Sphex dorsalis* | **kukai šuš** | EN 118151 |
| Apoidea |  |  |
| Halictidae |  |  |
| sp. | **suk** | EN 118099, 118101, 118177 |
| *Augochloropsis* sp | **šyaš ʔič** | EN 118098, 118100 |
| *Pseudaugochloropsis* sp. | **suʔsiwal** | EN 118097 |
| Megachilidae |  |  |
| *Megachile* sp. | **suʔsiwal** | EN 118096 |
| Anthophoridae |  |  |
| Anthophorinae |  |  |
| *Anthophora* sp. | **suʔsiwal** | EN 118094–118095 |
| *Melissodes* sp. | **ʔaha čab** | EN 118088 |
| Xylocopinae |  |  |
| *Xylocopa* spp. | **nucnuc** | EN 118090–118093 |
| Apidae |  |  |
| Euglossinae |  |  |
| *Eulaema* sp. | **honon teʔ** | EN 118078 |
| Bombinae |  |  |
| *Bombus* sp. 1 | **čʼin honon, meʔ honon** | EN 118075–118077, 118081– |

|  |  | 118083 |
|---|---|---|
| *Bombus* sp. 2 | c'irin honon | EN 118079–118080, 118084 |
| Apinae |  |  |
| *Apis mellifera* | ʔaha čab | EN 118085–118087, 118089 |
| *Trigona* spp. | sunul, šoy, ʔinam čab, šenen čab, ʔus čab | EN 118102–118116, 118118– 118119, 118121–118124, 118126–118127, 1002358– 10023559 |

**CHORDATA**
**PISCES**
  **CHONDRICHTHYES**

| Rajiformes | HLF |  |
|---|---|---|

  **OSTEICHTHYES**
    Anguilliformes

| Anguillidae | čan čay |  |
|---|---|---|

    Siluriformes
      Pimelodidae

| *Rhamdia* sp. | ʔisim čay |  |
|---|---|---|

    Antheriniformes

| Exocoetidae⁻ | HLF |  |
|---|---|---|
| Poeciliidae | č'uhč'ul čay | EH 151, 183 |

    Perciformes
      Cichlidae

| *Cichlasoma* sp. | muháro |  |
|---|---|---|
| Scombridae | peskáro | P |

**AMPHIBIA**
  Gymnophiona
    Caeciliidae

| *Gymnophis* spp. | herínka lukum |  |
|---|---|---|

  Caudata
    Plethodontidae

| *Bolitoglossa hartwegi* | c'uhkuton | Sp: MVZ |
|---|---|---|
| *B. mexicana* | c'uhkuton | Sp: MVZ |
| *B. resplendens* | c'uhkuton | Sp: MVZ |
| *B. rostrata* | c'uhkuton | Sp: MVZ |

  Anura
    Leptodactylidae

| *Eleutherodactylus* sp. | č'ulul haʔ, šč'uč' | MVZ 99537–99538 |
|---|---|---|
| *Leptodactylus* spp. | č'ulul haʔ |  |

    Bufonidae

| *Bufo bocourti* | pokok | MVZ 99524 |
|---|---|---|
| *B. marinus* | henhen | P |
| *B. valliceps* | pokok | MVZ 99521–99523 |
| *Bufo* sp. | šʔenkenek | MVZ 99536 |

    Hylidae

| *Hyla* sp. larva | šʔabuy | EH 125 |
|---|---|---|
| *Hyla microcephala* | stok'ob | MVZ 99528 |
| *H. regilla* | stok'ob | S |
| *H. walkeri* | stok'ob | MVZ 99526–99527 |
| *Smilisca baudinii* | stok'ob | MVZ 99525 |

    Ranidae

| *Rana* sp. larvae | šberon, šʔabuy | EH 124, 137–138, 151? |
|---|---|---|
| *Rana pipiens* | šč'uč' | MVZ 99529–99533 |

    Microhylidae

| *Hypopachus* sp. larva | šʔabuy | EH 144 |
|---|---|---|
| *Hypopachus barberi* | šʔenkenek | MVZ 99534–99535 |

**REPTILIA**
  Crocodilia
    Alligatoridae

| *Caiman crocodilus* | šʔain | Z |
|---|---|---|

Crocodylidae
   *Crocodylus acutus*            *š ʔain*              Z
   *C. moreletii*              *š ʔain*              Z
Testudinata
  Testudinidae
   *Chrysemys scripta*      *š ʔahk'*
  Kinosternidae
   *Kinosternon cruentatum*  *š ʔahk'*            JFC
   *K. leucostomum*         *š ʔahk'*
   *Staurotypus triporcatus*  *š ʔahk'*
Squamata
  Lacertilia
   Gekkonidae
    *Coleonyx elegans*     *c' uhkuton*
   Iguanidae
    *Anolis anisolepis*     *k' intun*
    *A. crassulus*         *k' intun*          MVZ 99539–99541
    *A. sericeus*          *k' intun*
    *A. tropidonotus*      *k' intun*
    *Basiliscus vittatus*    *ʔečeh*            P
    *Ctenosaura pectinata*   *š ʔiwána*
    *C. similis*           *š ʔiwána*
    *Iguana iguana*       *š ʔiwána*
    *Sceloporus malachiticus* *ʔohkoc*           P
    *S. serrifer*          *ʔohkoc*           P
    *S. teapensis*        *ʔohkoc, k' intun*   Sp:MAT
    *S. variabilis*       *ʔohkoc, k' intun*   S
   Scincidae
    *Leiolopisma incertum*   *ʔuhc' ʔuhc' niʔ*   Sp:MVZ
   Teiidae
    *Ameiva undulata*     *k' alel čan*       S
    *Cnemidophorus* sp.     *k' alel čan*       Sp:JFC
   Helodermatidae
    *Heloderma horridum*    *š ʔiwána*
   Anguidae
    *Abronia lythrochila*    *č' iš čikin*      P
    *Barisia moreleti*     *k' alel čan*       Sp:MVZ
    *Gerrhonotus liocephalus* *ʔohkoc čan*     Sp:JFC
  Ophidia
   Leptotyphlopidae
    *Leptotyphlops goudotii* *lukum čan*, HLS
    *L. humilis*        *lukum čan*      Sp:JFC
   Boidae
    *Boa constrictor*     *masakwáto*
    *Loxocemus bicolor*    HLS            Sp:JFC
   Colubridae
    *Adelphicos veraepacis*  *mokoč čan*       Sp:JFC
    *Coniophanes imperialis* *meʔ k' apal*     MVZ 99543
    *C. schmidti*        *c' ibal čan*      Sp:JFC
    *Conophis vittatus*    *c' ibal čan*      Sp:JFC
    *Dryadophis melanolomus* HLS
    *Drymarchon corais*    *ʔáwa kantil*    Sp:JFC
    *Drymobius margaritiferus* *k' ančo*, HLS    Sp
    *Elaphe triaspis*     *yaš ʔitah čan*   Sp:JFC
    *Ficimia* sp.        *mokoč čan*
    *Geophis* sp.       *mokoč čan*
    *Lampropeltis triangulum* *meʔ c' isim*, HLS  Sp:JFC
    *Leptodeira septentrionalis* *p' ehel nuhkul čan*
    *Leptophis ahaetulla*  *yaš ʔitah čan*
    *L. modestus*       *yaš ʔitah čan*

| | | |
|---|---|---|
| *Ninia diademata* | **pacan sihk'** | Sp |
| *N. sebae* | **meʔ čenek'** | P |
| *Oxybelis aeneus* | **šč'oš čan** | |
| *O. fulgidus* | **yaš ʔitah čan** | |
| *Pituophis lineaticollis* | **ʔahaw čan** | P |
| *Pliocercus elapoides* | HLS | |
| *Rhadinaea hempsteadae* | **meʔ ʔišim** | Sp:JFC |
| *Salvadora lemniscata* | HLS | Sp:JFC |
| *Spilotes pullatus* | **čihil čan** | Sp:JFC |
| *Stenorrhina freminvillii* | **mokoč čan** | Sp:JFC |
| *Tantilla* sp. | **meʔ čenek'** | |
| *Thamnophis cyrtopsis* | **haʔal čan** | MVZ 99542 |
| *T. proximus* | **haʔal čan** | Sp:MAT |
| *Trimorphodon biscutatus* | **p'ehel nuhkul čan** | Sp:JFC |
| *Tropidodipsas fischeri* | **p'ahsum čan** | Sp:JFC |
| *Xenodon rabdocephalus* | **p'ehel nuhkul čan** | |
| Elapidae | | |
| *Micrurus diastema* | **kantéla čan** | |
| *M. elegans* | **kantéla čan** | P |
| Crotalidae | | |
| *Agkistrodon bilineatus* | **kantil** | |
| *Bothrops asper* | HLS, **ʔik'os čan** | Sp:JFC |
| *B. godmani* | **c'in teʔ čan** | Sp:MVZ |
| *B. nigroviridis* | **yaš ʔitah čan** | Sp:JFC |
| *B. nummifer* | **ʔik'os čan** | |
| *Crotalus durissus* | **ʔahaw čan** | Sp:JFC |
| AVES | | |
| Tinamiformes | | |
| Tinamidae | | |
| *Crypturellus cinnamomeus* | **čiktawilon** | |
| Podicipediformes | | |
| Podicipedidae | | |
| *Podiceps dominicus* | **peč'ul haʔ** | S |
| *Podilymbus podiceps* | **peč'ul haʔ** | |
| Pelicaniformes | | |
| Fregatidae | | |
| *Fregata magnificens* | HLB | |
| Ciconiiformes | | |
| Ardeidae | | |
| *Ardea herodias* | **htiʔ čay** | S |
| *Butorides virescens* | **htiʔ čay** | S |
| *Florida caerulea* | **htiʔ čay** | S |
| *Egretta alba* | **htiʔ čay** | S |
| *E. thula* | **htiʔ čay** | S |
| *Nycticorax nycticorax* | HLB, **htiʔ čay** | Z |
| (bitterns) | **htiʔ čay** | |
| Threskiornithidae | **htiʔ čay** | |
| Anseriformes | | |
| Anatidae | | |
| *Anser* sp. (domestic) | **peč'** | S |
| *Dendrocygna autumnalis* | **peč'ul haʔ** | Z |
| *Cairina moschata* (domestic) | **peč'** | S |
| *Anas acuta* | **peč'ul haʔ** | S |
| *A. platyrhynchos* (domestic) | **peč'** | S |
| *A. discors* | **peč'ul haʔ** | S |
| *A. americana* | **peč'ul haʔ** | S |
| *Oxyura jamaicensis* | **peč'ul haʔ** | S |
| Falconiformes | | |
| Cathartidae | | |
| *Sarcoramphus papa* | **ʔusel** | |

| | | |
|---|---|---|
| *Coragyps atratus* | **ca ?los** | S |
| *Cathartes aura* | **šulem** | S |
| Accipitridae | | |
| *Elanus leucurus* | **me ? k῾ulub** | S |
| *Elanoides forficatus* | **tešereš ne** | S |
| *Ictinia misisippiensis* | **me ? k῾ulub** | |
| *I. plumbea* | **me ? k῾ulub** | |
| *Accipiter chionogaster* | **yan te ?tikil likawal** | S |
| *Buteo albicaudatus* | **sakil likawal** | S |
| *B. jamaicensis* | **cahal likawal, ?ihk῾al likawal** | S |
| *B. albonotatus* | **?ihk῾al likawal** | |
| *B. magnirostris* | **šik likawal** | S |
| *B. brachyurus* | **šik likawal** | S |
| *Leucopternis albicollis* | **sakil likawal** | |
| *Buteogallus anthracinus* | **?ihk῾al likawal** | |
| *B. urubitinga* | **?ihk῾al likawal** | |
| *Harpyhaliaetus solitarius* | **?ihk῾al likawal** | Z |
| *Harpia harpyja* | **kok mut** | Z |
| *Aquila chrysaetos* | **kok mut** | |
| Pandionidae | | |
| *Pandion haliaetus* | following **tešereš ne** | |
| Falconidae | | |
| *Herpetotheres cachinnans* | HLB | |
| *Falco sparverius* | **liklik** | S |
| Galliformes | | |
| Cracidae | | |
| *Ortalis vetula* | **hohkot** | S |
| *Penelope purpurascens* | **te ?tikil tuluk῾** | Z |
| *Penelopina nigra* | **č῾ekek** | |
| *Crax rubra* | **?is mut, te ?tikil tuluk῾** | |
| Phasianidae | | |
| *Gallus gallus* | **mut$_2$** | S |
| *Pavo cristatus* | **mo ?, tuluk῾** | |
| *Dendrortyx leucophrys* | **čiktawilon** | |
| *Colinus virginianus* | **č῾in š ?ub** | S |
| *Odontophorus guttatus* | **muk῾ul š ?ub** | |
| *Dactylortyx thoracicus* | **muk῾ul š ?ub** | |
| *Cyrtonyx ocellatus* | **muk῾ul š ?ub** | |
| Meleagridae | | |
| *Meleagris gallopavo* | **tuluk῾** | P |
| *Agriocharis ocellata* | **tuluk῾, mo ?** | |
| Gruiformes | | |
| Rallidae | | |
| *Rallus limicola* | **me ? c῾ahel** | |
| *Porzana carolina* | **me ? c῾ahel** | |
| *Fulica americana* | **peč῾ul ha ?** | S |
| Charadriiformes | | |
| Charadriidae | | |
| *Charadrius semipalmatus* | **c῾u ? lukum** | S |
| *C. vociferus* | **c῾u ? lukum** | S |
| Scolopacidae | | |
| *Tringa solitaria* | **c῾u ? lukum** | S |
| *Actitis macularia* | **c῾u ? lukum** | S |
| *Calidris minutilla* | **c῾u ? lukum** | S |
| *C. melanotos* | **c῾u ? lukum** | S |
| Phalaropodidae | | |
| *Steganopus tricolor* | **c῾u ? lukum** | S |
| Laridae | | |
| *Larus atricilla* | **hti ? čay** | S |
| *Sterna forsteri* | **hti ? čay** | S |

| | | |
|---|---|---|
| *Thalasseus elegans* | *hti<sup>ʔ</sup> čay* | S |
| Columbiformes | | |
| Columbidae | | |
| *Columba livia* (domestic) | *palomaš* | S |
| *C. flavirostris* | *kuč kuutik wo* | S |
| *C. fasciata* | *šč̓a bikil* | S |
| *Zenaida macroura* | *yalem scumut* | S |
| *Z. asiatica* | *kašlan scumut* | S |
| *Scardafella inca* | *kašlan špurowok* | S |
| *Columbina passerina* | *špurowok* | S |
| *C. minuta* | *špurowok* | |
| *C. talpacoti* | *cahal špurowok* | S |
| *Leptotila verreauxi* | *bac̓il scumut* | S |
| *Geotrygon albifacies* | *scumut* | |
| Psittaciformes | | |
| Psittacidae | | |
| *Ara militaris* | *mo<sup>ʔ</sup>* | |
| *A. macao* | *mo<sup>ʔ</sup>* | |
| *Aratinga holochlora* | *períko* | S |
| *A. canicularis* | *lorotíro, períko* | S |
| *Bolborhynchus lineola* | *puyuč̓* | |
| *Brotogeris jugularis* | *lorotíro* | |
| *Pionus senilis* | *puyuč̓* | |
| *Amazona albifrons* | *puyuč̓* | |
| *A. ochrocephala* | *períko* | Z |
| Cuculiformes | | |
| Cuculidae | | |
| *Coccyzus americanus* | *hti<sup>ʔ</sup> cuhkum* | S |
| *Piaya cayana* | *k̓ank̓an mut* | S |
| *Crotophaga sulcirostris* | *hti<sup>ʔ</sup> sip* | S |
| *Geococcyx velox* | *š<sup>ʔ</sup>uman* | S |
| Strigiformes | | |
| Tytonidae | | |
| *Tyto alba* | *šoč̓* | |
| Strigidae | | |
| *Otus trichopsis* | *kurunkuc* | S |
| *O. barbarus* | *kurunkuc* | |
| *O. guatemalae* | *kurunkuc* | |
| *Lophostrix cristata* | *škuh* | |
| *Bubo virginianus* | *tuhkulum pukuh* | |
| *Pulsatrix perspicillata* | *škuh* | |
| *Glaucidium gnoma* | *<sup>ʔ</sup>ahk̓ubal toytoy* | S |
| *G. brasilianum* | *k̓alel toytoy* | P |
| *Ciccaba virgata* | *škuh* | |
| *C. nigrolineata* | *škuh* | |
| *Strix occidentalis* | *k̓ahk̓al waš* | |
| *S. varia* | *k̓ahk̓al waš* | |
| *S. fulvescens* | *k̓ahk̓al waš* | |
| *Rhinoptynx clamator* | *škuh* | |
| *Asio stygius* | *škuh* | |
| *Aegolius ridgwayi* | *<sup>ʔ</sup>ahk̓ubal toytoy* | P |
| Caprimulgiformes | | |
| Nyctibiidae | | |
| *Nyctibius griseus* | HLB | |
| Caprimulgidae | | |
| *Chordeiles minor* | *pum cis* | |
| *C. acutipennis* | *pum cis* | S |
| *Nyctidromus albicollis* | *pu<sup>ʔ</sup>kuy* | Sp |
| *Caprimulgus carolinensis* | nightjar complex | |
| *C. vociferus* | *purkuwič̓* | S |

| | | |
|---|---|---|
| *C. salvini* | nightjar complex | |
| *C. ridgwayi* | nightjar complex | |
| Apodiformes | | |
| Apodidae | | |
| *Streptoprocne zonaris* | **muk`ul sik`** | S |
| *S. semicollaris* | **sik`** | |
| *Cypseloides rutilus* | **č`in sik`** | S |
| *C. niger* | **č`in sik`** | S |
| *Chaetura vauxi* | **č`in sik`** | S |
| *Aeronautes saxatalis* | **č`in sik`** | S |
| *Panyptila sanctihieronymi* | **sik`** | |
| Trochilidae | | |
| *Campylopterus rufus* | **c`unun** | |
| *Colibri thalassinus* | **kašlan c`unun** | P |
| *Chlorostilbon canivetii* | **kašlan c`unun** | S |
| *Hylocharis leucotis* | **c`ibal sit c`unun** | P |
| *Amazilia cyanocephala* | **sakil c`unun** | S |
| *A. beryllina* | **c`unun** | S |
| *Lampornis amethystinus* | **ʔihk`al c`unun** | P |
| *Lamprolaima rhami* | **ʔihk`al c`unun** | S |
| *Eugenes fulgens* | **kašlan c`unun, ʔihk`al c`unun** | P |
| *Heliomaster constantii* | **sakil c`unun** | S |
| *Doricha enicura* | **tešereš ne c`unun** | S |
| *Calothorax* sp. | **c`unun** | S |
| *Archilochus colubris* | **sakil c`unun** | S |
| *Atthis heloisa* | **c`unun** | |
| *A. ellioti* | **c`unun** | S |
| *Selasphorus platycercus* | **sakil c`unun** | S |
| Trogoniformes | | |
| Trogonidae | | |
| *Pharomachrus mocinno* | **k`uk`** | |
| *Trogon mexicanus* | **k`uk`** | S |
| *T. violaceus* | **k`uk`** | S |
| Coraciiformes | | |
| Alcedinidae | | |
| *Ceryle torquata* | **peč`ul haʔ** | S |
| *C. alcyon* | **peč`ul haʔ** | S |
| *Chloroceryle amazona* | **peč`ul haʔ** | S |
| Momotidae | | |
| *Aspatha gularis* | **šk`orin mut** | P |
| *Momotus mexicanus* | **kuckuc** | S |
| *M. momota* | **kuckuc** | S |
| Piciformes | | |
| Ramphastidae | | |
| *Ramphastos sulfuratus* | **pan** | |
| *Aulacorhynchus prasinus* | **pan** | |
| *Pteroglossus torquatus* | **pan** | S |
| Picidae | | |
| *Colaptes auratus* | **tukut** | S |
| *Piculus rubiginosus* | **k`anal c`ihtil** | S |
| *Dryocopus lineatus* | **tuncerek`** | S |
| *Melanerpes formicivorus* | **k`oročoč, tiʔ** | S |
| *Centurus aurifrons* | **tiʔ** | S |
| *Dendrocopos villosus* | **ʔihk`al c`ihtil** | S |
| *D. scalaris* | **c`irin c`ihtil** | S |
| *Campephilus guatemalensis* | **tuncerek`** | |
| Passeriformes | | |
| Dendrocolaptidae | | |
| *Xiphocolaptes promeropirhynchus* | **c`uhkin mut** | |
| *Xiphorhynchus flavigaster* | **c`uhkin mut** | S |

| | | |
|---|---|---|
| *Lepidocolaptes affinis* | *c'uhkin mut* | P |
| Furnariidae | | |
| *Synallaxis erythrothorax* | HLB | S |
| Formicariidae | | |
| *Thamnophilus doliatus* | HLB | S |
| Cotingidae | | |
| *Rhytipterna holerythra* | *wirin* | |
| *Platypsaris aglaiae* | HLB | S |
| *Tityra semifasciata* | *wirin* | S |
| Tyrannidae | | |
| *Sayornis nigricans* | *ʔihkʼal wirin* | S |
| *Pyrocephalus rubinus* | *cahal wirin* | S |
| *Muscivora forficata* | *wirin* | S |
| *Tyrannus tyrannus* | *kašlan wirin* | S |
| *T. vociferans* | *kašlan wirin* | S |
| *T. melancholicus* | *kašlan wirin* | S |
| *Myiodynastes luteiventris* | *wirin* | S |
| *Megarynchus pitangua* | *wirin, pahal macʼ* | |
| *Myiozetetes similis* | *pahal macʼ, wirin* | S |
| *Pitangus sulphuratus* | *pahal macʼ, wirin* | P |
| *Myiarchus tuberculifer* | *bacʼil wirin* | S |
| *Contopus virens* | *čʼin wirin* | S |
| *C. sordidulus* | *čʼin wirin* | S |
| *C. cinereus* | *čʼin wirin* | S |
| *C. pertinax* | *bacʼil wirin* | P |
| *Mitrephanes phaeocercus* | *cahal wirin* | S |
| *Empidonax albigularis* | *pʼitpʼit* | S |
| *E. affinis* | *pʼitpʼit* | P |
| *E. flavescens* | *pʼitpʼit* | S |
| *E. fulvifrons* | *pʼitpʼit* | S |
| Hirundinidae | | |
| *Tachycineta thalassina* | *ʔulič* | |
| *T. bicolor* | *ʔulič* | S |
| *T. albilinea* | *ʔulič* | S |
| *Notiochelidon pileata* | *ʔulič* | S |
| *Progne chalybea* | *ʔulič* | S |
| *Stelgidopteryx ruficollis* | *ʔulič* | S |
| *Riparia riparia* | *ʔulič* | S |
| *Hirundo rustica* | *ʔulič* | S |
| *Petrochelidon pyrrhonota* | *ʔulič* | S |
| *P. fulva* | *ʔulič* | S |
| Corvidae | | |
| *Corvus corax* | *hoh* | S |
| *Calocitta formosa* | *šulub mut* | S |
| *Psilorhinus morio* | *peyaʔ* | S |
| *Cyanocorax yncas* | *kʼan heš* | P |
| *Cyanolyca cucullata* | *sak hol heš* | Sp:MVZ |
| *C. pumilo* | *kastiyána heš* | P |
| *Aphelocoma unicolor* | *yaš heš* | S |
| *Cyanocitta stelleri* | *yaš heš* | P |
| Paridae | | |
| *Psaltriparus minimus* | *cʼircʼir pay* | P |
| Certhiidae | | |
| *Certhia familiaris* | *cʼirin mut* | S |
| Cinclidae | | |
| *Cinclus mexicanus* | HLB | |
| Troglodytidae | | |
| *Campylorhynchus zonatus* | *coʔkoy* | P |
| *Thryothorus modestus* | *čʼetet waš* | S |
| *T. pleurostictus* | *čʼetet waš* | S |

| | | |
|---|---|---|
| *T. maculipectus* | *č'etet waš* | S |
| *Troglodytes musculus* | *či?či? bulbul* | S |
| *T. ruficiliatus* | *či?či? bulbul* | |
| *Henicorhina leucophrys* | *č'etet waš* | P |
| *Catherpes mexicanus* | *č'etet waš* | S |
| Mimidae | | |
| *Melanotis hypoleucus* | *čulin* | P |
| *Dumetella carolinensis* | *šč'e?* | P |
| *Mimus gilvus* | *hti? cuhkum* | S |
| Turdidae | | |
| *Turdus migratorius* | *cahal toht* | S |
| *T. rufitorques* | *č'iš toht* | P |
| *T. assimilis* | *toht* | |
| *T. grayi* | *k'an toht* | P |
| *T. plebejus* | *yašal toht* | P |
| *T. infuscatus* | *?ihk'al toht* | S |
| *Myadestes obscurus* | *sian* | P |
| *M. unicolor* | *sian* | |
| *Hylocichla mustelina* | HLB | S |
| *Catharus ustulatus* | HLB | P |
| *C. frantzii* | *šluš* | P |
| *C. aurantiirostris* | *šluš* | S |
| *Sialia sialis* | *yaš mut* | S |
| Sylviidae | | S |
| *Polioptila caerulea* | HLB | S |
| *P. albiloris* | HLB | S |
| *Ramphocaenus rufiventris* | HLB | |
| Ptilogonatidae | | |
| *Ptilogonys cinereus* | *t'ok hol mut* | S |
| Cyclarhidae | | |
| *Cyclarhis gujanensis* | *yihkac te? mut* | P |
| Vireonidae | | |
| *Vireo griseus* | *šč'iht* | S |
| *V. huttoni* | *tahína mut* | P |
| *V. solitarius* | *tahína mut* | P |
| *V. flavoviridis* | *čayin* | S |
| *V. gilvus* | *šč'iht* | S |
| Coerebidae | | |
| *Diglossa baritula* | *nuk' ničim* | P |
| Parulidae | | |
| *Mniotilta varia* | HLB | S |
| *Vermivora peregrina* | *šč'iht* | S |
| *V. celata* | *šč'iht* | S |
| *V. ruficapilla* | *šč'iht* | S |
| *V. superciliosa* | *šč'iht* | S |
| *Parula pitiayumi* | *šč'iht* | S |
| *Peucedramus taeniatus* | *šč'iht, me? k'in ha?al* | S |
| *Dendroica petechia* | *šč'iht* | S |
| *D. magnolia* | *šč'iht* | S |
| *D. caerulescens* | *šč'iht* | P |
| *D. coronata* | *šč'iht* | S |
| *D. townsendi* | *šč'iht* | P |
| *D. virens* | *šč'iht* | P |
| *D. chrysoparia* | *šč'iht* | S |
| *D. occidentalis* | *šč'iht* | P |
| *D. fusca* | *šč'iht, ?ičil č'uht mut* | S |
| *D. dominica* | *šč'iht* | S |
| *D. graciae* | *šč'iht* | S |
| *D. pensylvanica* | *šč'iht* | S |
| *Seiurus aurocapillus* | *šmayil* | S |

| | | |
|---|---|---|
| *S. motacilla* | **šmayil** | P |
| *S. noveboracensis* | **šmayil** | S |
| *Oporornis philadelphia* | **šč'iht** | |
| *O. tolmiei* | **šč'iht** | P |
| *Geothlypis trichas* | **šč'iht** | S |
| *G. poliocephala* | HLB | S |
| *Icteria virens* | **šč'eʔ** | |
| *Wilsonia pusilla* | **šč'iht** | P |
| *W. canadensis* | **šč'iht** | S |
| *Myioborus picta* | **ʔičil č'uht mut** | P |
| *M. miniatus* | **ʔičil č'uht mut** | P |
| *Ergaticus versicolor* | **ʔičil mut, šč'iht** | P |
| *Basileuterus belli* | **c'irin hol mut, šč'iht** | P |
| *B. rufifrons* | **c'irin hol mut, šč'iht** | P |
| Ploceidae | | |
|    *Passer domesticus* | **kašlan čončiw** | P |
| Icteridae | | |
|    *Zarhynchus wagleri* | **bak hol mut** | Sp:MVZ |
|    *Amblycercus holosericeus* | **ʔotʔot** | S |
|    *Molothrus aeneus* | **sanáte** | S |
|    *Cassidix mexicanus* | **hoh mut** | S |
|    *Dives dives* | **wančil** | P |
|    *Icterus spurius* | **tu č'ič'** | S |
|    *I. wagleri* | **burúho mut** | S |
|    *I. mesomelas* | **burúho mut** | S |
|    *I. chrysater* | **tu č'ič'** | P |
|    *I. galbula* | **tu č'ič'** | P |
|    *I. sclateri* | **tu č'ič'** | S |
|    *Agelaius phoeniceus* | **kulkulína** | S |
|    *Sturnella magna* | **čiboriáno** | S |
| Thraupidae | | |
|    *Thraupis abbas* | HLB | S |
|    *Phlogothraupis sanguinolenta* | HLB | P |
|    *Piranga rubra* | **kaptan mut** | |
|    *P. flava* | **kaptan mut** | P |
|    *Habia fuscicauda* | **coʔkoy** | S |
|    *Chlorospingus ophthalmicus* | **pay sit mut** | P |
| Fringillidae | | |
|    *Saltator atriceps* | **čačalak' mut** | S |
|    *S. coerulescens* | **čohčowit** | S |
|    *Pheucticus chrysopeplus* | **wol niʔ mut, tu č'ič'** | P |
|    *P. ludovicianus* | **wol niʔ mut** | |
|    *Tiaris olivacea* | HLB, **cob nič ʔak** | S |
|    *Sporophila torqueola* | **cob nič ʔak** | S |
|    *Volatinia jacarina* | **šč'eʔ, cob nič ʔak** | S |
|    *Atlapetes albinucha* | **k'usin** | P |
|    *Pipilo erythrophthalmus* | **k'oweš** | S |
|    *Melozone biarcuatum* | **solsol** | P |
|    *Aimophila rufescens* | **meʔ čončiw** | P |
|    *Melospiza lincolnii* | **meba čončiw** | P |
|    *Zonotrichia capensis* | **bac'il čončiw** | P |
|    *Junco phaeonotus* | **tak'in sit mut** | P |
|    *Spinus pinus* | **meʔ k'in haʔal** | S |
|    *S. atriceps* | **meʔ k'in haʔal** | P |
|    *S. notatus* | **meʔ k'in haʔal** | P |
|    *S. psaltria* | **meʔ k'in haʔal** | S |
|    *Loxia curvirostra* | **šep ʔe mut** | Sp:MVZ |
| MAMMALIA | | |
|   Marsupialia | | |
|    Didelphidae | | |

| | | |
|---|---|---|
| *Didelphis virginiana* | **huyum ʔuč** | MVZ 141220, 141667, 141700–141701 |
| *D. marsupialis* | **bac'il ʔuč** | |
| *Philander opossum* | **ʔuč č'o** | Sp:MVZ |
| *Marmosa* sp. | opossum complex | |
| *Caluromys* sp. | opossum complex | |
| Insectivora | | |
| Soricidae | | |
| *Cryptotis micrura* | **yaʔal be** | MVZ 141668–141671 |
| *Sorex* spp. | **yaʔal be** | |
| Chiroptera | | |
| Phyllostomidae | | |
| *Anoura geoffroyi* | **soc'** | MVZ 141213–141214, 141672–141674 |
| *Carollia perspicillata* | **soc'** | MVZ 141675–141678 |
| *Sturnira ludovici* | **soc'** | MVZ 141216(?), 141679–141692 |
| *Artibeus jamaicensis* | **soc'** | MVZ 141693–141694 |
| Desmodontidae | | |
| *Desmodus rotundus* | **soc'** | MVZ 141695–141698 |
| Vespertilionidae | | |
| *Myotis nigricans* | **soc'** | MVZ 141699 |
| Primates | | |
| Cebidae | | |
| *Alouatta palliata* | **bac'** | |
| *A. pigra* | **bac'** | |
| *Ateles geoffroyi* | **maš** | Z |
| Hominidae | | |
| *Homo sapiens* | **čanbalam₁** | S |
| Edentata | | |
| Myrmecophagidae | | |
| *Tamandua tetradactyla* | **c'uhc'uneh čab** | |
| *Cyclopes didactylus* | **ʔuyoh** | Sp:MAT |
| Dasypodidae | | |
| *Dasypus novemcinctus* | **mayil tiʔbal** | MVZ 141222 |
| Lagomorpha | | |
| Leporidae | | |
| *Sylvilagus floridanus* | **bac'il t'ul** | MVZ 141218, 141706 |
| *S. brasiliensis* | **bac'il t'ul** | |
| *Oryctolagus cuniculus* (domestic) | **kašlan t'ul** | S |
| Rodentia | | |
| Sciuridae | | |
| *Sciurus aureogaster* | [R] **čuč** | MVZ 141707 |
| (> *S. griseoflavus*, *S. socialis*) | | |
| *S. deppei* | **c'eh** | S |
| *Glaucomys volans* | **pehpen čuč** | |
| Geomyidae | | |
| *Heterogeomys hispidus* | **ba** | MVZ 141219, 141708–141709 |
| *Macrogeomys underwoodi* | **č'uy pat ba** | |
| Heteromyidae | | |
| *Heteromys desmarestianus* | **k'iwoč č'o** | |
| Cricetidae | | |
| *Oryzomys palustris* | **sabin č'o** | MVZ 141800–141802 |
| *Tylomys bullaris* | **hseʔ teʔ** | MVZ 141786 |
| *Nyctomys sumichrasti* | **moin teʔ č'o** | |
| *Reithrodontomys megalotis* | **sin** | MVZ 141787–141792, 141794(?), 141795–141799 |
| *R. mexicanus* | **sin** | MVZ 141215–141793 |
| *Peromyscus boylii* | [white-footed mouse] | MVZ 141208–141210, 141718(?), 141719–141722 |

| | | |
|---|---|---|
| *P. mexicanus* | [white-footed mouse] | MVZ 141211–141212, 141723–141763 |
| *P. zarhynchus* | [white-footed mouse] | MVZ 141765, 141767–141776, 141777(?), 141778–141785 |
| *P. oaxacensis* | [white-footed mouse] | MVZ 141764(?) |
| *P. lophurus* | [white-footed mouse] | |
| *Peromyscus* sp. | [white-footed mouse] | MVZ 141712–141717 |
| *Sigmodon hispidus* | **čitam č'o** | MVZ 141803–141812 |
| *Neotoma mexicana* | **hse? te?** | |
| Muridae | | |
| *Rattus rattus* | **karánsa** | MVZ 141766, 141813–141815 |
| *R. norvegicus* | **karánsa** | |
| *Mus musculus* | **šlumil č'o** | MVZ 141206–141207 |
| Erethizontidae | | |
| *Coendou mexicanus* | **č'iš ?uhčum** | Sp |
| Dasyproctidae | | |
| *Cuniculus paca* | **halaw** | MVZ 141217, 141710–141711 |
| *Dasyprocta* sp. | **halaw** | Z |
| Carnivora | | |
| Canidae | | |
| *Canis latrans* | **?ok'il₁** | |
| *C. familiaris* (domestic) | **c'i?** | S |
| *Urocyon cinereoargenteus* | **waš** | MVZ 141702 |
| Procyonidae | | |
| *Procyon lotor* | **me?el** | MVZ 141221, 141703 |
| *Nasua narica* | **kohtom** | Z |
| *Potos flavus* | **?uyoh** | Z |
| Mustelidae | | |
| *Mustela frenata* | **sabin** | MVZ 141702 |
| *Eira barbara* | **sak hol** | Z |
| *Spilogale angustifrons* | **č'in pay** | Sp:MVZ |
| *Mephitis macroura* | **?ihk'al pay** | Sp:MVZ |
| *Conepatus mesoleucus* | **lem pat pay** | Sp:MVZ |
| *Lutra annectens* | **ha?al c'i?** | |
| Felidae | | |
| *Felis onca* | **balam** | Z |
| *F. concolor* | **čoh** | |
| *F. pardalis* | **cahal čoh** | Z |
| *F. wiedii* | **cis balam** | Z |
| *F. yagouaroundi* | **?ik' sab** | Z |
| *F. cattus* (domestic) | **šawin** | S |
| Perissodactyla | | |
| Tapiridae | | |
| *Tapirus bairdii* | **cemen** | |
| Equidae | | |
| *Equus asinus* (domestic) | **búro** | P |
| *E. caballus* (domestic) | **kawáyu** | S |
| Artiodactyla | | |
| Suiformes | | |
| Suidae | | |
| *Sus scrofa* (domestic) | **čitam** | P |
| Tayassuidae | | |
| *Tayassu pecari* | **wamal čitam** | Z |
| *Dicotyles tajacu* | **wamal čitam** | Z |
| Ruminantia | | |
| Cervidae | | |
| *Odocoileus virginianus* | **yašal te?tikil čih** | Z |
| *Mazama americana* | **cahal te?tikil čih** | MVZ 141705 |
| Bovidae | | |
| *Bos taurus* (domestic) | **wakaš** | S |
| *Ovis aries* (domestic) | **tunim čih** | S |
| *Capra hircus* (domestic) | **tencun** | S |

# REFERENCES

Acheson, N. H.
1966 Etnozoología Zinacanteca. In *Los Zinacantecos*, edited by E. Z. Vogt. México D. F.: Instituto National Indigenista.

Adams, R. N., and A. J. Rubel
1967 Sickness and social relations. In *Handbook of Middle-American Indians*. Vol. 6: *Social Anthropology*, edited by M. Nash. Austin: Univ. of Texas Press.

Alvarez del Toro, M.
1952 *Los animales silvestres de Chiapas*. Chiapas, México: Instituto de Ciencias y Artes de Chiapas.
1971 *Las aves de Chiapas*. Chiapas, México: Gobierno del Estado de Chiapas.
1973 *Los reptiles de Chiapas*. 2nd edition. Chiapas, México: Gobierno del Estado de Chiapas.

American Ornithologists' Union
1973 Thirty-second Supplement to the American Ornithologists' Union Checklist of North American Birds. *Auk* **90**: 411–419.

Anderson, R. M.
1965 *Methods of collecting and preserving vertebrate animals*. Ottawa: National Museum of Canada.

Antonio Castro, C.
1965 *Narraciones Tzeltales de Chiapas*. Cuadernos de la Facultad de Filosofía, Letras y Ciencias, Universidad Veracruzana, Xalapa, Veracruz, México, No. 27.

Berlin, B.
1962a Esbozo de la fonología del Tzeltal de Tenejapa, Chiapas. *Estudios de cultura Maya* **2**: 17–36.
1962b A Tzeltal origin myth. *Folklore* **73**: 230–233.
1967 Categories of eating in Tzeltal and Navaho. *International Journal of American Linguistics* **33**: 1–6.
1968 *Tzeltal numeral classifiers: A study in ethnographic semantics*. The Hague: Mouton.
1970 A universalist–evolutionary approach in ethnographic semantics. In *Current directions in anthropology*, edited by A. Fischer, *Bulletin of the American Anthropological Association* **3**, Part 2: 3–18.
1972 Speculations on the growth of ethnobotanical nomenclature. *Language in Society* **1**: 51–86.
1973 Folk systematics in relation to biological classification and nomenclature. *Annual Review of Ecology and Systematics* **4**: 259–271.

Berlin, B., D. E. Breedlove, R. M. Laughlin, and P. H. Raven
1973 Cultural significance and lexical retention in Tzeltal–Tzotzil ethnobotany. In *Meaning in Mayan languages*, edited by M. S. Edmonson. The Hague: Mouton. Pp. 143–164.

Berlin, B., D. E. Breedlove, and P. H. Raven
1966 Folk taxonomies and biological classification. *Science* **154**: 273–275.
1968 Covert categories and folk taxonomies. *American Anthropologist* **70**: 290–299.
1973 General principles of classification and nomenclature in folk biology. *American Anthropologist* **75**: 214–242.
1974 *Principles of Tzeltal plant classification: An introduction to the botanical ethnography of a Mayan-speaking community of highland Chiapas*. New York: Academic Press.

Berlin, B., and P. Kay
1969 *Basic color terms: Their universality and evolution*. Berkeley: Univ. of California Press.

Black, M. B.
1967 An ethnoscience investigation of Ojibwa ontology and world view. Unpublished doctoral dissertation, Stanford University, Stanford, California.

Black, M. B., and D. Metzger
1965 Ethnographic description and the study of law. *American Anthropologist* **67**: 141–165.

Blake, E. R.
1953 *Birds of Mexico: A guide for field identification*. Chicago: Univ. of Chicago Press.

Blom, F., and O. LaFarge
1927 *Tribes and temples*. Vols. 1 and 2. New Orleans, Louisiana: Tulane Univ. Press.

Borror, D. J., and R. E. White
1970 *A field guide to the insects of America north of Mexico*. Boston: Houghton Mifflin.

Bowes, A. L., and R. Castillo Perez
1964 *Birds of the Mayas*. Big Moose, New York: West-of-the-Wind Publications.

Branstetter, K.
1974 Tenejapans on clothing and vice versa; The social significance of clothing in a Mayan community in Chiapas, Mexico. Unpublished doctoral dissertation, University of California, Berkeley.

Bright, J. O., and W. Bright
1965 Semantic structures in northwestern California and the Sapir–Whorf hypothesis. In *Formal semantic analysis*, edited by E. A. Hammel, Special issue of *American Anthropologist* **67**, Part 2: 249–258.

Bruner, J. S., J. J. Goodnow, and G. A. Austin
1956 *A Study of thinking*. New York: Wiley.

Bulmer, R. N. H.
1970    Which came first, the chicken or the egg-head? In *Échanges et communications, mélanges offerts à Claude Lévi-Strauss à l'occasion de son 60-ème anniversaire*, edited by J. Pouillon and P. Maranda. The Hauge: Mouton. Pp. 1069–1091.

Bulmer, R. N. H., and M. J. Tyler
1968    Karam classification of frogs. *Journal of the Polynesian Society* 77: 333–385.

Burt, W. H. and R. P. Grossenheider
1964    *A field guide to the mammals.* Boston: Houghton Mifflin.

Cain, A. J.
1958    Logic and memory in Linnaeus's system of taxonomy. *Proceedings of the Linnaean Society of London* 169: 144–163.
1959    Deductive and inductive methods in post-Linnaean taxonomy. *Proceedings of the Linnaean Society of London* 170: 185–217.

Casagrande, J. B., and K. L. Hale
1967    Semantic relations in Papago folk definitions. In *Studies in southwestern ethnolinguistics*, edited by D. Hymes. The Hague: Mouton. Pp. 165–193.

Colby, B. N., and P. van den Berghe
1961    Ethnic relations in southeastern Mexico. *American Anthropologist* 63: 253–267.

Conklin, H. C.
1954    The relation of Hanunóo culture to the plant world. Unpublished doctoral dissertation, Yale University, New Haven, Connecticut.
1962    Lexicographical treatment of folk taxonomies. In *Problems in lexicography*, edited by F. W. Householder and S. Saporta, Bloomington, Indiana: Indiana Univ. Research Center in Anthropology, Folklore, and Linguistics.

Cooper, J. M.
1949    Traps. In *Handbook of South American Indians*, edited by J. Steward, *Bureau of American Ethnology, Bulletin 143*, Vol. 5. Pp. 265–276.

Corzo, A. M.
1946    *Geographia de Chiapas.* Chiapas, México: Editorial Protos.

Cowgill, U. M.
1962    An agricultral study of the southern Maya lowlands. *American Anthropologist* 64: 273–286.

Davis, L. I.
1972    *A field guide to the birds of Mexico and Central America.* Austin: Univ. of Texas Press.

Durkheim, E., and M. Mauss
1963    *Primitive classification*, translated and edited with an introduction by Rodney Needham. Chicago: Univ. of Chicago Press. Originally published 1903.

Edwards, E. P.
1972    *A field guide to the birds of Mexico.* Sweet Briar, Virginia: E. P. Edwards.

Eisenmann, E.
1971    Range expansion and population increase in north and middle America of the White-tailed Kite (*Elanus leucurus*). *American Birds* 25: 529–536.

Evans, H. E., and M. J. W. Eberhard
1970    *The wasps.* Ann Arbor: Univ. of Michigan Press.

Fabrega, H. Jr., and D. B. Silver
1973    *Illness and shamanistic curing in Zinacantan: An ethnomedical analysis.* Stanford, California: Stanford Univ. Press.

Farris, J. S.
1971    The hypothesis of nonspecificity and taxonomic congruence. *Annual Review of Ecology and Systematics* 2: 277–302.

Foster, G.
1969    The Mixe, Zoque, and Popoluca. In *Handbook of Middle-American Indians.* Vol. 7: *Ethnology*, edited by E. Z. Vogt. Austin: Univ. of Texas Press.

Frake, C. O.
1962    The ethnographic study of cognitive systems. In *Anthropology and human behavior*, edited by T. Gladwin and W. C. Sturtevant. Washington, D.C.: Anthropological Society of Washington, Pp. 72–93.

Friedrich, P.
1969    On the meaning of the Tarascan suffixes of space. *Supplement to the International Journal of American Linguistics* 35, Part 2: 1–48.

Gardner, A. L.
1973    *The systematics of the genus* Didelphis (*Marsupialia: Didelphidae*) *in North and Middle America.* Special Publications No. 4. The Museum, Texas Tech Univ., Lubbock, Texas.

Geoghegan, W.
1973    Polytypy in Folk Biological Taxonomics. Paper presented to the American Anthropological Association Annual Meeting, New Orleans, Louisiana.
1974    *Natural information processing rules: Theory and applications to ethnography.* Language-behavior Research Laboratory, Univ. of California (Berkeley). Monograph No. 3.

Gregg, J. R.
1954    *The language of taxonomy, an application of symbolic logic to the study of classificatory systems.* New York: Columbia Univ. Press.
1967    Finite Linnaean structures. *Bulletin of Mathematical Biophysics* 29: 191–206.

Hall, E. R., and K. R. Kelson
1959    *The mammals of North America*, Vols. 1 and 2. New York: Ronald Press.

Hays, T. E.
1974    Mauna: Explorations in Ndumba ethnobotany. Unpublished doctoral dissertation, Univ. of Washington, Seattle.

Heizer, R. F.
1949    Fish poisons. In *Handbook of South American Indians*, edited by J. Steward, *Bureau of American Ethnology, Bulletin 143*. Vol. 5, Pp. 277–281.

1960    Agriculture and the theocratic state in low-
        land southeastern Mexico. *American Anti-
        guity* **26**: 215–222.
Herdan, G.
1960    *Type-token mathematics.* Janua Linguarum
        Series Maior IV. The Hague: Mouton.
Hopkins, N. A.
1970    Estudio preliminar de los dialectos del Tzeltal
        y del Tzotzil. In *Ensayos de antropología en la
        zona central de Chiapas*, edited by N. A. Mc-
        Quown and J. Pitt-Rivers, México, D. F.:
        Instituto Nacional Indigenista. Pp. 185–214.
Hunn, E.
1973    Noteworthy bird observations from Chiapas,
        México. *The Condor* **75**:483.
1975a   A Measure of the degree of correspondence
        of folk to scientific biological classification.
        *American Ethnologist* **2**(2): 309–327.
1975b   Cognitive processes in folk-ornithology:
        The identification of gulls. Language-behavior
        Research Laboratory, Univ. of California
        (Berkeley). Working paper No. 42.
Kansas, University of
        Slide catalog of the Natural History Museum,
        University of Kansas, Lawrence, Kansas.
Katz, J. J., and J. A. Fodor
1963    The structure of a semantic theory. *Language*
        **39**: 170–210.
Kaufman, T. S.
1964    Materiales lingüísticos para el estudio de las
        relaciones internas y externas de la familia de
        idiomas Mayanos. In *Desarrollo cultural de los
        Mayas*, edited by E. Z. Vogt and A. Ruz. Pp.
        81–136.
Kay, P.
1971    Taxonomy and semantic contrast. *Language*
        **47**: 866–887.
Klots, A., and E. Klots
1971    *Insects of North America.* New York: Doubleday.
Land, H. C.
1970    *Birds of Guatemala.* Wynnewood, Pennsyl-
        vania: Livingston Publishing.
Laughlin, R. M.
1969    The Tzotzil. In *Handbook of Middle-American
        Indians.* Vol. 7: *Ethnology*, edited by E. Z.
        Vogt., Austin: Univ. of Texas Press.
n.d.    Tzotzil bird names: Zinacantan, Chiapas,
        Mexico. m.s.
Leopold, A. S.
1972    *Wildlife of Mexico: The game birds and mam-
        mals.* Berkeley: Univ. of California Press.
Lévi-Strauss, C.
1966    *The savage mind.* Chicago: Univ. of Chicago
        Press.
Lewis, H. L.
1973    *Butterflies of the world.* Chicago: Follett.
Mayr, E.
1970    *Populations, species, and evolution.* Cambridge,
        Massachusetts: Belknap Press. An abridgment
        of *Animal species and evolution*, 1963.
Mayr, E., E G. Linsley, and R. L. Usinger

1953    *Methods and principles of systematic zoology.*
        New York: McGraw–Hill.
Metzger, D., and G. E. Williams
1963    Tenejapa medicine: The curer. *Southwestern
        Journal of Anthropology* **19**: 216–234.
1966    Some procedures and results in the study of
        native categories: Tzeltal firewood. *American
        Anthropologist* **65**: 389–407.
Miller, G., E. Galanter, and K. Pribam
1960    *Plans and the structure of behavior.* New York:
        Holt–Dryden.
Montagu, R.
1969    The Tojolabal. In *Handbook of Middle-
        American Indians.* Vol. 7: *Ethnology*, edited
        by E. Z. Vogt. Austin: Univ. of Texas Press.
Musser, G. G.
1968    A systematic study of the Mexican and Guate-
        malan gray Squirrel, *Sciurus aureogaster* F.
        Cuvier (Rodentia: Sciuridae). *Miscellaneous
        Publications of the Museum of Zoology*
        No. 137. Univ. of Michigan, Ann Arbor, Mich.
Oakes, M.
1951    *The two crosses of Todos Santos.* Princeton,
        New Jersey: Princeton Univ. Press, Bollingen
        Series.
Parlem, A.
1955    The agricultural base of urban civilization in
        Mesoamerica. In *Irrigation civilizations:
        A comparative study*, edited by J. H. Steward.
        Washington, D. C.: Pan American Union,
        Social Science Monograph No. 1. Pp. 28–42.
1967    Agricultural systems and food patterns. In
        *Handbook of Middle-American Indians.* Vol. 6:
        *Social Anthropology*, edited by M. Nash.
        Austin: Univ. of Texas Press.
Perchonock, N., and O. Werner
1969    Navaho systems of classification: Some impli-
        cations for ethnoscience. *Ethnology* **8**: 229–
        242.
Peterson, R. T., and E. L. Chalif
1973    *A field guide to Mexican birds.* Boston:
        Houghton Mifflin.
Pimentel, R. A.
1967    *Invertebrate identification manual.* New York:
        Reinhold Publishing.
Radin, P.
1957    *Primitive man as philosopher.* New York:
        Dover Publications. Originally published 1927.
Rau, P.
1933    *The jungle bees and wasps of Barro Colorado
        Island.* Kirkwood, Missouri: P. Rau.
Redfield, R., and A. Villa Rojas
1934    *Chan Kom, a Maya village.* Washington, D.C.:
        Carnegie Institution of Washington, Publica-
        tion 448.
Richards, O. W., and M. J. Richards
1951    Observations on the social wasps of South
        America (Hymenoptera: Vespidae). *Trans-
        actions of the Royal Entomological Society of
        London* **102**, part 1:1–170.
Robbins, C. S., B. Bruun, and H. S. Zim

1966 *A guide to field identification: Birds of North America.* New York: Golden Press.

Ruddle, K.
1973 The human use of insects: Examples from the Yukpa. *Biotropica* **5**: 94–101.

Schwarz, H. F.
1948 Stingless bees (Meliponidae) of the western hemisphere. *Bulletin of the American Museum of Natural History* **90**.

Simpson, G. G.
1961 *Principles of animal taxonomy.* New York: Columbia Univ. Press.

Stross, B.
1973 Acquisition of botanical terminology by Tzeltal children. In *Meaning in Mayan languages*, edited by M. S. Edmonson. The Hague: Mouton. Pp. 107–141.
n.d. Variation and natural selection as factors in linguistic and cultural change. Austin: Univ. of Texas. m.s.

Stuart, L. C.
1963 *A checklist of the herpetofauna of Guatemala.* Miscellaneous Publication No. 122 of the Museum of Zoology, Ann Arbor: Univ. of Michigan.
1964 Fauna of Middle America. In *Handbook of Middle-American Indians.* Vol. 1: *Natural Environment and Early Cultures*, edited by R. O. West. Austin: Univ. of Texas Press.

Sturtevant, W. C.
1964 Studies in ethnoscience. *American Anthropologist* **66** (1), Part 2:99–131.

Trager, G.
1939 "Cottonwood = tree," a South-Western linguistic trait. *International Journal of American Linguistics* **9**: 117–118.

Triplehorn, C. A.
1972 *A Review of the Genus* Zopherus *of the world (Coleoptera: Tenebrionidae).* Washington, D.C.: Smithsonian Institution.

Tyler, S. A.
1969 *Cognitive anthropology.* New York: Holt, Rinehart and Winston.

University of Chicago
1964 *Social, cultural and linguistic change in the highlands of Chiapas.* Chicago: Univ. of Chicago, Department of Anthropology.

Villa Rojas, A.
1969 The Tzeltal. In *Handbook of Middle-American Indians.* Vol. 7: *Ethnology*, edited by E. Z. Vogt., Austin: Univ. of Texas Press.

Vogt, E. Z.
1969a *Zinacantan: a Maya community in the highlands of Chiapas.* Cambridge, Massachusetts: Belknap Press.
1969b Chiapas highlands. In *Handbook of Middle-American Indians.* Vol. 7: *Ethnology*, edited by E. Z. Vogt. Austin: Univ. of Texas Press.

Von Martens, E.
1890 *Biologia Centrali-Americana: Land and freshwater mollusca.* London: R. H. Porter.

Werner, O.
1969 The basic assumptions of ethnoscience. *Semiotica* **1**: 329–338.

Wilson, E. O.
1971 *The insect societies.* Cambridge, Massachusetts: Belknap Press.

Wyman, L. C., and F. L. Bailey
1964 *Navaho Indian ethnoentomology.* Publications in Anthropology No. 12. Albuquerque: Univ. of New Mexico.

# INDEX TO TZELTAL ANIMAL NAMES

*Italic page numbers indicate illustrations; boldface page numbers indicate main entry; boldface italic page numbers indicate main entry with illustration.*

# INDEX TO NON-TZELTAL ANIMAL NAMES

*Italic page numbers indicate illustrations; boldface page numbers indicate main entry; boldface italic page numbers indicate main entry with illustration.*

# GENERAL INDEX

## A

Agricultural pests, 214, 260, 262, 280, 289, 300–301, 302, 304, 306

Agriculture, 11, 12

Alvarez del Toro, M., 63, 153, 162, 190, 200, 227, 234, 236, 237, 240, 241, 242, 243, 244, 245, 246

Anatomical terminology, Tzeltal folk, 99–110, 299

Animal, *see* Apochryphal animals, Exotic animals, Immature animals, Introduced animals, Larval animals, Migratory animals, Parasitic animals, Protected animals, Venemous animals

Animal behavior in Tzeltal folk zoology, 22, 23, 25, 94–98, 131, 201, 209, 219, 257, 260, 262, 263, 264, 269, 271, 272, 279, 280, 286, 289, 294, 306

Animal husbandry, 12–13, 137, 146, 148, 151–152, 155, 166–167, 205, 215–218, 224, 225–231, 272, 274

Animal spirits, 219, 220, 284

Apochryphal animals, 220, 238, 246

Aquatic habitat, 136–140, 212, 232, 240, 242, 250, 270, 294

Archtypes of folk taxa, 55–56, 99, 131, 137–138, 143, 150, 152, 163, 171, 180–181, 187, 190, 194, 216, 235, 240, 242, 250, 258

Attributes, *see* features, attributes

Attributives in Tzeltal nomenclature, *see* Color, Tzeltal attributives of; Oldor, Tzeltal attributives of; Pattern and texture, Tzeltal attributives of; Shape, Tzeltal attributives of; Size, Tzeltal attributives of

## B

Basic ranges of folk taxa, 55–57, 138, 279

Beans, 12, 54, 164, 242, 300–301

Berlin, B., xiii, 3, 26, 37, 41, 44–45, 47, 48, 50, 53–55, 60, 61, 64, 65, 69, 70, 71, 75, 81, 82, 87, 91, 132, 134, 135, 181, 225, 228

Black, M., 3, 60–62

Branstetter, K., 228, 229, 281

Breedlove, D., 20, 146, 170, 182, 244, 245

Bruner, J., 41, 45–47, 59

Bulmer, R., 3, 45, 47, 48, 61, 64, 65, 69, 70, 81, 82

## C

Cancuc, 6, 9, 10, 34, 179, 228, 229, 232, 246

*Cargo* system, 9

Central highlands of Chiapas, xiii, 6, 14

Chamula, 6, 7, 9, 10, 228

Chiapas, *see* Central Highlands of Chiapas, Grijalva River valley, Gulf slope of Chiapas, Pacific coastal plain of Chiapas, Sierra Madre de Chiapas

Classification, folk, 19–21, 37, 41–75 scientific, 41, 43, 44, 55, 60, 71, 133

Coefficient of taxonomic dissimilarity, 63–74, 80–82

Cognitive anthropology, 4–5

Cold country, *see* Highlands

Color, Tzeltal attributives of, 37, 53, 58, 86–89, 137, 140, 146, 148, 152, 166, 179, 181, 185, 201–202, 206, 209, 210, 224, 228, 229, 230, 235, 236, 240, 242, 243, 248, 250, 260, 262, 263, 268, 281, 290, 295, 296, 298, 301, 302, 304, 305, 306, 309, 310

Complexes, Tzeltal folk zoological, 37, 55, 56, 80, 133, 295

Configurational categories, 46, 50, 58–59, 135

Conklin, H., 3, 26, 41, 116

Contrast, semantic, in taxonomies, 43–44

Contrast set, 43–44, 53

Copp, J., 32, 236, 240, 244, 245, 246, 247

Corn, xv, 12, 214, 243, 301, 302

Correspondence of folk to scientific classification, 19, 21, 22, 24–26, 36–37, 42, 47, 56, 58–75, 80–84, 202, 205, 210, 212, 264, 280–281, 285, 290

Covert categories, 29, 36–38, 44, 55, 56, 80, 133, 206, 210, 230–231, 234, 281, 285

Critical ratio of taxa, 51–53, 55, 72

Cultural significance of animals, 24, 56, 58–59, 60, 75, 81, 146, 148, 170, 214, 259, 264, 280, 285, 287, 304, 306, *see also* Agricultural pests; Fishing; Folklore, animals in; Honey, animal sources; Hunting; Material culture, animal products in; Medicinal uses of animals; Omens; Trapping; Venemous animals

Curers, 35

## D

Data collection, methods, 19–38

Data recording procedures, 28–29